Guide to U.S. Map Resources

Third Edition

Map and Geography Round Table (MAGERT) of the American Library Association

Edited by
Christopher J.J. Thiry

The Scarecrow Press, Inc.
Lanham, Maryland • Toronto • Oxford
2006

SCARECROW PRESS, INC.

Published in the United States of America
by Scarecrow Press, Inc.
A wholly owned subsidiary of
The Rowman & Littlefield Publishing Group, Inc.
4501 Forbes Boulevard, Suite 200, Lanham, Maryland 20706
www.scarecrowpress.com

PO Box 317
Oxford
OX2 9RU, UK

British Library Cataloguing in Publication Information Available

Library of Congress Cataloging-in-Publication Data

Guide to U.S. map resources / Map and Geography Round Table (MAGERT) of
the American library association ; edited by Christopher J.J. Thiry.— 3rd ed.
    p. cm.
 Rev. ed. of: Guide to U.S. map resources / David A. Cobb, 1990.
 Includes bibliographical references and index.
 ISBN 0-8108-5268-3 (pbk. : alk. paper)
 1. Map collections—United States—Directories. I. Thiry, Christopher John Joseph, 1966–
II. Cobb, David A., 1945– Guide to U.S. map resources. III. Map &
Geography Round Table (American Library Association)
GA193.U5C62 2005
026.912—dc22

                                                    2005010479

Contents

Acknowledgments

I tried my best to make this edition of the *Guide to U.S. Map Resources* easy to use and useful. I spent the majority of my time working on formatting and organizational issues. I hope I was successful. I want to thank all those who helped and guided me in the process of writing the original survey, constructing the *Guide*, and editing it. Steve Rogers of The Ohio State University fielded many e-mails and phone calls, and helped proof this edition. The Publications Committee of MAGERT was instrumental in creation of the survey. The regional editors did a great job. Thanks to each and every one of you! Lastly, this book is dedicated to my wife, Dr. Heather Thiry for her words of encouragement, love, and for putting up with all this "map stuff."

Foreword

Most librarians, researchers, and map users would agree that the appearance of this volume is long overdue. More than fourteen years have passed since the second edition of the Map and Geography Round Table's *Guide to U.S. Map Resources* appeared in 1990 (The first edition was published five years earlier in 1986). After the second edition was published, it was hoped that a newly revised *Guide* would be issued every five years or so. That schedule of regular revision was never achieved. However, after a lengthy interval, the third edition of the *Guide to U.S. Map Resources* at last has been realized. It offers the user a detailed snapshot of and guide to hundreds of map collections and cartographic resources in libraries and repositories throughout the nation.

Substantial changes have occurred within library map collections over the past decade and a half. The computer, not surprisingly, has been at the core of most of these innovations. Geographic information systems (GIS), the World Wide Web, e-mail, Portable Document Format, data sets, the Internet and digitization have all played revolutionary roles in transforming libraries—and map collections in particular—over the past fifteen years. Today's librarian who works with maps is no longer limited by the contents of his or her own map and atlas collection. In many cases and with relatively little effort, the librarian can turn to the Internet and locate a map or data set physically located in a library hundreds or thousands of miles away.

But not always. As we are all well aware, not *everything* is available through the Internet—at least not yet anyway. But knowing *which* collection might contain a needed cartographic item can be a valuable first step in locating the item in question. As map collections everywhere continue to grow, new maps, digital files, aerial photos, and atlases become available to users every day. A detailed, timely and reliable guide to these varied and still somewhat "hidden" cartographic collections—and their personnel—will serve as a very useful reference tool, especially in this digital age, when library online catalogues are immediately and readily accessible.

Christopher J.J. Thiry, map librarian at the Colorado School of Mines' Arthur Lakes Library, has taken on the challenging task of compiling and editing this third edition of the *Guide to U.S. Map Resources*. He has been assisted by several members of the Map and Geography Round Table, as well as other volunteers who have gathered detailed information from over 500 libraries and institutions holding collections of maps and other cartographic material.

This third edition of the *Guide*—the result of considerable efforts by Christopher and the many regional editors—should prove to be a beneficial and valuable reference tool for discovering and utilizing the cartographic riches and resources found in map collections located in every region of the country.

Stephen W. Rogers
The Ohio State University
Columbus, Ohio

Introduction

History

The first edition of the *Guide to U.S. Map Resources* was compiled by David Cobb with the help of 19 Regional and Specialist Editors, and published in 1986 by the Map and Geography Roundtable (MAGERT) of the American Library Association (ALA). It was over 200 pages, and contained information on 919 collections. The *Guide* was MAGERT's first publication, and conceived as an on-going title that would be produced every five years. On schedule, the second edition appeared in 1990. Once again, David Cobb compiled the *Guide,* with the help of 32 regional editors. This edition was based on a survey of map collections conducted in early 1989. Physically, the page size was smaller (10 × 7 in., as opposed to 11 × 8.5 in.), but was over 500 pages, and contained information on 974 collections, and 3 addition indexes. The formatting was dramatically improved so as to make the book more user-friendly.

Much has changed since then: most notably, the coming of the World Wide Web and the proliferation of e-mail. In addition, many area codes have changed, not to mention personnel. The number of collections listed in this edition is down, from 974 to 564 in this edition. This can be explained in many ways. First, the third edition established a threshold for inclusion: only collections with more than 1,000 maps, or those with significant or historical value, were included. Second, many collections that were in the previous edition were combined. Third, the number of people who work exclusively on maps has fallen; over the last decade, many map librarian positions have been eliminated or the duties of those positions have been merged. Thus, there were fewer librarians with detailed knowledge of a map collection willing or able to participate.

The Third Edition

Although the third edition of the *Guide to U.S. Map Resources* was planned to begin production in the early 1990s, nothing happened, although there were a couple of false starts. Finally, in the summer of 2001, things began to move when Christopher J.J. Thiry agreed to become the editor.

Over the next year, the new editor developed, with guidance and input from the Publications Committee of MAGERT, a revamped survey that would be used to compile the third edition. It was agreed that submissions would be emailed directly to the editor via an interactive survey on the web. The survey and its formatting took a long time to work out and went through many changes. The original or "long" survey was deemed too complex and time-consuming by some, and thus a pared-down version, the "short" survey, was developed. Institutions were allowed to chose which version they wished to submit. Despite the time needed to fill it out, 369 institutions filled out the "long" survey, while only 197 filled out the "short" survey. Both surveys are reproduced in the appendices and yielded in-depth information regarding the map collections in the U.S.

Forty-six people volunteered or were asked to act as regional editors of this edition. They were chosen on the basis of their geographic location, and asked to be in charge of certain areas of the country. Their job was to announce the existence of the survey via local means such as List-Servs. Many regional editors also made phone calls or wrote directly to institutions to encourage them to complete the survey, and thus be included in this book.

All was going well until 2002 when a major roadblock was hit when ALA decided not to publish this book. After a short period of time, Steve Rogers and others found Scarecrow Press, and things were ready to begin.

The Survey and the Work on the Third Edition Begins

The survey, whose results were used to create the 3rd Edition of the *Guide to U.S. Map Resources*, was launched in late October 2003 and remained open until April 2004. The interactive survey was hosted on the Colorado School of Mines, Map Room's website. The responses were directly emailed to the editor in a text format. These were manipulated in Microsoft Word, then transferred to a Microsoft Excel database, manipulated more, and finally brought back in to Microsoft Word.

The survey was posted exclusively on the web, but unlike earlier editions, there were no mass mailings, although some regional editors did distribute hard copies of the surveys. Because it was acceptable for the institutions to leave answers blank or to estimate holdings, and because so much of the survey was free-text, the editor spent a great deal of time carefully formatting each section in order to produce an easy-to-use book. Although much of the free-text was left intact in the "Collection Directory" section, a painstaking effort was made to standardize the terms in the Geographic/Subject/Special Collection index.

This edition includes listings for all the large and/or important map collections in the United States that responded to the survey. However, no surveys were received from 7 Regional Federal Depository Libraries, nor any institution in Mississippi, thus they were not included in this book.

One of the noteworthy discoveries was the dramatic rise in the number of collections with over 300,000 maps. In the second edition, only 16 had so many maps, while in this edition, 28 do. Also, 56 collections now report having over 200,000 maps.

Using the Guide

The institutions were self-identified into six general categories—Academic, Federal, Private, Public, State, and Other.

The "Collection Directory," or main part of the *Guide*, is organized alphabetically by state, then by city, then by institution within each city. An accession number was assigned to each institution responding. Those accession numbers are used in the indexes. The entries have the following subheading structures (for a complete list of field entries, see "Appendix B: Long Survey"):

- **Name**—Institution name, year founded, address, phone number, fax number, e-mail address, web page address.
- **Personnel**—Person responsible for the collection, title, e-mail address, phone number, other personnel, number of full-time professionals and para-professionals, number of student workers, number of student worker hours per week, number of volunteers, and number of volunteer hours per month.
- **Holdings**—Geographic strengths, special collections, subject strengths (see "Long Survey" for complete list of choices), maps from various agencies (i.e., USGS) received via the Federal Depository Library Program and the percentage received, number of printed maps, manuscript maps, raised relief maps, microfiche, microfilms, aerial photographs, satellite images, globes, gazetteers, printed atlases, manuscript atlases, books (map and cartographic materials only) (excluding atlases and gazetteers), serials titles (active), serials titles (inactive), CD-ROMs, computer programs, if the institution is collecting digital data, chronological coverage of the collection, annual budget over the last 5 years, and on-going publications.
- **Access**—Openness of collection, number of reference questions per year, availability of reference services via the Internet, number of patrons per month, hours, circulation policies, and circulation statistics.
- **Geographic Information Systems (GIS)**—Availability of GIS, types of software available, availability of GIS help, and access to a scanner and plotter.
- **Collection services**—Percentages of the collection classified, cataloged, and available on the institution's public catalog, status of cataloging datasets, classification schemes, cataloging utilities, location of catalog, preservation techniques, and percentage of items gone through preservation process.
- **Physical facilities**—Availability of Internet, square footage, number of computers, printers, map cases, file cabinets, and atlas stands, linear feet of book and atlas shelves, number of stereoscopes, microform reader/printers, and light tables, and copying facilities.
- **Notes**—Many added notes regarding their collections, services and/or institutions.

The following indexes were included:

- Library/Institution, alphabetical by name
- Names and contact information of people listed in the "Collection Directory"
- Geographic/Subject/Special Collection
- Regional Federal Depository Libraries
- Depository library collections (institutions that receive items distributed through the Federal Depository Library Program)

All index numbers refer to institution accession numbers, not page numbers.

Additional resources

Hundreds of good map library resources are available on the Internet. These web sites' information are kept up-to-date by their owners. It was believed that reprinting the information from those sites in this book would be redundant and obsolete. Some Websites of note:

- **http://www.waml.org/maptools.html** The Map Librarians Toolbox by the Western Association of Map Librarians (WAML). This web site lists various links to resources including vendors, and bibliographic tools that may help map collections.
- **http://oregonstate.edu/~reeset/html/tools.html** Map Cataloging Tools. This site offers a range of tools that are useful in cataloging maps.
- **http://infomine.ucr.edu/cgi-bin/search?category=maps** Infomine, Scholarly Internet Resources Collections. This is a virtual library of Internet resources relevant to faculty, students, and research staff at the university level.
- **http://www.maphistory.info/** Map History / History of Cartography This site offers links to historic maps.
- **http://www.evergreen.edu/library/govdocs/statemaps.html** 50 States Government Sources: State Maps. This web site contains links to state mapping agencies.
- **http://ngmdb.usgs.gov/** National Geologic Mapping Database. This site, by the US Geological Survey, is an index to geologic and earth science maps.
- **http://oddens.geog.uu.nl/index.php** Oddens' Bookmarks, The Fascinating World of Maps and Mapping. This web site contains over 22,000 links to sites about maps and mapping.

Christopher J.J. Thiry
Editor
Map Librarian
Colorado School of Mines
cthiry@mines.edu

Please notify the editor, if you believe this edition lacks specific institutional entries.

Regional Editors

Jerry Adams
Earth Sciences Librarian
Brigham Young University

Marcy M. Allen
Government Information Librarian
Western Illinois University

John M. Anderson
Map Librarian and Director
Cartographic Information Center
Department of Geography & Anthropology
Louisiana State University

Paige G. Andrew
Faculty Maps Cataloger
The Pennsylvania State University

HelenJane Armstrong
Head, Map & Imagery Library
University of Florida Libraries

David Cobb
Curator, Harvard Map Collection
Harvard University

Jim Coombs
Map Librarian
Southwest Missouri State University

Angie Cope
Academic Map Librarian
American Geographical Society Library UW Milwaukee

Carlos A. Diaz
Government Documents Specialist
Daniel J. Evans Library
The Evergreen State College

Janet B. Dixon
Geosciences Librarian
University of Arkansas Libraries

Travis Dolence
Assistant Professor, Map/GIS Librarian
University of Tennessee

Carol Doyle
Head, Government Documents and Maps
California State University, Fresno

Megan Dreger
Government Publications & Map Librarian
San Diego State University

Sue Ann Gardner
Associate Professor/Cataloger
University of Nebraska-Lincoln

Lucinda M. Hall
Reference Bibliographer
Dartmouth College

Julie Hoff
Map Librarian
Arizona State Library, Archives and Public Records

Jenny Marie Johnson
Map and Geography Librarian and Associate Professor
   of Library Administration
University of Illinois at Urbana—Champaign

Carolyn Kadri
Special Collections Librarian/Cataloger
University of Texas at Arlington
Arlington, Texas

Christine Kollen
Geography and Sociology Librarian
University of Arizona

Kimberly C. Kowal
Curator of Digital Mapping
The British Library, Map Library

Matt Knutzen
Assistant Chief, Map Division
New York Public Library

Kathryn Lage
Map Librarian
University of Colorado at Boulder
Jerry Crail Johnson Earth Sciences &
   Map Library

Peter Linberger
Business, Geography and Maps Bibliographer,
   Associate Prof. of Bibliography
University Libraries, The University of Akron

Becky Lutkenhaus
Documents and Maps Reference Librarian
   and Bibliographer
Rod Library, University of Northern Iowa

Brenda G. Mathenia
Assistant Professor/Reference Librarian
   & Instruction Coordinator
Montana State University—Bozeman

Cheryl S. McCoy
Documents/Maps Librarian
University of South Florida, Tampa Library

Mary McInroy
Map Librarian/Interim Head, Government Publications
University of Iowa Libraries

Christopher H. Mixon
Information Technology Specialist, Maps & GIS
Auburn University Libraries

Riley Moffat
Head of Reference
Brigham Young University—Hawaii

Susan Moore
Catalog Librarian/Bibliographer
University of Northern Iowa

Robert Morris
Acquisitions Librarian
Geography and Map Division
Library of Congress

John Olson
Maps/GIS Librarian
Syracuse University

Liz Paulus
Board Member
Special Library Organization, Oregon Chapter

John C. Phillips
Map Librarian
The University of Toledo

Ed Redmond
Reference Specialist
Geography and Map Division, Library of Congress

Stephen W. Rogers
Map Librarian
Ohio State University

Earl Roy
Catalog Librarian, Map Collection
History and Social Sciences Team
Sterling Memorial Library
Yale University

Bruce Sarjeant
Reference/Documents and Maps Librarian
Northern Michigan University

Robert Sathrum
Natural Resources Librarian
Humboldt State University

Tsering Wangyal Shawa
Geographic Information Systems Librarian
Princeton University

Michele D. Shular
Geosciences Librarian
State University of New York at Buffalo

Lorre Smith
Librarian for Digital Library Initiatives
University at Albany

Julie Sweetkind-Singer
Head, Branner Earth Sciences Library & Map Collections
Stanford University

Deborah Yerkes
Assistant Documents Librarian
University of South Carolina-Thomas Cooper Library

Dawn Youngblood
Director
Edwin J. Foscue Map Library
Southern Methodist University

Linda Zellmer
Head, Geology Library
Indiana University Libraries

Collection Directory

1 *Auburn University, AL*

Auburn University

Library
231 Mell Street
Auburn University, AL 36849-5606
Telephone: 334-844-1759
Fax: 334-844-4461
Email: mixonch@auburn.edu
Web: www.lib.auburn.edu/govdocs/

Personnel:
Responsible person: Christopher H. Mixon, Curator, *email:* mixonch@auburn.edu
Assistants: Kitty Siu, Library Assistant
Number of student workers hours per week: 12

Holdings:
Geographic strengths: Alabama, Southeast
Special collections: Sanborn Fire Insurance maps for Alabama, and Georgia, rare and early maps for Alabama and Southeast
Subject strengths: aerial photos, aeronautical, agriculture, geology, hydrology, nautical charts, political geography, recreation, soil
Map depositories and percentages: USGS topos (100%), USGS geology maps (100%), USGS other (100%), Department of Transportation, NOAA, GPO, CIA, National Forest Service, NIMA nautical, NIMA aeronautical, BLM, State
98,091 printed maps
50 manuscript maps
15 wall maps
17 raised relief maps
55,117 aerial photos
106 satellite images
145 gazetteers
1,332 printed atlases
237 books
18 inactive serials
140 CD-ROMs
Collecting digital data
Chronological coverage:
1900–1939: 40%
1940–present: 60%
Average budget over the last 5 years: $300

Access:
Maps in separate area
Collection is open to the public
Reference questions per year: 800
Answers email questions
Patrons per month: 50
Hours:
Monday–Friday: 7:45 A.M.–2 A.M.
Saturday: 9 A.M.–9 P.M.
Sunday: 1 P.M.–2 A.M.
Total hours per week opened: 66.25
Maps circulate
Circulation policies apply
Map circulation duration: 1 week
Atlas circulation duration: 23 days
Book circulation duration: 1 week
Number of maps circulated annually: 142

Geographic Information Systems:
GIS services available in an open environment
GIS software: ArcView, ArcGIS
GIS assistance available for Census mapping, geocoding, and image analysis
General GIS questions answered
Plotter available
Scans maps for patrons

Collection services:
Maps cataloged: 85%
Maps classified: 85%
Maps in OPAC: 85%
Datasets are cataloged
Classification schemes: LC, SuDocs
Cataloging utilities: OCLC
Catalog accessibility: online
Preservation techniques: encapsulation, deacidification, book tape
Percent of items that have gone through the preservation process: 12%

Physical facilities:
Internet access available
Square footage: 1,500
Number of map cases: 150
Number of vertical files (file cabinets): 17
Linear book shelving: 30 ft.
Linear atlas shelving: 321 ft.

Other map storage: 2 rolled map cases
Number of microform readers: 13
Copying facilities available: copier, microform copier
Notes: Under GIS services, we do not require appointments but the facility is monitored by staff and student workers.

2 *Birmingham, AL*

Birmingham Public Library

Linn-Henley Research Library
Rucker Agee Map Collection, founded 1964
2100 Park Place
Birmingham, AL 35203-2794
Telephone: 205-226-3665
Fax: 205-226-3663
Email: yvonne@bham.lib.al.us
Web: www.bplonline.org
Personnel:
   Responsible person: Yvonne Crumpler, Curator, *email:*
      yvonne@bham.lib.al.us
Holdings:
   Geographic strengths: Alabama, Southeast
   Special collections: Sanborn Fire Insurance maps for
      Alabama
   Subject strengths: aerial photos, early cartography,
      modern cartography, caves, celestial, city, economic
      geography, genealogy, geology, historical geography,
      mineral resources, roads, antique maps
   Map depositories:: USGS topos, USGS geology maps,
      State
   3,750 printed maps
   14 wall maps
   26 microfiche
   127 aerial photos
   36 gazetteers
   705 printed atlases
   2,568 books
   Chronological coverage:
      1800–1899: 30%
      1900–1939: 40%
      1940–present: 25%
Access:
   Maps in separate area
   Collection is partially open to the public
   Reference questions per year: 2,000
   Answers email questions
   Patrons per month: 40
   Hours:
      Monday–Saturday: by appointment
Geographic Information Systems:
   No GIS services available
   Scans maps for patrons
Collection services:
   Maps cataloged: 10%

Maps classified: 10%
Maps in OPAC: 10%
Classification schemes: LC
Cataloging utilities: OCLC
Catalog accessibility: online, printout
Preservation techniques: encapsulation
Percent of items that have gone through the preservation process: 70%
Physical facilities:
   Internet access available
   Square footage: 315
   Linear book shelving: 316 ft.
   Linear atlas shelving: 165 ft.
   Other map storage: mobile roll case
   Copying facilities available: copier, microform copier

3 *Birmingham, AL*

Samford University

Samford University Library
800 Lakeshore Drive
Birmingham, AL 35229
Telephone: 205-726-2749
Fax: 205-726-2642
Email: scdept@samford.edu
Web: library.samford.edu
Holdings:
   Geographic strengths: Alabama, Southeast, Ireland
   Special collections: Casey Collection of Irish History
      and Genealogy, Brantley Collection (Alabama and
      Southeast), Sanborn Fire Insurance maps (Alabama
      only)
   Subject strengths: geology, historical geography,
      roads
   Map depositories:: USGS topos, USGS geology maps,
      USGS other
   4,497 printed maps
   10 manuscript maps
   15 wall maps
   41 raised relief maps
   335 microfiche
   13 microfilms
   76 gazetteers
   299 printed atlases
   191 books
   129 CD-ROMs
   Chronological coverage:
      1800–1899: 10%
      1900–1939: 10%
      1940–present: 76%
   On-going publications: Maps in the Samford University Library: An Annotated List (1977), inactive
Access:
   Collection is partially open to the public
   Answers email questions

Hours:
Monday–Friday: 8 A.M.–4:30 P.M.
Total hours per week opened: 42.5
Maps circulate
Circulation policies apply
Map circulation duration: 4 weeks
Atlas circulation duration: 4 weeks
Book circulation duration: 4 weeks
Geographic Information Systems:
No GIS services available
Collection services:
Maps cataloged: 85%
Maps classified: 85%
Maps in OPAC: 38%
Classification schemes: LC, SuDocs, Local
Cataloging utilities: OCLC
Catalog accessibility: online, printout
Preservation techniques: encapsulation, edging
Percent of items that have gone through the preservation process: 5%
Physical facilities:
Internet access available
Linear book shelving: 15 ft.
Linear atlas shelving: 20 ft.
Copying facilities available: copier, color copier, large-format copier, microform copier

4 *Mobile, AL*

University of South Alabama

University Library
307 University Boulevard
Mobile, AL 36688-0002
Telephone: 251-460-7024
Fax: 251-461-1628
Email: docref@jaguar1.usouthal.edu
Web: www.library.southalabama.edu
Personnel:
Responsible person: Vicki Tate, Head, Documents/ Serials, *email:* vtate@jaguar1.usouthal.edu
Assistants: Nancy Pugh, LTA, Maps/Fiche
FTE para-professionals: 0.5
Holdings:
Geographic strengths: Southeast
Special collections: Flood Insurance Rate maps of Mobile County, Alabama
Subject strengths: aerial photos, modern cartography, climatology, forestry, geology, hydrology, map catalogs, mineral resources, nautical charts, population, soil, waterways
Map depositories and percentages: USGS topos (10%), USGS geology maps (50%), USGS other, Department of Transportation, NOAA, GPO, CIA, National Forest Service, NIMA nautical
9,250 printed maps

1,090 microfiche
130 aerial photos
56 satellite images
50 gazetteers
410 printed atlases
20,000 books
375 active serials
50 CD-ROMs
Chronological coverage:
1940–present: 95%
Access:
Collection is open to the public
Answers email questions
Hours:
Monday–Friday: 8 A.M.–10:30 P.M.
Saturday: 9:30 A.M.–5 P.M.
Sunday: 1 P.M.–10:30 P.M.
Total hours per week opened: 76
Maps circulate
Circulation policies apply
Map circulation duration: 1 week
Book circulation duration: 4 weeks
Interlibrary loan available
Geographic Information Systems:
No GIS services available
Collection services:
Maps cataloged: 100%
Maps classified: 100%
Maps in OPAC: 20%
Classification schemes: LC, SuDocs
Cataloging utilities: OCLC, Marcive
Catalog accessibility: online, cards
Preservation techniques: lamination
Physical facilities:
Internet access available
Square footage: 650
Linear book shelving: 600 ft.
Linear atlas shelving: 90 ft.
Copying facilities available: copier, microform copier

5 *Montgomery, AL*

Alabama Department of Archives and History

P.O. Box 300100
624 Washington Avenue
Montgomery, AL 36130
Telephone: 334-242-4363
Fax: 334-240-3433
Email: cluckie@archives.state.al.us
Web: www.archives.state.al.us
Personnel:
Responsible person: Cynthia A. Luckie, *email:* cluckie@archives.state.al.us
Number of volunteer hours per month: 20

Holdings:

Geographic strengths: Alabama

Special collections: Insurance maps of Alabama municipalities from Sanborn and from local companies, Civil War manuscript maps, state and county highway maps from the Alabama Department of Transportation, pre-1980 USGS Geological Survey maps of Alabama, General Land Office plat maps

Subject strengths: aerial photos, city, military, political geography, railroads, roads, soil

6,000 printed maps

686 manuscript maps

17 wall maps

1,800 aerial photos

97 printed atlases

10 books

Chronological coverage:

1800–1899: 20%

1900–1939: 30%

1940–present: 49%

Average budget over the last 5 years: $200

Access:

Collection is paged

Reference questions per year: 20

Answers email questions

Hours:

Tuesday–Saturday: 8:30 A.M.–4:30 P.M.

Sunday: closed

Total hours per week opened: 32

Geographic Information Systems:

No GIS services available

Scans maps for patrons

Collection services:

Maps cataloged: 70%

Maps classified: 70%

Maps in OPAC: 70%

Classification schemes: Local

Cataloging utilities: RLG, Local, A few in RLG, most in local database

Catalog accessibility: online

Preservation techniques: encapsulation

Percent of items that have gone through the preservation process: 30%

Physical facilities:

Internet access available

Square footage: 800

Number of map cases: 14

Linear book shelving: 300

Copying facilities available: copier, arranged through outside vendor

Notes: Some maps are cataloged in MARC in our online catalog and in RLIN. About 70% are available through a local database on our website (http://www.archives.state.al.us/mapbase/mapbase.cfm). Several hundred have been digitized and are viewable at Alabama Maps

(http://alabamamaps.ua.edu), maintained by the Cartographic Research Lab at the University of Alabama.

6 *Tuscaloosa, AL*

Geological Survey of Alabama

Library

Founded 1874

P.O. Box 869999

Tuscaloosa, AL 35486-6999

Telephone: 205-247-3634

Fax: 205-349-2861

Email: library@gsa.state.al.us

Web: www.gsa.state.al.us

Personnel:

Responsible person: Lewis S. Dean, *email:* ldean@gsa.state.al.us

Holdings:

Geographic strengths: Alabama, Southeast

Special collections: Geologic maps of Alabama

Subject strengths: aerial photos, agriculture, caves, geodetic surveys, geology, historical geography, hydrology, mineral resources, mining, nautical charts, railroads, roads, satellite imagery, soil, waterways, Alabama county highway maps

Map depositories and percentages: USGS topos (100%), USGS geology maps (75%), USGS other (75%), Alabama Department of Transportation

10,000 printed maps

200 manuscript maps

100 wall maps

10 raised relief maps

200 microfilms

12,000 aerial photos

200 satellite images

12 gazetteers

25 printed atlases

200 CD-ROMs

Chronological coverage:

1800–1899: 25%

1900–1939: 25%

1940–present: 50%

On-going publications: Publications of the Geological Survey of Alabama

Access:

Maps in separate area

Collection is open to the public

Reference questions per year: 100

Answers email questions

Patrons per month: 20

Hours:

Total hours per week opened: 40

Maps circulate

Circulation policies apply

Map circulation duration: 2 weeks

Atlas circulation duration: 2 weeks

Book circulation duration: 4 weeks
Number of maps circulated annually: 50
Number of books circulated annually: 200
Interlibrary loan available

Geographic Information Systems:
GIS services available by appointment
Plotter available
Scans maps for patrons

Collection services:
Maps cataloged: 50%
Maps classified: 50%
Maps in OPAC: 50%
Datasets are cataloged
Classification schemes: SuDocs, Dewey
Catalog accessibility: online, cards
Preservation techniques: encapsulation
Percent of items that have gone through the preservation process: 25%

Physical facilities:
Internet access available
Copying facilities available: copier, scanner

7 *Tuscaloosa, AL*

University of Alabama

W. S. Hoole Special Collections Library
Box 870266
Tuscaloosa, AL 35487-0266
Telephone: 205-348-0500
Fax: 205-348-1699
Email: archives@bama.ua.edu
Web: www.lib.ua.edu/libraries/hoole/

Personnel:
Responsible person: Clark E. Center, Jr., Curator, *email:* ccenter@bama.ua.edu
Assistants: Jessica Lacher-Feldman, Public and Outreach Services Librarian; Donnelly Lancaster, Archival Access Coordinator; Thomas S. Land, Institutional Records Analyst; Allyson Holliday, Library Assistant; Angela Kao, Archival Technician; Kevin Ray, Institutional Records Assistant; Holli Connell, Office Associate

Holdings:
Geographic strengths: Alabama, Southeast
Special collections: Sanborn Fire Insurance maps, soil survey maps, Warner Map Collection
934 printed maps
36 books
Maps cataloged: 98%
Maps in OPAC: 98%
Classification schemes: LC

Access:
Hours:
Monday–Wednesday: 8 A.M.–5 P.M.

Thursday: 8 A.M.–9 P.M.
Friday: 8 A.M.–5 P.M.

Physical facilities:
Public computers: 2
Map cases: 12

Notes: Maps kept in climate-controlled stack areas with other materials; used in controlled-access reading room.

8 *Tuscaloosa, AL*

University of Alabama

Map Library
P.O. Box 870322
Tuscaloosa, AL 35487
Telephone: 205-348-6028
Email: maplib@bama.ua.edu
Web: maplibrary.ua.edu

Personnel:
Responsible person: Thomas Kallsen, Map Library Supervisor, *email:* maplib@bama.ua.edu
FTE professionals: 1

Holdings:
Geographic strengths: Alabama, United States, Europe
Special collections: Placenames Research Center
Map depositories: USGS topos, Department of Transportation, NOAA, National Forest Service, NGA nautical, NGA aeronautical, BLM
278,689 printed maps
78,260 aerial photos
210 atlases
642 books
315 CD-ROMs

Access:
Hours:
Monday–Friday: 8 A.M.–4:45 P.M.
Saturday–Sunday: closed
Items circulate
Interlibrary loan available

Collection Services:
Maps cataloged: 10%
Maps classified: 50%
Maps in OPAC: 10%
Classification schemes: LC, SuDocs

Physical facilities:
Maps in separate area
Map cases: 202
Vertical files: 35

9 *Anchorage, AK*

Alaska Resources Library and Information Services (ARLIS)

3211 Providence Drive
Suite 111
Anchorage, AK 99508

Telephone: 907-272-7547
Fax: 907-271-4742
Web: www.arlis.org
Personnel:
Responsible person: Kevin Keating, Reference Librarian, *email:* ankmk@uaa.alaska.edu
FTE professionals: 0   *FTE para-professionals:* 0
Holdings:
Geographic strengths: Alaska (natural resources, transportation, land status, oil and gas development)
Special collections: Exxon Valdez Oil Spill collection
Map depositories: USGS topos, BLM
7,200 printed maps
450 aerial photos
45 atlases
80 books
15 active serials
75 CD-ROMs
Access:
Hours:
Monday–Friday: 8 A.M.–5 P.M.
Interlibrary loan available
Collection Services:
Maps cataloged: 30%
Maps in OPAC: 30%
Classification schemes: LC, Local
Physical facilities:
Public computers: 0
Map cases: 5
Vertical files: 4

10 *Anchorage, AK*

University of Alaska, Anchorage

UAA/APU Consortium Library
3211 Providence Drive
Anchorage, AK 99508
Telephone: 907-786-1825
Fax: 907-786-1834
Web: www.lib.uaa.alaska.edu
Personnel:
Responsible person: Kevin Keating, Reference Librarian, *email:* ankmk@uaa.alaska.edu
FTE professionals: 0   *FTE para-professionals:* 0
Holdings:
Geographic strengths: Alaska
Map depositories: USGS topos, NOAA, CIA, National Forest Service
5,900 printed maps
450 aerial photos
2 globes
100 atlases
225 books
12 active serials

Access:
Hours:
Monday–Friday: 7:30 A.M.–11 P.M.
Saturday: 10 A.M.–6 P.M.
Sunday: noon–10 P.M.
Collection Services:
Maps cataloged: 15%
Maps in OPAC: 15%
Classification schemes: LC, SuDocs
Physical facilities:
Map cases: 4
Vertical files: 5

11 *Douglas, AK*

Bureau of Land Management, Juneau—John Rishel Information Center

Juneau—John Rishel Information Center
100 Savikko Road
Douglas, AK 99824
Telephone: 907-364-1553
Fax: 907-364-1574
Email: jalbrech@ak.blm.gov
Web: juneau.ak.blm.gov/library/library.html
Personnel:
Responsible person: Jane Albrecht, Librarian, *email:* jalbrech@ak.blm.gov
Holdings:
Geographic strengths: Alaska
Subject strengths: geology, mineral resources
1,400 printed maps
Chronological coverage:
1940–present: 100%
On-going publications: List of U.S. Geological Survey geologic and water-supply reports and maps for Alaska. Publications of the U.S. Geological Survey.
Access:
Collection is partially open to the public
Answers email questions
Patrons per month: 45
Hours:
Monday–Friday: 8 A.M.–4:30 P.M.
Total hours per week opened: 40
Circulation policies apply
Geographic Information Systems:
No GIS services available
Collection services:
Maps cataloged: 85%
Percentage of maps in OPAC: 85%
Classification schemes: Local
Cataloging utilities: OCLC, Local
Catalog accessibility: online
Physical facilities:
Internet access available
Copying facilities available: copier

12 *Fairbanks, AK*

Alaska Division of Geological and Geophysical Surveys

Library, founded 1962
3354 College Road
Fairbanks, AK 99709-3707
Telephone: 907-451-5020
Fax: 907-451-5050
Email: dggspubs@dnr.state.ak.us
Web: www.dggs.dnr.state.ak.us
Personnel:
Responsible person: Dawn Roberts, Natural Resource Technician, *email:* dawn_roberts@dnr.state.ak.us
Holdings:
Geographic strengths: Alaska
Special collections: Territorial Department of Mines
Subject strengths: geology, geospatial data, mineral resources, mining, travel books, geophysics, geologic hazards
Map depositories:: USGS geology maps, BLM, State 7,000 printed maps
Chronological coverage:
  1900–1939: 10%
  1940–present: 89%
Access:
Reference questions per year: 700
Answers email questions
Patrons per month: 100
Hours:
  Monday–Friday: 8 A.M.–5 P.M.
  Total hours per week opened: 45
Geographic Information Systems:
No GIS services available
Collection services:
Maps cataloged: 50%
Maps classified: 5%
Maps in OPAC: 45%
Classification schemes: Local
Cataloging utilities: Local
Catalog accessibility: online, printout
Physical facilities:
Internet access available
Square footage: 2,000
Number of vertical files (file cabinets): 30
Linear book shelving: 2,700 ft.
Other map storage: rolled map cases
Copying facilities available: copier

13 *Fairbanks, AK*

University of Alaska, Fairbanks

Elmer E. Rasmuson Library
Documents and Maps Collection, founded 1975

P.O. Box 756817
Fairbanks, AK 99775-6817
Telephone: 907-474-7624
Fax: 907-474-1155
Email: ffjdk@uaf.edu
Web: www.uaf.edu/library
Personnel:
Responsible person: John Kawula, Government Documents and Maps Librarian, *email:* ffjdk@uaf.edu
Assistants: Lori Boone, Library Technician
Number of student workers hours per week: 10
Holdings:
Geographic strengths: Alaska, Northern Canada, Polar regions
Subject strengths: aeronautical, archaeology, biology, climatology, city, forestry, geology, land use, language, map catalogs, mineral resources, mining, nautical charts, raised relief models, recreation, soil, vegetation
Map depositories: and percentage: USGS topos (100%) (Alaska only), USGS geology maps (100%), USGS other (100%), Department of Transportation, NOAA, GPO, CIA, National Forest Service, NIMA topos, NIMA aeronautical, BLM
30,000 printed maps
40 raised relief maps
50 satellite images
1,000 printed atlases
10 CD-ROMs
Chronological coverage:
  1940–present: 90%
Average budget over the last 5 years: $3,000
Access:
Collection is open to the public
Reference questions per year: 40
Answers email questions
Hours:
  Monday–Friday: 8 A.M.–5 P.M.
  Total hours per week opened: 40
Maps circulate
Interlibrary loan available
Geographic Information Systems:
No GIS services available
Scans maps for patrons
Collection services:
Maps cataloged: 100%
Maps classified: 100%
Maps in OPAC: 100%
Classification schemes: LC, SuDocs
Cataloging utilities: OCLC
Catalog accessibility: online
Physical facilities:
Internet access available
Square footage: 1,800
Number of map cases: 19

Linear atlas shelving: 135 ft.
Copying facilities available: copier, color copier, microform copier

14 *Juneau, AK*

Alaska State Library

Historical Collections
P.O. Box 110571
Juneau, AK 99811-0571
Telephone: 907-465-2925
Fax: 907-465-2990
Web: www.library.state.ak.us/hist/hist.html
Personnel:
Responsible person: Kathryn H. Shelton
Holdings:
Geographic strengths: Alaska
Special collections: Sanborn Fire Insurance maps, USGS topographical maps of Alaska 1940s–1970s, early explorers
Subject strengths: geology, map catalogs, mineral resources, mining, nautical charts
Map: USGS topos, USGS geology maps, NOAA
6,000 printed maps
608 manuscript maps
300 microfiche
1,500 aerial photos
65 manuscript atlases
500 books
Chronological coverage:
Pre-1800: 10%
1800–1899: 30%
1900–1939: 30%
1940–present: 30%
Access:
Maps in separate area
Collection is paged
Answers email questions
Hours:
Monday–Friday: 1 P.M.–5 P.M.
Total hours per week opened: 20
Geographic Information Systems:
No GIS services available
Collection services:
Maps cataloged: 95%
Maps classified: 75%
Maps in OPAC: 95%
Classification schemes: LC, Local
Cataloging utilities: OCLC, Local
Catalog accessibility: online, fiche
Preservation techniques: encapsulation, encapsulation in mylar
Percent of items that have gone through the preservation process: 90%

Physical facilities:
No Internet access
Square footage: 1,250
Linear atlas shelving: 175 ft.
Copying facilities available: copier, microform copier

15 *Ketchikan, AK*

Ketchikan Public Library

Adult Division
629 Dock Street
Ketchikan, AK 99901
Telephone: 907 225 3331
Fax: 907-225 0153
Email: library@firstcitylibraries.org
Web: www.firstcitylibraries.org
Personnel:
Responsible person: Bridgit Stearns, *email:* bridgits@firstcitylibraries.org
FTE professionals: 1
Holdings:
Geographic strengths: Alaska
Map depositories: USGS
1,500 printed maps
1 globe
10 atlases
5 CD-ROMs
Collection Services:
Maps cataloged: 0%
Maps classified: 90%
Maps in OPAC: 5%
Classification schemes: Local
Access:
Hours:
Monday–Saturday: 10 A.M.–6 P.M.
Sunday: 1 P.M.–5 P.M.
Interlibrary loan available
Physical facilities:
Maps in separate area
Public computers: 12
Map cases: 2
Vertical files: 1

16 *Flagstaff, AZ*

Flagstaff City—Coconino County Public Library

Main Library
300 West Aspen Avenue
Flagstaff, AZ 86001
Telephone: 928-779-7670
Fax: 928-774-9573
Web: flagstaffpubliclibrary.org

Personnel:

Responsible person: Dawn Gardner, Public Services Manager, *email:* dgardner@fpl.lib.az.us

FTE professionals: 0.05   *FTE para-professionals:* 0.05

Holdings:

Geographic strengths: Flagstaff, Arizona

Special collections: Sanborn Fire Insurance maps for Flagstaff ((paper)1943, 1916, 1977, (microfilm) 1890, 1892, 1895, 1901, 1910, 1916, 1948), topos of Arizona, Flagstaff street and water maps, older topos of Arizona

1,500 printed maps

4 aerial photos

1 globes

75 atlases

Access:

Hours:

Monday–Thursday: 10 A.M.–7 or 9 P.M.

Friday: 10 A.M.–7 P.M.

Saturday: 10 A.M.–6 P.M.

Collection Services:

Maps cataloged: 50%

Maps classified: 50%

Maps in OPAC: 50%

Classification schemes: Dewey

Physical facilities:

Maps in separate area

Map cases: 2

Notes: The cataloged local historical maps are in the library archive; the Arizona and other western states topos are in the public area and are not cataloged.

17 *Flagstaff, AZ*

Northern Arizona University

Cline Library

Map Collection

P.O. Box 6022

Flagstaff, AZ 86011

Telephone: 928-523-6805

Fax: 928-523-3770

Web: www.nau.edu/library

Personnel:

Responsible person: Susan Beard, Government Information Specialist, *email:* Susan.Beard@nau.edu

Number of student workers hours per week: 8

Holdings:

Geographic strengths: Arizona, Southwest

Subject strengths: aerial photos, aeronautical, celestial, climatology, city, forestry, geology, hydrology, land ownership, land use, map catalogs, mineral resources, mining, nautical charts, political geography,

population, recreation, roads, satellite imagery, soil, travel books, vegetation

Map depositories and percentages: USGS topos (15%), USGS geology maps (15%), Department of Transportation, GPO, CIA, National Forest Service, NIMA nautical, BLM

45,000 printed maps

400 aerial photos

50 printed atlases

50 CD-ROMs

Chronological coverage:

1900–1939: 15%

1940–present: 80%

Average budget over the last 5 years: $100

Access:

Collection is open to the public

Answers email questions

Hours:

Monday–Thursday: 7:30 A.M.–11:30 P.M.

Friday: 7:30 A.M.–7 P.M.

Saturday: 10:30 A.M.–7 P.M.

Sunday: 10:30 A.M.–11:30 P.M.

Total hours per week opened: 83.5

Geographic Information Systems:

No GIS services available

Collection services:

Maps cataloged: 70%

Maps classified: 40%

Maps in OPAC: 70%

Datasets are cataloged

Classification schemes: LC, SuDocs

Cataloging utilities: OCLC

Catalog accessibility: online, cards

Preservation techniques: encapsulation, lamination

Physical facilities:

No Internet access

Square footage: 500

Number of map cases: 35

Number of vertical files (file cabinets): 10

Linear atlas shelving: 12 ft.

Copying facilities available: copier, color copier, large-format copier

18 *Flagstaff, AZ*

Northern Arizona University

Cline Library

Special Collections and Archives Department

Box 6022

Flagstaff, AZ 86011-6022

Telephone: 928-523-5551

Fax: 928-523-3770

Email: special.collections@nau.edu

Web: www.nau.edu/library/speccoll

Personnel:

Responsible person: Karen J. Underhill, *email:* karen.underhill@nau.edu

Assistants: Todd Welch, Digital Access Librarian; Richard Quartaroli, Special Collections Librarian; Jill Koelling, Curator of Visual Materials; Bee Valvo, Library Specialist; Jess Vogelsang, Library Specialist; Susan McGlothlin, Library Specialist; Pamela Piatchek, Library Specialist

FTE professionals: 1

Holdings:

Geographic strengths: Coconino County, Northern Arizona, Colorado Plateau, Southern Utah

Special collections: Arizona Woolgrowers, Harvey Butchart Grand Canyon hiking maps, (Timber) Arizona Lumber and Timber Company, (Timber) Saginaw and Manistee Lumber Company, General Land Office, Colorado River plan and profile, Brad Washburn National Geographic Bright Angel Trail (Grand Canyon), Coconino County Plats, Wheeler Atlas

Map depositories: USGS topos, Department of Transportation, National Forest Service, BLM

2,000 printed maps

1,000 aerial photos

10 atlases

Access:

Hours:

Monday–Friday: 9 A.M.–6 P.M.

Saturday: closed

Sunday: 1 P.M.–4 P.M.

Collection Services:

Maps cataloged: 50%

Maps classified: 50%

Maps in OPAC: 50%

Classification schemes: LC, Local

Physical facilities:

Maps in separate area

Public computers: 1

Map cases: 11

Vertical files: 1

19 *Kingman, AZ*

Mohave Museum of History and Art

Founded 1986

400 West Beale Street

Kingman, AZ 86401

Telephone: 928-753-3195

Fax: 928-718-1562

Email: mocohist@citlink.net

Web: www.mohavemuseum.org

Personnel:

Responsible person: email: mmdirector@citlink.net

Assistants: Roseanne Rosenberg, Librarian

Number of volunteer hours per month: 10

Holdings:

Geographic strengths: Mohave County, Arizona

Special collections: Sanborn Fire, Wheeler, USGS

Subject strengths: aerial photos, modern cartography, city, engineering, land ownership, mineral resources, mining, railroads, roads, soil

9,000 printed maps

1,000 manuscript maps

40 aerial photos

Chronological coverage:

1800–1899: 1%

1900–1939: 75%

1940–present: 24%

Access:

Collection is paged

Reference questions per year: 200

Answers email questions

Patrons per month: 20

Hours:

Monday–Friday: 9 A.M.–5 P.M.

Total hours per week opened: 40

Geographic Information Systems:

No GIS services available

Collection services:

Maps cataloged: 100%

Maps classified: 100%

Classification schemes: Local

Cataloging utilities: Local

Catalog accessibility: printout

Preservation techniques: encapsulation, flexible backing

Percent of items that have gone through the preservation process: 5%

Physical facilities:

No Internet access

Square footage: 3,000

Other map storage: 1 rolled map case

Copying facilities available: copier

20 *Mesa, AZ*

City of Mesa Library

64 East First Street

Mesa, AZ 85201

Telephone: 480-644-2207

Web: www.mesalibrary.org

Personnel:

Responsible person: Rebecca Allen, Librarian II, *email:* rebecca.allen@cityofmesa.org

Holdings:

Geographic strengths: Arizona.

Subject strengths: aerial photos, aeronautical, city, engineering, forestry, land ownership, raised relief models, recreation, roads, travel books

Map depositories and percentages: USGS topos (0.5%), USGS geology maps (0.1%), USGS other

(0.1%), Department of Transportation, CIA, National Forest Service, State
3,445 printed maps
458 manuscript maps
20 wall maps
21 raised relief maps
1,988 aerial photos
98 gazetteers
246 printed atlases
35 CD-ROMs
Chronological coverage:
    1940–present: 97%
Average budget over the last 5 years: $3,400
Access:
Collection is open to the public
Answers email questions
Hours:
    Monday–Friday: 9:30 A.M.–9 P.M.
    Saturday: 9:30 A.M.–5:30 P.M.
    Sunday: 1:30 P.M.–5:30 P.M.
    Total hours per week opened: 58
Geographic Information Systems:
No GIS services available
Number of public GIS workstations: 133
Collection services:
Classification schemes: SuDocs, Dewey, Local
Cataloging utilities: OCLC, Local
Catalog accessibility: online
Preservation techniques: encapsulation
Physical facilities:
Internet access available
Number of public computers: 133
Number of vertical map cases: 10
Copying facilities available: copier, large-format copier, microform copier

21 *Phoenix, AZ*

Arizona Department Mines and Mineral Resources

Arizona Mines and Mineral Resource Library
1502 West Washington
Phoenix, AZ 85007
Telephone: 602-255-3795
Fax: 602-255-3777
Web: www.admmr.state.az.us
Personnel:
Responsible person: Nyal Niemuth, *email:* njn22r@hotmail.com
Assistants: Diane Bain
Holdings:
Geographic strengths: Arizona
Special collections: US Department of Energy "NURE" maps, Arizona mine, surface and underground, geology, claim, and land status maps of Arizona,

10,000 printed maps
100 aerial photos
100 CD-ROMs
Access:
Hours:
    Monday–Friday: 8 A.M.–5 P.M.
Collection Services:
Maps cataloged: 75%
Maps classified: 50%
Maps in OPAC: 5%
Classification schemes: Other (subject, place)
Physical facilities:
Maps in separate area
Public computers: 1
Map cases: 10
Vertical files: 25

22 *Phoenix, AZ*

Arizona State Library, Archives and Public Records

Arizona State Library Law and Research Division
Map Collection, founded 1983
1700 West Washington
Phoenix, AZ 85007
Telephone: 602-542-4343
Fax: 602-542-4400
Email: research@lib.az.us
Web: www.lib.az.us
Personnel:
Responsible person: Julie Hoff, Map Librarian, *email:* jhoff@lib.az.us
Holdings:
Geographic strengths: Arizona, Southwest
Special collections: Arizona Sanborn Fire Insurance maps, ADOT County atlas series (1937–1993), Arizona Forest atlases, Salt River Project Irrigation atlases, Maricopa County Land Ownership atlases (1903–1929), Maricopa County plat maps (1889–1958), FEMA maps for Arizona (1985–present)
Subject strengths: aeronautical, agriculture, early cartography, city, engineering, forestry, geology, geospatial data, historical geography, hydrology, land ownership, land use, mineral resources, nautical charts, political geography, population, railroads, raised relief models, roads, soil
Map depositories and percentages: USGS topos (100%), USGS geology maps (100%), USGS other (100%), Department of Transportation, NOAA, GPO, CIA, National Forest Service, NIMA topos, NIMA nautical, NIMA aeronautical, BLM, State
86,000 printed maps
100 manuscript maps
95 wall maps
54 raised relief maps
2,460 microfiche

16 microfilms
3,378 aerial photos
563 gazetteers
559 printed atlases
180 books
750 CD-ROMs
Collecting digital data
Chronological coverage:
    1940–present: 95%
Average budget over the last 5 years: $500

Access:

Maps in separate area
Collection is open to the public
Reference questions per year: 900
Answers email questions
Patrons per month: 45

Hours:

Monday–Friday: 8 A.M.–5 P.M.
Total hours per week opened: 40

Geographic Information Systems:

GIS services available by appointment
GIS software: ArcView
GIS assistance available for Census mapping
Scans maps for patrons

Collection services:

Maps cataloged: 16%
Maps classified: 100%
Maps in OPAC: 16%
Classification schemes: LC, SuDocs
Cataloging utilities: OCLC
Catalog accessibility: online
Preservation techniques: encapsulation
Percent of items that have gone through the preservation process: 2%

Physical facilities:

Internet access available
Square footage: 3,200
Number of map cases: 28
Number of vertical map cases: 17
Linear book shelving: 147 ft.
Linear atlas shelving: 222 ft.
Other map storage: 1 rolled map case
Copying facilities available: copier, microform copier

23 *Phoenix, AZ*

Maricopa County Assessor's Office

Parcel Maps
Founded 1955
301 West Jefferson Street Ste 330
Phoenix, AZ 85003
Telephone: 602-372-1627
Fax: 602-506-3394
Email: rheisin@mail.maricopa.gov
Web: www.maricopa.gov/assessor/gis

Personnel:

Responsible person email: rheisin@mail.maricopa.gov

Holdings:

Subject strengths: aerial photos, modern cartography, city, geospatial data, land ownership, land use, political geography, projections, railroads, recreation, roads
Collecting digital data
Chronological coverage:
    1940–present: 100%

Notes: Office has 2,500 CAD files of 1.4 million parcels in county. Maps are printed on demand. No papaer copies are held.

24 *Phoenix, AZ*

Phoenix Public Library

Burton Barr Central Library
Founded 1934
1221 North Central Avenue
Phoenix, AZ 85004
Telephone: 602-262-4636
Fax: 602-261-8751
Email: theresa.peterson@phxlib.org
Web: www.phxlib.org

Personnel:

Responsible person: Theresa Peterson, Map Librarian, *email:* theresa.peterson@phxlib.org

Holdings:

Geographic strengths: Arizona
Special collections: Sanborn Fire Insurance maps, Arizona Collection
Subject strengths: aerial photos, archaeology, early cartography, modern cartography, city, geology, historical geography, hydrology, land ownership, land use, map catalogs, military, mineral resources, mining, political geography, railroads, raised relief models, recreation, roads, soil, travel books, views, waterways
Map depositories:: USGS topos, GPO, CIA, National Forest Service, BLM
50 gazetteers
250 printed atlases
100 books
Chronological coverage:
    1940–present: 100%
Average budget over the last 5 years: $2,000

Access:

Collection is open to the public
Reference questions per year: 950
Answers email questions
Patrons per month: 300

Hours:

Monday–Friday: 10 A.M.–9 P.M.
Friday: 10 A.M.–9 P.M.

Saturday–Sunday: 10 A.M.–6 P.M.
Total hours per week opened: 66

Geographic Information Systems:

Number of public GIS workstations: 25

Collection services:

Maps cataloged: 75%

Maps classified: 75%

Maps in OPAC: 75%

Classification schemes: LC, SuDocs, Dewey, Local

Cataloging utilities: OCLC

Catalog accessibility: online

Preservation techniques: encapsulation, lamination, edging

Percent of items that have gone through the preservation process: 15%

Physical facilities:

No Internet access

Square footage: 900

Number of map cases: 10

Linear book shelving: 75 ft.

Linear atlas shelving: 100 ft.

Copying facilities available: copier, color copier

---

25 *Prescott, AZ*

Sharlot Hall Museum

Archives
415 West Gurley Street
Prescott, AZ 86301
Telephone: 928-445-3122
Fax: 928-776-9053
Web: www.sharlot.org/archives

Personnel:

Responsible person: Susan Alden, Archivist, *email:* susan@sharlot.org

FTE professionals: 0.1   *FTE para-professionals:* 0.1

Holdings:

Geographic strengths: Yavapai County, Arizona

Special collections: Waara Collection, William Collection

4,000 printed maps

100 aerial photos

20 atlases

Maps cataloged: 80%

Maps classified: 80%

Maps in OPAC: 10%

Classification schemes: LC

Access:

Hours:

Tuesday–Friday: noon–4 P.M.

Saturday: 10 A.M.–2 P.M.

Physical facilities:

Maps in separate area

Public computers: 1

Map cases: 3

Notes: We have a graphical maps database at www.sharlot.org/archives/map

---

26 *Prescott, AZ*

Yavapai College

Library
1100 East Sheldon Street
Prescott, AZ 86301
Telephone: 928-776-2261
Fax: 928-776-2275
Email: Library_Reference_Desk@yc.edu
Web: www.yc.edu/library.nsf

Personnel:

Responsible person: Mollie Gugler, Senior Library Analyst, *email:* mollie_gugler@yc.edu

FTE para-professionals: 0.25

Holdings:

Geographic strengths: Arizona

Subject strengths: forestry, geology, topographic

Map depositories: USGS topos, CIA

1,900 printed maps

Chronological coverage:

1940–present: 100%

Access:

Collection is open to the public

Reference questions per year: 25

Answers email questions

Hours:

Monday–Friday: 7 A.M.–9 P.M.

Saturday–Sunday: noon–4 P.M.

Total hours per week opened: 73

Geographic Information Systems:

No GIS services available

Collection services:

Maps cataloged: 15%

Maps classified: 100%

Maps in OPAC: 15%

Classification schemes: LC, SuDocs

Cataloging utilities: OCLC

Catalog accessibility: online

Preservation techniques: lamination

Physical facilities:

Internet access available

Number of public computers: 30

Copying facilities available: copier, microform copier

---

27 *Tempe, AZ*

Arizona State University

Hayden Library
Arizona Historical Foundation
P.O. Box 871006
Tempe, AZ 85287-1006
Telephone: 480-966-8331

Fax: 480-966-1077
Email: azhistoryinfo@arizonahistoricalfoundation
.org
Web: www.arizonahistoricalfoundation.org
Personnel:
Responsible person: Jack August, Director, *email:*
jack.august@asu.edu
Assistants: Cory Hatch, Interim Curator; Jared Jackson,
Library Specialist
FTE professionals: 2
Holdings:
Geographic strengths: Arizona, Southwest
600 printed maps
50 atlases
20 books
Access:
Hours:
Monday–Friday: 8 A.M.–5 P.M.
Collection Services:
Maps cataloged: 100%
Maps classified: 0%
Maps in OPAC: 100%
Classification schemes: LC, Dewey, Local
Physical facilities:
Maps in separate area
Public computers: 3
Vertical files: 20

28 *Tempe, AZ*

Arizona State University

Noble Science and Engineering Library
Map Collection, founded 1970
P.O. Box 871006
Tempe, AZ 85287-1006
Telephone: 480-965-3582
Fax: 480-965-0883
Email: Map-eref@asu.edu
Web: www.asu.edu/lib/hayden/govdocs/maps/
mapcoll.htm
Personnel:
Responsible person: Hillery Oberle, Maps Assistant
Archivist, *email:* hillery.oberle@asu.edu
Assistants: Frank Stieber, Library Specialist Senior;
Miriam Glanz, Library Specialist Senior
FTE professionals: 1   *FTE para-professionals:* 2
Number of student workers hours per week: 10
Holdings:
Geographic strengths: Phoenix Metropolitan region,
Arizona, Southwest, Mexico
Special collections: Sanborn Fire Insurance, historical
Arizona aerial photography
Subject strengths: aerial photos, geology
Map depositories and percentages: USGS topos
(100%), USGS geology maps (100%), USGS other

(100%), Department of Transportation, NOAA,
GPO, CIA, National Forest Service, NIMA nautical,
NIMA aeronautical, BLM, State
210,000 printed maps
3,340 manuscript maps
40 wall maps
250 raised relief maps
250 microfiche
30 microfilms
20,500 aerial photos
75 satellite images
350 gazetteers
2,000 printed atlases
3,350 manuscript atlases
500 books
12 inactive serials
500 CD-ROMs
Collecting digital data
Chronological coverage:
1900–1939: 12%
1940–present: 85%
Average budget over the last 5 years: $6,600
Access:
Collection is open to the public
Reference questions per year: 11,500
Answers email questions
Hours:
Monday–Thursday: 8 A.M.–8 P.M.
Friday: 8 A.M.–5 P.M.
Saturday–Saturday: closed
Total hours per week opened: 57
Maps circulate
Circulation policies apply
Map circulation duration: 2 weeks
Number of maps circulated annually: 6,000
Interlibrary loan available
Geographic Information Systems:
GIS services available by appointment
GIS software: ArcGIS, ArcView
GIS assistance available for Census mapping, and im-
age analysis
Collection services:
Maps cataloged: 10%
Maps classified: 98%
Maps in OPAC: 100%
Classification schemes: LC
Cataloging utilities: OCLC, Local
Catalog accessibility: online, online local database for
maps
Preservation techniques: encapsulation, deacidification
Physical facilities:
Internet access available
Square footage: 5,800
Number of map cases: 263
Number of vertical files (file cabinets): 10
Linear book shelving: 250 ft.

Linear atlas shelving: 250 ft.

Copying facilities available: copier, color copier, large-format copier, microform copier

Notes: Maps are LC classified but in a local online map index; all other materials, monographs, CD, etc. are in main catalog.

29 *Tucson, AZ*

Arizona Geological Survey

416 West Congress
Tucson, AZ 85701
Telephone: 520-770-3500
Fax: 520-770-3505
Email: tom.mcgarvin@azgs.az.gov
Web: www.azgs.az.gov
Personnel:
Responsible person: Tom McGarvin, Geologist, *email:* tom.mcgarvin@azgs.az.gov
Holdings:
Geographic strengths: Arizona
Map depositories: USGS topos, BLM
2,000 printed maps
Access:
Hours:
Monday–Friday: 8 A.M.–5 P.M.
Saturday–Sunday: closed
Collection Services:
Classification schemes: Other (alphabetical, numerical)
Physical facilities:
Vertical files: 10

30 *Tucson, AZ*

Arizona State Museum

Archives, founded 1964
University of Arizona
Tucson, AZ 85721-0026
Telephone: 520-621-2970
Fax: 520-621-2976
Email: ferg@email.arizona.edu
Web: www.statemuseum.arizona.edu/library
Personnel:
Responsible person: Alan Ferg, Archivist, *email:* ferg@email.arizona.edu
FTE professionals: 0.1
Holdings:
Geographic strengths: Arizona, New Mexico, Colorado, Sonora, Chihuahua, California
Subject strengths: aerial photos, archaeology, city, historical geography, land ownership, roads
Map depositories and percentages: USGS topos, Department of Transportation
6,000 printed maps

Chronological coverage:
1940–present: 90%
Access:
Collection is paged
Reference questions per year: 25
Answers email questions
Patrons per month: 50
Hours:
Monday–Friday: by appointment
Geographic Information Systems:
No GIS services available
Collection services:
Classification schemes: Local, Other (ASM site numbers)
Catalog accessibility: cards
Preservation techniques: storage in acid-free map folders.
Physical facilities:
No Internet access
Square footage: 150
Number of vertical map cases: 4
Copying facilities available: copier
Notes: Access to many of our maps may be refused unless researcher has legitimate need of information related to archaeological site locations, which is exempt from FOIA.

31 *Tucson, AZ*

Tucson—Pima Public Library

Joel D. Valdez Main Library
Reference Department
101 North Stone Avenue
Tucson, AZ 85701
Telephone: 520-791-4393
Web: www.tppl.org
Personnel:
Responsible person: Mary Ann O'Neil, *email:* moneil1@ci.tucson.az.us
FTE professionals: 1   *FTE para-professionals:* 1
Holdings:
Geographic strengths: Arizona
Special collections: Arizona Collection
Subject strengths: aerial photos, archaeology, biology, city, Arizona USGS maps
Map depositories:: USGS topos, GPO, State
1,100 printed maps
8 gazetteers
50 printed atlases
Access:
Collection is open to the public
Reference questions per year: 50
Answers email questions
Patrons per month: 5,000
Hours:
Monday–Wednesday: 9 A.M.–8 P.M.

Thursday: 9 A.M.–6 P.M.
Friday: 8 A.M.–6 P.M.
Saturday: 10 A.M.–5 P.M.
Sunday: 1 P.M.–5 P.M.
Total hours per week opened: 61

Geographic Information Systems:
GIS services available in an open environment
GIS software: Map Guide
Number of public GIS workstations: 7
Number of GIS stations (not monitored): 7

Collection services:
Maps cataloged: 5%
Maps classified: 5%
Maps in OPAC: 5%
Classification schemes: SuDocs, Dewey
Cataloging utilities: OCLC
Catalog accessibility: online
Preservation techniques: encapsulation, lamination
Percent of items that have gone through the preservation process: 80%

Physical facilities:
Internet access available
Square footage: 15,000
Number of public computers: 7
Number of public printers: 1
Number of map cases: 3
Number of atlas stands: 2
Number of microform readers: 8
Number of microform printers: 7
Copying facilities available: copier, color copier, microform copier

32 *Tucson, AZ*

University of Arizona

Library
Founded 1955
1510 East University
Tucson, AZ 85721
Telephone: 520-621-6441
Fax: 520-621-9733
Web: www.library.arizona.edu

Personnel:
Responsible person: Chris Kollen, *email:* kollenc@u.library.arizona.edu
Assistants: Wendy Begay
FTE professionals: 0.4
Number of student works: 90

Holdings:
Geographic strengths: Arizona, Southwest, Northwest Mexico, Sonoran Desert region
Special collections: Arizona Sanborn Fire Insurance maps, LANDSAT Satellite Imagery for 1975–1977, Frank Schilling military maps

Subject strengths: agriculture, early cartography, geology, historical geography, hydrology, mineral resources, political geography, population, roads, soil
Map depositories:: USGS topos, USGS geology maps, USGS other, Department of Transportation, NOAA, GPO, CIA, National Forest Service, NIMA topos, NIMA nautical, NIMA aeronautical, BLM, United Nations
238,525 printed maps
42 wall maps
176 raised relief maps
26,945 microfiche
20 microfilms
17,000 aerial photos
2,200 satellite images
20 globes
431 gazetteers
2,500 printed atlases
1,100 books
50 CD-ROMs
Collecting digital data
Chronological coverage:
1900–1939: 30%
1940–present: 68%
Average budget over the last 5 years: $16,000

Access:
Maps in separate area
Collection is partially open to the public
Answers email questions
Hours:
Monday–Friday: noon–9 P.M.
Saturday: 9 A.M.–9 P.M.
Sunday: 11 A.M.–midnight
Total hours per week opened: 142
Maps circulate
Map circulation duration: 3 weeks
Interlibrary loan available

Geographic Information Systems:
GIS services available in an open environment
GIS software: ArcView, ArcMap
Number of GIS stations (not monitored): 220
GIS assistance available for Census mapping, and geocoding
Plotter available

Collection services:
Maps cataloged: 90%
Maps classified: 10%
Maps in OPAC: 90%
Datasets are cataloged
Classification schemes: LC
Cataloging utilities: OCLC
Catalog accessibility: online

Physical facilities:
Internet access available
Square footage: 4,200

Number of map cases: 90
Linear book shelving: 105 ft.
Linear atlas shelving: 495 ft.
Other map storage: 5 rolled map cases
Number of microform printers: 10
Copying facilities available: copier, color copier, large-format copier, microform copier
Notes: We have not had a separate map collection since about 1993.

33 *Yuma, AZ*

Arizona Western College

Academic Library
P.O. Box 929
Yuma, AZ 85366
Telephone: 928-344-7777
Fax: 928-344-7751
Email: library@azwestern.edu
Web: www.azwestern.edu/library/
Personnel:
Responsible person: Camille O'Neill, Reference Librarian, *email:* camille.oneill@azwestern.edu
Assistants: Alan Schuck, Information Technology Librarian
FTE para-professionals: 0.5
Holdings:
Geographic strengths: Arizona
Subject strengths: Arizona topographical maps
Map depositories and percentages: USGS topos, CIA, NIMA topos
2,729 printed maps
10 gazetteers
238 printed atlases
25 CD-ROMs
Chronological coverage:
1900–1939: 10%
1940–present: 80%
Average budget over the last 5 years: $100
Access:
Collection is open to the public
Reference questions per year: 74
Answers email questions
Hours:
Total hours per week opened: 76
Maps circulate
Circulation policies apply
Map circulation duration: 3 weeks
Atlas circulation duration: 3 weeks
Book circulation duration: 3 weeks
Number of maps circulated annually: 20
Number of books circulated annually: 10
Interlibrary loan available
Geographic Information Systems:
Number of public GIS workstations: 19

Collection services:
Maps classified: 95%
Datasets are cataloged
Classification schemes: LC, SuDocs
Cataloging utilities: OCLC, Local
Catalog accessibility: online, cards
Physical facilities:
Internet access available
Number of public computers: 19
Number of staff computers: 23
Number of public printers: 10
Number of vertical files (file cabinets): 0.5
Linear book shelving: 15 ft.
Linear atlas shelving: 30 ft.
Copying facilities available: copier, color copier, microform copier

34 *Conway, AR*

University of Central Arkansas

Torreyson Library
Archives Map Collection
201 Donaghey
Conway, AR 72035
Telephone: 501-450-3418
Fax: 501-450-5208
Email: jimmyb@uca.edu
Web: www.uca.edu
Personnel:
Responsible person: Jimmy Bryant, *email:* jimmyb@uca.edu
Assistants: Betty Osborn
FTE professionals: 1   *FTE para-professionals:* 4
Holdings:
Geographic strengths: Arkansas
1,000 printed maps
20 aerial photos
15 atlases
20 books
Maps cataloged: 100%
Maps classified: 100%
Maps in OPAC: 0%
Classification schemes: Local
Access:
Hours:
Monday–Thursday: 8 A.M.–9 P.M.
Friday: 8 A.M.–5 P.M.
Saturday: 8:30 A.M.–noon
Sunday: closed
Physical facilities:
Maps in separate area
Public computers: 1
Map cases: 2
Notes: All of our maps are about the state of Arkansas between 1750 and 2000. Most of the maps are of the

entire state, however, some maps are of the individual counties

35 *Fayetteville, AR*

University of Arkansas

University Libraries
Government Documents/Map Collection
365 North Ozark Avenue
Fayetteville, AR 72701
Telephone: 479-575-5516
Fax: 479-575-6656
Web: libinfo.uark.edu/gis/

Personnel:
Responsible person: Janet B. Dixon, Geosciences Librarian, *email:* jbdixon@uark.edu
Assistants: Sarah Santos, Head, Government Documents
FTE professionals: 1
Number of student workers hours per week: 15

Holdings:
Geographic strengths: Arkansas
Special collections: Arkansas historical maps, Arkansas Sanborn Fire Insurance maps
Subject strengths: aeronautical, early cartography, geology
Map depositories and percentages: USGS topos (100%), USGS geology maps (100%), USGS other (100%), Department of Transportation, NOAA, GPO, CIA, National Forest Service, NIMA topos, NIMA nautical, NIMA aeronautical, BLM, State
120,000 printed maps
150 wall maps
2,300 microfiche
10 microfilms
6,000 aerial photos
500 gazetteers
150 printed atlases
1,520 books
31 active serials
45 inactive serials
450 CD-ROMs
Chronological coverage:
1940–present: 90%
Average budget over the last 5 years: $500
On-going publications: guides: *University of Arkansas Libraries—Arkansas Maps, U.S. Topographic Maps, Geologic Maps, World Maps*

Access:
Collection is partially open to the public
Reference questions per year: 200
Answers email questions
Patrons per month: 20
Hours:
Monday–Thursday: 7 A.M.–midnight

Friday: 7:30 A.M.–7 P.M.
Saturday: 9 A.M.–6 P.M.
Sunday: noon–midnight
Total hours per week opened: 88
Maps circulate
Circulation policies apply
Map circulation duration: 1 week
Atlas circulation duration: 1 week
Book circulation duration: 16 weeks
Number of maps circulated annually: 400
Number of books circulated annually: 360
Number of other items circulated annually: 50
Interlibrary loan available

Geographic Information Systems:
GIS services available by appointment
GIS software: ArcGIS
General GIS questions answered

Collection services:
Maps cataloged: 40%
Maps classified: 100%
Maps in OPAC: 40%
Classification schemes: LC, SuDocs, Dewey, Local
Cataloging utilities: OCLC, Local
Catalog accessibility: online, cards
Preservation techniques: mylar sleeves

Physical facilities:
Internet access available
Square footage: 1,800
Number of map cases: 60
Number of vertical files (file cabinets): 13
Linear book shelving: 45 ft.
Linear atlas shelving: 132 ft.
Other map storage: 1 rolled map case
Copying facilities available: copier, microform copier

36 *Little Rock, AR*

Arkansas Geological Commission

Geological Library
3815 West Roosevelt Road
Little Rock, AR 72204
Telephone: 501-296-1877
Fax: 501-663-7360
Email: agc@mail.state.ar.us
Web: www.state.ar.us/agc/agc.htm

Personnel:
Responsible person: Susan Young, Cartographer Supervisor, *email:* susan.young@mail.state.ar.us

Holdings:
Geographic strengths: Arkansas
Special collections: USGS topographic maps of Arkansas
Subject strengths: aerial photos, early cartography, modern cartography, geology, geospatial data, historical geography, hydrology, map catalogs, map collecting, mineral resources, mining, projections, roads, soil

Map depositories:: USGS topos, USGS other
Chronological coverage:
    1900–1939: 15%
    1940–present: 80%
Access:
Maps in separate area
Collection is partially open to the public
Answers email questions
Patrons per month: 15
Hours:
    Monday–Friday: 8 A.M.–4:30 P.M.
    Total hours per week opened: 40
Interlibrary loan available
Geographic Information Systems:
GIS services available in an open environment
GIS assistance available for image analysis
Scans maps for patrons
Collection services:
Preservation techniques: encapsulation, lamination, edging
Percent of items that have gone through the preservation process: 25%
Physical facilities:
No Internet access
Number of vertical files (file cabinets): 20
Copying facilities available: copier
Notes: This is a technical library used by staff geologists and other patrons interested in Arkansas geology and earth science issues. We do allow patrons to use our library with staff assistance.

37 *Little Rock, AR*

Arkansas State Library

Document Services
One Capitol Mall
Little Rock, AR 72201
Telephone: 501-682-2869
Fax: 501-681-1532
Web:www.asl.lib.ar.us
Personnel:
Responsible person: Mary Brewer, *email:* mbrewer@asl.li.ar.us
Holdings:
Map depositories: USGS topos, Department of Transportation, NOAA, CIA, National Forest Service, NGA nautical, NGA aeronautical, BLM
60,000 printed maps
Access:
Hours:
    Monday–Friday: 8 A.M.–5 P.M.
    Saturday–Sunday: closed
Collection Services:
Maps cataloged: 100%
Maps classified: 100%

Maps in OPAC: 100%
Classification schemes: SuDocs, Local
Physical facilities:
Public computers: 5
Map cases: 43
Notes: We do not maintain a separate map collection. All maps received are through the Federal Depository Library Program and are housed in the federal documents collection. We have no staff allocated to the a map collection.

38 *Little Rock, AR*

Central Arkansas Library System

Main Library
Reference Services
100 Rock Street
Little Rock, AR 72201
Telephone: 501-918-3000
Fax: 501-376-1830
Email: sarahz@cals.lib.ar.us
Web: www.cals.lib.ar.us
Personnel:
Responsible person: Sarah Ziegenbein, *email:* sarahz@cals.lib.ar.us
FTE professionals: 1   *FTE para-professionals:* 0.25
Holdings:
Geographic strengths: Arkansas
Special collections: Arkansas topos
Map depositories:: USGS topos, CIA, National Forest Service
800 printed maps
1 globe
25 atlases
Access:
Hours:
    Monday–Thursday: 9 A.M.–8 P.M.
    Friday–Saturday: 9 A.M.–6 P.M.
    Sunday: 1 P.M.–5 P.M.
Collection services:
Maps cataloged: 100%
Maps classified: 100%
Maps in OPAC: 0%
Classification schemes: Local
Physical facilities:
Public computers: 16
Map cases: 2
Vertical files: 4

39 *Little Rock, AR*

University of Arkansas, Little Rock

Ottenhimer Library
2801 South University Avenue
Little Rock, AR 72204

Telephone: 501-569-8806
Fax: 501-569-3017
Web: library1.ualr.edu
Personnel:
Responsible person: email: kmruss@uar.edu
Assistants: Linda Pine, Archivist
FTE professionals: 0.5   *FTE para-professionals:* 0.5
Holdings:
Geographic strengths: Arkansas
Special collections: Arkansas topos
Map depositories: USGS topos, CIA
1,500 printed maps
4 globes
39 atlases
108 books
7 active serials
3 CD-ROMs
Collection Services:
Maps cataloged: 50%
Maps classified: 100%
Maps in OPAC: 50%
Classification schemes: LC, SuDocs, Local
Access:
Hours:
Monday–Friday: 8 A.M.–9 P.M.
Saturday: 8 A.M.–5 P.M.
Sunday: 1 P.M.–9 P.M.
Physical facilities:
Public computers: 42
Map cases: 10
Vertical files: 1

40 *Russellville, AR*

Arkansas Tech University

Pendergraft Library and Technology Center
305 West Q Street
Russellville, AR 72801
Telephone: 479-968-0289
Fax: 479-964-0559
Email: frances.hager@mail.atu.edu
Web: library.atu.edu
Personnel:
Responsible person: Frances Hager, Acquisitions Librarian, *email:* frances.hager@mail.atu.edu
FTE professionals: 0.05   *FTE para-professionals:* 0.1
Holdings:
Geographic strengths: Arkansas
Special collections: Arkansas, FEMA maps of Arkansas
Map depositories: USGS
224 printed maps
2 globes
43 atlases

55 books
1 active serial
2 CD-ROMs
Maps cataloged: 75%
Maps classified: 100%
Maps in OPAC: 75%
Classification schemes: SuDocs, Dewey
Access:
Hours:
Monday–Thursday: 7:30 A.M.–11 P.M.
Friday: 7:30 A.M.–6 P.M.
Saturday: 10 A.M.–6 P.M.
Sunday: 2 P.M.–11 P.M.
Interlibrary loan available
Physical facilities:
Public computers: 250
Map cases: 3
Vertical files: 3
Notes: We have only recently started collection maps, so our collection is small.

41 *Arcata, CA*

Humboldt State University

University Library
1 Harpst Street
Arcata, CA 95521
Telephone: 707-442-3418
Fax: 707-442-4900
Web: library.humboldt.edu/infoservices/atmapcoll.htm
Personnel:
Responsible person: Robert Sathrum, Natural Resources Librarian, *email:* rls2@humboldt.edu
FTE professionals: 0.1
Holdings:
Geographic strengths: Northwest California
Special collections: Timber maps (Lumber industry: Hammond/Vance/Georgia Pacific/Louisiana Pacific)
Subject strengths: forestry, historical geography, soil, vegetation
Map depositories and percentages: USGS topos (10%), USGS geology maps (100%), USGS other (75%), Department of Transportation, NOAA, GPO, CIA, National Forest Service, NIMA topos, NIMA aeronautical, BLM
27,363 printed maps
750 manuscript maps
12 wall maps
15 raised relief maps
25 microfilms
5,000 aerial photos
625 printed atlases
15 CD-ROMs
Collecting digital data

Chronological coverage:
    1940–present: 90%
Average budget over the last 5 years: $600
Access:
Collection is open to the public
Answers email questions
Hours:
    Monday–Friday: 7:30 A.M.–11 P.M.
    Saturday: 11 A.M.–5 P.M.
    Sunday: 11 A.M.–10 P.M.
    Total hours per week opened: 94
Maps circulate
Circulation policies apply
    Map circulation duration: 3 weeks
    Number of maps circulated annually: 90
Interlibrary loan available
Geographic Information Systems:
GIS services available in an open environment
GIS software: ArcView
Number of public GIS workstations: 2
GIS assistance available for Census mapping, and geocoding
Scans maps for patrons
Collection services:
Maps cataloged: 50%
Maps classified: 50%
Maps in OPAC: 100%
Datasets are cataloged
Classification schemes: LC
Cataloging utilities: OCLC
Catalog accessibility: online
Preservation techniques: encapsulation, cartex, lamination
Physical facilities:
Internet access available
Square footage: 1,000
Number of map cases: 34
Linear book shelving: 30 ft.
Linear atlas shelving: 109 ft.
Copying facilities available: copier, microform copier

42 *Bakersfield, CA*

Kern County Library

Beale Memorial Library
Geology—Mining—Petroleum Room
701 Truxtun Avenue
Bakersfield, CA 93301
Telephone: 661-868-0783
Web: www.kerncountylibrary.org
Personnel:
Responsible person: Katherine Bradley, Reference Librarian, *email:* katherine.bradley@kerncounty library.org

Number of volunteer hours per month: 12
Holdings:
Geographic strengths: California
Special collections: Alquist-Priolo/fault maps
Subject strengths: city, geology, topographic maps
Map depositories and percentages: USGS topos (15%)
2,100 printed maps
10 wall maps
100 books
Chronological coverage:
    1940–present: 99%
Access:
Maps in separate area
Collection is partially open to the public
Reference questions per year: 52
Patrons per month: 100
Hours:
    Total hours per week opened: 58
Geographic Information Systems:
No GIS services available
Collection services:
Maps classified: 0.5%
Classification schemes: Local
Catalog accessibility: cards
Physical facilities:
No Internet access
Square footage: 200
Linear book shelving: 20 ft.
Copying facilities available: copier, color copier, microform copier

43 *Berkeley, CA*

Berkeley Public Library

2090 Kittredge Street
Berkeley, CA 94704
Telephone: 510-981-6148
Fax: 510-981-6246
Web: www.berkeleypubliclibrary.org
Personnel:
Responsible person: Robert Saunderson, *email:* bos2@ ci.berkeley.ca.us
FTE professionals: 0.25
Holdings:
Special collections: Berkeley historical maps
Subject strengths: city, mining, political geography, roads, travel books
2,000 printed maps
25 gazetteers
50 printed atlases
Chronological coverage:
    1940–present: 97%
Access:
Collection is partially open to the public

Reference questions per year: 300

Hours:

Monday–Friday: 9am–10 P.M.

Saturday: 10 A.M.–6 P.M.

Sunday: 1 P.M.–5 P.M.

Total hours per week opened: 64

Geographic Information Systems:

Number of public GIS workstations: 20

Collection services:

Maps cataloged: 10%

Maps in OPAC: 10%

Classification schemes: Dewey

Cataloging utilities: OCLC

Catalog accessibility: online

Preservation techniques: deacidification

Physical facilities:

Internet access available

Copying facilities available: copier, microform copier

44 *Berkeley, CA*

University of California, Berkeley

Bancroft Library

Map Collection

Berkeley, CA 94720

Telephone: 510-642-6481

Fax: 510-642-7589

Personnel:

Responsible person: Susan Snyder, Head of Public Services, *email:* ssnyder@library.berkeley.edu

Assistants: Theresa Salazar, Curator of Western Americana; Anthony Bliss, Curator of Rare Books; David Farrell, Acting University Archivist; Randal Brandt, Head of Cataloging

FTE professionals: 0.25   *FTE para-professionals:* 0.3

Holdings:

Geographic strengths: California, West, Mexico, Europe

Special collections: Sanborn Insurance maps, Carl Wheat Map Collection, Land Case maps, C. H. Merriam Map Collection, Emil Bronimann Map Collection, Alfred H. de Vries Atlas and Map Collection, University Archives maps

Subject strengths: early cartography, city, historical geography, land ownership, land use, language, map catalogs, mining, nautical charts, railroads, travel books, views, waterways, University of California related maps

14,100 printed maps

2,825 manuscript maps

520 wall maps

250 printed atlases

Chronological coverage:

1800–1899: 55%

1900–1939: 30%

1940–present: 10%

On-going publications: Integrated into list of *Bancroft Library's New Acquisition Lists*

Access:

Maps in separate area

Collection is paged

Reference questions per year: 35

Answers email questions

Patrons per month: 65

Hours:

Monday–Friday: 9 A.M.–5 P.M.

Saturday: 1 P.M.–5 P.M.

Total hours per week opened: 44

Geographic Information Systems:

No GIS services available

Scans maps for patrons

Collection services:

Maps cataloged: 98%

Maps classified: 98%

Maps in OPAC: 98%

Classification schemes: LC, Local

Cataloging utilities: OCLC, Local

Catalog accessibility: online

Preservation techniques: encapsulation, deacidification, mending

Percent of items that have gone through the preservation process: 15%

Physical facilities:

Internet access available

Square footage: 545

Number of map cases: 52

Linear book shelving: 59 ft.

Other map storage: rolled map cases

Copying facilities available: outside vendor provides copying services

Notes: The map collection in integrated into the Bancroft Library's subject collections. There is no dedicated staff for the collection.

45 *Berkeley, CA*

University of California, Berkeley

Department of Geography

Map Collection

507 McCone Hall #4740

Berkeley, CA 94720

Telephone: 510-642-4368

Fax: 510-642-3370

Email: dplum@socrates.berkeley.edu

Web: geography.berkeley.edu

Personnel:

Responsible person: Daniel Plumlee, Equipment/Collections Manager, *email:* dplum@socrates.berkeley.edu

Holdings:

Geographic strengths: West, World

Subject strengths: agriculture, early cartography, modern cartography, climatology, city, economic geography, forestry, geodetic surveys, geology, historical geography, hydrology, industries, land use, language, military, mineral resources, mining, nautical charts, oceanography, political geography, population, projections, railroads, raised relief models, religion, roads, satellite imagery, soil, vegetation, views, waterways

1,600 printed maps
715 wall maps
30 raised relief maps
10 satellite images
25 printed atlases
Chronological coverage:
  1900–1939: 20%
  1940–present: 75%
Average budget over the last 5 years: $2,000
On-going publications: Departmental Web Site: geography.berkeley.edu

Access:
  Maps in separate area
  Reference questions per year: 100
  Answers email questions
  Patrons per month: 10
Hours:
  Monday–Friday: 9 A.M.–6 P.M.
  Total hours per week opened: 44
Geographic Information Systems:
  No GIS services available
Collection services:
  Maps cataloged: 80%
  Datasets are cataloged
  Classification schemes: Local
  Cataloging utilities: Local
  Catalog accessibility: online, printout
Physical facilities:
  No Internet access
  Square footage: 300
  Number of map cases: 13
  Copying facilities available: copier
Notes: The departmental map collection focuses on wall maps for instructional use throughout the university. We have a collection of topographic maps and general purpose flat maps to aid in teaching and student research.

46 *Berkeley, CA*

University of California, Berkeley

Earth Sciences and Map Library
50 McCone Hall
Berkeley, CA 94720-6000
Telephone: 510-642-2997
Fax: 510-643-6576

Email: eartmaps@library.berkeley.edu
Web: www.lib.berkeley.edu/EART/
Personnel:
  Responsible person: John A. Creaser, Information/Map Specialist, *email:* jcreaser@library.berkeley.edu
  Assistants: Fatemah Van Buren, Acting Head, Map Cataloger
  Number of student works: 9
  Number of student workers hours per week: 30
Holdings:
  Geographic strengths: San Francisco Bay region, California, United States
  Special collections: California aerial photography, California Sanborn Fire Insurance maps, German and Japanese captured maps
  Subject strengths: aerial photos, aeronautical, early cartography, modern cartography, city, forestry, geology, geospatial data, historical geography, hydrology, land ownership, land use, map catalogs, map collecting, mineral resources, nautical charts, oceanography, political geography, population, projections, railroads, roads, views, waterways
  Map depositories and percentages: USGS topos (100%), USGS geology maps (100%), USGS other (100%), Department of Transportation, NOAA, GPO, CIA, National Forest Service, NIMA topos, NIMA nautical, NIMA aeronautical, BLM, State, California Geological Survey
  376,852 printed maps
  50 wall maps
  200 raised relief maps
  84,103 total microfiche
  500 microfilms
  69,328 aerial photos
  200 satellite images
  900 gazetteers
  6,900 printed atlases
  1,766 CD-ROMs
  50 computer programs
  Collecting digital data
  Chronological coverage:
    1900–1939: 48%
    1940–present: 48%
  Average budget over the last 5 years: $40,570
Access:
  Maps in separate area
  Collection is open to the public
  Maps off site: 11%
  Reference questions per year: 3,000
  Answers email questions
  Patrons per month: 8,757
Hours:
  Total hours per week opened: 60
  Maps circulate
  Circulation policies apply
    Map circulation duration: 7 days

Atlas circulation duration: 1 day
Book circulation duration: 30 days
Interlibrary loan available

Geographic Information Systems:

GIS services available in an open environment
GIS software: ArcView
Number of public GIS workstations: 11
GIS assistance available for Census mapping, and image analysis
Scans maps for patrons

Collection services:

Maps cataloged: 100%
Maps classified: 100%
Maps in OPAC: 100%
Datasets are cataloged
Classification schemes: LC
Cataloging utilities: OCLC, Local
Catalog accessibility: online
Preservation techniques: encapsulation, older maps on linen

Physical facilities:

Internet access available
Square footage: 5,400
Number of public computers: 12
Number of staff computers: 11
Number of map cases: 305
Number of vertical files (file cabinets): 34
Linear book shelving: 9,228 ft.
Linear atlas shelving: 254 ft.
Other map storage: rolled map cases, microfiche/film cabinet, cd-rom/dvd cabinet
Copying facilities available: copier, microform copier, networked printers

47 *Berkeley, CA*

University of California, Berkeley

Water Resources Center Archives
Founded 1957
410 O'Brien Hall
Berkeley, CA 94720-1718
Telephone: 510-642-2666
Fax: 510-642-9143
Email: waterarc@library.berkeley.edu
Web: www.lib.berkeley.edu/WRCA/

Personnel:

Responsible person: Linda Vida, Director, *email:* lvida@library.berkeley.edu
Assistants: Paul Atwood, Assistant Librarian
FTE professionals: 0.25   *FTE para-professionals:* 0.25
Number of student works: 0.5
Number of student workers hours per week: 18

Holdings:

Geographic strengths: California, West

Special collections: William Hammond Hall maps
Subject strengths: aerial photos, agriculture, climatology, engineering, forestry, hydrology, land ownership, land use, map catalogs, military, mining, nautical charts, soil, waterways
Map depositories and percentages: USGS topos, NOAA, State
2,500 printed maps
2,500 manuscript maps
10 wall maps
25,000 aerial photos
10 gazetteers
20 printed atlases
125,000 books
500 active serials
1,500 inactive serials
100 CD-ROMs
25 computer programs
Chronological coverage:
   1800–1899: 10%
   1900–1939: 55%
   1940–present: 35%
Average budget over the last 5 years: $500
On-going publications: Bi-monthly acquisition lists & newsletter, published three times a year.

Access:

Maps in separate area
Collection is paged
Reference questions per year: 750
Answers email questions
Patrons per month: 600

Hours:

   Monday–Friday: 9 A.M.–5 P.M.
   Saturday–Saturday: closed
   Total hours per week opened: 40
Circulation policies apply
   Map circulation duration: 1 day
   Atlas circulation duration: 1 day
   Book circulation duration: 30 days
   Number of maps circulated annually: 150
   Number of books circulated annually: 7,000
   Number of other items circulated annually: 200
Interlibrary loan available

Geographic Information Systems:

No GIS services available
Scans maps for patrons

Collection services:

Maps cataloged: 65%
Maps classified: 75%
Maps in OPAC: 65%
Datasets are cataloged
Classification schemes: Local
Cataloging utilities: OCLC, Local
Catalog accessibility: online
Preservation techniques: encapsulation, cartex

Percent of items that have gone through the preservation process: 5%

Physical facilities:
Internet access available
Square footage: 375
Linear book shelving: 6,000 ft.
Linear atlas shelving: 300 ft.
Copying facilities available: copier

Notes: The map collection is a part of the archives collection of reports, books and manuscript collections.

48 *Carlsbad, CA*

Nederlof Historical Library

Founded 1941
P.O.Box 130880
Carlsbad, CA 92013-0880
Telephone: 760-634-2960
Fax: 760-635-8641
Email: larryn@microseconds.com
Personnel:
Responsible person: J. Larry Nederlof, *email:* larryn@ microseconds.com
Holdings:
Geographic strengths: Netherlands, Belgium, Netherlands Colonies, Indonesia
Subject strengths: agriculture, early cartography, modern cartography, climatology, city, economic geography, forestry, genealogy, geology, historical geography, land use, language, map catalogs, map collecting, military, mining, nautical charts, political geography, population, railroads, religion, roads, satellite imagery, soil, travel books, vegetation, views, waterways, Dutch colonial history
1,100 printed maps
10 wall maps
50 printed atlases
400 books
Chronological coverage:
Pre-1800: 50%
1800–1899: 30%
1900–1939: 15%
On-going publications: website coming early 2004
Access:
Collection is paged
Reference questions per year: 100
Answers email questions
Patrons per month: 25
Geographic Information Systems:
No GIS services available
Scans maps for patrons
Collection services:
Maps cataloged: 100%
Maps classified: 100%

Classification schemes: Other
Catalog accessibility: printout
Preservation techniques: deacidification, lamination
Percent of items that have gone through the preservation process: 25%

Physical facilities:
No Internet access
Square footage: 1,000
Linear book shelving: 150 ft.
Linear atlas shelving: 100 ft.
Copying facilities available: copier, color copier, large-format copier, computerized micro-scanning

Notes: Our library is sponsored by MicroSeconds International, Inc., a Dutch/American software company

49 *Chico, CA*

California State University, Chico

Meriam Library
Maps founded 1962
400 West First Street
Chico, CA 95926
Telephone: 539-898-5710
Fax: 530-898-4443
Email: bjones2@csuchico.edu
Web: www.csuchico.edu/lbib/maps/maps_page1.html
Personnel:
Responsible person: William A. Jones, *email:* bjones2@ csuchico.edu
FTE professionals: 0.05   *FTE para-professionals:* 0.1
Number of student workers hours per week: 10
Holdings:
Geographic strengths: Northeast California
Special collections: historic maps of Butte, Plumas, Tehama, Shasta, Trinity, Glenn, Colusa, Sutter, Yuba, Siskiyou, Modoc, and Lassen counties.
Subject strengths: agriculture, hydrology, land ownership, soil, Northeastern California
Map depositories:: USGS topos, USGS geology maps, USGS other, CIA, National Forest Service
300,000 printed maps
100 aerial photos
5 globes
Chronological coverage:
1940–present: 70%
Average budget over the last 5 years: $750
Access:
Maps in separate area
Collection is open to the public
Answers email questions
Hours:
Total hours per week opened: 88
Geographic Information Systems:
No GIS services available

Number of public GIS workstations: 3
Scans maps for patrons
Collection services:
Maps cataloged: 10%
Maps classified: 10%
Maps in OPAC: 3%
Classification schemes: LC
Cataloging utilities: OCLC
Catalog accessibility: online, cards
Preservation techniques: encapsulation
Percent of items that have gone through the preservation process: 5%
Physical facilities:
No Internet access
Square footage: 2,000
Number of map cases: 56
Number of vertical files (file cabinets): 25
Copying facilities available: microform copier
Notes: Some maps from Special Collections are being scanned and placed on 2 web sites: California Historic Topography Map Collection (http://cricket.csuchico.edu/portfolio/topo_search.html) and Digital Geographic Data Collection (http://maps.csuchico.edu)

50 *Claremont, CA*

Claremont University Center, Claremont Colleges

Honnold/Mudd Library
800 North Dartmouth Ave
Claremont, CA 91711
Telephone: 909-621-8045
Fax: 909-621-8681
Web: libraries.claremont.edu/hm
Personnel:
Responsible person: Sheri Irvin, Government Publications Librarian; Carrie Marsh, Special Collections Librarian, *email:* sheri.irvin@libraries.claremont.edu,carrie.marsh@libraries.claremont.edu
FTE para-professionals: 2.5
Number of student works: 0.5
Holdings:
Geographic strengths: California, Southern California, Northwest coast of United States, contiguous States
Special collections: Wagner (Henry Raup) Collection
Subject strengths: agriculture, early cartography, celestial, engineering, forestry, geodetic surveys, geology, geospatial data, hydrology, military, waterways
Map depositories and percentages: USGS topos, USGS geology maps (50%), USGS other, GPO, CIA, National Forest Service, NIMA topos
12,000 printed maps
500 manuscript maps
20 gazetteers
55 printed atlases
1,000 CD-ROMs

4 computer programs
Chronological coverage:
Pre-1800: 10%
1900–1939: 20%
1940–present: 65%
Access:
Collection is partially open to the public
Maps off site: 25%
Reference questions per year: 100
Answers email questions
Hours:
Monday–Friday: 8 A.M.–8 P.M.
Saturday: 9 A.M.–8 P.M.
Sunday: 11 A.M.–midnight
Total hours per week opened: 84
Geographic Information Systems:
GIS services available by appointment
GIS software: ESRI
GIS assistance available for Census mapping
Plotter available
Collection services:
Maps cataloged: 10%
Maps classified: 95%
Maps in OPAC: 10%
Datasets are cataloged
Classification schemes: LC, SuDocs
Cataloging utilities: OCLC
Catalog accessibility: online
Preservation techniques: deacidification, lamination, encapsulation in mylar
Physical facilities:
No Internet access
Number of map cases: 15
Copying facilities available: copier, color copier, large-format copier, microform copier

51 *Davis, CA*

University of California, Davis

Peter J. Shields Library
Government Information and Maps, founded 1957
100 NW Quad
Davis, CA 95616
Telephone: 530-752-1689
Fax: 530-752-3148
Email: govdocref@ucdavis.edu
Web: www.lib.ucdavis.edu/govdoc/MapCollection/map_about.html
Personnel:
Responsible person: Kathleen Stroud, Map/GIS Librarian *email:* kpstroud@ucdavis.edu
Assistants: Pauline Roddan, Library Assistant III
Number of student workers hours per week: 24
Holdings:
Geographic strengths: Central Valley of California, Mediterranean

Special collections: Agri-land surveys for California, Sanborn Fire Insurance maps for the Central Valley of California

Subject strengths: aerial photos, agriculture, climatology, forestry, geology, land ownership, land use, nautical charts, soil, vegetation, viticulture, enology

Map depositories and percentages: USGS geology maps (25%), USGS other (100%), Department of Transportation, NOAA, GPO, CIA, NIMA nautical, NIMA aeronautical, BLM

130,000 printed maps
20 manuscript maps
511 wall maps
50 raised relief maps
42,000 microfiche
75,000 aerial photos
1,000 satellite images
300 gazetteers
650 printed atlases
500 books
90 CD-ROMs
Collecting digital data
Chronological coverage:
    1900–1939: 16%
    1940–present: 75%
Average budget over the last 5 years: $11,500

Access:
Maps in separate area
Collection is open to the public
Reference questions per year: 550
Answers email questions
Patrons per month: 150

Hours:
    Monday–Friday: 9 A.M.–5 P.M.
    Total hours per week opened: 40
Interlibrary loan available

Geographic Information Systems:
No GIS services available
Scans maps for patrons

Collection services:
Maps cataloged: 80%
Maps classified: 80%
Maps in OPAC: 80%
Datasets are cataloged
Classification schemes: LC
Cataloging utilities: OCLC
Catalog accessibility: online, cards
Preservation techniques: encapsulation, cartex
Percent of items that have gone through the preservation process: 10%

Physical facilities:
Internet access available
Square footage: 4,000
Number of map cases: 48
Number of vertical files (file cabinets): 17

Linear book shelving: 135 ft.
Linear atlas shelving: 125 ft.
Other map storage: 18 rolled map cases
Copying facilities available: copier, color copier, microform copier, scanner

52 *Fresno, CA*

California State University, Fresno

Henry Madden Library
Map Library, founded 1985
5200 West Barton Avenue
M/S ML34
Fresno, CA 93740-8014
Telephone: 559-278-2405
Fax: 559-278-6952
Web: www.lib.csufresno.edu/subjectresources/maps/

Personnel:
Responsible person: Carol Doyle, Head, Government Documents and Maps, *email:* carol_doyle@csufresno.edu
Assistants: Rebecca Reid–Johansson, Library Assistant
Number of student works: 1.8
Number of student workers hours per week: 73

Holdings:
Geographic strengths: California, Fresno County
Special collections: Fresno County aerial photos, California historical USGS topos
Subject strengths: aerial photos, aeronautical, geology, historical geography, nautical charts
Map depositories and percentages: USGS topos (40%), USGS geology maps, USGS other, Department of Transportation, NOAA, GPO, CIA, National Forest Service, NIMA topos, NIMA nautical, NIMA aeronautical

122,404 printed maps
46 raised relief maps
22,995 microfiche
58 microfilms
16,386 aerial photos
340 gazetteers
1,372 printed atlases
45 books
Average budget over the last 5 years: $4,500

Access:
Maps in separate area
Collection is partially open to the public
Reference questions per year: 2,045
Answers email questions
Patrons per month: 170

Hours:
    Monday–Tuesday: 8 A.M.–8 P.M.
    Wednesday–Friday: 8 A.M.–5 P.M.
    Saturday: closed

Sunday: 1 P.M.–5 P.M.
Total hours per week opened: 55
Maps circulate
Circulation policies apply
 Map circulation duration: 2 weeks
 Number of maps circulated annually: 750
 Number of other items circulated annually: 537
Interlibrary loan available

Geographic Information Systems:
No GIS services available

Collection services:
Maps cataloged: 95%
Maps classified: 95%
Maps in OPAC: 95%
Classification schemes: LC
Cataloging utilities: OCLC
Catalog accessibility: online
Preservation techniques: encapsulation

Physical facilities:
Internet access available
Square footage: 3,264
Number of map cases: 93
Number of vertical files (file cabinets): 28
Linear book shelving: 125 ft.
Linear atlas shelving: 245 ft.
Copying facilities available: copier, color copier, microform copier

53 *Irvine, CA*

University of California, Irvine

Langson Library
P.O. Box 19557
Irvine, CA 92623-9557
Telephone: 949-824-7290
Fax: 949-824-3644
Email: kcollins@lib.uci.edu
Web: www.lib.uci.edu/libraries/collections/gis.html
Assistants: Julia Gelfand; Yvonne Wilson; Kay Collins; Judy Ruttenberg
FTE professionals: 0.1   *FTE para-professionals:* 0.05

Holdings:
Geographic strengths: Orange County, California, and adjacent states
Special collections: Sanborn Fire maps on microfi'm, late 19th Century to 1990, Orange County California aerial surveys
Subject strengths: aerial photos, biology, modern cartography, climatology, economic geography, forestry, geology, geospatial data, land use, map catalogs, mineral resources, mining, oceanography, political geography, population, recreation, roads, satellite imagery, soil, travel books, vegetation, views, waterways, zoogeography

Map depositories:: USGS topos, GPO, CIA, National Forest Service, BLM, State, United Nations
1,100 printed maps
Chronological coverage:
 1940–present: 95%
Average budget over the last 5 years: $1,000

Access:
Collection is open to the public
Answers email questions

Hours:
Monday–Friday: 7:30 A.M.–11 P.M.
Saturday: 10 A.M.–9 P.M.
Sunday: 10 A.M.–11 P.M.
Total hours per week opened: 98.5

Geographic Information Systems:
GIS services available by appointment
GIS software: ArcGIS
Number of public GIS workstations: 81
GIS assistance available for Census mapping

Collection services:
Maps cataloged: 50%
Maps classified: 75%
Maps in OPAC: 50%
Datasets are cataloged
Classification schemes: LC, SuDocs, Local
Cataloging utilities: OCLC
Catalog accessibility: online, fiche, cards, printout
Preservation techniques: encapsulation
Percent of items that have gone through the preservation process: 10%

Physical facilities:
Internet access available
Linear book shelving: 420 ft.
Linear atlas shelving: 420 ft.
Copying facilities available: copier, color copier, large-format copier, microform copier, CD-ROMs and web copying available

54 *La Jolla, CA*

Scripps Institution of Oceanography

University of California, San Diego
Map and Chart Collection, founded 1948
8755 Biological Grade
La Jolla, CA 92093
Telephone: 858-534-1228
Fax: 858-534-5269
Email: pleverenz@ucsd.edu
Web: scilib.ucsd.edu/sio/guide/map.html

Personnel:
Responsible person: Paul Leverenz, *email:* pleverenz@ UCSD.EDU

Holdings:
Geographic strengths: North America, Pacific Rim, oceans

Special collections: British Admiralty nautical charts, France Service Hydrographique nautical charts, older generation U.S. Hydrographic Office and Coast and Geodetic Survey bathymetric charts

Subject strengths: aeronautical, geodetic surveys, geology, hydrology, land use, mineral resources, nautical charts, oceanography, waterways

Map depositories and percentages: USGS topos, USGS geology maps, USGS other, NOAA, NIMA nautical, NIMA aeronautical

81,646 printed maps

Chronological coverage:
    1940–present: 90%

Access:

Maps in separate area

Collection is partially open to the public

Answers email questions

Hours:
    Monday–Friday: 8 A.M.–4 P.M.

Maps circulate

Interlibrary loan available

Geographic Information Systems:

No GIS services available

Physical facilities:

No Internet access

Square footage: 1,769

Number of map cases: 111

Number of vertical files (file cabinets): 24

Linear atlas shelving: 270 ft.

Copying facilities available: large-format copier

Notes: Our mailing address is different: 9500 Gilman Drive 0219, La Jolla, CA 92093

55 *La Jolla, CA*

University of California, San Diego

Social Sciences and Humanities Library, founded 1970
9500 Gilman Drive 0175R
La Jolla, CA 92093
Telephone: 858-534-1248
Fax: 858-534-7548
Email: lcruse@ucsd.edu
Web: govinfo.ucsd.edu/maps/index.html

Personnel:

Responsible person: Larry Cruse, Map Bibliographer, *email:* lcruse@ucsd.edu

Assistants: Ngan Le, Library Assistant

Number of student workers hours per week: 24

Holdings:

Subject strengths: aerial photos, aeronautical, agriculture, archaeology, biology, early cartography, modern cartography, caves, celestial, climatology, city, economic geography, engineering, forestry, genealogy, geodetic surveys, geology, geospatial data, historical geography, hydrology, industries, land ownership, land use, language, map catalogs, map collecting, military, mineral resources, mining, nautical charts, oceanography, political geography, population, projections, railroads, raised relief models, recreation, religion, roads, satellite imagery, soil, travel books, vegetation, views, waterways, zoogeography

Map depositories and percentages: USGS topos (10%), GPO, CIA, National Forest Service, NIMA topos, NIMA aeronautical, BLM, State, Auto Club

100,000 printed maps

100 wall maps

1,000 raised relief maps

10,000 microfiche

1,000 microfilms

10,000 aerial photos

100 satellite images

1,000 gazetteers

1,000 printed atlases

2,000 books

200 active serials

100 inactive serials

1,000 CD-ROMs

100 computer programs

Collecting digital data

Chronological coverage:
    Pre-1800: 25%
    1800–1899: 25%
    1900–1939: 25%
    1940–present: 25%

Average budget over the last 5 years: $10,000

Access:

Maps in separate area

Collection is open to the public

Maps off site: 50%

Reference questions per year: 300

Answers email questions

Patrons per month: 300

Hours:
    Monday–Friday: 8 A.M.–midnight
    Saturday: 10 A.M.–6 P.M.
    Sunday: 10 A.M.–midnight
    Total hours per week opened: 102

Maps circulate

Circulation policies apply
    Map circulation duration: 30 days
    Atlas circulation duration: 30 days
    Book circulation duration: 30 days
    Number of maps circulated annually: 300
    Number of books circulated annually: 3,000

Interlibrary loan available

Geographic Information Systems:

GIS services available by appointment

GIS software: ESRI

Number of GIS stations (monitored): 10

GIS assistance available for Census mapping, geocoding, and image analysis

Plotter available
Scans maps for patrons

Collection services:
Maps cataloged: 100%
Maps classified: 100%
Maps in OPAC: 100%
Datasets are cataloged
Classification schemes: LC, SuDocs
Cataloging utilities: OCLC
Catalog accessibility: online
Preservation techniques: encapsulation, deacidification
Percent of items that have gone through the preservation process: 10%

Physical facilities:
Internet access available
Square footage: 3,000
Number of map cases: 24
Linear book shelving: 400 ft.
Linear atlas shelving: 240 ft.
Copying facilities available: copier, color copier, large-format copier, microform copier, microform scanner

56 *Los Angeles, CA*

Los Angeles Public Library

Richard J. Riordan Central Library
History and Genealogy Department, founded 1945
630 West 5th Street
Los Angeles, CA 90065
Telephone: 213-228-7414
Fax: 213-228-7409
Email: gcreaso@lapl.org
Web: www.lapl.org/guides/map_coll.html

Personnel:
Responsible person: Glen Creason, Map Librarian, email: gcreaso@lapl.org
Number of volunteer hours per month: 20

Holdings:
Geographic strengths: Los Angeles, Southern California, California, West
Special collections: Sanborn Fire Insurance atlases for the state of California (Library of Congress microfilm collection), Historic street guides of Los Angeles, Obsolete USGS topos of California
Subject strengths: aeronautical, early cartography, modern cartography, city, genealogy, historical geography, map catalogs, map collecting, military, nautical charts, projections, raised relief models, roads, travel books, views, pictorial maps
Map depositories and percentages: USGS topos (100%), USGS other (100%), Department of Transportation, NOAA, GPO, CIA, National Forest Service, NIMA topos, NIMA nautical, NIMA aeronautical, BLM, State
80,000 printed maps
100 wall maps

10 raised relief maps
5,000 microfiche
200 microfilms
600 aerial photos
1,000 gazetteers
2,000 printed atlases
5,000 books
10 active serials
50 CD-ROMs
Chronological coverage:
1800–1899: 10%
1900–1939: 50%
1940–present: 38%
Average budget over the last 5 years: $25,000

Access:
Collection is open to the public
Reference questions per year: 2,500
Answers email questions
Patrons per month: 250

Hours:
Monday–Friday: 10 A.M.–8 P.M.
Saturday: 10 A.M.–6 P.M.
Sunday: 1 P.M.–5 P.M.
Total hours per week opened: 61
Maps circulate
Circulation policies apply
Atlas circulation duration: 3 weeks
Book circulation duration: 3 weeks
Interlibrary loan available

Geographic Information Systems:
No GIS services available

Collection services:
Maps cataloged: 10%
Maps in OPAC: 10%
Classification schemes: Dewey
Cataloging utilities: OCLC
Catalog accessibility: online
Preservation techniques: encapsulation

Physical facilities:
Internet access available
Number of public computers: 12
Number of map cases: 300
Number of vertical map cases: 10
Number of vertical files (file cabinets): 60
Number of microform readers: 20
Number of microform printers: 20
Copying facilities available: copier, color copier, microform copier

57 *Los Angeles, CA*

Loyola Marymount University

Charles Von der Ahe Library
Department of Archives and Special Collections
One LMU Drive
MS 8200

Los Angeles, CA 90045-2659
Telephone: 310-338-3048
Fax: 310-338-5895
Email: estevens@lmu.edu
Personnel:
Responsible person: Errol Stevens, *email:* estevens@lmu.edu
Holdings:
Geographic strengths: Southern California
Special collections: Surveys and tract maps of Southern California
Subject strengths: city, land use
500 printed maps
Chronological coverage:
    1800–1899: 50%
    1900–1939: 50%
Access:
Collection is paged
Answers email questions
Hours:
    Monday–Friday: 9 A.M.–4 P.M.
    Total hours per week opened: 35
Geographic Information Systems:
No GIS services available
Scans maps for patrons
Collection services:
Maps cataloged: 40%
Physical facilities:
No Internet access
Copying facilities available: copier
Notes: Ours is a late-nineteenth and early-twentieth century collection of survey maps and surveyors note books.

58 *Los Angeles, CA*

University of California, Los Angeles

Young Research Library
Henry J. Bruman Map Collection, founded 1961
Room A4510
P.O. Box 951575
Los Angeles, CA 90095-1575
Telephone: 310-825-1088
Fax: 310-825-6795
Email: yrl-ref@library.ucla.edu
Web: www.library.ucla.edu/libraries/yrl/referenc/rco/geographic.htm
Personnel:
Responsible person: David Deckelbaum, Cartographic Information Librarian, *email:* ddeckelb@library.ucla.edu
Number of student workers hours per week: 15
Holdings:
Geographic strengths: Los Angeles Metropolitan region, California, United States, Latin America, Pacific Rim, Near East
Special collections: Sanborn Fire Insurance maps

Subject strengths: aerial photos, aeronautical, archaeology, early cartography, modern cartography, celestial, climatology, city, economic geography, forestry, geospatial data, historical geography, hydrology, industries, land ownership, land use, language, map catalogs, map collecting, military, mineral resources, mining, nautical charts, oceanography, political geography, population, projections, railroads, raised relief models, recreation, religion, roads, soil, vegetation, views, waterways, zoogeography
Map depositories and percentages: USGS topos (100%), USGS other, Department of Transportation, NOAA, GPO, CIA, NIMA topos, NIMA nautical, NIMA aeronautical, BLM, United Nations
613,512 printed maps
Collecting digital data
Chronological coverage:
    1800–1899: 10%
    1900–1939: 10%
    1940–present: 75%
Average budget over the last 5 years: $40,000
Access:
Maps in separate area
Collection is partially open to the public
Maps off site: 50%
Answers email questions
Hours:
    Monday–Friday: 9 A.M.–5 P.M.
    Total hours per week opened: 40
Interlibrary loan available
Geographic Information Systems:
GIS services available in an open environment
GIS assistance available for Census mapping, and geocoding
Collection services:
Maps cataloged: 70%
Maps classified: 100%
Maps in OPAC: 70%
Classification schemes: LC, Other (local modification of LC)
Cataloging utilities: OCLC
Catalog accessibility: online
Preservation techniques: encapsulation
Physical facilities:
Internet access available
Number of map cases: 224
Other map storage: 1,954 vertical files
Copying facilities available: copier, color copier, large-format copier, microform copier

59 *Menlo Park, CA*

United States Geological Survey, Menlo Park

Library
Founded 1951
345 Middlefield Road

MS 955
Menlo Park, CA 94025
Telephone: 650-329-5027
Fax: 650-329-5132
Email: men_lib@usgs.gov
Web: library.usgs.gov
Personnel:
Responsible person: Emily Shen-Torbik, Head Librar-
ian, *email:* eshen-torbik@usgs.gov
FTE professionals: 0.25   *FTE para-professionals:* 0.25
Holdings:
Geographic strengths: United States, World
Special collections: Collection of data in California
water, climate, geology, soil, topo maps, and aerial
photos
Subject strengths: aerial photos, agriculture, biology,
modern cartography, caves, city, geodetic surveys,
geology, geospatial data, historical geography, hydrology, mineral resources, mining, nautical charts,
oceanography, railroads, raised relief models, recreation, soil, travel books, waterways
Map depositories and percentages: USGS topos
(90%), USGS geology maps (90%), USGS other
(90%), NOAA, GPO, CIA, NIMA nautical, BLM,
State
500 gazetteers
500 printed atlases
Chronological coverage:
1900–1939: 30%
1940–present: 68%
On-going publications: New acquisitions of all types of
material (provided by OCLC available from USGS
library website)
Access:
Collection is open to the public
Reference questions per year: 1,000
Answers email questions
Patrons per month: 250
Hours:
Monday–Friday: 8:30 A.M.–4:30 P.M.
Total hours per week opened: 40
Maps circulate
Circulation policies apply
Map circulation duration: 1 month
Atlas circulation duration: 1 month
Book circulation duration: 1 month
Number of maps circulated annually: 2,000
Interlibrary loan available
Geographic Information Systems:
No GIS services available
Collection services:
Maps cataloged: 80%
Maps classified: 80%
Maps in OPAC: 80%
Classification schemes: Local, Other (USGS)
Cataloging utilities: OCLC

Catalog accessibility: online, cards, printout
Preservation techniques: lamination
Physical facilities:
Internet access available
Number of map cases: 400
Copying facilities available: copier

60 *Mill Valley, CA*

Mill Valley Public Library

Lucretia Little History Room
Founded 1979
375 Throckmorton Avenue
Mill Valley, CA 94941
Telephone: 415-389-4292 x104
Web: www.millvalleylibrary.org
Personnel:
Responsible person: Joyce Crews, History Room Li-
brarian, *email:* jcrews@cityofmillvalley.org
Holdings:
Geographic strengths: Mill Valley, Marin County
Special collections: Sanborn Fire Insurance maps of
Mill Valley (1903, 1908, 1924. 1933), Tamalpais
Land and Water Company maps for Mill Valley
Subject strengths: aerial photos, agriculture, early car-
tography, modern cartography, city, forestry, geol-
ogy, historical geography, hydrology, land owner-
ship, railroads, roads
493 printed maps
50 aerial photos
Chronological coverage:
1800–1899: 10%
1900–1939: 45%
1940–present: 45%
Average budget over the last 5 years: $100
Access:
Maps in separate area
Collection is open to the public
Answers email questions
Patrons per month: 100
Hours:
Monday–Friday: 10 A.M.–noon, 2 P.M.–4 P.M.,
7 P.M.–9 P.M.
Saturday–Sunday: 2 P.M.–4 P.M.
Total hours per week opened: 12
Geographic Information Systems:
No GIS services available
Collection services:
Maps cataloged: 100%
Catalog accessibility: cards
Preservation techniques: encapsulation
*Percent of items that have gone through the preserva-
tion process:* 25%
Physical facilities:
No Internet access

Other map storage: 1 rolled map case
Copying facilities available: copier

61 *Monterey, CA*

Monterey Public Library

California History Room
Map Collection, founded 1930
625 Pacific Street
Monterey, CA 93940
Telephone: 831-646-3741
Fax: 831-646-5618
Email: copeland@ci.monterey.ca.us
Web: www.co.monterey.ca.us/library
Personnel:
Responsible person: Dennis Copeland, Archivist, *email:* copeland@ci.monterey.ca.us
Holdings:
Geographic strengths: Monterey, Monterey Peninsula, Monterey County, California
Special collections: U.S. Geological Survey Map Collection, Sanborn Map Collection (original and microfilm), Early California Exploration maps and Coastal Surveys, Monterey City maps, Monterey County maps, Del Monte Properties maps, Geological and Seismological maps (Monterey Region)
Subject strengths: early cartography, city, geology, historical geography, mineral resources, projections, roads, soil, travel books, views, Topography
Map depositories and percentages: USGS topos (20%)
611 printed maps
40 aerial photos
10 books
Chronological coverage:
1800–1899: 20%
1900–1939: 35%
1940–present: 40%
On-going publications: Printed index. Online descriptive cataloging planned.
Access:
Maps in separate area
Reference questions per year: 25
Answers email questions
Hours:
Monday–Friday: by appointment
Geographic Information Systems:
No GIS services available
Scans maps for patrons
Collection services:
Maps cataloged: 25%
Maps in OPAC: Planned
Classification schemes: LC, Dewey
Cataloging utilities: OCLC
Catalog accessibility: fiche, printout

Preservation techniques: encapsulation, archival
Percent of items that have gone through the preservation process: 20%
Physical facilities:
No Internet access
Square footage: 79
Linear book shelving: 0.5 ft.
Copying facilities available: copier, microform copier, large-format copying available through vendor
Notes: The map collection forms part of the archives of the local history collection

62 *Nevada City, CA*

Nevada County Library System

Doris Foley Library for Historic Research
Map Collection
211 North Pine Street
Nevada City, CA 95959
Telephone: 530-265-4606
Fax: 530-478-9751
Email: maria.brower@co.nevada.ca.us
Web: new.mynevadacounty.com/library/
Holdings:
Geographic strengths: Nevada County
Special collections: Sanborn Fire Insurance maps, Mining Collection Assessment maps of Nevada County
Subject strengths: aerial photos, city, geology, mining, roads, travel books
550 printed maps
200 aerial photos
Chronological coverage:
1800–1899: 60%
1900–1939: 10%
1940–present: 30%
Access:
Collection is partially open to the public
Reference questions per year: 200
Answers email questions
Patrons per month: 400
Hours:
Monday–Wednesday: 10 A.M.–4 P.M.
Friday–Saturday: 10 A.M.–4 P.M.
Sunday: closed
Total hours per week opened: 30
Geographic Information Systems:
No GIS services available
Collection services:
Maps cataloged: 50%
Maps classified: 50%
Classification schemes: Dewey
Cataloging utilities: OCLC
Catalog accessibility: online, cards
Preservation techniques: encapsulation

Percent of items that have gone through the preservation process: 50%

Physical facilities:
No Internet access
Number of map cases: 2
Copying facilities available: copier, microform copier

63 *Oakland, CA*

Oakland Public Library

125 14th Street
Oakland, CA 94612
Telephone: 510-238-3136
Fax: 510-238-2125
Email: amhl@oaklandlibrary.org
Web: www.oaklandlibrary.org/Seasonal/Sections/
amhl.html#maps

Personnel:
Responsible person: Kathleen Leles DiGiovanni, Librarian II, *email:* amhl@oaklandlibrary.org
FTE para-professionals: 0.07

Holdings:
Geographic strengths: Oakland, San Francisco Bay region
Special collections: Sanborn Fire Insurance maps, Alameda County Tax Assessor's Block Books
Subject strengths: aerial photos, city, forestry, historical geography, land ownership, land use, mining, nautical charts, political geography, railroads, roads, soil, travel books, views
Map depositories and percentages: USGS topos (40%), NOAA, GPO, CIA, National Forest Service, NIMA topos, NIMA nautical, BLM, State
Average budget over the last 5 years: $150
On-going publications: A map help guide for staff use

Access:
Collection is partially open to the public
Answers email questions

Hours:
Total hours per week opened: 50
Maps circulate
Circulation policies apply
Map circulation duration: 3 weeks
Atlas circulation duration: 3 weeks
Book circulation duration: 3 weeks

Geographic Information Systems:
No GIS services available

Collection services:
Classification schemes: SuDocs, Dewey, Local
Cataloging utilities: OCLC
Catalog accessibility: online, cards

Physical facilities:
No Internet access
Number of map cases: 12
Other map storage: 2 rolled map cases
Copying facilities available: copier

64 *Pasadena, CA*

California Institute of Technology

Geological and Planetary Sciences Library
Map Room
Geology Library 100-23
Pasadena, CA 91125
Telephone: 626-395-6699
Fax: 626-568-0935
Web: library.caltech.edu

Personnel:
Responsible person: Jim O'Donnell, Geological and Planetary Sciences Librarian, *email:* jimodo@caltech.edu
FTE para-professionals: 0.25

Holdings:
Geographic strengths: West, Pacific Rim
Subject strengths: aeronautical, celestial, geology
Map depositories and percentages: USGS topos (25%), USGS geology maps (100%), USGS other (100%), NOAA, GPO, CIA, NIMA aeronautical
70,000 printed maps
50 printed atlases
25 books
Chronological coverage:
1900–1939: 20%
1940–present: 80%

Access:
Maps in separate area
Collection is partially open to the public
Maps off site: 20%
Reference questions per year: 50
Answers email questions
Patrons per month: 25

Hours:
Monday–Friday: 1 P.M.–3 P.M.
Total hours per week opened: 10
Maps circulate
Map circulation duration: 4 weeks
Number of maps circulated annually: 175
Interlibrary loan available

Collection services:
Maps cataloged: 15%
Maps classified: 35%
Maps in OPAC: 10%
Classification schemes: LC, SuDocs
Cataloging utilities: OCLC
Catalog accessibility: online
Preservation techniques: encapsulation

Physical facilities:
No Internet access
Square footage: 594
Number of map cases: 51
Number of vertical files (file cabinets): 19
Other map storage: 3 rolled map stands (24 tubes apiece)
Copying facilities available: copier, large-format copier

65 *Pleasant Hill, CA*

Contra Costa County Library

Central Library
1750 Oak Park Boulevard
Pleasant Hill, CA 94523-4497
Telephone: 925-646-6434
Fax: 925-646-6040
Email: ask@ccclib.org
Web: ccclib.org
Personnel:
Responsible person: Carol Yuke, Documents Specialist, *email:* cyuke@ccclib.org
Assistants: Rebecca Malin, Documents Assistant
FTE professionals: 0.5   *FTE para-professionals:* 0.5
Holdings:
Geographic strengths: Contra Costa County
Special collections: historical geography, land ownership, land use, California soil surveys, Sanborn Fire Insurance maps for Contra Costa County
Map depositories: USGS topos, CIA
6,630 printed maps
540 aerial photos
1 globe
218 atlases
45 CD-ROMs
Access:
  Hours:
    Monday–Tuesday: noon–8 P.M.
    Wednesday: 10 A.M.–6 P.M.
    Thursday: noon–8 P.M.
    Friday–Saturday: 10 A.M.–6 P.M.
    Sunday: Closed
  Interlibrary loan available
Collection Services:
  Maps cataloged: 16%
  Maps classified: 16%
  Maps in OPAC: 16%
  Classification schemes: SuDocs, Dewey, Local
Physical facilities:
  Maps in separate area
  Public computers: 25
  Map cases: 6
  Vertical files: 1

66 *Redwood City, CA*

San Mateo County History Museum

Archives
777 Hamilton Street
Redwood City, CA 94063
Telephone: 650-299-0104 x22
Fax: 650-299-0141
Email: carol@samhist.com
Web: www.sanmateocountyhistory.com
Personnel:
Responsible person: Carol Peterson, Archivist, *email:* carol@samhist.com
Holdings:
Geographic strengths: San Mateo County
1,750 printed maps
Access:
  Hours:
    Tuesday–Thursday: 10 A.M.–noon, 12:30 P.M.–4 P.M.
    Sunday: noon–4 P.M.
Collection Services:
  Maps cataloged: 100%
  Classification schemes: Other (place)
Physical facilities:
  Map cases: 12

67 *Riverside, CA*

University of California, Riverside

Science Library
Information Services / Map Collection
P. O. Box 5900
Riverside, CA 92517
Telephone: 909-787-6423
Fax: 909-787-6378
Email: wendie@citrus.ucr.edu
Web: library.ucr.edu/?view=collections/maps/
Personnel:
Responsible person: Wendie Helms, Map Curator, GIS Coordinator, *email:* wendie@citrus.ucr.edu
Assistants: Margarita Yonezawa, Map Collection Assistant
Number of student workers hours per week: 20
Holdings:
Geographic strengths: Riverside County, San Bernardino County, California
Subject strengths: aerial photos, geology, geospatial data
Map depositories and percentages: USGS topos, USGS geology maps (90%), Department of Transportation
100,000 printed maps
40 raised relief maps
9,000 microfiche
4,000 aerial photos
1,700 printed atlases
Collecting digital data
Access:
  Maps in separate area
  Collection is open to the public
  Answers email questions
  Hours:
    Monday–Friday: 9 A.M.–5 P.M.
    Total hours per week opened: 40
  Maps circulate
  Circulation policies apply
    Map circulation duration: 3 days
    Atlas circulation duration: 3 days

Geographic Information Systems:

GIS services available by appointment

GIS software: ArcGIS, ArcView, ArcInfo

GIS assistance available for Census mapping, and geocoding

Plotter available

Scans maps for patrons

Collection services:

Maps cataloged: 20%

Maps classified: 95%

Classification schemes: LC

Cataloging utilities: OCLC

Catalog accessibility: online

Preservation techniques: encapsulation

Physical facilities:

Internet access available

Square footage: 6,400

Number of map cases: 125

Copying facilities available: copier, large-format copier

68 *Sacramento, CA*

California State Library

California History Section

900 N Street

Room 200

Sacramento, CA 95814

Telephone: 916 654-0176

Fax: 916 654-8777

Email: cslcal@library.ca.gov

Web: www.library.ca.gov

Personnel:

Responsible person: Kathleen Correia, Supervising Librarian, *email:* cslcal@library.ca.gov

FTE professionals: 0.75   *FTE para-professionals:* 0.25

Holdings:

Geographic strengths: California

Special collections: Sanborn Fire Insurance maps, automobile club maps, Chamber of Commerce maps, manuscript maps of mining operations

5,200 printed maps

4,500 aerial photos

1,500 atlases

Access:

Hours:

Monday–Friday: 9:30 A.M.–4 P.M.

Saturday–Sunday: closed

Collection services:

Maps cataloged: 90%

Maps classified: 90%

Maps in OPAC: 85%

Classification schemes: Local

Physical facilities:

Maps in separate area

Public computers: 2

Map cases: 37

Vertical files: 2

69 *Sacramento, CA*

California State Library

Government Publications Section

914 Capitol Mall

Sacramento, CA 95814

Telephone: 916-654-0069

Fax: 916-653-6114

Email: cslgps@library.ca.gov

Web: www.library.ca.gov

Personnel:

Responsible person: Debbie Weber, *email:* dweber@library.ca.gov

FTE professionals: 0.25   *FTE para-professionals:* 0.5

Number of student workers hours per week: 100

Holdings:

Geographic strengths: California

Subject strengths: aeronautical, modern cartography, climatology, geology, land use, map catalogs, mineral resources, mining, nautical charts, population, recreation, soil, vegetation

Map depositories and percentages: USGS topos (100%), USGS geology maps (100%), USGS other (100%), Department of Transportation, NOAA, GPO, CIA, National Forest Service, NIMA topos, NIMA nautical, NIMA aeronautical, BLM, State, United Nations

80,000 printed maps

50,000 microfiche

Access:

Maps in separate area

Collection is paged

Answers email questions

Patrons per month: 20

Hours:

Monday–Friday: 9:30 A.M.–4 P.M.

Saturday–Saturday: closed

Total hours per week opened: 32.5

Circulation policies apply

Book circulation duration: 5 weeks

Geographic Information Systems:

Scans maps for patrons

Collection services:

Maps cataloged: 100%

Maps classified: 100%

Classification schemes: SuDocs, Local

Cataloging utilities: RLG

Catalog accessibility: online, cards

Preservation techniques: encapsulation

Physical facilities:

Internet access available

Square footage: 1,200
Number of map cases: 84
Copying facilities available: copier, microform copier

70 *San Bruno, CA*

National Archives and Records Administration, Pacific Region, San Francisco

1000 Commodore Drive
San Bruno, CA 94066
Telephone: 650-238-3501
Fax: 650-238-3510
Email: sanbruno.archives@nara.gov
Web: www.archives.gov/facilities/ca/san_francisco
.html
Holdings:
Geographic strengths: Northern and Central California, Nevada, Hawai`i, Trust Territory of Pacific
Subject strengths: aerial photos, agriculture, modern cartography, engineering, forestry, geodetic surveys, hydrology, land ownership, land use, vegetation, Naval Bases, National Parks, National Forests, Indian Reservations, Corps of Engineers Civil Works Projects
1,000 printed maps
5,000 manuscript maps
10,000 aerial photos
Chronological coverage:
1900–1939: 60%
1940–present: 35%
On-going publications: Guide to Archival Holdings at NARA's Pacific Region (San Francisco). In-house finding aids by RG
Access:
Collection is partially open to the public
Patrons per month: 100
Hours:
Monday–Friday: 8 A.M.–4 P.M.
Total hours per week opened: 40
Geographic Information Systems:
Scans maps for patrons
Collection services:
Maps cataloged: 30%
Classification schemes: Other (NARA Record Group/ Originating Office)
Cataloging utilities: NARA
Preservation techniques: encapsulation
Percent of items that have gone through the preservation process: 10%
Physical facilities:
No Internet access
Number of staff computers: 10
Number of map cases: 150
Copying facilities available: large-format copier
Notes: NARA Pacific Region does not have separate map collections or reference facilities for maps per se. All maps are integrated with textual records and/or engineering drawings for particular Federal sites of particular Federal Agency offices. The maps are dispersed among holdings dated approximately 1850–1980, depending upon the dates for a particular RG or office.

71 *San Diego, CA*

San Diego State University

Library and Information Access
5500 Campanile Drive
San Diego, CA 92182
Telephone: 619-594-6724
Fax: 619-594-3270
Web: infodome.sdsu.edu/research/guides/maps/
index.shtml
Personnel:
Responsible person: Megan Dreger, *email:* mdreger@
mail.sdsu.edu
FTE professionals: 0.25   *FTE para-professionals:* 0.25
Holdings:
Geographic strengths: Southern California
Map depositories: USGS topos, Department of Transportation, NOAA, CIA, National Forest Service, NGA nautical, NGA aeronautical, BLM
138,000 printed maps
200 aerial photos
3 globes
1,200 atlases
100 books
15 CD-ROMs
Access:
Hours:
Monday–Thursday: 7 A.M.–1am
Friday: 7 A.M.–6 P.M.
Saturday: 10 A.M.–6 P.M.
Sunday: noon–1am
Collection Services:
Maps cataloged: 5%
Maps classified: 80%
Maps in OPAC: 5%
Classification schemes: Local
Physical facilities:
Public computers: 4
Map cases: 100

72 *San Francisco, CA*

California Academy of Sciences

J.W. Mailliard, Jr. Library
Donald C. Heckman Memorial Map Collection
55 Concourse Drive
Golden Gate Park
San Francisco, CA 94118

Telephone: 415-750-7102
Fax: 415-750-7106
Email: library@calacademy.org
Web: www.calacademy.org/research/library/
Personnel:
Responsible person: Lawrence W. Currie, Associate Librarian for User Services, *email:* lcurrie@calacademy.org
FTE professionals: 0.05
Holdings:
Geographic strengths: West
Special collections: Baja California
Subject strengths: geology, mineral resources
Map depositories and percentages: USGS topos (15%), USGS geology maps (10%), USGS other, NOAA, National Forest Service
55,000 printed maps
24 raised relief maps
20 microfiche
12 aerial photos
200 gazetteers
100 printed atlases
650 books
25 active serials
100 inactive serials
50 CD-ROMs
10 computer programs
Chronological coverage:
Pre-1800: <1%
1800–1899: <1%
1900–1939: <1%
1940–present: 98%
Average budget over the last 5 years: $500
On-going publications: General library brochure and handout "U.S. Geological Survey maps at the California Academy of Sciences Library".
Access:
Collection is open to the public
Reference questions per year: 150
Answers email questions
Hours:
Monday–Friday: 10 A.M.–5 P.M.
Total hours per week opened: 35
Interlibrary loan available
Geographic Information Systems:
No GIS services available
GIS software: ArcView GIS
Scans maps for patrons
Collection services:
Maps cataloged: 100%
Maps classified: 10%
Maps in OPAC: 10%
Classification schemes: LC
Cataloging utilities: OCLC
Catalog accessibility: online, cards

Physical facilities:
Internet access available
Square footage: 800
Number of map cases: 36
Linear book shelving: 150 ft.
Linear atlas shelving: 50 ft.
Copying facilities available: copier, color copier

73 *San Francisco, CA*

California Historical Society

North Baker Research Library
678 Mission Street
San Francisco, CA 94105
Telephone: 415-357-1848
Fax: 415-357-1850
Email: reference@calhist.org
Web: www.californiahistoricalsociety.org
Personnel:
Responsible person: Mary Morganti, Director of Library and Archives, *email:* mary@calhist.org
FTE professionals: 0   *FTE para-professionals:* 0
Holdings:
Geographic strengths: San Francisco, California
Special collections: Sanborn Fire Insurance maps
2,500 printed maps
25 atlases
Access:
Hours:
Wednesday–Friday: noon–4:30 P.M.
Collection Services:
Maps cataloged: 0%
Maps classified: 90%
Maps in OPAC: 0%
Classification schemes: Local
Physical facilities:
Public computers: 2
Map cases: 3

74 *San Francisco, CA*

David Rumsey Collection

Founded 1980
Cole Valley
San Francisco, CA 94117
Telephone: 415-386-1750
Fax: 415-386-1781
Email: rumsey@luna-img.com
Web: www.davidrumsey.com
Personnel:
Responsible person: David M. Rumsey, President, *email:* rumsey@luna-img.com
FTE professionals: 1.35   *FTE para-professionals:* 2.6

Holdings:

Geographic strengths: North and South America

Special collections: American school geographies and atlases, West, works of John Melish, Henry Tanner, S.A. Mitchell, J.H. Colton, online collection of 10,000 images from the collection

Subject strengths: aeronautical, city, land ownership, map/atlas catalogs, railroads, views

Map depositories and percentages: USGS topos

3,100 printed maps

25 manuscript maps

650 wall maps

10 raised relief maps

49 globes

160 gazetteers

2,300 printed atlases

1,400 books

20 CD-ROMs

10 computer programs

Chronological coverage:

Pre-1800: 10%

1800–1899: 65%

1900–1939: 12%

1940–present: 13%

Average budget over the last 5 years: $30,000

On-going publications: Irregular list of new images added to website (electronic); Monthly list of newly created MARC records for online images (electronic)

Access:

Collection is partially open to the public

Reference questions per year: 1,200

Answers email questions

Patrons per month: 5

Hours:

Monday–Friday: by appointment

Geographic Information Systems:

GIS software: ArcView, ArcIMS modified by Telemorphic for online

Geocoding, Image analysis help available

Collection services:

Maps cataloged: 95%

Maps in OPAC: 95%

Cataloging utilities: Local, OCLC for online images

Catalog accessibility: online

Preservation techniques: deacidification, encapsulation in mylar

Percent of items that have gone through the preservation process: 80%

Physical facilities:

Square footage: 3,000

Linear book shelving: 441 ft.

Linear atlas shelving: 56 ft.

Other map storage: 5 wall map cases

Copying facilities available: copier, scanner

75 *San Francisco, CA*

Presidio Trust

34 Graham Street

San Francisco, CA 94129

Telephone: 415-561-5343

Email: bjanis@presidiotrust.gov

Web: www.presidio.gov

Personnel:

Responsible person: Barbara Janis, *email:* bjanis@presidiotrust.gov

FTE professionals: 1

Holdings:

Geographic strengths: Presidio of San Francisco

100 printed maps

80 aerial photos

Access:

Hours:

Monday–Friday: 8 A.M.–5 P.M.

Saturday–Sunday: closed

Interlibrary loan available

Physical facilities:

Public computers: 1

76 *San Francisco, CA*

San Francisco Maritime National Historical Park

J Porter Shaw Library

Building E Fort Mason Center

San Francisco, CA 94123

Telephone: 415-561-7030

Email: steve_davenport@nps.gov

Web: www.nps.gov/safr/local/lib/libtop.html

Personnel:

Responsible person: Steve Davenport, Reference Librarian, *email:* steve_davenport@nps.gov

Assistants: Heather Hernandez, Tech Services Librarian

Holdings:

Geographic strengths: San Francisco Bay, California coast, United States west coast, Pacific Basin

Special collections: maps of Early San Francisco, Charts of the San Francisco Bay, Sanborn Fire Insurance maps for cities of the Bay, early Pacific Exploration charts

Subject strengths: archaeology, early cartography, modern cartography, celestial, city, engineering, geodetic surveys, geospatial data, historical geography, hydrology, land ownership, land use, map catalogs, map collecting, military, nautical charts, oceanography, travel books, views, waterways

4,200 printed maps

175 books

Chronological coverage:

1800–1899: 35%

1900–1939: 55%
1940–present: 10%

Access:

Collection is paged

Reference questions per year: 15

Answers email questions

Patrons per month: 45

Hours:

Tuesday–Friday: 1 A.M.–5 P.M. by appointment

Saturday: 10 A.M.–5 P.M.

Sunday: closed

Total hours per week opened: 40

Interlibrary loan available

Geographic Information Systems:

No GIS services available

Scans maps for patrons

Collection services:

Maps cataloged: 90%

Maps classified: 100%

Classification schemes: LC, SuDocs

Cataloging utilities: OCLC, Local

Catalog accessibility: online, cards

Preservation techniques: encapsulation, deacidification, edging

Percent of items that have gone through the preservation process: 20%

Physical facilities:

No Internet access

Copying facilities available: copier, large-format copier, microform copier

77 *San Francisco, CA*

San Francisco Municipal Railway

Library

Founded 1975

1145 Market Street

Suite 402

San Francisco, CA 94103-1545

Telephone: 415-934-3977

Fax: 415-934-5747

Email: marc_hofstadter@ci.sf.ca.us

Personnel:

Responsible person: Dr. Marc Hofstadter, Librarian, *email:* marc_hofstadter@ci.sf.ca.us

Holdings:

Geographic strengths: San Francisco

Subject strengths: city, engineering, historical geography, land use, railroads, roads, Transit and transportation; urban planning

200 printed maps

10 manuscript maps

Chronological coverage:

1900–1939: 20%

1940–present: 80%

Access:

Collection is open to the public

Answers email questions

Hours:

Tuesday: 1 P.M.–6 P.M.

Friday: 1 P.M.–6 P.M.

Total hours per week opened: 10

Physical facilities:

No Internet access

Square footage: 60

Copying facilities available: copier

78 *San Francisco, CA*

San Francisco Public Library

General Collections Department

100 Larkin Street

San Francisco, CA 94102

Telephone: 415-557-4401

Fax: 415-437-4831

Email: info@sfpl.org

Web: www.sfpl.org

Personnel:

Responsible person: Joan Haskell, *email:* jhaskell@sfpl.org

FTE professionals: 1

Holdings:

Geographic strengths: California

Special collections: City street maps of major international cities, world atlases from 1880s to the present

491 printed maps

3 globes

71 atlases

Access:

Hours:

Monday–Friday: 9 A.M.–6 P.M.

Saturday: 10 A.M.–6 P.M.

Sunday: noon–5 P.M.

Collection Services:

Maps cataloged: 20%

Maps classified: 100%

Maps in OPAC: 20%

Classification schemes: Dewey

Physical facilities:

Public computers: 90

Vertical files: 8

79 *San Francisco, CA*

San Francisco Public Library

Government Information Center

100 Larkin Street

San Francisco, CA 94102

Telephone: 415-557-4500
Fax: 415-557-4475
Email: governmentinfo@sfpl.org
Web: sfpl.org/librarylocations/main/gic/gic.htm
Personnel:
Responsible person: Carol Coon, Documents Manager, *email:* ccoon@sfpl.org
Holdings:
Subject strengths: nautical charts, soil
Map depositories and percentages: USGS topos, USGS geology maps, USGS other, NOAA, GPO, CIA, National Forest Service, BLM
188,139 printed maps
Access:
Collection is partially open to the public
Answers email questions
Hours:
Monday: 10 A.M.–6 P.M.
Tuesday–Thursday: 9 A.M.–8 P.M.
Friday: noon–6 P.M.
Saturday: 10 A.M.–6 P.M.
Sunday: noon–5 P.M.
Total hours per week opened: 60
Geographic Information Systems:
Number of public GIS workstations: 14
Collection services:
Classification schemes: SuDocs
Catalog accessibility: cards
Preservation techniques: encapsulation
Physical facilities:
Internet access available
Copying facilities available: copier, color copier, microform copier

80 *San Francisco, CA*

San Francisco State University

Alfred Rockwell Sumner Memorial Map Library
Founded 1962
1600 Holloway Avenue
HSS 289
San Francisco, CA 94132
Telephone: 415-338-1145
Fax: 415-338-6243
Email: nancyw@sfsu.edu
Web: bss.sfsu.edu/geog/maplib.htm
Personnel:
Responsible person: Dr. Nancy Wilkinson, Geography Department Chair, *email:* nancyw@sfsu.edu
Assistants: Jeremy Bailey, Aaron Mount
Number of student workers hours per week: 40
Holdings:
Geographic strengths: California, West
Special collections: 1937 Airphotos US Forest Service of Tahoe, Eldorado, and Lassen National forests

Subject strengths: aerial photos, aeronautical, early cartography, modern cartography, celestial, city, forestry, geology, geospatial data, historical geography, hydrology, land use, map catalogs, military, mineral resources, nautical charts, oceanography, raised relief models, roads, satellite imagery, soil, travel books, waterways
Map depositories and percentages: USGS topos (100%)
42,201 printed maps
500 manuscript maps
875 wall maps
500 raised relief maps
500 aerial photos
200 satellite images
10 gazetteers
204 printed atlases
1,216 books
15 active serials
Collecting digital data
Chronological coverage:
1900–1939: 10%
1940–present: 85%
Access:
Maps in separate area
Collection is partially open to the public
Reference questions per year: 55
Answers email questions
Patrons per month: 135
Hours:
Monday–Friday: 8:30 A.M.–4:30 P.M.
Total hours per week opened: 40
Maps circulate
Circulation policies apply
Map circulation duration: 2 weeks
Atlas circulation duration: 2 weeks
Book circulation duration: 2 weeks
Geographic Information Systems:
GIS services available by appointment
GIS software: ArcGIS/ ERDAS
GIS assistance available for Census mapping, geocoding, and image analysis
Collection services:
Maps cataloged: 20%
Maps classified: 80%
Maps in OPAC: 5%
Classification schemes: Local
Cataloging utilities: Local
Catalog accessibility: online, printout
Preservation techniques: lamination
Percent of items that have gone through the preservation process: 3%
Physical facilities:
Internet access available
Square footage: 1,400
Number of map cases: 72

Linear book shelving: 420 ft.
Linear atlas shelving: 20 ft.
Other map storage: wall map storage room
Number of stereoscopes: 20
Copying facilities available: none

81 *San Francisco, CA*

San Francisco State University

J. Paul Leonard Library
Government Publications/Maps Department
1630 Holloway Avenue
San Francisco, CA 94132
Telephone: 415-338-6953
Fax: 415-338-1504
Web: www.library.sfsu.edu/servcoll/maps.html
Personnel:
Responsible person: LaVonne Jacobsen, Collection Access and Management Services Division, Head, *email:* lavonne@sfsu.edu
FTE professionals: 0.1   *FTE para-professionals:* 0.25
Number of student works: 0.5
Holdings:
Geographic strengths: California
Map depositories:: USGS geology maps, USGS other, NOAA, GPO, CIA, National Forest Service, United Nations, Old AMS collection
14,366 printed maps
25 raised relief maps
100 gazetteers
Chronological coverage:
1940–present: 95%
Access:
Collection is open to the public
Answers email questions
Hours:
Monday–Friday: 8 A.M.–5 P.M.
Saturday: 1 P.M.–5 P.M.
Sunday: closed
Total hours per week opened: 49
Maps circulate
Circulation policies apply
Map circulation duration: 4 weeks
Atlas circulation duration: 2 days
Book circulation duration: 4 weeks
Number of maps circulated annually: 150
Collection services:
Maps cataloged: 100%
Maps classified: 60%
Maps in OPAC: 40%
Classification schemes: LC, SuDocs
Cataloging utilities: OCLC
Catalog accessibility: online, cards
Physical facilities:
Internet access available
Square footage: 900

Number of map cases: 35
Linear book shelving: 63 ft.
Linear atlas shelving: 312 ft.
Copying facilities available: copier, color copier, large-format copier, microform copier

82 *San Jose, CA*

History San Jose

Research Library
1650 Senter Road
San Jose, CA 95112-2599
Telephone: 408-287-2290
Fax: 408-287-2291
Email: research@historysanjose.org
Web: www.historysanjose.org/research/library
Personnel:
Responsible person: Senior Archivist, *email:* pjabloner@historysanjose.org
FTE professionals: 0.05   *FTE para-professionals:* 0.05
Holdings:
Geographic strengths: San Jose, Santa Clara County, California
Special collections: Sanborn Fire Insurance maps for San Jose and Santa Clara, New Almaden Mines maps, early Santa Clara County aerial photographs, Wall maps for Santa Clara County, San Jose Real Estate and Tax Assessment maps
Subject strengths: aerial photos, agriculture, city, economic geography, historical geography, land ownership, land use, map catalogs, mining, railroads, roads, views
600 printed maps
400 manuscript maps
100 wall maps
500 aerial photos
10 printed atlases
50 books
Chronological coverage:
1800–1899: 29%
1900–1939: 40%
1940–present: 30%
Access:
Maps in separate area
Collection is paged
Maps off site: 40%
Reference questions per year: 100
Answers email questions
Patrons per month: 25
Hours:
Wednesday: 1 P.M.–4 P.M.
Monday–Friday: by appointment
Geographic Information Systems:
No GIS services available
Collection services:
Maps cataloged: 20%

Classification schemes: LC, Local

Catalog accessibility: cards, Pastperfect (museum database)

Percent of items that have gone through the preservation process: 20%

Physical facilities:

No Internet access

Square footage: 180

Number of map cases: 13

Linear atlas shelving: 24 ft.

Other map storage: hanging horizontal rolled maps on textile racks

Copying facilities available: copier, microform copier

83 *San Jose, CA*

San Jose State University

Department of Geology

San Jose, CA 95192-0102

Telephone: 408-924-5050

Fax: 408-924-5053

Web: www.geosun.sjsu.edu

Personnel:

FTE professionals: 0   *FTE para-professionals:* 0

Holdings:

Geographic strengths: California, West

Special collections: USGS folios, older topographic maps, 15' topographic maps

17,000 printed maps

Access:

Hours:

Monday–Friday: by appointment

Collection services:

Maps in OPAC: 0%

Classification schemes: Other (departmental)

Physical facilities:

Maps in separate area

Vertical files: 50

Notes: We have an extensive map collection, mostly topographic, but including geologic maps and folios, some quite old. Actually no one really knows what we have!

84 *San Jose, CA*

San Jose State University

Dr. Martin Luther King Jr. Library

1 Washington Square

San Jose, CA 95192-0028

Telephone: 408-808-2000

Email: hmeserve@sjsu.edu

Web: www.sjlibrary.org

Personnel:

Responsible person: Harry C. Meserve, *email:* hmeserve@sjsu.edu

FTE professionals: 0.25   *FTE para-professionals:* 0.25

Holdings:

Geographic strengths: California, West

Special collections: Sanborn Fire Insurance maps

Subject strengths: aeronautical, early cartography, modern cartography, climatology, city, economic geography, genealogy, historical geography, land use, nautical charts, political geography, population, raised relief models, recreation, roads, waterways

Map depositories and percentages: USGS topos (100%), GPO, State

3,000 printed maps

Access:

Collection is open to the public

Reference questions per year: 75

Answers email questions

Hours:

Monday–Friday: 8 A.M.–6 P.M.

Saturday: 9 A.M.–6 P.M.

Sunday: noon–7 P.M.

Total hours per week opened: 66

Circulation policies apply

Book circulation duration: 3 weeks

Interlibrary loan available

Geographic Information Systems:

No GIS services available

Collection services:

Classification schemes: LC, SuDocs

Catalog accessibility: online

Percent of items that have gone through the preservation process: 10%

Physical facilities:

Internet access available

Number of map cases: 10

Copying facilities available: copier, microform copier

85 *San Leandro, CA*

San Leandro Public Library

Map File

300 Estudillo Avenue

San Leandro, CA 94577

Telephone: 510-577-3971

Fax: 510-577-3987

Web: www.ci.san-leandro.ca/us/sllibrary.html

Personnel:

Responsible person: Cheryl Mouton, *email:* cmouton@ci.san-leandro.ca.us

FTE professionals: 1   *FTE para-professionals:* 0.25

Holdings:

Geographic strengths: California, United States

Map depositories: USGS topos, CIA, BLM

1,200 printed maps

60 atlases

14 books

1 CD-ROM

Access:

Items circulate

Collection services:
Maps cataloged: 0%
Maps classified: 100%
Maps in OPAC: 0%
Classification schemes: Other (subject)

Physical facilities:
Public computers: 67
Map cases: 1
Vertical files: 4

86 *San Luis Obispo, CA*

California Polytechnic State University

Robert E. Kennedy Library
Reference Department
San Luis Obispo, CA 93407
Telephone: 805-756-2649
Web: www.lib.calpoly.edu

Personnel:
Responsible person: email: sfujitan@calpoly.edu
FTE professionals: 0.125   *FTE para-professionals:* 0.125

Holdings:
Map depositories: USGS topos, Department of Transportation, CIA, National Forest Service, BLM
10,200 printed maps
555 aerial photos
4 globes
588 atlases

Access:
Hours:
Monday–Thursday: 7 A.M.–midnight
Friday: 7 A.M.–5 P.M.
Saturday: 10 A.M.–5 P.M.
Sunday: 10 A.M.–midnight

Collection services:
Maps cataloged: 100%
Maps in OPAC: 100%
Classification schemes: LC

Physical facilities:
Maps in separate area
Public computers: 2
Map cases: 26
Vertical files: 5

87 *Santa Barbara, CA*

Santa Barbara Museum of Natural History

Library
2559 Puesta del Sol Road
Santa Barbara, CA 93105
Telephone: 805-682-4711
Fax: 805-569-3170
Web: www.sbnature.org/library/index.htm

Personnel:
Responsible person: Terri Sheridan, Librarian, *email:* tsheridan@sbnature2.org
Assistants: Lena Simms, Library Assistant
FTE para-professionals: 0.1

Holdings:
Geographic strengths: California
Special collections: Channel Islands Archive, Dibblee Geologic Collection
Subject strengths: archaeology, biology, early cartography, climatology, city, forestry, geodetic surveys, geology, geospatial data, hydrology, land ownership, land use, mineral resources, mining, nautical charts, political geography, population, roads, soil, vegetation, views
Map depositories:: USGS topos, USGS geology maps, USGS other, National Forest Service, BLM, State
2,300 printed maps
25 manuscript maps
10 wall maps
10 aerial photos
12 printed atlases
Chronological coverage:
1900–1939: 57%
1940–present: 40%

Access:
Maps in separate area
Collection is paged
Reference questions per year: 25
Answers email questions
Hours:
Monday–Saturday: 10 A.M.–5 P.M.
Total hours per week opened: 42

Collection services:
Maps cataloged: 97%
Maps in OPAC: 97%
Classification schemes: LC, Local
Cataloging utilities: Local
Catalog accessibility: online, MARC/ProCite
Preservation techniques: acid-free folders

Physical facilities:
No Internet access
Square footage: 40
Number of map cases: 12
Copying facilities available: copier

88 *Santa Barbara, CA*

University of California, Santa Barbara

Davidson Library
Map and Imagery Laboratory, founded 1967
Santa Barbara, CA 93106-9010
Telephone: 805-893-2779
Fax: 805-893-8799

Email: milrefdesk@library.ucsb.edu
Web: www.sdc.ucsb.edu
Personnel:
Responsible person: Larry Carver, Head, *email:* carber@library.ucsb.edu
Assistants: Mary Lynette Larsgaard, Assistant Head; Rusty Brown (LA IV); Deborah Lupo (LA II); Ann Hefferman (LA IV), Office Manager and Student Supervisor; Heather Alexander (LA II); Marilyn Treusdellm (LA II) Cataloger; Clayton Burnham, Head of Davidson Library and MIL systems, (Programmer III); Catherine Masi (Programmer III), Head of Operational Alexandria Digital Library; Greg Hajic (Programmer II); David Valentine (Programmer III); Carolyn Jones (Lab Tech II), Scanning Supervisor; Cian Phillips (Programmer II), Web programmer, Davidson Library and ADL
FTE professionals: 0   *FTE para-professionals:* 12.4
Number of student works: 20
Number of student workers hours per week: 200
Holdings:
Geographic strengths: Santa Barbara, California, World
Special collections: Maximus Collection, Antique maps Collection, maps of U.S. during Civil War, Landsat 1, 2, and 3, Teledyne Air Photo Collection, Mark Hurd Air surveys
Subject strengths: aerial photos, aeronautical, modern cartography, city, geology, geospatial data, historical geography, map catalogs, nautical charts, roads, satellite imagery, soil, travel books, views
Map depositories and percentages: USGS topos (100%), USGS geology maps (100%), USGS other (100%), Department of Transportation, NOAA, GPO, CIA, National Forest Service, NIMA topos, NIMA nautical, NIMA aeronautical, BLM, State
464,000 printed maps
500 manuscript maps
300 raised relief maps
47,000 microfiche
3,300 microfilms
3,200,000 aerial photos
1,200,000 satellite images
23 globes
300 gazetteers
6,000 printed atlases
3,500 books
10 active serials
40 inactive serials
3,300 CD-ROMs
Collecting digital data
Chronological coverage:
  Pre-1800: 0.001%
  1800–1899: 0.001%
  1940–present: 95%
Average budget over the last 5 years: $51,000

Access:
Maps in separate area
Collection is partially paged, partially open to the public
Maps off site: 30%
Reference questions per year: 18,000
Answers email questions
Patrons per month: 640
Hours:
  Monday–Thursday: 8 A.M.–5 P.M., 7 P.M.–10 P.M.
  Total hours per week opened: 40
Maps circulate
Circulation policies apply
  Map circulation duration: special permission
  Atlas circulation duration: 3 weeks
  Book circulation duration: 3 weeks
  Number of maps circulated annually: 200
Geographic Information Systems:
GIS services available by appointment
GIS software: Arc/Info, ArcView, ERDAS
GIS assistance available for Census mapping, geocoding, and image analysis
Scans maps for patrons
Collection services:
Maps cataloged: 60%
Maps classified: 100%
Maps in OPAC: 40%
Datasets are cataloged
Classification schemes: LC, Local, Other (provenance [air photo and satellite images])
Cataloging utilities: OCLC
Catalog accessibility: online
Preservation techniques: encapsulation
Percent of items that have gone through the preservation process: 15%
Physical facilities:
Internet access available
Square footage: 18,000
Number of staff computers: 12
Number of map cases: 350
Number of vertical files (file cabinets): 26
Linear book shelving: 900 ft.
Linear atlas shelving: 1,200 ft.
Other map storage: linear shelving for air photos
Copying facilities available: copier, color copier, large-format copier, microform copier, large-format scanner, plotter

89 *Santa Cruz, CA*

University of California, Santa Cruz

Science and Engineering Library
Map Room, founded 1965
1156 High Street
Santa Cruz, CA 95064
Telephone: 831-459-2364

Fax: 831-459-4187
Email: cjahns@ucsc.edu
Web: library.ucsc.edu/maps/
Personnel:
Responsible person: Cynthia Jahns, Head, Maps Unit, *email:* cjahns@ucsc.edu
Assistants: Laura Campbell, Library Assistant/Public Service
Number of student workers hours per week: 25
Holdings:
Geographic strengths: Monterey Bay region, California
Special collections: F.A. Hihn Archive maps of Santa Cruz County
Subject strengths: aerial photos, agriculture, city, geology, historical geography, hydrology, land ownership, mineral resources, nautical charts, political geography, population, recreation, roads, soil
Map depositories:: USGS topos, USGS geology maps, USGS other, NOAA, GPO, CIA, NIMA topos, NIMA nautical, NIMA aeronautical, State
136,964 printed maps
687 manuscript maps
425 wall maps
22 raised relief maps
42,525 microfiche
30 microfilms
96,386 aerial photos
2,362 books
974 CD-ROMs
Chronological coverage:
  1900–1939: 17%
  1940–present: 75%
Average budget over the last 5 years: $12,000
On-going publications: Web page updated regularly, which includes holdings of Sanborn maps on glass slides, aerial photos indexed by location, photos of wall maps, etc.
Access:
Maps in separate area
Collection is partially open to the public
Reference questions per year: 2,000
Answers email questions
Patrons per month: 153
Hours:
  Monday–Friday: 9 A.M.–noon, 1 P.M.–5 P.M.
  Total hours per week opened: 35
  Number of other items circulated annually: 3,800
  Interlibrary loan available
Geographic Information Systems:
GIS services available in an open environment
GIS software: ArcGIS , ArcView 3.2
GIS assistance available for Census mapping
Scans maps for patrons
Collection services:
Maps cataloged: 60%

Maps classified: 100%
Maps in OPAC: 60%
Datasets are cataloged
Classification schemes: LC, SuDocs
Cataloging utilities: OCLC
Catalog accessibility: online
Preservation techniques: encapsulation, acid-free folders
Physical facilities:
Internet access available
Square footage: 2,600
Number of map cases: 84
Number of vertical files (file cabinets): 19
Linear book shelving: 180 ft.
Linear atlas shelving: 744 ft.
Other map storage: 2 oversize map cases, 425 wall maps
Copying facilities available: copier, microform copier, scanner with CD-burner

90 *Santa Rosa, CA*

Sonoma County Library

3rd and E Street
Santa Rosa, CA 95404
Telephone: 707-545-0831
Fax: 707-575-0437
Email: salcorta@sonoma.lib.ca.us
Web: www.sonomalibrary.org
Personnel:
Responsible person: Steven Alcorta, Librarian II, *email:* salcorta@sonoma.lib.ca.us
Assistants: Tony Hoskins, History, Genealogy and Archives Librarian
FTE professionals: 0.1
Holdings:
Geographic strengths: Sonoma County, California
Special collections: Sanborn Fire Insurance of Sonoma County
Subject strengths: aerial photos, aeronautical, early cartography, modern cartography, city, genealogy, historical geography, land ownership, land use, language, political geography, railroads, raised relief models, roads, travel books, views, waterways
Map depositories and percentages: USGS topos (100% (California and Oregon only)), CIA, State
1,100 printed maps
52 aerial photos
Chronological coverage:
  Pre-1800: 0.01%
  1800–1899: 10%
  1900–1939: 15%
  1940–present: 75%
On-going publications: Online list of topos of California
Access:
Collection is open to the public

Reference questions per year: 520
Answers email questions
Patrons per month: 18
Hours:
Monday–Saturday: 9:30 A.M.–6 P.M.
Sunday: 2 P.M.–6 P.M.
Total hours per week opened: 55
Collection services:
Classification schemes: Dewey, Other (alphabetical)
Physical facilities:
No Internet access
Number of public computers: 20
Number of map cases: 2
Copying facilities available: copier, microform copier

91 *Stanford, CA*

Stanford University

Branner Earth Sciences Library and Map Collections
Mitchell Earth Sciences Building
397 Panama Mall
Stanford, CA 94305
Telephone: 650-725-1103
Fax: 650-725-2534
Email: branner@pangea.stanford.edu
Web: www-sul.stanford.edu/depts/branner/brief_map
.html
Personnel:
Responsible person: Julie Sweetkind—Singer, GIS and
Map Librarian, *email:* sweetkind@stanford.edu
Assistants: Jane Ingalls, Assistant Map Librarian
FTE professionals: 1.5
Number of student workers hours per week: 20
Holdings:
Geographic strengths: California, Africa, Europe, So-
viet Union, Australia, Canada, Japan, China, South
America
Special collections: Central Geological Survey, Bro-
ken Hill NSW mining plans, Jahns (Richard H.)
map archives, Hoover Library map collection, East
Asian map collection, Robert and William Moran
map collection
Subject strengths: aeronautical, geodetic surveys, geology, geospatial data, military, mineral resources, political geography, roads, Geophysics
Map depositories and percentages: USGS topos
(100%), USGS geology maps (100%), USGS other
(50%), CIA, NIMA topos, BLM, State, DMA Aeronautical
270,000 printed maps
300 manuscript maps
160 wall maps
25 raised relief maps
6,000 aerial photos

300 satellite images
100 gazetteers
688 printed atlases
550 books
20 active serials
250 CD-ROMs
20 computer programs
Collecting digital data
Chronological coverage:
1900–1939: 35%
1940–present: 60%
Average budget over the last 5 years: $40,000
Access:
Maps in separate area
Collection is open to the public
Maps off site: 10%
Reference questions per year: 1,300
Answers email questions
Patrons per month: 200
Hours:
Monday–Thursday: 9 A.M.–9 P.M.
Friday: 9 A.M.–5 P.M.
Saturday: 1 A.M.–5 P.M.
Sunday: 4 P.M.–9 P.M.
Total hours per week opened: 65
Maps circulate
Circulation policies apply
Map circulation duration: 1 quarter
Atlas circulation duration: 1 quarter
Book circulation duration: 1 quarter
Interlibrary loan available
Geographic Information Systems:
GIS services available in an open environment
GIS software: ArcView, ArcGIS, ArcIMS
*GIS assistance available for Census mapping, geocod-
ing, and image analysis*
Collection services:
Maps cataloged: 70%
Maps classified: 80%
Maps in OPAC: 60%
Datasets are cataloged
Classification schemes: LC, Dewey
Cataloging utilities: OCLC, RLG
Catalog accessibility: online, cards
Preservation techniques: encapsulation, deacidification
Physical facilities:
Internet access available
Square footage: 2,522
Number of map cases: 1,120
Number of vertical files (file cabinets): 233
Linear book shelving: 252 ft.
Linear atlas shelving: 458 ft.
Other map storage: wall maps held in off site storage
Copying facilities available: copier, large-format
copier, microform copier, 36" plotter, 40" scanner

92 *Stanford, CA*

Stanford University

Green Library
Historic Map Collection
Department of Special Collections and University Archives
Green Library
Stanford, CA 94305
Telephone: 650-725-1022
Fax: 650-723-8690
Email: speccoll@stanford.edu
Web:www.sul.stanford.edu/depts/spc/maps/index.html

Personnel:
Responsible person: Roberto Trujillo, Head, Department of Special Collections, Frances and Charles Field Curator of Special Collections, *email:* trujillo@stanford.edu
FTE professionals: 0   *FTE para-professionals:* 0

Holdings:
Geographic strengths: Stanford University region, Africa
Special collections: Dr. Oscar I. Norwich Collection of the Maps of Africa and its Islands, Antiquarian Map Collection, Southern Pacific Company—drawings and maps (ca. 1870–1965), Stanford University Archives Map Collection (1853–1997)
6,000 printed maps
3 globes
120 atlases
320 books
1 active serial

Access:
Hours:
Monday–Friday: 10 A.M.–5 P.M.
Saturday–Sunday: closed

Collection Services:
Maps cataloged: 1%
Maps classified: 99%
Maps in OPAC: 1%
Classification schemes: LC, Local

Notes: Maps are kept off-site, with no one admitted. We have three computer terminals in our reading room. The collection is browsable through the libraries' web site.

93 *Ventura, CA*

Ventura County Museum of History and Art

Research Library
100 E. Main Street
Ventura, CA 93001
Telephone: 805-653-0323
Fax: 805-653-5267

Email: library@vcmha.org
Web: www.vcmha.org

Personnel:
Responsible person: Charles Johnson, Librarian, *email:* library@vcmha.org

Holdings:
Geographic strengths: Ventura County region, Santa Barbara County
Special collections: Sanborn Fire Insurance maps (1880–1950), Hale Collection of regional maps (1860–1989)
Subject strengths: aerial photos, city, engineering, historical geography, hydrology, industries, land ownership, land use, mining, railroads, raised relief models, views
4,000 printed maps

Access:
Collection is paged
Answers email questions

Hours:
Monday–Friday: 10 A.M.–5 P.M.
Saturday: 10 A.M.–1 P.M.
Total hours per week opened: 38

Physical facilities:
No Internet access
Copying facilities available: copier

Notes: Presently processing approximately 4,000 maps, anticipated to be made available to the general public in 2007. The library is open free to the public.

94 *Boulder, CO*

Boulder Public Library

Carnegie Branch Library for Local History
Map Collection
1125 Pine Street
Boulder, CO 80302
Telephone: 303-441-3110
Fax: 720-406-7452
Web: www.boulder.lib.co.us

Personnel:
Responsible person: Marti Anderson, Archivist, *email:* andersonma@boulder.lib.co.us
FTE professionals: 0.5

Holdings:
Geographic strengths: Boulder County
Special collections: Sanborn Fire Insurance maps, Marden Plat maps, Drumm maps of the County and City of Boulder
Subject strengths: aerial photos, city, geology, historical geography, land ownership, land use, mineral resources, mining, population, roads, views, waterways
207 printed maps
150 aerial photos

Chronological coverage:
  1800–1899: 20%
  1900–1939: 50%
  1940–present: 30%
Average budget over the last 5 years: $100

Access:
  Maps in separate area
  Collection is paged
  Reference questions per year: 120
  Answers email questions
  Patrons per month: 250

Hours:
  Total hours per week opened: 40

Collection services:
  Maps cataloged: 85%
  Maps classified: 85%
  Maps in OPAC: 85%
  Classification schemes: Local
  Cataloging utilities: OCLC
  Catalog accessibility: online
  Preservation techniques: encapsulation
  Percent of items that have gone through the preservation process: 85%

Physical facilities:
  Internet access available
  Square footage: 100
  Copying facilities available: copier

Notes: Our map collection is not separated from the rest of our collection, in that one single individual is responsible for it. It is integrated into the library's photograph and document collection.

95 *Boulder, CO*

University of Colorado, Boulder

Jerry Crail Johnson Earth Sciences and Map Library
Map Library
184 UCB
Boulder, CO 80309
Telephone: 303-492-7578
Fax: 303-735-4879
Email: maplib@colorado.edu
Web: www-libraries.colorado.edu/ps/map/

Personnel:
  Responsible person: Kathryn Lage, Map Librarian, *email:* katie.lage@colorado.edu
  Assistants: Naomi Heiser, Library Technician III; Ilene Raynes, Library Technician III
  Number of student workers hours per week: 80

Holdings:
  Geographic strengths: Colorado, West
  Special collections: Sanborn Fire Insurance maps of Colorado on microfiche, Historical Aerial Photographs of Colorado (1938 to ~1970)

Subject strengths: aerial photos, aeronautical, city, geology, geospatial data, nautical charts, recreation, roads, views
Map depositories and percentages: USGS topos (100%), USGS geology maps (100%), USGS other (100%), Department of Transportation, NOAA, GPO, CIA, National Forest Service, NIMA topos, NIMA nautical, NIMA aeronautical, BLM
190,000 printed maps
10 wall maps
50 microfiche
15,000 aerial photos
50 satellite images
22 gazetteers
370 printed atlases
1,159 books
669 CD-ROMs
Collecting digital data
Chronological coverage:
  Pre-1800: 0.5%
  1900–1939: 3.5%
  1940–present: 94%
Average budget over the last 5 years: $6,000
On-going publications: Web page. Collection handout. 2001Williams, Elisabeth Filar. "University of Colorado at Boulder, Map Library," Map Library Bulletin Board, *Cartographic Perspectives*, No. 39, Spring 2001. p. 47–50.

Access:
  Collection is open to the public
  Reference questions per year: 1,404
  Answers email questions

Hours:
  Monday–Thursday: 8 A.M.–10 P.M.
  Friday: 8 A.M.–5 P.M.
  Saturday: noon–5 P.M.
  Sunday: noon–10 P.M.
  Total hours per week opened: 80
  Maps circulate
  Circulation policies apply
    Map circulation duration: 2 weeks
    Number of maps circulated annually: 2,400

Geographic Information Systems:
  GIS services available in an open environment
  GIS software: ArcView 3.x, ArcGIS 8.x

Collection services:
  Maps cataloged: 60%
  Maps classified: 60%
  Maps in OPAC: 60%
  Datasets are cataloged
  Classification schemes: LC, SuDocs, Local, Other (Colorado State document numbers)
  Cataloging utilities: OCLC
  Catalog accessibility: online
  Preservation techniques: encapsulation, deacidification

Items that have gone through the preservation process: 0.5%

Physical facilities:
Internet access available
Square footage: 2,600
Number of map cases: 128
Linear book shelving: 360 ft.
Linear atlas shelving: 1,260 ft.
Copying facilities available: copier, large-format copier, microform copier

96 *Boulder, CO*

University of Colorado, Boulder

University Libraries Archives, founded 1917
184 UCB
Boulder, CO 80309-0184
Telephone: 303-492-7242
Fax: 303-492-3960
Email: arv@colorado.edu
Web: www.libraries.colorado.edu/ps/arv/frontpage.htm
Personnel:
Responsible person: Bruce P. Montgomery, Curator/ Head
Assistants: David M. Hays, Archivist
Number of student works: 14
Number of student workers hours per week: 10
Holdings:
Geographic strengths: Colorado, West
Special collections: Bent–Hyde (1830s–1910s), McLeod, Warren (1864–1944), William Carey Brown (1871–1930), Cobb, Harrison (1890s–1950s), Hall, Babitt and Thayer 1884–1921, Sanborn Insurance maps (1883–1937)
Subject strengths: aerial photos, agriculture, city, historical geography, military, mineral resources, mining, railroads, recreation, roads, travel books, views, waterways
Map depositories and percentages: USGS topos, National Forest Service
6,415 printed maps
Chronological coverage:
1800–1899: 20%
1900–1939: 40%
1940–present: 40%
Access:
Collection is open to the public
Reference questions per year: 40
Answers email questions
Patrons per month: 5
Hours:
Monday: 11 A.M.–5 P.M.
Wednesday: 11 A.M.–5 P.M.
Friday: 11 A.M.–5 P.M.
Total hours per week opened: 18
Geographic Information Systems:

No GIS services available
Collection services:
Maps cataloged: 90%
Catalog accessibility: cards
Physical facilities:
No Internet access
Number of map cases: 13
Other map storage: 2 rolled map cases
Copying facilities available: copier, color copier
Notes: Only 50% of our maps are in maps are in map cases, the rest are in or near their manuscript collection. Maps are either catalogued in a separate card file or in manuscript guides. There is no discrete map division in the archives, no special staffing, and few special resources.

97 *Colorado Springs, CO*

Colorado College

Tutt Library
Government Documents/Maps
1021 North Cascade Avenue
Colorado Springs, CO 80903
Telephone: 719-389-6660
Fax: 719-389-6082
Web: www2.coloradocollege.edu/Library/
Personnel:
Responsible person email: msielaff@coloradocollege.edu
Holdings:
Map depositories: USGS topos, CIA, National Forest Service, BLM
20,300 printed maps
1 globe
1,200 atlases
100 books
75 CD-ROMs
Maps cataloged: 40%
Maps classified: 100%
Maps in OPAC: 40%
Classification schemes: LC, SuDocs
Physical facilities:
Public computers: 1
Map cases: 35
Notes: Our collection is small. There are no set hours for working on it. The collection is available all hours the library is open. Some of the more rare maps are located in the government documents enclosed collection.

98 *Colorado Springs, CO*

Pikes Peak Library District

Carnegie Library
Special Collections
20 North Cascade Avenue
Colorado Springs, CO 80903
Telephone: 719-531-6333 x2253

Fax: 719-389-8161
Web: ppld.org
Personnel:
Responsible person: Tim Blevins, Manager, *email:* tblevins@mail.ppld.org
Assistants: Jody Jones, Local History Specialist
FTE para-professionals: 1
Holdings:
Geographic strengths: Colorado Springs, El Paso County, Pikes Peak region
Map depositories: USGS topos, National Forest Service
1,500 printed maps
10,000 aerial photos
20 atlases
30 books
Access:
Hours:
Monday–Friday: 10 A.M.–9 P.M.
Saturday: 10 A.M.–6 P.M.
Sunday: 1 P.M.–5 P.M.
Collection services:
Maps cataloged: 99%
Maps in OPAC: 99%
Classification schemes: Dewey
Physical facilities:
Public computers: 5
Map cases: 5
Vertical files: 1
Notes: Aerial photos are not in online catalog unless scanned in digital photo archive, which is online.

99 *Colorado Springs, CO*

University of Colorado, Colorado Springs

Kraemer Family Library
1420 Austin Bluffs Parkway
Colorado Springs, CO 80918
Telephone: 719-262-3295
Fax: 719-528-5227
Email: refdesk@uccs.edu
Web: web.uccs.edu/library/
Personnel:
Responsible person: Judith Rice-Jones, Social Sciences Librarian, *email:* jricejon@uccs.edu
FTE professionals: 0.2   *FTE para-professionals:* 0.2
Holdings:
Geographic strengths: El Paso County
Map depositories: USGS topos, CIA, National Forest Service, BLM
10,929 printed maps
30 aerial photos
1 globe
200 atlases
1,400 books
3 active serials
Access:

Hours:
Monday–Friday: 8 A.M.–11 P.M.
Saturday: 11 A.M.–7 P.M.
Sunday: noon–8 P.M.
Items circulate
Interlibrary loan available
Collection services:
Maps cataloged: 100%
Maps classified: 100%
Maps in OPAC: 10%
Classification schemes: LC, SuDocs
Physical facilities:
Public computers: 4
Map cases: 6
Vertical files: 7
Notes: Library hours vary with academic schedule. Check website or call for hours.

100 *Denver, CO*

Colorado Historical Society

Stephen H. Hart Library
1300 Broadway
Denver, CO 80224
Telephone: 303-866-4600
Fax: 303-866-5739
Web: www.coloradohistory.org
Personnel:
Responsible person: Patrick J. Fraker, *email:* patrick.fraker@chs.state.co.us
FTE professionals: 1
Holdings:
Geographic strengths: Colorado, West, Southwest
Special collections: Sanborn Fire Insurance maps, mines in Colorado, roads in Colorado
2,500 printed maps
30 atlases
30 books
Maps cataloged: 95%
Maps classified: 95%
Maps in OPAC: 95%
Classification schemes: Dewey
Access:
Hours:
Tuesday–Saturday: 10 A.M.–4:30 P.M.
Sunday: closed
Physical facilities:
Maps in separate area
Map cases: 15
Vertical files: 5

101 *Denver, CO*

Colorado State Archives

1313 Sherman Street
Room 1B-20
Denver, CO 80203

Telephone: 303-866-2550
Fax: 303-866-2257
Email: archives@state.co.us
Web: www.colorado.gov/dpa/doit/archives/
geography.htm
Personnel:
Responsible person: Terry Ketelsen, State Archivist,
FTE professionals: 0.25
Holdings:
Geographic strengths: Colorado
Special collections: School District boundary maps,
State Land Board Maps
125 printed maps
Collection services:
Maps cataloged: 90%
Maps classified: 100%
Classification schemes: Other (archival)

102 *Denver, CO*

Denver Public Library

Central Branch
Government Publications/GOVPUBS Maps
10 West 14th Avenue Parkway
Denver, CO 80204-2731
Telephone: 720-865-1721
Fax: 720-865-1785
Email: rtaht@denver.lib.co.us
Web: www.denverlibrary.org
Personnel:
Responsible person: Rose Ann Taht, *email:* rtaht@denver
.lib.co.us
Assistants: Rob Jackson, Senior Collection Specialist
Holdings:
Geographic strengths: United States, World
Special collections: AMS, Forest Service, USGS topos,
Colorado State Highway maps
Subject strengths: aerial photos, aeronautical, agricul-
ture, archaeology, early cartography, modern cartog-
raphy, celestial, climatology, city, economic geogra-
phy, forestry, genealogy, geodetic surveys, geology,
geospatial data, historical geography, hydrology,
land ownership, land use, map catalogs, map collecting, military, mineral resources, mining, nautical
charts, population, railroads, raised relief models,
recreation, roads, satellite imagery, soil, vegetation,
waterways
Map depositories and percentages: USGS topos
(100%), USGS geology maps (100%), USGS other,
Department of Transportation, NOAA, GPO, CIA,
National Forest Service, NIMA topos, NIMA nautical, NIMA aeronautical, BLM, State
85,000 printed maps
1,000 aerial photos
50 satellite images

300 gazetteers
1,000 printed atlases
On-going publications: In-house flyers.
Access:
Collection is open to the public
Reference questions per year: 400
Answers email questions
Patrons per month: 40
Hours:
Total hours per week opened: 40
Maps circulate
Map circulation duration: 1 week
Collection services:
Classification schemes: LC, SuDocs, Dewey, Local
Cataloging utilities: OCLC, Local
Catalog accessibility: online, fiche, cards, printout
Preservation techniques: encapsulation
Items that have gone through the preservation process:
10%
Physical facilities:
No Internet access
Number of map cases: 60
Copying facilities available: copier, microform copier

103 *Denver, CO*

Denver Public Library

Western History Collection, founded 1935
10 West 14th Avenue Parkway
Denver, CO 80204
Telephone: 720-865-1821
Fax: 720-865-1880
Web: www.denver.lib.co.us
Personnel:
Responsible person: Philip J. Panum, Special Collec-
tions Librarian, *email:* ppanum@denver.lib.co.us
Number of volunteer hours per month: 12
Holdings:
Geographic strengths: Colorado, Rocky Mountain region, Trans-Mississippi West
Special collections: Sanborn fire of Denver, and Colorado, New Mexico and Wyoming, historic USGS
topos for Colorado, State Highway map Collection
for Colorado from beginning, maps from serial sets
pertaining to exploration in the West, 19th century
mining maps for Colorado, maps of Denver
Subject strengths: aerial photos, aeronautical, agriculture, archaeology, early cartography, modern cartography, city, forestry, geology, historical geography,
hydrology, land ownership, land use, language, map
catalogs, mineral resources, mining, political geography, population, railroads, recreation, religion, roads,
satellite imagery, soil, travel books, vegetation,
views, waterways
Map depositories: USGS topos, National Forest Service

7,000 printed maps
100 manuscript maps
100 wall maps
50 microfilms
50 printed atlases
Chronological coverage:
Pre-1800: 10%
1800–1899: 40%
1900–1939: 30%
1940–present: 20%
Average budget over the last 5 years: $15,000
Access:
Collection is open to the public
Maps offsite: 10%
Answers email questions
Hours:
Total hours per week opened: 55
Geographic Information Systems:
No GIS services available
Scans maps for patrons
Collection services:
Maps cataloged: 100%
Maps classified: 100%
Maps in OPAC: 100%
Classification schemes: LC
Cataloging utilities: OCLC
Catalog accessibility: online
Preservation techniques: encapsulation, deacidification
Items that have gone through the preservation process: 50%
Physical facilities:
No Internet access
Square footage: 3,000
Number of map cases: 100
Linear book shelving: 300 ft.
Other map storage: rolled map cases
Copying facilities available: copier, color copier, large-format copier, microform copier

104 *Denver, CO*

National Archives and Records Administration, Rocky Mountain Region

P.O. Box 25307
Building 48
Denver Federal Center
Denver, CO 80225
Telephone: 303-407-5740
Fax: 303-407-5707
Email: archives@denver.nara.gov
Web: www.archives.gov/facilities/rocky_mountain_region.html
Personnel:
Responsible person: Eileen Bolger, Director, Archival Operations, *email:* eileen.bolger@nara.gov

Holdings:
Geographic strengths: Colorado, Montana, New Mexico, North Dakota, South Dakota, Utah, Wyoming
Special collections: permanently valuable records from over 75 federal agencies (1840s–1990s), includes copies of census bureau maps for entire county
48,000 printed maps
Access:
Hours:
Monday–Friday: 7:30 A.M.–3:45 P.M.
Physical facilities:
Public computers: 3
Map cases: 14

105 *Denver, CO*

United States Geological Survey, Denver

Central Region Library
Box 25046
Federal Center
Mail Stop 914
Denver, CO 80225
Telephone: 303-236-1000
Fax: 303-236-0015
Email: den_lib@usgs.gov
Web: library.usgs.gov
Personnel:
Responsible person: Cheryl Sund, *email:* csund@usgs.gov
Holdings:
Geographic strengths: United States, North America, Central America, South America
Special collections: USGS topographic maps
Subject strengths: aeronautical, agriculture, modern cartography, climatology, geology, hydrology, mineral resources, mining, projections, soil, vegetation, waterways
Map depositories and percentages: USGS topos (100%), USGS geology maps (100%), USGS other (100%)
150,000 printed maps
10 globes
400 gazetteers
250 printed atlases
Chronological coverage:
1900–1939: 14%
1940–present: 85%
Access:
Collection is open to the public
Answers email questions
Hours:
Monday–Friday: 8 A.M.–4 P.M.
Total hours per week opened: 40
Maps circulate
Circulation policies apply
Map circulation duration: 2 weeks

Atlas circulation duration: 2 weeks
Book circulation duration: 2 weeks
Interlibrary loan available
Geographic Information Systems:
No GIS services available
Collection services:
Maps cataloged: 80%
Maps classified: 100%
Maps in OPAC: 75%
Classification schemes: Other (USGS)
Cataloging utilities: OCLC
Catalog accessibility: online, cards
Preservation techniques: encapsulation, edging
Physical facilities:
Internet access available
Square footage: 2,300
Number of map cases: 254
Number of vertical files (file cabinets): 21
Linear atlas shelving: 297 ft.
Other map storage: 2 rolled map cases
Copying facilities available: copier

106 *Durango, CO*

Fort Lewis College

John F. Reed Library and the Center for Southwest
Studies
Map Collection
Durango, CO 81303
Telephone: 970-247-7551
Email: arbeeny_p@fortlewis.edu
Web: library.fortlewis.edu/reference/mapgovweb/
maps.html swcenter.fortlewis.edu/SpecialCollections
.htm#Guides
Personnel:
Responsible person: Pamela Arbeeny, Reed Library.
Todd Ellison, Center for SW Studies, *email:* arbeeny_p@fortlewis.edu
FTE professionals: 1.1   *FTE para-professionals:* 0.2
Number of student workers hours per week: 22
Holdings:
Geographic strengths: Colorado, New Mexico, Arizona, Utah
Special collections: Cutter World Map Collection,
Hayden Survey maps, Sanborn maps of selected
Southwest cities on microfilm
Subject strengths: geology
Map depositories and percentages: USGS topos (20%),
USGS geology maps (15%), USGS other, BLM, State
39,000 printed maps
12 wall maps
200 microfilms
36 satellite images
18 gazetteers

138 printed atlases
75 books
Chronological coverage:
Pre-1800: 0.2%
1940–present: 90.8%
Access:
Collection is open to the public
Answers email questions
Hours:
Monday–Friday: 7:30 A.M.–10 P.M.
Saturday: 1 P.M.–5 P.M.
Sunday: 1 P.M.–10 P.M.
Total hours per week opened: 80
Circulation policies apply
Map circulation duration: 3 weeks
Geographic Information Systems:
No GIS services available
Collection services:
Maps cataloged: 10%
Classification schemes: LC, Local
Cataloging utilities: OCLC
Catalog accessibility: online
Preservation techniques: lamination
Physical facilities:
Internet access available
Number of map cases: 30
Copying facilities available: copier, microform copier

107 *Fort Collins, CO*

Colorado State University

Morgan Library
Karen W. Jacob Map Collection
Fort Collins, CO 80523-1019
Telephone: 970-491-1836
Fax: 970-491-5817
Web: lib.colostate.edu
Personnel:
Responsible person: Suzanne N. Taylor, Reference Librarian, *email:* staylor@manta.colostate.edu
FTE professionals: 0.1   *FTE para-professionals:* 0.3
Number of student works: 1.5
Number of student workers hours per week: 15
Holdings:
Geographic strengths: Colorado
Subject strengths: aeronautical, forestry, geology, mineral resources, political geography
Map depositories and percentages: USGS topos
(100%), USGS geology maps (100%), USGS other
(100%), Department of Transportation, NOAA,
GPO, CIA, National Forest Service, NIMA topos,
NIMA nautical, NIMA aeronautical, BLM, State
70,000 printed maps
12 wall maps

15 raised relief maps
1,000 printed atlases
200 books
200 CD-ROMs
Collecting digital data
Chronological coverage:
   1940–present: 95%
Average budget over the last 5 years: $3,000
Access:
Collection is open to the public
Maps off site
Hours:
   Monday–Friday: 7:30 A.M.–midnight
   Saturday: 9 A.M.–10 P.M.
   Sunday: noon–midnight
   Total hours per week opened: 105.5
Maps circulate
Circulation policies apply
   Map circulation duration: 2 weeks
   Atlas circulation duration: 2 weeks
   Book circulation duration: 2 weeks
   Number of maps circulated annually: 1,500
Interlibrary loan available
Geographic Information Systems:
GIS services available in an open environment
GIS software: ArcGIS
Scans maps for patrons
Collection services:
Maps cataloged: 70%
Maps classified: 100%
Maps in OPAC: 70%
Datasets are cataloged
Classification schemes: LC, SuDocs
Cataloging utilities: OCLC
Catalog accessibility: online
Preservation techniques: encapsulation, deacidification, lamination, edging
Items that have gone through the preservation process: 15%
Physical facilities:
Square footage: 2,500
Number of map cases: 58
Linear book shelving: 612 ft.
Linear atlas shelving: 228 ft.
Other map storage: 3 rolled map cases
Copying facilities available: copier, color copier, microform copier
Notes: Our map collection is not located in a separate room, just in a separate area.

108 *Golden, CO*

American Alpine Club

Henry S. Hall, Jr. Library
710 Tenth Street

Suite 15
Golden, CO 80401
Telephone: 303-384-0112
Fax: 303-384-0113
Email: library@americanalpineclub.org
Web: www.americanalpineclub.org/knowledge/aaclibrary.asp
Personnel:
Responsible person: Daniel Farnbach, Library Assistant, *email:* serials@americanalpineclub.org
Assistants: Bridget Burke, Library Director; Maria Borysiewicz, Cataloging Librarian
Holdings:
Geographic strengths: Colorado, Alaska, Peru, Switzerland, Himalayas, Nepal, Karakoram Mountains
Subject strengths: aeronautical, early cartography, forestry, geology, raised relief models, recreation, roads, travel books, views, waterways, mountaineering maps
3,400 printed maps
11 raised relief maps
36 gazetteers
51 printed atlases
15 books
18 CD-ROMs
Chronological coverage:
   1900–1939: 33%
   1940–present: 65%
Average budget over the last 5 years: $200
On-going publications: Friends of the Library Newsletter.
Access:
Collection is partially open to the public
Answers email questions
Patrons per month: 100
Hours:
   Total hours per week opened: 30
Maps circulate
Circulation policies apply
   Map circulation duration: 4 weeks
   Book circulation duration: 4 weeks
   Number of books circulated annually: 3,000
Geographic Information Systems:
No GIS services available
Scans maps for patrons
Collection services:
Maps classified: 100%
Classification schemes: LC
Cataloging utilities: OCLC
Catalog accessibility: online
Preservation techniques: encapsulation
Physical facilities:
Internet access available
Square footage: 400

Linear book shelving: 24 ft.
Copying facilities available: copier, scanner

109 *Golden, CO*

Colorado School of Mines

Arthur Lakes Library
Map Room, founded 1957
1400 Illinois
Golden, CO 80401
Telephone: 303-273-3697
Fax: 303-273-3199
Email: cthiry@mines.edu
Web: www.mines.edu/library/maproom

Personnel:

Responsible person: Christopher J.J. Thiry, Map Librarian, *email:* cthiry@mines.edu
Assistants: Cheryl Livingston, Library Technician III
FTE professionals: 1   *FTE para-professionals:* 0.25
Number of student workers hours per week: 15

Holdings:

Geographic strengths: Colorado, Rocky Mountains
Special collections: Colorado topographic maps, mining maps of Colorado and the Rocky Mountains
Subject strengths: aerial photos, engineering, geology, hydrology, mineral resources, mining
Map depositories and percentages: USGS topos (100%), USGS geology maps (100%), USGS other (100%), Department of Transportation, GPO, CIA, National Forest Service, NIMA topos, NIMA aeronautical, BLM, State
202,800 printed maps
75 raised relief maps
54 microfiche
46,767 aerial photos
1,000 printed atlases
6,675 books
15 inactive serials
54 CD-ROMs
Chronological coverage:
    1800–1899: 10%
    1900–1939: 20%
    1940–present: 70%
Average budget over the last 5 years: $4,000

Access:

Collection is open to the public
Reference questions per year: 600
Answers email questions

Hours:

    Monday–Thursday: 7:30 A.M.–midnight
    Friday: 7:30 A.M.–6 P.M.
    Saturday: 10 A.M.–5 P.M.
    Sunday: 1 P.M.–10 P.M.
    Total hours per week opened: 92.5
Maps circulate
Circulation policies apply

Map circulation duration: 3 weeks
Atlas circulation duration: 3 weeks
Book circulation duration: 3 weeks
Interlibrary loan available

Geographic Information Systems:
No GIS services available

Collection services:
Maps cataloged: 100%
Maps classified: 100%
Maps in OPAC: 100%
Classification schemes: LC
Cataloging utilities: OCLC
Catalog accessibility: online
Preservation techniques: encapsulation, deacidification
Items that have gone through the preservation process: 10%

Physical facilities:
Internet access available
Square footage: 5,000
Number of public computers: 1
Number of staff computers: 2
Number of map cases: 192
Number of vertical files (file cabinets): 34
Number of atlas stands: 3
Linear book shelving: 411 ft.
Linear atlas shelving: 339 ft.
Other map storage: rolled map case
Number of light tables: 2
Copying facilities available: copier, microform copier

Notes: Reference help only available Monday–Friday, 8 A.M.–5 P.M.

110 *Greeley, CO*

University of Northern Colorado

James A. Michener Library
Campus Box 48
Greeley, CO 80639
Telephone: 970-351-2671
Fax: 970-351-2963
Web: www.unco.edu/library/

Personnel:

Responsible person: Adonna Fleming, Assistant Professor University Libraries, *email:* adonna.fleming@unco.edu
FTE professionals: 0.092

Holdings:

Map depositories: USGS topos, CIA, National Forest Service, BLM
55,000 printed maps
4 globes
1,016 atlases
349 books
27 active serials
54 CD-ROMs

Access:

Hours:
Monday–Thursday: 7:30 A.M.–midnight
Friday: 7:30-6 P.M.
Saturday: noon–5 P.M.
Sunday: noon–midnight

Collection services:
Items circulate
Maps cataloged: 10%
Maps classified: 100%
Maps in OPAC: 10%
Classification schemes: LC, SuDocs

Physical facilities:
Public computers: 1
Map cases: 24
Vertical files: 4

Notes: The map collection is part of the reference collection. The map collection is open all hours that the library is open. Hours vary during intersession, summer sessions, and holidays.

111 *Lakewood, CO*

Jefferson County Public Library

Lakewood Library
Government Documents
10200 West 20th Avenue
Lakewood, CO 80215
Telephone: 303-232-9507
Fax: 303-275-2234
Web: jefferson.lib.co.us

Personnel:
Responsible person: Sharon Partridge, Government Documents Librarian, *email:* sharonp@jefferson.lib.co.us
FTE professionals: 0.25   *FTE para-professionals:* 0.25

Holdings:
Geographic strengths: Colorado, Wyoming, New Mexico, Utah, Arizona
Map depositories: USGS topos, NOAA, CIA, National Forest Service, BLM
5,000 printed maps
100 aerial photos
1 globe
50 atlases
50 books
30 CD-ROMs

Access:
Hours:
Monday–Thursday: 10 A.M.–9 P.M.
Friday: 10 A.M.–5 P.M.
Sunday: noon–5 P.M.
Items circulate
Interlibrary loan available

Collection services:
Maps cataloged: 50%
Maps classified: 100%
Maps in OPAC: 50%

Classification schemes: SuDocs, Dewey, Local
Physical facilities:
Public computers: 40
Vertical files: 6

112 *Loveland, CO*

Loveland Public Library

Map Vertical File
300 North Adams
Loveland, CO 80537
Telephone: 970-962-2402
Fax: 970-962-2905
Web: www.ci.loveland.co.us/library

Personnel:
Responsible person: Susan Linden, Librarian I, *email:* lindes@ci.loveland.co.us
FTE para-professionals: 0.5
Number of student workers hours per week: 0.25

Holdings:
Geographic strengths: Loveland, Larimer County
Special collections: Robert P. Markham Collection of USGS topographic maps, USGS 1:100,000 topographic maps
Subject strengths: city, travel books, Loveland, Colorado
2,200 printed maps
1 aerial photo
4 globes
12 gazetteers
223 printed atlases
25 books
1 active serial
4 CD-ROMs
Average budget over the last 5 years: $40

Access:
Answers email questions
Hours:
Monday–Friday: 10 A.M.–9 P.M.
Saturday: 10 A.M.–6 P.M.
Sunday: 1 A.M.–5 P.M.

Collection services:
Maps cataloged: 1%
Maps classified: 95%
Maps in OPAC: 1%
Classification schemes: Dewey, Local

Physical facilities:
Number of public computers: 16
Number of map cases: 1
Number of vertical files (file cabinets): 2

113 *Pueblo, CO*

Pueblo City—County Library District

Robert Hoag Rawlings Public Library
Western Research Map Collection

100 East Abriendo Avenue
Pueblo, CO 81004
Telephone: 719-562-5626
Fax: 719-553-0327
Web: www.pueblolibrary.org
Personnel:
Responsible person: Noreen Riffe, *email:* noreen@
pueblolibrary.org
FTE professionals: 1   *FTE para-professionals:* 0.5
Holdings:
Geographic strengths: Colorado, Pueblo, Southeastern
Colorado
Special collections: Sanborn Fire Insurance maps for
Pueblo (1883, 1886, 1893, 1904-5, 1941, 1951) and
for various other Southeastern Colorado towns
Map depositories: USGS topos, CIA
2,100 printed maps
10 aerial photos
275 atlases
5 CD-ROMs
Access:
Hours:
Monday–Thursday: 9 A.M.–9 P.M.
Friday–Saturday: 9 A.M.–6 P.M.
Sunday: 1 P.M.–5 P.M.
Collection services:
Maps cataloged: 95%
Maps classified: 95%
Maps in OPAC: 75%
Classification schemes: SuDocs, Dewey, Local
Physical facilities:
Maps in separate area
Public computers: 1
Map cases: 5
Vertical files: 6 archive boxes

114 *Hartford, CT*

Connecticut Historical Society Library

1 Elizabeth Street
Hartford, CT 06105
Telephone: 860-236-5621
Fax: 860-236-2664
Web: www.chs.org
Personnel:
Responsible person: Nancy Milnor, Library Director,
email: nancy_milnor@chs.org
Holdings:
Geographic strengths: Connecticut, New England
Subject strengths: agriculture, early cartography, city,
economic geography, forestry, genealogy, geology,
historical geography, hydrology, industries, land
ownership, land use, map catalogs, nautical charts,
political geography, population, railroads, roads,
vegetation, views, waterways

1,200 printed maps
51 manuscript maps
40 wall maps
100 printed atlases
35 books
Chronological coverage:
Pre-1800: 15%
1800–1899: 60%
1900–1939: 20%
1940–present: 5%
Access:
Maps in separate area
Collection is paged
Answers email questions
Hours:
Tuesday–Saturday: 10 A.M.–5 P.M.
Total hours per week opened: 35
Geographic Information Systems:
No GIS services available
Scans maps for patrons
Collection services:
Maps cataloged: 60%
Maps classified: 60%
Maps in OPAC: 25%
Classification schemes: Dewey, Local
Cataloging utilities: OCLC
Catalog accessibility: online, cards
Preservation techniques: encapsulation, deacidifica-
tion, lamination
Items that have gone through the preservation process:
10%
Physical facilities:
Internet access available
Linear atlas shelving: 30 ft.
Other map storage: 4 rolled map cases
Copying facilities available: copier, microform copier

115 *Hartford, CT*

Connecticut State Library

History and Genealogy Unit
231 Capitol Avenue
Hartford, CT 06106
Telephone: 860-757-6580
Fax: 860-757-6677
Email: isref@cslib.org
Web: www.cslib.org
Personnel:
Responsible person: Carolyn M. Picciano, Library Spe-
cialist, *email:* cpicciano@cslib.org
Number of student workers hours per week: 20
Holdings:
Geographic strengths: Connecticut
Special collections: Sanborn Fire Insurance maps of
Connecticut, City Directory maps of Connecticut,

William B. Goodwin Collection of early maps of America, Aerial Photograph Collection of Connecticut (1932–1995)

Subject strengths: aerial photos, early cartography, city, genealogy, railroads, roads, views

24,000 printed maps

300 manuscript maps

250 wall maps

750 microfiche

27 microfilms

53,000 aerial photos

25 gazetteers

350 printed atlases

75 books

Chronological coverage:
  1900–1939: 30%
  1940–present: 65%

Access:
  Collection is partially open to the public
  Reference questions per year: 3,000
  Answers email questions
  Patrons per month: 125

Hours:
  Monday–Friday: 9 A.M.–5 P.M.
  Saturday: 9 A.M.–2 P.M.
  Total hours per week opened: 45

Geographic Information Systems:
  No GIS services available

Collection services:
  Maps cataloged: 30%
  Maps classified: 30%
  Classification schemes: LC, Dewey, Local
  Cataloging utilities: OCLC
  Catalog accessibility: online, cards
  Preservation techniques: encapsulation, deacidification
  Items that have gone through the preservation process: 10%

Physical facilities:
  Internet access available
  Square footage: 300
  Number of map cases: 27
  Linear atlas shelving: 50 ft.
  Other map storage: shelving for boxed aerial photographs and rolled maps
  Copying facilities available: copier, color copier, microform copier

116 *Hartford, CT*

Trinity College

Watkinson Library
300 Summit Street
Hartford, CT 06106
Telephone: 860-297-2268
Fax: 860-297-2251

Web: www.trincoll.edu/depts/library/watkinson/

Personnel:
  Responsible person: Jeffrey H. Kaimowitz, *email:* jeffrey.kaimowitz@trincoll.edu

Holdings:
  Geographic strengths: East
  Special collections: Barnard Textbook collection with over 600 school atlases and geographies, Hakluyt Society Publications, Enders Ornithology Collection
  Subject strengths: early cartography, land use, travel books, Ornithology atlases
  700 printed maps
  300 printed atlases
  Chronological coverage:
    Pre-1800: 15%
    1800–1899: 75%
    1900–1939: 10%
  On-going publications: Kaimowitz, Jeffrey H. "American School Atlases and Geographies with Maps in the Barnard Collection." *Meridian*, no. 18 (1998), p. 13–22.

Access:
  Maps in separate area
  Collection is paged
  Answers email questions

Hours:
  Monday–Friday: 9:30 A.M.–4:30 P.M.
  Sunday: closed
  Total hours per week opened: 35

Collection services:
  Maps cataloged: 95%
  Maps classified: 95%
  Maps in OPAC: 50%
  Classification schemes: LC, Local
  Cataloging utilities: OCLC
  Catalog accessibility: online, cards
  Preservation techniques: encapsulation, deacidification

Physical facilities:
  No Internet access
  Square footage: 88
  Copying facilities available: face-up scanning copier

Notes: This only applies to the Watkinson Library, Trinity College's special collections.

117 *Mystic, CT*

Mystic Seaport

G.W. Blunt White Library
Charts and Maps Collection
75 Greenmanville Avenue
Mystic, CT 06355
Telephone: 860-572-0711
Fax: 860-572-5394
Email: inquiries@mysticseaport.org
Web: schooner.mysticseaport.org

Personnel:

Responsible person: Leah Prescott, Manuscripts and Archives Librarian, *email:* leah.prescott@mystic seaport.org

Holdings:

Geographic strengths: Oceans

Special collections: Sanborn Fire Insurance maps for Mystic, Connecticut, F.W. Beers maps for Southeastern Connecticut, Oyster ground charts for the Connecticut coast

Subject strengths: nautical charts, waterways, track charts for maritime voyages

10,000 printed maps

Access:

Maps in separate area

Collection is paged

Answers email questions

Hours:

Monday–Friday: noon–5 P.M.

Total hours per week opened: 25

Geographic Information Systems:

No GIS services available

Scans maps for patrons

Collection services:

Maps cataloged: 0.75%

Maps classified: 1%

Maps in OPAC: 1%

Classification schemes: LC, Other (Boggs and Lewis)

Cataloging utilities: OCLC, Local, LC

Catalog accessibility: online, cards

Preservation techniques: encapsulation

Items that have gone through the preservation process: 1%

Physical facilities:

No Internet access

Number of map cases: 10

Copying facilities available: copier, scanners

118 *New Haven, CT*

New Haven Colony Historical Society

Whitney Library

114 Whitney Avenue

New Haven, CT 06510

Telephone: 203-562-4183, x15

Fax: 203-562-2002

Personnel:

Responsible person: James W. Campbell, Library Services Manager

FTE professionals: 2

Holdings:

Geographic strengths: New Haven, Connecticut

Subject strengths: city, genealogy, historical geography, nautical charts, railroads

300 printed maps

60 manuscript maps

20 wall maps

20 gazetteers

30 printed atlases

60 CD-ROMs

Chronological coverage:

Pre-1800: 10%

1800–1899: 50%

1900–1939: 35%

Access:

Collection is open to the public

Reference questions per year: 250

Patrons per month: 100

Hours:

Wednesday–Friday: 10 A.M.–5 P.M.

Total hours per week opened: 21

Geographic Information Systems:

Number of public GIS workstations: 0

Scans maps for patrons

Collection services:

Maps cataloged: 100%

Maps classified: 100%

Maps in OPAC: 0%

Classification schemes: LC

Catalog accessibility: cards

Preservation techniques: encapsulation, deacidification

Items that have gone through the preservation process: 25%

Physical facilities:

No Internet access

Number of map cases: 40

Linear book shelving: 61 ft.

Other map storage: rolled map cases

Copying facilities available: copier, microform copier

119 *New Haven, CT*

Yale University

Sterling Memorial Library

Map Collection

130 Wall Street

P.O. Box 208240

New Haven, CT 06520

Telephone: 203-432-1867

Fax: 203-432-8527

Email: maps@yale.edu

Web: www.library.yale.edu/MapColl

Personnel:

Responsible person: Fred Musto, Curator, *email:* fred.musto@yale.edu

Assistants: Abraham Parrish, GIS Specialist; Margit Kaye, Library Assistant

FTE professionals: 2.5   *FTE para-professionals:* 1.5
Number of student workers hours per week: 25

Holdings:

Geographic strengths: Connecticut, New England, Colonial America (18th century), United States (19th century), West, Africa

Special collections: Sanborn Fire Insurance maps for Connecticut, Seaver Collection of road maps

Subject strengths: early cartography, modern cartography, city, geospatial data, historical geography, land ownership, map collecting, nautical charts, roads

Map depositories and percentages: USGS topos (100%), CIA, National Forest Service, NIMA topos, BLM

225,000 printed maps
525 manuscript maps
550 wall maps
50 raised relief maps
25 aerial photos
50 satellite images
33 globes
3,400 printed atlases
750 books
15 active serials
10 inactive serials
50 CD-ROMs
Collecting digital data

Chronological coverage:
1800–1899: 15%
1900–1939: 20%
1940–present: 60%

Access:

Maps in separate area
Collection is partially open to the public
Maps off site
Reference questions per year: 1,200
Answers email questions
Patrons per month: 150

Hours:

Monday–Friday: 10 A.M.–5 P.M.
Saturday–Saturday: closed
Total hours per week opened: 35

Geographic Information Systems:

GIS services available by appointment
GIS software: ArcGIS (ArcView, ArcSDE, ArcIMS)
GIS assistance available for Census mapping, geocoding, and image analysis
Plotter available
Scans maps for patrons

Collection services:

Maps cataloged: 95%
Maps classified: 99%
Maps in OPAC: 40%

Classification schemes: LC, Local
Cataloging utilities: OCLC, RLG, Local
Catalog accessibility: online, cards
Preservation techniques: encapsulation, deacidification
Items that have gone through the preservation process: 10%

Physical facilities:

Internet access available
Square footage; 3,500
Number of map cases: 125
Linear book shelving: 258 ft.
Linear atlas shelving: 1,600 ft.
Other map storage: 265 pamphlet boxes; 978 linear feet of flat map shelving
Copying facilities available: copier, large-format copier, microform copier, Large-format scanner, color plotter

120 *Somers, CT*

Broer Map Library

74 Hampden Road
Somers, CT 06071
Telephone: 413-221-4642
Email: dave@broermaps.org
Web: www.broermaps.org/

Personnel:

Responsible person: David F Broer, *email:* dave@broermaps.org

Holdings:

Geographic strengths: New England, Labrador, Tuvalu, European Theater World War II

Subject strengths: aeronautical, caves, celestial, climatology, city, economic geography, engineering, forestry, geodetic surveys, geology, geospatial data, historical geography, hydrology, land ownership, land use, language, map catalogs, map collecting, military, mineral resources, mining, nautical charts, oceanography, population, projections, railroads, raised relief models, recreation, roads, travel books, vegetation, views, waterways

35,500 printed maps
16 raised relief maps
56 gazetteers
344 printed atlases
1,032 books
6,700 CD-ROMs

Chronological coverage:
1800–1899: 1.5%
1900–1939: 9.1%
1940–present: 89.4%

Average budget over the last 5 years: $12,500
On-going publications: http://www.broermaps.org/

Access:

Maps in separate area

Collection is partially open to the public

Answers email questions

Maps circulate

Circulation policies apply

Map circulation duration: 3 weeks

Atlas circulation duration: 3 weeks

Book circulation duration: 3 weeks

Number of maps circulated annually: 150

Number of books circulated annually: 75

Interlibrary loan available

Geographic Information Systems:

No GIS services available

Scans maps for patrons

Collection services:

Maps cataloged: 100%

Maps classified: 100%

Maps in OPAC: 100%

Datasets are cataloged

Classification schemes: Other

Catalog accessibility: online

Physical facilities:

Internet access available

Square footage: 450

Linear book shelving: 64 ft.

Linear atlas shelving: 64 ft.

Notes: Our collection is private. Available to the public through a co-operative that lends its maps and atlases to members. The collection is in the process of being digitized for public terminal access without having to ship the actual map to a requesting member.

---

121 *Storrs, CT*

University of Connecticut

Homer Babbidge Library

Map and Geographic Information Center, founded 1972

369 Fairfield Road

Storrs, CT 06269-0584

Telephone: 860-486-4589

Fax: 486-4100

Email: Bill.Miller@uconn.edu

Web: magic.lib.uconn.edu/

Personnel:

Responsible person: Patrick McGlamery, *email:* patrick.mcglamery@uconn.edu

Assistants: Bill Miller, Assistant to the Map Librarian

FTE para-professionals: 0.75

Number of student works: 10

Number of student workers hours per week: 70

Holdings:

Geographic strengths: Connecticut, Southern New England, New England, Middle Atlantic, Europe

Special collections: Petersen Collection of New England villages, Images of the U.S. Coast Survey

Subject strengths: aerial photos, agriculture, archaeology, biology, early cartography, modern cartography, celestial, city, economic geography, engineering, forestry, genealogy, geodetic surveys, geology, geospatial data, historical geography, hydrology, industries, land ownership, land use, map catalogs, map collecting, military, mineral resources, mining, political geography, population, railroads, raised relief models, recreation, religion, roads, soil, travel books, vegetation, views, waterways

Map depositories and percentages: USGS topos (90%), USGS geology maps (80%), USGS other (75%), GPO, CIA, National Forest Service, NIMA topos, BLM, State

190,000 printed maps

58 raised relief maps

130 aerial photos

10,000 satellite images

351 gazetteers

1,300 printed atlases

33 books

550 CD-ROMs

Collecting digital data

Chronological coverage:

1800–1899: 25%

1900–1939: 25%

1940–present: 50%

Average budget over the last 5 years: $15,000

Access:

Maps in separate area

Collection is open to the public

Answers email questions

Hours:

Monday–Friday: 9 A.M.–noon, 1 P.M.–5 P.M.

Total hours per week opened: 45

Maps circulate

Map circulation duration: 2 weeks

Atlas circulation duration: 2 weeks

Book circulation duration: 2 weeks

Interlibrary loan available

Geographic Information Systems:

GIS assistance available for Census mapping, geocoding, and image analysis

Data capture, georeferencing help available

Plotter available

Scans maps for patrons

Collection services:

Maps cataloged: 75%

Maps classified: 90%

Maps in OPAC: 98%

Classification schemes: LC

Cataloging utilities: OCLC

Catalog accessibility: online
Preservation techniques: encapsulation, deacidification, lamination
Physical facilities:
Internet access available
Copying facilities available: copier, color copier, large-format copier, microform copier

122 *Newark, DE*

University of Delaware

Hugh M. Morris Library
Map Room
181 South College Avenue
Newark, DE 19717-526
Telephone: 302-831-6664
Fax: 302-831-1046
Web: www.lib.udel.edu/ud/digital/microcopy/gis/ and www.lib.udel.edu/ud/spec/findaids/hist_map/index.htm
Personnel:
Responsible person: Shelly McCoy, Head, Digital User Services Department, *email:* smccoy@udel.edu
FTE professionals: 1   *FTE para-professionals:* 6
Holdings:
Geographic strengths: United States
Special collections: Sanborn Fire Insurance maps for Delaware, New Jersey, Maryland, Pennsylvania, and Washington DC (microfilm), Historic Map Collection of 993 maps (1561–1995)
Map depositories: USGS topos, NOAA, CIA, National Forest Service, NGA nautical, NGA aeronautical, BLM
100,000 printed maps

123 *Washington, DC*

District of Columbia Public Library

Martin Luther King Jr. Memorial Library
Washingtoniana Division #307
901 G Street NW
Washington, DC 20001
Telephone: 202-727-1213
Fax: 202-727-1129
Email: wash.dcpl@dc.gov
Web: www.dclibrary.org
Personnel:
Responsible person: Karen Blackman-Mills, *email:* karen.blackman-mills@dc.gov
Assistants: Mohammed Jaleel
FTE professionals: 0.25   *FTE para-professionals:* 0
Holdings:

Geographic strengths: Washington, DC
Special collections: Sanborn Fire Insurance maps
400 printed maps
5 aerial photos
1 globe
1 book
Maps cataloged: 75%
Maps classified: 75%
Maps in OPAC: 0%
Classification schemes: Local
Access:
Hours:
Monday–Friday: 9:30 A.M.–9 P.M.
Saturday: 9:30 A.M.–5:30 P.M.
Sunday: 1 P.M.–5 P.M.
Physical facilities:
Map cases: 7
Vertical files: 1

124 *Washington, DC*

Folger Shakespeare Library

201 East Capitol Street SE
Washington, DC 20003
Telephone: 202-544-4600
Fax: 202-675-0313
Email: reference@folger.edu
Web: www.folger.edu
Assistants: Dr. Georgianna Ziegler, Head of Reference; Rachel Doggett, Curator of Rare Books; Dr. Erin Blake, Curator of Art; Dr. Heather Wolf, Curator of Manuscripts
Holdings:
Geographic strengths: Great Britain (especially London and Warwickshire), Europe
Subject strengths: early cartography, celestial, city, historical geography, land ownership, map catalogs, map collecting, travel books, views, imaginary places
350 printed maps
70 printed atlases
Chronological coverage:
Pre-1800: 95%
On-going publications: Printed catalogs of books, art and manuscripts. Items acquired since 1996 are listed in online catalog, Hamnet
Access:
Maps in separate area
Collection is partially open to the public
Answers email questions
Hours:
Monday–Friday: 8:45 A.M.–4:45 P.M.
Saturday: 9 A.M.–noon, 1 P.M.–4:30 P.M.
Total hours per week opened: 46

Geographic Information Systems:
No GIS services available
Scans maps for patrons
Collection services:
Maps cataloged: 85%
Maps classified: 100%
Maps in OPAC: 10%
Classification schemes: LC, Local
Cataloging utilities: RLG
Catalog accessibility: online, cards, printout
Preservation techniques: encapsulation, deacidification, acid-free folders
Physical facilities:
Internet access available
Copying facilities available: copier, microform copier, Photography Department
Notes: Many of the maps are in early printed books (1475–1700). Most of those books are cataloged, but the maps within them are not cataloged separately. Many of the separate maps in the collection are of Great Britain.

125 *Washington, DC*

Library of Congress

Geography and Map Division
Founded 1897
101 Independence Avenue SE
Madison Building
Room LM B01
Washington, DC 20540-4650
Telephone: 202-707-6277
Fax: 202-707-8531
Email: www.loc.gov/rr/askalib/ask-geogmap.html
Web: www.loc.gov/rr/geogmap/
Personnel:
Responsible person: John Hébert
Assistants: Michael Buscher, Collection Management Team Leader; Kathryn Engstrom, Reference Team Leader
FTE professionals: 38   *FTE para-professionals:* 16
Holdings:
Subject strengths: aeronautical, agriculture, archaeology, biology, early cartography, modern cartography, caves, celestial, climatology, city, economic geography, engineering, forestry, genealogy, geodetic surveys, geology, geospatial data, historical geography, hydrology, industries, land ownership, land use, language, map catalogs, map collecting, military, mineral resources, mining, nautical charts, oceanography, political geography, population, projections, railroads, raised relief models, recreation, religion, roads, soil, travel books, vegetation, views, waterways, zoogeography

Map depositories and percentages: USGS topos (100%), USGS geology maps (100%), USGS other (100%), Department of Transportation, NOAA, GPO, CIA, National Forest Service, NIMA topos, NIMA nautical, NIMA aeronautical, BLM, State, United Nations
4,800,000 printed maps
40,000 manuscript maps
100 wall maps
2,600 raised relief maps
97,000 microfiche
5,800 microfilms
500 aerial photos
500 satellite images
550 globes
1,500 gazetteers
65,000 printed atlases
20 manuscript atlases
6,000 books
10 active serials
40 inactive serials
14,000 CD-ROMs
Collecting digital data
Chronological coverage:
  1800–1899: 20%
  1900–1939: 40%
  1940–present: 35%
On-going publications: Philip Lee Phillips Society Newsletter, Philip Lee Phillips Society Occasional Paper Series, List of officially published works, http://lcweb.loc.gov/rr/geogmap/published.html
Access:
Maps in separate area
Collection is paged
Reference questions per year: 16,000
Answers email questions
Patrons per month: 250
Hours:
  Monday–Friday: 8:30 A.M.–5 P.M.
  Saturday–Saturday: closed
  Total hours per week opened: 42.5
Interlibrary loan available
Geographic Information Systems:
Scans maps for patrons
Collection services:
Maps cataloged: 50%
Maps classified: 60%
Maps in OPAC: 50%
Datasets are cataloged
Classification schemes: LC
Cataloging utilities: Local
Catalog accessibility: online
Preservation techniques: encapsulation, deacidification, repair, humidification
Physical facilities:
Internet access available

Square footage: 95,000
Number of staff computers: 60
Number of map cases: 8,000
Number of vertical files (file cabinets): 30
Linear book shelving: 1,000 ft.
Linear atlas shelving: 55,000 ft.
Copying facilities available: copier, color copier, large-format copier, microform copier

126 *Washington, DC*

National Geographic Society

Harold A. Hanson Map Library
National Geographic Maps
1145 17th Street NW
Washington, DC 20036
Telephone: 202-857-7083
Web: www.nationalgeographic.com
Personnel:
Responsible person: Eric Lindstrom, Map Library Director, *email:* elindstr@ngs.org
Number of student workers hours per week: 10
Holdings:
Special collections: National Geographic maps
Subject strengths: aeronautical, archaeology, celestial, city, historical geography, nautical charts, oceanography, recreation, satellite imagery
45,000 printed maps
2,000 printed atlases
500 books
Chronological coverage:
1940–present: 94%
Access:
Maps in separate area
Maps off site: 10%
Collection services:
Maps cataloged: 90%
Maps in OPAC: 90%
Classification schemes: LC, Local
Cataloging utilities: OCLC, Local
Catalog accessibility: online
Notes: The National Geographic map library is only occasionally open to the public and by appointment only.

127 *Washington, DC*

Smithsonian Institution

Regional Planetary Image Facility
Planetary Maps
6th and Independence Avenue SW
Washington, DC 20560
Telephone: 202-633-2480
Fax: 202-786-2566
Email: rsteinat@nasm.si.edu
Web: www.nasm.si.edu/research/ceps/imagery.cfm

Personnel:
Responsible person: Jim Zimbelman, *email:* jrz@nasm.si.edu
Assistants: Rosemary Steinat, Data Manager
FTE professionals: 1   *FTE para-professionals:* 1
Holdings:
Geographic strengths: Moon, Mars, Mercury, Venus, Jupiter/Moons, Saturn/Moons
Special collections: Lunar orthophoto and topophoto maps
Map depositories: USGS topos, NGA aeronautical
1,200 printed maps
500 aerial photos
4 globes
25 atlases
Access:
Hours:
Monday–Friday: 8 A.M.–5 P.M.
Physical facilities:
Public computers: 1
Vertical files: 3

128 *Washington, DC*

World Bank

Library and Archives Development
1818 H Street
Washington, DC 20433
Telephone: 202-473-8670
Fax: 202-522-1160
Personnel:
Responsible person: L. Wilson, Information Assistant, *email:* lwilson@worldbank.org
Holdings:
Geographic strengths: World
Subject strengths: agriculture, climatology, economic geography, geodetic surveys, geology, historical geography, hydrology, industries, land use, language, mineral resources, mining, oceanography, political geography, population, railroads, religion, roads, satellite imagery, soil, vegetation, waterways
9,600 printed maps
Access:
Maps in separate area
Collection is partially paged, partially open to the public
Hours:
Monday–Friday: 9 A.M.–5:30 P.M.
Geographic Information Systems:
Scans maps for patrons
Collection services:
Classification schemes: LC, Local
Cataloging utilities: OCLC, Local
Catalog accessibility: online
Physical facilities:
Copying facilities available: copier

129 *Boca Raton, FL*

Florida Atlantic University

S.E. Wimberly Library
777 Glades Road
Boca Raton, FL 33431
Telephone: 561-297-3760
Fax: 561-338-3863
Web: www.fau.edu/library
Personnel:
Responsible person: Dawn Smith, Department Head, Reference and Government Documents, *email:* dsmith@fau.edu
Assistants: Bruce Barron, Government Documents Librarian; Weina Luo, Senior Library Technical Assistant; Larry Mello, Senior Library Technical Assistant
FTE professionals: 2   *FTE para-professionals:* 2
Holdings:
Geographic strengths: Palm Beach, Broward County, Miami–Dade County, Florida
Special collections: Census 2000 Tract Outline Maps and Census 2000 Block maps for Palm Beach, Broward, and Miami-Dade counties
Map depositories: USGS topos, CIA, National Forest Service, BLM
36,493 printed maps
8 globes
230 atlases
1,449 books
29 active serials
Access:
Hours:
Monday–Thursday: 8 A.M.–midnight
Friday: 8 A.M.–7 P.M.
Saturday: 9 A.M. 8 P.M.
Sunday: noon–midnight
Items circulate
Interlibrary loan available
Collection services:
Maps cataloged: 20%
Maps classified: 25%
Maps in OPAC: 20%
Classification schemes: SuDocs, Local
Physical facilities:
Public computers: 2
Map cases: 13
Vertical files: 20

130 *Coral Gables, FL*

University of Miami

Otto G. Richter Library
Archives and Special Collection Department
1300 Memorial Drive
Coral Gables, FL 33124-0320
Telephone: 305-284-3247

Fax: 305-284-4027
Web: www.library.miami.edu/archives/intro.html
Personnel:
Responsible person: Craig S. Likness, Head, Archives and Special Collections, *email:* clikness@miami.edu
Holdings:
Geographic strengths: Florida, United States, South America, West Indies
Special collections: Boyd (Mark F.) Early maps of Florida, Eder (Phanor J.) maps of Colombia, Venezuela and Mexico, Karpinski (Louis) maps of South America and West Indies, Kelleher (Joseph) maps of Lesser Antilles, Bahamas, and Bermuda, Roney Early maps of America, Florida, West Indies and Southeast, Willson (M.M.) maps of Florida
Subject strengths: aerial photos, historical geography
7,000 printed maps
500 aerial photos
Chronological coverage:
Pre-1800: 10%
1800–1899: 60%
1900–1939: 30%
Access:
Maps in separate area
Collection is partially open to the public
Reference questions per year: 50
Hours:
Monday–Friday: 9 A.M.–4 P.M.
Saturday–Saturday: closed
Total hours per week opened: 35
Geographic Information Systems:
No GIS services available
Collection services:
Maps classified: 100%
Classification schemes: Local
Preservation techniques: encapsulation
Items that have gone through the preservation process: 25%
Physical facilities:
No Internet access
Square footage: 150
Number of map cases: 16
Other map storage: acid-free boxes
Copying facilities available: copier, color copier, microform copier

131 *Coral Gables, FL*

University of Miami

Otto G. Richter Library
Cuban Heritage Collection, founded 1998
1300 Memorial Drive
Coral Gables, FL 33124-0320
Telephone: 305-284-4008
Fax: 305-284-4901
Email: edevaron@miami.edu

Web: www.library.miami.edu/umcuban/cuban.html

Personnel:

Responsible person: Esperanza B. de Varona, Department Head, *email:* edevaron@miami.edu

Assistants: Lesbia Varona, Collection Development Librarian

Holdings:

Geographic strengths: Cuba

256 printed maps

Chronological coverage:

1800–1899: 17%

1900–1939: 15%

1940–present: 60%

Access:

Collection is paged

Reference questions per year: 50

Answers email questions

Hours:

Monday–Tuesday: 9 A.M.–4 P.M.

Wednesday: 9 A.M.–7 P.M.

Thursday–Friday: 9 A.M.–4 P.M.

Saturday–Saturday: closed

Total hours per week opened: 38

Geographic Information Systems:

No GIS services available

Scans maps for patrons

Collection services:

Maps classified: 100%

Classification schemes: Local

Catalog accessibility: printout

Preservation techniques: encapsulation, deacidification

Items that have gone through the preservation process: 100%

Physical facilities:

Internet access available

Square footage: 15

Copying facilities available: copier, color copier

132 *Coral Gables, FL*

University of Miami

Otto G. Richter Library

Government Information and Special Formats Department, founded 1983

1300 Memorial Drive

Coral Gables, FL 33124-0320

Telephone: 305-284-3155

Fax: 305-284-4027

Web: www.library.miami.edu/library/mapcollection.html

Personnel:

Responsible person: Terri J. Robar, Special Formats Librarian, *email:* trobar@miami.edu

Holdings:

Geographic strengths: Florida, Caribbean, Latin America

Subject strengths: city, roads

Map depositories and percentages: USGS topos (58%), USGS geology maps (100%), USGS other (100%), GPO, CIA, National Forest Service, BLM, State

49,000 printed maps

42 raised relief maps

Chronological coverage:

1900–1939: 19%

1940–present: 80%

Average budget over the last 5 years: $3,000

Access:

Collection is partially open to the public

Reference questions per year: 250

Answers email questions

Patrons per month: 15

Hours:

Monday–Friday: 8 A.M.–9 P.M.

Saturday: 9 A.M.–5 P.M.

Sunday: noon–midnight

Total hours per week opened: 85

Maps circulate

Circulation policies apply

Map circulation duration: 2 weeks

Number of maps circulated annually: 700

Interlibrary loan available

Geographic Information Systems:

No GIS services available

Collection services:

Maps cataloged: 25%

Maps classified: 100%

Maps in OPAC: 25%

Classification schemes: Local

Cataloging utilities: OCLC

Catalog accessibility: online

Preservation techniques: encapsulation

Physical facilities:

No Internet access

Square footage: 1,660

Number of map cases: 42

Copying facilities available: copier, color copier, microform copier

133 *DeLand, FL*

Stetson University

duPont-Ball Library

Government Documents Department

421 North Woodland Boulevard

DeLand, FL 32723

Telephone: 386-822-7185

Fax: 386-740-3626

Web: www.stetson.edu/library

Personnel:

Responsible person: Barbara Costello, Documents Librarian, *email:* bcostell@stetson.edu

FTE professionals: 1   *FTE para-professionals:* 1

Holdings:
Geographic strengths: Florida
Map depositories: USGS topos, CIA
2,121 printed maps
1 globe
275 atlases
219 CD-ROMs
Access:
Hours:
Monday–Friday: 8 A.M.–midnight
Saturday: 11 A.M.–5 P.M.
Sunday: 11 A.M.–midnight
Collection services:
Maps cataloged: 70%
Maps classified: 70%
Maps in OPAC: 50%
Classification schemes: LC, SuDocs
Physical facilities:
Map cases: 6

134 *Gainesville, FL*

University of Florida

George A. Smathers Library
Historical Florida Map Collection
Department of Special and Area Studies Collections
2nd Floor
Library East
Gainesville, FL 32611
Telephone: 352-392-9075
Web: web.uflib.ufl.edu/spec/pkyonge/index. html
Personnel:
Responsible person: Dr. James G. Cusick, *email:* jamcusi@mail.uflib.ufl.edu
Number of student workers hours per week: 12
Holdings:
Geographic strengths: Florida, Gulf of Mexico, Caribbean, Southeast
Special collections: Second Seminole War (1835–1842) military maps, Florida Ephemera Collection (railroad, steamship, and road maps)
Subject strengths: agriculture, archaeology, early cartography, city, forestry, geodetic surveys, geology, historical geography, land ownership, land use, map catalogs, military, nautical charts, population, railroads, recreation, roads, soil, travel books, vegetation, views, waterways
Map depositories and percentages: USGS topos, USGS geology maps, State
1,120 printed maps
800 manuscript maps
Chronological coverage:
Pre-1800: 40%
1800–1899: 40%
1900–1939: 20%

Access:
Collection is partially paged, partially open to the public
Reference questions per year: 50
Answers email questions
Patrons per month: 10
Hours:
Monday–Friday: 9 A.M.–5 P.M.
Saturday–Saturday: closed
Total hours per week opened: 40
Collection services:
Maps cataloged: 80%
Maps classified: 80%
Maps in OPAC: 80%
Classification schemes: Local
Cataloging utilities: Local
Catalog accessibility: online
Preservation techniques: encapsulation, deacidification
Items that have gone through the preservation process: 30%
Physical facilities:
Internet access available
Square footage: 225
Other map storage: rolled map cases, oversize map cases
Copying facilities available: copier, microform copier, scanner

135 *Gainesville, FL*

University of Florida

George A. Smathers Libraries
Map and Imagery Library, founded 1973
P.O. Box 11701
110 Marston Science Library
Gainesville, FL 32611-7011
Telephone: 352-392-2825
Fax: 352-392-4787
Email: mapsref@uflib.ufl.edu
Web: web.uflib.ufl.edu/maps
Personnel:
Responsible person: Dr. HelenJane Armstrong, Map and Imagery Librarian, *email:* hjarms@uflib.ufl.edu
Assistants: Jennifer Farrington, Senior Archivist; Carol McAuliffe, Senior Library Technician; Susan Remer, Senior Librarian Technician
FTE professionals: 1.1   *FTE para-professionals:* 3.1
Number of student workers hours per week: 55
Number of volunteers: 6
Number of volunteer hours per month: 60
Holdings:
Geographic strengths: Florida, Southeast, Africa, Caribbean, Latin America, Israel, Holy Lands, Western Europe, Nepal, Southeast Asia
Special collections: Florida Sanborn Fire Insurance maps (copyright collection), Simmons Antique maps of the Holy Lands, ASCS Archival Aerial Photos of

Florida, CARTA (Antique maps of Africa and Latin America), NASA/Kennedy Space Center Aerial Film Library, Erwin Raisz Personal maps and Books, Florida Geographic Data Library

Subject strengths: aerial photos, aeronautical, agriculture, biology, early cartography, modern cartography, celestial, climatology, city, economic geography, engineering, forestry, genealogy, geodetic surveys, geology, geospatial data, historical geography, hydrology, industries, land ownership, land use, language, map collecting, military, mineral resources, mining, nautical charts, oceanography, political geography, population, projections, railroads, raised relief models, recreation, roads, satellite imagery, soil, travel books, vegetation, views, waterways, zoogeography

Map depositories and percentages: USGS topos (100%), USGS geology maps (100%), USGS other (100%), Department of Transportation, NOAA, GPO, CIA, National Forest Service, NIMA topos, NIMA nautical, NIMA aeronautical, BLM, State, United Nations, European Union

513,514 printed maps

165 manuscript maps

30 wall maps

148 raised relief maps

7,459 microfiche

435 microfilms

297,938 aerial photos

4,997 satellite images

42 globes

926 gazetteers

3,726 printed atlases

5,057 books

2,134 CD-ROMs

Collecting digital data

Chronological coverage:
1940–present: 90%

Average budget over the last 5 years: $68,000

On-going publications: Published book; *Antique maps of the Holy Land in the University of Florida Libraries*, featuring the James C. and Adina P. Simmons of Tel-Aviv, Israel and Tallahassee, Florida Collection of Antique Maps of the Holy Land; an annotated cartobibliography by HelenJane Armstrong.

Access:

Maps in separate area

Collection is partially paged, partially open to the public

Maps off site

Reference questions per year: 15,400

Answers email questions

Patrons per month: 367

Hours:

Monday–Friday: 8:30 A.M.–5 P.M.

Saturday–Saturday: closed

Total hours per week opened: 42.5

Maps circulate

Circulation policies apply

Map circulation duration: 1 week

Atlas circulation duration: 2 hours by special permission

Book circulation duration: 2 hours by special permission

Number of maps circulated annually: 10,463

Number of other items circulated annually: 10,496

Geographic Information Systems:

GIS services available in an open environment

GIS software: ArcView 3.2, ArcGIS, MapInfo, ERDAS Imagine

GIS assistance available for Census mapping, geocoding, and image analysis

Collection services:

Maps cataloged: 91%

Maps classified: 100%

Maps in OPAC: 91%

Datasets are cataloged

Classification schemes: LC, Local

Cataloging utilities: OCLC, RLG

Catalog accessibility: online

Preservation techniques: encapsulation, deacidification, cartex, acid-free folders

Items that have gone through the preservation process: 25%

Physical facilities:

Internet access available

Square footage: 4,990

Number of map cases: 312

Number of vertical files (file cabinets): 48

Number of atlas stands: 20

Linear book shelving: 1,071 ft.

Linear atlas shelving: 474 ft.

Other map storage: CD cabinet, 9 rolled film storage, aerial index files, microform cabinets

Copying facilities available: copier, microform copier, scanner, cd burner, color printer

136 *Miami, FL*

Historical Museum of Southern Florida

Charlton W. Tebeau Research Library

101 West Flagler Street

Miami, FL 33130

Telephone: 305-375-1492

Fax: 305-372-6313

Web: www.historical-museum.org

Personnel:

Responsible person: Rebecca A. Smith, Curator of Research Materials, *email:* hasf@historical-museum.org

Holdings:

Geographic strengths: Florida, Bahamas, Caribbean

Subject strengths: city
2,000 printed maps
300 manuscript maps
10 wall maps
5,000 aerial photos
10 gazetteers
100 books
Chronological coverage:
    Pre-1800: 10%
    1800–1899: 35%
    1900–1939: 30%
    1940–present: 25%
Average budget over the last 5 years: $3,000

Access:
Collection is partially open to the public
Reference questions per year: 500
Answers email questions
Patrons per month: 40

Hours:
    Monday–Friday: 10 A.M.–4:30 P.M.
    Saturday–Saturday: closed
    Total hours per week opened: 32.5

Geographic Information Systems:
No GIS services available
Scans maps for patrons

Collection services:
Maps classified: 100%
Classification schemes: Local
Catalog accessibility: online
Preservation techniques: encapsulation

Physical facilities:
No Internet access
Square footage: 100
Number of map cases: 17
Copying facilities available: copier, on-request reproductions

Notes: Presenters of the Annual Miami International Map Fair.

137 *Miami, FL*

Miami–Dade Public Library System

Main Library
Social Science and the Florida Room
101 West Flagler Street
Miami, FL 33130
Telephone: 305-375-5575
Fax: 305-375-3048
Email: eref@mdpls.org
Web: www.mdpls.org

Personnel:
Responsible person: Mary Garcia, Government Documents Librarian, *email:* garciam@mdpls.org
Assistants: Mark Plotkin, Librarian

Holdings:

Special collections: Sanborn Fire Insurance maps of Florida
Subject strengths: aerial photos, archaeology, modern cartography, city, genealogy, geodetic surveys, historical geography, hydrology, land ownership, land use, map catalogs, military, political geography, population, railroads, recreation, roads, soil, travel books, vegetation, waterways
Map depositories and percentages: USGS topos (100% [Florida only]), GPO, CIA, State, FEMA Flood Maps for Florida
4,000 printed maps
20 wall maps
6,000 microfiche
32 microfilms
900 aerial photos
22 gazetteers
269 printed atlases
88 books
Chronological coverage:
    1800–1899: 10%
    1900–1939: 35%
    1940–present: 50%

Access:
Collection is open to the public
Answers email questions

Hours:
    Monday–Wednesday: 9 A.M.–6 P.M.
    Thursday: 9 A.M.–9 P.M.
    Friday–Saturday: 9 A.M.–6 P.M.
    Sunday: 1 P.M.–5 P.M.
    Total hours per week opened: 61
Maps circulate
Circulation policies apply
    Atlas circulation duration: 4 weeks
    Book circulation duration: 4 weeks
Interlibrary loan available

Geographic Information Systems:
No GIS services available
Number of public GIS workstations: 22

Collection services:
Maps cataloged: 100%
Percentage of maps classified: 100
Maps in OPAC: 100%
Classification schemes: SuDocs, Dewey
Cataloging utilities: OCLC
Catalog accessibility: online
Preservation techniques: encapsulation, deacidification, lamination
Items that have gone through the preservation process: 5%

Physical facilities:
Internet access available
Square footage: 1,000
Number of public computers: 22

Number of vertical files (file cabinets): 12
Linear book shelving: 60 ft.
Number of microform readers: 14
Copying facilities available: copier, microform copier

138 *Miami, FL*

University of Miami

Rosenstiel School of Marine and Atmospheric Science
  Library
4600 Rickenbacker Causeway
Miami, FL 33149-1098
Telephone: 305-361-4060
Fax: 305-361-9306
Web: www.rsmas.miami.edu/support/lib/
Personnel:
  Responsible person: Roberta Y. Rand, Library Director,
    email: rrand@rsmas.miami.edu
Holdings:
  Geographic strengths: Florida, Atlantic Coast, Gulf
    Coast, Caribbean
  Subject strengths: nautical charts, oceanography
  Map depositories and percentages: NOAA, NIMA
    nautical
  1,500 printed maps
  500 printed atlases
  Chronological coverage:
    1940–present: 90%
Access:
  Collection is open to the public
  Reference questions per year: 100
  Patrons per month: 15
  Hours:
    Monday–Thursday: 8:30 A.M.–10 P.M.
    Friday: 8:30 A.M.–5 P.M.
    Saturday: 1 P.M.–5 P.M.
    Sunday: 1 P.M.–10 P.M.
    Total hours per week opened: 75.5
  Maps circulate
  Circulation policies apply
    Map circulation duration: 2 weeks
    Number of maps circulated annually: 200
  Interlibrary loan available
Geographic Information Systems:
  GIS services available by appointment
  GIS software: ArcView
Collection services:
  Maps cataloged: 80%
  Percentage of maps classified: 90
  Maps in OPAC: 80%
  Classification schemes: SuDocs, Local
  Cataloging utilities: OCLC
  Catalog accessibility: online
Physical facilities:
  Internet access available

Square footage: 1,200
Copying facilities available: copier

139 *Tampa, FL*

University of South Florida

Tampa Library
Reference/Documents—Map Collection
4202 East Fowler Avenue
LIB 122
Tampa, FL 33620-5400
Telephone: 813-974-2729
Fax: 813-974-9875
Email: docsmail@lib.usf.edu
Web: www.lib.usf.edu/tampa/govdocs/
Personnel:
  Responsible person: Cheryl McCoy, University Librar-
    ian, *email:* cmccoy@lib.usf.edu
  Assistants: Julie Sayles, Sr. Library Technical Assistant
  FTE professionals: 0.05   *FTE para-professionals:* 0.25
Holdings:
  Geographic strengths: West Central Florida, Southeast
  Map depositories: USGS topos, CIA, National Forest
    Service, BLM
  85,500 printed maps
  12 globes
  358 atlases
  995 books
  11 active serials
  368 CD-ROMs
Access:
  Hours:
    Monday–Friday: 7:30 A.M.–midnight
    Saturday: 10 A.M.–5 P.M.
    Sunday: noon–midnight
  Items circulate
  Interlibrary loan available
Collection services:
  Maps cataloged: 35%
  Maps classified: 75%
  Maps in OPAC: 35%
  Classification schemes: LC, SuDocs, Local
Physical facilities:
  Map cases: 125

140 *Americus, GA*

Georgia Southwestern State University

James Earl Carter Library
800 Wheatley Street
Americus, GA 31709
Telephone: 229-931-2259
Fax: 229-931-2265
Web: www.gsw.edu/~library/

Personnel:

FTE professionals: 1 *FTE para-professionals:* 1

Holdings:

Special collections: CIA maps, US Geological Survey maps

Map depositories: USGS topos, CIA

1,474 printed maps

1 globe

145 atlases

Access:

Hours:

Monday–Thursday: 8 A.M.–10 P.M.

Friday: 8 A.M.–5 P.M.

Saturday: noon–4 P.M.

Sunday: 3 P.M.–9 P.M.

Interlibrary loan available

Collection services:

Maps cataloged: 100%

Maps classified: 0%

Maps in OPAC: 95%

Classification schemes: LC, SuDocs

Physical facilities:

Public computers: 14

Map cases: 4

Notes: The cataloging librarian is responsible for the atlases and maps in the general collection. Government Documents is responsible for the Government Documents atlases and maps.

141 *Athens, GA*

University of Georgia

Libraries

Map Collection

Athens, GA 20602

Telephone: 706-542-0690

Fax: 706-542-6523

Email: jsutherl@uga.edu

Web: www.libs.uga.edu/maproom/index.html

Personnel:

Responsible person: Johnnie D. Sutherland, Curator of Maps, *email:* jsutherl@uga.edu

Assistants: Tom Hardaway, Map Room Assistant; Tom Cutshall, Map Cataloger

FTE professionals: 1.5

Number of student works: 1.5

Number of student workers hours per week: 30

Holdings:

Geographic strengths: Georgia, Southeast, United States, Latin America, Europe, World

Special collections: Sanborn Fire Insurance maps, Aerial Photography of Georgia, Hudgens Company maps, Historical maps of Georgia

Subject strengths: aerial photos, aeronautical, agriculture, early cartography, modern cartography, climatology, city, forestry, geology, geospatial data, historical geography, hydrology, land ownership, land use, map catalogs, mineral resources, nautical charts, railroads, recreation, roads, satellite imagery, soil, vegetation, views, waterways, zoogeography

Map depositories and percentages: USGS topos (100%), USGS geology maps (100%), USGS other (100%), Department of Transportation, NOAA, GPO, CIA, National Forest Service, NIMA topos, NIMA nautical, NIMA aeronautical, BLM, State

400,000 printed maps

400 manuscript maps

300 wall maps

50 raised relief maps

20,000 microfilms

225,000 aerial photos

500 satellite images

10 globes

300 gazetteers

3,500 printed atlases

500 books

1,400 CD-ROMs

Collecting digital data

Chronological coverage:

1940–present: 94%

Average budget over the last 5 years: $30,000

On-going publications: All printed publication transferred to web pages. Several lists and bibliographies maintained online and accessed through the web pages.

Access:

Collection is open to the public

Reference questions per year: 4,800

Answers email questions

Patrons per month: 400

Hours:

Monday–Friday: 8 A.M.–5 P.M.

Saturday: 1 P.M.–5 P.M.

Sunday: closed

Total hours per week opened: 49

Maps circulate

Circulation policies apply

Map circulation duration: 2 weeks

Atlas circulation duration: 4 weeks

Book circulation duration: 4 weeks

Number of maps circulated annually: 52,000

Number of books circulated annually: 250

Number of other items circulated annually: 100

Interlibrary loan available

Geographic Information Systems:

GIS services available in an open environment

GIS software: ArcView

GIS assistance available for geocoding

GIS assistance available for image analysis

Scans maps for patrons

Collection services:

Maps cataloged: 90%

Maps classified: 90%

Maps in OPAC: 90%

Classification schemes: LC, SuDocs

Cataloging utilities: OCLC

Catalog accessibility: online

Preservation techniques: encapsulation, cartex

Physical facilities:

Internet access available

Square footage: 8,000

Number of map cases: 289

Number of vertical files (file cabinets): 44

Linear book shelving: 57 ft.

Linear atlas shelving: 600 ft.

Other map storage: 224 linear feet of flat archival shelving, 2 rolled map cases

Copying facilities available: copier, microform copier, scanner

Notes: The Map Collection has an active program to make its holdings available online. Photo indexes and about 50,000 air photos of Georgia are currently available in an online database, Georgia Aerial Photographs. The collection's Sanborn maps will go up in another online database.

142 *Atlanta, GA*

Atlanta–Fulton Public Library

Central Library

Special Collections/Georgia Local and Family History

One Margaret Mitchell Square

Atlanta, GA 30303

Telephone: 404-730-1896 or 1897

Fax: 404-730-1895

Email: ReferenceLine@co.fulton.ga.us

Web: www.af.public.lib.ga.us./central/gagen/index.html

Personnel:

Responsible person: William A. Montgomery

Holdings:

Geographic strengths: Atlanta, Georgia

Subject strengths: city, economic geography, genealogy, historical geography, land use, military, political geography, roads, travel books

900 printed maps

10 gazetteers

20 printed atlases

Chronological coverage:

1800–1899: 35%

1900–1939: 30%

1940–present: 30%

Average budget over the last 5 years: $100

On-going publications: Finding Aid for Map Collection is updated by staff

Access:

Collection is open to the public

Reference questions per year: 100

Hours:

Monday–Thursday: 9 A.M.–9 P.M.

Friday–Saturday: 9 A.M.–6 P.M.

Sunday: 2 P.M.–6 P.M.

Total hours per week opened: 70

Geographic Information Systems:

No GIS services available

Collection services:

Maps classified: 100%

Classification schemes: Dewey

Cataloging utilities: OCLC

Catalog accessibility: online, printed finding aid to Map Collection

Physical facilities:

Internet access available

Other map storage: 1 rolled map case

Copying facilities available: copier, microform copier

Notes: Our map collection is an integral part of the holdings of the Special Collections/Georgia Local and Family History Department. Other departments and/or branches of the library system have additional materials.

143 *Atlanta, GA*

Emory University

Robert W. Woodruff Library

540 Asbury Circle

Atlanta, GA 30322

Telephone: 404 727-6875

Web: web.library.emory.edu/subjects/maps/maps.html

Personnel:

Responsible person: Eric Nitschke, Reference Librarian, email:* liben@emory.edu

FTE para-professionals: 1

Holdings:

Geographic strengths: Atlanta, Georgia

Special collections: Southeast United States topo maps

Map depositories: USGS

105,000 printed maps

1,274 atlases

Access:

Hours:

Monday–Friday: 8 A.M.–9 P.M.

Saturday: 9 A.M.–8 P.M.

Sunday: noon–9 P.M.

Collection services:

Maps cataloged: 10%

Maps in OPAC: 10%

Classification schemes: LC, SuDocs

Physical facilities:

Public computers: 3

Map cases: 3

144 *Atlanta, GA*

Georgia Institute of Technology

Library and Information Center
Special Formats and Maps Department
704 Cherry Street
Atlanta, GA 30332-0900
Telephone: 404-385-0226
Fax: 404-894-8190
Web: www.library.gatech.edu
Personnel:
Responsible person: Barbara J. Walker, *email:* barbara
.walker@library.gatech.edu
Holdings:
Geographic strengths: Southeast
Special collections: Sanborn Fire Insurance maps of
Georgia
Subject strengths: aerial photos, aeronautical, city, en-
gineering, geodetic surveys, geology, hydrology,
land ownership, land use, map catalogs, mineral re-
sources, nautical charts, oceanography, political ge-
ography, raised relief models, roads, soil, travel
books, vegetation
Map depositories and percentages: USGS topos
(100%), USGS geology maps (100%), Department
of Transportation, NOAA, GPO, CIA, NIMA nauti-
cal, NIMA aeronautical, BLM
193,000 printed maps
60 raised relief maps
10 microfilms
14 aerial photos
Access:
Maps in separate area
Collection is open to the public
Answers email questions
Hours:
Saturday: 9 A.M.–6 P.M.
Sunday: noon–midnight
Total hours per week opened: 87
Maps circulate
Circulation policies apply
  Map circulation duration: 1 semester
  Book circulation duration: 1 semester
Interlibrary loan available
Geographic Information Systems:
No GIS services available
GIS assistance available for Census mapping, and im-
age analysis
Scans maps for patrons
Collection services:
Maps cataloged: 100%
Maps classified: 100%
Maps in OPAC: 99%
Datasets are cataloged
Classification schemes: LC

Cataloging utilities: OCLC, RLG, Local
Catalog accessibility: online
Preservation techniques: deacidification, lamination
Physical facilities:
No Internet access
Number of map cases: 66
Linear book shelving: 278 ft.
Linear atlas shelving: 70 ft.
Copying facilities available: copier, color copier, mi-
croform copier

145 *Atlanta, GA*

Georgia State University

University Library
Information Services Department
100 Decatur Street SE
Atlanta, GA 30303-3202
Telephone: 404-463-9934
Fax: 404-651-4315
Email: gchristian@gsu.edu
Web: www.library.gsu.edu/maps
Personnel:
Responsible person: Gayle Christian, Government
Information/Map Librarian, *email:* gchristian@
gsu.edu
FTE professionals: 0.06   *FTE para-professionals:* 0.06
Holdings:
Geographic strengths: Atlanta, Georgia
Map depositories: USGS topos, NOAA, CIA, National
Forest Service, BLM
27,000 printed maps
1 globe
Access:
Hours:
Monday–Thursday: 7:30 A.M.–11 P.M.
Friday: 7:30-6 P.M.
Saturday: 9 A.M.–6 P.M.
Sunday: noon–8 P.M.
Collection services:
Maps cataloged: 95%
Maps classified: 100%
Maps in OPAC: 95%
Classification schemes: LC, SuDocs
Physical facilities:
Public computers: 75
Map cases: 31
Vertical files: 2

146 *Augusta, GA*

Augusta State University

Reese Library
2500 Walton Way
Augusta, GA 30904-2200

Telephone: 706-737-1748
Fax: 706-667-4415
Web: www.aug.edu
Personnel:
Responsible person: Joseph Schneider, Government Documents Librarian, *email:* jschneider@aug.edu
Assistants: Miriam Zecharias, Government Documents Assistant
FTE professionals: 1   *FTE para-professionals:* 1.5
Holdings:
Geographic strengths: Augusta, Georgia
Special collections: Sanborn Fire Insurance maps
Map depositories: USGS topos, Department of Transportation, NOAA, CIA, National Forest Service, NGA nautical, NGA aeronautical, BLM
10,100 printed maps
171 aerial photos
2 globes
810 atlases
10,030 books
123 CD-ROMs
Access:
Hours:
Monday–Friday: 7:30 A.M.–10:30 P.M.
Saturday: 9 A.M.–5 P.M.
Sunday: 1:30 P.M.–9:30 P.M.
Items circulate
Interlibrary loan available
Collection services:
Maps cataloged: 70%
Maps classified: 70%
Maps in OPAC: 70%
Classification schemes: LC, SuDocs
Physical facilities:
Public computers: 35
Map cases: 8

147 *Carrollton, GA*

State University of West Georgia

Irvine Sullivan Ingram Library
1600 Maple Street
Carrollton, GA 30118
Telephone: 770-830-2357
Fax: 770-836-6626
Web: www.westga.edu/~library/
Personnel:
Responsible person: Michael Aldrich, Government Documents Librarian, *email:* maldrich@westga.edu
Assistants: Lori Lester, Documents Associate
FTE professionals: 0.25   *FTE para-professionals:* 0.25
Holdings:
Geographic strengths: Georgia
Special collections: Sanborn Fire Insurance maps
Map depositories: USGS topos, CIA, BLM

50,000 printed maps
2 globes
30 atlases
Access:
Hours:
Monday–Thursday: 7:30 A.M.–10 P.M.
Friday: 7:30 A.M.–6 P.M.
Saturday: 10 A.M.–6 P.M.
Sunday: 2 P.M.–10 P.M.
Items circulate
Interlibrary loan available
Collection services:
Maps cataloged: 75%
Maps classified: 100%
Maps in OPAC: 75%
Classification schemes: LC, SuDocs, Local
Physical facilities:
Map cases: 29
Vertical files: 1

148 *Macon, GA*

Middle Georgia Archives

Washington Memorial Library
Map Collection
1180 Washington Avenue
Macon, GA 31201
Telephone: 478-744-0820
Fax: 478-744-0893
Email: jacksonm@mail.bibb.public.lib.ga.us
Web: www.co.bibb.public.lib.ga.us
Personnel:
Responsible person: Willard Rocer, Head of Genealogy, *email:* rockerw@mailb.bibb.public.lib.ga.us
Assistants: Muriel M. Jackson, Archivist
FTE professionals: 3   *FTE para-professionals:* 3
Holdings:
Geographic strengths: Macon, Bibb County, Georgia
Special collections: Sanborn Fire Insurance maps for the State of Georgia, Camp Wheeler Military Map Collection, City of Macon Ward Maps
Map depositories: USGS
259 printed maps
57 atlases
75 books
Access:
Hours:
Monday: 9 A.M.–9 P.M.
Tuesday–Saturday: 9 A.M.–6 P.M.
Sunday: closed
Collection services:
Maps cataloged: 100%
Maps classified: 100%
Maps in OPAC: 0%
Classification schemes: Local

Physical facilities:
Maps in separate area
Public computers: 6
Map cases: 12

149 *Milledgeville, GA*

Georgia College and State University

Ina Dillard Russell Library
CBX 043
Milledgeville, GA 31061
Telephone: 478-445-4047
Fax: 478-445-6847
Email: lisa.ennis@gcsu.edu
Web: library.gcsu.edu
Personnel:
Responsible person: Lisa Ennis, Government Docu-
ments Librarian, *email:* lisa.ennis@gcsu.edu
Assistants: Donna Gautier, Government Documents
Associate
FTE professionals: 0.5   *FTE para-professionals:* 1
Holdings:
Geographic strengths: Georgia
Special collections: Sanborn Fire Insurance maps for
Georgia [microform] (1884-1950)
Map depositories: USGS topos, CIA, National Forest
Service, BLM
2,000 printed maps
Access:
Hours:
Monday–Thursday: 7:30 A.M.–11 P.M.
Friday: 7:30 A.M.–5 P.M.
Saturday: 10 A.M.–6 P.M.
Sunday: 1 P.M.–11 P.M.
Items circulate
Interlibrary loan available
Collection services:
Maps cataloged: 100%
Maps classified: 100%
Maps in OPAC: 100%
Classification schemes: LC, SuDocs, Other (topos al-
phabetical)
Physical facilities:
Public computers: 25
Map cases: 2

150 *Rome, GA*

Sara Hightower Regional Library

Rome–Floyd County Public Library
Special Collections
205 Riverside Parkway
Rome, GA 30161
Telephone: 706-236-4607
Fax: 706-236-4605
Email: barkleya@mail.floyd.public.lib.ga.us

Web: www.floyd.public.lib.ga.us
Personnel:
Responsible person: Dawn Hampton, Coordinator,
Special Collections, *email:* hamptond@mail.floyd
.public.lib.ga.us
Assistants: Allison Limbrick Barkley, Assistant Coordi-
nator
Number of volunteer hours per month: 48
Holdings:
Geographic strengths: Rome County, Floyd County,
Georgia
Special collections: Sanborn Fire Insurance maps,
FIRM Flood Insurance Program maps, Civil War
maps (all of Rome and Floyd County, Georgia), aerial photographs of Floyd and surrounding counties,
historical blueprints of buildings, including schools
and factories in Rome, Georgia
Subject strengths: aerial photos, agriculture, archaeology, modern cartography, city, forestry, genealogy, geodetic surveys, geology, industries, land
ownership, map catalogs, military, mineral re-
sources, mining, political geography, railroads,
raised relief models, roads, soil, travel books, wa-
terways
Map depositories and percentages: State, United Na-
tions
220 printed maps
101 aerial photos
Chronological coverage:
1900–1939: 10%
1940–present: 80%
Access:
Collection is open to the public
Reference questions per year: 160
Answers email questions
Patrons per month: 14
Hours:
Monday–Thursday: 8:30 A.M.–8:30 P.M.
Friday: 8:30 A.M.–6 P.M.
Saturday: 10 A.M.–5 P.M.
Sunday: 1:30 P.M.–5:30 P.M.
Total hours per week opened: 69.5
Geographic Information Systems:
No GIS services available
Scans maps for patrons
Collection services:
Maps classified: 85%
Classification schemes: Dewey
Cataloging utilities: Local
Catalog accessibility: cards, printout
Preservation techniques: lamination, acid-free folders
Items that have gone through the preservation process:
80%
Physical facilities:
Internet access available
Square footage: 2,140

Other map storage: storage cylinders
Copying facilities available: copier, color copier, large-format copier, microform copier

151 *Mangilao, GU*

University of Guam

Robert F. Kennedy Memorial Library
Government Documents
UOG Station
Mangilao, GU 96923
Telephone: 671-735-2321
Fax: 671-734-6882
Email: stbell@uog9.uog.edu
Web: www.uog.edu/rfk/
Personnel:
Responsible person: Suzanne T. Bell, *email:* stbell@uog9.uog.edu
Assistants: Walfrid C. Benavente, Library Technician II
Holdings:
Geographic strengths: Northern Hemisphere, Asia
Subject strengths: nautical charts
143 printed maps
Chronological coverage:
1940–present: 100%
Access:
Collection is partially open to the public
Hours:
Monday–Friday: 8 A.M.–5 P.M.
Total hours per week opened: 40
Geographic Information Systems:
GIS services available in an open environment
GIS assistance available for Census mapping
Scans maps for patrons
Collection services:
Maps classified: 100%
Classification schemes: SuDocs
Physical facilities:
Internet access available
Copying facilities available: copier

152 *Honolulu, HI*

Hawai'i State Archives

Map Collection
Iolani Palace Grounds
Honolulu, HI 96813
Telephone: 808-586-0329
Fax: 808-586-0330
Email: archives@Hawaii.gov
Web: statearchives.lib.Hawaii.edu/
Holdings:
Geographic strengths: Hawai'i
Subject strengths: aerial photos, aeronautical, agriculture, biology, early cartography, modern cartography, climatology, city, forestry, geology, historical geog-

raphy, land ownership, land use, mineral resources, nautical charts, oceanography, political geography, population, raised relief models, recreation, roads, soil, travel books, vegetation, views, waterways
1,500 printed maps
300 manuscript maps
10 wall maps
10 raised relief maps
50 microfilms
1,000 aerial photos
20 books
Chronological coverage:
1800–1899: 24%
1900–1939: 40%
1940–present: 35%
Access:
Maps in separate area
Collection is paged
Reference questions per year: 500
Answers email questions
Patrons per month: 40
Hours:
Monday–Friday: 9 A.M.–3:30 P.M.
Total hours per week opened: 32.5
Geographic Information Systems:
No GIS services available
Collection services:
Maps cataloged: 100%
Maps classified: 100%
Maps in OPAC: 100%
Classification schemes: LC
Cataloging utilities: Local
Catalog accessibility: online
Preservation techniques: encapsulation, lamination
Physical facilities:
No Internet access
Square footage: 160
Number of map cases: 25
Linear book shelving: 15 ft.
Linear atlas shelving: 40 ft.
Other map storage: 20 rolled map tubes
Copying facilities available: copier, large-format copier, microform copier

153 *Honolulu, HI*

Hawai'i State Public Library System

Hawai'i and Pacific Section
478 South King Street
Honolulu, HI 96813
Telephone: 808-586-3535
Fax: 808-586-3586
Web: www.Hawaii.gov/hidocs
Personnel:
Responsible person: Patrick McNally, Section Head, *email:* hslhp@libariesHawaii.org

FTE professionals: 0.1   *FTE para-professionals:* 0.1
Holdings:
Geographic strengths: Hawai'i
400 printed maps
50 aerial photos
12 atlases
7 books
Access:
Hours:
Monday–Saturday: 9 A.M.–5 P.M.
Interlibrary loan available
Collection services:
Maps cataloged: 5%
Maps classified: 5%
Maps in OPAC: 5%
Classification schemes: Dewey
Physical facilities:
Public computers: 2
Map cases: 2
Vertical files: 2
Notes: Very eclectic collection of maps as a part of a primarily monographic public library collection.

154 *Honolulu, HI*

University of Hawai'i at Manoa

Hamilton Library
Map Collection
2550 McCarthy Mall
Honolulu, HI 96822
Telephone: 808-956-6199
Fax: 808-956-5968
Email: mapcoll@Hawaii.edu
Web: libweb.Hawaii.edu/libdept/maps/index.html
Personnel:
Responsible person: Ross R. Togashi, *email:* rtogashi@Hawaii.edu
Number of student workers hours per week: 40
Holdings:
Geographic strengths: Hawai'i, Pacific region, East Asia
Special collections: Trust Territory of the Pacific Islands Archives (maps and aerial photographs), U.S. Navy aerial photographs of the Western Pacific and East Asia, Sanborn Fire Insurance maps, Historic Hawai'i USGS topographic maps, Aerial photographs of Hawai'i
Subject strengths: aerial photos, aeronautical, geology, nautical charts, roads
Map depositories and percentages: USGS topos (100%), USGS geology maps (100%), USGS other (100%), Department of Transportation, NOAA, GPO, CIA, National Forest Service, NIMA topos, NIMA nautical, NIMA aeronautical, BLM, United Nations
164,000 printed maps
113 wall maps

58 raised relief maps
90,475 aerial photos
180 gazetteers
50 books
12 CD-ROMs
Chronological coverage:
Pre-1800: 0.25%
1800–1899: 0.75%
1940–present: 97%
Average budget over the last 5 years: $1,000
Access:
Maps in separate area
Collection is paged
Reference questions per year: 800
Answers email questions
Patrons per month: 70
Hours:
Monday–Friday: 10 A.M.–5 P.M.
Total hours per week opened: 35
Maps circulate
Circulation policies apply
Map circulation duration: 1 week
Number of maps circulated annually: 220
Geographic Information Systems:
No GIS services available
Scans maps for patrons
Collection services:
Maps cataloged: 75%
Maps classified: 100%
Maps in OPAC: 10%
Classification schemes: LC, SuDocs
Cataloging utilities: OCLC
Catalog accessibility: online, cards
Preservation techniques: encapsulation
Items that have gone through the preservation process: 1%
Physical facilities:
Internet access available
Square footage: 4,732
Number of map cases: 140
Number of vertical files (file cabinets): 15
Linear book shelving: 84 ft.
Other map storage: raised relief planhold racks; rolled wall map stands
Copying facilities available: copier, color copier, large-format copier, microform copier, photographic reproduction services
Note: These figures apply to the map collection before the devastating October 2004 flood.

155 *Laie, HI*

Brigham Young University—Hawai'i Campus

Joseph F. Smith Library
Founded 1987

55-220 Kulanui Street
Laie, HI 96762
Telephone: 808-293-3884
Fax: 808-293-3877
Email: moffatr@byuh.edu
Personnel:
Responsible person: Riley Moffat, Head of Reference, *email:* moffatr@byuh.edu
FTE professionals: 0.1
Holdings:
Geographic strengths: Hawai'i, Pacific Islands, Polynesia
Subject strengths: aerial photos, aeronautical, early cartography, modern cartography, celestial, climatology, city, economic geography, genealogy, geology, historical geography, hydrology, land ownership, land use, language, map catalogs, map collecting, military, mineral resources, nautical charts, oceanography, political geography, population, raised relief models, recreation, religion, roads, satellite imagery, travel books, vegetation
Map depositories and percentages: USGS topos (10%), USGS geology maps, Department of Transportation, NOAA, GPO, CIA, NIMA topos, NIMA nautical, NIMA aeronautical, State
14,000 printed maps
10 wall maps
10 raised relief maps
100 aerial photos
20 satellite images
50 gazetteers
300 printed atlases
20 books
Chronological coverage:
1940–present: 93%
Average budget over the last 5 years: $1,000
Access:
Collection is open to the public
Reference questions per year: 200
Answers email questions
Patrons per month: 50
Hours:
Monday–Friday: 7 A.M.–midnight
Saturday: 9 A.M.–9 P.M.
Sunday: closed
Total hours per week opened: 91
Maps circulate
Circulation policies apply
Map circulation duration: 2 weeks
Book circulation duration: 2 weeks
Number of maps circulated annually: 100
Number of books circulated annually: 50
Geographic Information Systems:
No GIS services available
Collection services:

Maps cataloged: 100%
Maps classified: 100%
Maps in OPAC: 100%
Classification schemes: LC
Cataloging utilities: OCLC
Catalog accessibility: online
Preservation techniques: encapsulation, lamination
Physical facilities:
Internet access available
Square footage: 200
Number of public computers: 10
Linear atlas shelving: 60 ft.
Copying facilities available: copier, color copier, microform copier

156 *Boise, ID*

Boise State University

Albertsons Library
Hollenbaugh Map Collection, founded 1973
1910 University Drive
Boise, ID 83725
Telephone: 208-426-1264
Email: nbazemor@boisestate.edu
Web: library.boisestate.edu/Maps/
Personnel:
Responsible person: Norris Bazemore, Jr., Reference/ Map Librarian, *email:* nbazemor@boisestate.edu
FTE professionals: 0.5
Holdings:
Geographic strengths: Idaho, Pacific Northwest, United States
Special collections: City maps of Boise, Idaho
Subject strengths: city, geology, land ownership, land use, mineral resources
Map depositories and percentages: USGS topos (100%), BLM
99,439 printed maps
10 manuscript maps
96 raised relief maps
36 satellite images
68 books
10 CD-ROMs
Chronological coverage:
1940–present: 94%
Average budget over the last 5 years: $1,500
Access:
Maps in separate area
Collection is open to the public
Answers email questions
Patrons per month: 150
Hours:
Monday–Thursday: 7:30 A.M.–11 P.M.
Friday: 7:30 A.M.–6 P.M.

Saturday: 10 A.M.–6 P.M.

Sunday: 10 A.M.–11 P.M.

Total hours per week opened: 98.5

Maps circulate

Circulation policies apply

  Map circulation duration: 2 weeks

  Atlas circulation duration: 2 weeks

  Book circulation duration: 2 weeks

  Number of maps circulated annually: 301

Geographic Information Systems:

GIS services available by appointment

Number of public GIS workstations: 80

Collection services:

Maps cataloged: 100%

Maps classified: 100%

Classification schemes: LC

Cataloging utilities: OCLC

Catalog accessibility: cards

Preservation techniques: lamination

Physical facilities:

No Internet access

Square footage: 2,500

Number of map cases: 19

Number of vertical map cases: 22

Linear book shelving: 19 ft.

Other map storage: rolled map case

Copying facilities available: copier, large-format copier, microform copier

Notes: The answers to this survey do not include any maps, etc. housed in other departments. Older historical maps, especially in reference to Idaho, are retained in Special Collections. Also, maps received through the depository system, such as Forest Service, CIA, and USGS reports, are kept in Government Documents. In addition, numerous maps are catalogued and included as part of the general collection. Of the over 99,000 maps in our collection, 86,336 are topographic and the majority of the remainder relate to Idaho and the states of the Pacific Northwest, as well as BLM and Canadian topos.

157 *Boise, ID*

Idaho State Historical Society

Historical Library and State Archives

450 North Fourth Street

Boise, ID 83702

Telephone: 208-334-3356

Fax: 208-334-3198

Email: sbarrett@ishs.state.id.us

Web: www.idahohistory.net/library_archives.html

Personnel:

Responsible person: Linda Morton-Keithley, Administrator, *email:* lindamk@ishs.state.id.us

Assistants: Dylan McDonald, Archivist

FTE professionals: 1.2   *FTE para-professionals:* 0.3

Number of volunteer hours per month: 20

Holdings:

Geographic strengths: Idaho, Pacific Northwest

Special collections: Sanborn Fire Insurance maps, Idaho Surveying and Rating Bureau maps, Carey Act maps, road/highway maps

Subject strengths: city, forestry, genealogy, historical geography, industries, land ownership, land use, military, mineral resources, mining, railroads, recreation, roads, waterways

20,000 printed maps

Chronological coverage:

  1800–1899: 33%

  1900–1939: 33%

  1940–present: 33%

Average budget over the last 5 years: $1,000

On-going publications: A quarterly in-house newsletter— News from the Library and Archives—does regularly list new map acquisitions.

Access:

Maps in separate area

Collection is paged

Maps off site: 60%

Answers email questions

Hours:

Wednesday–Saturday: 9 A.M.–5 P.M.

Sunday: closed

Total hours per week opened: 32

Geographic Information Systems:

No GIS services available

Scans maps for patrons

Collection services:

Maps cataloged: 40%

Maps classified: 40%

Maps in OPAC: 40%

Classification schemes: LC

Cataloging utilities: OCLC, Local

Catalog accessibility: online, local use only

Preservation techniques: encapsulation

Items that have gone through the preservation process: 20%

Physical facilities:

No Internet access

Square footage: 700

Number of map cases: 30

Copying facilities available: copier, large-format copier, microform copier

Notes: Please note that although maps are stored in two separate areas (one in the Library and the other at the Archives storage facility), they are brought to the Library reading room for public access.

158 *Moscow, ID*

University of Idaho

Library

Reference Department

Box 442350
Moscow, ID 83844-2350
Telephone: 208-885-6584
Fax: 208-885-6718
Email: libref@uidaho.edu
Web: www.lib.uidaho.edu OR www.insideidaho
.org
Personnel:
Responsible person: email: dbaird@uidaho.edu
Number of student workers hours per week: 10
Holdings:
Geographic strengths: Idaho, Pacific Northwest
Special collections: Historic Air Photo for Northern Idaho
Subject strengths: aerial photos, aeronautical, agriculture, modern cartography, climatology, city, economic geography, forestry, geology, geospatial data, historical geography, hydrology, land ownership, land use, mineral resources, nautical charts, political geography, population, recreation, satellite imagery, soil, travel books, vegetation, waterways
Map depositories and percentages: USGS topos (100%), USGS geology maps (100%), USGS other (100%), Department of Transportation, NOAA, GPO, CIA, National Forest Service, NIMA topos, NIMA nautical, NIMA aeronautical, BLM, State
350,000 printed maps
250 satellite images
Collecting digital data
Average budget over the last 5 years: $500
Access:
Maps in separate area
Collection is open to the public
Answers email questions
Hours:
Total hours per week opened: 40
Maps circulate
Circulation policies apply
Interlibrary loan available
Geographic Information Systems:
GIS services available in an open environment
GIS software: INSIDE Idaho
Number of public GIS workstations: 120
Number of GIS stations (not monitored): 120
GIS assistance available for Census mapping
General GIS questions answered on web site
Collection services:
Datasets are cataloged
Classification schemes: LC, SuDocs
Cataloging utilities: OCLC
Catalog accessibility: online
Preservation techniques: lamination
Items that have gone through the preservation process: 0.005%
Physical facilities:
Internet access available

Square footage: 10,000
Number of public computers: 120
Number of map cases: 665
Number of vertical files (file cabinets): 84
Linear atlas shelving: 360 ft.
Copying facilities available: copier, color copier, microform copier

159 *Moscow, ID*

University of Idaho

Library
Government Documents Department
Box 442353
Moscow, ID 83844-2353
Telephone: 208-885-6344
Fax: 208-885-6817
Email: lib-ref@uidaho.edu
Web: www.insideidaho.org
Personnel:
Responsible person: Dennis Baird, Head of Reference Service, *email:* dbaird@uidaho.edu
FTE professionals: 0.05%   *FTE para-professionals:* 0.05%
Holdings:
Geographic strengths: Idaho
Special collections: Digital Geospatial Data Clearinghouse for Idaho (website www.insideidaho.org)
Map depositories: USGS topos, NOAA, CIA, National Forest Service, NGA nautical, NGA aeronautical, BLM
300,000 printed maps
5 globes
Maps cataloged: 5%
Maps classified: 5%
Maps in OPAC: 5%
Classification schemes: LC, SuDocs
Access:
Hours:
Monday–Friday: 8 A.M.–5 P.M.
Items circulate
Interlibrary loan available
Physical facilities:
Maps in separate area
Public computers: 1

160 *Carbondale, IL*

Southern Illinois University, Carbondale

Morris Library
Map Library, founded 1953
605 Agriculture Drive
Carbondale, IL 62901-6636
Telephone: 618-453-2705
Fax: 618-453-2704

Email: hdavis@lib.siu.edu
Web: www.lib.siu.edu/hp/divisions/sci/maplib.shtml
Personnel:
Responsible person: Harry O. Davis, Map Librarian,
  email: hdavis@lib.siu.edu
Assistants: Janice Fiorino, Map Library Assistant
FTE professionals: 0.75   *FTE para-professionals:* 0.75
Number of student workers hours per week: 35
Number of volunteer hours per month: 27
Holdings:
Geographic strengths: Illinois, United States, Europe
Special collections: Sang Collection of Early maps
  (Mississippi Valley focus) (1584–1899), Rutledge
  Illinois coal Mine Map Collection, Crown Collection
  of Photographs of American maps
Subject strengths: aerial photos, caves, city, geology, hydrology, land ownership, land use, map collecting, mineral resources, raised relief models, roads, waterways
Map depositories and percentages: USGS topos
  (100%), USGS geology maps (95%), USGS other
  (95%), Department of Transportation, NOAA, GPO,
  CIA, National Forest Service, NIMA topos, NIMA
  nautical, NIMA aeronautical, BLM, State
249,054 printed maps
125 manuscript maps
200 wall maps
325 raised relief maps
665 microfiche
85,214 aerial photos
25 satellite images
335 gazetteers
1,575 printed atlases
1,738 books
26 active serials
36 inactive serials
41 CD-ROMs
Chronological coverage:
  Pre-1800: 0.25%
  1800–1899: 1.5%
  1900–1939: 15%
  1940–present: 83%
Average budget over the last 5 years: $4,262
Access:
Collection is partially open to the public
Maps off site
Reference questions per year: 945
Answers email questions
Patrons per month: 1,715
Hours:
  Monday–Friday: 8:45 A.M.–5 P.M.
  Saturday–Saturday: closed
  Total hours per week opened: 44
Maps circulate
Circulation policies apply
  Map circulation duration: 2 weeks

Atlas circulation duration: 4 weeks
Book circulation duration: 4 weeks
Number of maps circulated annually: 7,287
Number of other items circulated annually: 1,165
Interlibrary loan available
Geographic Information Systems:
GIS services available by appointment
Scans maps for patrons
Collection services:
Maps cataloged: 92%
Maps classified: 92%
Classification schemes: LC, Dewey
Cataloging utilities: OCLC, Local
Catalog accessibility: online, cards
Preservation techniques: encapsulation
Physical facilities:
Internet access available
Square footage: 3,050
Number of map cases: 155
Number of vertical files (file cabinets): 49
Linear book shelving: 555 ft.
Linear atlas shelving: 465 ft.
Copying facilities available: copier, color copier
Notes: The library's GIS unit is on a separate floor and
separately staffed.

161 *Champaign, IL*

Illinois State Geological Survey

Library and Map Room
615 East Peabody Drive
Champaign, IL 61820
Telephone: 217-333-5110
Fax: 217-333-2830
Email: library@isgs.uiuc.edu
Web: www.isgs.uiuc.edu/library/index.html
Personnel:
Responsible person: Mary Krick, Head Librarian,
  email: krick@isgs.uiuc.edu
Assistants: Chiawen Liu, Assistant Librarian
FTE professionals: 0.25   *FTE para-professionals:* 0.25
Number of volunteer hours per month: 20
Holdings:
Geographic strengths: Illinois, Illinois Basin
Special collections: Chicago lakeshore aerial photos,
  Illinois coal mine maps, ISGS researchers' original
  field notebooks
Subject strengths: aerial photos, biology, geology, land
  ownership, mineral resources, mining, soil
14,200 printed maps
9,800 manuscript maps
10 wall maps
10 microfilms
7,500 aerial photos

20 printed atlases
100 CD-ROMs
Chronological coverage:
  1900–1939: 20%
  1940–present: 79%
Average budget over the last 5 years: $100
Access:
Maps in separate area
Collection is open to the public
Reference questions per year: 50
Answers email questions
Patrons per month: 60
Hours:
  Monday–Friday: 8 A.M.–noon, 1 P.M.–5 P.M.
  Total hours per week opened: 40
Interlibrary loan available
Collection services:
Maps cataloged: 50%
Maps classified: 66%
Maps in OPAC: 40%
Classification schemes: LC, Local
Cataloging utilities: OCLC, Local
Catalog accessibility: online, cards
Physical facilities:
Internet access available
Square footage: 900
Number of map cases: 47
Number of vertical files (file cabinets): 28
Other map storage: 1 rolled map case, 5 field notebook
  shelving units, 2 oversize air photo cases
Copying facilities available: copier

162 *Charleston, IL*

Eastern Illinois University

Booth Library
Government Documents, founded 1965
600 Lincoln Avenue
Charleston, IL 61920
Telephone: 217-581-6072
Fax: 217-581-6066
Web: www.library.eiu.edu
Personnel:
Responsible person: Jocelyn Tipton, Government Doc-
  uments Coordinator, *email:* cfjtt@eiu.edu
Assistants: Lois Dickenson, Library Operations Assistant
FTE professionals: 0.1   *FTE para-professionals:* 0.2
Holdings:
Subject strengths: Regional Topography
Map depositories and percentages: USGS topos (33%),
  GPO, CIA, NIMA topos, NIMA nautical, NIMA
  aeronautical, State, Census, National Climate Data
  Center (CD-ROMS)
27,486 printed maps

Chronological coverage:
  1940–present: 95%
Access:
Collection is open to the public
Reference questions per year: 120
Answers email questions
Patrons per month: 10
Hours:
  Monday–Thursday: 8 A.M.–midnight
  Friday: 8 A.M.–5 P.M.
  Saturday: 9 A.M.–5 P.M.
  Sunday: noon–midnight
  Total hours per week opened: 93
Maps circulate
Circulation policies apply
  Map circulation duration: 2 weeks
  Number of maps circulated annually: 25
Interlibrary loan available
Geographic Information Systems:
No GIS services available
Collection services:
Maps cataloged: 80%
Maps classified: 80%
Maps in OPAC: 25%
Datasets are cataloged
Classification schemes: LC, SuDocs
Cataloging utilities: OCLC
Catalog accessibility: online, cards
Preservation techniques: lamination
Physical facilities:
Internet access available
Number of map cases: 30
Linear book shelving: 72 ft.
Copying facilities available: copier, microform copier

163 *Chicago, IL*

Adler Planetarium and Astronomy Museum

History of Astronomy Research Center
1300 South Lake Shore Drive
Chicago, IL 60605
Telephone: 312-322-0594
Fax: 312-341-9935
Email: astrohistory@adlernet.org
Web: www.adlerplanetarium.org
Personnel:
Responsible person: Devon Pyle-Vowles, Collections
  Manager, *email:* astrohistory@adlernet.org
Assistants: Anna Friedman, Assistant Curator
FTE professionals: 1   *FTE para-professionals:* 1
Holdings:
Geographic strengths: Celestial
Special collections: Comet maps, star atlases, eclipse
  maps

100 printed maps
50 globes
100 atlases
4,000 books
5 active serials

Access:

Hours:

Monday–Friday: by appointment, 10 A.M.–4 P.M.
Saturday–Sunday: closed

Collection services:

Maps cataloged: 100%
Maps classified: 100%
Maps in OPAC: 50%
Classification schemes: LC, Local

Physical facilities:

Maps in separate area
Public computers: 2
Map cases: 4
Vertical files: 1

164 *Chicago, IL*

Chicago Public Library

Harold Washington Library Center
Government Publications Department
400 South State Street
Chicago, IL 60605
Telephone: 312-747-4508
Fax: 312-747-4516
Email: gneumann@chipublib.org
Web: chipublib.org

Personnel:

Responsible person: Glenn Neumann, *email:* gneumann@chipublib.org

Assistants: Lynne Kiviluoma, Department Head; Tom Mikula, Librarian I; Tom Edwards, Librarian II; Patricia Magierski, Librarian I; Inanama Santos, Librarian; Shah Tiwana, Librarian III

FTE professionals: 2

Holdings:

Geographic strengths: Illinois
Special collections: Sanborn Fire Insurance maps
Subject strengths: aerial photos, aeronautical, agriculture, celestial, climatology, city, forestry, geology, hydrology, mineral resources, mining, nautical charts, recreation, roads, soil, views, waterways
Map depositories and percentages: USGS topos (100%), USGS geology maps (100%), USGS other (100%), Department of Transportation, NOAA, GPO, CIA, National Forest Service, NIMA topos, NIMA nautical, NIMA aeronautical, BLM, State
94,200 printed maps
Chronological coverage:
1900–1939: 23%

1940–present: 75%
Average budget over the last 5 years: $700

Access:

Maps in separate area
Collection is partially open to the public

Hours:

Monday–Tuesday: 9 A.M.–5 P.M.
Wednesday–Thursday: 9 A.M.–7 P.M.
Friday–Saturday: 9 A.M.–5 P.M.
Sunday: 1 P.M.–5 P.M.
Total hours per week opened: 58

Geographic Information Systems:

No GIS services available

Collection services:

Maps cataloged: 100%
Maps classified: 100%
Maps in OPAC: 15%
Classification schemes: SuDocs
Cataloging utilities: OCLC, Local
Catalog accessibility: online
Preservation techniques: lamination
Items that have gone through the preservation process: 25%

Physical facilities:

Internet access available
Number of vertical files (file cabinets): 35
Copying facilities available: copier, color copier, large-format copier, microform copier

165 *Chicago, IL*

Illinois Institute of Technology

Paul V. Galvin Library
Government Documents
35 West 33rd Street
Chicago, IL 60616
Telephone: 312-567-3614
Fax: 312-567-3955
Email: ahrens@iit.edu
Web: www.gl.iit.edu/govdocs/

Personnel:

Responsible person: Aric Ahrens, Government Documents Depository Coordinator, *email:* ahrens@iit.edu
FTE professionals: 1

Holdings:

Geographic strengths: Illinois, United States
Map depositories: USGS topos, CIA, NGA nautical, NGA aeronautical
60,000 printed maps
200 atlases

Access:

Hours:

Monday–Saturday: 8:30 A.M.–5 P.M.
Sunday: 2 P.M.–10 P.M.

Collection services:
Maps cataloged: 20%
Maps classified: 95%
Maps in OPAC: 20%
Classification schemes: SuDocs
Physical facilities:
Map cases: 30
Vertical files: 1

166 *Chicago, IL*

University of Chicago

Joseph Regenstein Library
Map Collection, founded 1929
1100 East 57th Street
Chicago, IL 60637
Telephone: 773-702-8761
Fax: 773-702-6623
Email: wintersc@uchicago.edu
Web: www.lib.uchicago.edu/e/su/maps
Personnel:
Responsible person: Christopher Winters, *email:* wintersc@uchicago.edu
FTE professionals: 0.5
Number of student workers hours per week: 26
Holdings:
Geographic strengths: United States, Western Europe, Russia, India
Subject strengths: city, geology, topographic
Map depositories and percentages: USGS topos (100%), USGS geology maps (100%), USGS other (100%), Department of Transportation, NOAA, GPO, CIA, National Forest Service, NIMA topos, NIMA nautical, NIMA aeronautical, BLM, State, European Union, Canada
410,379 printed maps
400 manuscript maps
20 wall maps
50 raised relief maps
1,000 microfiche
10 microfilms
9,778 aerial photos
500 gazetteers
1,750 printed atlases
800 books
75 inactive serials
633 CD-ROMs
50 computer programs
Collecting digital data
Chronological coverage:
Pre-1800: 2%
1800–1899: 8%
1900–1939: 50%
1940–present: 40%
Average budget over the last 5 years: $14,000

Access:
Maps in separate area
Collection is partially open to the public
Reference questions per year: 1,200
Answers email questions
Patrons per month: 100
Hours:
Monday–Friday: noon–5 P.M.
Number of maps circulated annually: 8,000
Interlibrary loan available
Geographic Information Systems:
GIS services available by appointment
GIS software: ArcView, ArcGIS
GIS assistance available for Census mapping, geocoding, and image analysis
General GIS questions answered
Plotter available
Collection services:
Maps cataloged: 50%
Maps classified: 60%
Maps in OPAC: 50%
Datasets are cataloged
Classification schemes: LC
Cataloging utilities: OCLC, RLG
Catalog accessibility: online
Preservation techniques: encapsulation
Items that have gone through the preservation process: 5%
Physical facilities:
Internet access available
Square footage: 5,000
Number of map cases: 378
Number of vertical files (file cabinets): 40
Linear book shelving: 268 ft.
Linear atlas shelving: 240 ft.
Other map storage: 3 older cabinets
Copying facilities available: copier, microform copier, scanner
Notes: ILL: copies only. GIS workstations are monitored but appointment not needed.

167 *Chicago, IL*

University of Illinois, Chicago

Richard J. Daley Library
Map Section, founded 1957
801 South Morgan Street
Chicago, IL 60607
Telephone: 312-996-2738
Fax: 312-413-0424
Email: lib-maps@uic.edu
Web: www.uic.edu/depts/library/
Personnel:
Responsible person: Marsha L. Selmer, Map Librarian, *email:* lib-maps@uic.edu

Assistants: Harvey Huie, Library Technical Assistant II

Number of student workers hours per week: 15

Holdings:

Geographic strengths: Chicago metropolitan region, Illinois, United States

Special collections: Chicago metropolitan area aerial photographs and photomaps, Chicago and Illinois (19th century), Great Lakes region (17th–18th century), Eastern Europe and the Russian Empire (16th–19th century), fire insurance maps of Chicago (19th–20th century)

Subject strengths: aerial photos, aeronautical, early cartography, modern cartography, city, geology, geospatial data, hydrology, land ownership, land use, map catalogs, mineral resources, political geography, population, projections, religion, roads, soil, views, fire insurance maps

Map depositories and percentages: USGS topos (99%), USGS geology maps (100%), USGS other (100%), Department of Transportation, GPO, CIA, National Forest Service, NIMA topos, NIMA aeronautical, BLM, State

179,000 printed maps

245 microfiche

153 microfilms

4,000 aerial photos

100 gazetteers

1,300 printed atlases

100 books

Collecting digital data

Chronological coverage:
1940–present: 97%

Access:

Collection is partially open to the public

Reference questions per year: 3,200

Answers email questions

Hours:

Monday–Friday: 8 A.M.–5 P.M.

Total hours per week opened: 45

Maps circulate

Circulation policies apply

Map circulation duration: 1 week

Number of maps circulated annually: 760

Interlibrary loan available

Geographic Information Systems:

GIS services available by appointment

GIS software: ArcView

GIS assistance available for Census mapping, geocoding, and image analysis

Plotter available

Collection services:

Maps cataloged: 99%

Maps classified: 99%

Datasets are cataloged

Classification schemes: LC, SuDocs

Cataloging utilities: OCLC

Catalog accessibility: online, cards

Preservation techniques: encapsulation

Physical facilities:

Internet access available

Number of map cases: 86

Number of vertical files (file cabinets): 22

Linear book shelving: 210 ft.

Linear atlas shelving: 500 ft.

Copying facilities available: copier, microform copier

168 *Edwardsville, IL*

Southern Illinois University Edwardsville

Lovejoy Library

Map Library

P.O. Boz 1063

Edwardsville, IL 62026-2063

Telephone: 618-650-2632

Fax: 618-650-2717

Email: gdenue@siue.edu

Web: www.library.siue.edu/lib/

Personnel:

Responsible person: Gary N. Denue, U.S. Documents/ Map Librarian, *email:* gdenue@siue.edu

Assistants: Melissa Kenney, Library Technical Assistant

FTE professionals: 0.25   *FTE para-professionals:* 0.33

Holdings:

Geographic strengths: Southwestern Illinois, Illinois

Map depositories: USGS topos, CIA, National Forest Service, BLM

146,500 printed maps

3,400 aerial photos

1 globe

412 atlases

829 books

150 CD-ROMs

Access:

Hours:

Monday–Friday: 7:30 A.M.–11:30 P.M.

Saturday: 10 A.M.–6 P.M.

Sunday: 1 P.M.–9 P.M.

Items circulate

Collection services:

Maps cataloged: 40%

Maps classified: 40%

Maps in OPAC: 10%

Classification schemes: LC, SuDocs

Physical facilities:

Maps in separate area

Public computers: 2

Map cases: 81

Vertical files: 10

169 *Evanston, IL*

Northwestern University

Main Library (Evanston Campus)
Government Publications and Maps Department,
founded 1948
1970 Campus Drive
Evanston, IL 60202
Telephone: 847-491-3130
Fax: 847-491-8306
Email: govpubs@northwestern.edu
Web: www.library.northwestern.edu/govpub/
Personnel:
Responsible person: Michael L. Smith, *email:* mls@
northwestern.edu
Number of student workers hours per week: 10
Holdings:
Geographic strengths: Illinois, Chicago, Great Lakes
States, North America, Africa, Europe
Special collections: Antique maps of Africa
Subject strengths: aeronautical, agriculture, early car-
tography, modern cartography, climatology, city,
economic geography, forestry, genealogy, geodetic
surveys, geology, geospatial data, historical geography, hydrology, land use, language, map catalogs,
map collecting, military, mineral resources, mining,
nautical charts, oceanography, political geography,
population, projections, railroads, recreation, religion, roads, satellite imagery, soil, travel books, vegetation, views, waterways
Map depositories and percentages: USGS topos
(100%), USGS geology maps (100%), USGS other
(100%), Department of Transportation, NOAA,
GPO, CIA, National Forest Service, NIMA topos,
NIMA nautical, NIMA aeronautical, BLM, State,
United Nations, European Union, OAS, World
Tourism Organization
200,000 printed maps
250 manuscript maps
500 wall maps
20 raised relief maps
100 aerial photos
250 satellite images
200 gazetteers
2,000 printed atlases
10 manuscript atlases
500 books
20 active serials
10 CD-ROMs
Collecting digital data
Chronological coverage:
1900–1939: 15%
1940–present: 79%
Average budget over the last 5 years: $2,500
Access:

Collection is partially open to the public
Maps off site: 30%
Reference questions per year: 500
Answers email questions
Patrons per month: 1,000
Hours:
Monday–Friday: 8:30 A.M.–9 P.M.
Saturday: 8:30 A.M.–5 P.M.
Total hours per week opened: 71
Maps circulate
Circulation policies apply
Map circulation duration: 3 weeks
Atlas circulation duration: 3 weeks
Book circulation duration: 3 weeks
Number of maps circulated annually: 50
Number of books circulated annually: 50
Interlibrary loan available
Geographic Information Systems:
GIS services available in an open environment
GIS software: ArcVIew
Number of public GIS workstations: 10
GIS assistance available for Census mapping, geocod-
ing, and image analysis
Scans maps for patrons
Collection services:
Maps cataloged: 95%
Maps classified: 95%
Maps in OPAC: 10%
Datasets are cataloged
Classification schemes: LC, SuDocs, Dewey
Cataloging utilities: OCLC
Catalog accessibility: online, cards
Preservation techniques: encapsulation, deacidifica-
tion
Physical facilities:
Internet access available
Copying facilities available: copier, color copier, large-
format copier, microform copier

170 *Macomb, IL*

Western Illinois University

Leslie F. Malpass Library
Government and Legal Information Unit
1 University Circle
Macomb, IL 61455
Telephone: 309-298-2700
Fax: 309-298-2791
Email: mm-allen@wiu.edu
Web: www.wiu.edu/library/govpubs/maps/
Personnel:
Responsible person: Marcy M. Allen, *email:* mm-allen@
wiu.edu
FTE professionals: 0.25   *FTE para-professionals:* 0.1

Holdings:

Geographic strengths: Illinois, United States

Map depositories: USGS topos, Department of Transportation, NOAA, CIA

300,000 printed maps

12,000 aerial photos

2 globes

2,208 atlases

3,800 books

20 active serials

3,600 CD-ROMs

Access:

Hours:

Monday–Friday: 8 A.M.–midnight

Saturday: 9 A.M.–9 P.M.

Sunday: 12:30 P.M.–midnight

Items circulate

Collection services:

Maps cataloged: 3%

Maps classified: 95%

Maps in OPAC: 0%

Classification schemes: LC, SuDocs, Local

Physical facilities:

Public computers: 12

Map cases: 105

Vertical files: 4

171 *Normal, IL*

Illinois State University

Milner Library

Social Sciences Division

Campus Box 8900

Normal, IL 61790-8900

Telephone: 309-438-3486

Fax: 309-438-3676

Email: vmschwa@ilstu.edu

Web: www.mlb.ilstu.edu

Personnel:

Responsible person: Vanette Schwartz, Social Sciences and Maps Librarian, *email:* vmschwa@ilstu.edu

Number of student workers hours per week: 10

Holdings:

Geographic strengths: United States, Canada, Australia, Great Britain

Map depositories and percentages: USGS topos, USGS geology maps, CIA, National Forest Service, BLM

300,000 printed maps

20,000 aerial photos

500 printed atlases

Chronological coverage:

1900–1939: 15%

1940–present: 80%

Access:

Collection is open to the public

Answers email questions

Hours:

Monday–Friday: 8 A.M.–5 P.M.

Saturday–Saturday: closed

Total hours per week opened: 40

Maps circulate

Circulation policies apply

Map circulation duration: 2 weeks

Atlas circulation duration: 4 weeks

Book circulation duration: 4 weeks

Interlibrary loan available

Geographic Information Systems:

No GIS services available

Number of public GIS workstations: 12

Collection services:

Maps cataloged: 10%

Maps classified: 10%

Maps in OPAC: 10%

Classification schemes: LC, SuDocs

Cataloging utilities: OCLC

Catalog accessibility: online

Preservation techniques: encapsulation, deacidification

Physical facilities:

Internet access available

Square footage: 3,000

Number of map cases: 105

Number of vertical files (file cabinets): 40

Copying facilities available: copier, color copier, microform copier

172 *Oglesby, IL*

Illinois Valley Community College

Jacobs Library

815 North Orlando Smith Avenue

Oglesby, IL 61348

Telephone: 815 224-0306

Fax: 815 224-9147

Email: jeanne_struna@ivcc.edu

Web: www.ivcc.edu/library/

Personnel:

Responsible person: Jane Norem, Librarian, *email:* jane_norem@ivcc.edu

Assistants: Jeanne A. Struna, Library Technician

FTE professionals: 0.25

Holdings:

Map depositories: USGS topos, CIA, National Forest Service, NGA aeronautical

8,421 printed maps

321 atlases

Access:

Hours:

Monday–Thursday: 7:30 A.M.–8 P.M.

Friday: 7:30 A.M.–6 P.M.

Saturday: 10 A.M.–2 P.M.

Items circulate
Interlibrary loan available
Collection services:
Maps cataloged: 75%
Maps classified: 0%
Maps in OPAC: 75%
Classification schemes: LC, SuDocs
Physical facilities:
Map cases: 1

173 *Peoria, IL*

Bradley University

Cullom-Davis Library
1501 West Bradley Avenue
Peoria, IL 61625
Telephone: 309-677-2840
Fax: 309-677-2558
Email: johnson@bradley.edu
Web: library.bradley.edu
Personnel:
Responsible person: Peggy Scott, Documents Assistant, *email:* scott @bumail.bradley.edu
Holdings:
Special collections: Sanborn Fire Insurance maps online
Map depositories: USGS topos, CIA, National Forest Service
10,000 printed maps
Access:
Hours:
Monday–Friday: 9 A.M.–5 P.M.
Collection services:
Maps cataloged: 5%
Maps classified: 5%
Maps in OPAC: 5%
Classification schemes: LC, SuDocs
Physical facilities:
Maps in separate area
Public computers: 4
Notes: USGS maps are held in a separate location, and must be requested. On request, USGS maps will be brought to the main library for study. Other depository and purchased maps are in the library's map cabinets and government documents areas, and are available all hours the library is open. Special Collections is open limited hours, and should be called prior to visiting.

174 *Rock Island, IL*

Augustana College

Thomas Tredway Library
Loring Map Collection, founded 1945
639 38th Street
Rock Island, IL 61201
Telephone: 309-794-7318

Fax: 309-794-7564
Email: ggmoline@augustana.edu
Web: www.augustana.edu/library
Personnel:
Responsible person: Dr. Norm Moline, *email:* ggmoline@augustana.edu
FTE professionals: 0.1
Number of student workers hours per week: 15
Holdings:
Geographic strengths: Illinois, Iowa, Wisconsin, Minnesota, East Asia, China
Special collections: Sanborn Fire Insurance maps for Illinois (1867–1970)
Subject strengths: celestial, geology, hydrology, mineral resources, nautical charts, raised relief models, zoogeography
Map depositories and percentages: USGS topos (40%), USGS geology maps (100%), USGS other, NOAA, NIMA topos, NGA maps
100,000 printed maps
100 manuscript maps
300 wall maps
400 raised relief maps
5,400 aerial photos
50 satellite images
15 globes
110 printed atlases
20 books
Chronological coverage:
1940–present: 90%
Average budget over the last 5 years: $1,000
Access:
Maps in separate area
Collection is partially open to the public
Reference questions per year: 100
Answers email questions
Patrons per month: 50
Hours:
Monday–Friday: 8 A.M.–midnight
Saturday: 10 A.M.–5 P.M.
Sunday: noon–midnight
Total hours per week opened: 95
Maps circulate
Circulation policies apply
Atlas circulation duration: 3 weeks
Book circulation duration: 3 weeks
Number of maps circulated annually: 150
Geographic Information Systems:
GIS services available by appointment
GIS software: Atlas GIS, Atlas Graphics, GS Menu 1.0
Scans maps for patrons
Collection services:
Maps cataloged: 20%
Maps classified: 100%
Classification schemes: LC, Local

Cataloging utilities: OCLC, Local
Catalog accessibility: online, index sheets
Items that have gone through the preservation process: 0

Physical facilities:
No Internet access
Square footage: 2,056
Number of map cases: 119
Number of vertical files (file cabinets): 11
Linear atlas shelving: 21 ft.
Other map storage: 5 rolled map cases, 1 flat shelf for oversize maps
Copying facilities available: copier, microform copier

175 *Springfield, IL*

Illinois State Archives

MC Norton Building
Springfield, IL 62756
Telephone: 217-782-3501
Fax: 217-524-3930
Web: www.cyberdriveillinois.com

Personnel:
Responsible person: Wayne C. Temple
FTE professionals: 0.2

Holdings:
Geographic strengths: Illinois
Special collections: Illinois original federal township plats with field notes
Subject strengths: aerial photos, agriculture, archaeology, biology, early cartography, city, forestry, genealogy, hydrology, land ownership, map catalogs, military, mineral resources, mining, vegetation, waterways
40,000 printed maps
50 printed atlases
Chronological coverage:
1800–1899: 90%
1900–1939: 10%
On-going publications: Descriptive Inventory of the Archives of the State of Illinois (2nd edition), 1997

Access:
Collection is paged
Patrons per month: 15
Hours:
Monday–Friday: 8 A.M.–4:30 P.M.
Saturday: 8 A.M.–3:30 P.M.
Sunday: closed
Total hours per week opened: 50

Geographic Information Systems:
GIS services available by appointment

Collection services:
Maps cataloged: 100%
Maps classified: 100%

Classification schemes: LC
Cataloging utilities: OCLC
Catalog accessibility: online
Preservation techniques: encapsulation, deacidification, lamination, digitization
Items that have gone through the preservation process: 75%

Physical facilities:
Internet access available
Number of staff computers: 20
Copying facilities available: copier, large-format copier

Notes: Annual hits at our federal township plats website now exceed 2 million.

176 *Springfield, IL*

Illinois State Library

300 South Second Street
Springfield, IL 62701
Telephone: 217-782-5823
Fax: 217-557-6737
Email: islinformationline@ilsos.net
Web: www.cyberdriveillinois.com/library/isl/ref/islmaps.html

Personnel:
Responsible person: Arlyn Booth, Map Coordinator, email: abooth@ilsos.net
FTE para-professionals: 0.25

Holdings:
Geographic strengths: Illinois
Special collections: Illinois Sanborn atlases, Illinois land ownership atlases, Illinois state and county road maps, Illinois city maps, Illinois aerial photos, Illinois DOQs and DRGs, Illinois census maps, Illinois topo and geologic maps
Subject strengths: aerial photos, aeronautical, agriculture, archaeology, modern cartography, celestial, climatology, city, engineering, forestry, genealogy, geology, geospatial data, historical geography, hydrology, land ownership, land use, map catalogs, map collecting, military, mineral resources, mining, nautical charts, political geography, population, railroads, recreation, roads, soil, travel books, waterways
Map depositories and percentages: USGS topos (100%), USGS geology maps (100%), USGS other (100%), Department of Transportation, NOAA, GPO, CIA, National Forest Service, NIMA topos, NIMA nautical, NIMA aeronautical, BLM, State
185,000 printed maps
200 manuscript maps
16 wall maps
27,000 aerial photos
1,500 gazetteers

5,000 printed atlases
500 books
50 active serials
40 CD-ROMs
Collecting digital data
Chronological coverage:
    1800–1899: 10%
    1900–1939: 20%
    1940–present: 70%
Average budget over the last 5 years: $1,500
On-going publications: Acquisition list generated quarterly from OCLC and posted on web site. Inventories of Illinois topos, Illinois county atlases, Illinois county highway maps, and Illinois DOQs available in hardcopy or on web site.

Access:
Maps in separate area
Collection is paged
Reference questions per year: 4,000
Answers email questions
Patrons per month: 80
Hours:
    Monday–Friday: 8 A.M.–4:30 P.M.
    Total hours per week opened: 42.5
Maps circulate
Circulation policies apply
    Map circulation duration: 4 weeks
    Atlas circulation duration: 4 weeks
    Book circulation duration: 4 weeks
    Number of maps circulated annually: 500
Interlibrary loan available

Geographic Information Systems:
GIS services available by appointment
GIS software: ArcView
Scans maps for patrons

Collection services:
Maps cataloged: 100%
Maps classified: 100%
Maps in OPAC: 100%
Classification schemes: LC, SuDocs, Dewey
Cataloging utilities: OCLC
Catalog accessibility: online
Preservation techniques: encapsulation, deacidification, archival tape repair
Items that have gone through the preservation process: 30%

Physical facilities:
Internet access available
Square footage: 1,250
Number of map cases: 93
Number of vertical files (file cabinets): 14
Linear book shelving: 15 ft.
Linear atlas shelving: 52,160 ft.
Other map storage: 1 wall map rack

Copying facilities available: copier, color copier, large-format copier, microform copier
Notes: The map collection is semi-separate from the rest of the library. We have a separate reference desk and a lot of separate shelving, but our atlases, most of the fiche and CDs and the general book collection is scattered throughout the library. We have a public room, a work room/map cabinet room, and 2 more separate map cabinet rooms.

177 *Urbana, IL*

University of Illinois, Urbana–Champaign

Illinois Historical Survey
346 Library
1408 West Gregory Drive
Urbana, IL 61801
Telephone: 217-333-1777
Web: www.library.uiuc.edu/ihx
Personnel:
Responsible person: John Hoffmann, *email:* jmhoffma@uiuc.edu
Holdings:
Geographic strengths: Illinois, Northwest Territory, Mississippi Valley, Great Lakes
Special collections: County Atlases of Illinois (1870–1920), Karpinski Collection of maps of North America (17–19th century), Rascher {fire insurance} Atlases of Chicago (ca. 1890)
Subject strengths: historical geography, land ownership
1,800 printed maps
10 manuscript maps
10 wall maps
35 aerial photos
10 gazetteers
300 printed atlases
Chronological coverage:
    Pre-1800: 10%
    1800–1899: 50%
    1900–1939: 30%
    1940–present: 10%
Access:
Collection is paged
Answers email questions
Hours:
    Monday–Friday: 8:30 A.M.–5 P.M.
    Total hours per week opened: 42.5
Collection services:
Maps cataloged: 90%
Maps classified: 90%
Maps in OPAC: 30%
Classification schemes: LC, Local
Cataloging utilities: OCLC

Catalog accessibility: online, cards
Physical facilities:
Linear atlas shelving: 50 ft.
Copying facilities available: copier

178 *Urbana, IL*

University of Illinois, Urbana—Champaign

Map and Geography Library
418 Library
MC-522
1408 West Gregory Drive
Urbana, IL 61801
Telephone: 217-333-0827
Fax: 217-333-2214
Email: mapgeo@cliff.library.uiuc.edu
Web: www.library.uiuc.edu/max
Personnel:
Responsible person: Jenny Marie Johnson, Map and Geography Librarian, *email:* jmj@uiuc.edu
Assistants: Katelyn Dyani Swan, Library Technical Specialist
FTE professionals: 1   *FTE para-professionals:* 1
Holdings:
Geographic strengths: Illinois, Canada, Great Britain, Latin America
Special collections: Illinois aerial photography, Sanborn Fire Insurance maps for Illinois cities
Map depositories: USGS topos, Department of Transportation, NOAA, CIA, National Forest Service, NGA nautical, NGA aeronautical, BLM, Illinois Department of Transportation
403,400 printed maps
259,700 aerial photos
8 globes
19,600 books
240 active serials
620 CD-ROMs
Access:
Hours:
Monday–Friday: 8:30 A.M.–5 P.M.
Saturday: 1 P.M.–5 P.M.
Sunday: closed
Items circulate
Interlibrary loan available
Collection services:
Maps cataloged: 75%
Maps classified: 100%
Maps in OPAC: 50%
Classification schemes: LC
Physical facilities:
Maps in separate area
Public computers: 2
Map cases: 229
Vertical files: 37

Notes: Additional depository: Pre-1960 imprints do not circulate nor do materials that have been encapsulated or mounted on fabric.

179 *Urbana, IL*

University of Illinois, Urbana—Champaign

Rare Book and Special Collections Library
1408 West Gregory Drive
Room 346
Urbana, IL 61801
Telephone: 217-333-3777
Fax: 217-333-2214
Web: www.library.uiuc.edu/rbx/
Personnel:
Responsible person: Alvan Bregman, Rare Book Collections Librarian, *email:* abregman@uiuc.edu
Holdings:
Geographic strengths: North America, South America, Europe
Subject strengths: early cartography, celestial
1,250 printed maps
300 printed atlases
Chronological coverage:
Pre-1800: 95%
Access:
Collection is paged
Reference questions per year: 20
Answers email questions
Hours:
Monday–Friday: 8:30 A.M.–5 P.M.
Total hours per week opened: 42.5
Collection services:
Maps cataloged: 75%
Maps classified: 75%
Maps in OPAC: 50%
Classification schemes: LC, Dewey
Cataloging utilities: OCLC
Catalog accessibility: online, cards
Preservation techniques: encapsulation
Items that have gone through the preservation process: 10%
Physical facilities:
Copying facilities available: copier, flatbed, overhead scanner

180 *Urbana, IL*

Urbana Free Library

Champaign County Historical Archives
Founded 1980
201 South Race Street
Urbana, IL 61801
Telephone: 217-367-0807
Fax: 217-367-4061

Web: urbanafreelibrary.org/archives.htm

Personnel:

Responsible person: Howard C. Grueneberg, *email:* hcgruen@hotmail.com

FTE professionals: 0.25

Holdings:

Geographic strengths: Champaign, Urbana, Champaign County, Illinois

Special collections: Sanborn Fire Insurance maps for Champaign and Urbana (complete: paper and microfilm), Sidwell plat book/parcel number set for Champaign County (complete: 1979–present), historic Illinois Central Railroad Company maps for the Champaign/Mattoon districts

Subject strengths: aerial photos, city, land ownership, railroads, roads

1,500 printed maps

20 wall maps

400 aerial photos

65 printed atlases

150 books

Chronological coverage:
1900–1939: 20%
1940–present: 75%

Access:

Collection is paged

Maps off site; *Percentage offsite:* 25%

Reference questions per year: 150

Answers email questions

Patrons per month: 400

Hours:
Monday–Saturday: 9 A.M.–5 P.M.
Sunday: 1 P.M.–5 P.M.
Total hours per week opened: 52

Geographic Information Systems:

No GIS services available

Collection services:

Maps cataloged: 10%

Maps classified: 30%

Classification schemes: LC, Local

Cataloging utilities: OCLC

Catalog accessibility: online, printout

Physical facilities:

No Internet access

Square footage: 24

Linear book shelving: 35 ft.

Linear atlas shelving: 30 ft.

Copying facilities available: copier, microform copier

181 *Bloomington, IN*

Indiana University, Bloomington

Geography and Map Library
Founded 1973
701 East Kirkwood

015 Student Building
Bloomington, IN 47405

Telephone: 812-855-1108

Email: libgm@indiana.edu

Web: www.indiana.edu/~libgm

Personnel:

Responsible person: Lou Malcomb, Librarian for Geography and Map Library, *email:* malcomb@indiana.edu

Assistants: Heiko Muehr, Geography and Map Library Coordinator

FTE professionals: 0.2

Number of student workers hours per week: 60

Number of volunteer hours per month: 10

Holdings:

Special collections: Indiana Historic maps, Sanborn Fire Insurance maps for Indiana, Kinsey (Alfred C.) map collection

Subject strengths: aerial photos, climatology, city, economic geography, geospatial data, historical geography, land use, political geography, population, roads, satellite imagery

Map depositories and percentages: USGS topos (90%), (35%), USGS other (50%), GPO, CIA

250,000 printed maps

25 manuscript maps

100 wall maps

50 raised relief maps

10,000 microfiche

30 microfilms

7,000 aerial photos

10 satellite images

45 gazetteers

2,000 printed atlases

18,000 books

185 active serials

135 inactive serials

245 CD-ROMs

Chronological coverage:
1800–1899: 10%
1900–1939: 30%
1940–present: 60%

Average budget over the last 5 years: $10,000

Access:

Collection is open to the public

Reference questions per year: 623

Answers email questions

Patrons per month: 400

Hours:
Monday–Thursday: 8 A.M.–10 P.M.
Friday: 8 A.M.–5 P.M.
Saturday: 1 P.M.–5 P.M.
Sunday: 1 P.M.–10 P.M.
Total hours per week opened: 67

Maps circulate

Circulation policies apply

Map circulation duration: 30 days
Atlas circulation duration: 30 days
Book circulation duration: 30 days
Number of maps circulated annually: 1,702
Number of books circulated annually: 10,984
Number of other items circulated annually: 34
Interlibrary loan available

Geographic Information Systems:

GIS services available by appointment
GIS assistance available for Census mapping
Plotter available

Collection services:

Maps cataloged: 50%
Maps classified: 100%
Maps in OPAC: 45%
Datasets are cataloged
Classification schemes: LC, Local
Cataloging utilities: OCLC
Catalog accessibility: online
Preservation techniques: encapsulation, atlases and books boxed as needed
Items that have gone through the preservation process: 10%

Physical facilities:

Internet access available
Square footage: 3,946
Number of map cases: 173
Linear book shelving: 1,000 ft.
Linear atlas shelving: 62 ft.
Other map storage: hanging rolled maps: 12 linear feet
Copying facilities available: microform copier

182 *Bloomington, IN*

Indiana University, Bloomington

Geology Library
1001 East Tenth Street
Bloomington, IN 47405-1405
Telephone: 812-855-1494
Fax: 812-855-6614
Email: libgeol@indiana.edu

Personnel:

Responsible person: Linda R. Zellmer *email:* libgeol@indiana.edu
FTE professionals: 0.1 *FTE para-professionals:* 0.3

Holdings:

Geographic strengths: Indiana, Central States, United States
Special collections: Indiana Geological Survey
Subject strengths: aeronautical, caves, engineering, geology, geospatial data, hydrology, land ownership, land use, mineral resources, mining, nautical charts, raised relief models, soil, waterways
Map depositories and percentages: USGS topos (100%), USGS geology maps (100%), USGS other

(100%), Department of Transportation, NOAA, NIMA nautical, NIMA aeronautical, BLM, State
200,000 printed maps
20 wall maps
700 CD-ROMs
Collecting digital data
Chronological coverage:
1800–1899: 10%
1900–1939: 20%
1940–present: 70%
Average budget over the last 5 years: $1,000

Access:

Maps in separate area
Collection is open to the public
Answers email questions

Hours:

Monday–Thursday: 8 A.M.–11 P.M.
Friday: 8 A.M.–5 P.M.
Saturday: 1 P.M.–5 P.M.
Sunday: 1 P.M.–10 P.M.
Total hours per week opened: 82
Maps circulate
Circulation policies apply
Interlibrary loan available

Geographic Information Systems:

GIS services available in an open environment
GIS software: ArcGIS
GIS assistance available for Census mapping, and geocoding
Plotter available
Scans maps for patrons

Collection services:

Maps classified: 40%
Datasets are cataloged
Classification schemes: LC, SuDocs
Cataloging utilities: OCLC
Catalog accessibility: online, Librarian's memory
Preservation techniques: encapsulation, deacidification

Physical facilities:

Internet access available
Number of map cases: 44
Number of vertical files (file cabinets): 15
Linear book shelving: 1,878 ft.
Copying facilities available: copier, large-format copier. Scanners are oversize and page-size.

183 *Bloomington, IN*

Indiana University, Bloomington

Government Information, Microforms, and Statistical Services
Founded 1881
1320 East 10th Street
c264 IUB Main Library
Bloomington, IN 47405
Telephone: 812-855-6924

Fax: 812-855-3460
Email: libgpd@indiana.edu
Web: www.indiana.edu/~libgpd
Personnel:

Responsible person: Lou Malcomb, Head Government Information, Microforms and Statistical Services, *email:* malcomb@indiana.edu

Number of student workers hours per week: 15

Holdings:

Special collections: U.S. Census maps

Subject strengths: agriculture, climatology, city, forestry, geospatial data, hydrology, land use, political geography, population, recreation, roads, satellite imagery, soil, vegetation, waterways

Map depositories and percentages: GPO, CIA, National Forest Service, BLM, State, United Nations, European Union

15,000 printed maps

287 gazetteers

45 printed atlases

1,800 CD-ROMs

Chronological coverage:

1800–1899: 10%

1900–1939: 40%

1940–present: 50%

Average budget over the last 5 years: $1,000

On-going publications: http://www.indiana.edu/~libgm

Access:

Maps in separate area

Collection is open to the public

Maps off site: 10%

Answers email questions

Hours:

Monday–Thursday: 8 A.M.–midnight

Friday: 8 A.M.–9 P.M.

Saturday: 10 A.M.–9 P.M.

Sunday: 11 A.M.–12m

Total hours per week opened: 107

Maps circulate

Circulation policies apply

Map circulation duration: 30 days

Atlas circulation duration: 30 days

Book circulation duration: 30 days

Interlibrary loan available

Geographic Information Systems:

GIS services available by appointment

GIS assistance available for Census mapping

Plotter available

Collection services:

Maps cataloged: 50%

Maps classified: 100%

Maps in OPAC: 45%

Datasets are cataloged

Classification schemes: LC, Local

Cataloging utilities: OCLC

Catalog accessibility: online

Preservation techniques: encapsulation, atlases and books boxed as needed

Items that have gone through the preservation process: 10%

Physical facilities:

Internet access available

Square footage: 3,946

Number of map cases: 173

Linear book shelving: 1,000 ft.

Linear atlas shelving: 62 ft.

Other map storage: hanging rolled maps: 12 linear feet

Copying facilities available: microform copier

184 *Evansville, IN*

University of Evansville

Libraries
1800 Lincoln Avenue
Evansville, IN 47722
Telephone: 812-479-2482
Fax: 812-471-6996
Web: libraries.evansville.edu/
Personnel:

Responsible person: Margaret Atwater, Singer, Reference/Instruction Librarian, *email:* ma35@evansville.edu

FTE professionals: 0.1

Holdings:

Geographic strengths: Vanderburgh County, Indiana

500 printed maps

100 aerial photos

100 atlases

Access:

Hours:

Monday–Friday: 8 A.M.–11 P.M.

Saturday: 9 A.M.–8 P.M.

Sunday: noon–11 P.M.

Collection services:

Maps cataloged: 100%

Maps classified: 100%

Maps in OPAC: 100%

Classification schemes: LC

Physical facilities:

Map cases: 1

185 *Fort Wayne, IN*

Indiana University—Purdue University, Fort Wayne

Helmke Library
Geosciences Department Map Collection
SB 230
2101 East Coliseum Boulevard
Fort Wayne, IN 46805
Telephone: 260-481-6514
Fax: 260-481-6509
Email: truesdel@ipfw.edu

Web: www.lib.ipfw.edu

Personnel:

Responsible person: Solomon Isiorho, Associate Professor of Geosciences, *email:* isiorho@ipfw.edu

Assistants: Cheryl Truesdell, Assistant Director and Head of Document Delivery Services and Government Documents

FTE professionals: 0.5   *FTE para-professionals:* 0.5

Holdings:

Geographic strengths: Indiana, Illinois, Kentucky, Michigan, Ohio

Map depositories: USGS topos, NOAA, CIA, National Forest Service, BLM

4,222 printed maps

2 globes

108 atlases

81 CD-ROMs

Access:

Hours:

Monday–Friday: 8 A.M.–5 P.M.

Collection services:

Maps cataloged: 95%

Maps classified: 95%

Maps in OPAC: 95%

Classification schemes: LC, SuDocs, Local

Physical facilities:

Maps in separate area

Public computers: 18

Map cases: 25

Vertical files: 2

Notes: Most federal depository map materials are housed in the Geosciences Department Map Collection separate from Helmke Library, and catalog records for these items appear in the IUCAT library catalog.

186 *Gary, IN*

Indiana University, Northwest

Library

Government Publications Department, founded 1966

3400 Broadway

Gary, IN 46408

Telephone: 219-980-6608

Fax: 219-980-6558

Email: sutherla@iun.edu

Web: www.iun.edu/~lib

Personnel:

Responsible person: Government Publications Librarian, *email:* sutherla@iun.edu

FTE professionals: 0.2   *FTE para-professionals:* 0.1

Holdings:

Geographic strengths: United States

Subject strengths: geology, geospatial data

Map depositories and percentages: USGS topos (100%), USGS geology maps (100%), BLM, State

25,000 printed maps

20 wall maps

100 printed atlases

50 books

Collecting digital data

Chronological coverage:

1940–present: 100%

Average budget over the last 5 years: $1,500

Access:

Collection is open to the public

Reference questions per year: 100

Answers email questions

Patrons per month: 50

Hours:

Monday–Thursday: 8 A.M.–8 P.M.

Friday: 8 A.M.–5 P.M.

Saturday: 10 A.M.–5 P.M.

Sunday: 1 P.M.–5 P.M.

Total hours per week opened: 82

Maps circulate

Circulation policies apply

Map circulation duration: 2 weeks

Number of maps circulated annually: 50

Number of books circulated annually: 50

Interlibrary loan available

Geographic Information Systems:

GIS services available by appointment

GIS software: ArcGIS

Number of GIS stations (monitored): 17

GIS assistance available for Census mapping, and geocoding

Scans maps for patrons

Collection services:

Maps cataloged: 80%

Maps classified: 10%

Maps in OPAC: 80%

Datasets are cataloged

Classification schemes: LC, SuDocs

Cataloging utilities: OCLC

Catalog accessibility: online

Physical facilities:

Internet access available

Number of map cases: 100

Number of vertical map cases: 20

Linear book shelving: 10 ft.

Linear atlas shelving: 20 ft.

Copying facilities available: copier, microform copier

187 *Greencastle, IN*

DePauw University

Prevo Science Library

602 South College

Greencastle, IN 46135

Telephone: 765-658-4306

Web: www.depauw.edu/library

Personnel:

Responsible person: Caroline L. Gilson, Coordinator, Prevo Science Library, *email:* cgilson@depauw.edu

Assistants: Kathryn C. Millis, Coordinator, Reference and Government Documents

FTE professionals: 0.05   *FTE para-professionals:* 0.05

Holdings:

Map depositories and percentages: USGS topos (90%), USGS geology maps (50%), USGS other (10%), GPO, CIA, National Forest Service

65,000 printed maps

50 wall maps

15 gazetteers

100 printed atlases

2,000 books

50 active serials

2,000 CD-ROMs

Chronological coverage:

1940–present: 90%

Access:

Maps in separate area

Collection is open to the public

Reference questions per year: 25

Answers email questions

Hours:

Monday–Friday: 7:45 A.M.–midnight

Saturday: 10 A.M.–5 P.M.

Sunday: noon–midnight

Total hours per week opened: 96

Maps circulate

Circulation policies apply

Map circulation duration: 30 days

Atlas circulation duration: 1 day

Book circulation duration: 30 days

Number of maps circulated annually: 100

Number of books circulated annually: 45

Number of other items circulated annually: 10

Interlibrary loan available

Geographic Information Systems:

No GIS services available

GIS assistance available for image analysis

Scans maps for patrons

Collection services:

Maps cataloged: 1%

Maps classified: 5%

Maps in OPAC: 1%

Classification schemes: LC, SuDocs

Cataloging utilities: OCLC

Catalog accessibility: online

Physical facilities:

Internet access available

Square footage: 480

Number of vertical map cases: 24

Number of vertical files (file cabinets): 12

Linear book shelving: 1,000 ft.

Copying facilities available: copier, color copier, microform copier

188 *Hanover, IN*

Hanover College

Duggan Library

P.O. Box 287

Hanover, IN 47243

Telephone: 812-866-7165

Fax: 812-866-7172

Web: www.hanover.edu/Library

Personnel:

Responsible person: Grace Ireland, Government Documents Assistant, *email:* ireland@hanover.edu

FTE para-professionals: 0.5

Holdings:

Geographic strengths: Indiana, Illinois, Arizona, Colorado, Kentucky, Michigan, New Mexico, Ohio, Oregon, Utah, Wisconsin

Map depositories: USGS topos, NGA nautical

20,000 printed maps

14 atlases

Access:

Hours:

Monday–Friday: 7:30 A.M.–midnight

Saturday: 10 A.M.–10 P.M.

Sunday: 1 P.M.–midnight

Collection services:

Maps cataloged: 0%

Maps classified: 0%

Maps in OPAC: 0%

Physical facilities:

Map cases: 15

Vertical files: 15

189 *Indianapolis, IN*

Indiana Historical Society

William Henry Smith Memorial Library

450 West Ohio Street

Indianapolis, IN 46202-3269

Telephone: 317-232-1879

Fax: 317-234-0169

Web: www.indianahistory.org

Personnel:

Responsible person: Eric L. Mundell, Director, Printed Collections and Artifacts, *email:* emundell@indianahistory.org

Assistants: Rebecca Renz, Senior Cataloger; Erin Kirchhoff, Cataloger

FTE professionals: 2   *FTE para-professionals:* 1

Holdings:

Geographic strengths: Indiana, Midwest, Northwest Territory, North America

Special collections: Sanborn Fire Insurance maps, Baist Real Estate maps, Ohio River Army Corps of Engineers maps

1,150 printed maps

2 globes
320 atlases
800 books
4 active serials

Access:

Hours:

Monday–Saturday: 10 A.M.–5 P.M.
Sunday: closed

Collection services:

Maps cataloged: 15%
Maps classified: 85%
Maps in OPAC: 15%
Classification schemes: LC

Physical facilities:

Maps in separate area
Public computers: 6
Map cases: 6

190 *Indianapolis, IN*

Indiana State Library

140 North Senate Avenue
Indianapolis, IN 46204-2296
Telephone: 317-232-3685
Fax: 317-232-3728
Web: www.statelib.lib.in.us

Personnel:

Responsible person: Doug Conrads

Holdings:

Geographic strengths: Indiana
Special collections: Indiana Sanborn Fire Insurance
Subject strengths: city, genealogy, historical geography, population, railroads, roads, Census
Map depositories and percentages: USGS topos (100%), USGS geology maps (100%), USGS other (100%), Department of Transportation, NOAA, GPO, CIA, National Forest Service, NIMA topos, NIMA nautical, NIMA aeronautical, BLM
113,135 printed maps

Access:

Maps in separate area
Collection is paged
Answers email questions

Hours:

Monday–Friday: 8 A.M.–4:30 P.M.
Total hours per week opened: 42.5

Geographic Information Systems:

GIS services available by appointment
Number of public GIS workstations: 21
GIS assistance available for Census mapping
Scans maps for patrons

Collection services:

Maps cataloged: 100%
Maps classified: 100%
Classification schemes: LC, SuDocs, Dewey, Local
Cataloging utilities: OCLC

Catalog accessibility: online, cards
Preservation techniques: encapsulation

Physical facilities:

Number of map cases: 136
Number of vertical files (file cabinets): 13
Copying facilities available: copier, color copier, large-format copier, microform copier

191 *Indianapolis, IN*

Indianapolis—Marion County Public Library

Central Library
40 East Street Clair Street
Indianapolis, IN 46202
Telephone: 317-269-1700
Fax: 317-268-5229
Email: munrue@imcpl.org
Web: imcpl.org

Personnel:

Responsible person: Laura Bramble, Central Library Director, *email:* lbramble@imcpl.org
Assistants: Penny Pace-Cannon, Manager 4th Floor Reference; Kathy Diehl, Manager 3rd Floor Reference; Michille Unrue, 4th Floor Reference Librarian; Matt Hannigan, 3rd Floor Reference Librarian
FTE professionals: 15

Holdings:

Geographic strengths: Indianapolis, Indiana
Special collections: Indianapolis Sanborn Fire Insurance maps (1887, 1898, 1914–1950), Indianapolis Baists Real Estate Atlas (1901, 1908, 1909, 1916, 1927, 1941)
Subject strengths: city, geodetic surveys, historical geography
Map depositories and percentages: GPO, CIA
5,274 printed maps
120 gazetteers
280 printed atlases

Access:

Collection is open to the public
Answers email questions

Hours:

Monday–Friday: 9 A.M.–9 P.M.
Saturday: 9 A.M.–5 P.M.
Sunday: 1 P.M.–5 P.M.
Total hours per week opened: 72
Maps circulate
Circulation policies apply
Map circulation duration: 3 weeks
Atlas circulation duration: 3 weeks
Book circulation duration: 3 weeks
Interlibrary loan available

Geographic Information Systems:

No GIS services available
GIS assistance available for geocoding

Collection services:

Maps cataloged: 10%
Maps in OPAC: 90%
Datasets are cataloged
Classification schemes: Dewey, Local
Cataloging utilities: OCLC
Catalog accessibility: online
Physical facilities:
Internet access available
Linear book shelving: 50 ft.
Copying facilities available: copier, microform copier

192 *Indianapolis, IN*

Indiana University—Purdue University, Indianapolis

University Library
775 West Michigan Street
Indianapolis, IN 46202-5195
Telephone: 317-274-8278
Fax: 317-278-2300
Web: www.ulib.iupui.edu
Holdings:
Geographic strengths: Central Indiana
Special collections: Electronic Atlas of Central Indiana (http://atlas.ulib.iupui.edu/)—a web-based repository of spatially referenced data for the Indianapolis Metropolitan Statistical Area (MSA)
Map depositories: USGS
3,000 printed maps
1,800 atlases
2,064 books
5 active serials
Collection services:
Maps cataloged: 100%
Maps classified: 100%
Maps in OPAC: 100%
Classification schemes: LC, SuDocs
Physical facilities:
Public computers: 300
Map cases: 2
Notes: Our print map collection consists primarily of Indiana-related maps. Concerning USGS topographical maps, we retain Indiana-related topos only. We do collect selected USGS publications that include maps.

193 *Muncie, IN*

Ball State University

Bracken
Geospatial Center and Map Collection, founded 1975
University Libraries
Muncie, IN 47306
Telephone: 765-285-1097
Fax: 765-285-2644
Web: www.bsu.edu/library/collections/gcmc
Personnel:

Number of student workers hours per week: 35
Holdings:
Geographic strengths: Indiana, United States
Special collections: Sanborn Fire Insurance maps of parts of Indiana
Subject strengths: aeronautical, city, nautical charts, recreation, roads, soil, travel books, views
Map depositories and percentages: USGS topos, USGS geology maps, Department of Transportation, NOAA, CIA, National Forest Service, NIMA aeronautical, BLM
118,000 printed maps
23 raised relief maps
600 aerial photos
190 gazetteers
2,358 printed atlases
208 books
90 CD-ROMs
Collecting digital data
Chronological coverage:
1940–present: 98%
Average budget over the last 5 years: $1,000
Access:
Maps in separate area
Collection is partially open to the public
Reference questions per year: 1,800
Answers email questions
Patrons per month: 620
Hours:
Monday–Friday: 8 A.M.–5 P.M.
Total hours per week opened: 45
Maps circulate
Circulation policies apply
Map circulation duration: 2 weeks
Atlas circulation duration: 4 weeks
Number of maps circulated annually: 1,362
Interlibrary loan available
Geographic Information Systems:
GIS services available in an open environment
GIS software: ArcView3.5, ArcGIS 3.8, GeoMedia 5.1.
GIS assistance available for Census mapping, geocoding, and image analysis
Plotter available
Collection services:
Maps cataloged: 70%
Maps classified: 100%
Maps in OPAC: 70%
Classification schemes: LC
Cataloging utilities: OCLC
Catalog accessibility: online
Preservation techniques: encapsulation, lamination
Physical facilities:
Internet access available
Square footage: 1,820
Number of map cases: 55
Linear book shelving: 405 ft.

Linear atlas shelving: 783 ft.
Copying facilities available: copier, microform copier

194 *New Albany, IN*

New Albany-Floyd County Public Library

180 West Spring Street
New Albany, IN 47150
Telephone: 812-949-3527
Fax: 812-949-3733
Email: ind.staff@nafcpl.lib.in.us
Web: www.nafcpl.lib.in.us
Personnel:
  Responsible person: Lynn Rueff, Manager Indiana History, *email:* lrueff@nafcpl.lib.in.us
  Assistants: Cynthia Froman, Library Associate I
  FTE professionals: 1   *FTE para-professionals:* 1
Holdings:
  Geographic strengths: Clark County, Floyd County, Harrison County, Indiana
  Special collections: Sanborn Fire Insurance maps, Early Plat Maps, Clark's Grant (Illinois Grant), Civil War maps, Census maps of various Indiana counties
  Map depositories: USGS
  1,736 printed maps
  1 CD-ROM
Access:
  Hours:
    Monday–Friday: 9 A.M.–8:30 P.M.
    Saturday: 9 A.M.–5:30 P.M.
    Sunday: closed
Collection services:
  Maps classified: 100%
Physical facilities:
  Public computers: 2
  Map cases: 1
  Vertical files: 4
Notes: Maps are stored on 3 series of deep shelves in the department. Fragile and historical maps are in the storage area in a map cabinet.

195 *Richmond, IN*

Earlham College

Wildman Science Library
P.O. Box 72
Richmond, IN 47374
Telephone: 765-983-1245
Web: www.earlham.edu/~libr/wildman/
Personnel:
  Responsible person: Sara Penhale, Reference Librarian, *email:* sarap@earlham.edu
  Assistants: Mary Bogue, Library Manager
  Number of student works: 15

Number of student workers hours per week: 10
Holdings:
  Geographic strengths: Midwest
  Subject strengths: geology, land use, political geography, soil
  Map depositories and percentages: USGS topos (95%), USGS geology maps, USGS other, CIA
  16,400 printed maps
  32 printed atlases
  35 books
  Chronological coverage:
    1940–present: 90%
Access:
  Collection is open to the public
  Reference questions per year: 15
  Hours:
    Monday–Thursday: 8 A.M.–midnight
    Friday: 8 A.M.–10 P.M.
    Saturday: 10 A.M.–8 P.M.
    Sunday: noon–midnight
    Total hours per week opened: 100
  Maps circulate
  Circulation policies apply
    Map circulation duration: 2 weeks
    Book circulation duration: 2 weeks
    Number of maps circulated annually: 70
    Number of books circulated annually: 10
  Interlibrary loan available
Geographic Information Systems:
  GIS services available in an open environment
  GIS software: ArcView
Collection services:
  Maps cataloged: 100%
  Maps classified: 100%
  Classification schemes: LC, SuDocs, Other (AGS)
  Cataloging utilities: OCLC
  Catalog accessibility: online, cards
Physical facilities:
  Internet access available
  Square footage: 350
  Number of map cases: 20
  Linear atlas shelving: 40 ft.
  Other map storage: 3 rolled map stands
  Copying facilities available: copier

196 *Terre Haute, IN*

Indiana State University

Geography, Geology and Anthropology Department Map Library
Founded 1961
Science 151
Terre Haute, IN 47809
Telephone: 812-237-2266
Web: lib.indstate.edu

Personnel:
Number of student workers hours per week: 10
Holdings:
Subject strengths: aerial photos, early cartography, modern cartography, city, forestry, geology, geospatial data, historical geography, hydrology, map catalogs, mineral resources, raised relief models, satellite imagery, soil
Map depositories: USGS topos, USGS geology maps, USGS other, NOAA
290,400 printed maps
400 wall maps
4 globes
Chronological coverage:
1800–1899: 20%
1900–1939: 20%
1940–present: 60%
Access:
Maps in separate area
Collection is partially open to the public
Answers email questions
Patrons per month: 40
Hours:
Monday–Friday: 9 A.M.–4 P.M.
Total hours per week opened: 35
Maps circulate
Circulation policies apply
Map circulation duration: 1 month
Geographic Information Systems:
No GIS services available
Collection services:
Maps cataloged: 50%
Maps classified: 100%
Classification schemes: SuDocs, Local
Catalog accessibility: cards
Preservation techniques: controlled environment
Physical facilities:
Internet access available
Square footage: 400
Number of vertical map cases: 230

197 *Valparaiso, IN*

Valparaiso University

Christopher Center for Library and Information Resources
1410 Chapel Drive
Valparaiso, IN 46383
Telephone: 219 464-5771
Fax: 219 464-5792
Email: becky.byrum@valpo.edu
Web: www.valpo.edu/library/map
Personnel:
Responsible person: Rebecca H. Byrum, *email:* becky.byrum@valpo.edu

FTE professionals: 1
Holdings:
Map depositories: USGS topos, Department of Transportation, CIA, National Forest Service
75,000 printed maps
Access:
Hours:
Monday–Friday: 8 A.M.–midnight
Saturday: 10 A.M.–6 P.M.
Sunday: noon–midnight
Items circulate
Interlibrary loan available
Collection services:
Maps cataloged: 0%
Maps classified: 0%
Maps in OPAC: 0%
Physical facilities:
Map cases: 20
Vertical files: 8

198 *West Lafayette, IN*

Purdue University

Earth and Atmospheric Sciences (EAS) Library
EAS Map Room
Civil Engineering Building
Room 2253
West Lafayette, IN 47907
Telephone: 765-494-0202
Email: easlib@purdue.edu
Web: www.lib.purdue.edu/eas/inmaps.html
Personnel:
Responsible person: Carolyn Lafoon, Professional Librarian, *email:* carolyn@purdue.edu
Assistants: Claire Alexander, Map Curator
FTE professionals: 1   *FTE para-professionals:* 1
Holdings:
Geographic strengths: Indiana, Canada
Special collections: Indiana Aerial Photos, Natural Resources Canada, USGS topographic overall USGS topos, DMA/NIMA/National Geospatial Intelligence Agency, NOAA, FEMA Flood Insurance, CIA, US Forest Service, Census Bureau Population Census, U.S. Congressional Serial Set
Map depositories: USGS topos, Department of Transportation, NOAA, CIA, National Forest Service, NGA nautical, NGA aeronautical
201,000 printed maps
150,000 aerial photos
2 globes
5,000 atlases
24 active serials
380 CD-ROMs
Access:
Hours:

Monday–Friday: 8 A.M.–5 P.M.
Items circulate
Interlibrary loan available
Collection services:
Maps cataloged: 5%
Maps classified: 100%
Maps in OPAC: 7%
Classification schemes: SuDocs, Dewey
Physical facilities:
Maps in separate area
Public computers: 5
Map cases: 33
Vertical files: 32
Notes: Most maps are kept in Purdue's Earth and Atmospheric Sciences Library but some maps, such as Census, CIA, and the U.S. Congressional Serial Set, are kept in the Humanities, Social Science, and Education Library.

199 *Ames, IA*

Iowa State University

Parks Library
Map Room
281 Parks Library
Ames, IA 50011-2140
Telephone: 515-294-3956
Fax: 515-294-5525
Email: slshuman@iastate.edu
Web: www.lib.iastate.edu/libinfo/dept/maproom.html
Personnel:
Responsible person: Kathy A. Parsons, Head Stacks and Service Desks, *email:* kap@iastate.edu
Assistants: Steve Shuman, Map Room Supervisor
FTE professionals: 0.2
Number of student workers hours per week: 41
Holdings:
Geographic strengths: Iowa
Subject strengths: agriculture, city, forestry, geology, land ownership, land use, political geography, recreation, roads, soil
Map depositories and percentages: USGS topos (100%), USGS geology maps (75%), USGS other (10%), Department of Transportation, NOAA, GPO, CIA, National Forest Service, BLM
105,289 printed maps
984 microfiche
2,323 aerial photos
10 satellite images
13 globes
306 gazetteers
1,460 printed atlases
524 books
136 CD-ROMs
Chronological coverage:
1900–1939: 20%

1940–present: 75%
Average budget over the last 5 years: $6,290
Access:
Collection is open to the public
Reference questions per year: 1,800
Answers email questions
Patrons per month: 225
Hours:
Monday–Thursday: 8 A.M.–8 P.M.
Friday: 8 A.M.–5 P.M.
Saturday–Sunday: 1 P.M.–5 P.M.
Total hours per week opened: 65
Maps circulate
Circulation policies apply
Map circulation duration: 2 weeks
Atlas circulation duration: 2 weeks
Book circulation duration: 2 weeks
Number of maps circulated annually: 650
Number of books circulated annually: 190
Number of other items circulated annually: 10
Interlibrary loan available
Geographic Information Systems:
GIS services available by appointment
GIS software: ArcView
GIS assistance available for Census mapping
Collection services:
Maps cataloged: 55%
Maps classified: 50%
Maps in OPAC: 40%
Classification schemes: LC, SuDocs
Cataloging utilities: OCLC
Catalog accessibility: online, cards, printout
Preservation techniques: encapsulation
Items that have gone through the preservation process: 1%
Physical facilities:
Internet access available
Square footage: 1,500
Number of map cases: 71
Linear book shelving: 250 ft.
Linear atlas shelving: 45 ft.
Copying facilities available: copier, microform copier

200 *Cedar Falls, IA*

University of Northern Iowa

Rod Library
Documents and Maps Collection
1227 West 27th Street
Cedar Falls, IA 50613-3675
Telephone: 319-273-2838
Fax: 319-273-2913
Email: refdesk@uni.edu
Web: www.library.uni.edu/gov/
Personnel:

Responsible person: Becky Lutkenhaus, Documents and Maps Librarian, *email:* becky.lutkenhaus@uni.edu

Assistants: Susan Moore, Cataloging Librarian

FTE professionals: 0.5   *FTE para-professionals:* 0.5

Number of student workers hours per week: 20

Holdings:

Geographic strengths: Cedar Falls, Waterloo, Black Hawk County, Iowa

Subject strengths: aerial photos, city, soil

Map depositories: USGS topos, USGS geology maps, USGS other, CIA, National Forest Service, BLM, State

40,866 printed maps

1,002 aerial photos

63 gazetteers

1,631 printed atlases

30 CD-ROMs

112 computer programs

Chronological coverage:

1900–1939: 38%

1940–present: 61%

Average budget over the last 5 years: $2,500

Access:

Collection is open to the public

Reference questions per year: 250

Answers email questions

Patrons per month: 200

Hours:

Monday–Thursday: 7:30 A.M.–midnight

Friday: 7:30 A.M.–9 P.M.

Saturday: noon–10 P.M.

Sunday: noon–midnight

Total hours per week opened: 101.5

Maps circulate

Circulation policies apply

Map circulation duration: 3 weeks

Number of maps circulated annually: 175

Interlibrary loan available

Geographic Information Systems:

No GIS services available

Collection services:

Maps cataloged: 85%

Maps classified: 65%

Maps in OPAC: 70%

Datasets are cataloged

Classification schemes: LC, SuDocs, Local

Cataloging utilities: OCLC

Catalog accessibility: online, cards

Preservation techniques: encapsulation, edging

Items that have gone through the preservation process: 10%

Physical facilities:

Internet access available

Number of map cases: 17

Number of vertical files (file cabinets): 11

Copying facilities available: copier, microform copier

201 *Dubuque, IA*

Loras College

Loras College Library

1450 Alta Vista

Dubuque, IA 52001

Telephone: 563-588-7042

Fax: 563-588-7292

Email: kristen.smith@loras.edu

Web: www.loras.edu/~LIB/

Holdings:

5,500 printed maps

202 *Grinnell, IA*

Grinnell College

Burling Library

1111 6th Avenue

Grinnell, IA 50112

Telephone: 641-269-4234

Fax: 641-269-4283

Email: engelk@grinnell.edu

Web: www.lib.grin.edu/Places/govdocs/

Personnel:

Responsible person: Kevin Engel, Librarian, *email:* engelk@grinnell.edu

Assistants: Debra Martzahn, Library Assistant

Number of student workers hours per week: 0.5

Holdings:

Geographic strengths: Iowa

Map depositories and percentages: USGS topos (20%), GPO, CIA

3,089 printed maps

Chronological coverage:

1940–present: 98%

Access:

Collection is open to the public

Reference questions per year: 75

Answers email questions

Patrons per month: 225

Hours:

Monday–Friday: 8 A.M.–1 A.M.

Saturday: 10 A.M.–10 P.M.

Sunday: 11 A.M.–1 A.M.

Total hours per week opened: 107

Geographic Information Systems:

GIS services available in an open environment

GIS software: ArcGIS 8.3

GIS assistance available for Census mapping, geocoding, and image analysis

Plotter available

Scans maps for patrons

Collection services:

Datasets are cataloged

Physical facilities:
No Internet access
Linear atlas shelving: 60 ft.
Copying facilities available: copier, color copier, microform copier
Notes: Our map collection is not separate from the rest of the library. It is covered by the general reference librarians. Nearly all the maps are depository or National Geographic types.

203 *Iowa City, IA*

State Historical Society of Iowa, Department of Cultural Affairs

Special Collections/Map Collection, founded 1857
402 Iowa Avenue
Iowa City, IA 52240
Telephone: 319-335-3916
Fax: 319-335-3935
Email: bennettm@blue.weeg.uiowa.edu
Web: www.iowahistory.org
Personnel:
Responsible person: Mary Bennett, Special Collections Coordinator, *email:* bennettm@blue.weeg.uiowa.edu
Assistants: Kevin Knoot, Special Collections Archivist
Number of student workers hours per week: 40
Number of volunteer hours per month: 30
Holdings:
Geographic strengths: Iowa, Upper Mississippi Valley, North America
Special collections: Sanborn Fire Insurance maps for Iowa towns (1970s–1940s), Iowa county atlases
Subject strengths: aerial photos, archaeology, early cartography, modern cartography, city, genealogy, historical geography, land ownership, land use, map catalogs, map collecting, mineral resources, population, railroads, religion, roads, travel books, vegetation, views, waterways
3,000 printed maps
30 manuscript maps
4,000 microfiche
20 microfilms
800 aerial photos
906 printed atlases
Chronological coverage:
1800–1899: 28%
1900–1939: 19%
1940–present: 50%
On-going publications: Checklist of Printed Maps of the Middle West to 1900—Iowa, Volume 8, Compiled by Diana J. Fox (Boston, G.K. Hall Co., 1981); plan to launch database for collection on SHSI website: iowahistory.org
Access:
Maps in separate area

Collection is open to the public
Reference questions per year: 100
Answers email questions
Hours:
Tuesday–Friday: 9 A.M.–4:30 P.M.
Sunday: closed
Total hours per week opened: 37.5
Geographic Information Systems:
No GIS services available
Collection services:
Maps cataloged: 65%
Maps classified: 100%
Classification schemes: LC
Cataloging utilities: OCLC
Catalog accessibility: online, fiche, cards, printout
Preservation techniques: encapsulation, deacidification, cartex
Items that have gone through the preservation process: 15%
Physical facilities:
No Internet access
Square footage: 1,000
Linear book shelving: 20 ft.
Linear atlas shelving: 275 ft.
Other map storage: 4 rolled map drawers
Copying facilities available: copier, microform copier, patrons may use camera
Notes: This describes holdings in the Iowa City library of the State Historical Society of Iowa. Additional holdings in the Des Moines library of the State Historical Society of Iowa.

204 *Iowa City, IA*

University of Iowa

Geoscience Library
136 Trowbridge Hall
Iowa City, IA 52242
Telephone: 319-335-3084
Fax: 319-335-3419
Email: lib-geoscience@uiowa.edu
Web: www.lib.uiowa.edu/geoscience
Personnel:
Responsible person: Leo Clougherty, Head, *email:* leo-clougherty@uiowa.edu
Assistants: Nancy Ritchey, Geoscience Library Assistant
FTE professionals: 0.2
Number of student works: 1.5
Number of student workers hours per week: 57
Holdings:
Geographic strengths: United States
Subject strengths: geology
Map depositories and percentages: USGS topos (100%), USGS geology maps (100%), USGS other (50%), State

73,153 printed maps
50 printed atlases
100 books
500 CD-ROMs
Chronological coverage:
   1800–1899: 10%
   1900–1939: 10%
   1940–present: 80%

Access:
Collection is open to the public
Reference questions per year: 20
Answers email questions
Patrons per month: 15
Hours:
   Monday–Thursday: 9 A.M.–8 P.M.
   Friday: 9 A.M.–5 P.M.
   Saturday: noon–5 P.M.
   Total hours per week opened: 57
Circulation policies apply
   Atlas circulation duration: 4 weeks
   Book circulation duration: 4 weeks
   Number of books circulated annually: 6,250
   Number of other items circulated annually: 60
Interlibrary loan available
Geographic Information Systems:
No GIS services available
Collection services:
Maps cataloged: 35%
Maps classified: 25%
Maps in OPAC: 10%
Classification schemes: LC, Local
Cataloging utilities: OCLC
Catalog accessibility: online, cards
Items that have gone through the preservation process:
   1%
Physical facilities:
Internet access available
Square footage: 4,700
Number of map cases: 52
Number of vertical files (file cabinets): 14
Linear book shelving: 2,100 ft.
Linear atlas shelving: 60 ft.
Copying facilities available: none

205 *Iowa City, IA*

University of Iowa

Map Collection, founded 1965
3111 Main Library
Iowa City, IA 52242-1420
Telephone: 319-335-5920
Fax: 319-335-5900
Email: lib-maps@uiowa.edu
Web: www.lib.uiowa.edu/maps
Personnel:

Responsible person: Mary McInroy, *email:* mary-mcinroy@uiowa.edu
Assistants: Jane Carlson, Library Assistant III
FTE professionals: 0.5
Number of student workers hours per week: 44.5
Holdings:
Geographic strengths: Iowa
Special collections: Fire insurance maps for Iowa, Iowa county atlases, aerial photography of Iowa, Iowa plat books, WW II captured German and Japanese maps, AMS foreign topographic maps, earlier editions of USGS topographic maps
Subject strengths: aerial photos, aeronautical, land ownership, nautical charts, US and Canadian topos
Map depositories and percentages: USGS other (100%), Department of Transportation, NOAA, GPO, CIA, National Forest Service, NIMA nautical, NIMA aeronautical, BLM, State
188,341 printed maps
66 wall maps
20 raised relief maps
7,708 microfiche
25 microfilms
146,250 aerial photos
55 satellite images
535 gazetteers
2,020 printed atlases
2,725 books
287 CD-ROMs
Chronological coverage:
   Pre-1800: 0.5%
   1900–1939: 12.5%
   1940–present: 86%
Average budget over the last 5 years: $20,500
Access:
Maps in separate area
Collection is partially open to the public
Reference questions per year: 737
Answers email questions
Patrons per month: 897
Hours:
   Monday–Friday: 8:30 A.M.–5:30 P.M.
   Saturday–Saturday: closed
   Total hours per week opened: 44.5
Maps circulate
Circulation policies apply
   Map circulation duration: 1 week
   Atlas circulation duration: 2 weeks
   Book circulation duration: 2 weeks
   Number of books circulated annually: 128
   Number of other items circulated annually: 665 (aerial photos, etc.)
Interlibrary loan available
Geographic Information Systems:
GIS services available by appointment

GIS software: ArcView, Maptitude
GIS assistance available for Census mapping
Scans maps for patrons
Collection services:
Maps cataloged: 39%
Maps classified: 39%
Maps in OPAC: 10%
Classification schemes: LC, SuDocs, Local
Cataloging utilities: OCLC, RLG, MARCIVE tapeloads
Catalog accessibility: online, cards, FileMaker Pro data-
  bases
Preservation techniques: encapsulation, deacidifica-
  tion, edging
Physical facilities:
Internet access available
Square footage: 3,817
Number of map cases: 165
Number of vertical files (file cabinets): 23
Linear book shelving: 670.5 ft.
Linear atlas shelving: 286 ft.
Copying facilities available: copier, large-format copier,
  microform copier, microdex (digitizes microforms)

206 *Sioux City, IA*

Sioux City Public Library

529 Pierce Street
Sioux City, IA 51101-1203
Telephone: 712-255-2933 x221
Fax: 712-279-6432
Email: govdocs@siouxcitylibrary.org
Web: www.siouxcitylibrary.org
Personnel:
Responsible person: Connie McKnight, Manager, Ref-
  erence and Reader Services, *email:* cmcknight@
  siouxcitylibrary.org
FTE professionals: 0.025   *FTE para-professionals:*
  0.025
Holdings:
Geographic strengths: Sioux City region, Missouri
  River
Special collections: Sanborn Fire Insurance maps for
  Sioux City on microfilm (1924-1968)
Map depositories: USGS topos, CIA
1,650 printed maps
1 globe
210 atlases
7 active serials
Access:
  Hours:
    Monday–Thursday: 9 A.M.–9 P.M.
    Friday–Saturday: 9 A.M.–5 P.M.
    Sunday: 1 P.M.–5 P.M.
Collection services:
Maps cataloged: 5%

Maps classified: 5%
Maps in OPAC: 5%
Classification schemes: SuDocs, Dewey
Physical facilities:
Public computers: 28
Map cases: 2
Vertical files: 17

207 *Emporia, KS*

Emporia State University

William Allen White Library
Information and Instructional Services
1200 Commercial
Campus Box 4051
Emporia, KS 66801
Telephone: 620-341-5207
Fax: 620-341-5997
Email: libref01@emporia.edu
Web: www.emporia.edu/libsv
Personnel:
Responsible person: Cynthia Akers, Head of Informa-
  tion and Instructional Services, *email:* akerscyn@
  emporia.edu
Assistants: Karen Nordgren, Government Documents
  Librarian
FTE para-professionals: 0.5
Number of student workers hours per week: 10
Holdings:
Geographic strengths: Kansas, Great Plains
Subject strengths: celestial, U.S. Interior Department
  maps and atlases
Map depositories and percentages: USGS topos (90%),
  USGS geology maps, USGS other, GPO, CIA,
  BLM, State
20,000 printed maps
100 aerial photos
50 satellite images
65 gazetteers
918 printed atlases
18 CD-ROMs
Chronological coverage:
  1940–present: 95%
Average budget over the last 5 years: $1,500
Access:
Collection is open to the public
Maps off site
Reference questions per year: 40
Answers email questions
  Hours:
    Monday–Thursday: 7:30 A.M.–11 P.M.
    Friday: 7:30 A.M.–6 P.M.
    Saturday: 9 A.M.–6 P.M.
    Sunday: noon–11 P.M.
    Total hours per week opened: 92.5

Maps circulate
Circulation policies apply
  Map circulation duration: 4 weeks
  Book circulation duration: 4 weeks
  Number of maps circulated annually: 75
  Number of books circulated annually: 200
Interlibrary loan available

Geographic Information Systems:
No GIS services available

Collection services:
Maps cataloged: 20%
Maps classified: 100%
Maps in OPAC: 20%
Classification schemes: SuDocs, Dewey, Local
Cataloging utilities: OCLC, Local
Catalog accessibility: online, cards
Preservation techniques: encapsulation, lamination
Items that have gone through the preservation process:
  1%

Physical facilities:
Internet access available
Linear book shelving: 37 ft.
Linear atlas shelving: 37 ft.

208 *Emporia, KS*

Emporia State University

William Allen White Library
Physical Science Division/Geology Map Library,
  founded 1984
1200 Commercial
Campus Box 4051
Emporia, KS 66801
Telephone: 620-341-5207
Fax: 620-341-5997
Email: libref01@emporia.edu
Web: www.emporia.edu/earthsci/amber/maplibrary.htm

Personnel:
Responsible person: Cynthia Akers, Head of Infor-
  mation and Instruction, Associate Professor, *email:*
  akerscyn@emporia.edu
FTE para-professionals: 0.5
Number of student workers hours per week: 10

Holdings:
Geographic strengths: Kansas, Great Plains
Map depositories and percentages: USGS topos (90%),
  USGS geology maps, USGS other, BLM, State
20,000 printed maps
25 wall maps
100 aerial photos
10 printed atlases
Chronological coverage:
  1940–present: 95%
On-going publications: Limited information on the
  web site.

Access:
Maps in separate area
Collection is open to the public
Reference questions per year: 25
Answers email questions
Patrons per month: 100

Hours:
Monday–Friday: 8 A.M.–5 P.M.
Saturday–Saturday: closed
Total hours per week opened: 45
Maps circulate
Circulation policies apply
  Map circulation duration: 2 weeks
  Number of maps circulated annually: 20
Interlibrary loan available

Geographic Information Systems:
No GIS services available

Collection services:
Maps cataloged: 0.2%
Maps in OPAC: 0.99%
Classification schemes: SuDocs, Local
Cataloging utilities: OCLC, Local
Catalog accessibility: online
Preservation techniques: encapsulation, lamination
Items that have gone through the preservation process:
  0.01%

Physical facilities:
Internet access available
Square footage: 480
Number of staff computers: 2
Number of map cases: 33
Linear book shelving: 28 ft.
Other map storage: 15 map large tubes
Copying facilities available: copier

Notes: This is primarily a small teaching collection and
  Federal Map Depository. Most clients are earth science
  and geography students and faculty.

209 *Hays, KS*

Fort Hays State University

Forsyth Library
600 Park Street
Hays, KS 67601
Telephone: 785-628-4340
Fax: 785-628-4096
Web: www.fhsu.edu/forsyth_lib.

Personnel:
Responsible person: Mac Reed, *email:* mreed@fhsu.edu
FTE para-professionals: 0.5

Holdings:
Subject strengths: geology, soil
Map depositories: USGS topos, USGS geology maps,
  GPO, CIA, BLM
2,100 printed maps

126 CD-ROMs
Collecting digital data
Chronological coverage:
  1900–1939: 10%
  1940–present: 90%
Access:
  Collection is open to the public
  Reference questions per year: 25
  Answers email questions
  Hours:
    Monday–Thursday: 7:30 A.M.–midnight
    Friday: 7:30 A.M.–5 P.M.
    Saturday: 10 A.M.–5 P.M.
    Sunday: 1 P.M.–midnight
  Maps circulate
  Circulation policies apply
    Map circulation duration: 3 weeks
  Interlibrary loan available
Geographic Information Systems:
  GIS services available in an open environment
  GIS software: ArcView
  Number of public GIS workstations: 50
  Number of GIS stations (not monitored): 10
Collection services:
  Maps cataloged: 75%
  Maps classified: 75%
  Maps in OPAC: 75%
  Classification schemes: SuDocs, Local
  Cataloging utilities: OCLC, Marcive
  Catalog accessibility: online
Physical facilities:
  Internet access available
  Number of map cases: 12
  Copying facilities available: copier, microform copier

210 *Lawrence, KS*

University of Kansas

Anschutz Library
Thomas R. Smith Map Collections, founded 1947
1301 Hoch Auditoria Drive
Lawrence, KS 66045
Telephone: 785-864-4420
Fax: 785-864-4420
Email: mapsref@ku.edu
Web: www2.lib.ku.edu/mapscoll/
Personnel:
  Responsible person: Scott R. McEathron, Map Librarian, *email:* macmap68@ku.edu
  Assistants: Rhonda S. Houser, GIS and Data Services Specialist; Alex Slater, Operations Manager
  Number of student works: 10
  Number of student workers hours per week: 110
Holdings:

Geographic strengths: Costa Rica, Central America, Japan, Europe, North America
Special collections: U.S. Congressional Serial Set
Subject strengths: aerial photos, aeronautical, agriculture, climatology, city, economic geography, forestry, geodetic surveys, geology, geospatial data, historical geography, hydrology, industries, military, mineral resources, mining, nautical charts, political geography, population, railroads, raised relief models, recreation, roads, soil, vegetation, waterways
Map depositories and percentages: USGS topos (100%), USGS geology maps (100%), USGS other (100%), Department of Transportation, NOAA, GPO, CIA, National Forest Service, NIMA topos, NIMA nautical, NIMA aeronautical, BLM, State, United Nations
333,426 printed maps
123 manuscript maps
23 wall maps
27 raised relief maps
2,285 microfiche
122,500 aerial photos
113 satellite images
17 globes
387 gazetteers
3,100 printed atlases
350 books
15 active serials
1,200 CD-ROMs
30 computer programs
Collecting digital data
Chronological coverage:
  1900–1939: 15%
  1940–present: 80%
Average budget over the last 5 years: $8,000
On-going publications: Koepp, Donna P. *CIS U.S. Serial Set Index. Part XIV, Index and Carto-bibliography of Maps, 1789–1969.* Bethesda, MD. Congressional Information Service, 1995 . Kuchler, A. W., ed. *International Bibliography of Vegetation Maps.* Lawrence. University of Kansas Libraries, 1965–1980. Palmerlee, Albert E. *Maps of Costa Rica. An Annotated Cartobibliography.* Lawrence. University of Kansas Libraries, 1965.
Access:
  Maps in separate area
  Collection is partially open to the public
  Reference questions per year: 1,750
  Answers email questions
  Patrons per month: 2,500
  Hours:
    Monday–Thursday: 9 A.M.–8 P.M.
    Friday: 9 A.M.–5 P.M.
    Saturday–Sunday: 1 P.M.–5 P.M.

Total hours per week opened: 60

Maps circulate

Circulation policies apply

  Map circulation duration: 6 weeks

  Atlas circulation duration: 6 weeks

  Book circulation duration: 6 weeks

Number of maps circulated annually: 1,500

Number of books circulated annually: 200

Interlibrary loan available

Geographic Information Systems:

GIS services available in an open environment

GIS software: ArcMap

GIS assistance available for Census mapping, geocoding, and image analysis

Plotter available

Scans maps for patrons

Collection services:

Maps cataloged: 85%

Maps classified: 85%

Maps in OPAC: 30%

Datasets are cataloged

Classification schemes: LC, SuDocs, Dewey, Local, Other (T. R. Smith Classification)

Cataloging utilities: OCLC

Catalog accessibility: online, cards

Preservation techniques: encapsulation, deacidification

Physical facilities:

Internet access available

Square footage: 7,700

Number of map cases: 309

Number of vertical files (file cabinets): 32

Linear book shelving: 340 ft.

Linear atlas shelving: 540 ft.

Copying facilities available: copier, microform copier

211 *Lawrence, KS*

University of Kansas

Kenneth Spencer Research Library

Special Collections

1450 Poplar Lane

Lawrence, KS 66045-7616

Telephone: 785-864-4334

Fax: 785-864-5803

Web: spencer.lib.ku.edu/sc/index.htm

Personnel:

Responsible person: Richard Clement, Head of Special Collections, *email:* rclement@ku.edu

Assistants: Karen S. Cook, Assistant Special Collections Librarian (Manuscripts)

Holdings:

Geographic strengths: United States, Europe

Special collections: Orbis Collection (history of cartography)

Subject strengths: early cartography

5,500 printed maps

375 manuscript maps

200 printed atlases

650 books

Chronological coverage:

  Pre-1800: 97%

On-going publications: Smith, Thomas R. and Bradford L. Thomas. *Maps of the 16th to 19th centuries in the University of Kansas Libraries* (Lawrence: University of Kansas Libraries, 1963)

Access:

Collection is paged

Reference questions per year: 15

Answers email questions

Patrons per month: 2

Hours:

  Monday–Friday: 8 A.M.–5 P.M.

  Saturday: noon–4 P.M.

  Total hours per week opened: 49

Geographic Information Systems:

No GIS services available

Scans maps for patrons

Collection services:

Maps cataloged: 80%

Maps classified: 80%

Maps in OPAC: 20%

Classification schemes: Local

Cataloging utilities: OCLC

Catalog accessibility: online, cards

Preservation techniques: encapsulation, deacidification

Items that have gone through the preservation process: 5%

Physical facilities:

Internet access available

Square footage: 550

Number of public computers: 3

Number of staff computers: 2

Number of public printers: 1

Number of map cases: 14

Linear book shelving: 100 ft.

Linear atlas shelving: 25 ft.

Number of light tables: 1 portable

Copying facilities available: copier, large-format copier, microform copier, overhead copier, scanner, digital photography in building, conventional photography by arrangement

212 *Manhattan, KS*

Kansas State University

Hale Library

Government Publications Division

Manhattan, KS 66502-1200

Telephone: 785-532-7448
Fax: 785-532-6144
Email: jlj@ksu.edu
Web: www.lib.ksu.edu/depts/govpubs/mainmap.html
Personnel:
Responsible person: John Johnson, Documents Reference Librarian, *email:* jlj@ksu.edu
FTE professionals: 0.1   *FTE para-professionals:* 0.1
Holdings:
Geographic strengths: Great Plains, United States
Subject strengths: aerial photos, aeronautical, agriculture, city, economic geography, geology, hydrology, nautical charts, political geography, roads, satellite imagery, travel books
Map depositories and percentages: USGS topos (95%), USGS geology maps (75%), USGS other (75%), GPO, CIA, National Forest Service, NIMA aeronautical, BLM, State
120,000 printed maps
10 wall maps
500 aerial photos
65 satellite images
30 gazetteers
850 printed atlases
60 books
Chronological coverage:
1900–1939: 10%
1940–present: 85%
Average budget over the last 5 years: $1,500
Access:
Collection is open to the public
Maps off site: 25%
Patrons per month: 125
Hours:
Total hours per week opened: 82
Maps circulate
Map circulation duration: 1 week
Atlas circulation duration: 30 days
Number of maps circulated annually: 2,500
Geographic Information Systems:
GIS services available in an open environment
Collection services:
Maps cataloged: 75%
Maps in OPAC: 75%
Classification schemes: LC, SuDocs
Cataloging utilities: Local
Catalog accessibility: online
Preservation techniques: lamination
Items that have gone through the preservation process: 0.05%
Physical facilities:
Internet access available
Square footage: 1,200
Number of map cases: 116
Number of vertical files (file cabinets): 21

Linear book shelving: 135 ft.
Linear atlas shelving: 2,268 ft.
Copying facilities available: copier, microform copier

213 *Overland Park, KS*

Johnson County Library

9875 West 87th Street
Overland Park, KS 66212
Telephone: 913-495-2400
Fax: 913-495-9104
Email: childersm@jocolibrary.org
Web: www.jocolibrary.org
Personnel:
Responsible person: Martha Childers, Government Documents Librarian, *email:* childersm@jocolibrary.org
Holdings:
Geographic strengths: Johnson County, Kansas, Missouri
Special collections: topographic maps for Kansas and Missouri, Sanborn Fire Insurance maps, Kansas
Subject strengths: genealogy, population, roads, soil, travel books
Map depositories and percentages: USGS topos (10%), GPO, CIA, BLM, State
3,267 printed maps
26 gazetteers
268 printed atlases
81 CD-ROMs
Chronological coverage:
1940–present: 100%
Access:
Collection is open to the public
Reference questions per year: 1,400
Answers email questions
Patrons per month: 50
Hours:
Monday–Thursday: 9 A.M.–9 P.M.
Friday: 9 A.M.–6 P.M.
Saturday: 9 A.M.–5 P.M.
Sunday: 1 P.M.–5 P.M.
Total hours per week opened: 69
Maps circulate
Circulation policies apply
Map circulation duration: 3 weeks
Atlas circulation duration: 3 weeks
Book circulation duration: 3 weeks
Number of maps circulated annually: 45
Number of books circulated annually: 350
Interlibrary loan available
Geographic Information Systems:
GIS services available in an open environment
Number of public GIS workstations: 85
GIS assistance available for Census mapping
Collection services:
Maps cataloged: 75%

Maps classified: 75%

Maps in OPAC: 75%

Classification schemes: SuDocs, Dewey, Local

Cataloging utilities: OCLC, Local

Catalog accessibility: online

Physical facilities:

Internet access available

Copying facilities available: copier, color copier, microform copier

214 *Pittsburg, KS*

Pittsburg State University

Leonard H. Axe Library

Government Documents

1605 South Joplin

Pittsburg, KS 66762

Telephone: 620-235-4889

Fax: 620-235-4090

Web: library.pittstate.edu

Personnel:

Responsible person: Jo Anne Beezley, *email:* beezley@pittstate.edu

Number of student workers hours per week: 15

Holdings:

Subject strengths: projections

Map depositories and percentages: USGS topos (12%), CIA, National Forest Service, BLM

5,750 printed maps

Access:

Reference questions per year: 25

Answers email questions

Hours:

Monday–Friday: 7:45 A.M.–11 P.M.

Saturday: 9 A.M.–5 P.M.

Sunday: 3 P.M.–11 P.M.

Total hours per week opened: 89

Maps circulate

Circulation policies apply

Map circulation duration: 3 weeks

Book circulation duration: 3 weeks

Interlibrary loan available

Geographic Information Systems:

No GIS services available

Scans maps for patrons

Collection services:

Maps cataloged: 90%

Maps classified: 100%

Maps in OPAC: 90%

Classification schemes: SuDocs, Dewey

Cataloging utilities: OCLC

Catalog accessibility: online

Preservation techniques: encapsulation

Items that have gone through the preservation process: 0%

Physical facilities:

Internet access available

Square footage: 60

Number of public computers: 52

Number of staff computers: 26

Linear book shelving: 20 ft.

Linear atlas shelving: 10 ft.

Copying facilities available: copier, microform copier

215 *Topeka, KS*

Kansas State Historical Society

Center for Historical Research

Library and Archives Division, founded 1875

6425 SW 6th Avenue

Topeka, KS 66615-1099

Telephone: 785-272-8681 x116

Fax: 785-272-8682

Email: reference@kshs.org

Web: www.kshs.org

Personnel:

Responsible person: Bob Knecht, Curator of Maps, *email:* bknecht@kshs.org

FTE professionals: 0.333

Holdings:

Geographic strengths: Kansas, Great Plains, United States

Special collections: Atchison, Topeka and Santa Fe Railway maps, architectural drawings from State agencies and several firms, Sanborn Fire Insurance maps, manuscript maps created to document roads authorized by Kansas Territorial and State governments, maps created by State agencies

Subject strengths: modern cartography, city, historical geography, land ownership, military, railroads, roads, Kansas counties, trails, Indians and their lands, exploration

Map depositories and percentages: USGS topos (10%), State

16,000 printed maps

500 manuscript maps

50 wall maps

105,285 microfiche

70,000 microfilms

5,000 aerial photos

30 gazetteers

400 printed atlases

50 books

Chronological coverage:

1800–1899: 59%

1900–1939: 15%

1940–present: 25%

Average budget over the last 5 years: $500

Access:

Collection is paged

Reference questions per year: 175
Answers email questions
Patrons per month: 802
Hours:
Total hours per week opened: 37.5
Interlibrary loan available
Geographic Information Systems:
No GIS services available
Scans maps for patrons
Collection services:
Maps cataloged: 75%
Maps classified: 80%
Classification schemes: Dewey, Local, Other (modified LC)
Cataloging utilities: OCLC, Local
Catalog accessibility: online, cards, printout, special lists
Preservation techniques: encapsulation, deacidification
Physical facilities:
Internet access available
Square footage: 1,188
Number of map cases: 39
Linear book shelving: 42,000 ft.
Linear atlas shelving: 240 ft.
Other map storage: rolled map boxes, flat boxes, upright archives boxes, high security storage area
Number of microform readers: 31
Copying facilities available: copier, large-format copier, microform copier, scanners, oversize plotter, photograph and imaging and microfilm labs
Notes: We are a state agency but not the state library. We loan microforms, but not originals, through interlibrary loan. We have a shared research room, where researchers use all formats of materials; equipment listed is not exclusive to maps.

216 *Wichita, KS*

Wichita Public Library

Reference Services Division, founded 1980
223 South Main Street
Wichita, KS 67202
Telephone: 316-261-8500
Fax: 316-262-4540
Web: www.wichita.lib.ks.us
Personnel:
Responsible person: Larry Vos, Coordinator of Reference Services, *email:* lvos@wichita.gov
Holdings:
Geographic strengths: Kansas
Special collections: Sanborn Fire Insurance maps for Wichita and some other Kansas cities
Subject strengths: city, recreation, roads, travel books
6,255 printed maps
15 microfilms
25 gazetteers

445 printed atlases
Chronological coverage:
1940–present: 95%
Average budget over the last 5 years: $1,200
Access:
Collection is open to the public
Answers email questions
Hours:
Total hours per week opened: 63
Collection services:
Maps cataloged: 80%
Maps classified: 80%
Maps in OPAC: 80%
Classification schemes: LC, Dewey
Cataloging utilities: OCLC
Catalog accessibility: online
Preservation techniques: encapsulation
Physical facilities:
Number of map cases: 15
Copying facilities available: copier

217 *Wichita, KS*

Wichita State University

Ablah Library
Department of Special Collections, founded 1969
1845 Fairmount
Wichita, KS 67260
Telephone: 316-978-3590
Fax: 316-978-3048
Email: michael.kelly@wichita.edu
Web: specialcollections.wichita.edu/collections/maps/index.asp
Personnel:
Responsible person: Michael Kelly, Curator of Special Collections, *email:* Michael.kelly@wichita.edu
Assistants: Mary Nelson, Library Assistant
FTE professionals: 0.1   *FTE para-professionals:* 0.1
Holdings:
Geographic strengths: Kansas, Transmississippi West
Special collections: Baughman Collection of Kansas maps
Subject strengths: historical geography, railroads, roads, views, waterways
Map depositories: USGS other
1,000 printed maps
10 manuscript maps
10 wall maps
10 printed atlases
Chronological coverage:
Pre-1800: 20%
1800–1899: 50%
1900–1939: 20%
1940–present: 10%
Average budget over the last 5 years: $5,000
Access:

Collection is paged
Reference questions per year: 1,000
Answers email questions
Patrons per month: 200
Hours:
Monday–Friday: 8 A.M.–5 P.M.
Total hours per week opened: 45
Geographic Information Systems:
No GIS services available
Scans maps for patrons
Collection services:
Maps cataloged: 20%
Maps in OPAC: 75%
Datasets are cataloged
Classification schemes: LC
Cataloging utilities: OCLC
Catalog accessibility: online
Preservation techniques: encapsulation, deacidification
Items that have gone through the preservation process: 20%
Physical facilities:
Internet access available
Number of map cases: 20
Linear atlas shelving: 20 ft.
Copying facilities available: copier, color copier

218 *Berea, KY*

Berea College

Hutchins Library
Berea, KY 40404
Telephone: 850-985-3172
Web: www.berea.edu/hutchinslibrary
Personnel:
Responsible person: Ed Poston, Reference and Instruction Librarian, *email:* ed_poston@berea.edu
Holdings:
Geographic strengths: Appalachia
Subject strengths: agriculture, celestial, climatology, city, geology, historical geography, land use, language, mineral resources, mining, soil
1,200 printed maps
55 printed atlases
Chronological coverage:
1800–1899: 20%
1900–1939: 30%
1940–present: 50%
Average budget over the last 5 years: $100
Access:
Collection is partially open to the public
Reference questions per year: 18
Hours:
Monday–Friday: 8 A.M.–11 P.M.
Saturday: 10 A.M.–6 P.M.
Sunday: 2 P.M.–11 P.M.
Circulation policies apply

Map circulation duration: do not circulate
Atlas circulation duration: some for 3 weeks
Book circulation duration: 3 weeks
Interlibrary loan available
Geographic Information Systems:
No GIS services available
Collection services:
Maps cataloged: 10%
Maps classified: 10%
Maps in OPAC: 10%
Classification schemes: Dewey
Cataloging utilities: OCLC
Catalog accessibility: online
Physical facilities:
No Internet access
Linear atlas shelving: 40 ft.
Copying facilities available: none

219 *Bowling Green, KY*

Western Kentucky University

Helm–Cravens Library
Maps and Atlases Collection
1 Big Red Way
Bowling Green, KY 42101-3576
Telephone: 270-745-6125
Fax: 270-745-6175
Web: www.wku.edu/library/
Personnel:
Responsible person: Charles H. Smith, Science Librarian, *email:* charles.smith@wku.edu
Assistants: Dewayne Stovall
FTE professionals: 0.05
Holdings:
Geographic strengths: Kentucky
Special collections: Geologic Atlas of the United States, Kentucky County geologic maps, CIA maps, USGS maps
Subject strengths: caves, political geography, recreation, religion, roads, soil, travel books
Map depositories and percentages: USGS topos (100%), USGS geology maps (100%), GPO, CIA, National Forest Service, NIMA topos, State
10,000 printed maps
200 aerial photos
2 globes
76 gazetteers
375 printed atlases
800 books
80 CD-ROMs
Chronological coverage:
1940–present: 100%
Average budget over the last 5 years: $2,000
Access:
Collection is open to the public
Reference questions per year: 150

Answers email questions

Hours:

Monday–Friday: 7:45 A.M.–midnight

Saturday: 9 A.M.–midnight

Sunday: 1 P.M.–midnight

Total hours per week opened: 105

Interlibrary loan available

Geographic Information Systems:

No GIS services available

Number of public GIS workstations: 12

GIS assistance available for Census mapping

Collection services:

Maps cataloged: 85%

Maps classified: 100%

Maps in OPAC: 85%

Classification schemes: LC, SuDocs

Cataloging utilities: OCLC

Catalog accessibility: online

Preservation techniques: encapsulation, lamination

Physical facilities:

Internet access available

Number of public computers: 12

Linear atlas shelving: 336 ft.

Copying facilities available: copier, color copier, microform copier

220 *Frankfort, KY*

Kentucky Division of Mines and Minerals

Mine Map Information Center

Mine Map Repository, founded 1884

P.O. 2244

Frankfort, KY 40601

Telephone: 502-573-0140

Email: john.hiett@ky.gov

Web: minemaps.ky.gov

Personnel:

Responsible person: John Hiett, Program Manager, *email:* john.hiett@ky.gov

Assistants: Dan O'Canna, Tech III

Number of student workers hours per week: 20

Holdings:

Geographic strengths: Kentucky

Subject strengths: economic geography, geology, geospatial data, land ownership, mineral resources, mining

164,000 printed maps

163,000 manuscript maps

8,000 microfilms

Collecting digital data

Chronological coverage:

1940–present: 85%

Access:

Maps in separate area

Collection is open to the public

Reference questions per year: 1,200

Answers email questions

Patrons per month: 150

Hours:

Monday–Friday: 9 A.M.–5 P.M.

Total hours per week opened: 40

Geographic Information Systems:

GIS services available in an open environment

GIS assistance available for geocoding

GIS assistance available for image analysis

Scans maps for patrons

Collection services:

Maps cataloged: 90%

Maps classified: 90%

Maps in OPAC: 100%

Datasets are cataloged

Classification schemes: Local

Catalog accessibility: online

Physical facilities:

Internet access available

Square footage: 1,000

Linear book shelving: 600 ft.

Copying facilities available: copier, scanner

221 *Frankfort, KY*

Kentucky Historical Society

Thomas D. Clark Library and Special Collections

100 West Broadway

Frankfort, KY 40601

Telephone: 502-564-1792

Fax: 502-564-4701

Email: refdesk@ky.gov

Web: history.ky.gov/

Personnel:

Responsible person: Mary E. Winter, Special Collections Branch Manager, *email:* mary.winter@ky.gov

Assistants: Brenda J. Smith, Rare Imprints Cataloger

Holdings:

Geographic strengths: Kentucky, Tennessee, East

Special collections: Kentucky Geological Survey maps, 1850-1980

Subject strengths: agriculture, caves, celestial, city, economic geography, forestry, genealogy, geology, historical geography, hydrology, industries, land ownership, land use, map catalogs, map collecting, military, mineral resources, mining, political geography, population, railroads, recreation, roads, satellite imagery, soil, travel books, views, waterways

2,000 printed maps

20 manuscript maps

30 wall maps

20 microfiche

30 aerial photos

20 gazetteers

60 printed atlases
50 books
Chronological coverage:
1800–1899: 35%
1900–1939: 40%
1940–present: 20%

Access:
Maps in separate area
Collection is paged
Reference questions per year: 200
Answers email questions
Patrons per month: 60

Hours:
Tuesday–Friday: 8 A.M.–4 P.M.
Total hours per week opened: 32

Geographic Information Systems:
No GIS services available
Scans maps for patrons

Collection services:
Maps cataloged: 70%
Classification schemes: Local
Cataloging utilities: OCLC, Local
Catalog accessibility: online, printout
Preservation techniques: encapsulation, deacidification, edging

Physical facilities:
Internet access available
Square footage: 2,600
Number of map cases: 30
Linear book shelving: 27 ft.
Linear atlas shelving: 21 ft.
Number of microform readers: 10
Copying facilities available: copier, large-format copier

222 *Highland Heights, KY*

Northern Kentucky University

Steely Library
Map Collection
Louie B. Nunn Drive
Highland Heights, KY 40199-6101
Telephone: 859-572-5456
Fax: 859-572-5390
Web: library.nku.edu/welcome.html

Personnel:
Responsible person: Philip A. Yannarella, Documents Librarian, *email:* yannarella@exchange.nku.edu
Assistants: Judy Brueggen, Library Specialist II

Holdings:
Geographic strengths: Kentucky
Map depositories: USGS topos
6,449 printed maps
64 printed atlases
Collecting digital data

Access:

Collection is open to the public
Answers email questions

Hours:
Monday–Friday: 8 A.M.–midnight
Saturday: 11 A.M.–6 P.M.
Sunday: 1 P.M.–midnight
Total hours per week opened: 89
Circulation policies apply

Geographic Information Systems:
No GIS services available

Collection services:
Maps cataloged: 80%
Maps classified: 100%
Maps in OPAC: 90%
Classification schemes: LC, SuDocs, Local
Cataloging utilities: OCLC, Local
Catalog accessibility: online

Physical facilities:
Internet access available
Square footage: 150
Linear atlas shelving: 12 ft.
Copying facilities available: copier, microform copier

Notes: The NKU map collection is physically one part of the library reference collection, which is also "just part of" the general reference functions.

223 *Lexington, KY*

University of Kentucky

Pirtle Geological Sciences Library and Map Collection
410 King Library Addition
Lexington, KY 40506-0039
Telephone: 859-257-5730
Fax: 859-323-3225
Web: www.uky.edu/Libraries

Personnel:
Responsible person: Gwen Curtis, Map Collection Manager, *email:* gscurt00@uky.edu
Assistants: Mary Spencer, Geology Library Manager; Sharon McGuire, Senior Technician
Number of student workers hours per week: 65

Holdings:
Geographic strengths: Kentucky
Special collections: Sanborn Fire Insurance maps of Kentucky cities, Kentucky Geological Survey maps and publications
Subject strengths: aerial photos, aeronautical, city, forestry, geology, historical geography, hydrology, mineral resources, nautical charts, railroads, roads, views, Topography
Map depositories and percentages: USGS topos (100%), USGS geology maps (100%), USGS other (100%), Department of Transportation, NOAA, GPO, CIA, National Forest Service, NIMA topos, NIMA nautical, NIMA aeronautical, BLM, European Union

200,750 printed maps
22 raised relief maps
25,300 microfiche
500 microfilms
36,600 aerial photos
275 gazetteers
1,300 printed atlases
19,500 books
341 active serials
1,500 inactive serials
868 CD-ROMs
Chronological coverage:
  1900–1939: 10%
  1940–present: 80%
Average budget over the last 5 years: $2,250
On-going publications: monthly new book list

Access:
Collection is partially open to the public
Reference questions per year: 700
Answers email questions
Patrons per month: 175

Hours:
  Monday–Tuesday: 8 A.M.–9 P.M.
  Wednesday–Friday: 8 A.M.–4:30 P.M.
  Saturday: closed
  Sunday: 1 P.M.–5 P.M.
  Total hours per week opened: 55.5
Circulation policies apply
  Atlas circulation duration: 4 weeks
  Book circulation duration: 4 weeks
  Number of books circulated annually: 4,480
Interlibrary loan available

Geographic Information Systems:
No GIS services available
Scans maps for patrons

Collection services:
Maps cataloged: 50%
Maps classified: 50%
Maps in OPAC: 50%
Classification schemes: LC, SuDocs, Dewey, Local
Cataloging utilities: OCLC
Catalog accessibility: online, cards
Preservation techniques: encapsulation, edging, archival repair tape
Items that have gone through the preservation process: 10%

Physical facilities:
Internet access available
Square footage: 11,000
Number of map cases: 159
Number of vertical files (file cabinets): 31
Linear book shelving: 7,956 ft.
Linear atlas shelving: 576 ft.
Number of microform printers: 2

Copying facilities available: copier, microform copier
Notes: Pirtle Geological Sciences Library and MIK Library Map Collection merged in 2002. Responses reflect newly combined staff, collections, etc.

224 *Louisville, KY*

University of Louisville

Ekstrom Library
2301 S Third Street
Louisville, KY 40292
Telephone: 502-852-6747
Fax: 502-852-8736
Email: caspro01@louisville.edu
Web: library.louisville.edu/ekstrom/collections/maps.htm

Personnel:
Responsible person: Claudene Sproles, Government Documents Reference Librarian, *email:* caspro01@louisville.edu
FTE professionals: 0.3

Holdings:
Geographic strengths: Kentucky
Special collections: Kentucky Sanborn Fire Insurance maps
Subject strengths: Kentucky topographic maps
Map depositories and percentages: USGS topos (20%), USGS geology maps (100%), USGS other (75%), GPO, CIA, National Forest Service, NIMA topos, State
8,000 printed maps
200 gazetteers
1,000 printed atlases
Chronological coverage:
  1900–1939: 10%
  1940–present: 86%

Access:
Collection is open to the public
Reference questions per year: 24
Answers email questions

Hours:
  Monday–Friday: 7:30 A.M.–midnight
  Saturday: 9 A.M.–6 P.M.
  Sunday: noon–midnight
  Total hours per week opened: 78
Maps circulate
Circulation policies apply
  Map circulation duration: 1 week
  Atlas circulation duration: 3 weeks
  Book circulation duration: 3 weeks
  Number of maps circulated annually: 50
  Number of books circulated annually: 354,000
Interlibrary loan available

Geographic Information Systems:

No GIS services available
Number of public GIS workstations: 160
Collection services:
Maps classified: 100%
Classification schemes: LC, SuDocs, Local
Cataloging utilities: OCLC, Local
Catalog accessibility: online, local database
Physical facilities:
Internet access available
Square footage: 112
Number of vertical files (file cabinets): 14
Linear atlas shelving: 90 ft.
Copying facilities available: copier, color copier, microform copier

225 *Morehead, KY*

Morehead State University

Camden-Carroll Library
Morehead, KY 40351
Telephone: 606-783-5491
Fax: 606-783-2799
Web: www.moreheadstate.edu/library/
Personnel:
FTE professionals: 0.5 *FTE para-professionals:* 0.5
Holdings:
Special collections: Sanborn Fire Insurance maps of Kentucky (microfilm)
Map depositories: USGS topos, CIA, National Forest Service
1,418 printed maps
21 aerial photos
40 globes
48 atlases
Access:
Hours:
Monday–Friday: 7:30 A.M.–11 P.M.
Saturday: 9 A.M.–5 P.M.
Sunday: 1 P.M.–11 P.M.
Items circulate
Collection services:
Classification schemes: SuDocs, Dewey
Physical facilities:
Map cases: 7
Vertical files: 1

226 *Richmond, KY*

Eastern Kentucky University

John Grant Crabbe Library
University Archives Map Collection, founded 2003
521 Lancaster Avenue
Richmond, KY 40475

Telephone: 859-622-1792
Fax: 859-622-1174
Email: archives.library@eku.edu
Web: www.library.eku.edu/collections/sca/
Personnel:
Responsible person: Chuck Hill, University Archivist, *email:* archives.library@eku.edu
Assistants: Deborah Whalen, Special Collections Librarian; Jackie Couture, University Records Officer
Number of student workers hours per week: 60
Holdings:
Geographic strengths: Kentucky
Subject strengths: early cartography, modern cartography, geology, topographic
658 printed maps
Chronological coverage:
1800–1899: 14%
1900–1939: 50%
1940–present: 34%
Access:
Collection is paged
Reference questions per year: 30
Answers email questions
Hours:
Monday–Friday: 9 A.M.–5 P.M.
Total hours per week opened: 40
Geographic Information Systems:
No GIS services available
Collection services:
Maps cataloged: 100%
Maps classified: 100%
Maps in OPAC: 100%
Classification schemes: Local
Cataloging utilities: Local
Catalog accessibility: online, printout
Preservation techniques: encapsulation
Physical facilities:
Internet access available
Square footage: 20
Number of map cases: 25
Copying facilities available: copier, microform copier

227 *Baton Rouge, LA*

Louisiana State University

Cartographic Information Center
Founded 1954
313 Howe-Russell Building
Baton Rouge, LA 70803
Telephone: 225-578-6247
Fax: 225-578-4420
Email: janders@lsu.edu
Web: www.cic.lsu.edu

Personnel:

Responsible person: John M. Anderson, Map Librarian and Director, *email:* janders@lsu.edu

Number of student workers hours per week: 24

Holdings:

Geographic strengths: Louisiana, Gulf South, Mississippi Valley, Mexico, Latin America

Special collections: Robert C. West Latin American Slides and Photographs, Russell Reprint Collection, James P. Morgan Coastal Geomorphology Collection, Roger T. Saucier Collection

Subject strengths: aerial photos, aeronautical, archaeology, modern cartography, celestial, climatology, city, economic geography, forestry, geodetic surveys, geology, geospatial data, historical geography, hydrology, land use, map catalogs, military, mineral resources, mining, nautical charts, oceanography, political geography, population, projections, roads, soil, vegetation, waterways, zoogeography

Map depositories and percentages: USGS topos (100%), USGS geology maps (100%), USGS other (100%), Department of Transportation, NOAA, GPO, National Forest Service, NIMA topos, NIMA nautical, NIMA aeronautical, BLM

311,770 printed maps

381 wall maps

81 raised relief maps

832 microfiche

108,024 aerial photos

400 satellite images

40 gazetteers

220 printed atlases

4,065 books

22 inactive serials

1,680 CD-ROMs

12 computer programs

Collecting digital data

Chronological coverage:

1900–1939: 15%

1940–present: 80%

Access:

Collection is paged

Reference questions per year: 50

Answers email questions

Patrons per month: 40

Hours:

Monday–Friday: 8 A.M.–4:30 P.M.

Total hours per week opened: 40

Maps circulate

Circulation policies apply

Map circulation duration: 2 hours

Atlas circulation duration: 2 hours

Book circulation duration: 2 hours

Number of maps circulated annually: 330

Number of books circulated annually: 20

Geographic Information Systems:

GIS services available in an open environment

GIS software: ArcGIS, GeoMedia

Collection services:

Maps cataloged: 10%

Maps classified: 100%

Maps in OPAC: 10%

Classification schemes: SuDocs, Local

Catalog accessibility: online, local databases

Preservation techniques: edging

Physical facilities:

Internet access available

Square footage: 3,900

Number of map cases: 138

Number of vertical map cases: 39

Number of vertical files (file cabinets): 10

Linear book shelving: 150 ft.

Linear atlas shelving: 75 ft.

Other map storage: 10 rolled map racks

Copying facilities available: 11" × 17" scanner

228 *Baton Rouge, LA*

Louisiana State University

Hill Memorial Library

Special Collections, founded 1935

Baton Rouge, LA 70803

Telephone: 225-578-6551

Fax: 225-578-9425

Email: fphilli@lsu.edu

Web: www.lib.lsu.edu/special

Personnel:

Responsible person: Elaine Smyth, Curator of Special Collections, *email:* esmyth@lsu.edu

FTE professionals: 0.05   *FTE para-professionals:* 1.5

Number of student workers hours per week: 15

Holdings:

Geographic strengths: Louisiana, Gulf Coast, lower Mississippi Valley, Mississippi River, Gulf Coast

Special collections: Sanborn Fire Insurance maps, Louisiana official state maps, Civil War maps, historical Louisiana maps, Louisiana Collection maps, Louisiana State University collection

Subject strengths: aerial photos, early cartography, city, historical geography, hydrology, land ownership, land use, map collecting, military, population, railroads, roads, travel books, waterways

Map depositories: Department of Transportation, National Forest Service, State

1,500 printed maps

Access:

Collection is open to the public

Reference questions per year: 100

Answers email questions

Hours:

Monday: 9 A.M.–5 P.M.

Tuesday: 9 A.M.–8 P.M.

Wednesday–Friday: 9 A.M.–5 P.M.

Saturday: 9 A.M.–1 P.M.

Total hours per week opened: 47

Geographic Information Systems:

No GIS services available

Scans maps for patrons

Collection services:

Maps cataloged: 0.5%

Maps classified: 0.5%

Maps in OPAC: 0.5%

Datasets are cataloged

Classification schemes: LC, Local

Cataloging utilities: OCLC, Local

Catalog accessibility: online

Preservation techniques: encapsulation, deacidification

Items that have gone through the preservation process: 0.25%

Physical facilities:

Internet access available

Number of staff computers: 30

Number of map cases: 14

Linear atlas shelving: 20 ft.

Other map storage: rolled map cases

Copying facilities available: copier, microform copier, scanner

229 *Baton Rouge, LA*

Louisiana State University

Troy H. Middleton Library

Government Documents/Microforms Department

53 Middleton

Baton Rouge, LA 70803

Telephone: 225-578-2570

Fax: 225-578-6535

Email: docslib@lsu.edu

Web: www.lib.lsu.edu/govdocs

Personnel:

Responsible person: Maureen Olle, Government Information/Microforms Librarian, *email:* molle@lsu.edu

Assistants: Doris Hutson, Library Technician; Bambi Hernandez, Library Assistant; Paulette Rogers, Library Technician; Elissa Plank, Library Assistant

Number of student works: 13

Number of student workers hours per week: 89

Holdings:

Special collections: Sanborn Fire Insurance maps

Map depositories: Department of Transportation, GPO, CIA

6,035 printed maps

Chronological coverage:

1940–present: 90%

Access:

Collection is open to the public

Answers email questions

Patrons per month: 90

Hours:

Monday–Thursday: 7:15 A.M.–10 P.M.

Friday: 7:15 A.M.–8 P.M.

Saturday: 10 A.M.–5 P.M.

Sunday: noon–10 P.M.

Total hours per week opened: 88.75

Maps circulate

Circulation policies apply

Book circulation duration: 4 weeks

Number of books circulated annually: 4,031

Number of other items circulated annually: 5,000

Interlibrary loan available

Geographic Information Systems:

GIS services available by appointment

GIS software: ArcView

GIS assistance available for Census mapping, geocoding, and image analysis

Collection services:

Maps classified: 100%

Maps in OPAC: 30%

Classification schemes: SuDocs, Local

Cataloging utilities: OCLC

Catalog accessibility: online, cards

Physical facilities:

Internet access available

Number of staff computers: 10

Copying facilities available: copier, color copier, microform copier, scanner

230 *Lake Charles, LA*

McNeese State University

Frazar Memorial Library

Government Documents Department

300 Beauregard Drive

Lake Charles, LA 70609

Telephone: 337-475-5736

Fax: 337-475-5719

Email: governmentinfo@mcneese.edu

Web: library.mcneese.edu/depts/docs/index.htm

Personnel:

Responsible person: R. Brantley Cagle, Documents Librarian, *email:* governmentinfo@mcneese.edu

Number of student workers hours per week: 12

Holdings:

Special collections: 7.5 minute topographic series

Subject strengths: modern cartography, economic geography, geology, map catalogs, nautical charts, soil

Map depositories and percentages: USGS topos (100%), NOAA, GPO, CIA

1,000 printed maps

150 gazetteers
120 books
50 CD-ROMs
Chronological coverage:
   1800–1899: 0.5%
   1940–present: 92.5%
Access:
   Collection is partially open to the public
   Reference questions per year: 25
   Answers email questions
   Patrons per month: 10
Hours:
   Monday–Friday: 7:45 A.M.–10 P.M.
   Saturday: 1 A.M.–5 P.M.
   Sunday: 2 A.M.–10 P.M.
   Total hours per week opened: 83
   Maps circulate
   Circulation policies apply
      Map circulation duration: 3 days
      Book circulation duration: 3 days
      Number of books circulated annually: 10
   Interlibrary loan available
Geographic Information Systems:
   GIS services available by appointment
   GIS assistance available for Census mapping, geocoding, and image analysis
Collection services:
   Maps cataloged: 75%
   Maps classified: 100%
   Maps in OPAC: 75%
   Datasets are cataloged
   Classification schemes: SuDocs
   Cataloging utilities: OCLC
   Catalog accessibility: online
Physical facilities:
   Internet access available
   Square footage: 80
   Copying facilities available: copier, microform copier

231 *New Orleans, LA*

United States Army Corps of Engineers, NOD

Library and Map Collection
IMO
704 Leale Avenue
New Orleans, LA 70118-3651
Telephone: 504-862-1775
Fax: 504-862-1721
Email: nathaniel.griffin@mvn02.usace.army.mil
Personnel:
   Responsible person: Nathaniel Grifin, *email:* Nathaniel
      .Grifin@mvn02.usace.army.mil
Holdings:
   Geographic strengths: New Orleans, Louisiana
   Subject strengths: aerial photos, aeronautical, early cartography, modern cartography, city, engineering, ge-

odetic surveys, historical geography, hydrology, map collecting, nautical charts, waterways
670 printed maps
1,325 microfiche
1,120 microfilms
6,100 aerial photos
12 computer programs
Collecting digital data
Chronological coverage:
   1900–1939: 18%
   1940–present: 59%
Access:
   Maps in separate area
   Collection is open to the public
   Reference questions per year: 55
   Answers email questions
Hours:
   Total hours per week opened: 40
   Maps circulate
Geographic Information Systems:
   No GIS services available
Collection services:
   Classification schemes: Local
   Catalog accessibility: online, fiche
Physical facilities:
   Internet access available
   Copying facilities available: copier, color copier, large-format copier
Note: These figures apply to the map collection before Hurricane Katrina and the subsequent flood.

232 *New Orleans, LA*

United States Department of the Interior, Minerals Management Service

Library
1201 Elmwood Park Boulevard
New Orleans, LA 70123
Telephone: 504-736-2521
Fax: 504-736-2525
Email: stephen.pomes@mms.gov
Web: www.mms.gov/library/
Personnel:
   Responsible person: Stephen Pomes, *email:* stephen
      .pomes@mms.gov
   Number of student workers hours per week: 20
Holdings:
   Geographic strengths: Gulf of Mexico
   Subject strengths: biology, modern cartography, geodetic surveys, geology, hydrology, land use, map catalogs, mineral resources, oceanography
200 printed maps
2,000 microfiche
20 printed atlases
10,000 books
174 active serials

100 inactive serials
250 CD-ROMs
20 computer programs
Chronological coverage:
  1940–present: 96%
Average budget over the last 5 years: $20

Access:

Collection is open to the public
Reference questions per year: 40
Answers email questions
Patrons per month: 120

Hours:

  Monday–Friday: 7 A.M.–4 P.M.
  Total hours per week opened: 40
Maps circulate
Circulation policies apply
  Map circulation duration: 10 days
  Atlas circulation duration: 20 days
  Book circulation duration: 30 days
  Number of maps circulated annually: 20
  Number of books circulated annually: 700
  Number of other items circulated annually: 46
Interlibrary loan available

Geographic Information Systems:

No GIS services available

Collection services:

Maps cataloged: 20%
Maps classified: 20%
Maps in OPAC: 20%
Classification schemes: LC
Cataloging utilities: OCLC, Local
Catalog accessibility: online

Physical facilities:

No Internet access
Square footage: 10
Number of staff computers: 50
Linear book shelving: 500 ft.
Linear atlas shelving: 10 ft.
Copying facilities available: copier, color copier, large-format copier, microform copier

Note: These figures apply to the map collection before Hurricane Katrina and the subsequent flood.

233 *Ruston, LA*

Louisiana Tech University

Prescott Memorial Library
Everett Street at the Columns
Ruston, LA 71272
Telephone: 318-257-4989
Fax: 318-257-2579
Web: www.latech.edu/tech/library/maps.htm

Personnel:

Responsible person: Donna L. Vavrek, Documents/Reference Librarian, *email:* dvavrek@library.latech.edu

FTE professionals: 1   *FTE para-professionals:* 0.25

Holdings:

Geographic strengths: Louisiana
Special collections: Sanborn Fire Insurance maps of Louisiana (online, 1867-1970)
Map depositories: USGS topos, Department of Transportation, NOAA, CIA, National Forest Service, NGA nautical, NGA aeronautical, BLM
35,400 printed maps
3 globes
120 atlases
200 CD-ROMs

Access:

Hours:

  Monday–Friday: 7:30 A.M.–11 P.M.
  Saturday: 10 A.M.–6 P.M.
  Sunday: 1 P.M.–11 P.M.

Collection services:

Maps cataloged: 99.9%
Maps classified: 100%
Classification schemes: LC, SuDocs

Physical facilities:

Public computers: 22
Map cases: 38
Vertical files: 2

Note: These figures apply to the map collection before Hurricane Katrina and the subsequent flood.

234 *Castine, ME*

Maine Maritime Academy

Nutting Memorial Library
Founded 1969
Battle Avenue
Castine, ME 04420
Telephone: 207-326-2265
Fax: 207-326-2261
Email: chudson@mma.edu
Web: www.bell.mma.edu/~library

Personnel:

Responsible person: Caroline Clark Hudson, Librarian Assistant, *email:* chudson@mma.edu
FTE para-professionals: 0.05
Number of student workers hours per week: 2

Holdings:

Geographic strengths: United States, Europe, Asia
Subject strengths: aeronautical, nautical charts
Map depositories and percentages: USGS topos (1%), USGS geology maps (1%), Department of Transportation, NOAA, NIMA topos, NIMA nautical, NIMA aeronautical
2,333 printed maps
50 printed atlases
Chronological coverage:
  1940–present: 100%

Access:

Maps in separate area
Collection is open to the public
Reference questions per year: 100
Patrons per month: 10
Hours:
   Monday–Friday: 8 A.M.–11 P.M.
   Saturday: 10 A.M.–6 P.M.
   Sunday: 2 P.M.–10 P.M.
   Total hours per week opened: 65
   Book circulation duration: 1 week
Geographic Information Systems:
   Number of public GIS workstations: 11
Collection services:
   Classification schemes: LC, SuDocs
   Cataloging utilities: OCLC
   Catalog accessibility: online
Physical facilities:
   No Internet access
   Number of public computers: 0
   Number of staff computers: 0
   Number of public printers: 0
   Copying facilities available: copier, microform copier

235 *New Gloucester, ME*

United Society of Shakers

Shaker Library
Map Collection
707 Shaker Road
New Gloucester, ME 04260
Telephone: 207-926-4597
Email: brooks1@shaker.lib.me.us
Web: www.shaker.lib.me.us
Personnel:
   Responsible person: Leonard L. Brooks, Director, *email:* brooks1@shaker.lib.me.us
   Assistants: Tina S. Agren, Librarian/Archivist
Holdings:
   Geographic strengths: Maine, Shaker Villages
   Subject strengths: aerial photos, agriculture, modern cartography, forestry, genealogy, geodetic surveys, historical geography, industries, land ownership, land use, recreation, religion, roads, satellite imagery, travel books, views
   94 printed maps
   65 manuscript maps
   19 printed atlases
   400 linear ft books
   Chronological coverage:
      Pre-1800: 10%
      1800–1899: 25%
      1900–1939: 10%
      1940–present: 55%
Access:

Maps in separate area
Collection is open to the public
Answers email questions
Patrons per month: 12
Hours:
   Tuesday–Thursday: by appointment
   Total hours per week opened: 24
Collection services:
   Maps cataloged: 100%
   Maps classified: 100%
   Classification schemes: LC
   Cataloging utilities: OCLC
   Catalog accessibility: cards
   Preservation techniques: archival folders
Physical facilities:
   Square footage: 16
   Other map storage: 3 rolled maps
   Copying facilities available: no copying allowed

236 *Orono, ME*

University of Maine

Raymond H. Fogler Library
Government Documents and Microforms Department, founded 1986
Orono, ME 04469-5729
Telephone: 207-581-1680
Fax: 207-581-1653
Email: ref_questions@umit.maine.edu
Web: www.library.umaine.edu/govdoc/default.htm
Personnel:
   Responsible person: Frank Wihbey, *email:* frankw@umit.maine.edu
   FTE para-professionals: 1.5
   Number of student workers hours per week: 20
Holdings:
   Geographic strengths: Maine, New England, Eastern Canada
   Special collections: Sanborn Fire Insurance maps, U.S. Congressional Serial Set bound and loose maps, local special purpose mapping
   Subject strengths: aerial photos, aeronautical, agriculture, modern cartography, celestial, climatology, city, economic geography, forestry, genealogy, geodetic surveys, geology, geospatial data, historical geography, hydrology, land use, language, map catalogs, map collecting, mineral resources, nautical charts, oceanography, political geography, population, projections, railroads, raised relief models, recreation, religion, roads, soil, vegetation, views, waterways
   Map depositories and percentages: USGS topos (100%), USGS geology maps (100%), Department of Transportation, NOAA, GPO, CIA, National Forest Service, NIMA topos, NIMA nautical, NIMA aeronautical, BLM

65,000 printed maps
14 raised relief maps
30,000 microfiche
500 microfilms
250 aerial photos
300 gazetteers
470 printed atlases
1,050 books
25 active serials
300 CD-ROMs
10 computer programs
Collecting digital data
Chronological coverage:
   1940–present: 92%
Average budget over the last 5 years: $1,000
Access:
Collection is partially open to the public
Maps off site
Reference questions per year: 700
Answers email questions
Patrons per month: 60
   Hours:
   Monday–Friday: 8 A.M.–midnight
   Saturday: 10 A.M.–6 P.M.
   Sunday: 10 A.M.–midnight
   Total hours per week opened: 102
Maps circulate
Circulation policies apply
   Map circulation duration: 4 weeks
   Atlas circulation duration: 4 weeks
   Book circulation duration: 4 weeks
   Number of maps circulated annually: 650
   Number of books circulated annually: 105
   Number of other items circulated annually: 30
Interlibrary loan available
Geographic Information Systems:
GIS services available by appointment
Number of public GIS workstations: 30
GIS assistance available for Census mapping, geocoding, and image analysis
Social science and natural resource mapping help available
Plotter available
Scans maps for patrons
Collection services:
Maps cataloged: 100%
Maps classified: 100%
Maps in OPAC: 100%
Datasets are cataloged
Classification schemes: LC, SuDocs, Local, Other (Canadian document)
Cataloging utilities: OCLC, RLG
Catalog accessibility: online
Physical facilities:
Internet access available

Square footage: 1,650
Number of public computers: 30
Number of map cases: 15
Linear book shelving: 400 ft.
Linear atlas shelving: 112 ft.
Number of microform readers: 10
Number of microform printers: 12
Copying facilities available: copier, microform copier, microform scanner (all microformats)

237 *Portland, ME*

Maine Historical Society

Research Library
489 Congress Street
Portland, ME 04101
Telephone: 207-774-1822
Fax: 207-775-4301
Email: rdesk@mainehistory.org
Web: www.mainehistory.org
Personnel:
Responsible person: Nicholas Noyes, Head of Library Services, *email:* nnoyes@mainehistory.org
FTE professionals: 0.25
Number of volunteer hours per month: 10
Holdings:
Geographic strengths: Maine, Northeast
Special collections: Thomas Barclay/Northeast Boundary, Kennebec Proprietors, Pejepscot Proprietors, Sanborn Fire Insurance maps
Subject strengths: archaeology, early cartography, modern cartography, city, economic geography, engineering, forestry, genealogy, geodetic surveys, geology, historical geography, land ownership, land use, map catalogs, map collecting, military, mineral resources, nautical charts, political geography, population, railroads, recreation, religion, roads, travel books, vegetation, views, waterways
4,500 printed maps
1,000 manuscript maps
80 wall maps
50 gazetteers
120 printed atlases
70 books
Chronological coverage:
   Pre-1800: 15%
   1800–1899: 55%
   1900–1939: 10%
   1940–present: 20%
Access:
Maps in separate area
Collection is paged
Reference questions per year: 100
Answers email questions
Patrons per month: 500

Hours:

Tuesday–Saturday: 10 A.M.–4 P.M.

Total hours per week opened: 30

Geographic Information Systems:

Scans maps for patrons

Collection services:

Maps cataloged: 80%

Maps classified: 80%

Classification schemes: Local

Cataloging utilities: Triple I

Catalog accessibility: online, cards

Preservation techniques: encapsulation, deacidification

Physical facilities:

Internet access available

Number of map cases: 50

Linear atlas shelving: 75 ft.

Other map storage: rolled map case

Copying facilities available: copier, microform copier, scanner, digital photography

238 *Portland, ME*

University of Southern Maine

Glickman Family Library

Osher Map Library and Smith Center for Cartographic Education, founded 1994

P.O. Box 9301

Portland, ME 04104-9301

Telephone: 207-780-4850

Fax: 207-780-5310

Email: oml@usm.maine.edu

Web: www.usm.maine.edu/maps

Personnel:

Responsible person: Yolanda Theunnissen, Curator, *email:* curator@usm.maine.edu

Number of student workers hours per week: 30

Number of volunteer hours per month: 16

Holdings:

Geographic strengths: Maine, New England, World

Special collections: maps of Spain and the Iberian Peninsula (1482–1828), American road maps, 19th century School geographies, cartographic ephemera, Early English sea charts of the Atlantic Northeast

Subject strengths: early cartography, celestial, map catalogs, map collecting, nautical charts, views

15,165 printed maps

14 manuscript maps

110 wall maps

47 reels microfilms

170 globes

892 printed atlases

1,213 books

Chronological coverage:

Pre-1800: 35%

1800–1899: 31%

1900–1939: 20%

1940–present: 14%

On-going publications: 1. *Maps, Globes, Atlases and Geographies through the year 1800: The Eleanor Houston and Lawrence M.C. Smith Cartographic Collection.* 2. *Norumbega News* (newsletter). 3. *Maine 175:A Celebration of Maine Statehood* (exhibition catalog). 4. *Jerusalem 3000: Three Millenia of History* (exhibition catalog). 5. *Charting Neptune's Realm: From Classical Mythology to Satellite Imagery* (exhibition catalog).

Access:

Maps in separate area

Collection is partially open to the public

Collection services:

Maps cataloged: 19%

Maps classified: 20%

Maps in OPAC: 19%

Classification schemes: LC

Cataloging utilities: OCLC, Local

Catalog accessibility: online

Preservation techniques: deacidification, encapsulation in mylar

Physical facilities:

Internet access available

Square footage: 300

Number of map cases: 29

Number of vertical files (file cabinets): 14

Linear book shelving: 401 ft.

Linear atlas shelving: 948 ft.

Other map storage: map tubes

Copying facilities available: copier, microform copier

239 *Searsport, ME*

Penobscot Marine Museum

Stephen Phillips Memorial Library

P.O. Box 498

9 Church Street

Searsport, ME 04974

Telephone: 207-548-2529 x212

Fax: 207-548-2520

Email: library@penobscotmarinemuseum.org

Web: www.penobscotmarinemuseum.org

Personnel:

Responsible person: John G. Arrison, *email:* library@penobscotmarinemuseum.org

FTE professionals: 0.1   *FTE para-professionals:* 0.1

Number of volunteer hours per month: 15

Holdings:

Geographic strengths: New England, China Seas, South America, Europe

Subject strengths: modern cartography, genealogy, geodetic surveys, land ownership, nautical charts

Chronological coverage:
1800–1899: 55%
1900–1939: 32%
1940–present: 10%
On-going publications: Annual Report
3,250 printed maps

Access:
Maps in separate area
Collection is paged
Reference questions per year: 25
Answers email questions

Hours:
Tuesday–Friday: By appointment

Geographic Information Systems:
No GIS services available
Scans maps for patrons

Collection services:
Maps cataloged: 95%
Maps in OPAC: 95%
Classification schemes: Local
Cataloging utilities: Local
Catalog accessibility: online
Preservation techniques: encapsulation, edging, humidification and flattening, storage in acid-free folders

Physical facilities:
No Internet access
Square footage: 500
Number of map cases: 16
Linear atlas shelving: 15 ft.
Other map storage: rolled map case
Copying facilities available: copier, microform copier

240 *Baltimore, MD*

Enoch Pratt Free Library

Enoch Pratt Free Library
Maryland Department/Map Collection
400 Cathedral Street
Baltimore, MD 21201
Telephone: 410-396-5468
Fax: 410-396-9537
Email: mdx@epfl.net
Web: www.epfl.net/slrc/md/

Personnel:
Responsible person: Don Bonsteel, Librarian, *email:* bonsteel@epfl.net
FTE professionals: 1

Holdings:
Geographic strengths: Baltimore, Maryland, Chesapeake Bay
Special collections: Sanborn Fire Insurance maps, 1927 Baltimore aerial photographic atlas, 1897 Baltimore topographic atlas
Subject strengths: aerial photos, aeronautical, agriculture, climatology, city, forestry, geodetic surveys, geology, historical geography, hydrology, industries, land ownership, land use, map catalogs, military, mineral resources, mining, nautical charts, political geography, population, railroads, raised relief models, recreation, religion, roads, satellite imagery, soil, vegetation, views, waterways

2,100 printed maps
32 microfilms
80 aerial photos
10 satellite images
15 gazetteers
25 printed atlases
Chronological coverage:
Pre-1800: 10%
1800–1899: 30%
1900–1939: 20%
1940–present: 40%

Access:
Collection is open to the public
Answers email questions

Hours:
Monday–Thursday: 10 A.M.–8 P.M.
Friday–Saturday: 10 A.M.–5 P.M.
Sunday: 1 P.M.–5 P.M.
Total hours per week opened: 54

Geographic Information Systems:
No GIS services available
GIS assistance available for Census mapping
Scans maps for patrons

Collection services:
Maps cataloged: 90%
Maps classified: 90%
Classification schemes: Local
Cataloging utilities: Local
Catalog accessibility: cards
Preservation techniques: encapsulation, lamination

Physical facilities:
Internet access available
Number of map cases: 39
Copying facilities available: copier, color copier, microform copier

241 *Baltimore, MD*

Enoch Pratt Free Library

Social Science and History Department
400 Cathedral Street
Baltimore, MD 21201
Telephone: 410-396-5320
Fax: 410-396-1413
Email: ssh@epfl.net
Web: www.epfl.net

Personnel:
Responsible person: Michael Donnelly, *email:* ssh@epfl.net

Holdings:

Geographic strengths: Maryland, Middle Atlantic, East Asia, Europe, Great Britain, Scotland, Wales

Special collections: USGS topographic maps, NOAA Coastal Charts

Subject strengths: city, geology, nautical charts, roads

Map depositories and percentages: USGS topos (20%), NOAA, CIA, United Nations

100,000 printed maps

2,000 wall maps

500 satellite images

30 gazetteers

200 printed atlases

Chronological coverage:

1800–1899: 13%

1900–1939: 20%

1940–present: 65%

Average budget over the last 5 years: $1,500

On-going publications: 15-page map guide to the collection written by staff and updated over the years.

Access:

Maps in separate area

Collection is partially open to the public

Maps off site: 95%

Reference questions per year: 500

Answers email questions

Patrons per month: 300

Hours:

Monday–Wednesday: 10 A.M.–8 P.M.

Thursday:–Saturday: 10 A.M.–5 P.M.

Sunday: 1 P.M.–5 P.M.

Total hours per week opened: 55

Maps circulate

Circulation policies apply

Map circulation duration: 3 weeks

Atlas circulation duration: 3 weeks

Book circulation duration: 3 weeks

Number of maps circulated annually: 1,000

Interlibrary loan available

Geographic Information Systems:

No GIS services available

Collection services:

Maps classified: 0%

Classification schemes: LC, SuDocs, Local

Cataloging utilities: OCLC

Catalog accessibility: online

Physical facilities:

Internet access available

Square footage: 3,000

Number of map cases: 15

Number of vertical map cases: 20

Number of vertical files (file cabinets): 20

Linear atlas shelving: 100 ft.

Copying facilities available: copier, microform copier

242 *Baltimore, MD*

Johns Hopkins University

Eisenhower Library

Government Publications/Maps/Law Library, founded 1964

3400 North Charles Street

Baltimore, MD 21212

Telephone: 410-516-8360

Fax: 410-516-6029

Email: jeg@jhu.edu

Web: www.library.jhu.edu/gpm/

Personnel:

Responsible person: Jim Gillispie, Head, Government Publications/Maps/Law Library, *email:* jeg@jhu.edu

Assistants: Sharon Morris, Assistant Head, Government Publications/Maps/Law Library; Lynne Stuart, Government Publications/Maps/Law Librarian; Bonni Wittstadt, Maps and GIS Specialist

FTE professionals: 2.75 *FTE para-professionals:* 2.5

Number of student workers hours per week: 80

Holdings:

Geographic strengths: Maryland, Baltimore, United States

Special collections: GIS data sets for Baltimore and Maryland, Electronic Sanborn for Maryland

Subject strengths: early cartography, modern cartography, city, geology, geospatial data, land ownership, nautical charts, political geography, population, railroads

Map depositories and percentages: USGS topos (99%), USGS geology maps (99%), USGS other (99%), Department of Transportation, NOAA, GPO, CIA, National Forest Service, NIMA topos, NIMA nautical, NIMA aeronautical, BLM, State, United Nations, Maryland Geological Survey

208,000 printed maps

100 wall maps

50 raised relief maps

2,862 microfilms

50 aerial photos

1,000 satellite images

1,500 printed atlases

10 active serials

3,076 CD-ROMs

12 computer programs

Collecting digital data

Chronological coverage:

1800–1899: 10%

1900–1939: 10%

1940–present: 80%

Average budget over the last 5 years: $30,000

On-going publications: 15 page map guide to the collection written by staff and updated over the years.

Access:

Collection is open to the public

Answers email questions

Patrons per month: 1,437

Hours:

Monday–Friday: 8:30 A.M.–10 P.M.

Friday: 8:30 A.M.–10 P.M.

Saturday–Sunday: 1 P.M.–5 P.M.

Total hours per week opened: 72

Maps circulate

Circulation policies apply

Map circulation duration: 1 week

Geographic Information Systems:

GIS services available by appointment

GIS software: ArcGIS, ArcIMS

GIS assistance available for Census mapping, geocoding, and image analysis

General GIS questions answered

Scans maps for patrons

Collection services:

Maps cataloged: 0.5%

Maps classified: 100%

Maps in OPAC: 50%

Datasets are cataloged

Classification schemes: LC, SuDocs

Cataloging utilities: OCLC

Catalog accessibility: online, cards

Preservation techniques: encapsulation, deacidification, cartex

Physical facilities:

Internet access available

Square footage: 10,700

Number of map cases: 69

Number of vertical files (file cabinets): 13

Linear book shelving: 36 ft.

Linear atlas shelving: 54 ft.

Other map storage: 2 (16' long × 7" deep)

Copying facilities available: copier, color copier, large-format copier, microform copier

Notes: Staffing and some space/equipment information refer to the entire Government Publications/Maps/Law Library area. Collection size and funding is just for maps, atlas, GIS, images and cartographic reference materials.

243 *College Park, MD*

National Archives and Records Administration

Special Media Archives Services Division

Cartographic Section, founded 1937

8601 Adelphi Road

Room 3320

College Park, MD 20740-6001

Telephone: 301-837-0564

Fax: 301-837-3622

Email: carto@nara.gov

Web: www.archives.gov

Personnel:

Responsible person: Suzanne Adamko, *email:* suzanne.adamko@nara.gov

FTE professionals: 11

Holdings:

Subject strengths: aerial photos, aeronautical, agriculture, early cartography, modern cartography, city, economic geography, engineering, forestry, genealogy, geodetic surveys, geology, historical geography, hydrology, land use, military, mineral resources, mining, nautical charts, oceanography, population, railroads, roads, soil, vegetation, waterways

Map depositories and percentages: USGS topos (100%), USGS geology maps (100%), USGS other (100%), Department of Transportation, NOAA, CIA, National Forest Service, NIMA topos, NIMA nautical, NIMA aeronautical, BLM

2,000,000 printed maps

1,000,000 manuscript maps

50,000 microfiche

1,000,000 microfilms

18,000,000 aerial photos

Chronological coverage:

1800–1899: 30%

1900–1939: 25%

1940–present: 40%

Access:

Maps in separate area

Collection is paged

Maps off site: 10%

Reference questions per year: 5,000

Answers email questions

Patrons per month: 100

Hours:

Monday–Friday: 8:45 A.M.–5 P.M.

Saturday: 8:45 A.M.–4:45 P.M.

Sunday: closed

Total hours per week opened: 60

Geographic Information Systems:

No GIS services available

Scans maps for patrons

Collection services:

Maps in OPAC: 10%

Classification schemes: Other (record group and series)

Cataloging utilities: Archival Research Catalog

Catalog accessibility: online

Preservation techniques: encapsulation, deacidification

Items that have gone through the preservation process: 25%

Physical facilities:

Internet access available

Number of map cases: 8,000
Copying facilities available: copier, color copier, large-format copier, microform copier

244 *College Park, MD*

University of Maryland, College Park

Hornbake Library
Maryland Map Collection, founded 1950
College Park, MD 20742
Telephone: 301-410-9212
Fax: 301-314-2709
Email: rb302@umail.umd.edu
Web: www.lib.umd.edu/RARE/MarylandCollection/Maps/MdMaps.html
Personnel:
Responsible person: Douglas McElrath, Curator of Marylandia and Rare Books, *email:* dmcelrat@umd.edu
Assistants: Ann Hudak, Assistant Curator
Number of student workers hours per week: 80
Number of volunteer hours per month: 40
Holdings:
Geographic strengths: Maryland, Virginia, Delaware, District of Columbia, Middle Atlantic
Special collections: Sanborn Fire Insurance maps for Maryland and DC
Subject strengths: agriculture, archaeology, biology, early cartography, modern cartography, caves, climatology, city, economic geography, forestry, geodetic surveys, geology, geospatial data, historical geography, hydrology, industries, land ownership, land use, military, mineral resources, mining, nautical charts, oceanography, political geography, population, projections, railroads, recreation, religion, roads, soil, travel books, vegetation, views, waterways, zoogeography
Map depositories: State
3,500 printed maps
20 manuscript maps
20 microfilms
50 gazetteers
200 printed atlases
500 books
10 inactive serials
Chronological coverage:
Pre-1800: 15%
1800–1899: 25%
1900–1939: 40%
1940–present: 20%
Average budget over the last 5 years: $300
Access:
Collection is paged
Reference questions per year: 20

Answers email questions
Patrons per month: 700
Hours:
Monday–Friday: 10 A.M.–5 P.M.
Saturday: noon–5 P.M.
Total hours per week opened: 40
Geographic Information Systems:
No GIS services available
Scans maps for patrons
Collection services:
Maps cataloged: 10%
Maps classified: 20%
Maps in OPAC: 95%
Classification schemes: LC, Local
Cataloging utilities: OCLC
Catalog accessibility: online, printout
Preservation techniques: encapsulation, deacidification
Items that have gone through the preservation process: 15%
Physical facilities:
Internet access available
Square footage: 2,400
Number of map cases: 24
Number of vertical files (file cabinets): 14
Linear book shelving: 2,880 ft.
Linear atlas shelving: 300 ft.
Copying facilities available: copier, microform copier, scanner

245 *College Park, MD*

University of Maryland, College Park

McKeldin Library
Government Documents and Maps, founded 1925
4118 McKeldin Library
College Park, MD 20742
Telephone: 301-405-9165
Fax: 301-314-5651
Email: govdocs@umd.edu
Web: www.lib.umd.edu/gov/maproom.html
Personnel:
Responsible person: Marianne Ryan, *email:* mryan1@umd.edu
Assistants: Michael Fry, Librarian; Kim Ricker, Graduate Assistant
FTE para-professionals: 0.5
Holdings:
Geographic strengths: Maryland, Middle Atlantic, United States
Special collections: National Geographic maps
Subject strengths: aeronautical, climatology, forestry, geology, geospatial data, military, nautical charts, population, recreation, roads, soil

Map depositories and percentages: USGS topos (100%), USGS geology maps (100%), USGS other (100%), Department of Transportation, NOAA, GPO, CIA, National Forest Service, NIMA topos, NIMA nautical, NIMA aeronautical, BLM

400,000 printed maps

20 wall maps

120 raised relief maps

3,000 microfiche

250 satellite images

200 gazetteers

550 printed atlases

350 books

800 CD-ROMs

Collecting digital data

Chronological coverage:
1900–1939: 30%
1940–present: 65%

Average budget over the last 5 years: $1,000

Access:

Collection is open to the public

Reference questions per year: 320

Answers email questions

Patrons per month: 60

Hours:

Monday–Friday: 8 A.M.–11 P.M.

Saturday: 10 A.M.–8 P.M.

Sunday: noon–11 P.M.

Total hours per week opened: 83

Geographic Information Systems:

GIS services available in an open environment

GIS software: ArcView 3.2, ArcView 8.3, ArcGIS 8.3, GEOMedia, Map Point

GIS assistance available for Census mapping, geocoding, and image analysis

Data identification and retrieval, spatial analysis, text-to-spatial data conversion help available

Collection services:

Maps classified: 50%

Datasets are cataloged

Classification schemes: LC, SuDocs, Local

Cataloging utilities: OCLC, MarciveWeb DOCS

Catalog accessibility: online, cards

Preservation techniques: encapsulation, deacidification, edging

Items that have gone through the preservation process: 0.1%

Physical facilities:

Internet access available

Square footage: 2,500

Number of map cases: 141

Number of atlas stands: 20

Linear book shelving: 720 ft.

Linear atlas shelving: 150 ft.

Copying facilities available: copier, color copier, large-format copier, microform copier

246 *Frostburg, MD*

Frostburg State University

Lewis J. Ort Library

User Services Division, founded 1968

1 Stadium Drive

Frostburg, MD 21532

Telephone: 301-687-4887

Fax: 301-687-7069

Email: libref@mail.frostburg.edu

Web: www.frostburg.edu/dept/library/library.htm

Personnel:

Responsible person: Pamela S. Williams, *email:* pwilliams@frostburg.edu

Assistants: Virginia Williams, Cataloger; Jennifer Price, Government Document Technical Assistant

Holdings:

Geographic strengths: Maryland, West Virginia, Virginia, Delaware, Pennsylvania, New York, Canada

Special collections: J.J. Rutledge coal mine maps collection for Western Maryland, Sanborn Fire Insurance maps, PrEx series maps

Subject strengths: aerial photos, aeronautical, celestial, geology, historical geography, hydrology, land use, map catalogs, military, mineral resources, mining, nautical charts, oceanography, population, railroads, raised relief models, roads, satellite imagery, soil

Map depositories: USGS topos, USGS geology maps, GPO, CIA, National Forest Service, NIMA topos, NIMA nautical

40,276 printed maps

17 raised relief maps

3,297 aerial photos

16 satellite images

150 printed atlases

936 books

58 CD-ROMs

18 computer programs

Chronological coverage:
1900–1939: 15%
1940–present: 84%

Average budget over the last 5 years: $100

Access:

Collection is open to the public

Reference questions per year: 60

Answers email questions

Hours:

Monday–Thursday: 8 A.M.–midnight

Friday: 8 A.M.–8 P.M.

Saturday: 11 A.M.–8 P.M.

Sunday: 1 P.M.–midnight
Total hours per week opened: 96
Maps circulate
Circulation policies apply
  Map circulation duration: 4 weeks
  Atlas circulation duration: 4 weeks
  Book circulation duration: 4 weeks
  Number of maps circulated annually: 127

Geographic Information Systems:
Number of public GIS workstations: 36

Collection services:
Maps cataloged: 16%
Maps classified: 95%
Maps in OPAC: 16%
Classification schemes: LC, SuDocs, Local
Cataloging utilities: OCLC
Catalog accessibility: online
Preservation techniques: lamination, microfilm, digital
  images
Items that have gone through the preservation process:
  7%

Physical facilities:
Internet access available
Number of map cases: 54
Linear book shelving: 124 ft.
Linear atlas shelving: 15 ft.
Other map storage: map index display rack, rolled map
  containers for circulating maps
Copying facilities available: copier, microform copier,
  11" × 17" sheets available on microfilm copier and
  photocopier

Notes: Circulation of map collection restricted to Frostburg State University faculty, staff, students, and local
residents.

247 *Rockville, MD*

Montgomery College

Department of Applied Technology
Applied Geography
51 Mannakee Street
Rockville, MD 20850
Telephone: 301-251-7614
Fax: 301-279-5001
Email: tanya.allison@montgomerycollege.edu
Web: www.montgomerycollege.edu/library

Personnel:
Responsible person: Tanya Allison, Associate Professor and Program Coordinator, *email:* tanya.allison@
  montgomerycollege.edu
Number of student workers hours per week: 20

Holdings:
Geographic strengths: Russia, USSR, Baltic,
  Afghanistan, Japan, Mongolia, China, North Korea,
  South Korea, Philippines

Subject strengths: aerial photos, early cartography,
  modern cartography, celestial, climatology, city, economic geography, geodetic surveys, geospatial data,
  historical geography, land ownership, map catalogs,
  map collecting, military, nautical charts, political geography, population, raised relief models, recreation,
  roads, satellite imagery, travel books, views, waterways, globes

Map depositories and percentages: USGS topos (50%),
  USGS other, NOAA, GPO, CIA, NIMA topos,
  NIMA aeronautical, State
3,000 printed maps
Collecting digital data

Access:
Maps in separate area
Collection is paged
Answers email questions

Hours:
  Monday–Friday: 9 A.M.–5 P.M.
  Total hours per week opened: 40
Circulation policies apply

Geographic Information Systems:
GIS services available by appointment
GIS software: ArcGIS, MapInfo
Number of GIS stations (monitored): 24
GIS assistance available for Census mapping, geocod-
  ing, and image analysis
Plotter available

Collection services:
Preservation techniques: lamination

Physical facilities:
No Internet access
Number of staff computers: 24
Other map storage: map shelves, tubes
Number of stereoscopes: 10
Copying facilities available: copier, color copier, large-
  format copier

248 *Suitland, MD*

Smithsonian Institution

National Anthropological Archives
4210 Silver Hill Road
Suitland, MD 20746
Telephone: 301-238-2873
Fax: 301-238-2883
Email: naa@nmnh.si.edu
Web: www.nmnh.si.edu/naa

Personnel:
Responsible person: Dr. Jake Homiak, Director, *email:*
  homiak.jake@nmnh.si.edu

Holdings:
Geographic strengths: North America
Special collections: Bureau of American Ethnology
  Map Collection

Subject strengths: aerial photos, archaeology, language, Ethnology

1,000 printed maps

2,000 manuscript maps

300 aerial photos

Access:

Collection is paged

Answers email questions

Hours:

Monday–Friday: by appointment

Geographic Information Systems:

Scans maps for patrons

Collection services:

Maps cataloged: 25%

Maps in OPAC: 25%

Classification schemes: Local

Cataloging utilities: Local

Catalog accessibility: online, cards

Preservation techniques: encapsulation, deacidification, lamination

Physical facilities:

Copying facilities available: copier, microform copier

249 *Amherst, MA*

University of Massachusetts, Amherst

W.E.B. Du Bois Library

Map Collection

154 Hicks Way

Amherst, MA 01003

Telephone: 413-545-2397

Fax: 413-545-1399

Email: slillydahl@libraray.umass.edu

Web: www.library.umass.edu/maps/index/html

Personnel:

Responsible person: Sandy Lillydahl, Map Supervisor, *email:* slillydahl@library.umass.edu

Number of student workers hours per week: 30

Holdings:

Geographic strengths: Massachusetts, Western Massachusetts, United States, WW II, Moon

Special collections: FEMA, Massachusetts Historic, WW II, Lunar, CIS, Forestry, local aerial surveys

Subject strengths: agriculture, modern cartography, caves, celestial, city, forestry, geology, historical geography, land use, political geography, recreation, roads, soil, travel books, vegetation

Map depositories and percentages: USGS topos (100%), USGS geology maps (100%), USGS other, GPO, CIA, National Forest Service, BLM, State

115,000 printed maps

Chronological coverage:

1800–1899: 10%

1900–1939: 20%

1940–present: 70%

Average budget over the last 5 years: $2,500

Access:

Maps in separate area

Collection is open to the public

Reference questions per year: 1,365

Answers email questions

Patrons per month: 300

Hours:

Monday–Friday: 10 A.M.–5 P.M.

Total hours per week opened: 35

Geographic Information Systems:

GIS services available in an open environment

Collection services:

Maps cataloged: 66%

Maps classified: 66%

Maps in OPAC: 66%

Classification schemes: LC

Cataloging utilities: OCLC

Catalog accessibility: online

Preservation techniques: encapsulation, lamination

Items that have gone through the preservation process: 10%

Physical facilities:

Internet access available

Number of map cases: 117

Number of vertical files (file cabinets): 10

Linear book shelving: 99 ft.

Linear atlas shelving: 12 ft.

Copying facilities available: copier, color copier, large-format copier, microform copier

250 *Boston, MA*

Boston Athenaeum

10 1/2 Beacon Street

Boston, MA 02108

Telephone: 617-227-0270

Fax: 617-227-5266

Email: lannon@bostonathenaeum.org

Web: bostonathenaeum.org

Personnel:

Responsible person: John Lannon, Curator of Maps, *email:* lannon@bostonathenaeum.org

Number of volunteer hours per month: 12

Holdings:

Geographic strengths: New England, North America

Special collections: Bromley, Walker, Sanborn (other) city, county and state atlases, Des Barre-Atlantic Neptune, English Pilots

Subject strengths: early cartography, city, geodetic surveys, geology, land use, map catalogs, military, nautical charts, travel books, views

Map depositories: USGS topos, NOAA, GPO

3,000 printed maps

24 wall maps

12 raised relief maps
50 gazetteers
625 printed atlases
25 CD-ROMs
Chronological coverage:
  Pre-1800: 25%
  1800–1899: 40%
  1900–1939: 25%
  1940–present: 10%

Access:
  Collection is partially open to the public
  Answers email questions
  Hours:
    Monday–Friday: 9 A.M.–5 P.M.
    Saturday: 9 A.M.–4 P.M.
    Sunday: closed
    Book circulation duration: 2 weeks
  Interlibrary loan available
Geographic Information Systems:
  Number of public GIS workstations: 20
  Scans maps for patrons
Collection services:
  Maps cataloged: 90%
  Classification schemes: LC, Other (cutter)
  Cataloging utilities: OCLC, RLG
  Catalog accessibility: online, cards
  Preservation techniques: encapsulation, deacidification
Physical facilities:
  Internet access available
  Square footage: 97,000
  Number of public computers: 20
  Number of staff computers: 50
  Number of stereoscopes: 3
  Copying facilities available: copier
Notes: The facility data entered above refers to the entire building. We do not have a separate map room and collections are dispersed throughout the building.

251 *Boston, MA*

Boston Public Library

Boston Public Library
Norman Leventhal Map Center, founded 2003
Copley Square
Boston, MA 02116
Telephone: 617-536-5400
Web: www.bpl.org
Personnel:
  Assistants: Additional support to collection provided by various subject departments
Holdings:
  Geographic strengths: Boston, Massachusetts
  Special collections: Sanborn Fire Insurance maps, Land ownership maps U.S. (19th century), Boston

Ward maps (19th century), Bromley atlas collection, American manuscript maps in British repositories (microform sets), Baedeker's handbooks for travelers (microform set), City Plan Index—hand drawn street plans for the City of Boston (1850–1895), Fairchild survey of aerial photos of Boston and vicinity (part of the Boston Pictorial Archive)
  Subject strengths: aerial photos, early cartography, city, genealogy, geology, historical geography, land ownership, military, soil, views
  Map depositories and percentages: USGS topos (100%), USGS geology maps (100%), USGS other (100%), Department of Transportation, NOAA, GPO, National Forest Service, NIMA topos
1,400,000 printed maps
4,000 microfiche
1,600 microfilms
700 gazetteers
1,500 printed atlases
2,500 books
Chronological coverage:
  1800–1899: 15%
  1900-present: 80%
Access:
  Answers email questions
  Hours:
    Monday–Thursday: 9 A.M.–9 P.M.
    Friday–Saturday: 9 A.M.–5 P.M.
    Sunday: 1 P.M.–5 P.M.
    Total hours per week opened: 68
  Interlibrary loan available
Geographic Information Systems:
  No GIS services available
Collection services:
  Classification schemes: LC, SuDocs, Local
  Cataloging utilities: OCLC, Local
  Catalog accessibility: online, fiche, cards
  Preservation techniques: encapsulation
Physical facilities:
  Internet access available
  Number of map cases: 129
  Linear atlas shelving: 717 ft.
  Number of microform readers: 30
  Copying facilities available: copier, large-format copier, microform copier

252 *Boston, MA*

Bostonian Society

Library and Special Collections
206 Washington Street
Boston, MA 02109
Telephone: 617-720-1713 x12

Fax: 617-720-3289
Email: library@bostonhistory.org
Web: www.bostonhistory.org
Personnel:
Responsible person: Nancy Richard, Director of the Library and Special Collections
Holdings:
Geographic strengths: Boston region
Special collections: Sanborn Fire Insurance maps, G.W. Bromley and Company
Subject strengths: aerial photos, modern cartography, city, map catalogs, travel books, zoogeography
Map depositories: State, United Nations
400 printed maps
375 manuscript maps
100 aerial photos
15 gazetteers
25 printed atlases
Chronological coverage:
    Pre-1800: 22%
    1800–1899: 40%
    1900–1939: 20%
    1940–present: 20%
Access:
Collection is paged
Maps off site
Reference questions per year: 50
Answers email questions
Patrons per month: 30
Hours:
    Friday–Sunday: closed
    Total hours per week opened: 25
Geographic Information Systems:
No GIS services available
Scans maps for patrons
Collection services:
Maps cataloged: 100%
Classification schemes: Local
Cataloging utilities: Rediscovery
Catalog accessibility: cards
Preservation techniques: encapsulation
Physical facilities:
No Internet access
Number of map cases: 4
Linear book shelving: 10 ft.
Linear atlas shelving: 110 ft.
Other map storage: 2 rolled map cases
Copying facilities available: copier, scanner

253 *Boston, MA*

State Library of Massachusetts

341 State House
Boston, MA 02139
Telephone: 617-727-2590

Fax: 617-727-9730
Email: reference.department@state.ma.us
Web: www.mass.gov/lib
Personnel:
Responsible person: Betsy Lowenstein, *email:* betsy.lowenstein@state.ma.us
Holdings:
Geographic strengths: Massachusetts
Special collections: Sanborn Fire Insurance maps
Subject strengths: city, geodetic surveys, nautical charts, railroads, views
Map depositories: USGS topos
4,000 printed maps
150 manuscript maps
40 wall maps
465 printed atlases
Access:
Collection is paged
Reference questions per year: 250
Answers email questions
Patrons per month: 20
Hours:
    Monday–Friday: 9 A.M.–1 A.M
    Total hours per week opened: 20
Collection services:
Maps cataloged: 75%
Maps classified: 75%
Maps in OPAC: 75%
Classification schemes: LC, Local
Cataloging utilities: OCLC
Catalog accessibility: online, cards
Preservation techniques: encapsulation
Physical facilities:
Internet access available
Number of map cases: 20
Linear atlas shelving: 1,600 ft.
Copying facilities available: copier, microform copier

254 *Cambridge, MA*

Harvard University

Pusey Library
Harvard Map Collection, founded 1818
Cambridge, MA 02138
Telephone: 617-495-2417
Fax: 617-496-0440
Email: maps@harvard.edu
Web: hcl.harvard.edu/maps
Personnel:
Responsible person: David A. Cobb, *email:* cobb@fas.harvard.edu
Assistants: Reference; Digital Cartography Specialist; Geographic Information Systems Specialist
FTE para-professionals: 0.5
Number of student workers hours per week: 70

Holdings:

Geographic strengths: Boston, New England, United States, North America, Europe

Special collections: Sanborn Fire Insurance maps for New England states, Massachusetts Military Order of the Loyal Legion of the United States Civil War maps, McBey Collection of maps of Gibraltar and North Africa, Parkman Collection of Early American maps

Subject strengths: aerial photos, aeronautical, early cartography, modern cartography, celestial, climatology, city, economic geography, forestry, genealogy, geodetic surveys, geospatial data, historical geography, land ownership, land use, language, map catalogs, map collecting, military, nautical charts, oceanography, political geography, population, projections, railroads, recreation, religion, roads, satellite imagery, soil, vegetation, views, waterways, zoogeography

Map depositories: USGS topos, Department of Transportation, NOAA, GPO, CIA, National Forest Service, NIMA topos, NIMA nautical, NIMA aeronautical, BLM, State, Canada; various cartographic publishers

400,000 printed maps
250 manuscript maps
750 wall maps
5,000 microfiche
1,000 microfilms
2,000 aerial photos
100 satellite images
15 globes
1,500 gazetteers
9,000 printed atlases
4,000 books
52 active serials
1,200 CD-ROMs
15 computer programs
Collecting digital data

Chronological coverage:
1800–1899: 20%
1900–1939: 25%
1940–present: 52%

Average budget over the last 5 years: $75,000

Access:

Maps in separate area
Collection is paged
Maps off site
Reference questions per year: 2,500
Answers email questions
Patrons per month: 200

Hours:

Monday–Friday: 9 A.M.–5 P.M.
Saturday–Saturday: closed
Total hours per week opened: 35

Geographic Information Systems:

GIS services available by appointment

GIS assistance available for Census mapping, geocoding, and image analysis
Plotter available
Scans maps for patrons

Collection services:

Maps classified: 90%
Datasets are cataloged
Classification schemes: LC, Local
Cataloging utilities: OCLC
Catalog accessibility: online, cards
Preservation techniques: encapsulation, deacidification

Physical facilities:

Internet access available
Number of map cases: 482
Number of vertical files (file cabinets): 15
Copying facilities available: large-format copier

255 *Cambridge, MA*

Massachusetts Institute of Technology

Science Library
Map Collection
14S–134
77 Massachusetts Avenue
Cambridge, MA 02139-4307
Telephone: 617-253-5685
Web: libraries.mit.edu/science

Personnel:

Responsible person: Michael M. Noga, *email:* mnoga@mit.edu
FTE professionals: 0.1   *FTE para-professionals:* 0.1

Holdings:

Map depositories: USGS
81,000 printed maps
26 atlases
35 books
285 active serials

Access:

Hours:

Monday–Friday: 7 A.M.–midnight
Saturday: 8 A.M.–midnight
Sunday: 10 A.M.–midnight
Items circulate
Interlibrary loan available

Collection services:

Maps cataloged: 1%
Maps classified: 80%
Maps in OPAC: 1%
Classification schemes: LC

Physical facilities:

Maps in separate area
Map cases: 44

Notes: CIA maps are kept in the Dewey Library. Aeronautical are kept in the Aeronautics and Astronautics Library. The Lindgren Library collects geoscience maps.

256 *Dartmouth, MA*

University of Massachusetts, Dartmouth

Library
Map Collection, founded 1972
285 Old Westport Road
Dartmouth, MA 02747
Telephone: 508-999-8886
Fax: 508-999-9240
Email: pgibbs@umassd.edu
Web: www.lib.umassd.edu/Reference/Maps.html
Personnel:
Responsible person: Paige Gibbs, Librarian, *email:* pgibbs@umassd.edu
Holdings:
Special collections: Sanborn Fire Insurance maps of towns in southeastern Massachusetts, entire NOAA coastal chart series
Subject strengths: aeronautical, celestial, economic geography, engineering, historical geography, hydrology, industries, land use, map collecting, mining, nautical charts, oceanography, political geography, population, recreation, roads, satellite imagery, travel books, views, waterways
Map depositories and percentages: USGS topos (0.5%), USGS geology maps (0.1%), Department of Transportation, NOAA, GPO, CIA, National Forest Service, State
3,867 printed maps
20 satellite images
10 printed atlases
1,023 books
Chronological coverage:
1940–present: 92%
Average budget over the last 5 years: $300
On-going publications: http://www.lib.umassd.edu/Reference/Maps.html
Access:
Collection is open to the public
Reference questions per year: 500
Answers email questions
Patrons per month: 120
Hours:
Total hours per week opened: 77.9
Geographic Information Systems:
No GIS services available
Number of public GIS workstations: 50
Collection services:
Maps classified: 90%
Classification schemes: SuDocs
Cataloging utilities: OCLC
Catalog accessibility: online
Physical facilities:
No Internet access
Number of map cases: 16

Linear book shelving: 26 ft.
Linear atlas shelving: 15 ft.
Copying facilities available: copier, microform copier

257 *Springfield, MA*

Springfield City Library

220 State St
Springfield, MA 01103
Telephone: 413-263-6828
Web: www.springfieldlibrary.org
Personnel:
Responsible person: Ed Lonergan, Documents Coordinator, *email:* elonergan@spfldlibmus.org
FTE professionals: 1
Holdings:
Geographic strengths: New England, New York
Special collections: topographic maps
Map depositories: USGS topos, CIA, NGA aeronautical, BLM
1,200 printed maps
30 atlases
Access:
Hours:
Monday: 11 A.M.–8 P.M.
Tuesday: 9 A.M.–6 P.M.
Wednesday: 11 A.M.–8 P.M.
Thursday: 9 A.M.–6 P.M.
Friday–Saturday: 9 A.M.–5 P.M.
Sunday: noon–4 P.M.
Collection services:
Classification schemes: Local
Physical facilities:
Map cases: 2
Vertical files: 2

258 *Weston, MA*

Boston College

Thomas P. O'Neill Jr. Library
Catherine O'Connor Library
381 Concord Road
Weston, MA 02493
Telephone: 617-552-8300
Fax: 617-552-8388
Email: khans@bc.edu
Web: www.bc.edu/libraries/centers/weston/
Personnel:
Responsible person: Kathleen Berry, *email:* berryka@bc.edu
FTE professionals: 0.29   *FTE para-professionals:* 0.285
Holdings:
Geographic strengths: New England, New York

Map depositories: USGS topos, Department of Transportation, NOAA, CIA, BLM

12,000 printed maps

Access:

Items circulate

Collection services:

Classification schemes: LC, SuDocs

Physical facilities:

Maps in separate area

Public computers: 1

Map cases: 6

Vertical files: 4

Notes: Maps are located in 2 different libraries. We are in the process of inventorying our collection.

259 *Woods Hole, MA*

Woods Hole Oceanographic Institution

MBL/WHOI Library

Data Library and Archives, founded 1956

266 Woods Hole Road

MS 8

Woods Hole, MA 02543

Telephone: 508-289-2497

Fax: 508-289-2183

Email: archives@whoi.edu

Web: www.mblwhoilibrary.mbl.edu

Personnel:

Responsible person: Lisa Raymond, Catalog Librarian, *email:* lraymond@whoi.edu

Holdings:

Geographic strengths: Oceans, Coastal regions.

Subject strengths: geology, oceanography, hydrography, bathymetry, ocean floor photography

40,000 printed maps

Chronological coverage:

1940–present: 94%

Access:

Collection is paged

Answers email questions

Hours:

Monday–Friday: 8 A.M.–5 P.M.

Total hours per week opened: 45

Maps circulate

Circulation policies apply

Map circulation duration: 2 weeks

Number of maps circulated annually: 584

Interlibrary loan available

Geographic Information Systems:

No GIS services available

Collection services:

Maps cataloged: 98%

Maps classified: 98%

Maps in OPAC: 98%

Classification schemes: LC

Cataloging utilities: OCLC

Catalog accessibility: online

Preservation techniques: encapsulation

Items that have gone through the preservation process: 0.5%

Physical facilities:

No Internet access

Square footage: 6,888

Number of map cases: 417

Linear book shelving: 1282 ft.

Linear atlas shelving: 192 ft.

Other map storage: rolled map cases

Copying facilities available: copier, microform copier

Notes: Maps circulated to Woods Hole Scientific Community only. Books and some atlases available on ILL. Circulation periods listed are for Woods Hole Scientific Community.

260 *Worcester, MA*

American Antiquarian Society

185 Salisbury Street

Worcester, MA 01609

Telephone: 508-755-5221

Fax: 508-753-3311

Web: www.americanantiquarian.org

Personnel:

Responsible person: Georgia B. Barnhill, Curator of Graphic Arts, *email:* gbarnhill@mwa.org

Assistants: Therasa Tremblay, Assistant Curator of Graphic Arts

Holdings:

Geographic strengths: New England, United States

Subject strengths: historical geography, railroads, travel books

9,500 printed maps

200 manuscript maps

200 wall maps

500 printed atlases

Chronological coverage:

Pre-1800: 15%

1800–1899: 90%

Average budget over the last 5 years: $1,000

Access:

Collection is paged

Reference questions per year: 24

Answers email questions

Hours:

Monday–Friday: 9 A.M.–5 P.M.

Total hours per week opened: 40

Collection services:

Classification schemes: Local

Cataloging utilities: RLG

Catalog accessibility: handwritten index to the map collection, atlases printed through 1830 are fully cataloged

Preservation techniques: acid-free folders

Physical facilities:
No Internet access
Number of map cases: 60
Copying facilities available: copier, large-format copier, microform copier

261 *Allendale, MI*

Grand Valley State University

James H. Zumberge Library
1 Campus Drive
Allendale, MI 49401
Telephone: 616-331-3500
Web: www.gvsu.edu/library/govdoc
Personnel:
FTE professionals: 1   *FTE para-professionals:* 1.5
Holdings:
Map depositories: USGS topos, Department of Transportation, NOAA, CIA
61,000 printed maps
Collection services:
Maps cataloged: 99%
Maps in OPAC: 98%
Classification schemes: LC, SuDocs
Physical facilities:
Map cases: 60

262 *Ann Arbor, MI*

University of Michigan

Bentley Historical Library
Founded 1935
1150 Beal Avenue
Ann Arbor, MI 48109-2113
Telephone: 734-764-3482
Fax: 734-936-1333
Web: www.umich.edu/~bhl
Personnel:
Responsible person: Leonard A. Coombs, *email:* coombs@umich.edu
Holdings:
Geographic strengths: Michigan, Great Lakes region
Special collections: Manuscript field notes and maps of early state geologists of Michigan, photolithographic copies of original land surveys of Michigan, military maps relating to U.S. intervention in North Russia, 1918–1919
Subject strengths: genealogy, historical geography, land ownership, railroads, roads
7,000 printed maps
1,500 manuscript maps
100 wall maps
50 microfiche
25 microfilms
1,500 aerial photos
35 gazetteers

400 printed atlases
Chronological coverage:
1800–1899: 48%
1900–1939: 30%
1940–present: 20%
Average budget over the last 5 years: $100
Access:
Maps in separate area
Collection is paged
Answers email questions
Hours:
Monday–Friday: 9 A.M.–5 P.M.
Saturday: 9 A.M.–12:30 P.M.
Total hours per week opened: 43.5
Geographic Information Systems:
Scans maps for patrons
Collection services:
Maps cataloged: 100%
Maps classified: 100%
Maps in OPAC: 100%
Classification schemes: Local
Cataloging utilities: OCLC, RLG, Local
Catalog accessibility: online
Preservation techniques: encapsulation, deacidification, lamination
Items that have gone through the preservation process: 20%
Physical facilities:
Internet access available
Number of map cases: 30
Linear atlas shelving: 350 ft.
Other map storage: 2 rolled map cases
Copying facilities available: copier, microform copier

263 *Ann Arbor, MI*

University of Michigan

Map Library, founded 1902
Hatcher Graduate Library 825
Ann Arbor, MI 48109-1205
Telephone: 734-764-0407
Fax: 734-763-5080
Email: map.library@umich.edu
Web: www.lib.umich.edu/maplib
Personnel:
Responsible person: Karl Longstreth, Head and Map Librarian, *email:* karleric@umich.edu
Assistants: Tim Utter, Cataloguer
FTE professionals: 2
Number of student workers hours per week: 40
Holdings:
Geographic strengths: North America, Canada, United States, Mexico, Great Lakes region, Michigan, Eurasia, Europe, Mediterranean region, Italy, France, Great Britain, Germany, Netherlands, Belgium, Luxembourg, Poland, Spain, Greece, Eastern Europe,

East Asia, Japan, Southeast Asia, Central and South America, Africa, South Africa

Special collections: Vignaud collection of early maps and atlases, Hubbard collection of early maps, Leverett geology collection, Great Lakes and Michigan maps before 1900

Subject strengths: aeronautical, archaeology, early cartography, modern cartography, celestial, climatology, city, forestry, geology, geospatial data, historical geography, hydrology, land use, map catalogs, map collecting, mineral resources, mining, nautical charts, political geography, projections, roads, views, history of cartography

Map depositories and percentages: USGS topos (100%), USGS geology maps (100%), USGS other (100%), Department of Transportation, NOAA, GPO, CIA, National Forest Service, NIMA topos, NIMA nautical, NIMA aeronautical, BLM

328,700 printed maps

350 manuscript maps

220 wall maps

50 raised relief maps

10 microfiche

4,300 aerial photos

590 satellite images

450 gazetteers

4,800 printed atlases

3,850 books

51 active serials

12 inactive serials

950 CD-ROMs

52 computer programs

Collecting digital data

Chronological coverage:
1940–present: 86%

Access:

Collection is partially open to the public

Maps off site

Reference questions per year: 1,800

Answers email questions

Patrons per month: 220

Hours:

Monday–Friday: 10 A.M.–6 P.M. or by appointment

Sunday: 1 A.M.–4 P.M.

Total hours per week opened: 43

Maps circulate

Circulation policies apply

Map circulation duration: 1 week

Atlas circulation duration: 2 weeks

Book circulation duration: 3 weeks

Number of maps circulated annually: 200

Number of books circulated annually: 550

Interlibrary loan available

Geographic Information Systems:

GIS services available in an open environment

GIS software: ArcGIS, ArcView, PCI Geomatica, BoundarySeer, ClusterSeer, TerraSeer, SpaceStat, TerraViva, TimeMap, statistical packages (SAS, SPlus, SPSS, Stata, etc.)

GIS assistance available for Census mapping, geocoding, and image analysis

Assistance for all spatial data—with preparation for publication, with socio-economic, demographic and environmental data, with database development, etc.

Plotter available

Scans maps for patrons

Collection services:

Maps cataloged: 100%

Maps classified: 80%

Maps in OPAC: 100%

Datasets are cataloged

Classification schemes: LC

Cataloging utilities: OCLC, RLG, Local

Catalog accessibility: online

Preservation techniques: encapsulation, deacidification, custom enclosures, full conservation treatments, rebinding, and boxes for rare and special materials, digital reformatting

Items that have gone through the preservation process: 1%

Physical facilities:

Internet access available

Square footage: 4,450

Number of map cases: 428

Number of vertical files (file cabinets): 32

Linear book shelving: 360 ft.

Linear atlas shelving: 1,302 ft.

Other map storage: 2 rolled map cases, 3 custom cases for special materials (126 ln ft of shelves or drawers), CD-ROM cabinet

Copying facilities available: copier, color copier, large-format copier, microform copier

Notes: Most serials (journals) are in the Graduate or other libraries—667 titles in geography or cartography, 99 of these are cartography. We have over 48,000 titles in all formats in the map library; large sets (like all of the 1,24,000 US topos) are one title. We are counting books and atlases by individual volumes, and these include bound serials, and counting only those in the map collection. There are 1.5 FTE (3 half-time professional positions) in Numeric and Spatial Data Services (NSDS); those staff members and facilities are in the Map Library, but we do not consider that part of the map collection. There are three grad students also in NSDS, working 30 hours a week. Our GIS lab is open but monitored. The total number of public workstations, 9, includes the GIS stations (8); all have a full suite of other software, and can be used for any applications. Assistance provided for GIS is similar to our in-depth assistance for all questions.

264 *East Lansing, MI*

Michigan State University

Main Library
Map Library
100 Library W308
East Lansing, MI 48854
Telephone: 517-432-6277
Email: weessie2@msu.edu
Web: www.lib.msu.edu/coll/main/maps/index.htm
Personnel:
Responsible person: Kathleen Weessies, Head, *email:*
weessie2@msu.edu
FTE para-professionals: 0.5
Number of student workers hours per week: 97
Holdings:
Geographic strengths: Michigan, Canada, Africa
Subject strengths: aeronautical, agriculture, modern
cartography, city, forestry, geospatial data, land ownership, land use, nautical charts
Map depositories and percentages: USGS topos
(100%), USGS other (50%), Department of Transportation, NOAA, GPO, CIA, National Forest Service, NIMA topos, NIMA nautical, NIMA aeronautical, BLM, State, United Nations, EU
200,000 printed maps
25 manuscript maps
50 wall maps
500 microfiche
15 satellite images
10 globes
450 gazetteers
3,000 printed atlases
500 books
10 active serials
10 inactive serials
500 CD-ROMs
30 computer programs
Collecting digital data
Chronological coverage:
1900–1939: 20%
1940–present: 75%
Average budget over the last 5 years: $5,500
Access:
Maps in separate area
Collection is open to the public
Reference questions per year: 600
Answers email questions
Patrons per month: 45
Hours:
Total hours per week opened: 91
Interlibrary loan available
Geographic Information Systems:
GIS services available by appointment
GIS software: ArcGIS

GIS assistance available for Census mapping
Assistance finding data sets available
Scans maps for patrons
Collection services:
Maps classified: 95%
Datasets are cataloged
Classification schemes: LC, Other (AGS)
Cataloging utilities: OCLC
Catalog accessibility: online, cards
Preservation techniques: encapsulation, deacidifica-
tion, tape, boxes
Items that have gone through the preservation process:
30%
Physical facilities:
Internet access available
Square footage: 7,500
Number of map cases: 156
Number of vertical files (file cabinets): 12
Linear book shelving: 240 ft.
Linear atlas shelving: 330 ft.
Copying facilities available: copier, color copier, mi-
croform copier

265 *Flint, MI*

Flint District Library

Flint Public Library
Maps
1026 East Kearsley
Flint, MI 48502
Telephone: 810-232-7111
Fax: 810-249-2635
Web: www.flint.lib.mi.us
Personnel:
Responsible person: Grace Tucker, Head of Reference,
email: gtucker@flint.lib.mi.us
Holdings:
Geographic strengths: Genesee County, Michigan
Special collections: Sanborn Fire Insurance maps
Subject strengths: aerial photos, aeronautical, agricul-
ture, modern cartography, celestial, climatology, city,
economic geography, genealogy, geodetic surveys,
geology, geospatial data, historical geography, hydrology, industries, land ownership, land use, language, map catalogs, map collecting, military, mineral resources, mining, nautical charts, political
geography, population, projections, railroads, recreation, religion, roads, satellite imagery, soil, travel
books, vegetation, views, waterways, zoogeography
Map depositories: USGS topos, USGS geology maps,
USGS other, NOAA, GPO, CIA, National Forest
Service, NIMA topos, NIMA nautical, NIMA aeronautical, BLM, State, United Nations
1,000 printed maps

Access:

Collection is open to the public

Reference questions per year: 125

Answers email questions

Patrons per month: 12

Hours:

Monday–Friday: 9 A.M.–9 P.M.

Saturday: 9 A.M.–6 P.M.

Total hours per week opened: 63

Maps circulate

Circulation policies apply

Map circulation duration: 3 week

Atlas circulation duration: 3 week

Book circulation duration: 3 week

Number of maps circulated annually: 1,000

Interlibrary loan available

Geographic Information Systems:

GIS assistance available for Census mapping, geocoding, and image analysis

Scans maps for patrons

Collection services:

Maps cataloged: 100%

Maps classified: 100%

Maps in OPAC: 100%

Datasets are cataloged

Classification schemes: SuDocs, Dewey

Cataloging utilities: OCLC

Catalog accessibility: online

Physical facilities:

Internet access available

Copying facilities available: copier, color copier, large-format copier, microform copier

266 *Grand Rapids, MI*

Grand Rapids Public Library

Grand Rapids History and Special Collections Center (GRHSCC)

111 Library Street NE

Grand Rapids, MI 49503

Telephone: 616-988-5400

Fax: 616-988-5421

Email: mi@grpl.org

Web: www.grpl.org

Personnel:

Responsible person: Rebecca Mayne, Archivist, *email:* rmayne@grpl.org

FTE professionals: 0.05

Holdings:

Geographic strengths: Grand Rapids, Kent County, Michigan

Special collections: Sanborn Fire Insurance maps of Grand Rapids, Michigan Railroads

Map depositories: USGS

1,500 printed maps

200 aerial photos

60 atlases

25 books

Access:

Hours:

Monday–Thursday: 9 A.M.–9 P.M.

Friday–Saturday: 9 A.M.–5:30 P.M.

Sunday: 1 P.M.–5 P.M.

Collection services:

Maps cataloged: 0%

Maps classified: 90%

Maps in OPAC: 0%

Classification schemes: SuDocs, Local

Physical facilities:

Maps in separate area

Public computers: 6

Map cases: 9

Vertical files: 1

267 *Houghton, MI*

Michigan Technological University

J.R. Van Pelt Library

Map Room

1400 Townsend Drive

Houghton, MI 49931

Telephone: 906-487-2698

Fax: 906-487-2357

Web: www.lib.mtu.edu

Personnel:

Responsible person: Joan Goodbody, Government Documents Coordinator/Instruction/Reference Librarian, *email:* goodbody@mtu.edu

FTE professionals: 0.25   *FTE para-professionals:* 0.25

Number of student works: 1

Number of student workers hours per week: 2

Holdings:

Geographic strengths: Keweenaw, Upper Peninsula of Michigan, Great Lakes

Subject strengths: early cartography, climatology, city, economic geography, forestry, geodetic surveys, geology, geospatial data, hydrology, land ownership, land use, mineral resources, mining, nautical charts, roads

Map depositories and percentages: USGS topos (55%), USGS geology maps (90%), USGS other, Department of Transportation, NOAA, GPO, CIA, National Forest Service, NIMA topos, NIMA nautical, NIMA aeronautical, BLM, State, United Nations

100,000 printed maps

21 gazetteers

52 printed atlases

6 manuscript atlases

53 books
Collecting digital data
Chronological coverage:
1800–1899: 2%
1900–1939: 20%
1940–present: 88%
Access:
Collection is open to the public
Maps off site: 100%
Reference questions per year: 260
Answers email questions
Maps circulate
Circulation policies apply
Map circulation duration: 3 days
Atlas circulation duration: 17 weeks
Book circulation duration: 17 weeks
Interlibrary loan available
Geographic Information Systems:
Number of public GIS workstations: 21
Collection services:
Maps cataloged: 20%
Datasets are cataloged
Classification schemes: LC, SuDocs, Dewey
Cataloging utilities: OCLC
Catalog accessibility: online
Items that have gone through the preservation process: 1%
Physical facilities:
Internet access available
Copying facilities available: copier, color copier, large-format copier, microform copier
Notes: At this time, we are in flux. I am in the process of decreasing the numbers in the collection. Currently, all maps are stored off-site until construction is done.

268 *Kalamazoo, MI*

Kalamazoo Public Library

Central Branch
Adult Services/History Room
315 South Rose St
Kalamazoo, MI 49009
Telephone: 269-553-7801
Fax: 269-342-0414
Web: www.kpl.gov
Personnel:
Responsible person: Kathryn Steadman, Head of Adult Services, *email:* Katy@kpl.gov
Holdings:
Geographic strengths: Kalamazoo County, Michigan
Special collections: Sanborn Fire Insurance maps (Kalamazoo County), Plat maps (Michigan, with emphasis on Kalamazoo County), Historic maps of Kalamazoo County

Subject strengths: city, land ownership, Michigan topographical maps
700 printed maps
Access:
Collection is partially open to the public
Answers email questions
Hours:
Monday–Thursday: 9 A.M.–9 P.M.
Friday: 9 A.M.–6 P.M.
Saturday: 9 A.M.–5 P.M.
Sunday: 1 P.M.–5 P.M.
Total hours per week opened: 69
Circulation policies apply
Atlas circulation duration: 3 weeks
Book circulation duration: 3 weeks
Geographic Information Systems:
Number of public GIS workstations: 10
Collection services:
Classification schemes: SuDocs, Dewey
Cataloging utilities: OCLC, Local
Catalog accessibility: online, cards
Preservation techniques: lamination
Physical facilities:
Internet access available
Other map storage: wall mount
Copying facilities available: copier, large-format copier, microform copier

269 *Kalamazoo, MI*

Western Michigan University

Waldo Library
Map Department
1903 West Michigan Avenue
Kalamazoo, MI 49008
Telephone: 269-387-5047
Email: Michael.McDonnell@wmich.edu
Web: www.wmich.edu/library/depts/maps/index.html
Personnel:
Responsible person: Michael McDonnell, Reference Librarian for Maps and Documents, *email:* michael.mcdonnell@wmich.edu
Assistants: Stefan Sarenius, Coordinator, Maps and Microforms
FTE professionals: 0.1   *FTE para-professionals:* 0.75
Number of student workers hours per week: 12
Holdings:
Geographic strengths: Great Lakes, United States
Subject strengths: aeronautical, modern cartography, climatology, city, geology, historical geography, hydrology, land ownership, map collecting, nautical charts, political geography, population, recreation, roads, soil, waterways

Map depositories and percentages: USGS topos (75%), USGS geology maps (80%), USGS other (50%), Department of Transportation, NOAA, GPO, CIA, National Forest Service

190,000 printed maps

70 gazetteers

600 printed atlases

300 books

20 CD-ROMs

Chronological coverage:
1940–present: 90%

Average budget over the last 5 years: $3,500

Access:

Maps in separate area

Collection is open to the public

Reference questions per year: 500

Answers email questions

Patrons per month: 200

Hours:

Monday–Friday: 8 A.M.–5 P.M.

Saturday: closed

Sunday: 6 P.M.–9 P.M.

Total hours per week opened: 50

Geographic Information Systems:

No GIS services available

Collection services:

Maps cataloged: 25%

Maps classified: 90%

Maps in OPAC: 25%

Classification schemes: LC, SuDocs

Cataloging utilities: OCLC

Catalog accessibility: online

Preservation techniques: encapsulation, acid-free folders

Items that have gone through the preservation process: 10%

Physical facilities:

Internet access available

Square footage: 5,200

Number of map cases: 148

Number of vertical files (file cabinets): 15

Linear book shelving: 570 ft.

Linear atlas shelving: 432 ft.

Copying facilities available: copier, color copier, large-format copier, microform copier

270 *Lansing, MI*

Library of Michigan

Public Services

702 West Kalamazoo

Lansing, MI 48909

Telephone: 517-373-1300

Fax: 517-373-5853

Email: librarian@michigan.gov

Web: michigan.gov/libraryofmichigan

Personnel:

Responsible person: Leelyn Johnson, Reference/Federal Documents Coordinator, *email:* ljohnson@michigan.gov

FTE professionals: 0.5

Holdings:

Geographic strengths: Michigan, Great Lakes

Special collections: USGS topographical maps, Sanborn Fire Insurance maps, Michigan Census Tract maps, Michigan Highway Department road maps, Trygg Composite Maps of U.S. Land Surveyor's Original Plats and Field Notes

Map depositories: USGS topos, Department of Transportation, NOAA, CIA, National Forest Service, NGA nautical, NGA aeronautical, BLM

9,100 printed maps

1,100 atlases

100 books

Access:

Hours:

Monday–Friday: 8 A.M.–6 P.M.

Saturday: 9 A.M.–5 P.M.

Sunday: 1 P.M.–5 P.M.

Collection services:

Maps cataloged: 85%

Maps classified: 85%

Maps in OPAC: 85%

Classification schemes: LC, SuDocs, Dewey

Physical facilities:

Map cases: 20

271 *Lansing, MI*

State Archives of Michigan

P.O. Box 30740

Lansing, MI 48909

Telephone: 517-373-1408

Fax: 517-241-1658

Email: archives@mi.gov

Web: www.michigan.gov/statearchives

Personnel:

Responsible person: Helen Taylor, Processing Archivist, *email:* archives@mi.gov

Assistants: Mark Harvey, Reference Archivist

Holdings:

Geographic strengths: Michigan

Subject strengths: aerial photos, agriculture, archaeology, forestry, genealogy, geology, hydrology, land ownership, land use, mining, nautical charts, railroads, raised relief models, roads, soil, vegetation, views, waterways

Map depositories and percentages: Department of Transportation, State

300,000 printed maps

200,000 manuscript maps

20 wall maps
10 raised relief maps
200 aerial photos
Chronological coverage:
    Pre-1800: 10%
    1800–1899: 30%
    1900–1939: 30%
    1940–present: 30%

Access:
    Collection is open to the public
    Reference questions per year: 1,000
    Answers email questions
    Patrons per month: 300

Hours:
    Monday–Friday: 10 A.M.–4 P.M.

Geographic Information Systems:
    No GIS services available
    Scans maps for patrons

Collection services:
    Maps cataloged: 80%
    Maps in OPAC: 65%
    Classification schemes: LC
    Cataloging utilities: OCLC
    Catalog accessibility: online
    Preservation techniques: encapsulation
    Items that have gone through the preservation process:
        15%

Physical facilities:
    No Internet access
    Copying facilities available: copier, digital camera

272 *Mount Pleasant, MI*

Central Michigan University

Charles V. Park Library
Founded 1958
300 East Preston Street
Mount Pleasant, MI 48859
Telephone: 989-774-3414
Fax: 989-774-1350
Web: www.cmich.edu/libraries.htm

Personnel:
    Responsible person: David B. Shirley, Documents and
        Map Librarian, *email:* David.B.Shirley@cmich.edu
    FTE professionals: 0.5   *FTE para-professionals:* 0.5
    Number of student workers hours per week: 20

Holdings:
    Geographic strengths: Michigan, United States
    Subject strengths: geology, political geography, popu-
        lation
    Map depositories and percentages: USGS topos (98%),
        USGS geology maps (98%), USGS other (100%),
        GPO, CIA, National Forest Service, NIMA topos, State
    43,908 printed maps
    60 gazetteers

508 printed atlases
100 books
26 CD-ROMs
GIS programs available in GIS Center, Geography De-
    partment computer programs
Chronological coverage:
    1940–present: 98%
Average budget over the last 5 years: $5,000

Access:
    Collection is open to the public
    Answers email questions

Hours:
    Monday–Friday: 8 A.M.–midnight
    Saturday: 9 A.M.–6 P.M.
    Sunday: noon–midnight
    Circulation policies apply
        Atlas circulation duration: 3 weeks
        Book circulation duration: 3 weeks
    Interlibrary loan available

Geographic Information Systems:
    GIS services available by appointment
    Number of public GIS workstations: 380
    GIS assistance available in GIS Center, Geography
        Department
    Plotter available
    Scans maps for patrons

Collection services:
    Maps cataloged: 100%
    Maps classified: 100%
    Maps in OPAC: 100%
    Datasets are cataloged
    Classification schemes: LC
    Cataloging utilities: OCLC
    Catalog accessibility: online
    Preservation techniques: encapsulation, lamination

Physical facilities:
    Internet access available
    Number of public computers: 20
    Number of public printers: 4
    Number of map cases: 120
    Number of vertical files (file cabinets): 20
    Linear book shelving: 32 ft.
    Linear atlas shelving: 162 ft.
    Number of microform printers: 2
    Copying facilities available: copier, color copier, large-
        format copier, microform copier

Notes: Map collection is housed in semicircular area on
2nd floor of new library addition.

273 *Ypsilanti, MI*

Eastern Michigan University

Bruce T. Halle Library
Maps, founded 1965
Ypsilanti, MI 48197

Telephone: 734-487-0020 x2115, x2116
Fax: 734-487-8861
Email: joanne.hansen@emich.edu
Web: www.emich.edu/halle
Personnel:
Responsible person: Joanne Hansen, Map Librarian,
email: joanne.hansen@emich.edu
Assistants: Diane Browning, Map Assistant
FTE professionals: 0.5
Number of student workers hours per week: 10
Holdings:
Special collections: Tourist and Road Map File cover-
ing all countries (37,500 items)
Map depositories and percentages: USGS topos (85%),
USGS geology maps (100%), USGS other (100%),
NOAA, GPO, CIA, National Forest Service, NIMA
topos, NIMA nautical, NIMA aeronautical, BLM,
State, Michigan Wetlands
54,651 printed maps
26 raised relief maps
1,796 microfiche
200 satellite images
220 gazetteers
2,458 printed atlases
25 books
30 CD-ROMs
Chronological coverage:
1940–present: 94%
Access:
Maps in separate area
Collection is partially open to the public
Answers email questions
Hours:
Monday–Wednesday: 8 A.M.–6 P.M.
Thursday–Friday: 8 A.M.–5 P.M.
Total hours per week opened: 48
Geographic Information Systems:
GIS services available in an open environment
Number of public GIS workstations: 355
Number of GIS stations (not monitored): 22
Plotter available
Scans maps for patrons
Collection services:
Maps cataloged: 99%
Maps classified: 99%
Maps in OPAC: 85%
Datasets are cataloged
Classification schemes: LC, SuDocs, Local
Cataloging utilities: OCLC, Local
Catalog accessibility: online, cards
Preservation techniques: encapsulation, lamination,
acid free tape
Physical facilities:
Internet access available
Square footage: 1,168

Number of map cases: 64
Number of vertical files (file cabinets): 23
Linear book shelving: 162 ft.
Linear atlas shelving: 363 ft.
Other map storage: 13 horizontal map drawers
Copying facilities available: copier, color copier, large-
format copier, microform copier
Notes: While the maps and atlases in the map room do not
circulate, we have the maps and items in the tourist and
road map file and a circulating collection of atlases of
approximately 650 that do and would be available for
ILL.

274 *Bemidji, MN*

Bemidji State University

Map Library
HS 244
Bemidji, MN 56601
Telephone: 218-755-2804
Fax: 218-755-2822
Web: www.bemidjistate.edu/library
Personnel:
Responsible person: Dr. Michael Garrett, *email:*
mgarrett@bemidjistate.edu
Number of student workers hours per week: 30
Holdings:
Geographic strengths: United States, Great Britain
Subject strengths: early cartography, modern cartogra-
phy, climatology, city, economic geography, forestry,
geology, land use, nautical charts, political geogra-
phy, population, raised relief models, religion, roads,
soil, travel books, vegetation
Map depositories: USGS topos, State
48,000 printed maps
160 wall maps
22 raised relief maps
15 globes
10 printed atlases
Chronological coverage:
1900–1939: 25%
1940–present: 70%
Access:
Maps in separate area
Collection is open to the public
Hours:
Monday–Friday: 9 A.M.–5 P.M.
Total hours per week opened: 40
Maps circulate
Circulation policies apply
Map circulation duration: 2 days
Geographic Information Systems:
No GIS services available
Collection services:

Maps cataloged: 80%
Datasets are cataloged
Classification schemes: LC
Cataloging utilities: Local
Catalog accessibility: cards, printout
Physical facilities:
No Internet access
Square footage: 1,200
Number of map cases: 45
Copying facilities available: none

275 *Chisholm, MN*

Iron Range Research Center

Maps, founded 1979
801 SW Highway 169
Suite 1
Chisholm, MN 55719
Telephone: 218-254-7959
Fax: 218-254-7971
Email: aimee.brown@ironworld.com
Web: www.ironrangeresearchcenter.org
Personnel:
Responsible person: Aimee Brown, Archivist, *email:* aimee.brown@ironworld.com
Holdings:
Geographic strengths: Minnesota Iron Range
Special collections: Sanborn Fire Insurance, early state atlases and plat maps, mine cross-sections, regional geology, underground mine excavations
Subject strengths: aerial photos, city, economic geography, engineering, forestry, genealogy, geodetic surveys, geology, geospatial data, historical geography, industries, land ownership, land use, map catalogs, mineral resources, mining
10,000 printed maps
5,000 microfilms
Chronological coverage:
1900–1939: 48%
1940–present: 50%
Access:
Collection is paged
Answers email questions
Hours:
Monday–Friday: 8 A.M.–4:30 P.M.
Total hours per week opened: 40
Collection services:
Classification schemes: LC
Cataloging utilities: OCLC, Local
Catalog accessibility: online
Preservation techniques: encapsulation, deacidification
Physical facilities:
No Internet access
Square footage: 1,500
Number of map cases: 58

Number of microform readers: 11
Copying facilities available: copier

276 *Collegeville, MN*

Saint John's University

Alcuin Library
Collegeville, MN 56321
Telephone: 320-363-2122
Fax: 320-363-2126
Web: www.csbsju.edu/library
Personnel:
Responsible person: Jim Parsons, Associate Director for Public Services, *email:* jparsons@csbsju.edu
Assistants: Paul Jasmer
FTE professionals: 0.2   *FTE para-professionals:* 0.2
Holdings:
Geographic strengths: Minnesota
Map depositories: USGS topos, CIA
16,000 printed maps
200 atlases
500 books
100 CD-ROMs
Access:
Hours:
Monday–Thursday: 8 A.M.–midnight
Friday: 8 A.M.–10 P.M.
Saturday: 10 A.M.–10 P.M.
Sunday: 10 A.M.–midnight
Items circulate
Interlibrary loan available
Collection services:
Maps cataloged: 95%
Maps classified: 100%
Maps in OPAC: 95%
Classification schemes: LC, SuDocs
Physical facilities:
Public computers: 12
Map cases: 14
Notes: Our library is actually the Joint Libraries of the College of St. Benedict and St. John's University.

277 *Duluth, MN*

University of Minnesota, Duluth

Library
416 Library Drive
Duluth, MN 55812-3001
Telephone: 218-726-8100
Fax: 218-726-6205
Email: tzogg@d.umn.edu
Web: www.d.umn.edu/lib/
Personnel:
Responsible person: Thomas R. Zogg, Geography Librarian, *email:* tzogg@d.umn.edu

Holdings:

Geographic strengths: Minnesota, Wisconsin

Subject strengths: aeronautical, geology, hydrology, land ownership, land use, nautical charts, oceanography, political geography, roads, satellite imagery, soil, topographic

Map depositories and percentages: USGS topos, Department of Transportation, NOAA, GPO

3,000 printed maps

100 printed atlases

Chronological coverage:
   1940–present: 100%

Average budget over the last 5 years: $50

Access:

Collection is open to the public

Reference questions per year: 100

Answers email questions

Patrons per month: 100

Hours:

Monday–Thursday: 7:30–midnight

Friday: 7 A.M.–7 P.M.

Saturday: 9 A.M.–5 P.M.

Sunday: noon–midnight

Total hours per week opened: 97.5

Maps circulate

Circulation policies apply

   Map circulation duration: 4 weeks

   Number of maps circulated annually: 100

Interlibrary loan available

Geographic Information Systems:

No GIS services available

Number of public GIS workstations: 20

Collection services:

Maps cataloged: 10%

Maps classified: 1%

Maps in OPAC: 10%

Datasets are cataloged

Classification schemes: LC, SuDocs

Cataloging utilities: OCLC

Catalog accessibility: online

Physical facilities:

Internet access available

Square footage: 100

Linear atlas shelving: 30 ft.

Copying facilities available: copier, color copier, large-format copier, microform copier, computer print stations

Notes: Map collection is part of reference area that includes general reference and federal government documents areas. Atlases are partly in general reference collection, and government documents maps are partly in government documents area; both are adjacent to visible map case/atlas stand/vertical files/three CD-ROM stations that do form a loosely definable maps/atlases area.

278 *Mankato, MN*

Minnesota State University, Mankato

Memorial Library

P.O. Box 8419

Mankato, MN 56002-8419

Telephone: 507-389-5952

Fax: 507-389-5155

Web: www.lib.mnsu.edu

Personnel:

Responsible person: Evan Rusch, Government Documents/Instruction Librarian, *email:* evan.rusch@mnsu.edu

Assistants: Harry Perkins, Maps/Government Documents Technician

Number of student workers hours per week: 20

Holdings:

Geographic strengths: Minnesota

Special collections: Sanborn Fire Insurance maps for Minnesota, FEMA Flood Insurance Rate maps, Minnesota Lake maps, Minnesota Recreational maps, Minnesota Aerial Photos

Subject strengths: aerial photos, agriculture, modern cartography, celestial, climatology, city, economic geography, forestry, geodetic surveys, geology, geospatial data, historical geography, hydrology, industries, land ownership, land use, mineral resources, oceanography, political geography, population, projections, railroads, raised relief models, recreation, roads, soil, travel books, vegetation, waterways

Map depositories and percentages: USGS topos (99%), USGS geology maps (65%), USGS other (65%), Department of Transportation, NOAA, GPO, CIA, National Forest Service, NIMA topos, NIMA nautical, NIMA aeronautical, BLM

80,000 printed maps

57 wall maps

40 raised relief maps

128 microfilms

24,000 aerial photos

10 satellite images

22 globes

70 gazetteers

900 printed atlases

300 books

Chronological coverage:
   1900–1939: 15%
   1940–present: 84%

Average budget over the last 5 years: $1,700

Access:

Collection is open to the public

Reference questions per year: 400

Answers email questions

Hours:

Total hours per week opened: 93

Maps circulate
Circulation policies apply
  Map circulation duration: 3 weeks
  Book circulation duration: 3 weeks
Interlibrary loan available

Geographic Information Systems:
No GIS services available

Collection services:
Maps cataloged: 100%
Maps classified: 100%
Maps in OPAC: 100%
Classification schemes: LC
Cataloging utilities: OCLC
Catalog accessibility: online
Preservation techniques: encapsulation, lamination
Items that have gone through the preservation process: 5%

Physical facilities:
Internet access available
Square footage: 3,300
Number of map cases: 70
Number of atlas stands: 27
Linear book shelving: 228 ft.
Other map storage: 2 rolled map cases
Number of stereoscopes: 10
Copying facilities available: copier, color copier, microform copier

279 *Minneapolis, MN*

East View Cartographic, Inc.

Corporate Library
3020 Harbor Lane North
Minneapolis, MN 55447-8956
Telephone: 763-550-0965
Fax: 763-559-2931
Email: maps@cartographic.com
Web: www.cartographic.com

Personnel:
Responsible person: Xiao-Hong Zhang, GIS/Map Librarian, *email:* xzhang@cartographic.com
Assistants: Geoffrey Forbes, Director of Operations; Lisa Watson, GIS/Map Library Assistant
FTE professionals: 2   *FTE para-professionals:* 1

Holdings:
Geographic strengths: Russia, USSR, Baltic nations, Afghanistan, Japan, Mongolia, China, North Korea, South Korea, Philippines, Australia, India, Iran, Iraq, Egypt, Libya, Somalia, Angola, Sierra Leone, Yugoslavia and the newly independent countries, France, Mexico, Cuba, Haiti, Dominican Republic, Colombia, Brazil, Argentina, Antarctica, Arctic Ocean, Ecuador, Bolivia, Guyana, Trinidad and Tobago, Indonesia, Malaysia, United Arab Emirates, Burma (Myanmar), Taiwan, Botswana, Madagascar, Ethiopia, Eritrea, Kenya, Uganda, Tanzania, Democratic Republic of Congo, Nigeria, Cameroon, Liberia, Syria, Jordan, Saudi Arabia, Greece, Turkey, Israel, Vietnam, Cambodia, Laos, Thailand, New Zealand

Special collections: Russian Topographic maps (global collection, all scales), American Topographic maps (global collection, all scales), Russian nautical charts (global collection, all scales), American nautical charts (global collection, all scales), Russian language cartography book collection

Subject strengths: aeronautical, early cartography, modern cartography, celestial, climatology, city, geodetic surveys, geology, geospatial data, historical geography, industries, language, military, mineral resources, mining, nautical charts, oceanography, political geography, population, railroads, raised relief models, roads, satellite imagery, soil, travel books, waterways

Map depositories: Russian language cartography books
100,000 printed maps
100 manuscript maps
200 wall maps
200 raised relief maps
200 microfiche
100 microfilms
30,000 aerial photos
1,000 satellite images
3 globes
100 gazetteers
100 printed atlases
1,000 books
50 active serials
50 inactive serials
6,000 CD-ROMs
10 computer programs
Collecting digital data
Chronological coverage:
  1900–1939: 2%
  1940–present: 98%

Access:
Maps in separate area
Collection is partially open to the public
Reference questions per year: 4,000
Answers email questions
Patrons per month: 10

Hours:
Monday–Friday: 9 A.M.–5 P.M.
Saturday–Saturday: closed
Total hours per week opened: 40

Geographic Information Systems:
GIS services available by appointment
GIS software: MapInfo, ArcIMS, ArcGIS
Number of GIS stations (monitored): 15

GIS assistance available for geocoding
GIS assistance available for image analysis
DEM creation and vectorizing assistance available
Plotter available
Scans maps for patrons

Collection services:

Maps cataloged: 70%

Maps classified: 10%

Maps in OPAC: 60%

Datasets are cataloged

Classification schemes: LC, Local

Cataloging utilities: OCLC, Local

Catalog accessibility: online, EVC vector index

Physical facilities:

Internet access available

Square footage: 1,000

Number of public computers: 0

Number of staff computers: 30

Number of vertical files (file cabinets): 3

Number of atlas stands: 1

Linear book shelving: 250 ft.

Linear atlas shelving: 20 ft.

Other map storage: 5 rolled map cases

Number of microform readers: 1

Copying facilities available: copier, color copier, large-format copier, microform copier, scanner

280 *Minneapolis, MN*

Minneapolis Public Library

300 Nicollet Mall
Minneapolis, MN 55401
Telephone: 612-630-6000
Fax: 612-630-6220
Email: askus@mplib.org
Web: www.mplib.org

Personnel:

Responsible person: Helen Burke, Government Documents Coordinator, *email:* hburke@mplib.org

Assistants: Carrie Brunsberg, Librarian II

Holdings:

Geographic strengths: Minneapolis, Minnesota, United States

Special collections: Sanborn Fire Insurance maps, Historic Minneapolis Real Property

Subject strengths: city, genealogy, geology, land ownership, military, recreation, roads, soil, travel books, waterways

Map depositories and percentages: USGS topos (100%), CIA, National Forest Service, NIMA nautical

100,000 printed maps

50 gazetteers

1,500 printed atlases

40 CD-ROMs

Chronological coverage:

1800–1899: 10%
1900–1939: 15%
1940–present: 75%

Access:

Collection is partially open to the public

Reference questions per year: 200

Answers email questions

Patrons per month: 16

Hours:

Monday–Saturday: 10 A.M.–5 P.M.
Total hours per week opened: 40

Maps circulate

Circulation policies apply

Map circulation duration: 3 weeks

Atlas circulation duration: 3 weeks

Book circulation duration: 3 weeks

Geographic Information Systems:

No GIS services available

Scans maps for patrons

Collection services:

Maps cataloged: 25%

Maps classified: 75%

Maps in OPAC: 50%

Classification schemes: LC, SuDocs, Local

Cataloging utilities: OCLC

Catalog accessibility: online, cards, printout

Preservation techniques: encapsulation, deacidification, lamination

Physical facilities:

Internet access available

Number of map cases: 15

Copying facilities available: copier, microform copier

281 *Minneapolis, MN*

University of Minnesota

O.M. Wilson Library
John R. Borchert Map Library, founded 1945
309 19th Avenue South
Minneapolis, MN 55455
Telephone: 612-624-4549
Fax: 612-626-9353
Email: mapref@umn.edu
Web: map.lib.umn.edu

Personnel:

Responsible person: Brent Allison, Director, *email:* b-alli@umn.edu

Assistants: Hallie Pritchett, Library Assistant III

Number of student workers hours per week: 120

Holdings:

Geographic strengths: Minnesota, Upper Midwest, North America, Canada, Scandinavia

Special collections: Ames Library of South Asia map collection (700 pre-1900 maps of south Asia)

Subject strengths: aerial photos, aeronautical, agriculture, archaeology, biology, early cartography, modern cartography, celestial, climatology, city, economic geography, engineering, forestry, genealogy, geodetic surveys, geology, geospatial data, historical geography, hydrology, industries, land ownership, land use, map catalogs, map collecting, military, mineral resources, mining, nautical charts, political geography, population, projections, railroads, recreation, roads, soil, vegetation, views, waterways

Map depositories and percentages: USGS topos (100%), Department of Transportation, NOAA, GPO, CIA, National Forest Service, NIMA topos, NIMA nautical, NIMA aeronautical, State, Canadian topographic maps

335,481 printed maps
41 manuscript maps
12 raised relief maps
5,037 microfiche
48 microfilms
410,545 aerial photos
24 satellite images
18 globes
1,125 gazetteers
9,568 printed atlases
4,822 books
35 active serials
11 inactive serials
1,014 CD-ROMs
72 computer programs
Collecting digital data

Chronological coverage:
  1800–1899: 10%
  1900–1939: 35%
  1940–present: 50%

Average budget over the last 5 years: $40,000
On-going publications: Minnesota Aerial Photography Index; Minnesota County Plat Books

Access:

Maps in separate area
Collection is open to the public
Reference questions per year: 15,000
Answers email questions
Patrons per month: 2,000

Hours:

Monday–Wednesday: 9 A.M.–8 P.M.
Thursday–Friday: 9 A.M.–5 P.M.
Saturday: 1 P.M.–5 P.M.
Sunday: closed
Total hours per week opened: 53

Maps circulate
Circulation policies apply
  Map circulation duration: 2 weeks
  Atlas circulation duration: 1 month
  Book circulation duration: 1 month

Number of maps circulated annually: 50
Number of books circulated annually: 725
Number of other items circulated annually: 15,880
  (aerial photos)
Interlibrary loan available

Geographic Information Systems:

GIS services available in an open environment
Number of public GIS workstations: 10
Number of GIS stations (not monitored): 10
GIS assistance available for Census mapping, geocoding, and image analysis
Plotter available
Scans maps for patrons

Collection services:

Maps cataloged: 100%
Maps classified: 75%
Maps in OPAC: 75%
Datasets are cataloged
Classification schemes: LC
Cataloging utilities: OCLC, RLG, Local
Catalog accessibility: online, cards
Preservation techniques: encapsulation, lamination
Items that have gone through the preservation process:
  15%

Physical facilities:

Internet access available
Square footage: 8,916
Number of public computers: 11
Number of map cases: 240
Linear book shelving: 820 ft.
Linear atlas shelving: 2,085 ft.
Copying facilities available: copier, color copier, microform copier

282 *Minneapolis, MN*

University of Minnesota

Science and Engineering Library
Geologic Map Collection
206 Walter Library
117 Pleasant Street SE
Minneapolis, MN 55455
Telephone: 612-624-0224
Email: sciref@umn.edu
Web: sciweb.lib.umn.edu/subject/earthsci.html

Personnel:

Responsible person: Janice Jaguszewski, *email:* j-jagu@umn.edu
Assistants: Robert Filipek
FTE professionals: 0.1   *FTE para-professionals:* 0.2

Holdings:

Geographic strengths: Minnesota and surrounding states
Map depositories: USGS
80,000 printed maps
20 atlases

Access:

Hours:

Monday–Friday: 8 A.M.–9 P.M.

Saturday: 9 A.M.–9 P.M.

Sunday: noon–9 P.M.

Items circulate

Collection services:

Maps cataloged: 5%

Maps classified: 5%

Maps in OPAC: 5%

Classification schemes: LC

Physical facilities:

Maps in separate area

Public computers: 47

Map cases: 60

Vertical files: 15

283 *Northfield, MN*

Carleton College

Laurence McKinley Gould Library

Map Collection

One North College Street

Northfield, MN 55057

Telephone: 507-646-4260

Fax: 507-646-4087

Email: csanford@carleton.edu

Web: www.carleton.edu/campus/library/collections/
overview.html#maps

Personnel:

Responsible person: Carolyn Sanford, Head of Reference and Instruction, Documents Librarian, Map Librarian, *email:* csanford@carleton.edu

FTE professionals: 0.2   *FTE para-professionals:* 0.2

Number of student works: 0.5

Holdings:

Geographic strengths: United States

Subject strengths: geology, hydrology, land use

Map depositories and percentages: USGS topos (95%), USGS geology maps (40%), USGS other (25%), NOAA, GPO, CIA, National Forest Service, State, Fish and Wildlife, Minerals Management Service, Census Bureau

80,000 printed maps

1,878 microfiche

155 gazetteers

1,489 printed atlases

8,761 books

84 CD-ROMs

Chronological coverage:

1940–present: 90%

Average budget over the last 5 years: $500

Access:

Collection is open to the public

Answers email questions

Hours:

Monday–Friday: 8 A.M.–1 A.M.

Saturday: 8 A.M.–midnight

Sunday: 10 A.M.–1 A.M.

Total hours per week opened: 116

Maps circulate

Circulation policies apply

Map circulation duration: 10 weeks

Atlas circulation duration: 10 weeks

Book circulation duration: 10 weeks

Number of maps circulated annually: 40

Number of books circulated annually: 1,800

Geographic Information Systems:

No GIS services available

Collection services:

Classification schemes: LC, SuDocs

Cataloging utilities: OCLC

Catalog accessibility: online

Preservation techniques: encapsulation

Items that have gone through the preservation process: 10%

Physical facilities:

Internet access available

Square footage: 2,000

Number of map cases: 141

Number of vertical files (file cabinets): 10

Linear book shelving: 1,583 ft.

Linear atlas shelving: 88 ft.

Copying facilities available: copier, color copier, microform copier

284 *Saint Cloud, MN*

Saint Cloud State University

James W. Miller Learning Resources Center

Government Documents/Maps

720 4th Avenue South

Saint Cloud, MN 56301

Telephone: 320-308-2063

Fax: 320-308-4778

Email: sqwilliams@stcloudstate.edu

Web: lrts.stcloudstate.edu

Personnel:

Responsible person: Sandra Q. Williams, *email:* sqwilliams@stcloudstate.edu

Assistants: Debbie Binsfeld

FTE professionals: 1   *FTE para-professionals:* 1

Holdings:

Geographic strengths: Central States

Map depositories: USGS

70,000 printed maps

2,500 aerial photos

1 globe

1,500 atlases

Access:

Hours:

Monday–Friday: 7:45 A.M.–11:45 P.M.

Saturday: 10 A.M.–5:45 P.M.

Sunday: 1 P.M.–11:45 P.M.

Items circulate

Interlibrary loan available

Collection services:

Maps cataloged: 5%

Maps classified: 5%

Maps in OPAC: 5%

Classification schemes: LC, SuDocs

Physical facilities:

Public computers: 625

Map cases: 24

285 *Saint Cloud, MN*

Stearns History Museum

Research Center and Archives

235 33rd Avenue South

Saint Cloud, MN 56301

Telephone: 320 253-8424

Fax: 320 253-2172

Email: info@stearns-museum.org

Web: www.stearns-museum.org

Personnel:

Responsible person: John Decker, Assistant Director— Archives, *email:* johnd@stearns-museum.org

FTE professionals: 0   *FTE para-professionals:* 0

Holdings:

Geographic strengths: Stearns County

Special collections: Sanborn Fire Insurance maps of Saint Cloud, Minnesota (1893–1966), Stearns County, Minnesota Highway maps (1927–1997)

200 printed maps

750 aerial photos

1 globe

68 atlases

5 books

3 active serials

2 CD-ROMs

Access:

Hours:

Monday–Saturday: 10 A.M.–4 P.M.

Sunday: noon–4 P.M.

Collection services:

Maps cataloged: 80%

Maps classified: 95%

Maps in OPAC: 80%

Classification schemes: LC

Physical facilities:

Public computers: 3

Map cases: 8

286 *Saint Paul, MN*

Minnesota Geological Survey

2642 University Avenue West

Saint Paul, MN 55114-1057

Telephone: 612-627-4780

Fax: 612-627-4778

Email: www.geo.umn.edu/mgs/

Web: www.geo.umn.edu/mgs/

Personnel:

Responsible person: Dr. Harvey Thorleifson, Director, *email:* thorleif@umn.edu

FTE professionals: 0.25

Holdings:

Geographic strengths: Minnesota

Map depositories: USGS

3,000 printed maps

3,000 aerial photos

22 atlases

30 active serials

Collection services:

Maps in OPAC: 0%

Physical facilities:

Maps in separate area

Map cases: 6

Notes: Our library is for staff use only. It is not available to the public.

287 Saint Paul, MN

Minnesota Historical Society

Library and Archives

345 Kellogg Boulevard West

Saint Paul, MN 55102-1906

Telephone: 651-296-2143

Fax: 651-297-7436

Email: reference@mnhs.org

Web: www.mnhs.org

Personnel:

Responsible person: Ruth Bauer Anderson, Reference Archivist, *email:* ruth.anderso@mnhs.org

FTE professionals: 0.5   *FTE para-professionals:* 0.5

Holdings:

Geographic strengths: Minnesota, Midwest, Northwest

Special collections: Sanborn Fire Insurance maps of Minnesota, Fire Underwriters Service Bureau, Great Northern and Northern Pacific Railway Collections, Minnesota State Archives including official state highway maps, Rascher Fire Insurance Maps

Map depositories: USGS

19,277 printed maps

5,700 aerial photos

1 globe

2,027 atlases

750 books

33 active serials

Access:

Hours:

Tuesday: noon–8 P.M.

Wednesday–Saturday: 9 A.M.–4 P.M.

Sunday: closed

Collection services:

Maps cataloged: 60%

Maps classified: 60%

Maps in OPAC: 60%

Classification schemes: LC, SuDocs

Physical facilities:

Maps in separate area

Public computers: 14

Map cases: 25

Vertical files: 1

288 *Saint Paul, MN*

Saint Paul Public Library

Central Library

90 West 4th Street

Saint Paul, MN 55102

Telephone: 651-266-7000

Fax: 651-266-7011

Web: www.sppl.org

Personnel:

Responsible person: Phyllis Kendig, Government Documents Librarian, *email:* phyllis.kendig@ci.stpaul.mn.us

Assistants: Erin Zolotukin-Ridgeway, Librarian I

FTE professionals: 0.07   *FTE para-professionals:* 0.02

Holdings:

Geographic strengths: St. Paul, Minnesota

Map depositories: USGS

2,600 printed maps

1 aerial photo

120 atlases

50 books

1 active serial

15 CD-ROMs

Access:

Hours:

Monday: 11:30 A.M.–8 P.M.

Tuesday–Wednesday: 9 A.M.–5:30 P.M.

Thursday: 9 A.M.–8 P.M.

Friday: 9 A.M.–5:30 P.M.

Saturday: 11 P.M.–4 P.M.

Interlibrary loan available

Collection services:

Maps cataloged: 5%

Maps classified: 100%

Maps in OPAC: 5%

Classification schemes: LC, SuDocs, Local

Physical facilities:

Public computers: 16

Map cases: 2

289 *Saint Peter, MN*

Gustavus Adolphus College

Bob Moline Map Library

800 West College Avenue

Saint Peter, MN 56082

Telephone: 507-933-7313

Fax: 507-933-7041

Email: bdouglas@gac.edu

Web: www.gustavus.edu/library

Personnel:

Responsible person: Bob Douglas, Professor of Geography, *email:* bdouglas@gac.edu

Assistants: Emily Grimshaw, Map Librarian

FTE professionals: 1   *FTE para-professionals:* 1

Holdings:

Geographic strengths: West, United States, Asia, Europe

Special collections: Japanese City Plans, Bureau of Soils

Map depositories: USGS topos, NOAA, CIA, National Forest Service, NGA nautical, NGA aeronautical, BLM

80,000 printed maps

5,000 aerial photos

10 globes

50 atlases

25 books

Access:

Hours:

Monday–Friday: 9 A.M.–noon, 2 P.M.–4 P.M.

Items circulate

Collection services:

Maps cataloged: 35%

Maps classified: 100%

Maps in OPAC: 0%

Classification schemes: LC

Physical facilities:

Maps in separate area

Public computers: 1

Map cases: 80

Vertical files: 9

290 *Joplin, MO*

Missouri Southern State University, Joplin

George A. Spiva Library

Tri-State Mining Collection, founded 1950

3950 East Newman Road

Joplin, MO 64801

Telephone: 417-625-9552

Fax: 417-625-9734

Email: nodler-c@mssu.edu

Web: www.mssu.edu/spivalib

Personnel:

Responsible person: Charles Nodler, Archivist, *email:* nodler-c@mail.mssu.edu

Number of student workers hours per week: 25

Number of volunteer hours per month: 11

Holdings:

Geographic strengths: Missouri, Kansas, Oklahoma

Special collections: Sanborn Fire Insurance maps

Subject strengths: aerial photos, biology, modern cartography, caves, city, geology, historical geography, industries, land ownership, land use, map catalogs, map collecting, mineral resources, mining, political geography, population, railroads, roads, soil, views, waterways

Map depositories: USGS topos, USGS geology maps, USGS other, GPO, NIMA topos, State

7,000 printed maps

700 books

Chronological coverage:
  1900–1939: 60%
  1940–present: 35%

On-going publications: Southern Footnotes Newsletter

Access:

Maps in separate area

Collection is open to the public

Reference questions per year: 200

Answers email questions

Patrons per month: 15

Hours:

  Total hours per week opened: 40

Circulation policies apply

Geographic Information Systems:

No GIS services available

Scans maps for patrons

Collection services:

Maps cataloged: 100%

Classification schemes: Local

Cataloging utilities: OCLC

Catalog accessibility: online

Preservation techniques: acid-free tape repair

Items that have gone through the preservation process: 50%

Physical facilities:

No Internet access

Copying facilities available: copier, microform copier

Notes: Our maps primarily document—*100 years of Lead and Zinc Mining in the Tri-State Area of SW Missouri, SE Kansas, and NE Oklahoma.*

291 *Rolla, MO*

University of Missouri, Rolla

Curtis Laws Wilson Library
A. C. Spreng Map Room
1870 Miner Circle
Rolla, MO 65409
Telephone: 573-341-4007
Fax: 573-341-4233
Web: campus.umr.edu/library
Holdings:

Geographic strengths: Missouri

Subject strengths: geology

Map depositories: USGS topos, USGS geology maps, USGS other, GPO, CIA, BLM

100,000 printed maps

65 printed atlases

294 CD-ROMs

Collecting digital data

Chronological coverage:
  1900–1939: 20%
  1940–present: 78%

Access:

Maps in separate area

Collection is open to the public

Reference questions per year: 35

Answers email questions

Patrons per month: 10

Hours:

  Monday–Sunday: 8 A.M.–midnight
  Total hours per week opened: 110

Maps circulate

Circulation policies apply

  Map circulation duration: 2 weeks

Interlibrary loan available

Geographic Information Systems:

GIS services available by appointment

GIS software: ArcView/Landat

GIS assistance available for Census mapping

Collection services:

Maps cataloged: 10%

Maps classified: 10%

Maps in OPAC: 10%

Classification schemes: LC, Dewey, Local

Cataloging utilities: OCLC

Catalog accessibility: online

Preservation techniques: encapsulation, cartex

Items that have gone through the preservation process: 2%

Physical facilities:

No Internet access

Square footage: 737

Number of map cases: 56

Number of vertical files (file cabinets): 13

Other map storage: 1 rolled map case

Copying facilities available: copier, microform copier

292 *Saint Louis, MO*

Saint Louis Public Library

Founded 1866
1301 Olive Street
Saint Louis, MO 63103
Telephone: 314-241-2288
Fax: 314-539-0393
Web: www.slpl.lib.mo.us

Personnel:

Responsible person: Joseph M. Winkler, Manager, Research Collections, *email:* jwinkler@slpl.lib.mo.us

FTE professionals: 0.05   *FTE para-professionals:* 0.1

Holdings:

Geographic strengths: United States, Europe, East Asia

Subject strengths: city, genealogy, historical geography, roads, travel books, Topographic

Map depositories and percentages: USGS topos (100%), GPO, CIA, National Forest Service, State

125,000 printed maps

20 wall maps

2,500 microfiche

200 gazetteers

800 printed atlases

400 books

40 CD-ROMs

Chronological coverage:

1900–1939: 20%

1940–present: 75%

Average budget over the last 5 years: $1,600

Access:

Maps in separate area

Collection is partially open to the public

Reference questions per year: 600

Answers email questions

Patrons per month: 30

Hours:

Monday: 10 A.M.–9 P.M.

Tuesday–Friday: 10 A.M.–6 P.M.

Saturday: 9 A.M.–5 P.M.

Total hours per week opened: 51

Maps circulate

Circulation policies apply

Map circulation duration: 3 weeks

Atlas circulation duration: 3 weeks

Book circulation duration: 3 weeks

Number of maps circulated annually: 200

Number of books circulated annually: 100

Geographic Information Systems:

No GIS services available

Collection services:

Maps cataloged: 0.01%

Maps classified: 99%

Maps in OPAC: 0.01%

Classification schemes: LC, SuDocs

Cataloging utilities: Local

Catalog accessibility: stand-alone file

Preservation techniques: encapsulation, cloth backing (not current)

Physical facilities:

No Internet access

Square footage: 1,500

Number of map cases: 30

Number of vertical map cases: 19

Number of vertical files (file cabinets): 11

Linear book shelving: 180 ft.

Linear atlas shelving: 300 ft.

Copying facilities available: copier, color copier, microform copier

293 *Saint Louis, MO*

Saint Louis University

Pius XII Memorial Library

3650 Lindell Blvd

Saint Louis, MO 63108

Telephone: 314-977-3590

Email: montrejr@slu.edu

Web: www.slu.edu/libraries/pius/

Personnel:

Responsible person: John Montre, *email:* montrejr@slu.edu

Holdings:

Geographic strengths: Missouri

Special collections: Missouri (1925–present), Illinois (1925–present)

Map depositories and percentages: USGS topos (10%), GPO

100,000 printed maps

500 aerial photos

100 satellite images

60 gazetteers

200 printed atlases

Chronological coverage:

1900–1939: 50%

1940–present: 50%

Access:

Collection is open to the public

Answers email questions

Patrons per month: 20

Hours:

Monday–Friday: 8:30 A.M.–5 P.M.

Geographic Information Systems:

No GIS services available

Physical facilities:

No Internet access

Number of map cases: 47

Number of vertical map cases: 10

Copying facilities available: copier, color copier, microform copier

294 *Saint Louis, MO*

Washington University

Earth and Planetary Sciences Library

One Brookings Drive

Saint Louis, MO 63130

Telephone: 314-935-5406

Fax: 314-935-4800

Email: eps@wulib.wustl.edu

Web: library.wustl.edu

Personnel:

Responsible person: Clara McLeod, EPSc Librarian, *email:* c P.M.cleod@wulib.wustl.edu

Assistants: Cheryl Moten

FTE professionals: 1   *FTE para-professionals:* 1

Holdings:

Geographic strengths: Missouri, United States

Map depositories: USGS topos, Department of Transportation, CIA, National Forest Service, NGA nautical, NGA aeronautical, BLM

113,000 printed maps

200 aerial photos

2 globes

150 atlases

40 CD-ROMs

Access:

Hours:

Monday–Friday: 8:30 A.M.–9 P.M.

Sunday: noon–3 P.M.

Collection services:

Maps classified: 100%

Maps in OPAC: 50%

Classification schemes: LC, SuDocs, Local

Physical facilities:

Maps in separate area

Public computers: 1

Map cases: 50

Vertical files: 13

295 *Springfield, MO*

Southwest Missouri State University

Duane G. Meyer Library

Maps, founded 1980

901 South National #175

Springfield, MO 65804

Telephone: 417-836-4534

Fax: 417-836-6799

Web: library.smsu.edu/meyer/maps/index.shtml

Personnel:

Responsible person: Jim Coombs, Map Librarian, *email:* jac324f@smsu.edu

Assistants: Amy Hankins, Maps Library Associate

FTE para-professionals: 1

Number of student workers hours per week: 20

Holdings:

Geographic strengths: Ozark Mountains, Missouri

Subject strengths: aerial photos, caves, recreation, travel books

Map depositories and percentages: USGS topos (100%), USGS geology maps (100%), USGS other (100%), NOAA, GPO, CIA, National Forest Service, NIMA topos, NIMA aeronautical, BLM, State, United Nations

121,000 printed maps

25 manuscript maps

18 wall maps

1,175 microfiche

55,000 aerial photos

12 globes

10 gazetteers

783 printed atlases

400 books

Chronological coverage:

1940–present: 94%

Access:

Collection is open to the public

Answers email questions

Patrons per month: 7,423

Hours:

Monday–Thursday: 7 A.M.–midnight

Friday: 7 A.M.–6 P.M.

Saturday: 10 A.M.–6 P.M.

Sunday: noon–midnight

Total hours per week opened: 99

Maps circulate

Circulation policies apply

Map circulation duration: 2 weeks

Atlas circulation duration: 2 weeks

Book circulation duration: 2 weeks

Number of maps circulated annually: 1,132

Number of books circulated annually: 600

Interlibrary loan available

Geographic Information Systems:

GIS services available by appointment

GIS software: MapArt

General GIS questions answered

Scans maps for patrons

Collection services:

Maps cataloged: 30%

Maps classified: 90%

Maps in OPAC: 90%

Classification schemes: LC

Cataloging utilities: OCLC

Catalog accessibility: online

Preservation techniques: encapsulation

Physical facilities:

Internet access available

Number of map cases: 75

Number of vertical files (file cabinets): 19

Linear book shelving: 24 ft.

Number of stereoscopes: 20

Copying facilities available: copier, color copier, large-format copier, microform copier

296 *Bozeman, MT*

Montana State University, Bozeman

Roland R. Renne Library

The Libraries

P.O. Box 173320
Bozeman, MT 59717-3320
Telephone: 406-994-3171
Fax: 406-994-2851
Web: www.lib.montana.edu
Personnel:

Responsible person: Brenda Mathenia, Assistant Professor/Reference Librarian, *email:* mathenia@montana.edu

Assistants: Nancy Williams, Library Assistant; Tommye Warren, Library Assistant

FTE professionals: 2   *FTE para-professionals:* 4

Holdings:

Geographic strengths: Montana, Intermountain West

Map depositories: USGS topos, CIA, National Forest Service, BLM

80,000 printed maps
2 globes
100 atlases
53 CD-ROMs

Access:

Hours:

Monday–Friday: 8 A.M.–midnight
Saturday: 10 A.M.–5 P.M.
Sunday: 1 P.M.–midnight

Items circulate
Interlibrary loan available

Collection services:

Maps cataloged: 20%
Maps classified: 20%
Maps in OPAC: 20%
Classification schemes: LC, SuDocs

Physical facilities:

Public computers: 6
Map cases: 75
Vertical files: 14

Notes: Only some of our maps circulate and are available for interlibrary loan. Flat maps housed in our map cases do not circulate. If maps are folded or in government documents or are available through the regular stacks, they circulate and ILL.

297 *Butte, MT*

Montana Tech of the University of Montana

Library
1300 West Park Street
Butte, MT 59701
Telephone: 406-496-4281
Fax: 406-496-4133
Email: astclair@mtech.edu
Web: www.mtech.edu/library
Personnel:

Responsible person: Elizabeth Harper, Reference/Documents Librarian, *email:* eharper@mtech.edu

FTE professionals: 0   *FTE para-professionals:* 0

Holdings:

Geographic strengths: Montana, West

Special collections: Montana Bureau of Mines and Geology maps, Montana mining maps

Map depositories: USGS topos, BLM

84,000 printed maps
17 atlases
10 books

Access:

Hours:

Monday–Friday: 8 A.M.–10 P.M.
Sunday: 1 P.M.–9 P.M.

Items circulate
Interlibrary loan available

Collection services:

Maps cataloged: 7%
Maps classified: 75%
Maps in OPAC: 33%
Classification schemes: LC, SuDocs, Local

Physical facilities:

Public computers: 1
Map cases: 49
Vertical files: 23

298 *Helena, MT*

Montana Historical Society

Research Center
225 North Roberts
P.O. Box 201201
Helena, MT 59620
Telephone: 406-444-2681
Fax: 406-444-5297
Email: mhslibrary@state.mt.us
Web: www.montanahistoricalsociety.org
Personnel:

Responsible person: Brian Shovers, Reference Historian, *email:* bshovers@state.mt.us

Assistants: Rich Aarstad, Reference Historian

FTE professionals: 0.25

Holdings:

Geographic strengths: Montana

Special collections: Sanborn Fire Insurance maps of 302 Montana towns, Montana mine map, USGS topo maps (1894–present), Chicago, Milwaukee, and St. Paul Right of Way Maps (Montana), Montana National Forest maps, Montana county–city maps (1864–present), Montana State Highway Commission maps (1920–present)

Map depositories: USGS

7,100 printed maps
50 atlases

Access:

Hours:

Tuesday–Friday: 8 A.M.–5 P.M.
Saturday: 9 A.M.–1 P.M.

Collection services:

Maps cataloged: 80%

Maps classified: 80%

Maps in OPAC: 5%

Classification schemes: Local

Physical facilities:

Maps in separate area

Public computers: 1

Map cases: 31

Vertical files: 2

299 *Missoula, MT*

University of Montana

Maureen and Mike Mansfield Library

Documents/Maps Division

32 Campus Drive

Missoula, MT 59812-9936

Telephone: 406-243-6866

Web: www.lib.umt.edu

Personnel:

Number of student workers hours per week: 30

Holdings:

Geographic strengths: Missoula, Montana

Special collections: Sanborn Fire Insurance maps, General Land Office maps including homestead and mining plats, Montana Power Company maps, Montana Pest maps, Mineral Surveys of Montana, Western Montana townsite plats

Subject strengths: aerial photos, aeronautical, agriculture, early cartography, modern cartography, celestial, climatology, city, forestry, geology, historical geography, hydrology, land ownership, land use, map catalogs, mineral resources, mining, nautical charts, political geography, railroads, recreation, roads, soil

Map depositories and percentages: USGS topos (100%), USGS geology maps (100%), USGS other (100%), Department of Transportation, NOAA, GPO, CIA, National Forest Service, NIMA topos, NIMA nautical, NIMA aeronautical, BLM, State, Census, FEMA Flood Insurance, BIA, EIS, soil survey, prot series, serial set.

209,000 printed maps

25 manuscript maps

10 raised relief maps

25 microfilms

80 gazetteers

2,000 printed atlases

Chronological coverage:

1800–1899: 15%

1900–1939: 15%

1940–present: 70%

Average budget over the last 5 years: $300

Access:

Collection is partially open to the public

Reference questions per year: 9,000

Answers email questions

Patrons per month: 30

Hours:

Monday–Friday: 7:30 A.M.–11:30 P.M.

Saturday: 10:30 A.M.–7:30 P.M.

Sunday: 10:30 A.M.–11:30 P.M.

Total hours per week opened: 98

Circulation policies apply

Geographic Information Systems:

No GIS services available

GIS assistance available for geocoding

Collection services:

Maps cataloged: 90%

Maps classified: 46%

Maps in OPAC: 45%

Datasets are cataloged

Classification schemes: LC, SuDocs, Dewey, Local

Cataloging utilities: OCLC

Catalog accessibility: online

Preservation techniques: encapsulation

Physical facilities:

Internet access available

Square footage: 10,000

Number of map cases: 50

Number of vertical map cases: 18

Number of vertical files (file cabinets): 33

Linear atlas shelving: 382 ft.

Copying facilities available: copier, color copier, large-format copier, microform copier

300 *Crete, NE*

Doane College

Perkins Library

Vertical Files

1014 Boswell Avenue

Crete, NE 68333

Telephone: 402-826-8567

Fax: 402-826-8199

Web: www.doane.edu/library_new/index.asp

Personnel:

Responsible person: Roger Cross, Collection Development, *email:* rcross@doane.edu

Holdings:

1,500 printed maps

1 globe

45 atlases

Access:

Hours:

Monday–Friday: 8 A.M.–11 P.M.

Saturday: 10 A.M.–5 P.M.

Sunday: 5 P.M.–11 P.M.

Interlibrary loan available

Collection services:

Maps cataloged: 0%
Maps classified: 0%
Maps in OPAC: 0%

Physical facilities:
Public computers: 11
Vertical files: 4

301 *Fremont, NE*

Midland Lutheran College

Earth Science Department
900 North Clarkson
Fremont, NE 68025
Telephone: 402-941-6328
Web: www.mlc.edu/library

Personnel:
Responsible person: Gary A. Carlson

Holdings:
Geographic strengths: Nebraska, Glacier National Park, Grand Canyon National Park, Grand Teton National Park, Yellowstone National Park
Subject strengths: aerial photos, early cartography, celestial, economic geography, geology, historical geography, land use
Map depositories: USGS topos
5,300 printed maps
25 wall maps
25 raised relief maps
300 aerial photos
50 satellite images
60 globes
25 books
Chronological coverage:
1900–1939: 15%
1940–present: 80%

Access:
Collection is paged
Number of maps circulated annually: 50

Collection services:
Maps cataloged: 100%
Maps classified: 100%
Cataloging utilities: Local
Preservation techniques: lamination

Physical facilities:
Square footage: 500
Number of map cases: 10
Linear book shelving: 150 ft.
Number of stereoscopes: 30

302 *Kearney, NE*

University of Nebraska, Kearney

Calvin T. Ryan Library
Government Documents Department

2508 11th Avenue
Kearney, NE 68849-2240
Telephone: 308-865-8542
Fax: 308-865-8722
Email: keithdi@unk.edu
Web: www.unk.edu/acad/library/gov_doc/about.htm

Personnel:
Responsible person: Diana J. Keith, *email:* keithdi@unk.edu
Number of student workers hours per week: 30

Holdings:
Geographic strengths: Nebraska
Subject strengths: aeronautical, agriculture, soil
Map depositories and percentages: USGS topos (10%), USGS geology maps, Department of Transportation, GPO, CIA, National Forest Service, NIMA topos, NIMA aeronautical, BLM
2,390 printed maps
30 wall maps
26 gazetteers
46 printed atlases
Chronological coverage:
1940–present: 99%
On-going publications: Periodic new government documents list that includes maps and CDs added to collection http://www.unk.edu/acad/library/gov_doc/about.htm#linkn

Access:
Collection is open to the public
Answers email questions

Hours:
Monday–Friday: 7:30 A.M.–midnight
Saturday: 10 A.M.–5 P.M.
Sunday: 2 P.M.–midnight
Total hours per week opened: 93
Maps circulate
Circulation policies apply
Map circulation duration: 4 weeks
Atlas circulation duration: 4 weeks
Book circulation duration: 4 weeks
Number of maps circulated annually: 13
Interlibrary loan available

Geographic Information Systems:
No GIS services available

Collection services:
Maps cataloged: 30%
Maps classified: 100%
Maps in OPAC: 30%
Datasets are cataloged
Classification schemes: LC, SuDocs
Cataloging utilities: OCLC
Catalog accessibility: online

Physical facilities:
Internet access available
Square footage: 60

Copying facilities available: copier, microform copier

Notes: We have no separate map collection; maps/atlases are included in government documents collection, library non-book collection, and library reference collection.

303 *Kearney, NE*

University of Nebraska, Kearney

Geography Map Library
Department of Geography
Kearney, NE 68849
Telephone: 308-865-8682
Personnel:
Responsible person: Gordon E. Bennett
Holdings:
Geographic strengths: Nebraska
Special collections: Nebraska aerial photographs (1930s)
Map depositories: USGS topos, USGS geology maps
9,500 printed maps
50 manuscript maps
100 wall maps
100 raised relief maps
70,000 aerial photos
50 satellite images
20 globes
10 gazetteers
60 printed atlases
30 books
Chronological coverage:
　1800–1899: 10%
　1900–1939: 20%
　1940–present: 70%
Access:
Collection is paged
Patrons per month: 15
Hours:
　Monday–Friday: 9 A.M.–5 P.M.
Maps circulate
　Circulation policies apply
　Number of maps circulated annually: 100
　Number of books circulated annually: 10
Physical facilities:
Square footage: 800
Number of map cases: 15
Number of vertical files (file cabinets): 11
Copying facilities available: copier

304 *Lincoln, NE*

American Historical Society of Germans from Russia

631 D Street
Lincoln, NE 68502-1199
Telephone: 402-474-3363
Email: ahsgr@ahsgr.org
Web: www.ahsgr.org
Personnel:
Responsible person: Diane White, Office Manager
Holdings:
Geographic strengths: Germany, Russia, Nebraska
Subject strengths: genealogy
600 printed maps
10 printed atlases
Chronological coverage:
　Pre-1800: 50%
　1800–1899: 35%
　1900–1939: 10%
Access:
Collection is partially paged, partially open to the public
Hours:
　Monday–Friday: 9 A.M.–4 P.M.
　Saturday: 9 A.M.–1 P.M.
　Total hours per week opened: 45
Geographic Information Systems:
No GIS services available
Scans maps for patrons
Collection services:
Classification schemes: LC
Cataloging utilities: OCLC
Catalog accessibility: cards
Preservation techniques: lamination
Items that have gone through the preservation process: 25%
Physical facilities:
No Internet access
Square footage: 18
Copying facilities available: copier, microform copier

305 *Lincoln, NE*

Lincoln City Libraries

136 South 14th Street
Lincoln, NE 68508
Telephone: 402-441-8530
Fax: 402-441-8534
Web: www.lcl.lib.ne.us
Personnel:
Responsible person: Layne Pierce, Reference Librarian, *email:* l.pierce@mail.lcl.lib.ne.us
Assistants: Robert Boyce, Reference Librarian
FTE para-professionals: 0.1
Holdings:
Geographic strengths: Lincoln, Lancaster County
Special collections: Plat maps for Lancaster and surrounding counties (early 1900s), Lincoln and Lancaster County development plan maps (1951–present), state and city road and travel maps for United States

320 printed maps
2 globes
75 atlases
38 books
Access:
  Hours:
    Monday–Thursday: 10 A.M.–9 P.M.
    Friday–Saturday: 10 A.M.–6 P.M.
    Sunday: 1:30 P.M.–5:30 P.M.
  Items circulate
  Interlibrary loan available
Collection services:
  Maps cataloged: 22%
  Maps in OPAC: 22%
  Classification schemes: Dewey

306 *Lincoln, NE*

Nebraska Department of Natural Resources

Data Bank
Information Technology Division
301 Centennial Mall South
Lincoln, NE 68509
Telephone: 402-471-2363
Fax: 402-471-2900
Email: mbansal@dnr.state.ne.us
Web: www.dnr.state.ne.us
Personnel:
  Responsible person: email: mbansal@dnr.state.ne.us
Holdings:
  Geographic strengths: Nebraska
  Subject strengths: aerial photos, agriculture, climatology, city, engineering, geodetic surveys, geospatial data, hydrology, land use, political geography, population, projections, raised relief models, roads, soil, waterways
  Map depositories and percentages: USGS topos, State, GIS Spatial Data Coverages
  2,000 CD-ROMs
  Collecting digital data
  Chronological coverage:
    1940–present: 100%
Access:
  Collection is open to the public
  Reference questions per year: 1,100
  Answers email questions
  Hours:
    Monday–Friday: 8 A.M.–5 P.M.
    Total hours per week opened: 40
Geographic Information Systems:
  GIS services available by appointment
  GIS software: ArcGIS, ArcIMS Applications
  Number of GIS stations (monitored): 7
  GIS assistance available for Census mapping, geocoding, and image analysis

Collection services:
  Datasets are cataloged
  Classification schemes: Local
  Catalog accessibility: online
Physical facilities:
  Internet access available
  Number of staff computers: 7
  Copying facilities available: copier, color copier, size E plotter, scanner
Notes: Collection contains only digital maps. Paper copies are printed on demand. At nominal costs, interpretative maps are prepared on request from geo-spatial coverages that are available in the Data Bank, administered by the Nebraska Department of Natural Resources.

307 *Lincoln, NE*

Nebraska Department of Roads

GIS Map Library
P.O. Box 94759
Lincoln, NE 68509
Telephone: 402-479-4550
Fax: 402-479-3884
Email: dgenrich@dor.state.ne.us
Web: nebraskatransportation.org/maps/
Personnel:
  Responsible person email: dgenrich@dor.state.ne.us
Holdings:
  Geographic strengths: Nebraska
  Special collections: Highway Beautification maps, railroad maps, transportation maps
  Map depositories: USGS
  300 printed maps
  1 atlas
  1 book
Access:
  Hours:
    Monday–Friday: 8 A.M.–5 P.M.
    Saturday–Sunday: closed
Collection services:
  Maps cataloged: 0%
  Maps classified: 0%
  Maps in OPAC: 0%
  Classification schemes: LC, Local, Other (State and Federal Government Agencies, the Public, Department of Roads Divisions)
Physical facilities:
  Map cases: 4
  Vertical files: 10

308 *Lincoln, NE*

Nebraska Library Commission

Nebraska Publications Clearinghouse
1200 N Street

Suite 120
Lincoln, NE 68508
Telephone: 402-471-2045
Fax: 402-471-2083
Email: bgoble@nlc.state.ne.us
Web: www.nlc.state.ne.us/docs/clear.html
Personnel:
Responsible person: Beth Goble, Government Information Coordinator, *email:* bgoble@nlc.state.ne.us
Assistants: Lori Sailors, Federal Documents Librarian; Jennifer Wrampe, Documents Assistant
FTE professionals: 0.1   *FTE para-professionals:* 0.1
Holdings:
Geographic strengths: Lancaster County, Nebraska
Special collections: 1990 census block maps for all counties in Nebraska, 2000 census block maps for Lancaster County, Nebraska
Subject strengths: population
Map depositories: Census block maps (1990 and 2000) for Nebraska
2,545 printed maps
75 printed atlases
Chronological coverage:
1940–present: 100%
Access:
Collection is partially open to the public
Reference questions per year: 12
Answers email questions
Hours:
Monday–Friday: 8 A.M.–5 P.M.
Total hours per week opened: 45
Maps circulate
Circulation policies apply
Map circulation duration: 30 days
Interlibrary loan available
Geographic Information Systems:
No GIS services available
Scans maps for patrons
Collection services:
Maps cataloged: 100%
Maps classified: 100%
Classification schemes: SuDocs
Cataloging utilities: OCLC
Catalog accessibility: online
Physical facilities:
Internet access available
Copying facilities available: copier, microform copier

309 *Lincoln, NE*

Nebraska State Historical Society

Library/Archives
P.O. Box 82554
1500 R Street
Lincoln, NE 68501

Telephone: 402-471-4786
Fax: 402-471-8922
Email: nshs05@nebraskahistory.org
Web: www.nebraskahistory.org
Personnel:
Responsible person: Cindy S. Drake, Library Curator, *email:* nshs05@nebraskahistory.org
Assistants: Andrea Faling, Associate Director, Library/Archives; Ann Billesbach, Head of Reference
Holdings:
Geographic strengths: Nebraska, Midwest
Special collections: Nebraska Sanborn Fire Insurance maps
Subject strengths: agriculture, archaeology, city, economic geography, genealogy, geology, historical geography, industries, land ownership, land use, map catalogs, map collecting, military, population, projections, roads, soil, travel books, views
Map depositories: USGS topos, USGS geology maps, USGS other, NIMA nautical, State
1,500 printed maps
45 microfilms
2,000 aerial photos
22 gazetteers
Chronological coverage:
1800–1899: 65%
1900–1939: 25%
On-going publications: Checklist of Printed Maps of the Middle West to 1900, Vols. 12 and 13, Nebraska and Kansas (1981).
Access:
Collection is partially open to the public
Maps off site
Reference questions per year: 240
Answers email questions
Hours:
Monday: closed
Tuesday–Friday: 9 A.M.–noon, 1 P.M.–4 P.M.
Saturday: 8 A.M.–5 P.M.
Sunday: closed
Total hours per week opened: 33
Circulation policies apply
Interlibrary loan available
Geographic Information Systems:
No GIS services available
Scans maps for patrons
Collection services:
Maps cataloged: 85%
Maps classified: 85%
Maps in OPAC: 45%
Classification schemes: Dewey, Local, Other (modified Dewey)
Cataloging utilities: Local, Limited use of OCLC, CatExpress
Catalog accessibility: online, cards, printout

Preservation techniques: encapsulation, lamination, edging

Items that have gone through the preservation process: 80%

Physical facilities:

Internet access available

Square footage: 36

Number of map cases: 6

Linear atlas shelving: 50 ft.

Number of microform readers: 19

Copying facilities available: copier, microform copier, reproduce microfilm reels for negatives

Notes: We do not have "separate" staff to service our maps, and our reference staff (mainly 3 FTE) service maps as well as the rest of our library and archival collections. Of our pre-1920 Nebraska county plat books (atlases) on 9 rolls of microfilm (approximately 60 volumes), we have most of the originals. The atlases on this microfilm have been indexed by a volunteer, but the database is not available at this time. The microfilm count also includes the 10 reels for Nebraska of township plats from the U.S. General Land Office and 24 reels of Nebraska maps from the U.S. Surveyor General Collections (archival collection RG510). We also have 74 folders of original Nebraska land tract plats in the Land Office archival collection (RG509). The originals in the map collection do not circulate, except for items on microfilm. Internet access is limited since retrospective cataloging for maps is not complete. The majority of the maps are stored in our Reference Room, but some are stored in other areas within our building because of limited space in the room for oversize map cases.

310 *Lincoln, NE*

University of Nebraska, Lincoln

Conservation and Survey Division/SNR

102 Nebraska Hall

Lincoln, NE 68588-0517

Telephone: 402-472-7523 or 402-472-3471

Fax: 402-472-4542

Email: jotteman1@unl.edu

Web: csd.unl.edu/csd.htm

Personnel:

Responsible person: Judith G. Otteman, Staff Assistant, *email:* jotteman1@unl.edu

Holdings:

Geographic strengths: Nebraska

Subject strengths: aerial photos, agriculture, early cartography, modern cartography, celestial, city, geology, hydrology, land ownership, land use, mineral resources, railroads, recreation, roads, satellite imagery, soil, vegetation, miscellaneous publications and pamphlets

2,000 printed maps

Access:

Answers email questions

Hours:

Monday–Friday: 8 A.M.–5 P.M.

Total hours per week opened: 40

Physical facilities:

Internet access available

Copying facilities available: copier, large-format copier

311 *Lincoln, NE*

University of Nebraska, Lincoln

C.Y. Thompson Library

Founded 1965

38th and Holdrege Streets

East Campus

Lincoln, NE 68583-0717

Telephone: 402-472-4407

Fax: 402-472-7005

Email: cytmail@unlnotes.unl.edu

Web: www.unl.edu/libr/libs/cyt

Personnel:

Responsible person: Rebecca Bernthal, Head Librarian, *email:* rbernthal1@unl.edu

Assistants: Sharron Nagel

FTE para-professionals: 0.1

Number of student works: 33

Number of student workers hours per week: 255

Holdings:

Geographic strengths: Nebraska, United States

Subject strengths: agriculture, climatology, forestry, hydrology, land use, recreation, soil

Map depositories: National Forest Service, Agriculture and Soil Surveys

6,100 printed maps

7,400 microfiche

34 printed atlases

17 books

Chronological coverage:

1940–present: 95%

Average budget over the last 5 years: $100

Access:

Collection is open to the public

Reference questions per year: 50

Answers email questions

Patrons per month: 6,500

Hours:

Monday–Friday: 8 A.M.–midnight

Saturday: 9 A.M.–5 P.M.

Sunday: noon–midnight
Total hours per week opened: 96
Maps circulate
Circulation policies apply
 Map circulation duration: 1 week
 Atlas circulation duration: 4 weeks
 Book circulation duration: 4 weeks
 Number of maps circulated annually: 375
Interlibrary loan available
Geographic Information Systems:
No GIS services available
Collection services:
Maps cataloged: 70%
Maps classified: 95%
Maps in OPAC: 70%
Datasets are cataloged
Classification schemes: LC, SuDocs
Cataloging utilities: OCLC
Catalog accessibility: online
Physical facilities:
Internet access available
Square footage: 85
Number of public computers: 19
Number of staff computers: 12
Number of public printers: 15
Number of map cases: 6
Linear atlas shelving: 12 ft.
Copying facilities available: copier, microform copier

312 *Lincoln, NE*

University of Nebraska, Lincoln

Geology Library
10 Bessey Hall
Lincoln, NE 68588-0344
Telephone: 402-472-2653
Email: klogan-peters1@unl.edu
Web: www.unl.edu/libr/libs/geol/geol.html
Personnel:
Responsible person: Kay Logan-Peters, Chair of Access and Branch Services, *email:* klogan-peters1@unl.edu
Assistants: Jaci Groves, Library Assistant III
Holdings:
Geographic strengths: Nebraska, United States
Subject strengths: geology, mineral resources, mining, oceanography, projections, satellite imagery
Map depositories and percentages: USGS topos (100%), USGS geology maps (100%), USGS other (100%), GPO, BLM, State
200,000 printed maps
10 gazetteers
350 printed atlases

50 books
Chronological coverage:
 1900–1939: 10%
 1940–present: 90%
Access:
Collection is open to the public
Reference questions per year: 120
Answers email questions
Patrons per month: 1,500
Hours:
Monday–Friday: 8 A.M.–10 P.M.
Saturday–Sunday: 1 P.M.–4 P.M.
Total hours per week opened: 71
Maps circulate
Circulation policies apply
 Map circulation duration: 4 weeks
 Atlas circulation duration: 4 weeks
 Book circulation duration: 4 weeks
 Number of maps circulated annually: 750
Interlibrary loan available
Geographic Information Systems:
No GIS services available
Collection services:
Maps cataloged: 10%
Maps classified: 90%
Maps in OPAC: 10%
Classification schemes: LC, SuDocs
Cataloging utilities: OCLC
Catalog accessibility: online
Items that have gone through the preservation process: 0%
Physical facilities:
Internet access available
Number of map cases: 245
Copying facilities available: copier

313 *Lincoln, NE*

University of Nebraska, Lincoln

Love Memorial Library
Map Collection, founded 197-?
Lincoln, NE 68588-4100
Telephone: 402-472-3545
Fax: 402-472-2534
Email: sgardner2@unl.edu
Web: www.unl.edu/libr/gis/
Personnel:
Responsible person: Sue Ann Gardner, *email:* sgardner2@unl.edu
Assistants: Carol Niemann, Student Supervisor
FTE professionals: 0.2 *FTE para-professionals:* 0.2
Holdings:
Geographic strengths: Nebraska, Great Plains

Special collections: United States FIRM maps, aerial photos of some Nebraska counties, WW II *Time* magazine news maps, WW II Army news maps

Subject strengths: aerial photos, aeronautical, city, historical geography, nautical charts, World War II era maps

Map depositories: Department of Transportation, NOAA, GPO, CIA, NIMA nautical, NIMA aeronautical, State, United Nations

48,039 printed maps

10 raised relief maps

2,750 aerial photos

100 satellite images

40 gazetteers

1,225 printed atlases

750 books

15 CD-ROMs

Collecting digital data

Chronological coverage:
   1940–present: 90%

Average budget over the last 5 years: $300

Access:

Collection is open to the public

Reference questions per year: 150

Answers email questions

Patrons per month: 300

Hours:

Monday–Thursday: 8 A.M.–midnight

Friday: 8 A.M.–8 P.M.

Saturday: 9 A.M.–5 P.M.

Sunday: noon–midnight

Total hours per week opened: 96

Maps circulate

Circulation policies apply

   Map circulation duration: 1 week

   Atlas circulation duration: 4 weeks

   Book circulation duration: 4 weeks

Interlibrary loan available

Geographic Information Systems:

GIS services available in an open environment

GIS software: ArcGIS, ArcView

Number of public GIS workstations: 50

Collection services:

Maps cataloged: 0.15%

Maps in OPAC: 0.15%

Classification schemes: LC

Cataloging utilities: OCLC

Catalog accessibility: online

Preservation techniques: encapsulation, Old linen-backed

Items that have gone through the preservation process: 0.01%

Physical facilities:

Internet access available

Square footage: 800

Number of public computers: 75

Number of public printers: 75

Number of map cases: 66

Linear book shelving: 123 ft.

Linear atlas shelving: 32 ft.

Copying facilities available: copier

Notes: Patrons use a map-finding guide produced in 1998, which lists geographic regions, LC class numbers, and drawer numbers. We continue to work on cataloging the collection. The map collection is near the computer lab and reference area of the library, which explains the number of computers and printers available.

314 *Norfolk, NE*

Norfolk Public Library

Reference Department

308 Prospect Avenue

Norfolk, NE 68701

Telephone: 402-844-2100

Fax: 402-844-2102

Web: www.ci.norfolk.ne.us/library

Personnel:

Responsible person: Judy Hilkemann, Reference Supervisor

Assistants: JoAnn Steiger, Reference Assistant; Marcy Donner, Reference Assistant

FTE professionals: 0.1   *FTE para-professionals:* 0.1

Holdings:

Geographic strengths: Nebraska

800 printed maps

60 printed atlases

Chronological coverage:
   1940–present: 90%

Access:

Hours:

Monday–Thursday: 10 A.M.–9 P.M.

Friday–Saturday: 10 A.M.–5 P.M.

Sunday: 1:30 P.M.–4:30 P.M.

Total hours per week opened: 61

Maps circulate

Collection services:

Maps cataloged: 20%

Maps in OPAC: 20%

Classification schemes: Dewey

Cataloging utilities: OCLC

Catalog accessibility: online

Physical facilities:

No Internet access

Square footage: 20

Number of map cases: 2

Copying facilities available: copier, microform copier

315 *Omaha, NE*

Douglas County Historical Society Library

Library/Archives Center
Historical Maps
5730 North 30th Street
Omaha, NE 68111
Telephone: 402-451-1013
Fax: 402-453-9448
Email: archivist@omahahistory.org
Web: www.omahahistory.org
Personnel:
Responsible person: Joann Meyer, *email:* archivist@
omahahistory.org
Holdings:
Geographic strengths: Omaha, Douglas County
Special collections: Sanborn Fire Insurance maps of
Omaha
350 printed maps
Access:
Hours:
Tuesday–Friday: 10 A.M.–4 P.M.
Saturday–Sunday: by appointment
Collection services:
Maps cataloged: 90%
Maps classified: 90%
Maps in OPAC: 0%
Classification schemes: Dewey
Physical facilities:
Maps in separate area
Vertical files: 4
Notes: Our maps deal with the streets and land ownership
of Douglas County.

316 *Omaha, NE*

Omaha Public Library

W. Dale Clark Library
Business, Science, Technology
215 South 15th Street
Omaha, NE 68102-1629
Telephone: 402-444-4817
Fax: 402-444-4585
Email: mblackstone@omaha.lib.ne.us
Web: www.omaha.lib.ne.us
Personnel:
Responsible person: Margaret Blackstone, Government
Documents Librarian, *email:* mblackstone@omaha
.lib.ne.us
FTE professionals: 0.5
Number of student workers hours per week: 10
Holdings:
Geographic strengths: United States
Subject strengths: forestry, soil

Map depositories and percentages: USGS topos
(100%), National Forest Service, State
57,344 printed maps
Chronological coverage:
1900–1939: 12%
1940–present: 87%
Access:
Maps in separate area
Collection is open to the public
Reference questions per year: 100
Answers email questions
Patrons per month: 15
Hours:
Monday–Thursday: 10 A.M.–8 P.M.
Friday: 10 A.M.–6 P.M.
Total hours per week opened: 56
Geographic Information Systems:
No GIS services available
Collection services:
Classification schemes: Local
Catalog accessibility: online, fiche
Physical facilities:
Internet access available
Number of map cases: 45
Copying facilities available: copier, microform copier

317 *Omaha, NE*

University of Nebraska, Omaha

Department of Geography—Geology
Omaha, NE 68182-0199
Telephone: 402-554-3586
Personnel:
Responsible person: Marvin Barton
Holdings:
Geographic strengths: Nebraska, Upper Midwest
40,000 printed maps
400 aerial photos
2 globes
Collection services:
Maps classified: 100%
Physical facilities:
Map cases: 38
Vertical files: 12

318 *Omaha, NE*

University of Nebraska, Omaha

University Library
Government Documents
6001 Dodge Street
Omaha, NE 68182
Telephone: 402-554-2225

Fax: 402-554-3215
Email: jshaw@mail.unomaha.edu
Web: library.unomaha.edu
Personnel:
Responsible person: email: jshaw@mail.unomaha.edu
Number of student workers hours per week: 50
Holdings:
Geographic strengths: Nebraska, South Dakota, Iowa, Missouri, Kansas, Colorado, Wyoming
Special collections: Sanborn Fire Insurance maps on microfilm for Omaha, Nebraska and Council Bluffs, Iowa
Subject strengths: agriculture, celestial, forestry, geology, hydrology, political geography, population, soil, travel books
Map depositories and percentages: USGS topos (15%), USGS geology maps (15%), USGS other (30%), GPO, CIA, National Forest Service, NIMA aeronautical, BLM
20,000 printed maps
100 wall maps
4,000 microfiche
50 printed atlases
200 books
100 CD-ROMs
Chronological coverage:
1940–present: 95%
Access:
Collection is open to the public
Maps off site
Reference questions per year: 100
Answers email questions
Patrons per month: 10
Hours:
Monday–Friday: 7 A.M.–11 P.M.
Saturday: 10 A.M.–5 P.M.
Sunday: noon–11 P.M.
Total hours per week opened: 92
Geographic Information Systems:
No GIS services available
Collection services:
Maps cataloged: 25%
Maps classified: 25%
Maps in OPAC: 25%
Datasets are cataloged
Classification schemes: SuDocs
Cataloging utilities: OCLC
Catalog accessibility: online
Preservation techniques: encapsulation, lamination
Physical facilities:
No Internet access
Number of map cases: 23
Number of vertical files (file cabinets): 10
Linear book shelving: 12 ft.
Number of microform readers: 12

Copying facilities available: copier, microform copier, microform scanners
Notes: We are in the middle of a retrospective cataloging project for maps, so the numbers provided for our collection are rough estimates only.

319 *Carson City, NV*

Nevada State Library and Archives

100 North Stewart Street
Carson City, NV 89701-4285
Telephone: 775-684-3310
Fax: 775-684-3371
Email: archives@clan.lib.nv.us
Web: dmla.clan.lib.nv.us/docs/nsla/archives/
Personnel:
Responsible person: Jeffrey M. Kintop, *email:* jmkintop@clan.lib.nv.us
Assistants: Susan Searcy, Chris Driggs, Barbara Gray
FTE professionals: 3   *FTE para-professionals:* 1
Holdings:
Geographic strengths: Nevada
Special collections: State Library, Nevada USGS topographic maps, Sanborn Fire Insurance maps on microfilm, State Archives, Nevada Department of Transportation maps, US Land Office Survey Maps
Map depositories: USGS
8,870 printed maps
20 aerial photos
947 atlases
100 books
Access:
Hours:
Monday–Friday: 8 A.M.–5 P.M.
Collection services:
Classification schemes: Local, Other (USGS)
Physical facilities:
Public computers: 12
Map cases: 16
Vertical files: 4
Notes: Sanborn Maps are listed on http://dmla.clan.lib.nv.us/docs/nsla/sanborn_maps.htm Nevada USGS Topo maps are listed on http://dmla.clan.lib.nv.us/docs/nsla/fedpubs/map/maptopo.htm

320 *Reno, NV*

Nevada Historical Society

1650 North Virginia Street
Reno, NV 89503
Telephone: 775-688-1190
Fax: 775-688-2917
Web: www.nevadaculture.org
Personnel:

Responsible person: Michael Maher, Librarian, *email:* mpmaher@clan.lib.nv.us
Assistants: Eric Moody, Curator of Manuscripts
FTE professionals: 2   *FTE para-professionals:* 1

Holdings:
Geographic strengths: Nevada, Great Basin
Special collections: Nevada Mining, Nevada USGS topographic maps, Sanborn Fire Insurance maps of Nevada, Nevada Department of Transportation General Highway Maps
Map depositories: USGS
10,000 printed maps
34 aerial photos
30 atlases
30 books
1 active serial

Access:
Hours:
Tuesday–Saturday: noon–4 P.M.
Sunday: closed

Collection services:
Maps cataloged: 70%
Maps classified: 90%
Maps in OPAC: 0%
Classification schemes: Local

Physical facilities:
Maps in separate area
Map cases: 28

321 *Reno, NV*

University of Nevada, Reno

DeLaMare Library
Mary B. Ansari Map Library, founded 1969
DeLaMare Library
MS 262
Reno, NV 89557
Telephone: 775-784-6945 x230
Fax: 775-784-6949
Email: lnewman@unr.edu
Web: www.delamare.unr.edu/Maps/

Personnel:
Responsible person: Linda Newman, Geoscience and Map Librarian, *email:* lnewman@unr.edu
FTE professionals: 0.69   *FTE para-professionals:* 0.3
Number of student workers hours per week: 10

Holdings:
Geographic strengths: United States
Subject strengths: aeronautical, modern cartography, geology, hydrology, land use, mineral resources, mining, nautical charts, topographic U.S.
Map depositories and percentages: USGS topos (100%), USGS geology maps (100%), USGS other (100%), Department of Transportation, NOAA, National Forest Service, NIMA topos, NIMA nautical, NIMA aeronautical, BLM, State, Nevada Bureau of Mines and Geology maps
139,000 printed maps
190 gazetteers
1,425 printed atlases
58 books
1780 CD-ROMs
Collecting digital data
Chronological coverage:
1900–1939: 10%
1940–present: 85%
Average budget over the last 5 years: $2,500
On-going publications: "New Maps" posted monthly online on Map Library web site

Access:
Maps in separate area
Collection is open to the public
Maps off site
Answers email questions
Hours:
Monday–Friday: 8 A.M.–5 P.M.
Maps circulate
Circulation policies apply
Map circulation duration: 4 weeks
Atlas circulation duration: 4 weeks
Book circulation duration: 4 weeks
Interlibrary loan available

Geographic Information Systems:
GIS services available in an open environment
GIS software: ESRI
Number of public GIS workstations: 2
GIS assistance available for Census mapping, geocoding, and image analysis
Scans maps for patrons

Collection services:
Maps cataloged: 20%
Maps classified: 50%
Maps in OPAC: 25%
Datasets are cataloged
Classification schemes: LC, SuDocs, Local, Other (place)
Cataloging utilities: OCLC, Marcive
Catalog accessibility: online, cards
Preservation techniques: encapsulation

Physical facilities:
Internet access available
Square footage: 3,000
Number of public computers: 2
Number of map cases: 135
Number of vertical files (file cabinets): 21
Other map storage: locked cabinets
Copying facilities available: copier, large-format copier, microform copier

Notes: The majority of cartographic monographs and serials are shelved in the general book stacks or documents section of the [overall] library. Only map reference materials are on the map library floor. Other resources such as many additional public computers and printers are available within this building and accessible when the map library is open/available.

322 *Reno, NV*

University of Nevada, Reno

Getchell Library
Special Collections and Archives Department
1664 North Virginia Street
Reno, NV 89557-0044
Telephone: 775-784-6500 x327
Fax: 775-784-4529
Email: specoll@unr.edu
Web: www.library.unr.edu/specoll
Personnel:
 Responsible person: Robert E. Blesse, Head, Special Collections and Archives Department, *email:* blesse@unr.edu
 FTE para-professionals: 0.33
Holdings:
 Geographic strengths: Reno, Nevada, Eastern slope of the Sierra Nevada Mountains, Great Basin
 Special collections: Sanborn Fire Insurance maps, USGS topographic map, numerous manuscript maps within manuscript collections
 3,000 printed maps
 20 aerial photos
Access:
 Hours:
  Monday–Friday: 9 A.M.–5 P.M.
  Saturday: 1 P.M.–5 P.M.
  Sunday: closed
Collection services:
 Maps cataloged: 45%
 Maps classified: 33%
 Maps in OPAC: 33%
 Classification schemes: LC, Local
Physical facilities:
 Maps in separate area
 Public computers: 2
 Map cases: 10
Notes: Numerous maps (printed and manuscript) can be found within many of our manuscript collections. These are not cataloged or classified separately as "maps," but can be found via our manuscript finding aids as part of the collections.

323 *Concord, NH*

New Hampshire Historical Society

The Tuck Library
Special Collections

30 Park Street
Concord, NH 03301
Telephone: 603-228-6688
Fax: 603-224-0463
Email: library@nhhistory.org
Web: www.nhhistory.org
Personnel:
 Responsible person: David Smolen, Special Collections Librarian, *email:* dsmolen@nhhistory.org
 Assistants: Bill Copeley, Librarian
 Number of volunteers: 10
 Number of volunteer hours per month: 125
Holdings:
 Geographic strengths: New Hampshire, New England
 Special collections: Sanborn Fire Insurance maps and USGS maps for New Hampshire
 Subject strengths: city, genealogy, industries, land ownership, land use, railroads, recreation, roads, travel books, views, waterways
 2,000 printed maps
 300 manuscript maps
 50 wall maps
 30 gazetteers
 100 books
 Chronological coverage:
  Pre-1800: 20%
  1800–1899: 50%
  1900–1939: 20%
  1940–present: 10%
Access:
 Collection is partially open to the public
 Reference questions per year: 100
 Answers email questions
 Patrons per month: 15
 Hours:
  Total hours per week opened: 35
Geographic Information Systems:
 No GIS services available
 Scans maps for patrons
Collection services:
 Maps cataloged: 100%
 Maps classified: 100%
 Maps in OPAC: 100%
 Classification schemes: Dewey
 Cataloging utilities: OCLC
 Catalog accessibility: online, cards
 Preservation techniques: encapsulation, deacidification
Physical facilities:
 Internet access available
 Copying facilities available: copier

324 *Durham, NH*

University of New Hampshire

Dimond Library
Government Documents/Map Room

18 Library Way
Durham, NH 03824
Telephone: 603-862-1777
Fax: 603-862-3403
Web: docs.unh.edu
Personnel:
Responsible person: Thelma B. Thompson, Government Documents and Maps Librarian, *email:* thelmat@cisunix.unh.edu
FTE professionals: 0.6   *FTE para-professionals:* 0.1
Number of student workers hours per week: 3
Holdings:
Geographic strengths: New Hampshire, New England
Special collections: Historic topographic maps of New England and New York, digital collection of 1,500 scanned images covering 1890–1950
Subject strengths: aerial photos, geology, hydrology, nautical charts, soil
Map depositories and percentages: USGS topos (100%), USGS geology maps (100%), USGS other (100%), NOAA, GPO, CIA, National Forest Service, NIMA nautical, BLM
60,000 printed maps
Chronological coverage:
   1940–present: 90%
On-going publications: Indexing for digital historical topographic maps available online.
Access:
Maps in separate area
Collection is partially open to the public
Answers email questions
Hours:
   Monday–Tuesday: 9 A.M.–6:45 P.M.
   Wednesday–Friday: 9 A.M.–4 P.M.
   Saturday: 10 A.M.–3:45 P.M.
   Total hours per week opened: 33.25
Geographic Information Systems:
GIS services available by appointment
GIS software: ArcView 3.x
Discovery and initial evaluation of data sources help available
Collection services:
Datasets are cataloged
Classification schemes: LC, SuDocs, Local
Cataloging utilities: OCLC
Catalog accessibility: online
Items that have gone through the preservation process: 1%
Physical facilities:
Internet access available
Square footage: 1,300
Number of map cases: 28
Linear atlas shelving: 10 ft.
Copying facilities available: copier, microform copier
Notes: This does not include folded maps in documents, circulating collection, or microfiche. Nor does it in-clude atlases in general reference collection, or small number of historic maps in Special Collections. Map circulation is by special arrangement only.

325 *Hanover, NH*

Dartmouth College

Baker/Berry Library
Evans Map Room, founded 1945
HB 6025
Hanover, NH 03755
Telephone: 603-646-2579
Fax: 603-646-3628
Email: map.room@dartmouth.edu
Web: www.dartmouth.edu/~maproom/
Personnel:
Responsible person: Lucinda M. Hall, Reference Bibliographer for Geography and Maps, *email:* lucinda.m.hall@dartmouth.edu
Assistants: Joyce Ryerson and Peter Allen, Map Room Specialists
Number of student workers hours per week: 21
Holdings:
Geographic strengths: Hanover, New Hampshire, Vermont, New England, United States
Special collections: Sanborn Fire Insurance maps for New Hampshire, Crown Collection of photographs of American maps, Louis Charles Karpinski manuscript maps prior to 1800 relating to America (photographic facsimiles)
Subject strengths: historical geography, nautical charts, views
Map depositories and percentages: USGS topos (100%), Department of Transportation, NOAA, CIA, National Forest Service, NIMA topos, BLM, United Nations, Canadian topographic maps
196,148 printed maps
153 wall maps
227 raised relief maps
3,500 aerial photos
28 globes
264 gazetteers
200 printed atlases
1,458 books
621 CD-ROMs
12 computer programs
Collecting digital data
Chronological coverage:
   1800–1899: 11%
   1900–1939: 10%
   1940–present: 78%
Average budget over the last 5 years: $8,500
Access:
Maps in separate area
Collection is open to the public
Maps off site

Reference questions per year: 1,500
Answers email questions
Patrons per month: 125
Hours:
Monday–Friday: 8 A.M.–5 P.M.
Saturday–Saturday: closed
Total hours per week opened: 57
Maps circulate
Circulation policies apply
   Map circulation duration: 2 weeks
   Number of maps circulated annually: 70
Interlibrary loan available
Geographic Information Systems:
GIS services available in an open environment
GIS software: ArcGIS, BusinessMap
GIS assistance available for Census mapping, and geocoding
Plotter available
Scans maps for patrons
Collection services:
Maps cataloged: 50%
Maps classified: 90%
Maps in OPAC: 50%
Datasets are cataloged
Classification schemes: LC, Dewey, Local
Cataloging utilities: OCLC
Catalog accessibility: online, cards
Preservation techniques: encapsulation, deacidification
Items that have gone through the preservation process: 20%
Physical facilities:
Internet access available
Number of map cases: 148
Linear book shelving: 154 ft.
Linear atlas shelving: 93 ft.
Other map storage: roller map shelves
Copying facilities available: copier, large-format scanner, plotter

326 *Hanover, NH*

Dartmouth College

Kresge Physical Sciences Library
6115 Fairchild Center
Hanover, NH 3755
Telephone: 603-646-3563
Fax: 603-646-3681
Email: klr@dartmouth.edu
Web: www.dartmouth.edu/~krescook/index.shtml
Personnel:
Responsible person: Barbara DeFelice, Head Kresge Library, *email:* klr@dartmouth.edu
Assistants: Leslie Shahi, Physical Sciences Librarian responsible for Earth and Environmental Sciences
FTE professionals: 0.25   *FTE para-professionals:* 0.25

Holdings:
Geographic strengths: New Hampshire, Vermont, New England, United States
8,000 printed maps
400 atlases
300 books
70 active serials
15 CD-ROMs
Access:
Hours:
Monday–Friday: 8 A.M.–midnight
Saturday: 11 A.M.–8 P.M.
Sunday: 1 P.M.–midnight
Items circulate
Interlibrary loan available
Collection services:
Maps cataloged: 100%
Maps classified: 100%
Maps in OPAC: 100%
Classification schemes: LC, Dewey
Physical facilities:
Public computers: 16
Vertical files: 13

327 *Keene, NH*

Historical Society of Cheshire County

246 Main Street
P.O. Box 803
Keene, NH 3431
Telephone: 603-352-1895
Email: director@hsccnh.org
Web: www.hsccnh.org
Personnel:
Responsible person: Alan Rumrill, Director, *email:* diresctor@hsccnh.org
Assistants: Roxanne Roy, Administrative Assistant
FTE professionals: 0.2
Holdings:
Geographic strengths: Cheshire County
500 printed maps
15 aerial photos
20 atlases
Access:
Hours:
Monday–Tuesday: 9 A.M.–4 P.M.
Wednesday: 9 A.M.–9 P.M.
Thursday–Friday: 9 A.M.–4 P.M.
Saturday: 9 A.M.–noon
Collection services:
Maps cataloged: 85%
Maps classified: 98%
Maps in OPAC: 0%
Classification schemes: Local
Physical facilities:

Maps in separate area
Public computers: 1
Map cases: 5
Vertical files: 2

328 *Camden, NJ*

Rutgers University, Camden Campus

Paul Robeson Library
300 North 4th Street
Camden, NJ 8101
Telephone: 856-225-6034
Fax: 856-225-6428
Web: www.libraries.rutgers.edu/rul/libs/robeson_lib
Personnel:
Responsible person: John Maxymuk
FTE para-professionals: 0.5
Holdings:
Special collections: Local Census Tract and Block maps
Map depositories: CIA
1,200 printed maps
100 atlases
500 books
Access:
Hours:
Monday–Thursday: 8 A.M.–11 P.M.
Friday: 8 A.M.–5 P.M.
Saturday: 9 A.M.–5 P.M.
Sunday: 11 A.M.–7 P.M.
Collection services:
Maps cataloged: 0%
Maps classified: 100%
Maps in OPAC: 0%
Classification schemes: Local
Physical facilities:
Map cases: 4

329 *Piscataway, NJ*

Rutgers, The State University of New Jersey

Library of Science and Medicine
Founded 1970
165 Bevier Rd
Piscataway, NJ 08854-8009
Telephone: 732-445-2895
Fax: 732-44-5806
Email: www.libraries.rutgers.edu/rul/ask_a_lib/ask_
a_lib_form.shtml
Web: www.libraries.rutgers.edu/rul/index.shtml
Personnel:
Responsible person: Ellen Calhoun, Documents Librarian, *email:* calhoun@rci.rutgers.edu
FTE professionals: 0.25   *FTE para-professionals:* 0.25
Number of student workers hours per week: 10

Holdings:
Geographic strengths: New Jersey
Subject strengths: agriculture, forestry, geology, soil
Map depositories and percentages: USGS topos
(100%), USGS geology maps (100%), USGS other
(100%), GPO, CIA, National Forest Service, NIMA
topos
100,000 printed maps
145 gazetteers
220 printed atlases
100 books
Chronological coverage:
1940–present: 100%
Access:
Collection is open to the public
Reference questions per year: 12
Answers email questions
Hours:
Monday–Thursday: 8 A.M.–midnight
Friday: 8 A.M.–9 P.M.
Saturday: 10 A.M.–6 P.M.
Sunday: noon–midnight
Total hours per week opened: 117
Geographic Information Systems:
No GIS services available
Scans maps for patrons
Collection services:
Maps cataloged: 10%
Maps classified: 10%
Maps in OPAC: 10%
Classification schemes: LC, SuDocs
Cataloging utilities: OCLC, RLG, Local
Catalog accessibility: online
Preservation techniques: encapsulation in mylar
Items that have gone through the preservation process:
0.01%
Physical facilities:
Internet access available
Square footage: 1,050
Number of public computers: 40
Number of map cases: 58
Number of vertical map cases: 12
Linear book shelving: 48 ft.
Linear atlas shelving: 72 ft.
Copying facilities available: copier, color copier, microform copier

330 *Princeton, NJ*

Princeton University

Library
Historic Maps Collection, founded 1986
One Washington Road
Princeton, NJ 08544
Telephone: 609-258-3166

Fax: 609-258-2324
Email: rbsc@princeton.edu
Web: www.princeton.edu/~rbsc/department/maps
Personnel:
Responsible person: John Delaney, Curator, *email:* delaney@princeton.edu
FTE professionals: 0.33
Holdings:
Geographic strengths: New Jersey, United States, North America, France, Great Britain
Special collections: Sanborn Fire Insurance maps of New Jersey
Subject strengths: early cartography, modern cartography, celestial, city, land ownership, map catalogs, map collecting, travel books
3,500 printed maps
10 manuscript maps
10 globes
150 gazetteers
100 printed atlases
500 books
Chronological coverage:
Pre-1800: 35%
1800–1899: 55%
1900–1939: 10%
Average budget over the last 5 years: $15,000
Access:
Maps in separate area
Collection is paged
Reference questions per year: 100
Answers email questions
Patrons per month: 10
Hours:
Monday–Friday: 9 A.M.–5 P.M.
Total hours per week opened: 40
Collection services:
Maps cataloged: 25%
Maps classified: 25%
Maps in OPAC: 25%
Classification schemes: LC, Local
Cataloging utilities: Local, Endeavor's Voyager
Catalog accessibility: online
Preservation techniques: encapsulation, encapsulation in mylar
Items that have gone through the preservation process: 25%
Physical facilities:
Internet access available
Square footage: 800
Number of map cases: 84
Linear book shelving: 100 ft.
Copying facilities available: copier, microform copier
Notes: Difficult to separate Historic Map Collection from our Rare Books Division. The latter has most of the atlases and books.

331 *Albuquerque, NM*

Sandia National Laboratories

Technical Library
P.O. Box 5820
MS 0899
Albuquerque, NM 87185
Telephone: 505-845-8287
Fax: 505-844-3143
Web: infoserve.sandia.gov/
Personnel:
Responsible person: Lisa Wishard, *email:* lawisha@sandia.gov
FTE professionals: 0.25   *FTE para-professionals:* 0.25
Holdings:
Geographic strengths: United States, Asia, Russia
Map depositories: NGA aeronautical
8,500 printed maps
200 atlases
200 books
50 active serials
50 CD-ROMs
Maps cataloged: 85%
Maps in OPAC: 85%
Classification schemes: LC
Access:
Hours:
Monday–Friday: 8 A.M.–4:30 P.M.
Items circulate
Physical facilities:
Public computers: 1
Map cases: 12

332 *Albuquerque, NM*

University of New Mexico

Centennial Science and Engineering Library
Map and Geographic Information Center (aka The Map Room)
UNMGL/CSEL MSC05 3020 1
Albuquerque, NM 87131-0001
Telephone: 505-277-5738
Fax: 505-277-0702
Email: maproom@unm.edu
Web: elibrary2.unm.edu/csel
Personnel:
Responsible person: Mary T. Wyant, Map Librarian, *email:* mwyant@unm.edu
Assistants: Brian Freels-Stendel, GIS Librarian
FTE para-professionals: 0.05
Number of student workers hours per week: 60
Holdings:
Geographic strengths: Albuquerque, Bernalillo County, New Mexico, Southwest, Mexico

Special collections: Sanborn Fire Insurance maps of New Mexico, historical maps of New Mexico, road maps of New Mexico

Subject strengths: aerial photos, aeronautical, agriculture, biology, early cartography, modern cartography, celestial, city, forestry, genealogy, geodetic surveys, geology, geospatial data, historical geography, hydrology, land ownership, land use, map catalogs, military, mineral resources, mining, nautical charts, political geography, projections, railroads, raised relief models, roads, soil, vegetation, views, waterways

Map depositories and percentages: USGS topos (100%), USGS geology maps (100%), USGS other (100%), NOAA, GPO, CIA, National Forest Service, NIMA topos, NIMA nautical, NIMA aeronautical, BLM, State, Army Corps of Engineers, European Union

230,000 printed maps
45 wall maps
35 raised relief maps
3,700 microfiche
18,000 aerial photos
175 satellite images
17 globes
5,800 printed atlases
420 CD-ROMs

Average budget over the last 5 years: $7,000

Access:
Maps in separate area
Collection is partially open to the public
Reference questions per year: 2,300
Answers email questions
Patrons per month: 200

Hours:
Monday–Friday: 10 A.M.–6 P.M.
Saturday: 11 A.M.–5 P.M.
Sunday: closed
Total hours per week opened: 46
Maps circulate
Circulation policies apply
 Map circulation duration: 1 week
 Number of maps circulated annually: 450

Geographic Information Systems:
GIS services available in an open environment
GIS software: ArcGIS 8.3, ArcView 3.0
GIS assistance available for Census mapping, and geocoding
Scans maps for patrons

Collection services:
Maps cataloged: 10%
Maps classified: 100%
Maps in OPAC: 10%
Datasets are cataloged
Classification schemes: LC, SuDocs
Cataloging utilities: OCLC
Catalog accessibility: online

Preservation techniques: encapsulation, deacidification, acid-free tape

Physical facilities:
Internet access available
Square footage: 5,500
Number of map cases: 309
Number of vertical files (file cabinets): 16
Linear book shelving: 36 ft.
Linear atlas shelving: 24 ft.
Copying facilities available: copier, large-format copier, microform copier, color scanner, color printer

333 *Santa Fe, NM*

Laboratory of Anthropology

Library
Archeological Records Management System
708 Camino Lejo
Santa Fe, NM 87503
Telephone: 505-476-1275
Fax: 505-476-1320
Email: register@arms.state.nm.us
Web: potsuii.arms.state.nm.us

Personnel:
Responsible person: Tim Seaman, ARMS Program Manager, *email:* seaman@arms.state.nm.us
FTE professionals: 8

Holdings:
Geographic strengths: New Mexico
Map depositories: USGS
2,050 printed maps

Collection services:
Classification schemes: Other (USGS)

Notes: This is not a public resource. The Lab maintains a set of USGS 7.5' maps for the entire state annotated with archeological site locations. The info is protected from public release by the NM Cultural Properties act, so we are not a public library. Since we implemented GIS about 8 years ago, these maps are used for archival purposes only. We have several other map series here, similarly annotated and protected.

334 *Santa Fe, NM*

New Mexico State Library

1209 Camino Carlos Rey
Santa Fe, NM 87507
Telephone: 505-476-9702
Fax: 505-476-9703
Email: refer@stlib.state.nm.us
Web: www.stlib.state.nm.us/

Personnel:
Responsible person: Laurie Canepa, Federal Document Librarian, *email:* laurie@stlib.state.nm.us

Assistants: Nicodemus Montoya, Federal Documents Collection Manager; Jo Anne Jager, Southwest Librarian
FTE professionals: 0.5   *FTE para-professionals:* 0.5

Holdings:
Geographic strengths: New Mexico
Special collections: Sanborn Fire Insurance maps (1890s–1940s) of New Mexico, FEMA Flood Insurance Maps of New Mexico, Census Block and Tract Maps (full sized-paper)
Map depositories: USGS topos, Department of Transportation, NOAA, CIA, National Forest Service, NGA nautical, NGA aeronautical, BLM
100,000 printed maps
100 aerial photos
100 atlases
100 books
200 CD-ROMs

Access:
Hours:
Monday–Friday: 9 A.M.–5 P.M.
Saturday–Sunday: closed

Collection services:
Maps cataloged: 50%
Maps classified: 50%
Maps in OPAC: 50%
Classification schemes: SuDocs, Dewey, Local

Physical facilities:
Public computers: 20
Map cases: 250

335 *Santa Fe, NM*

Palace of the Governors

Angélico Chávez History Library
Map Collection
120 Washington Avenue
Santa Fe, NM 87501
Telephone: 505-476-5090
Fax: 505-476-5053
Email: histlib@mnm.state.nm.us
Web: www.palaceofthegovernors.org/library.html

Personnel:
Responsible person: Tomas Jaehn, Curator, *email:* tjaehn@mnm.state.nm.us
Assistants: Hazel Romero, Library Assistant
FTE professionals: 1   *FTE para-professionals:* 1

Holdings:
Geographic strengths: New Mexico, Southwest, Mexico
6,000 printed maps
50 atlases
200 books

Access:
Hours:
Monday–Tuesday: 1 P.M.–5 P.M.
Wednesday: 1 P.M.–8 P.M.

Thursday–Friday: 1 P.M.–5 P.M.

Collection services:
Maps cataloged: 60%
Maps classified: 90%
Maps in OPAC: 0%
Classification schemes: Dewey

Physical facilities:
Maps in separate area
Public computers: 3
Map cases: 30

Notes: Map copying services are available within the library. Digital images are available within the museum system.

336 *Socorro, NM*

New Mexico Tech, New Mexico Bureau of Geology and Mineral Resources

Geological Information Center Library
801 Leroy Place
Socorro, NM 87801
Telephone: 505-835 5322
Fax: 505-835 6333
Email: mwilks@gis.nmt.edu
Web: www.geoinfo.nmt.edu/data/home.html#gic

Personnel:
Responsible person: Dr. Maureen Wilks, *email:* mwilks@gis.nmt.edu
FTE para-professionals: 1

Holdings:
Geographic strengths: New Mexico
Map depositories: USGS
4,000 printed maps
1,000 aerial photos
50 atlases
50 books
10 active serials
150 CD-ROMs

Access:
Hours:
Monday–Friday: 8 A.M.–noon, 1 P.M.–5 P.M.
Saturday–Sunday: closed

Collection services:
Maps cataloged: 25%
Maps classified: 25%
Maps in OPAC: 0%
Classification schemes: Local

Physical facilities:
Map cases: 17
Vertical files: 10

337 *Brooklyn, NY*

Pratt Institute

Library
200 Willoughby Avenue

Brooklyn, NY 11205
Telephone: 718-636-3704
Fax: 718-399-4220
Web: lib.pratt.edu/public
Personnel:
Responsible person: Paul Schlotthauer, Librarian/ Assistant Professor, *email:* pschlott@pratt.edu
FTE professionals: 1
Holdings:
Geographic strengths: New York City, Brooklyn
Special collections: Sanborn Fire Insurance maps, USGS topographic maps
1,800 printed maps
33 atlases
67 books
Access:
Hours:
Monday–Thursday: 9 A.M.–11 P.M.
Friday: 9 A.M.–5 P.M.
Saturday: noon–6 P.M.
Sunday: noon–8 P.M.
Collection services:
Classification schemes: Dewey
Physical facilities:
Public computers: 14
Map cases: 9
Vertical files: 3

338 *Buffalo, NY*

Buffalo and Erie County Public Library

Central Library
Humanities and Social Sciences
1 Lafayette Square
Buffalo, NY 14203
Telephone: 716-858-8900
Fax: 716-858-6211
Web: www.buffalolib.org
Personnel:
Responsible person: Patricia M. Monahan, *email:* monahanp@buffalolib.org
FTE para-professionals: 0.5
Holdings:
Geographic strengths: Buffalo, New York State
Special collections: Sanborn Fire Insurance maps for Buffalo, Soil Surveys for New York and Pennsylvania, FEMA and Flood Insurance maps for Western New York
Subject strengths: aerial photos, agriculture, city, engineering, genealogy, geodetic surveys, geology, geospatial data, historical geography, hydrology, land ownership, land use, map catalogs, military, mineral resources, nautical charts, political geography, population, recreation, roads, soil, travel books, waterways

Map depositories and percentages: USGS topos (30%), USGS geology maps (10%), NOAA, CIA, National Forest Service, NIMA topos, NIMA nautical
80,000 printed maps
100 manuscript maps
25 wall maps
10 raised relief maps
100 aerial photos
300 gazetteers
200 printed atlases
Chronological coverage:
Pre-1800: 10%
1800–1899: 35%
1900–1939: 40%
1940–present: 15%
Average budget over the last 5 years: $500
On-going publications: "Map Collection of the BECPL" pamphlet and PowerPoint presentation
Access:
Maps in separate area
Collection is paged
Reference questions per year: 100
Answers email questions
Patrons per month: 20
Hours:
Monday–Saturday: 8:30 A.M.–6 P.M.
Sunday: 1 P.M.–5 P.M.
Total hours per week opened: 58
Interlibrary loan available
Geographic Information Systems:
No GIS services available
Scans maps for patrons
Collection services:
Maps cataloged: 30%
Maps classified: 100%
Maps in OPAC: 30%
Classification schemes: LC, Local
Cataloging utilities: OCLC
Catalog accessibility: online, cards
Preservation techniques: encapsulation, lamination
Physical facilities:
No Internet access
Square footage: 1,200
Number of map cases: 40
Copying facilities available: copier, color copier, large-format copier, microform copier

339 *Buffalo, NY*

State University of New York, Buffalo

Arts and Sciences Libraries
Map Collection
Capen Hall
Buffalo, NY 14260-1672
Telephone: 716-645-2947

Fax: 716-645-3710
Email: askasl@buffalo.edu
Web: ublib.buffalo.edu/libraries/asl/maps/map_room
.html
Personnel:
Responsible person: David J. Bertuca, Map Librarian,
email: dbertuca@buffalo.edu
Number of student workers hours per week: 20
Holdings:
Geographic strengths: Buffalo, Eire County, Niagara
County, New York State, Pennsylvania
Subject strengths: aerial photos, aeronautical, agriculture, biology, early cartography, modern cartography,
celestial, climatology, city, economic geography, engineering, forestry, geodetic surveys, geology,
geospatial data, historical geography, hydrology, industries, land use, language, map catalogs, map collecting, military, mineral resources, mining, nautical
charts, oceanography, political geography, population, projections, railroads, raised relief models, recreation, religion, roads, satellite imagery, soil, travel
books, vegetation, views, waterways, zoogeography
Map depositories and percentages: USGS topos
(100%), USGS geology maps (100%), USGS other
(100%), Department of Transportation, NOAA, CIA,
National Forest Service, NIMA topos, NIMA nautical, NIMA aeronautical, BLM, State, United Nations
320,300 printed maps
40 manuscript maps
30 wall maps
50 raised relief maps
10 microfilms
4,300 aerial photos
44 satellite images
50 gazetteers
510 printed atlases
42 books
32 CD-ROMs
16 computer programs
Chronological coverage:
1900–1939: 10%
1940–present: 85%
On-going publications: Website for Map Collection
provides ongoing updates. Also, Libraries Website
provides news.
Access:
Maps in separate area
Collection is partially open to the public
Maps off site: 15%
Answers email questions
Hours:
Total hours per week opened: 102
Maps circulate
Circulation policies apply
Number of maps circulated annually: 1,500

Interlibrary loan available
Geographic Information Systems:
GIS services available in an open environment
GIS software: ArcView, Topo US
GIS assistance available for Census mapping, and im-
age analysis
Scans maps for patrons
Collection services:
Maps cataloged: 95%
Maps classified: 60%
Maps in OPAC: 95%
Datasets are cataloged
Classification schemes: LC, SuDocs, Other
(alphabetical)
Cataloging utilities: OCLC, RLG
Catalog accessibility: online
Preservation techniques: encapsulation, edging, digi-
tization
Physical facilities:
Internet access available
Square footage: 1,200
Number of vertical files (file cabinets): 25
Number of atlas stands: 12
Linear book shelving: 30 ft.
Linear atlas shelving: 92 ft.
Other map storage: storage room
Copying facilities available: copier, microform copier

340 *Ithaca, NY*

Cornell University

John M. Olin Library
Map and Geospatial Information Collection, founded
1961
Ithaca, NY 14853-5301
Telephone: 607-255-7557
Fax: 607-255-9346
Email: olinmaps@cornell.edu
Web: www.library.cornell.edu/okuref/maps/map.htm
Personnel:
Responsible person: Susan Greaves, Map and GIS Li-
brarian, *email:* sjg4@cornell.edu
Assistants: Debra Bacon, Collection Assistant
Number of student workers hours per week: 30
Holdings:
Geographic strengths: Southeast Asia
Subject strengths: aerial photos, aeronautical, agricul-
ture, biology, early cartography, modern cartography,
celestial, climatology, city, economic geography, engineering, forestry, geodetic surveys, geology,
geospatial data, historical geography, hydrology, industries, land use, language, map catalogs, map collecting, military, mineral resources, mining, nautical
charts, oceanography, political geography, population, projections, railroads, raised relief models, recre-

ation, religion, roads, satellite imagery, soil, travel books, vegetation, views, waterways, zoogeography

Map depositories and percentages: USGS topos (100%), USGS geology maps (100%), USGS other (100%), NOAA, GPO, CIA, National Forest Service, NIMA topos, NIMA nautical, NIMA aeronautical, BLM, State

242,000 printed maps

100 wall maps

25 raised relief maps

110 aerial photos

100 satellite images

15 globes

360 gazetteers

3,126 printed atlases

500 CD-ROMs

Collecting digital data

Chronological coverage:
  1900–1939: 20%
  1940–present: 78%

Average budget over the last 5 years: $18,000

Access:

Maps in separate area

Collection is open to the public

Reference questions per year: 4,500

Answers email questions

Patrons per month: 300

Hours:

  Monday–Friday: 10 A.M.–5 P.M.

  Saturday: 1 P.M.–5 P.M.

  Total hours per week opened: 39

Interlibrary loan available

Geographic Information Systems:

GIS services available by appointment

GIS software: ESRI

GIS assistance available for Census mapping, and image analysis

General GIS questions answered, and assistance locating data available

Scans maps for patrons

Collection services:

Maps cataloged: 90%

Maps classified: 100%

Maps in OPAC: 70%

Datasets are cataloged

Classification schemes: LC

Cataloging utilities: OCLC

Catalog accessibility: online, cards

Preservation techniques: encapsulation, deacidification, cartex

Items that have gone through the preservation process: 10%

Physical facilities:

Internet access available

Square footage: 4,461

Number of map cases: 282

Number of vertical files (file cabinets): 25

Linear book shelving: 351 ft.

Linear atlas shelving: 1,056 ft.

Copying facilities available: copier, color copier, large-format copier, microform copier, digital camera, oversize scanner

341 *Jamaica, NY*

Queens Borough Public Library

Long Island Division

Founded 1912

89-11 Merrick Boulevard

Jamaica, NY 11432

Telephone: 718-990-0770

Fax: 718-658-8342

Web: queenslibrary.org

Holdings:

Geographic strengths: Long Island

Special collections: E. Belcher Hyde Map Company maps, Sanborn Company maps, DeBevoise Map Collection

Subject strengths: aerial photos, city, engineering, genealogy, historical geography, land ownership, nautical charts, population, railroads, roads, travel books

750 printed maps

450 aerial photos

112 printed atlases

Chronological coverage:
  1800–1899: 25%
  1900–1939: 30%
  1940–present: 40%

Access:

Collection is open to the public

Reference questions per year: 120

Patrons per month: 199

Hours:

  Monday–Saturday: 10 A.M.–5:30 P.M.

  Sunday: noon–5 P.M.

  Total hours per week opened: 50

Geographic Information Systems:

No GIS services available

Collection services:

Maps cataloged: 2%

Maps classified: 98%

Classification schemes: Local

Catalog accessibility: online

Preservation techniques: encapsulation, deacidification

Items that have gone through the preservation process: 20%

Physical facilities:

No Internet access

Number of map cases: 20

Linear atlas shelving: 100 ft.

Copying facilities available: copier, microform copier

342 *New York, NY*

Columbia University

Lehman Library Map Collection
420 West 118th Street
New York, NY 10027
Telephone: 212-854-5664
Fax: 212-854-1365
Email: jt2118@columbia.edu
Web: www.columbia.edu/cu/lweb/indiv/lehman/guides/maps.html

Personnel:

Responsible person: Jeremiah Trinidad-Christensen, GIS/Map Librarian, *email:* jt2118@columbia.edu
FTE professionals: 1   *FTE para-professionals:* 0.5

Holdings:

Geographic strengths: New York City, New York State
Map depositories: USGS topos, Department of Transportation, CIA, National Forest Service
116,500 printed maps
300 atlases
300 books

Access:

Hours:

Monday–Friday: 9 A.M.–midnight
Saturday: 10 A.M.–6 P.M.
Sunday: 11 A.M.–11 P.M.

Collection services:

Maps cataloged: 2%
Maps in OPAC: 2%
Classification schemes: LC, SuDocs, Other (alphabetical and conspectus)

Physical facilities:

Maps in separate area
Map cases: 160
Vertical files: 3

343 *New York, NY*

New York Public Library

Humanities and Social Sciences Library
Map Division, founded 1898
5th Ave and 42nd Street
Room 117
New York, NY 10018
Telephone: 212-930-0587
Fax: 212-930-0027
Email: mapref@nypl.org
Web: www.nypl.org/research/chss/map/map.html

Personnel:

Responsible person: Alice Hudson, Chief, *email:* ahudson@nypl.org
Assistants: Matthew Knutzen, Assistant Chief; Nancy Kandoian, Senior Cataloger; Alexandra Cabreja, Library Technical Assistant

Number of student workers hours per week: 17
Number of volunteer hours per month: 70

Holdings:

Geographic strengths: New York City, New York State, Northeast, Middle Atlantic, United States, North America
Special collections: Metropolitan New York City Real Estate Atlases, Road Map Collection (1890–), Lawrence H. Slaughter Collection of Middle Atlantic United States maps, Levine Collection of antique maps, postcard and holiday card maps, united states 19th-century county atlases
Subject strengths: aerial photos, aeronautical, archaeology, early cartography, modern cartography, city, economic geography, genealogy, geodetic surveys, geology, geospatial data, historical geography, land ownership, land use, map catalogs, map collecting, military, mineral resources, nautical charts, political geography, projections, railroads, recreation, religion, roads, travel books, views, waterways, Gazetteers, Dictionaries of Cartographic terms
Map depositories and percentages: USGS topos (100%), USGS geology maps (100%), USGS other (100%), Department of Transportation, NOAA, GPO, CIA, National Forest Service, NIMA topos, NIMA nautical, NIMA aeronautical
428,883 printed maps
100 manuscript maps
52 raised relief maps
40,227 microfiche
400 aerial photos
100 satellite images
20 globes
500 gazetteers
16,700 printed atlases
6,293 books
79 CD-ROMs
30 computer programs
Collecting digital data
Chronological coverage:
1800–1899: 25%
1900–1939: 20%
1940–present: 50%
Average budget over the last 5 years: $50,000
On-going publications: Dictionary Catalog of the Map Division (1971, 10 vol.)

Access:

Maps in separate area
Collection is paged
Maps off site
Reference questions per year: 9,484
Answers email questions
Patrons per month: 540

Hours:

Monday: closed

Tuesday: 1 P.M.–7:30 P.M.
Wednesday–Saturday: 1 P.M.–6 P.M.
Sunday: closed
Total hours per week opened: 26.5

Geographic Information Systems:

GIS services available by appointment

GIS assistance available for Census mapping, and geocoding

Scans maps for patrons

Collection services:

Maps cataloged: 80%

Maps classified: 100%

Maps in OPAC: 20%

Datasets are cataloged

Classification schemes: LC, Local

Cataloging utilities: OCLC, RLG

Catalog accessibility: online, printout

Preservation techniques: encapsulation, deacidification

Items that have gone through the preservation process: 20%

Physical facilities:

No Internet access

Square footage: 8,000

Number of map cases: 396

Number of vertical files (file cabinets): 17

Linear book shelving: 1,818 ft.

Linear atlas shelving: 1,263 ft.

Other map storage: 13 rolled map cases

Copying facilities available: copier, large-format copier, microform copier

Notes: NYPL Map Division is undergoing a complete renovation in 2005/6. Call or email before visiting

344 *New York, NY*

New York Historical Society

New York Historical Society Library
2 West 77th Street
New York, NY 10024
Telephone: 212-485-9225
Fax: 212-875-1591
Web: www.nyhistory.org

Holdings:

Geographic strengths: New York City Metropolitan region

Special collections: Erskine Dewitt Manuscript maps, (restricted access), Veiller's 1899 overcrowding maps, Sanborn Fire Insurance maps

Subject strengths: early cartography, modern cartography, city, geology, land ownership, population, railroads, roads, travel books, views

8,000 printed maps

3,500 manuscript maps

350 printed atlases

Chronological coverage:

Pre-1800: 13%

1800–1899: 60%

1900–1939: 18%

Average budget over the last 5 years: $1,500

Access:

Maps in separate area

Collection is paged

Hours:

Tuesday–Saturday: 10 A.M.–5 P.M.

Total hours per week opened: 35

Geographic Information Systems:

No GIS services available

Collection services:

Maps cataloged: 100%

Maps classified: 30%

Maps in OPAC: 100%

Classification schemes: LC

Cataloging utilities: OCLC, RLG

Catalog accessibility: online

Preservation techniques: encapsulation, deacidification

Physical facilities:

No Internet access

Copying facilities available: none

345 *Stony Brook, NY*

Stony Brook University

Melville Library
Map Collection, founded 1974
Stony Brook, NY 11790
Telephone: 631-632-7110
Web: www.sunysb.edu/library/ldmaps.htm

Personnel:

Responsible person: David Allen, Librarian

FTE para-professionals: 0.25

Number of student workers hours per week: 10

Holdings:

Geographic strengths: Long Island, New York State

Special collections: New York State Historical maps, United States Soil Survey Collection

Subject strengths: aerial photos, aeronautical, early cartography, modern cartography, celestial, city, economic geography, geodetic surveys, geology, geospatial data, historical geography, hydrology, land ownership, land use, language, map catalogs, nautical charts, oceanography, political geography, population, projections, railroads, recreation, religion, roads, soil, travel books, waterways

Map depositories and percentages: USGS topos (100%), USGS geology maps (100%), USGS other (100%), Department of Transportation, NOAA, GPO, CIA, National Forest Service, NIMA topos, NIMA nautical, NIMA aeronautical, BLM

134,000 printed maps
10 manuscript maps
15 wall maps
250 microfiche
1,000 microfilms
3,200 aerial photos
800 gazetteers
1,357 printed atlases
800 books
500 CD-ROMs
Collecting digital data
Chronological coverage:
    Pre-1800: >1%
    1940–present: 97%
Average budget over the last 5 years: $4,000

Access:

Collection is partially open to the public
Answers email questions

Hours:

Monday–Friday: 8:30 A.M.–midnight
Saturday: 10 A.M.–6 P.M.
Sunday: noon–2 P.M.
Total hours per week opened: 95
Maps circulate
Circulation policies apply
    Map circulation duration: 1 week
Interlibrary loan available

Geographic Information Systems:

GIS services available in an open environment
GIS software: ArcGIS, LandView
Number of public GIS workstations: 20
Number of GIS stations (not monitored): 50 (campus)
GIS assistance available for Census mapping, and image analysis
Scans maps for patrons

Collection services:

Maps cataloged: 60%
Maps classified: 100%
Maps in OPAC: 60%
Datasets are cataloged
Classification schemes: LC
Cataloging utilities: OCLC, RLG, Local
Catalog accessibility: online
Preservation techniques: encapsulation, deacidification
Items that have gone through the preservation process: 10%

Physical facilities:

Internet access available
Number of public computers: 20
Number of map cases: 82
Number of vertical files (file cabinets): 20
Number of atlas stands: 15
Linear book shelving: 540 ft.
Linear atlas shelving: 1,080 ft.
Number of microform readers: 10

Number of microform printers: 10
Copying facilities available: copier, color copier, microform copier

Notes: We are a dispersed collection with many services and much equipment located throughout the libraries.

346 *Syracuse, NY*

Syracuse University

Maps and Government Information, founded 1940?
Bird Library
Room 358
Syracuse, NY 13244
Telephone: 315-443-4176
Fax: 315-443-9510
Email: mapdocs@syr.edu
Web: libwww.syr.edu/information/mgi/index.html

Personnel:

Responsible person: John Olson, Maps/GIS Librarian, email: jaolson@syr.edu
FTE professionals: 0.5
Number of student workers hours per week: 30

Holdings:

Geographic strengths: Central New York
Special collections: New York City Sanborn Fire Insurance maps, Robert Burgess Vegetation Map Collection
Subject strengths: aerial photos, forestry, geology, geospatial data, mineral resources, nautical charts, recreation, roads, soil, travel books, vegetation
Map depositories and percentages: USGS topos (95%), USGS geology maps (67%), Department of Transportation, NOAA, GPO, CIA, National Forest Service, State, New York State
175,000 printed maps
10 manuscript maps
40 wall maps
50 raised relief maps
40,000 microfiche
800 microfilms
80,000 aerial photos
10 satellite images
250 gazetteers
3,500 printed atlases
1,000 books
10 active serials
50 inactive serials
150 CD-ROMs
30 computer programs
Collecting digital data
Chronological coverage:
    1900–1939: 30%
    1940–present: 65%

Access:

Maps in separate area
Collection is open to the public
Answers email questions
Patrons per month: 100
Hours:
    Monday–Friday: 8 A.M.–10 P.M.
    Saturday: 10 A.M.–6 P.M.
    Sunday: noon–10 P.M.
    Total hours per week opened: 88
Maps circulate
Circulation policies apply
    Map circulation duration: 4 weeks
Interlibrary loan available
Geographic Information Systems:
GIS services available by appointment
GIS software: ArcView, ArcGIS
GIS assistance available for Census mapping, and geocoding
Plotter available
Scans maps for patrons
Collection services:
Maps cataloged: 75%
Maps classified: 100%
Maps in OPAC: 75%
Datasets are cataloged
Classification schemes: LC, SuDocs, Local, Other (OSS)
Cataloging utilities: OCLC, RLG
Catalog accessibility: online, cards
Preservation techniques: encapsulation, deacidification
Physical facilities:
Internet access available
Square footage: 4,000
Number of map cases: 156
Number of vertical files (file cabinets): 14
Linear book shelving: 1,800 ft.
Linear atlas shelving: 800 ft.
Other map storage: 2 locked glass cabinets
Copying facilities available: copier, color copier, large-format copier, microform copier, film scanner to disk or paper

347 *Boone, NC*

Appalachian State University

Department of Geography and Planning
Boone, NC 28618
Telephone: 828-262-3000
Fax: 828-262-3067
Web: www.geo.appstate.edu
Personnel:
Responsible person: Dr. James Young, Chair and Associate Professor, *email:* youngje@appstate.edu
Number of student works: 4

Number of student workers hours per week: 36
Holdings:
Geographic strengths: North Carolina
Subject strengths: modern cartography, climatology, economic geography, geology, geospatial data, hydrology, population, roads, vegetation
Map depositories: USGS topos, USGS geology maps, USGS other, NOAA, National Forest Service, BLM
50,000 printed maps
400 wall maps
50 raised relief maps
250 printed atlases
50 books
200 CD-ROMs
Collecting digital data
Chronological coverage:
    1940–present: 95%
Access:
Maps in separate area
Collection is partially open to the public
Hours:
    Monday–Friday: 9 A.M.–3 P.M.
    Total hours per week opened: 30
Geographic Information Systems:
No GIS services available
Physical facilities:
Internet access available
Copying facilities available: copier
Notes: In the process of cataloging the collection, but it has been slow going.

348 *Buies Creek, NC*

Campbell University

Carrie Rich Memorial Library
Government Documents
227 Main Street
Buies Creek, NC 27506
Telephone: 910-893-1465
Fax: 910-893-1470
Email: pdavis@camel.campbell.edu
Web: www.lib.campbell.edu
Personnel:
Responsible person: Marie Berry, Reference Librarian, *email:* berry@camel.campbell.edu
Assistants: Pat Davis, Government Documents Assistant
FTE professionals: 0.2   *FTE para-professionals:* 1
Holdings:
Geographic strengths: North Carolina, South Carolina, Virginia
Map depositories: USGS
8,307 printed maps
1 globe
30 atlases

100 CD-ROMs

Access:

Hours:

Monday–Friday: 8 P.M.–4:30 P.M.

Saturday–Sunday: closed

Collection services:

Maps cataloged: 0%

Maps classified: 0%

Maps in OPAC: 0%

Classification schemes: SuDocs

Physical facilities:

Public computers: 2

Map cases: 5

349 *Chapel Hill, NC*

University of North Carolina, Chapel Hill

Academic Affairs Library

North Carolina Collection

CB #3930

Wilson Library

Chapel Hill, NC 27514-8890

Telephone: 919-962-1172

Fax: 919-962-4452

Email: nccref@email.unc.edu

Web: www.lib.unc.edu/ncc

Personnel:

Responsible person: Robert G. Anthony, Jr., Curator, *email:* nccref@email.unc.edu

Assistants: Eileen McGrath, Collection Management Librarian; Nicholas Graham, Head of Public Services; Jessica Efron, Maps Cataloger (a term appointment)

FTE professionals: 1.3   *FTE para-professionals:* 0.2

Holdings:

Geographic strengths: North Carolina, Southeast

Special collections: Sanborn Fire Insurance maps for North Carolina towns, Garland Stout maps of North Carolina counties, North Carolina maps from W.P. Cumming's the Southeast in Early maps

Subject strengths: city, political geography, railroads, roads, soil, travel books, University of North Carolina campus

5,000 printed maps

10 wall maps

10 raised relief maps

10 aerial photos

10 satellite images

20 printed atlases

20 CD-ROMs

Chronological coverage:

Pre-1800: 15%

1800–1899: 25%

1900–1939: 20%

1940–present: 40%

Average budget over the last 5 years: $400

Access:

Maps in separate area

Collection is paged

Answers email questions

Patrons per month: 50

Hours:

Monday–Friday: 8 A.M.–5 P.M.

Saturday: 9 A.M.–1 P.M.

Sunday: 1 P.M.–5 P.M.

Total hours per week opened: 53

Geographic Information Systems:

No GIS services available

Scans maps for patrons

Collection services:

Maps cataloged: 98%

Maps classified: 98%

Maps in OPAC: 35%

Classification schemes: Local

Cataloging utilities: OCLC

Catalog accessibility: online, cards

Preservation techniques: encapsulation, deacidification, lamination

Items that have gone through the preservation process: 90%

Physical facilities:

Internet access available

Square footage: 210

Number of map cases: 30

Copying facilities available: copier, large-format copier, microform copier, photographic reproduction, scanner

350 *Chapel Hill, NC*

University of North Carolina, Chapel Hill

Geological Sciences Library

CB #3315

Mitchell Hall

Chapel Hill, NC 27516

Telephone: 919-962-2386

Fax: 919-966-4519

Email: kennard@email.unc.edu

Web: www.lib.unc.edu/geolib/

Personnel:

Responsible person: Miriam L. Kennard, *email:* kennard@email.unc.edu

Assistants: Lynn Turner, Library Technical Assistant

FTE professionals: 1

Holdings:

Geographic strengths: United States

41,000 printed maps

3 globes

145 CD-ROMs

Access:

Hours:

Monday–Friday: 8 A.M.–5 P.M.

Items circulate

Interlibrary loan available

Collection services:

Maps cataloged: 0.01%

Maps classified: 65%

Maps in OPAC: 0.01%

Classification schemes: LC

Physical facilities:

Maps in separate area

Public computers: 4

Map cases: 35

Notes: Our library is in the process of transferring our map collection to the main library's map collection. The Geological Sciences Library's map collection is to be merged (defunct) by the end of the summer, 2004.

351 *Chapel Hill, NC*

University of North Carolina, Chapel Hill

John N. Couch Biology Library

Botany Section

CB #3280

Coker Hall

Chapel Hill, NC 27599-3280

Telephone: 919-962-3783

Fax: 919-843-8393

Email: billburk@email.unc.edu

Web: wwww.lib.unc.edu/biology

Personnel:

Responsible person: William R. Burk, *email:* billburk@email.unc.edu

Assistants: Jeffery S. Beam

FTE professionals: 1   *FTE para-professionals:* 1

Holdings:

Geographic strengths: North Carolina

Map depositories: USGS

2,086 printed maps

12 atlases

Access:

Hours:

Monday–Friday: 8 A.M.–5 P.M.

Items circulate

Collection services:

Maps cataloged: 100%

Maps classified: 0%

Maps in OPAC: 0%

Physical facilities:

Maps in separate area

Map cases: 4

352 *Chapel Hill, NC*

University of North Carolina, Chapel Hill

Wilson Library

Davis Reference/Maps Collection, founded 1968

CB #3928

Chapel Hill, NC 27514-8890

Telephone: 919-962-3028

Fax: 919-962-4452

Email: cd P.M.aps@email.unc.edu

Web: www.lib.unc.edu/maps and www.lib.unc.edu

Personnel:

Responsible person: Celia D. Pratt, Map Librarian, *email:* cd P.M.aps@email.unc.edu

Assistants: Jennifer Pendergast, Library Technical Assistant

Number of student workers hours per week: 31

Holdings:

Geographic strengths: North Carolina, Southeast, United States, East Africa, Latin America, North America, East Asia, South Asia, Europe

Special collections: Ancient World maps, Sanborn Fire Insurance maps of North Carolina (online access)

Subject strengths: aerial photos, aeronautical, archaeology, climatology, city, historical geography, map catalogs, nautical charts, political geography, population, railroads, raised relief models, roads, satellite imagery, vegetation, views, Classical history

Map depositories and percentages: USGS topos (100%), USGS geology maps (100%), USGS other (100%), Department of Transportation, NOAA, CIA, National Forest Service, NIMA topos, NIMA nautical, NIMA aeronautical, BLM, Fish and Wildlife, Census, US Army Corps of Engineers, Bureau of Indian Affairs

271,100 printed maps

100 wall maps

170 raised relief maps

2,600 microfiche

5,000 aerial photos

500 satellite images

550 gazetteers

1,910 printed atlases

1,150 books

26 active serials

70 CD-ROMs

Chronological coverage:

1940–present: 93%

Access:

Maps in separate area

Collection is open to the public

Reference questions per year: 900

Answers email questions

Patrons per month: 75

Hours:
>Monday–Friday: 8 A.M.–5 P.M.
>Saturday–Saturday: closed
>Total hours per week opened: 45
>*Maps circulate*
>*Circulation policies apply*
>>*Map circulation duration:* 1 week
>>*Number of maps circulated annually:* 2,600
>*Interlibrary loan available*

Geographic Information Systems:
>*No GIS services available*
>Plotter available
>Scans maps for patrons

Collection services:
>*Maps cataloged:* 55%
>*Maps classified:* 55%
>*Maps in OPAC:* 55%
>*Datasets are cataloged*
>*Classification schemes:* LC, SuDocs, Dewey
>*Cataloging utilities:* OCLC, Local
>*Catalog accessibility:* online, cards
>*Preservation techniques:* encapsulation, deacidification, Acid-free, lignon-free folders
>*Items that have gone through the preservation process:* 1%

Physical facilities:
>*Internet access available*
>*Square footage:* 5,100
>*Number of map cases:* 161
>*Number of vertical files (file cabinets):* 11
>*Linear book shelving:* 600 ft.
>*Linear atlas shelving:* 852 ft.
>*Copying facilities available:* copier, microform copier, scanner, color printer

353 *Charlotte, NC*

Public Library of Charlotte, Mecklenburg County

North Carolina Room Map Collection
310 North Tryon Street
Charlotte, NC 28202
Telephone: 704-336-2980
Fax: 704-336-6236
Email: ncrstaff@plcmc.org
Web: www.plcmc.org

Personnel:
>*Responsible person:* Valerie Burnie, Reference Librarian, *email:* ncrstaff@plcmc.org
>*FTE professionals:* 0.1

Holdings:
>*Geographic strengths:* Charlotte–Mecklenburg County, North Carolina, South Carolina, Virginia, Georgia, Tennessee
>*Map depositories:* USGS
>3,000 printed maps

50 aerial photos
25 atlases
25 books
5 CD-ROMs

Access:
>**Hours:**
>>Monday–Thursday: 9 A.M.–9 P.M.
>>Friday–Saturday: 9 A.M.–6 P.M.
>>Sunday: 1 P.M.–6 P.M.

Collection services:
>*Maps cataloged:* 100%
>*Maps classified:* 100%
>*Classification schemes:* SuDocs, Local

Physical facilities:
>Maps in separate area
>*Map cases:* 10
>*Vertical files:* 3

Notes: Our historic maps not copyrighted are available online through a link from the Char–Meck Story page to County Engineering.

354 *Charlotte, NC*

University of North Carolina, Charlotte

J. Murrey Atkins Library
9201 University City Boulevard
Charlotte, NC 282223
Telephone: 704-687-3601
Fax: 704-687-3050
Web: library.uncc.edu/

Personnel:
>*FTE professionals: FTE para-professionals:* 0.25

Holdings:
>*Geographic strengths:* Charlotte region, Charlotte–Mecklenburg County, North Carolina
>*Map depositories:* USGS topos, NOAA, CIA, NGA nautical
>54,099 printed maps
>1,330 aerial photos
>3 globes
>1,096 atlases
>1,466 books
>13 active serials
>642 CD-ROMs

Access:
>**Hours:**
>>Monday–Friday: 7:30 A.M.–midnight
>>Saturday: 10 A.M.–8 P.M.
>>Sunday: 11 A.M.–midnight

Collection services:
>*Maps cataloged:* 5%
>*Maps classified:* 90%
>*Maps in OPAC:* 5%
>*Classification schemes:* LC, SuDocs, Local

Physical facilities:

Map cases: 44
Vertical files: 6

355 *Cullowhee, NC*

Western Carolina University

Hunter Library
Map Room, founded 1982
176 Central Drive
Cullowhee, NC 28723
Telephone: 828-227-3394
Fax: 828-227-7380
Web: www.wcu.edu/library/research/maps/index.htm
Personnel:
Responsible person: Head, Map Room, *email:* aoser@ wcu.edu
Number of student workers hours per week: 24
Holdings:
Geographic strengths: North Carolina
Subject strengths: aeronautical
Map depositories and percentages: USGS topos (100%), USGS geology maps (100%), USGS other (100%), Department of Transportation, GPO, CIA, National Forest Service, NIMA topos, NIMA aeronautical, BLM, State
124,008 printed maps
11 raised relief maps
2396 microfiche
83 gazetteers
753 printed atlases
514 books
588 CD-ROMs
11 computer programs
Chronological coverage:
    1940–present: 99%
Average budget over the last 5 years: $2,000
Access:
Maps in separate area
Collection is open to the public
Reference questions per year: 500
Answers email questions
Hours:
    Monday–Friday: 11 A.M.–3 P.M.
    Saturday–Saturday: closed
    Total hours per week opened: 20
Maps circulate
Circulation policies apply
    Map circulation duration: 3 days
    Atlas circulation duration: 3 days
    Book circulation duration: 3 days
    Number of maps circulated annually: 90
Interlibrary loan available
Geographic Information Systems:
GIS services available in an open environment
GIS software: ArcGIS

GIS assistance available for Census mapping, geocoding, and image analysis
Collection services:
Maps classified: 100%
Datasets are cataloged
Classification schemes: LC
Cataloging utilities: OCLC
Catalog accessibility: online, cards
Preservation techniques: encapsulation
Items that have gone through the preservation process: 0%
Physical facilities:
Internet access available
Number of map cases: 33
Linear book shelving: 270 ft.
Linear atlas shelving: 99 ft.

356 *Durham, NC*

Duke University

Public Documents and Maps Department, founded 1945
025 Perkins Library
Durham, NC 27708-0177
Telephone: 919-660-5851
Fax: 919-684-2855
Email: perkins-docmaps@duke.edu
Web: docs.lib.duke.edu/maps/
Personnel:
Responsible person: Mark Thomas, Map and GIS Librarian, *email:* mark.thomas@duke.edu
Assistants: Melissa Raymer, Federal/Maps Assistant
FTE professionals: 0.375   *FTE para-professionals:* 0.25
Number of student workers hours per week: 20
Holdings:
Geographic strengths: Durham County, North Carolina, Southeast, Canada, South Asia
Subject strengths: aeronautical, geology, military, nautical charts, recreation, roads
Map depositories and percentages: USGS topos (100%), USGS geology maps (100%), USGS other (100%), Department of Transportation, GPO, CIA, National Forest Service, NIMA topos, NIMA nautical, NIMA aeronautical, State, European Union
134,000 printed maps
30 wall maps
44 raised relief maps
3,000 microfiche
61 microfilms
874 aerial photos
210 gazetteers
120 printed atlases
100 books
249 CD-ROMs
27 computer programs
Collecting digital data

Chronological coverage:
  1940–present: 94%
Average budget over the last 5 years: $5,500
Access:
  Maps in separate area
  Collection is open to the public
  Reference questions per year: 300
  Answers email questions
  Patrons per month: 50
Hours:
  Monday–Friday: 9 A.M.–5 P.M.
  Saturday–Sunday: 1 P.M.–5 P.M.
  Total hours per week opened: 48
  Maps circulate
  Circulation policies apply
    Map circulation duration: 1 week
    Number of maps circulated annually: 213
Geographic Information Systems:
  GIS services available in an open environment
  GIS software: ArcGIS, ArcView, MapInfo
  GIS assistance available for Census mapping, geocoding, and image analysis
  Scans maps for patrons
Collection services:
  Maps cataloged: 30%
  Maps classified: 40%
  Maps in OPAC: 30%
  Datasets are cataloged
  Classification schemes: LC, SuDocs, Dewey
  Cataloging utilities: OCLC
  Catalog accessibility: online
  Preservation techniques: encapsulation
Physical facilities:
  Internet access available
  Square footage: 1,400
  Number of map cases: 125
  Number of vertical files (file cabinets): 12
  Linear book shelving: 117 ft.
  Linear atlas shelving: 51 ft.
  Copying facilities available: copier, microform copier

357 *Durham, NC*

Duke University

Rare Book, Manuscript, and Special Collections Library
Map Collection
Box 90185
Durham, NC 27708-0185
Telephone: 919-660-5822
Fax: 919-660-5934
Email: special-collections@duke.edu
Web: scriptorium.lib.duke.edu
Holdings:
  Geographic strengths: North America

Subject strengths: aerial photos, early cartography, modern cartography, city, historical geography, land ownership, land use, map catalogs, military, political geography, railroads, roads, views, waterways
2,804 printed maps
360 manuscript maps
Access:
  Collection is paged
  Answers email questions
Hours:
  Monday–Thursday: 9 A.M.–9 P.M.
  Friday: 9 A.M.–5 P.M.
  Saturday: 1 A.M.–5 P.M.
  Sunday: closed
Geographic Information Systems:
  No GIS services available
  Scans maps for patrons
Collection services:
  Maps cataloged: 99%
  Maps in OPAC: 99%
  Classification schemes: Local
  Cataloging utilities: OCLC, Local
  Catalog accessibility: online
  Preservation techniques: encapsulation, deacidification
Physical facilities:
  Internet access available
  Copying facilities available: copier, large-format copier, microform copier

358 *Greensboro, NC*

Greensboro Public Library

North Carolina Collection
219 North Church Street
Greensboro, NC 27402-3178
Telephone: 336-335-5430
Fax: 336-335-5416
Email: helen.snow@greensboro-ci.gov
Web: www.greensborolibrary.org
Personnel:
  Responsible person: Helen Snow, North Carolina Librarian, *email:* helen.snow@greensboro-nc.gov
Holdings:
  Geographic strengths: Greensboro, Guilford County, North Carolina
  Subject strengths: city
  1,404 printed maps
  11 wall maps
  Chronological coverage:
    Pre-1800: 10%
    1800–1899: 10%
    1900–1939: 15%
    1940–present: 65%
  Average budget over the last 5 years: $200

On-going publications: Typed list

Access:

Collection is open to the public

Reference questions per year: 60

Answers email questions

Patrons per month: 20

Hours:

Monday–Friday: 9 A.M.–9 P.M.

Saturday: 9 A.M.–6 P.M.

Sunday: 2 P.M.–6 P.M.

Total hours per week opened: 73

Collection services:

Maps cataloged: 90%

Maps in OPAC: 50%

Classification schemes: Dewey

Cataloging utilities: OCLC

Catalog accessibility: online

Preservation techniques: encapsulation, lamination

Items that have gone through the preservation process: 10%

Physical facilities:

Internet access available

Copying facilities available: copier, color copier, microform copier

Notes: The Greensboro Public Library has an atlas collection appropriate for a public library of its size (not included in this survey), but the NC Collection houses the only map case in the library system.

359 *Greensboro, NC*

University of North Carolina, Greensboro

Jackson Library

Reference Department

P.O. Box 26170

Greensboro, NC 27402-6170

Telephone: 336-334-5419

Fax: 336-334-5097

Web: library.uncg.edu

Personnel:

Responsible person: Nancy Ryckman, Assistant Head Reference Librarian, *email:* nancy_ryckman@uncg.edu

Holdings:

Geographic strengths: Southeast

Map depositories: USGS topos, CIA

17,000 printed maps

10 globes

200 atlases

Access:

Hours:

Monday–Thursday: 8 A.M.–midnight

Friday: 8 A.M.–10 P.M.

Saturday: 10 A.M.–10 P.M.

Sunday: 10 A.M.–midnight

Collection services:

Maps cataloged: 5%

Maps classified: 0%

Maps in OPAC: 0%

Physical facilities:

Maps in separate area

Map cases: 12

Vertical files: 1

Notes: The books and serials relevant to the map collection are not kept in the map room. They are integrated with the rest of the library collection. Our maps are used primarily for recreation.

360 *Greenville, NC*

East Carolina University

Joyner Library

Government Documents and Microforms

E. 5th Street

Greenville, NC 27858-4353

Telephone: 252-328-0238

Fax: 252-328-2271

Email: govdocs@mail.ecu.edu

Web: www.lib.ecu.edu/govdoc/index.html

Personnel:

Responsible person: David Durant, Head of Documents and Microforms, *email:* durantd@mail.ecu.edu

Assistants: Janice Rice, Microforms Coordinator; Anna Dougherty, Documents Processing Specialist

FTE professionals: 1   *FTE para-professionals:* 3

Holdings:

Geographic strengths: North Carolina

Special collections: Army Mapping Service/Defense Mapping Agency, Geographical Section, General Staff (GSGS)

Map depositories: USGS topos, Department of Transportation, NOAA, CIA, National Forest Service, NGA nautical, NGA aeronautical

103,000 printed maps

2 globes

200 atlases

50 CD-ROMs

Access:

Hours:

Monday–Thursday: 8 A.M.–10 P.M.

Friday: 8 A.M.–5 P.M.

Saturday: 1 P.M.–5 P.M.

Sunday: 1 P.M.–10 P.M.

Items circulate

Interlibrary loan available

Collection services:

Maps cataloged: 15%

Maps classified: 80%

Maps in OPAC: 15%
Classification schemes: LC, SuDocs, Local
Physical facilities:
Public computers: 6
Map cases: 145
Vertical files: 12

361 *Raleigh, NC*

North Carolina Department Office of Archives and History

State Archives of North Carolina
4614 Mail Service Center
Raleigh, NC 27699-4614
Telephone: 919-807-7310
Fax: 919-733-1354
Email: archives@ncmail.net
Web: www.ah.dcr.state.nc.us/sections/archives/arch/
default.htm
Personnel:
Responsible person: James O. Sorrell, Head, Archival
Description Unit, *email:* james.sorrell@ncmail.net
Holdings:
Geographic strengths: North Carolina, Southeast
Special collections: Superintendent of Public Instruc-
tion Swamp Lands, Eric Norden Collection—surveys
lands in eastern North Carolina counties, Military
Collection World War I maps, State Highway Com-
mission Powell Bill maps, North Carolina Railroad
Company, North Carolina Wildlife Resources
Subject strengths: aerial photos, city, geodetic surveys,
historical geography, land ownership, land use, mil-
itary, mineral resources, mining, political geogra-
phy, population, railroads, recreation, roads, soil,
waterways
5,000 printed maps
Chronological coverage:
Pre-1800: 10%
1800–1899: 50%
1900–1939: 20%
1940–present: 20%
Access:
Collection is open to the public
Answers email questions
Hours:
Monday–Friday: 8 A.M.–5:30 P.M.
Saturday: 9 A.M.–5 P.M.
Sunday: closed
Total hours per week opened: 46
Geographic Information Systems:
No GIS services available
Scans maps for patrons
Collection services:
Maps cataloged: 75%
Maps classified: 75%
Maps in OPAC: 5%

Classification schemes: Other (Anglo-American)
Catalog accessibility: online, cards
Preservation techniques: encapsulation, deacidifica-
tion, edging
Items that have gone through the preservation process:
50%
Physical facilities:
Internet access available
Number of map cases: 11
Number of microform readers: 16
Copying facilities available: copier, large-format
copier, microform copier, digital scanner, printer

362 *Raleigh, NC*

North Carolina Geological Survey

1612 Mail Service Center
Raleigh, NC 27699-1612
Telephone: 919-715-9718
Fax: 9190733-0900
Email: paula.maynor@ncmail.net
Web: www.geology.enr.state.nc.us
Personnel:
Responsible person: Paula Maynor, Sales Office Man-
ager, *email:* paula.maynor@ncmail.net
FTE para-professionals: 1
Holdings:
Geographic strengths: North Carolina
Map depositories: USGS
1,600 printed maps
3,000 aerial photos
145 CD-ROMs
Access:
Hours:
Monday–Thursday: 9 A.M.–5 P.M.
Friday: 9 A.M.–5 P.M.
Physical facilities:
Maps in separate area
Map cases: 300
Vertical files: 10

363 *Raleigh, NC*

North Carolina State University

D.H. Hill Library
2205 Hillsborough Street
Campus Box 7111
Raleigh, NC 27695-7114
Telephone: 919-515-2935
Fax: 919-515-8264
Email: karrie_peterson@ncsu.edu
Web: www.lib.ncsu.edu/risd/govdocs
Personnel:
Responsible person: Karrie Peterson, *email:* karrie_
peterson@ncsu.edu
FTE professionals: 1   *FTE para-professionals:* 1

Holdings:

Geographic strengths: North Carolina, Southeast, United States

Map depositories: USGS topos, Department of Transportation, NOAA, CIA, National Forest Service, NGA nautical, NGA aeronautical, BLM

25,000 printed maps

1 globe

47 atlases

Access:

Hours:

Monday–Thursday: 7 A.M.–11 P.M.

Friday: 7 A.M.–6 P.M.

Saturday: 9 A.M.–6 P.M.

Sunday: 1 P.M.–11 P.M.

Collection services:

Classification schemes: LC, SuDocs

364 *Raleigh, NC*

North Carolina State University

Natural Resources Library

Founded 1989

Jordan Hall Room #1102

2800 Faucette Drive

Campus Box 7114

Raleigh, NC 27615

Telephone: 919-515-2306

Fax: 919-515-7802

Email: karen_ciccone@ncsu.edu

Web: www.lib.ncsu.edu/natural/

Personnel:

Responsible person: Karen Ciccone, *email:* karen_ciccone@ncsu.edu

Number of student works: 10

Number of student workers hours per week: 150

Holdings:

Subject strengths: forestry, geology, geospatial data, hydrology, mineral resources, oceanography, recreation

Map depositories and percentages: USGS topos (100%)

1,515 printed maps

114 printed atlases

82 CD-ROMs

Collecting digital data

Chronological coverage:

1940–present: 100%

On-going publications: Natural Resources Library, Monthly online newsletter, available at http://www.lib.ncsu.edu/news/nrl.php

Access:

Collection is open to the public

Answers email questions

Hours:

Monday–Thursday: 7:30 A.M.–11 P.M.

Friday: 7:30 A.M.–8 P.M.

Saturday: noon–10 P.M.

Sunday: 1 P.M.–11 P.M.

Total hours per week opened: 94.5

Geographic Information Systems:

GIS services available in an open environment

GIS software: ArcView 3.3, ArcGIS 8.3, MapInfo Professional 5.0

General GIS questions answered

Collection services:

Maps cataloged: 34%

Maps classified: 34%

Maps in OPAC: 34%

Datasets are cataloged

Classification schemes: LC

Catalog accessibility: online

Physical facilities:

Internet access available

Number of map cases: 3

Copying facilities available: copier, scanner

Notes: More equipment: VTI Auto Focus Magnification System, Proxima Ultralight XL2 computer projector (for lending), Dell laptop (3 units for lending), Nomadic Computing, wireless network

365 *Salisbury, NC*

Catawba College

Corriher–Linn–Black Library

2300 West Innes Street

Salisbury, NC 28144

Telephone: 704-637-4379

Fax: 704-637-4304

Email: jsims@catawba.edu

Web: www.lib.catawba.edu

Personnel:

Responsible person: Jacquelyn Sims, Head of Library Information, *email:* jsims@catawba.edu

Assistants: Mark Wurster, Library Technical Associate; Gail Sewell, Library Technical Associate

FTE professionals: 0.06   *FTE para-professionals:* 0.2

Holdings:

Geographic strengths: North Carolina, South Carolina, Virginia

Subject strengths: aerial photos, modern cartography, geology, historical geography, map catalogs, soil

Map depositories and percentages: USGS topos (15%), (20%), (10%), GPO

2,582 printed maps

18 gazetteers

322 printed atlases

482 books

96 CD-ROMs

250 computer programs

Collecting digital data

Chronological coverage:

1940–present: 100%

Average budget over the last 5 years: $120

Access:
Collection is open to the public
Answers email questions
Hours:
Monday–Thursday: 8 A.M.–11 P.M.
Friday: 8 A.M.–5 P.M.
Saturday: 10 A.M.–5 P.M.
Sunday: 1:30 P.M.–11 P.M.
Total hours per week opened: 85.5
Maps circulate
Circulation policies apply
Map circulation duration: 1 day
Book circulation duration: 30 days
Number of maps circulated annually: 25
Interlibrary loan available
Geographic Information Systems:
No GIS services available
Number of public GIS workstations: 10
Collection services:
Maps cataloged: 30%
Maps classified: 95%
Maps in OPAC: 30%
Datasets are cataloged
Classification schemes: SuDocs, Dewey
Cataloging utilities: OCLC
Catalog accessibility: online
Items that have gone through the preservation process: 0%
Physical facilities:
Internet access available
Number of map cases: 6
Linear book shelving: 14.2 ft.
Linear atlas shelving: 14.5 ft.
Copying facilities available: copier, microform copier, printers
Notes: Only the books that circulate are available via interlibrary loan.

366 *Wilmington, NC*

University of North Carolina, Wilmington

William Madison Randall Library
601 South College Road
Wilmington, NC 28403-5616
Telephone: 910-962-3270
Fax: 910-962-3078
Web: library.uncwil.edu
Holdings:
Map depositories: USGS topos, USGS geology maps, USGS other, NOAA, GPO, CIA, National Forest Service, BLM, State
17,000 printed maps
40 manuscript maps
10 wall maps
786,000 microfiche
30,000 microfilms

150 aerial photos
40 satellite images
40 gazetteers
400 printed atlases
50 computer programs
Chronological coverage:
1940–present: 97%
Average budget over the last 5 years: $1,000
Access:
Collection is partially open to the public
Reference questions per year: 1,000
Answers email questions
Patrons per month: 50
Hours:
Total hours per week opened: 98
Maps circulate
Circulation policies apply
Map circulation duration: 3 weeks
Atlas circulation duration: 1 day
Book circulation duration: 3 weeks
Number of maps circulated annually: 2,000
Interlibrary loan available
Geographic Information Systems:
No GIS services available
Number of public GIS workstations: 40
Collection services:
Maps cataloged: 98%
Maps classified: 98%
Maps in OPAC: 98%
Datasets are cataloged
Classification schemes: LC, SuDocs, Local
Cataloging utilities: OCLC
Catalog accessibility: online
Preservation techniques: encapsulation
Physical facilities:
Internet access available
Square footage: 300
Number of public computers: 40
Number of public printers: 10
Number of map cases: 35
Linear book shelving: 40 ft.
Linear atlas shelving: 50 ft.
Copying facilities available: copier, microform copier
Notes: We do not have a separate map room or separate map reference desk. Maps are stored in government documents area, reference area, and special collections.

367 Winston-Salem, NC

Moravian Archives

457 South Church Street
Winston–Salem, NC 27101
Telephone: 336-722-1742
Fax: 336-725-4514
Email: nblum@mcsp.org
Web: MoravianArchives.org

Personnel:

Responsible person: C. Daniel Crews, Archivist, *email:* nblum@mcsp.org

Assistants: Richard W. Starbuck, Assistant Archivist; L. Nicole Blum, Assistant Archivist

FTE professionals: 1

Holdings:

Geographic strengths: Forsyth County, North Carolina

600 printed maps

20 atlases

Access:

Hours:

Monday–Friday: 9:30–noon, 1:30 P.M.–4:30 P.M.

Saturday–Sunday: closed

Collection services:

Maps cataloged: 99%

Classification schemes: Local

Physical facilities:

Maps in separate area

Map cases: 4

368 *Fargo, ND*

North Dakota State University

Library

P.O. Box 5599

Fargo, ND 58105-5599

Telephone: 701-231-8863

Fax: 701-231-7138

Email: kathryn.thomas@ndsu.nodak.edu

Web: www.lib.ndsu.nodak.edu

Personnel:

Responsible person: Kathryn Thomas, Documents Librarian, *email:* Kathryn.Thomas@ndsu.nodak.edu

Assistants: Robert Jacobson, Documents Associate

FTE professionals: 0.1   *FTE para-professionals:* 0.25

Number of student workers hours per week: 15

Holdings:

Map depositories and percentages: USGS topos (100%), USGS geology maps (100%), USGS other (100%), GPO, CIA, National Forest Service, NIMA topos, NIMA nautical, NIMA aeronautical, BLM, State

100,000 printed maps

85 gazetteers

1,000 printed atlases

100 CD-ROMs

Chronological coverage:

1940–present: 100%

Average budget over the last 5 years: $200

Access:

Collection is open to the public

Reference questions per year: 500

Answers email questions

Patrons per month: 100

Hours:

Monday–Friday: 7:30 A.M.–midnight

Saturday: 11:30 A.M.–5 P.M.

Sunday: 1 P.M.–midnight

Total hours per week opened: 92

Maps circulate

Circulation policies apply

Map circulation duration: 4 weeks

Atlas circulation duration: 4 weeks

Book circulation duration: 4 weeks

Interlibrary loan available

Geographic Information Systems:

No GIS services available

Collection services:

Maps cataloged: 80%

Maps classified: 10%

Maps in OPAC: 80%

Classification schemes: LC, SuDocs

Cataloging utilities: OCLC

Catalog accessibility: online

Preservation techniques: encapsulation

Items that have gone through the preservation process: 1%

Physical facilities:

No Internet access

Number of vertical map cases: 25

Number of vertical files (file cabinets): 18

Other map storage: 1 rolled map case, 1 atlas case

Copying facilities available: copier, microform copier, scanner, color printer

Notes: The majority of our map collection is part of the Government Documents collection; atlases, gazetteers, etc. are integrated into the reference and circulating book collections. Computers, microfiche equipment, etc. are shared with other areas, such as microforms or reference. We are in the process of rebuilding our map collection after nearly all of it was destroyed in a flood in June 2000. Basic USGS maps have been replaced, but it will be years, if ever, before we're able to replace our specialized maps.

369 Minot, ND

Minot State University

Gordon B. Olson Library

Government Documents and Maps

500 University Avenue W

Minot, ND 58707

Telephone: 701-858-3200

Fax: 701-858-3581

Email: referenc@minotstateu.edu

Web: www.minotstateu.edu/library/

Personnel:

Responsible person: George C. Clark, Reference and Government Documents Librarian, *email:* clark@minotstateu.edu

Assistants: Donna Just, Government Documents Para-professional

FTE professionals: 0.2 *FTE para-professionals:* 0.4
Number of student works: 0.5

Holdings:

Geographic strengths: North Dakota, United States, Canada, Western Europe, South Africa

Subject strengths: aerial photos, aeronautical, forestry, geology, land use, nautical charts, roads, soil

Map depositories: USGS topos, USGS geology maps, USGS other, GPO, CIA, National Forest Service, NIMA topos, NIMA nautical, NIMA aeronautical, BLM, State

120,837 printed maps

13 gazetteers

128 printed atlases

Chronological coverage:
1940–present: 90%

Access:

Collection is open to the public

Maps off site

Answers email questions

Hours:

Monday–Thursday: 8 A.M.–10 P.M.

Friday: 8 A.M.–4:30 P.M.

Saturday: noon–4 P.M.

Sunday: 1 P.M.–9 P.M.

Total hours per week opened: 76

Map circulation duration: 1 week

Atlas circulation duration: 4 weeks

Book circulation duration: 4 weeks

Geographic Information Systems:

No GIS services available

Collection services:

Maps cataloged: 1%

Maps classified: 99%

Maps in OPAC: 1%

Classification schemes: LC, SuDocs, Local

Cataloging utilities: OCLC, Local

Catalog accessibility: online, cards, printout

Physical facilities:

Square footage: 1,800

Number of public computers: 13

Number of vertical map cases: 32

Linear book shelving: 75 ft.

Linear atlas shelving: 33 ft.

Number of microform readers: 11

Copying facilities available: copier, microform copier

370 *Akron, OH*

University of Akron

Bierce Library
Map Collection
Akron, OH 44325-1707
Telephone: 330-972-8176
Fax: 330-972-7225

Email: pl@uakron.edu
Web: www.uakron.edu/libraries/ul/subjects/look4maps.html

Personnel:

Responsible person: Peter Linberger, Business, Geography, and Maps Bibliographer, *email:* pl@uakron.edu

FTE professionals: 0.25

Holdings:

Geographic strengths: Akron, Ohio, United States

Special collections: Historic Urban Plans, Sanborn Fire Insurance maps of Ohio, USGS Topographic maps Series

Subject strengths: city, geology, historical geography, hydrology, political geography

Map depositories: USGS topos, USGS geology maps, USGS other, GPO, CIA, National Forest Service, State

21,000 printed maps

900 printed atlases

12 books

Chronological coverage:
1940–present: 90%

Access:

Maps in separate area

Collection is partially open to the public

Maps off site

Answers email questions

Hours:

Monday–Friday: 7:30 A.M.–midnight

Saturday: 9 A.M.–8 P.M.

Sunday: 12–midnight

Total hours per week opened: 102

Maps circulate

Atlas circulation duration: 5 days

Geographic Information Systems:

GIS services available by appointment

GIS software: ArcView

GIS assistance available for Census mapping

Scans maps for patrons

Collection services:

Maps cataloged: 95%

Maps classified: 75%

Maps in OPAC: 60%

Classification schemes: Local

Cataloging utilities: OCLC

Catalog accessibility: online, cards

Physical facilities:

No Internet access

Square footage: 1,578

Number of map cases: 36

Number of vertical files (file cabinets): 11

Linear book shelving: 450 ft.

Linear atlas shelving: 594 ft.

Copying facilities available: copier, microform copier

371 *Akron, OH*

University of Akron

Department of Geography and Planning
Map Room
Akron, OH 44325-5005
Telephone: 330-972-7620
Fax: 330-972-6080
Web: www.uakron.edu/libraries
Personnel:
Responsible person: Keith Pitts, Cartographer, *email:* kpitts@uakron.edu
Number of student workers hours per week: 10
Holdings:
Geographic strengths: Ohio
Special collections: National Geographic maps, relief maps
Subject strengths: aerial photos, aeronautical, modern cartography, climatology, city, historical geography, land use, raised relief models, roads, soil, vegetation
75,000 printed maps
100 wall maps
257 raised relief maps
320 aerial photos
40 satellite images
10 globes
Chronological coverage:
  1900–1939: 10%
  1940–present: 90%
Access:
Maps in separate area
Collection is open to the public
Answers email questions
Hours:
  Monday–Friday: 10 A.M.–11 P.M.
  Total hours per week opened: 10
Geographic Information Systems:
GIS services available in an open environment
Collection services:
Maps cataloged: 75%
Maps classified: 10%
Datasets are cataloged
Classification schemes: Local
Cataloging utilities: Local
Catalog accessibility: cards, printout
Physical facilities:
Internet access available
Square footage: 280
Number of map cases: 15
Copying facilities available: copier, color copier, large-format copier
Notes: Some of the collection (relief maps, wall maps) are soon to be cataloged for posting on department web page.

372 *Athens, OH*

Ohio University

Alden Library
Government Documents and Maps Collection
Park Place
Athens, OH 45701
Telephone: 740-593-2718
Fax: 740-593-2719
Web: www.library.ohiou.edu/libinfo/depts/maps/index.htm
Personnel:
Responsible person: Doreen Hockenberry, Head, *email:* hockenbe@ohio.edu
Assistants: Laura Burns, Sandy Seeley, Elizabeth Story
FTE professionals: 1   *FTE para-professionals:* 3
Holdings:
Geographic strengths: Athens County, Ohio, Indonesia, Malaysia
Map depositories: USGS topos, Department of Transportation, NOAA, CIA, National Forest Service, NGA nautical, NGA aeronautical, BLM
120,000 printed maps
4,500 aerial photos
7 globes
1,005 atlases
570 books
1 active serial
40 CD-ROMs
Access:
Hours:
  Monday–Friday: 8 A.M.–midnight
  Saturday: 10 A.M.–9 P.M.
  Sunday: noon–midnight
Items circulate
Interlibrary loan available
Collection services:
Maps cataloged: 30%
Maps classified: 100%
Maps in OPAC: 30%
Classification schemes: LC, SuDocs, Local
Physical facilities:
Maps in separate area
Public computers: 6
Map cases: 32
Vertical files: 30
Notes: Rare and fragile items do not circulate

373 *Bowling Green, OH*

Bowling Green State University

Jerome Library
Government Documents
Ridge Street
Bowling Green, OH 43403

Telephone: 419-372-2142
Fax: 419-372-7996
Email: parmer@bgnet.bgsu.edu
Web: www.bgsu.edu/colleges/library/services/govdocs/
index.html
Personnel:
Responsible person: Coleen Parmer, *email:* parmer@
bgnet.bgsu.edu
FTE professionals: 1   *FTE para-professionals:* 2.5
Holdings:
Geographic strengths: Ohio, Indiana, West Virginia,
Michigan, Pennsylvania, Kentucky, Colorado, New
Mexico, Great Lakes
Map depositories: USGS topos, CIA
22,000 printed maps
10 globes
200 atlases
15 CD-ROMs
Access:
Hours:
Monday–Friday: 8 A.M.–10 P.M.
Saturday: 9 A.M.–6 P.M.
Sunday: 1 P.M.–10 P.M.
Items circulate
Collection services:
Maps cataloged: 100%
Maps classified: 100%
Maps in OPAC: 100%
Classification schemes: LC, SuDocs
Physical facilities:
Public computers: 30
Map cases: 7

374 *Cincinnati, OH*

Cincinnati Museum Center

Cincinnati Historical Society Library
1301 Western Avenue
Cincinnati, OH 45203
Telephone: 513-287-7030
Fax: 513-287-7095
Web: www.cincymuseum.org
Personnel:
Responsible person: Barbara J. Dawson, *email:* bdaw-
son@cincymuseum.org
FTE professionals: 0.5
Holdings:
Geographic strengths: Cincinnati, Ohio, Northwest
Territory
Special collections: Sanborn Fire Insurance maps of
Cincinnati, Civil War maps
2,500 printed maps
190 atlases

Access:
Hours:
Monday–Friday: noon–5 P.M.
Saturday: 10 A.M.–5 P.M.
Collection services:
Maps cataloged: 90%
Maps classified: 90%
Maps in OPAC: 30%
Classification schemes: Dewey
Physical facilities:
Map cases: 3
Vertical files: 1

375 *Cincinnati, OH*

Public Library of Cincinnati and Hamilton County

History Department Map Collection
800 Vine Street
Cincinnati, OH 45230
Telephone: 513-369-6905
Fax: 513 369-3123
Email: history@cincinnatilibrary.org
Web: www.cincinnatilibrary.org
Personnel:
Responsible person: Doug Magee, Map Librarian,
email: doug.magee@cincinnatilibrary.org
Assistants: Sallie Mock, Map Assistant
FTE professionals: 1   *FTE para-professionals:* 1
Holdings:
Geographic strengths: Cincinnati, Hamilton County,
Ohio, Germany, England, Ireland
Special collections: Sanborn Fire Insurance maps for
all states bordering the Mississippi and Missouri
rivers and bordering the state of Ohio
10,300 printed maps
135 aerial photos
21 globes
2,500 atlases
270 books
44 active serials
2 CD-ROMs
Access:
Hours:
Monday–Wednesday: 9 A.M.–9 P.M.
Thursday–Saturday: 9 A.M.–6 P.M.
Sunday: 1 P.M.–5 P.M.
Items circulate
Collection services:
Maps cataloged: 50%
Maps classified: 50%
Maps in OPAC: 50%
Classification schemes: Dewey
Physical facilities:

Public computers: 10
Map cases: 7
Vertical files: 14

376 *Cincinnati, OH*

University of Cincinnati

Geology/Physics Library
Willis G. Meyer Map Collection
240 Braunstein Hall
M.L. 0153
Cincinnati, OH 45221
Telephone: 513-5561324
Fax: 513-5561930
Web: www.libraries.uc.edu/libraries/geol-phys/home
.html
Personnel:
Responsible person: Angela M. Gooden, *email:* angela
.gooden@uc.edu
Number of student workers hours per week: 20
Holdings:
Geographic strengths: Midwest, Latin America
Special collections: 1,500 various field guides and
guidebook some unique
Subject strengths: travel books
Map depositories and percentages: USGS topos (70%),
(30%), USGS other, National Forest Service, NIMA
nautical
130,000 printed maps
100 wall maps
200 gazetteers
40 printed atlases
132 CD-ROMs
Chronological coverage:
1940–present: 98%
Access:
Maps in separate area
Collection is open to the public
Answers email questions
Hours:
Monday–Thursday: 8 A.M.–8 P.M.
Friday: 8 A.M.–5 P.M.
Saturday–Sunday: 1 P.M.–5 P.M.
Total hours per week opened: 65
Maps circulate
Map circulation duration: 2 weeks
Book circulation duration: 1 quarter
Interlibrary loan available
Collection services:
Maps cataloged: 40%
Maps in OPAC: 40%
Classification schemes: LC
Cataloging utilities: OCLC

Catalog accessibility: online, printout
Preservation techniques: encapsulation
Physical facilities:
Internet access available
Square footage: 950
Number of map cases: 98
Copying facilities available: copier, large-format
copier, microform copier, scanner

377 *Cleveland, OH*

Case Western Reserve University

Kelvin Smith Library
11055 Euclid Avenue
Cleveland, OH 44106
Telephone: 216-368-6511
Fax: 216-368-3669
Email: kat4@cwru.edu
Web: library.case.edu/ksl/index.html
Personnel:
Responsible person: Karen Thornton, *email:* kat4@
cwru.edu
Assistants: Cheryl Burden
FTE professionals: 1   *FTE para-professionals:* 1
Holdings:
Map depositories: USGS topos, NOAA, CIA, National
Forest Service, NGA nautical, NGA aeronautical,
BLM
75,000 printed maps
15 books
50 CD-ROMs
Access:
Hours:
Monday–Friday: 8:30 A.M.–5 P.M.
Items circulate
Interlibrary loan available
Collection services:
Maps cataloged: 25%
Maps classified: 25%
Maps in OPAC: 25%
Classification schemes: SuDocs
Physical facilities:
Maps in separate area
Public computers: 1
Map cases: 30
Vertical files: 2

378 *Cleveland, OH*

Cleveland Public Library

Map Collection, founded 1884
325 Superior Avenue
Cleveland, OH 44114

Telephone: 216-623-2880
Fax: 216-902-4978
Email: maps@cpl.org
Web: www.cpl.org
Personnel:
Responsible person: Thomas Edwards, *email:* Thomas.Edwards@cpl.org
Number of student workers hours per week: 17
Holdings:
Geographic strengths: Cleveland, Ohio, Great Lakes region
Special collections: Sanborn Fire Insurance maps of Cleveland, G.M. Hopkins Plat Books of Cleveland and Cuyahoga County, Army Map Service maps (AMS), Environmental maps, Ohio County Atlases and Landownership maps (1841–1940), GPO Depository Collections
Subject strengths: aerial photos, aeronautical, agriculture, archaeology, biology, early cartography, modern cartography, caves, celestial, climatology, city, economic geography, engineering, forestry, genealogy, geodetic surveys, geology, geospatial data, historical geography, hydrology, industries, land ownership, land use, language, map catalogs, map collecting, military, mineral resources, mining, nautical charts, oceanography, political geography, population, projections, railroads, raised relief models, recreation, religion, roads, satellite imagery, soil, travel books, vegetation, views, waterways, zoogeography
Map depositories and percentages: USGS topos (100%), USGS geology maps (86%), Department of Transportation, NOAA, GPO, CIA, National Forest Service, NIMA topos, NIMA nautical, NIMA aeronautical, BLM, State
165,000 printed maps
16 wall maps
24 raised relief maps
40,600 microfiche
275 microfilms
2,034 aerial photos
400 gazetteers
1,625 printed atlases
1,300 books
62 active serials
10 inactive serials
700 CD-ROMs
Collecting digital data
Chronological coverage:
    1900–1939: 20%
    1940–present: 70%
Average budget over the last 5 years: $25,000
On-going publications: Annual report
Access:
Collection is open to the public

Maps off site; Percentage offsite: 15%
Reference questions per year: 1,000
Answers email questions
Patrons per month: 450
Hours:
    Monday–Saturday: 9 A.M.–6 P.M.
    Sunday: 1 P.M.–5 P.M.
    Total hours per week opened: 58
Geographic Information Systems:
No GIS services available
Scans maps for patrons
Collection services:
Maps cataloged: 0.2%
Maps classified: 0.3%
Maps in OPAC: 0.2%
Datasets are cataloged
Classification schemes: LC, SuDocs, Dewey, Local
Cataloging utilities: OCLC, Local
Catalog accessibility: online, fiche, cards, printout
Preservation techniques: encapsulation, deacidification, cartex, lamination, edging
Items that have gone through the preservation process: 0.8%
Physical facilities:
Internet access available
Square footage: 1,679
Number of map cases: 166
Number of vertical files (file cabinets): 25
Number of atlas stands: 19
Linear atlas shelving: 731 ft.
Copying facilities available: copier, color copier, large-format copier, microform copier, printers
Notes: We do circulate maps only per authorization of map librarian for increments of up to 3 weeks.

379 *Cleveland, OH*

Cleveland State University

Library
2121 Euclid Avenue
Cleveland, OH 44114
Telephone: 216-687-2475
Fax: 216-687-9380
Web: www.ulib.csuohio.edu
Personnel:
Responsible person: Janet Mongan, *email:* j.mongan@csuohio.edu
Holdings:
Geographic strengths: Ohio, United States
Map depositories: USGS topos, State
61,287 printed maps
Chronological coverage:
    1940–present: 100%
Access:

Collection is open to the public
Answers email questions
Hours:
Total hours per week opened: 83
Geographic Information Systems:
No GIS services available
Collection services:
Maps cataloged: 0%
Maps classified: 0%
Maps in OPAC: 0%
Physical facilities:
No Internet access
Number of map cases: 22
Linear book shelving: 12 ft.
Linear atlas shelving: 24 ft.
Copying facilities available: copier, large-format copier, microform copier

380 *Columbus, OH*

Columbus Metropolitan Library

Biography, History and Travel Division
96 South Grant Avenue
Columbus, OH 43215
Telephone: 614-645-2710
Fax: 614-645-2051
Email: mfrbht1@columbuslibrary.org
Web: www.columbuslibrary.org
Personnel:
Responsible person: John M. Newman, Manager, *email:* jnewman@cml.library.org
FTE professionals: 7   *FTE para-professionals:* 1
Holdings:
Geographic strengths: United States
Special collections: Historic Ohio county atlases with particular emphasis on Franklin County, Sanborn Fire Insurance maps for Columbus, Ohio
Map depositories: USGS
1,000 printed maps
1 globe
500 atlases
2,000 books
15 active serials
Access:
Hours:
Monday–Thursday: 9 A.M.–9 P.M.
Friday–Saturday: 9 A.M.–6 P.M.
Sunday: 1 P.M.–5 P.M.
Interlibrary loan available
Maps cataloged: 90%
Maps classified: 90%
Maps in OPAC: 90%
Physical facilities:
Public computers: 9

Map cases: 7
Vertical files: 10

381 *Columbus, OH*

Ohio Department of Natural Resources

Division of Geological Survey
4383 Fountain Square Drive
Columbus, OH 43224
Telephone: 614-265-6576
Fax: 614-447-1918
Email: geo.survey@dnr.state.oh.us
Web: www.dnr.ohiodnr.com/geosurvey/
Personnel:
Responsible person: Madge Fitak, *email:* madge.fitak@dnr.state.oh.us
FTE para-professionals: 1
Holdings:
Geographic strengths: Ohio
Map depositories: USGS
2,300 printed maps
1,000 aerial photos
2 atlases
10 books
5 active serials
10 CD-ROMs
Access:
Hours:
Monday–Friday: 8 A.M.–5 P.M.
Saturday–Sunday: closed
Collection services:
Maps cataloged: 0%
Maps classified: 0%
Maps in OPAC: 0%
Physical facilities:
Maps in separate area
Map cases: 30
Vertical files: 6

382 *Columbus, OH*

Ohio Historical Society

1982 Velma Avenue
Columbus, OH 43211-2497
Telephone: 614-297-2510
Fax: 614-297-2546
Email: ohsref@ohiohistory.org
Web: www.ohiohistory.org
Personnel:
Responsible person:
Holdings:
Geographic strengths: Ohio
14,000 printed maps
500 aerial photos
500 atlases

Access:
Hours:
Wednesday : 9 A.M.–5 P.M.
Thursday: 1 P.M.–9 P.M.
Saturday: 9 A.M.–5 P.M.
Collection services:
Classification schemes: Local
Physical facilities:
Maps in separate area
Public computers: 10
Map cases: 17
Vertical files: 1

383 *Columbus, OH*

Ohio State University

Orton Memorial Library of Geology
180 Orton Hall
155 South Oval Drive
Columbus, OH 43210
Telephone: 614-292-2428
Web: library.osu.edu/sites/geology
Personnel:
Responsible person: Mary W. Scott, Librarian, *email:* scott.36@osu.edu
Assistants: Patti Dittoe, Library Associate
FTE professionals: 0.1   *FTE para-professionals:* 0.1
Holdings:
Geographic strengths: United States
Map depositories: USGS
200,000 printed maps
300 atlases
1,000 books
100 CD-ROMs
Access:
Hours:
Monday–Friday: 8 A.M.–5 P.M.
Items circulate
Collection services:
Maps cataloged: 0.1%
Maps classified: 0.1%
Maps in OPAC: 0.1%
Classification schemes: LC, SuDocs, Other (filed by area until cataloged)
Physical facilities:
Public computers: 2
Map cases: 72
Vertical files: 5

384 *Columbus, OH*

Ohio State University

William Oxley Thompson (Main) Library
Map Room, founded 1950s
211 Main Library

1858 Neil Avenue Mall
Columbus, OH 43210
Telephone: 614-688-8774
Fax: 614-292-7859
Email: rogers.20@osu.edu
Web: library.osu.edu/sites/maps/
Personnel:
Responsible person: Steve Rogers, Map Librarian, *email:* rogers.20@osu.edu
Number of student workers hours per week: 10
Number of volunteer hours per month: 12
Holdings:
Geographic strengths: Columbus, Ohio, Canada
Special collections: Sanborn Fire Insurance maps of Ohio
Subject strengths: city, nautical charts, political geography, roads, views
Map depositories and percentages: USGS topos (14%), Department of Transportation, National Forest Service, NIMA nautical, NIMA aeronautical, BLM, Former Canadian map depository
80,000 printed maps
25 wall maps
15 raised relief maps
25 microfiche
75 microfilms
415 aerial photos
97 satellite images
250 gazetteers
2,000 printed atlases
1,250 books
15 active serials
25 inactive serials
50 CD-ROMs
Chronological coverage:
1940–present: 90%
Average budget over the last 5 years: $13,000
On-going publications: Map room new acquisitions list on web http://library.osu.edu/sites/maps/
Access:
Maps in separate area
Collection is open to the public
Reference questions per year: 800
Answers email questions
Patrons per month: 300
Hours:
Monday–Friday: 8 A.M.–5 P.M.
Total hours per week opened: 45
Geographic Information Systems:
GIS services available by appointment
GIS software: ArcExplorer, ArcView, Census Mapper
GIS assistance available for Census mapping
Scans maps for patrons
Collection services:
Maps cataloged: 10%
Maps classified: 35%

Maps in OPAC: 10%
Datasets are cataloged
Classification schemes: LC, SuDocs
Cataloging utilities: OCLC
Catalog accessibility: online
Preservation techniques: encapsulation, deacidification
Items that have gone through the preservation process:
  0.05%
Physical facilities:
Internet access available
Square footage: 1,500
Number of map cases: 111
Number of atlas stands: 15
Linear book shelving: 230 ft.
Linear atlas shelving: 33 ft.
Copying facilities available: copier

385 *Columbus, OH*

State Library of Ohio

Government Information Services
274 East First Avenue
Columbus, OH 43201
Telephone: 614-644-7051
Fax: 614-752-9178
Email: govinfo@sloma.state.oh.us
Web: winslo.state.oh.us
Personnel:
Responsible person: Gretchen Persohn, Head of Reference Services, *email:* gpersohn@sloma.state.oh.us
Assistants: Larry Walls, Library Assistant 2
FTE para-professionals: 1
Holdings:
Map depositories: USGS topos, Department of Transportation, NOAA, CIA, National Forest Service, NGA nautical, NGA aeronautical, BLM
90,600 printed maps
40 atlases
450 CD-ROMs
Access:
  Hours:
    Monday–Thursday: 8 A.M.–5 P.M.
    Friday: 8 A.M.–9 P.M.
    Saturday–Sunday: closed
  Items circulate
Collection services:
Maps cataloged: 75%
Maps classified: 75%
Maps in OPAC: 75%
Classification schemes: SuDocs
Physical facilities:
Public computers: 10
Map cases: 53
Vertical files: 4

386 *Dayton, OH*

Dayton Metro Library

215 East Third Street
Dayton, OH 45402
Telephone: 937-227-9500
Fax: 937-227-9548
Email: mag_ref@daytonmetrolibrary.org
Web: www.daytonmetrolibrary.org
Personnel:
Responsible person: James McQuinn, *email:* jmcquinn@daytonmetrolibrary.org
FTE professionals: 2   *FTE para-professionals:* 2
Holdings:
Geographic strengths: Dayton, Montgomery County, Ohio
Special collections: Sanborn Fire Insurance maps
Map depositories: USGS topos, CIA, NGA nautical, BLM
8,500 printed maps
20 aerial photos
1 globe
147 atlases
Access:
  Hours:
    Monday–Thursday: 9 A.M.–9 P.M.
    Friday–Saturday: 9 A.M.–5:30 P.M.
    Sunday: 1 P.M.–5 P.M.
Collection services:
Classification schemes: SuDocs, Dewey, Local
Physical facilities:
Public computers: 40
Map cases: 1
Vertical files: 25

387 *Dayton, OH*

Dayton Society of Natural History

Library and Map Collection
2600 DeWeese Parkway
Dayton, OH 45414
Telephone: 937-275-7431
Fax: 937-275-5811
Email: lsimonelli@boonshoftmuseum.org
Web: www.boonshoftmuseum.org
Personnel:
Responsible person: Lynn Simonelli, Curator of Anthropology/Collections Manager, *email:* lsimonelli@boonshoftmuseum.org
FTE professionals: 1
Holdings:
Geographic strengths: Dayton, Montgomery County, Ohio
Map depositories: USGS
25,000 printed maps

50 aerial photos
1 globe
25 atlases
2,000 books
1 CD-ROMs

Access:

Hours:

Monday–Thursday: 9 A.M.–4 P.M.

Collection services:

Maps cataloged: 99%

Maps classified: 95%

Maps in OPAC: 0%

Classification schemes: LC, Local

Physical facilities:

Maps in separate area

Public computers: 0

Map cases: 4

Vertical files: 6

Notes: Please note that this institution was formerly known as the Dayton Museum of Natural History. The name of the museum is now the Boonshoft Museum of Discovery, which is operated by the Dayton Society of Natural History.

388 *Dayton, OH*

Wright State University

University Libraries
Colonel Glenn Highway
Dayton, OH 45435
Telephone: 937-775-2925
Fax: 937-775-2356
Web: www.libraries.wright.edu

Personnel:

Responsible person: Cheryl Lauricella, Reference Specialist, *email:* cheryl.lauricella@wright.edu

FTE professionals: 1

Holdings:

Geographic strengths: Ohio, United States

Special collections: Sanborn Fire Insurance maps

Map depositories: USGS topos, CIA, National Forest Service, BLM

40,000 printed maps

Access:

Hours:

Monday–Friday: 8 A.M.–9 P.M.

Saturday: 10 A.M.–6 P.M.

Sunday: 1 P.M.–10 P.M.

Items circulate

Interlibrary loan available

Collection services:

Maps cataloged: 30%

Maps in OPAC: 30%

Classification schemes: LC, SuDocs, Local

Physical facilities:

Public computers: 16

Map cases: 32

Vertical files: 11

389 *Granville, OH*

Denison University

William Howard Doane Library
Geology Department/Government Documents
Granville, OH 43023
Telephone: 740-587-5644
Fax: 740-587-6285
Email: cortc@denison.edu
Web: www.denison.edu/library

Personnel:

Responsible person: Mary Prophet, Deputy Library Director, *email:* prophet@denison.edu

FTE para-professionals: 1

Holdings:

Geographic strengths: United States

Special collections: WW II newsmaps, Office of War Information

Map depositories: USGS topos, CIA

10,000 printed maps

Access:

Hours:

Monday–Friday: 9 A.M.–5 P.M.

Items circulate

Interlibrary loan available

Collection services:

Maps cataloged: 5%

Maps classified: 5%

Maps in OPAC: 5%

Classification schemes: SuDocs, Local

Physical facilities:

Public computers: 40

Map cases: 30

Vertical files: 6

Notes: We are in the middle of moving most of the maps from a classroom building into the library.

390 *Newark, OH*

Ohio State University, Newark and Central Ohio Technical College

Newark Campus Library
1179 University Dr.
Newark, OH 43055
Telephone: 740-366-9307
Fax: 740-366-9264
Email: crissinger.5@osu.edu
Web: www.newarkcampus.org/library

Personnel:

Responsible person: John D. Crissinger, *email:* crissinger.5@osu.edu

FTE para-professionals: 0

Holdings:

Geographic strengths: Ohio

1,200 printed maps

100 atlases

10 books

Access:

Hours:

Monday–Thursday: 8 A.M.–10 P.M.

Friday: 8 A.M.–5 P.M.

Saturday: 10 A.M.–4 P.M.

Sunday: 1 P.M.–5 P.M.

Items circulate

Collection services:

Maps cataloged: 0%

Maps classified: 0%

Maps in OPAC: 0%

Physical facilities:

Public computers: 23

Map cases: 2

391 *Oxford, OH*

Miami University

Brill Science Library

Map Collections

Oxford, OH 45056

Telephone: 513-529-1726

Fax: 513-529-1736

Email: grabacka@muohio.edu

Web: www.lib.muohio.edu/external

Personnel:

Responsible person: Kenneth A. Grabach, Maps Librarian, *email:* grabacka@muohio.edu

FTE professionals: 1

Number of student works: 2

Number of student workers hours per week: 20

Holdings:

Geographic strengths: Ohio, North Central States

Special collections: Kuchler Vegetation Maps Collection

Subject strengths: forestry, geology, soil, vegetation

Map depositories and percentages: USGS topos (100%), USGS geology maps (100%), USGS other (100%), GPO, CIA, National Forest Service, NIMA topos, NIMA nautical, NIMA aeronautical, BLM, State, European Union

152,000 printed maps

100 manuscript maps

5 wall maps

10,000 microfiche

3,000 aerial photos

3 globes

30 gazetteers

200 printed atlases

50 books

5 active serials

320 CD-ROMs

Chronological coverage:

1900–1939: 20%

1940–present: 80%

Average budget over the last 5 years: $2,000

Access:

Collection is partially open to the public

Reference questions per year: 100

Answers email questions

Patrons per month: 5

Hours:

Monday–Friday: 8 A.M.–5 P.M.

Total hours per week opened: 40

Interlibrary loan available

Geographic Information Systems:

GIS services available by appointment

GIS software: ESRI

Number of public GIS workstations: 40

Number of GIS stations (not monitored): 25

Number of GIS stations (monitored): 2

GIS assistance available for Census mapping, geocoding, and image analysis

Plotter available

Scans maps for patrons

Collection services:

Maps cataloged: 70%

Maps classified: 55%

Maps in OPAC: 70%

Classification schemes: LC, SuDocs

Cataloging utilities: OCLC

Catalog accessibility: online

Preservation techniques: encapsulation, deacidification

Items that have gone through the preservation process: 10%

Physical facilities:

Internet access available

Number of public computers: 40

Number of staff computers: 2

Number of public printers: 2

Number of map cases: 53

Number of vertical map cases: 10

Number of vertical files (file cabinets): 20

Number of atlas stands: 1

Linear book shelving: 6 ft.

Linear atlas shelving: 84 ft.

Number of microform readers: 1

Number of microform printers: 1

Number of light tables: 1

Copying facilities available: copier, microform copier, printer

Notes: Circulation of the map materials is by permission at point of use for research and class-related needs.

392 *Tiffin, OH*

Heidelberg College

Beeghly Library
10 Greenfield Street
Tiffin, OH 44883
Telephone: 419-448-2104
Fax: 419-448-2578
Web: www.heidelberg.edu/offices/library
Personnel:
Responsible person: Ed Krakora, *email:* ekrakora@
heidelberg.edu
Assistants: Linda Warren, Cataloging/Government
Documents Assistant
FTE professionals: 0.015   *FTE para-professionals:*
0.025
Holdings:
Geographic strengths: Ohio
Map depositories: USGS
637 printed maps
1 globe
21 CD-ROMs
Collection services:
Maps cataloged: 0%
Maps classified: 0%
Maps in OPAC: 0%
Physical facilities:
Public computers: 1
Map cases: 1
Vertical files: 1

393 *Toledo, OH*

Toledo–Lucas County Public Library

Main Library
325 Michigan Street
Toledo, OH 43624
Telephone: 419-259-5207
Web: www.toledolibrary.org
Personnel:
Responsible person: Donna Christian
Assistants: Amy Hartman; George Klein
Holdings:
Geographic strengths: Toledo County, Lucas County,
Ohio, Pennsylvania
Special collections: Ohio county atlases, Pennsylvania
archives maps, Sanborn Fire Insurance, area zoning
maps, Toledo and Lucas County maps
Subject strengths: city, genealogy, geodetic surveys,
historical geography, land use, military, World War
II, American and European history
Map depositories: USGS topos
75,000 printed maps
3,500 printed atlases
Chronological coverage:

1800–1899: 15%
1900–1939: 20%
1940–present: 60%
Access:
Collection is paged
Hours:
Monday–Friday: 9 A.M.–9 P.M.
Saturday: 9 A.M.–5:30 P.M.
Sunday: 1 P.M.–5:30 P.M.
Collection services:
Maps cataloged: 60%
Maps classified: 85%
Preservation techniques: deacidification, lamination
Physical facilities:
Square footage: 3,000
Copying facilities available: copier, microform copier

394 *Toledo, OH*

University of Toledo

William S. Carlson
Map Collection
2801 West Bancroft Street
Toledo, OH 43606-3390
Telephone: 419-530-2865
Fax: 419-530-2542
Email: john.phillips@utoledo.edu
Web: www.cl.utoledo.edu
Personnel:
Responsible person: John C. Phillips, Map Librarian,
email: John.Phillips@toledo.edu
Number of student workers hours per week: 12
Holdings:
Geographic strengths: United States, Europe, Asia
Special collections: Sanborn Fire Insurance maps,
LANDSAT 7 satellite image maps
Subject strengths: aeronautical, climatology, city, eco-
nomic geography, geology, nautical charts, roads,
Hydrographic maps
Map depositories and percentages: USGS topos (75%),
USGS other (25%), Department of Transportation,
NOAA, CIA, BLM
135,000 printed maps
20 wall maps
15 raised relief maps
115 aerial photos
15 satellite images
80 gazetteers
225 printed atlases
90 books
15 CD-ROMs
24 computer programs
Chronological coverage:
1900–1939: 24%
1940–present: 75%

Average budget over the last 5 years: $500
On-going publications: Newsletters, handouts, acquisition lists
Access:
Maps in separate area
Collection is open to the public
Reference questions per year: 400
Answers email questions
Patrons per month: 60
Hours:
Monday–Friday: 8 A.M.–5 P.M.
Total hours per week opened: 40
Geographic Information Systems:
No GIS services available
Scans maps for patrons
Collection services:
Maps cataloged: 20%
Maps classified: 60%
Maps in OPAC: 20%
Classification schemes: LC, Local
Cataloging utilities: OCLC, Local
Catalog accessibility: online, cards
Preservation techniques: lamination
Physical facilities:
Internet access available
Square footage: 2,025
Number of map cases: 98
Number of vertical map cases: 98
Number of vertical files (file cabinets): 16
Linear book shelving: 100 ft.
Linear atlas shelving: 250 ft.
Copying facilities available: copier, microform copier

395 *Westerville, OH*

Otterbein College

Courtright Memorial Library
1 Otterbein College
Westerville, OH 43081
Telephone: 614-823-1027
Fax: 614-823-1921
Web: library.otterbein.edu
Personnel:
Responsible person: email: jwu@otterbein.edu
FTE professionals: 0.25   *FTE para-professionals:* 0
Holdings:
Geographic strengths: Ohio
2,463 printed maps
1 globe
63 atlases
1,135 books
9 active serials
24 CD-ROMs
Access:
Hours:

Monday–Thursday: 7:45 A.M.–11 P.M.
Friday: 7:45 A.M.–6 P.M.
Saturday: 10 A.M.–5 P.M.
Sunday: noon–11 P.M.
Items circulate
Interlibrary loan available
Collection services:
Maps cataloged: 0.02%
Maps classified: 0.02%
Maps in OPAC: 0.02%
Classification schemes: LC, SuDocs
Physical facilities:
Map cases: 2
Vertical files: 3

396 *Durant, OK*

Southeastern Oklahoma State University

Henry G. Bennett Memorial Library
1405 North 4th Avenue
P.M.B 4105
Durant, OK 74701
Telephone: 580-745-2935
Fax: 580-745-7463
Email: bburnette@sosu.edu
Web: www.sosu.edu/govdocs/govdoc%20home.html
Personnel:
Responsible person: Brandon Burnette, Government Documents/Reference Librarian, *email:* bburnette@sosu.edu
FTE professionals: 1
Holdings:
Geographic strengths: Oklahoma
Map depositories: USGS topos, CIA, National Forest Service
391 printed maps
111 atlases
3 CD-ROMs
Access:
Hours:
Monday–Friday: 7:30 A.M.–10 P.M.
Saturday: 10 A.M.–4 P.M.
Sunday: 2 P.M.–10 P.M.
Collection services:
Maps cataloged: 65%
Maps classified: 100%
Maps in OPAC: 65%
Classification schemes: SuDocs, Dewey
Physical facilities:
Public computers: 16
Map cases: 1
Vertical files: 1
Notes: The CIA maps are located in one drawer of the government documents vertical file.

397 *Edmond, OK*

University of Central Oklahoma

Max Chambers Library
Map Collection, founded 1972
100 North University
Edmond, OK 73034
Telephone: 405-974-2906
Fax: 405-974-3806
Email: fbuckallew@ucok.edu
Web: www.ucok.edu
Personnel:
Responsible person: Fritz Buckallew, Map Librarian,
    email: fbuckallew@ucok.edu
FTE professionals: 0.3
Number of student workers hours per week: 15
Holdings:
Subject strengths: city, military, roads
Map depositories and percentages: USGS topos, CIA,
    National Forest Service, BLM, State
77,501 printed maps
Average budget over the last 5 years: $400
Access:
Collection is open to the public
Answers email questions
Hours:
    Monday–Friday: 7:30 A.M.–11 P.M.
    Saturday–Sunday: noon–11 P.M.
    Total hours per week opened: 99.5
Maps circulate
Interlibrary loan available
Geographic Information Systems:
No GIS services available
Collection services:
Maps cataloged: 100%
Maps classified: 100%
Maps in OPAC: 100%
Classification schemes: Other (Thomas Smith)
Cataloging utilities: OCLC
Catalog accessibility: online
Preservation techniques: encapsulation, edging
Physical facilities:
No Internet access
Number of map cases: 88
Copying facilities available: copier, color copier, mi-
    croform copier

398 *Tulsa, OK*

University of Tulsa

McFarlin Library
2933 East 6th Street
Tulsa, OK 74104-3123
Telephone: 918-631-2874

Fax: 918-631-3791
Email: ajl@utulsa.edu
Web: www.lib.utulsa.edu/govdocs/maps.htm
Personnel:
Responsible person: Andra Lupardus, Documents/Peri-
    odicals Librarian, *email:* ajl@utulsa.edu
Assistants: Lori Curtis, Director Special Collections
FTE professionals: 1   *FTE para-professionals:* 1
Holdings:
Geographic strengths: Indian Territory, Oklahoma,
    Texas, Pennsylvania, West
Special collections: Sanborn Fire Insurance maps of
    Oklahoma (microfilm), Crown Collection of Pho-
    tographs of American Maps
Map depositories: USGS topos, CIA, National Forest
    Service, BLM
30,000 printed maps
200 aerial photos
2 globes
700 atlases
500 books
2 active serials
400 CD-ROMs
Access:
    Hours:
        Monday–Friday: 8 A.M.–10 P.M.
        Saturday: 11 A.M.–8 P.M.
        Sunday: 1 P.M.–10 P.M.
Geographic Information Systems:
GIS services available in an open environment
Number of public GIS workstations: 1
Collection services:
Maps cataloged: 10%
Maps classified: 100%
Maps in OPAC: 10%
Classification schemes: LC, SuDocs, Dewey
Physical facilities:
Public computers: 14
Map cases: 30
Number of atlas stands: 5
Number of microform readers: 4
Number of microform printers: 4
Number of light tables: 1
Copying facilities available: copier, color copier

399 *Corvallis, OR*

Oregon State University

The Valley Library
Map Collection
121 The Valley Library
Corvallis, OR 97331-4501
Telephone: 541-737-7295
Fax: 541-737-8224

Email: valley.reference@oregonstate.edu
Web: osulibrary.oregonstate.edu/research/guides/maps/
maproom.htm
Personnel:
Responsible person: Jeanne Davidson, Physical Sciences
Librarian, *email:* jeanne.davidson@oregonstate.edu
Assistants: Larry Landis, Archivist; Elizabeth Nielsen,
Senior Staff Archivist; Karl McCreary, Archivist;
Faye Harkins, Archivist; Terry Reese, Cataloger
FTE professionals: 0.25
Number of student workers hours per week: 32
Holdings:
Geographic strengths: Oregon, Washington
Special collections: Oregon Sanborn Fire Insurance
maps, E.E. Wilson maps and papers, Washington and
Oregon historic forest maps, nautical charts for the
world, PAIGH topographic maps of Latin America,
Oregon Metsker Atlases, Oregon Historic topo-
graphic maps
Subject strengths: agriculture, climatology, city,
forestry, geology, hydrology, land ownership, land
use, nautical charts, oceanography, recreation, soil
Map depositories and percentages: USGS topos
(100%), USGS geology maps (100%), Department
of Transportation, NOAA, National Forest Service,
NIMA nautical, NIMA aeronautical, BLM, State
170,000 printed maps
11,000 aerial photos
280 gazetteers
800 printed atlases
Collecting digital data
Average budget over the last 5 years: $2,600
On-going publications: Map Collection Research
Guide (available online at http://osulibrary.oregon-
state.edu/research/guides/maps/maproom.htm
Access:
Maps in separate area
Collection is partially open to the public
Answers email questions
Hours:
Monday–Friday: 9 A.M.–5 P.M.
Saturday: 1 P.M.–5 P.M.
Sunday: 1 P.M.–9 P.M.
Total hours per week opened: 52
Maps circulate
Circulation policies apply
Map circulation duration: 3 weeks
Atlas circulation duration: 3 weeks
Book circulation duration: 3 weeks
Interlibrary loan available
Geographic Information Systems:
GIS services available in an open environment
GIS software: ArcGIS
Collection services:
Datasets are cataloged

Classification schemes: LC
Cataloging utilities: OCLC
Catalog accessibility: online, cards
Preservation techniques: encapsulation
Physical facilities:
No Internet access
Copying facilities available: copier, color copier, large-
format copier, microform copier, transparencies

400 *Eugene, OR*

University of Oregon

Knight Library
Document Center, founded 1967
1299 University of Oregon
Eugene, OR 97403-1299
Telephone: 541-346-4565
Fax: 541-346-1958
Email: map@darkwing.uoregon.edu
Web: libweb.uoregon.edu/map/
Assistants: Colin Kelly, Map and Aerial Photography
Technician
Number of student workers hours per week: 25
Number of volunteer hours per month: 10
Holdings:
Geographic strengths: Eugene–Springfield, Willamette
Valley, Oregon, Pacific Northwest
Special collections: Sanborn Fire Insurance maps of
Oregon Communities, Metsker Atlases for Oregon
counties, historic topographic maps of Oregon, other
Western States, Historic Transportation maps for
many Oregon communities (ODOT)
Subject strengths: aerial photos, aeronautical, agriculture,
early cartography, modern cartography, caves, celestial, climatology, city, economic geography, forestry,
genealogy, geodetic surveys, geology, geospatial data,
historical geography, hydrology, land ownership, land
use, language, map catalogs, map collecting, mineral
resources, mining, nautical charts, oceanography, political geography, population, projections, railroads,
raised relief models, recreation, religion, roads, soil,
vegetation, views, waterways
Map depositories and percentages: USGS topos
(100%), USGS geology maps (100%), Department
of Transportation, NOAA, GPO, CIA, National Forest Service, NIMA aeronautical, BLM, State, United
Nations
246,243 printed maps
60 raised relief maps
5,000 microfiche
300 microfilms
550,000 aerial photos
24 satellite images
75 gazetteers
85,000 printed atlases

5,780 books
12 active serials
25 CD-ROMs
10 computer programs
Chronological coverage:
  1900–1939: 20%
  1940–present: 70%
Average budget over the last 5 years: $8,000
Access:
  Collection is open to the public
  Reference questions per year: 675
  Answers email questions
  Patrons per month: 77
  Hours:
    Monday–Friday: 8 A.M.–midnight
    Saturday: 11 A.M.–6 P.M.
    Sunday: 11 A.M.–midnight
    Total hours per week opened: 104
  Maps circulate
  Circulation policies apply
    Map circulation duration: 1 week
  Interlibrary loan available
Geographic Information Systems:
  GIS services available by appointment
  GIS software: ESRI, ERDAS Imagine
  Number of public GIS workstations: 12
  GIS assistance available for Census mapping, geocoding, and image analysis
  Scans maps for patrons
Collection services:
  Maps cataloged: 25%
  Maps classified: 90%
  Maps in OPAC: 25%
  Datasets are cataloged
  Classification schemes: Uses LC classification
  Cataloging utilities: OCLC, Local
  Catalog accessibility: Catalog online, Catalog cards
  Preservation techniques: Encapsulation
  Items that have gone through the preservation process:
    25%
Physical facilities:
  Internet access available
  Number of public computers: 12
  Number of vertical files (file cabinets): 20
  Linear book shelving: 40 ft.
  Linear atlas shelving: 120 ft.
  Other map storage: 3 rolled map cases
  Number of microform readers: 10
  Copying facilities available: Copier available, color copier available, microform copier available

401 *Klamath Falls, OR*

Oregon Institute of Technology

Library
Maps

3201 Campus Dr.
Klamath Falls, OR 97601
Telephone: 541-885-1772
Fax: 541-885-1777
Web: www.oit.edu/lbry
Personnel:
  Responsible person: Larrisa John, Technical Service Librarian, *Assistants:* Deniece Davis, Acquisitions/Documents Manager
  FTE professionals: 1   *FTE para-professionals:* 1
Holdings:
  Geographic strengths: Oregon, California, Washington
  Map depositories: USGS topos, Department of Transportation, National Forest Service
  1,000 printed maps
  2 globes
  10 atlases
  10 CD-ROMs
Access:
  Hours:
    Monday–Friday: 7:30 A.M.–9 P.M.
    Saturday: 1 P.M.–5 P.M.
    Sunday: 1 P.M.–9 P.M.
  Items circulate
Collection services:
  Maps cataloged: 0%
  Maps classified: 0%
  Maps in OPAC: 0%
  Classification schemes: LC, SuDocs
Physical facilities:
  Public computers: 25
  Vertical files: 4

402 *La Grande, OR*

Eastern Oregon University

Pierce Library
1 University Boulevard
La Grande, OR 97850
Telephone: 541-962-3546
Fax: 541-962-3335
Web: pierce.eou.edu
Personnel:
  Responsible person: Ken Watson, Map Librarian, *email:* kwatson@eou.edu
  FTE professionals: 0.25
  Number of student works: 0.25
Holdings:
  Geographic strengths: Oregon
  Special collections: Sanborn Fire Insurance maps of Oregon
  Subject strengths: aerial photos, forestry, geology, mineral resources, roads, soil
  Map depositories and percentages: USGS topos, USGS geology maps
  3,578 printed maps

13 wall maps
24 raised relief maps
7,568 aerial photos
213 printed atlases
153 books
109 CD-ROMs
Average budget over the last 5 years: $300
Access:
Collection is open to the public
Reference questions per year: 115
Answers email questions
Patrons per month: 20
Hours:
Monday–Friday: 7:30 A.M.–11 P.M.
Saturday: 11 A.M.–7 P.M.
Sunday: 2 P.M.–11 P.M.
Total hours per week opened: 91.5
Circulation policies apply
Book circulation duration: 3 weeks
Interlibrary loan available
Geographic Information Systems:
GIS software: ARCGIS
Collection services:
Maps cataloged: 95%
Maps classified: 100%
Maps in OPAC: 95%
Datasets are cataloged
Classification schemes: LC, SuDocs, Local
Cataloging utilities: OCLC, Local
Catalog accessibility: online
Preservation techniques: encapsulation
Items that have gone through the preservation process: 1%
Physical facilities:
No Internet access
Square footage: 575
Number of map cases: 12
Linear book shelving: 20 ft.
Copying facilities available: copier, microform copier

403 *Pendleton, OR*

Blue Mountain Community College Library

Map Collection
2411 NW Carden Ave
Pendleton, OR 97801
Telephone: 541-278-5915
Fax: 541-276-6119
Email: ejensen@bluecc.edu
Web: www.bluecc.edu/library
Personnel:
Assistants: Erik Jensen, Library Assistant
Holdings:
Geographic strengths: Oregon, Washington, Idaho
Special collections: Oregon topographical maps (USGS), BLM maps

Subject strengths: geology, land use, mineral resources, political geography, recreation
Map depositories: USGS topos, CIA, BLM
1,100 printed maps
50 wall maps
3,900 microfiche
200 microfilms
13 gazetteers
83 printed atlases
150 CD-ROMs
Chronological coverage:
1940–present: 100%
Access:
Maps in separate area
Collection is open to the public
Reference questions per year: 10
Answers email questions
Hours:
Monday–Friday: 7:30 A.M.–9 P.M.
Total hours per week opened: 62.5
Maps circulate
Circulation policies apply
Map circulation duration: 3 weeks
Atlas circulation duration: 3 weeks
Book circulation duration: 3 weeks
Geographic Information Systems:
GIS services available in an open environment
GIS software: LandView, Tiger
Number of public GIS workstations: 14
GIS assistance available for Census mapping
Collection services:
Maps cataloged: 50%
Maps classified: 90%
Maps in OPAC: 50%
Classification schemes: SuDocs, Dewey
Cataloging utilities: OCLC
Catalog accessibility: online
Physical facilities:
Internet access available
Square footage: 500
Linear book shelving: 4,500 ft.
Linear atlas shelving: 100 ft.
Copying facilities available: copier, microform copier, printer
Notes: BMCC Library is currently in the process of reevaluating and updating the cataloging/classification of its map collection.

404 *Portland, OR*

Columbia River Inter-Tribal Fish Commission

StreamNet Library
Founded 1996
729 NE Oregon Street
Suite 190
Portland, OR 97232

Telephone: 503-731-1304
Fax: 503-731-1260
Email: fishlib@critfc.org
Web: www.fishlib.org
Personnel:
Assistants: Lenora A. Oftedahl, StreamNet Regional Librarian; Todd Hannon, Assistant Librarian; David Liberty, Library Technician; Alison Halfmoon, Library Technician
FTE professionals: 0.2   *FTE para-professionals:* 0.5
Holdings:
Geographic strengths: Pacific Northwest, Columbia Basin watershed
Subject strengths: agriculture, archaeology, biology, climatology, city, engineering, forestry, geospatial data, historical geography, hydrology, land ownership, land use, nautical charts, recreation, roads, soil, vegetation, waterways
200 printed maps
20 manuscript maps
49 printed atlases
20 CD-ROMs
Chronological coverage:
1900–1939: 10%
1940–present: 87%
Access:
Collection is open to the public
Answers email questions
Patrons per month: 20
Hours:
Monday–Friday: 8 A.M.–5 P.M.
Total hours per week opened: 40
Geographic Information Systems:
No GIS services available
Scans maps for patrons
Collection services:
Maps in OPAC: 90%
Cataloging utilities: OCLC
Catalog accessibility: online
Physical facilities:
No Internet access
Square footage: 50
Linear book shelving: 12 ft.
Linear atlas shelving: 12 ft.
Other map storage: 5 rolled map cases
Copying facilities available: copier, microform copier

405 *Portland, OR*

Lewis and Clark College

Aubrey Watzek Library
Special Collections
0615 SW Palatine Hill Road
Portland, OR 97219
Telephone: 503-768-7254

Fax: 5037687282
Email: archives@lclark.edu
Web: www.lclark.edu/~archives/specialcollections
Personnel:
Responsible person: Doug Erickson, Head of Special Collections College Archivist, *email:* dme@lclark.edu
Assistants: Jeremy Skinner, Assistant Archivist
FTE professionals: 2   *FTE para-professionals:* 1
Holdings:
Geographic strengths: Pacific Northwest, North America
Special collections: Maps carried or consulted by the Lewis and Clark Expedition
30 printed maps
15 atlases
20 books
Access:
Hours:
Monday–Friday: by appointment
Collection services:
Maps cataloged: 10%
Maps classified: 10%
Maps in OPAC: 10%
Physical facilities:
Maps in separate area
Public computers: 1
Map cases: 1
Vertical files: 1
Notes: We are in the process of cataloging the collection.

406 *Portland, OR*

Multnomah County Library

Central Library
801 SW 10th Avenue
Portland, OR 97205
Telephone: 503-988-5728
Fax: 503-988-5226
Web: www.multcolib.org
Personnel:
Responsible person: Michael Constan, Reference Librarian, *email:* michael.constan@co.multnomah.or.us
Holdings:
Geographic strengths: Oregon, Washington
Subject strengths: city
Map depositories and percentages: USGS topos (25%), Department of Transportation, NOAA, CIA, National Forest Service, State
40,000 printed maps
50 raised relief maps
12 microfilms
150 aerial photos
300 gazetteers
700 printed atlases
10 active serials
15 inactive serials
50 CD-ROMs

Chronological coverage:
  1900–1939: 20%
  1940–present: 80%
Average budget over the last 5 years: $4,000
On-going publications: Map Pathfinder

Access:
  Collection is open to the public
  Maps off site: 20%
  Reference questions per year: 1,500
  Answers email questions
  Patrons per month: 100

Hours:
  Monday–Thursday: 9 A.M.–9 P.M.
  Friday–Saturday: 9 A.M.–6 P.M.
  Sunday: 1 P.M.–5 P.M.
  Total hours per week opened: 70

Maps circulate
Circulation policies apply
  Map circulation duration: 3 weeks
  Atlas circulation duration: 3 weeks
  Book circulation duration: 3 weeks
Interlibrary loan available

Geographic Information Systems:
  No GIS services available
  Number of public GIS workstations: 12

Collection services:
  Maps cataloged: 80%
  Maps classified: 80%
  Maps in OPAC: 80%
  Classification schemes: SuDocs, Dewey, Local
  Cataloging utilities: OCLC, Local
  Catalog accessibility: online, cards

Physical facilities:
  No Internet access
  Square footage: 1,560
  Number of public computers: 12
  Number of map cases: 10
  Linear atlas shelving: 120 ft.
  Copying facilities available: copier, color copier, microform copier

407 *Portland, OR*

Oregon Department of Geology and Mineral Industries

800 NE Oregon Street #28
Portland, OR 97232
Telephone: 503-731-4100
Fax: 503-731-4066
Email: margi.jenks@dogami.state.or.us
Web: www.oregongeology.com

Personnel:
  Responsible person: Margaret D. Jenks, *email:* margi.jenks@dogami.state.or.us
  FTE professionals: 0.1

Holdings:

Geographic strengths: Oregon
Subject strengths: aerial photos, geology, geospatial data, hydrology, mineral resources, mining, soil
Map depositories and percentages: USGS topos (Oregon only) (100 %), USGS geology maps (100%), State

3,000 printed maps
10 atlases
6,000 books
200 CD-ROMs
4 active serials
6 inactive serials
Collecting digital data

Chronological coverage:
  1800–1899: 10%
  1900–1939: 40%
  1940–present: 50%
On-going publications: Our department has a publication list of our own publications that is available on our website.

Access:
  Collection is partially open to the public
  Reference questions per year: 75
  Answers email questions
  Patrons per month: 100

Hours:
  Monday–Friday: 7:30 A.M.–4:30 P.M.
  Saturday–Saturday: closed
  Total hours per week opened: 40

Interlibrary loan available

Geographic Information Systems:
  No GIS services available
  Scans maps for patrons

Physical facilities:
  No Internet access
  Square footage: 1,000
  Linear book shelving: 1,500 ft.
  Other map storage: rolled map cases, flat map storage
  Copying facilities available: copier

408 *Portland, OR*

Oregon Historical Society

Research Library
Maps Collection
1200 S. West Park Avenue
Portland, OR 97205
Telephone: 503-306-5240
Fax: 503-219-2040
Email: libreference@ohs.org
Web: www.ohs.org

Personnel:
  Responsible person: email: libreference@ohs.org

Holdings:
  Geographic strengths: Oregon, Pacific Northwest, North Pacific Rim

Special collections: Sanborn Fire Insurance maps of
  Portland, Oregon
Map depositories: USGS
25,000 printed maps
5,000 aerial photos
3 globes
115 atlases
71 books
4 active serials
Access:
  Hours:
    Monday–Saturday: 1 P.M.–5 P.M.
Collection services:
  Maps cataloged: 2.5%
  Maps classified: 2.5%
  Maps in OPAC: 2.5%
  Classification schemes: LC
Physical facilities:
  Public computers: 3
  Map cases: 21
  Vertical files: 4

409 *Portland, OR*

Portland State University

Millar Library
Founded 1946
P.O. Box 1151
Portland, OR 97207-1151
Telephone: 503-725-5874
Fax: 503-725-4524
Email: andrewsj@pdx.edu
Web: www.lib.pdx.edu/resources/maps_collection/in-
  dex.html
Personnel:
  Responsible person: Judy Andrews, Coordinator for
    Government Information, Data Sets and Maps,
    email: andrewsj@pdx.edu
  Assistants: Bertrand Robbins, Library Technician
  FTE professionals: 0.15   *FTE para-professionals:* 0.25
  Number of student workers hours per week: 10
  Number of volunteer hours per month: 20
Holdings:
  Geographic strengths: Portland Metropolitan region,
    Oregon, Washington
  Special collections: Portland Metropolitan area, Middle
    East (1970s, 1980s), Oregon state natural resources
  Subject strengths: city, geology
  Map depositories: USGS topos, USGS geology maps,
    NOAA, GPO, CIA, National Forest Service, NIMA
    topos, NIMA nautical, NIMA aeronautical, BLM,
    State
56,151 printed maps
24 wall maps

18 raised relief maps
253 aerial photos
206 gazetteers
1,102 printed atlases
30 books
623 CD-ROMs
Chronological coverage:
  1940–present: 98%
Average budget over the last 5 years: $2,000
Access:
  Collection is partially open to the public
  Reference questions per year: 428
  Answers email questions
  Patrons per month: 21
  Hours:
    Monday–Friday: 7:30 A.M.–midnight
    Saturday: 10 A.M.–7 P.M.
    Sunday: 11 A.M.–midnight
    Total hours per week opened: 105.5
  Maps circulate
  Circulation policies apply
    Map circulation duration: 3 days
    Book circulation duration: 3 weeks
  Interlibrary loan available
Geographic Information Systems:
  No GIS services available
  GIS assistance available for Census mapping
Collection services:
  Maps cataloged: 6%
  Maps classified: 6%
  Maps in OPAC: 6%
  Datasets are cataloged
  Classification schemes: LC, SuDocs, Other (alpha-
    betical)
  Cataloging utilities: OCLC
  Catalog accessibility: online
  Preservation techniques: encapsulation, lamination,
    fabric backing
  Items that have gone through the preservation process:
    1%
Physical facilities:
  Internet access available
  Square footage: 1,326
  Number of map cases: 20
  Number of vertical files (file cabinets): 12
  Linear book shelving: 54 ft.
  Linear atlas shelving: 259 ft.
  Copying facilities available: copier, microform copier
Notes: The hours given are for during our class terms.
  When school is not in session, the library is only open
  8 A.M.–5 P.M. Monday through Friday. Portland State
  University is the Regional Federal Depository Library
  for Oregon, so most of the maps come through that pro-
  gram. We keep superseded maps for Oregon and Wash-
  ington, but not for the other states.

410 Salem, OR

Oregon State Library

250 Winter Street NE
Salem, OR 97301
Telephone: 503-378-4277 x236
Fax: 503-588-7119
Web: www.oregon.gov/osl
Personnel:
Responsible person: Susan Westin, *email:* susan.b
.westin@state.or.us
Assistants: Merrialyce Blanchard
FTE professionals: 0.5   *FTE para-professionals:* 0.5
Holdings:
Geographic strengths: Oregon
Special collections: Metsker Maps of Oregon counties
Map depositories: USGS topos, National Forest Service, BLM
12,000 printed maps
10 atlases
25 CD-ROMs
Access:
  Hours:
    Monday–Friday: 8 A.M.–5 P.M.
  Items circulate
  Interlibrary loan available
Collection services:
Maps cataloged: 75%
Maps classified: 100%
Maps in OPAC: 75%
Classification schemes: SuDocs, Dewey, Local
Physical facilities:
Maps in separate area
Map cases: 10

411 Bethlehem, PA

Moravian College

Earth Science Collection
1200 Main Street
Bethlehem, PA 18018-6650
Telephone: 610-861-1440
Fax: 610-625-7918
Email: gerencher@moravian.edu
Web: home.moravian.edu/users/phys/mejjg01/interests/apparatus_pages/map_shelving.htm
Personnel:
Responsible person: Joseph Gerencher, *email:*
gerencher@moravian.edu
FTE professionals: 1
Holdings:
Geographic strengths: World War II European Theater
Special collections: DMA topographic maps
2,000 printed maps
300 aerial photos

14 globes
10 CD-ROMs
Access:
  Hours:
    Monday–Thursday: 8 A.M.–5 P.M.
    Friday: 8 A.M.–5 P.M.
Collection services:
Maps cataloged: 0%
Maps classified: 100%
Maps in OPAC: 0%
Physical facilities:
Maps in separate area
Map cases: 2
Vertical files: 3
Notes: Moravian College had been a DMA map depository since at least the 1960s and had kept the almost all of the collection of approximately 10,000 to 20,000 printed maps on seven stacks of specially constructed horizontal shelves that were housed in Reeves Library. However, about 10 years ago, the college needed the space within the library, so the collection was split into three unequal parts—topographic sheets of the local area were kept in Reeves library on two of the shelf stacks; five shelf stacks and most of the collection was donated to the main library at Penn State University; and selected portions of the collection were retained for the educational program at the college and are kept within three vertical map cases in the earth science classroom and in some other cases within the equipment area for the classroom. This response concerns only the portion of the collection that has been retained within the earth science area.

412 Bethlehem, PA

Moravian College

Reeves Library
1200 Main Street
Bethlehem, PA 18018
Telephone: 610-861-1540
Fax: 610-861-1577
Web: home.moravian.edu/public/reeves
Personnel:
Responsible person: Rita Berk, Library Director,
email: berkr@moravian.edu
FTE professionals: 0   *FTE para-professionals:* 0
Holdings:
1,724 printed maps
5 globes
30 atlases
Access:
  Hours:
    Monday–Friday: 8 A.M.–midnight
    Saturday: 10 A.M.–midnight
    Sunday: noon–midnight

Collection services:
Maps cataloged: 0%
Maps classified: 0%
Maps in OPAC: 0%
Physical facilities:
Maps in separate area
Public computers: 8
Map cases: 1

413 Bethlehem, PA

Lehigh University

Fairchild Martindale Library
Government Documents
8A East Packer Avenue
Bethlehem, PA 18015
Telephone: 610-758-5337
Web: www.lehigh.edu/library
Personnel:
Responsible person: Roseann Bowerman, Team Leader
Arts and Sciences Team, *email:* rb04@lehigh.edu
Assistants: Stefan Firtko
FTE professionals: 0.1   *FTE para-professionals:* 0.5
Holdings:
Geographic strengths: Pennsylvania
Map depositories: USGS topos, CIA, BLM
33,235 printed maps
100 aerial photos
75 atlases
Access:
Hours:
Monday–Friday: 8 A.M.–2 A.M.
Saturday: 10 A.M.–10 P.M.
Sunday: 10 A.M.–2 A.M.
Items circulate
Interlibrary loan available
Collection services:
Maps cataloged: 30%
Maps classified: 95%
Maps in OPAC: 30%
Classification schemes: SuDocs, Dewey
Physical facilities:
Public computers: 1
Map cases: 18
Vertical files: 2

414 Bryn Mawr, PA

Bryn Mawr College

Collier Science Library
Geologic Map Library
101 North Merion Avenue
Bryn Mawr, PA 19010
Telephone: 610-526-7462

Email: breese@brynmawr.edu
Web: www.brynmawr.edu/geology
Personnel:
Responsible person: Betsy Reese, Map Curator, *email:* breese@brynmawr.edu
Assistants: Dr. Maria Luisa Crawford, Professor
Number of student workers hours per week: 10
Number of volunteer hours per month: 12
Holdings:
Geographic strengths: Pennsylvania Piedmont
Special collections: Original maps of Florence Bascom, Dorothy Wyckoff and other women geologists from Bryn Mawr College
Subject strengths: aerial photos, agriculture, archaeology, biology, climatology, city, economic geography, engineering, forestry, geodetic surveys, geology, geospatial data, historical geography, hydrology, land use, map catalogs, mineral resources, mining, nautical charts, oceanography, projections, raised relief models, recreation, roads, satellite imagery, soil, vegetation, waterways
Map depositories and percentages: USGS topos (100%), USGS geology maps (40%), USGS other (20%), NOAA, State
10,000 printed maps
50 wall maps
12 raised relief maps
50 aerial photos
25 satellite images
25 printed atlases
25 books
40 CD-ROMs
Collecting digital data
Chronological coverage:
1900–1939: 30%
1940–present: 60%
Access:
Maps in separate area
Collection is partially open to the public
Reference questions per year: 100
Answers email questions
Hours:
Monday–Friday: 9 A.M.–5 P.M.
Saturday–Sunday: by appointment
Total hours per week opened: 40
Circulation policies apply
Book circulation duration: 2 weeks
Number of books circulated annually: 15
Geographic Information Systems:
GIS services available by appointment
GIS software: CARIS, ArcGIS
Number of public GIS workstations: 15
Number of GIS stations (monitored): 35
GIS assistance available for Census mapping, geocoding, and image analysis

Collection services:

Maps cataloged: 50%

Maps classified: 50%

Maps in OPAC: 50%

Classification schemes: LC, SuDocs, Local

Cataloging utilities: OCLC, Local

Catalog accessibility: online, cards

Preservation techniques: encapsulation, deacidification, lamination

Items that have gone through the preservation process: 10%

Physical facilities:

No Internet access

Square footage: 100

Number of map cases: 16

Copying facilities available: copier, color copier, large-format copier, microform copier, large-format scanner

415 *Harrisburg, PA*

Pennsylvania Department of Education

Bureau of State Library of Pennsylvania

Maps Collection

333 Market Street

Harrisburg, PA 17126-1745

Telephone: 717-783-5950

Fax: 717-787-9127

Email: ra-reference@state.pa.us

Web: www.statelibrary.state.pa.us

Personnel:

Responsible person: Richard Hill, Head of Main Reading Room, *email:* rhill@state.pa.us

Assistants: Dave Heueisen, Technician; Tim Kreider, Technicians

FTE professionals: 1   *FTE para-professionals:* 1

Holdings:

Geographic strengths: Pennsylvania, United States

Special collections: Pennsylvania state documents maps, Sanborn Fire Insurance maps, U.S. Federal depository maps

Map depositories: Department of Transportation, NOAA, CIA, National Forest Service

9,000 printed maps

2 globes

204 atlases

501 books

2 active serials

Access:

Hours:

Monday: 9 A.M.–4:30 P.M.

Tuesday: 9 A.M.–8 P.M.

Wednesday–Saturday: 9 A.M.–4:30 P.M.

Collection services:

Maps cataloged: 99%

Maps classified: 99%

Maps in OPAC: 99%

Classification schemes: SuDocs, Dewey, Local, Other (alphabetical)

Physical facilities:

Public computers: 28

Map cases: 15

416 *Harrisburg, PA*

Pennsylvania Historical and Museum Commission

Pennsylvania State Archives

Division of Archives and Manuscripts

350 North Street

Harrisburg, PA 17120-0090

Telephone: 717-783-3281

Fax: 717-787-4822

Email: ra-phmc-webmaster@state.pa.us

Web: www.phmc.state.pa.us/bah/dam/mg/mg11.htm

Personnel:

Responsible person: Michael Sherbon, *email:* msherbon@state.pa.us

FTE professionals: 1

Holdings:

Geographic strengths: Pennsylvania

Special collections: Penn land grant records, state aerial photography survey (1939), birds-eye views of T.M.Fowler (ca. 1875–1905), early USGS topo maps (to 1988), Aero Service Company photographs (ca. 1920–1940)

800 printed maps

15,000 aerial photos

100 atlases

Access:

Hours:

Monday–Friday: 9 A.M.–4 P.M.

Saturday–Sunday: closed

Collection services:

Maps cataloged: 90%

Maps in OPAC: 90%

Classification schemes: Local

Physical facilities:

Public computers: 1

Map cases: 45

417 *Kutztown, PA*

Kutztown University

Rohrbach Library

Maps Department

15200 Kutztown Road

Building 5
Kutztown, PA 19530
Telephone: 610-683-4813
Web: www.kutztown.edu/library/maps.htm
Personnel:
Responsible person: Sylvia Pham, Reference and Maps
    Librarian, *email:* spham@kutztown.edu
Assistants: Michael Weber, Cataloging Librarian
FTE professionals: 2
Holdings:
Geographic strengths: Pennsylvania
Special collections: Sanborn Fire Insurance maps of
    Pennsylvania (digital collection available online for
    Kutztown University Community only)
Map depositories: USGS topos, Department of Trans-
    portation, CIA, National Forest Service
40,379 printed maps
10 globes
13 CD-ROMs
Access:
Hours:
    Monday–Friday: 8 A.M.–midnight
    Saturday: 9 A.M.–5 P.M.
    Sunday: 2 P.M.–midnight
Items circulate
Collection services:
Maps cataloged: 99%
Maps classified: 99%
Maps in OPAC: 100%
Classification schemes: Other (Boggs and Lewis)
Physical facilities:
Maps in separate area
Public computers: 5
Vertical files: 30

418 *Lancaster, PA*

Franklin and Marshall College

Martin Library of the Sciences
P.O. Box 3003
Lancaster, PA 17604
Telephone: 717-291-3843
Fax: 717-291-4088
Web: library.fandm.edu
Personnel:
Responsible person: Dale B. Riordan, Science Librar-
    ian, *email:* dale.riordan@fandm.edu
FTE professionals: 0.1   *FTE para-professionals:*
    0.25
Holdings:
Geographic strengths: United States
Map depositories: USGS
57,000 printed maps
250 aerial photos
2 globes

251 atlases
79 books
31 CD-ROMs
Access:
Hours:
    Monday–Friday: 8 A.M.–2 A.M.
    Saturday: 9 A.M.–12 P.M.
    Sunday: 11 A.M.–2 A.M.
Items circulate
Collection services:
Maps cataloged: 2%
Maps classified: 2%
Maps in OPAC: 2%
Classification schemes: LC, SuDocs, Local
Physical facilities:
Public computers: 1
Map cases: 16
Vertical files: 4

419 *New Castle, PA*

New Castle Public Library

207 East North Street
New Castle, PA 16101
Telephone: 724-658-6659
Fax: 724-658-9012
Web: www.newcastle.lib.pa.us
Personnel:
Responsible person: Jennifer Joseph, Reference/
    Government Documents Librarian, *email:* librarian
    jen@msn.com
Assistants: Mike Orwell, Reference Librarian
FTE professionals: 2   *FTE para-professionals:* 0.25
Holdings:
Geographic strengths: New Castle, Pennsylvania, Ohio
Special collections: Historical maps
Map depositories: USGS
1,000 printed maps
2 globes
30 atlases
20 books
Access:
Hours:
    Monday: 3 P.M.–8:30 P.M.
    Tuesday–Friday: 8:30 A.M.–5 P.M.
    Saturday: 8:30 A.M.–2:30 P.M.
    Sunday: closed
Items circulate
Interlibrary loan available
Collection services:
Maps cataloged: 50%
Maps classified: 100%
Maps in OPAC: 25%
Classification schemes: SuDocs, Dewey

Physical facilities:
Public computers: 9
Map cases: 2
Vertical files: 4

420 *Philadelphia, PA*

Academy of Natural Sciences

Ewell Sale Stewart Library
James Bond Map Room
1900 Benjamin Franklin Parkway
Philadelphia, PA 19103
Telephone: 215-299-1040
Fax: 215-299-1144
Email: library@acnatsci.org
Web: www.acnatsci.org/library
Personnel:
Responsible person: Eileen Mathias, Information Services Librarian, *email:* mathias@acnatsci.org
Holdings:
Geographic strengths: Philadelphia, Pennsylvania, United States, World
Special collections: William Maclure Map Collection
Subject strengths: biology, early cartography, modern cartography, geodetic surveys, geology, geospatial data, historical geography, hydrology, land use, military, mineral resources, nautical charts, oceanography, political geography, soil, waterways, Maps of early exploration
Map depositories and percentages: USGS other, NOAA
25,000 printed maps
200 gazetteers
150 printed atlases
Chronological coverage:
1800–1899: 35%
1900–1939: 35%
1940–present: 25%
Access:
Maps in separate area
Collection is paged
Hours:
Tuesday–Friday: 1 P.M.–4:30 P.M.
Saturday–Saturday: closed
Total hours per week opened: 14
Geographic Information Systems:
No GIS services available
Scans maps for patrons
Collection services:
Maps cataloged: 25%
Maps classified: 100%
Maps in OPAC: 25%
Classification schemes: LC, Local
Cataloging utilities: OCLC, Local
Catalog accessibility: online, cards

Preservation techniques: encapsulation, deacidification, lamination, edging
Items that have gone through the preservation process: 1%
Physical facilities:
No Internet access
Square footage: 598
Number of map cases: 27
Linear book shelving: 34 ft.
Copying facilities available: copier, large-format copier, digital camera
Notes: The USGS Hydrologic and Water-resources Investigations Atlases are shelved in the regular library stacks, and are not kept in the map room.

421 *Philadelphia, PA*

Free Library of Philadelphia

Map Collection
Founded 1927
1901 Vine Street
Philadelphia, PA 19103-1189
Telephone: 215-686-5397
Fax: 215-563-3628
Web: www.library.phila.gov
Personnel:
Responsible person: Richard Boardman, Head, *email:* boardmanr@library.phila.gov
Holdings:
Geographic strengths: Philadelphia region, Pennsylvania, United States
Special collections: Sanborn Fire Insurance maps (Philadelphia area), Hexamer Fire Insurance maps (Philadelphia), Hexamer General Surveys (Philadelphia), insurance atlases (Philadelphia area), Pennsylvania county atlases, aerial photography (Philadelphia area), Baedeker travel guides
Subject strengths: aerial photos, aeronautical, early cartography, modern cartography, city, geology, industries, land ownership, land use, nautical charts, railroads, roads, travel books
Map depositories and percentages: USGS topos (100%), USGS geology maps (75%), NOAA, CIA, NIMA aeronautical, BLM
135,000 printed maps
15 manuscript maps
10 raised relief maps
15,000 microfiche
285 microfilms
1,000 aerial photos
15 globes
400 gazetteers
2,000 printed atlases
3,000 books

10 active serials
12 inactive serials
Chronological coverage:
  1800–1899: 20%
  1900–1939: 45%
  1940–present: 30%
Average budget over the last 5 years: $8,000
Access:
Collection is paged
Reference questions per year: 7,500
Answers email questions
Patrons per month: 225
Hours:
  Monday–Friday: 9 A.M.–5 P.M.
  Total hours per week opened: 40
Geographic Information Systems:
No GIS services available
Collection services:
Maps cataloged: 90%
Maps classified: 30%
Maps in OPAC: 30%
Classification schemes: Dewey
Cataloging utilities: OCLC
Catalog accessibility: online, cards
Preservation techniques: encapsulation, deacidification, acid-free boxes, folders
Physical facilities:
Internet access available
Square footage: 2,310
Number of map cases: 140
Number of vertical files (file cabinets): 12
Linear book shelving: 2,080 ft.
Linear atlas shelving: 2,446 ft.
Copying facilities available: copier, color copier, large-format copier, microform copier
Notes: Only monographs, atlases, gazetteers are classified and in the on-line catalog. Maps are cataloged with a local system but not in the public catalog.

422 *Philadelphia, PA*

Historical Society of Pennsylvania

Library Division
Archives
1300 Locust Street
Philadelphia, PA 19107
Telephone: 215-732-6200
Fax: 215-732-2680
Email: library@hsp.org
Web: www.hsp.org
Personnel:
Responsible person: Rachel Onuf, Director of Archives and Collections Management, *email:* ronuf@hsp.org
Holdings:

Geographic strengths: Delaware Valley region, Pennsylvania
Special collections: Hexamer Insurance atlases, Sanborn Fire Insurance maps
Subject strengths: city, historical geography, land ownership, map catalogs, military, travel books, views
5,000 printed maps
6,000 manuscript maps
300 printed atlases
Chronological coverage:
  Pre-1800: 10%
  1800–1899: 70%
  1900–1939: 20%
Access:
Maps in separate area
Collection is paged
Answers email questions
Hours:
  Monday–Tuesday: 1 P.M.–5:30 P.M.
  Wednesday: 1 P.M.–8:30 P.M.
  Thursday–Friday: 1 P.M.–5:30 P.M.
  Total hours per week opened: 25.5
Geographic Information Systems:
No GIS services available
Number of public GIS workstations: 10
Scans maps for patrons
Collection services:
Maps cataloged: 50%
Maps classified: 75%
Maps in OPAC: 75%
Classification schemes: LC, Local
Cataloging utilities: OCLC, Local
Catalog accessibility: online, cards
Preservation techniques: encapsulation, deacidification, encapsulation in mylar
Physical facilities:
No Internet access
Square footage: 450
Number of microform readers: 12
Copying facilities available: copier, large-format copier, overhead copier
Notes: We do not have a separate map department, map budget, map staff, or map reading room. Therefore, these figures are part of larger ones which cannot be easily separated (i.e., our flat files may also contain prints as well as maps; our microform equipment figures are for our Greenfield Microform Center).

423 *Philadelphia, PA*

Library Company of Philadelphia

Print and Photograph Department
1314 Locust Street
Philadelphia, PA 19107

Telephone: 215-546-8229
Fax: 215-546-5167
Email: printroom@librarycompany.org
Web: www.librarycompany.org
Personnel:
Responsible person: Sarah Weatherwax, Curator of Prints and Photographs, *email:* printroom@librarycompany.org
FTE professionals: 0.2
Holdings:
Geographic strengths: Philadelphia, Pennsylvania
Special collections: Strong collection of early American maps and atlases including many of the works described in Wheat and Brun's Maps and charts published in *America before 1800: A Bibliography* (New Haven and London, Yale University Press, 1969), maps published in 16th- to 19th-century European works on travel and exploration, 18th- and 19th-century Pennsylvania and Philadelphia maps, AeroService Corporation aerial photographs of the Delaware Valley (1930–1940)
2,000 printed maps
2,100 aerial photos
500 atlases
4,500 books
50 active serials
Access:
Hours:
Monday–Friday: 9 A.M.–4:45 P.M.
Collection services:
Classification schemes: Local

---

424 *Pittsburgh, PA*

Historical Society of Western Pennsylvania

1212 Smallman Street
Pittsburgh, PA 15222
Telephone: 412-454-6364
Fax: 412-454-6028
Web: www.pghhistory.org
Personnel:
Responsible person: Steve Doell, *email:* sdoell@hswp.org
Assistants: Art Louderback
FTE professionals: 2   *FTE para-professionals:* 0
Holdings:
Geographic strengths: Western Pennsylvania
Special collections: Sanborn Fire Insurance maps, Hopking maps, Geological Survey maps, historical maps
900 printed maps
20 aerial photos
100 atlases
100 books
Access:

Hours:
Tuesday–Saturday: 10 A.M.–5 P.M.
Sunday: closed
Collection services:
Maps cataloged: 10%
Maps classified: 100%
Maps in OPAC: 10%
Classification schemes: LC, Other (place)
Physical facilities:
Maps in separate area
Public computers: 6
Map cases: 5

---

425 *Pittsburgh, PA*

University of Pittsburgh

Hillman Library
Map Collection
3960 Forbes Avenue
Pittsburgh, PA 15260
Telephone: 412-648-7726; 412-648-7730
Fax: 412-648-7733
Email: wendym@pitt.edu;ttwiss@pitt.edu
Web: www.library.pitt.edu/libraries/maps/maps.html
Personnel:
Responsible person: Wendy Mann, Coordinator, Government Publications, *email:* wendym@pitt.edu
Assistants: Thomas Twiss, Government Information Librarian
FTE professionals: 0.5   *FTE para-professionals:* 0.5
Number of student works: 0.5
Number of student workers hours per week: 10
Holdings:
Geographic strengths: Pittsburgh, Pennsylvania, United States
Special collections: Sanborn Fire Insurance maps of the Pittsburgh area, Hopkins plat books of the Pittsburgh area, Consolidated Coal Company coal mine maps, mostly for Western Pennsylvania
Subject strengths: city, forestry, genealogy, geospatial data, historical geography, land ownership, land use, map collecting, military, mineral resources, political geography, population, recreation, roads, soil
Map depositories and percentages: USGS topos (100%), USGS geology maps (100%), USGS other (100%), Department of Transportation, NOAA, GPO, CIA, National Forest Service, NIMA topos, NIMA nautical, NIMA aeronautical, BLM, United Nations
95,000 printed maps
12 manuscript maps
2,690 microfiche
920 microfilms
45 satellite images
465 gazetteers

1,008 printed atlases
70 books
100 CD-ROMs
10 computer programs
Collecting digital data
Chronological coverage:
    1940–present: 96%
Average budget over the last 5 years: $2,500

Access:

Collection is partially open to the public
Maps off site
Reference questions per year: 500
Answers email questions
Patrons per month: 40

Hours:

Monday–Friday: 7:50 A.M.–2 A.M.
Saturday: 9 A.M.–midnight
Sunday: 10 A.M.–2 A.M.
Total hours per week opened: 118

Geographic Information Systems:

GIS services available in an open environment
GIS software: ArcGIS
GIS assistance available for Census mapping, and geocoding

Collection services:

Maps cataloged: 90%
Maps classified: 40%
Maps in OPAC: 50%
Datasets are cataloged
Classification schemes: LC, SuDocs
Cataloging utilities: OCLC
Catalog accessibility: online, fiche, cards
Preservation techniques: encapsulation, edging, reproduction on acid-free paper
Items that have gone through the preservation process: 1%

Physical facilities:

Internet access available
Square footage: 1,913
Number of map cases: 122
Copying facilities available: copier, microform copier

426 *University Park, PA*

Pennsylvania State University

Fletcher L. Byrom Earth and Mineral Sciences Library
105 Deike Building
University Park, PA 16802
Telephone: 814-865-9517
Fax: 814-865-1379
Email: ems@psulias.psu.edu
Web: www.libraries.psu.edu/emsl/

Personnel:

Responsible person: Linda Musser, Head, *email:* Lrm4@psu.edu

Holdings:

Geographic strengths: Pennsylvania
20,000 printed maps
1 globe
200 atlases
10,000 books
15 active serials
400 CD-ROMs

Access:

Hours:

Monday–Thursday: 7:30 A.M.–midnight
Friday: 7:30 A.M.–5 P.M.
Saturday: 9 A.M.–5 P.M.
Sunday: 1 P.M.–10 P.M.
Items circulate
Interlibrary loan available

Collection services:

Maps cataloged: 100%
Maps classified: 100%
Maps in OPAC: 100%
Classification schemes: LC, Local

Physical facilities:

Public computers: 28
Map cases: 8

Notes: There are two map collections in the PSU libraries. The primary collection is in the maps library. The EMS library houses the geologic maps collection. The local classification used is for our dissertations/theses only.

427 *University Park, PA*

Pennsylvania State University

University Libraries
Maps Library
001 Paterno Library
University Park, PA 16802
Telephone: 814-863-0094
Fax: 814-863-3560
Email: maproom@psu.edu
Web: www.libraries.psu.edu/maps

Personnel:

Responsible person: Joanne M. Perry, Maps Librarian and Head of Cartographic Information Services, *email:* jup4@psulias.psu.edu
Assistants: Derrick Beckner, Library Supervisor; Hilary Kleckner, Library Assistant
FTE professionals: 1   *FTE para-professionals:* 4

Holdings:

Geographic strengths: Pennsylvania, United States, Western Europe
Special collections: Warrantee Township maps of Pennsylvania
Map depositories: USGS topos, Department of Transportation, NOAA, CIA, National Forest Service, NGA nautical, NGA aeronautical, BLM

350,000 printed maps
2,000 aerial photos
11 globes
3,000 atlases
900 books
14 active serials
900 CD-ROMs

Access:

Hours:

Monday–Friday: 7:45 A.M.–10 P.M.
Saturday: 9 A.M.–5 P.M.
Sunday: noon–midnight

Items circulate
Interlibrary loan available

Collection services:

Maps cataloged: 80%
Maps classified: 90%
Maps in OPAC: 80%
Classification schemes: LC

Physical facilities:

Maps in separate area
Public computers: 6
Map cases: 190
Vertical files: 7

428 *West Chester, PA*

West Chester University

Francis Harvey Green Library
Dr. Sandra F. Pritchard Mather and Dr. John Russell
Mather Map Room., founded 1975
29 West Rosedale Avenue
West Chester, PA 19383
Telephone: 610-436-2869
Fax: 610-436-2251
Web: www.wcupa.edu/library.fhg/fhg_tour/maps.htm

Personnel:

Responsible person: Mary Anne Burns Duffy, Document
and Map Librarian, *email:* mburnsduff@wcupa.edu
Assistants: Eleanor Brennan, Library Technician
Number of student workers hours per week: 10

Holdings:

Geographic strengths: Chester County, Pennsylvania
Subject strengths: agriculture, city, population, views
Map depositories and percentages: USGS topos (30%),
USGS geology maps (10%), USGS other, GPO,
CIA, National Forest Service, State
4,500 printed maps
20 gazetteers
300 printed atlases
150 books
Collecting digital data
Chronological coverage:
1900–1939: 10%

1940–present: 87%
Average budget over the last 5 years: $2,000

Access:

Maps in separate area
Collection is open to the public
Reference questions per year: 250
Answers email questions
Patrons per month: 20

Hours:

Monday–Friday: 8 A.M.–10 P.M.
Saturday: noon–5 P.M.
Sunday: noon–midnight
Total hours per week opened: 85

Geographic Information Systems:

GIS services available by appointment
GIS assistance available for Census mapping, and image analysis
Scans maps for patrons

Collection services:

Maps cataloged: 100%
Maps classified: 100%
Maps in OPAC: 100%
Datasets are cataloged
Classification schemes: LC
Cataloging utilities: OCLC
Catalog accessibility: online
Preservation techniques: encapsulation, lamination

Physical facilities:

Internet access available
Square footage: 980
Number of map cases: 12
Copying facilities available: copier, microform copier

429 *Wilkes-Barre, PA*

**Office of Surface Mining
Reclamation and Enforcement**

Anthracite (Coal) Mine Map Repository
Branch of Anthracite—MMR
7 North Wilkes-Barre Boulevard
Suite 308
Wilkes-Barre, PA 18702-5293
Telephone: 570-830-1400
Fax: 570-830-1421
Email: jkomnath@osmre.gov
Web: mmr.osmre.gov

Personnel:

Responsible person: Michael "Mick" Kuhns, *email:*
mkuhns@osmre.gov
Assistants: Dave Philbin, Mining Engineer; Bob Bentz,
Program Specialist; Rollie Harper, Program Specialist
FTE professionals: 0.25   *FTE para-professionals:* 0.1

Holdings:

Geographic strengths: Northeastern Pennsylvania

Special collections: coal-mining collieries that mined anthracite coal in northeastern Pennsylvania, books on mining history, geologic survey maps (1800s–)

25,000 printed maps
200 aerial photos
100 books
50 CD-ROMs

Collection services:

Maps cataloged: 98%

Access:

Hours:

Monday–Friday: 7:30 A.M.–4 P.M.
Saturday–Sunday: closed

Physical facilities:

Maps in separate area
Map cases: 625 hangars
Vertical files: 150

Notes: Most maps in developed areas are made into overlying laminated folio (paper) format. Many of the more remote areas are in microfilm format only.

430 *Kingston, RI*

University of Rhode Island

University Library
Government Publications, founded 1993
15 Lippitt Road
Kingston, RI 02881
Telephone: 401-874-2606
Fax: 401-874-4608
Web: www.uri.edu/library/

Personnel:

Responsible person: Deborah Mongeau, *email:* dmongeau@uri.edu
FTE professionals: 0.2

Holdings:

Geographic strengths: Rhode Island, New England
Subject strengths: geodetic surveys, geology, nautical charts, population
Map depositories: USGS topos, USGS geology maps, NOAA, GPO, CIA

3,380 printed maps
Chronological coverage:
1900–1939: 10%
1940–present: 90%

Access:

Collection is open to the public
Reference questions per year: 100
Answers email questions

Hours:

Monday–Friday: 8 A.M.–midnight
Saturday: 10 A.M.–4 P.M.
Sunday: 1 P.M.–midnight
Total hours per week opened: 81

Collection services:

Maps cataloged: 50%

Maps classified: 50%
Maps in OPAC: 50%
Classification schemes: SuDocs
Cataloging utilities: OCLC
Catalog accessibility: online

Physical facilities:

Number of map cases: 10
Copying facilities available: copier, microform copier

431 *Providence, RI*

Providence Public Library

225 Washington Street
Providence, RI 02903
Telephone: 401-455-8000
Web: www.provlib.org

Personnel:

Assistants: Greg Frazier, Government Documents Librarian; Betty Fitzgerald, Rhode Island Collection Librarian
FTE professionals: 0.2

Holdings:

Geographic strengths: Rhode Island, New England, New York
Special collections: Sanborn Fire Insurance maps, Rhode Island historical maps, USGS maps for New England and New York
Subject strengths: early cartography, modern cartography, city, historical geography, map catalogs, nautical charts, topographic
Map depositories and percentages: USGS topos (10%), GPO, CIA

2,000 printed maps
50 microfilms
50 gazetteers
200 printed atlases
Chronological coverage:
Pre-1800: 10%
1800–1899: 15%
1900–1939: 25%
1940–present: 50%

Access:

Maps in separate area
Collection is paged
Reference questions per year: 300
Answers email questions
Patrons per month: 20

Hours:

Monday–Friday: 9 A.M.–8 P.M.
Saturday: 9 A.M.–5:30 P.M.
Sunday: 1 P.M.–5 P.M.
Total hours per week opened: 65

Geographic Information Systems:

No GIS services available
Number of public GIS workstations: 20
Scans maps for patrons

Collection services:

Maps cataloged: 40%

Maps classified: 100%

Maps in OPAC: 40%

Classification schemes: SuDocs, Dewey, Local

Cataloging utilities: OCLC

Catalog accessibility: online, cards

Preservation techniques: lamination

Items that have gone through the preservation process: 10%

Physical facilities:

No Internet access

Square footage: 200

Number of map cases: 12

Linear book shelving: 50 ft.

Linear atlas shelving: 50 ft.

Copying facilities available: copier, large-format copier, microform copier, scanner

432 *Providence, RI*

Rhode Island College

James P. Adams Library

600 Mount Pleasant Avenue

Providence, RI 2908

Telephone: 401-456-8125

Fax: 401-456-1915

Web: www.ric.edu/adamslibrary

Personnel:

Responsible person: Patricia B.M. Brennan, Head of the Reference Department, *email:* pbrennan@ric.edu

Assistants: Rachel Carpenter, Reference and Government Documents Librarian; Timothy Spindler, Reference and Information Technology Librarian; Carla Weiss, Reference and Collection Development Librarian

FTE professionals: 0   *FTE para-professionals:* 0

Holdings:

Geographic strengths: Rhode Island, New England

Special collections: Sanborn Fire Insurance maps of Rhode Island, Historical Outline Map Collection (1840–1980), Tübinger Atlas des Vorderen Orients

Map depositories: USGS topos, CIA, NGA aeronautical

2,100 printed maps

Access:

Hours:

Monday–Friday: 8 A.M.–midnight

Saturday: 9 A.M.–5 P.M.

Sunday: noon–midnight

Collection services:

Maps cataloged: 90%

Maps classified: 90%

Maps in OPAC: 90%

Classification schemes: LC, SuDocs

Physical facilities:

Public computers: 25

Map cases: 3

Vertical files: 1

Notes: Staffing: maps and atlases are a part of the main reference collection. There is no distinct staff for maps and atlases

433 *Providence, RI*

Rhode Island Historical Society

Graphics Collections

Founded 1969

121 Hope Street

Providence, RI 02906

Telephone: 401-273-8107 x20 or x21

Fax: 401-274-6852

Web: www.rihs.org/libraryhome.htm

Personnel:

Responsible person: Graphics Curator, *email:* acywin@rihs.org

Holdings:

Geographic strengths: Rhode Island

Special collections: Evert and Richards Atlas, Sanborn Fire Insurance, Walling

Subject strengths: aerial photos, early cartography, modern cartography, city, economic geography, engineering, genealogy, geology, historical geography, industries, land ownership, land use, map catalogs, map collecting, military, nautical charts, political geography, population, railroads, recreation, roads, soil, travel books, views

3,500 printed maps

200 aerial photos

50 printed atlases

Chronological coverage:

Pre-1800: 25%

1800–1899: 50%

1900–1939: 20%

Average budget over the last 5 years: $1,000

On-going publications: Online public access catalog to be launch 2004. In-house database catalog

Access:

Collection is open to the public

Answers email questions

Patrons per month: 100

Hours:

Tuesday–Monday: 9 A.M.–5 P.M.

Total hours per week opened: 40

Geographic Information Systems:

No GIS services available

Scans maps for patrons

Collection services:

Maps cataloged: 0.75%

Maps classified: 0.75%

Maps in OPAC: 0.75%

Classification schemes: LC

Cataloging utilities: Local

Preservation techniques: encapsulation

Items that have gone through the preservation process: 0.2%

Physical facilities:
No Internet access
Square footage: 750
Number of map cases: 10
Linear atlas shelving: 24 ft.
Copying facilities available: copier, microform copier

434 *Anderson, SC*

Anderson County Public Library

South Carolina Room
300 North McDuffie Street
Anderson, SC 29621
Telephone: 864-260-4500
Fax: 864-260-4098
Email: lholden@andersonlibrary.org
Web: www.andersonlibrary.org

Personnel:
Responsible person: Laura Holden, Head of Genealogy and Local History, *email:* lholden@andersonlibrary .org
Assistants: Jane Mears, LTA; Judy Brown, LA
FTE professionals: 1   *FTE para-professionals:* 2

Holdings:
Geographic strengths: Pendleton, Anderson County
Special collections: Sanborn Fire Insurance maps of city of Anderson and Belton, Dr. Linville Rich Collection (maps of areas in Georgia, Illinois, North and South Carolina, Pennsylvania, and Virginia)
100 printed maps
100 aerial photos
2 atlases
4 books

Access:
Hours:
Monday–Thursday: 9 A.M.–9 P.M.
Friday–Saturday: 9 A.M.–6 P.M.
Sunday: 2 P.M.–6 P.M.

Collection services:
Maps cataloged: 3%
Maps classified: 3%
Maps in OPAC: 3%
Classification schemes: Dewey, Local

Physical facilities:
Maps in separate area
Public computers: 2

435 *Beaufort, SC*

Beaufort County Public Library System

Beaufort Branch
South Carolina Room
311 Scott Street
Beaufort, SC 29902
Telephone: 843-525-4064
Email: gracec@bcgov.net
Web: www.bcgov.net/bftlib/normal.htm

Personnel:
Responsible person: email: gracec@bcgov.net
FTE professionals: 0.8

Holdings:
Geographic strengths: Beaufort, Beaufort County, Jasper County, Hampton County, Allendale County
525 printed maps
10 aerial photos
10 atlases
5 books

Access:
Hours:
Monday–Friday: 10 A.M.–5 P.M.
Saturday–Sunday: closed

Collection services:
Maps cataloged: 1%
Maps classified: 0%
Maps in OPAC: 0%

Physical facilities:
Map cases: 1

436 *Charleston, SC*

Charleston County Public Library

Main Library
68 Calhoun Street
Charleston, SC 29401
Telephone: 843-805-6930
Fax: 843-727-6752
Web: www.ccpl.org

Holdings:
Geographic strengths: Charleston, Charleston County, South Carolina
1,000 printed maps
50 printed atlases
Chronological coverage:
Pre-1800: 10%
1800–1899: 40%
1900–1939: 20%
1940–present: 30%

Access:
Collection is open to the public
Answers email questions
Hours:
Monday–Thursday: 9 A.M.–9 P.M.
Friday–Saturday: 9 A.M.–6 P.M.
Sunday: 2 P.M.–3 P.M.
Total hours per week opened: 69

Geographic Information Systems:
No GIS services available

Collection services:

Maps cataloged: 75%

Maps in OPAC: 75%

Classification schemes: Dewey

Catalog accessibility: online

Preservation techniques: encapsulation, deacidification, edging, lining or backing

Items that have gone through the preservation process: 60%

Physical facilities:

No Internet access

Square footage: 18.5

Copying facilities available: copier, color copier, microform copier

437 *Charleston, SC*

Charleston Library Society

164 King Street

Charleston, SC 29401

Telephone: 843-723-9912

Fax: 843-723-3500

Personnel:

Responsible person: Catherine Sandler, Head Librarian, *email:* chaslibsociety@aol.com

Holdings:

Geographic strengths: Charleston, South Carolina

Subject strength: Civil War

548 printed maps

1 globe

Chronological coverage:

Pre-1800: 30%

1800–1899: 42%

1900–present: 28%

Access:

Hours:

Monday–Thursday: 9:30 A.M.–5:30 P.M.

Friday: 9:30 A.M.–5:30 P.M.

Saturday: 9:30 A.M.–2 P.M.

Sunday: closed

Collection services:

Maps cataloged: 100%

Classification schemes: Other (modified Cutter)

Physical facilities:

Maps in separate area

Map cases: 2

Notes: This library is a membership library. Anyone can use it by paying $35 per year or $3 per day user fee.

438 *Charleston, SC*

Charleston Museum

Archives

360 Meeting Street

Charleston, SC 29403

Telephone: 843-722-2996

Fax: 843-722-1784

Web: www.charlestonmuseum.org

Personnel:

Responsible person: email: info@charlestonmuseum.org

Assistants: Assistant Archivist

Holdings:

200 printed maps

Access:

Hours:

Monday–Friday: by appointment

439 *Charleston, SC*

Citadel Military College

Daniel Library

171 Moultrie Street

Charleston, SC 29409

Telephone: 843-953-2569

Fax: 843-953-5190

Email: david.heisser@Citadel.edu

Web: www.citadel.edu/library/

Personnel:

Responsible person: David Heisser, Reference/Documents Librarian, *email:* David.Heisser@Citadel.edu

Assistants: Dwight Walsh, Library Specialist

FTE professionals: 0.5   *FTE para-professionals:* 0.5

Holdings:

Geographic strengths: South Carolina, World

Map depositories: USGS topos, CIA

1,500 printed maps

1 globe

100 atlases

10 CD-ROMs

Access:

Hours:

Monday–Thursday: 7:45 A.M.–10:30 P.M.

Friday: 7:45 A.M.–5 P.M.

Saturday: 8 A.M.–5 P.M.

Sunday: 2 P.M.–10:30 P.M.

Items circulate

Collection services:

Maps cataloged: 95%

Maps classified: 95%

Maps in OPAC: 95%

Classification schemes: LC, SuDocs

Physical facilities:

Public computers: 20

Map cases: 5

440 *Charleston, SC*

South Carolina Historical Society

100 Meeting Street

Charleston, SC 29401

Telephone: 843-723-3225
Fax: 843-723-8584
Email: lisa.reams@schistory.org
Web: www.schistory.org
Personnel:
Responsible person: Nic Butler, Archivist, *email:* nic
    .butler@schistory.org
Holdings:
Geographic strengths: South Carolina
Special collections: H.A.M. Smith Plat Collection
    (early South Carolina), Sanborn Fire Insurance maps
    (Microfilm)
Subject strengths: early cartography, city, genealogy,
    historical geography, land ownership
100 printed maps
2,000 manuscript maps
2,000 microfiche
50 aerial photos
15 printed atlases
25,000 books
10 inactive serials
Chronological coverage:
    Pre-1800: 20%
    1800–1899: 60%
    1900–1939: 15%
On-going publications: South Carolina Historical Mag-
    azine and The Carologue
Access:
Maps in separate area
Collection is partially open to the public
Reference questions per year: 20
Answers email questions
Hours:
    Monday: 9 A.M.–4 P.M.
    Tuesday: 9 A.M.–7:30 P.M.
    Wednesday–Friday: 9 A.M.–4 P.M.
    Saturday: 9 A.M.–2 P.M.
    Total hours per week opened: 43.5
Geographic Information Systems:
No GIS services available
Scans maps for patrons
Collection services:
Maps cataloged: 90%
Classification schemes: Dewey, Local
Cataloging utilities: OCLC
Catalog accessibility: online, fiche, cards
Preservation techniques: encapsulation, deacidification
Physical facilities:
No Internet access
Square footage: 200
Number of map cases: 10
Copying facilities available: copier, microform copier,
    outsourcing for large-format copying
Notes: We hope to have 100% of our map records in our
online catalog by 2006.

441 *Clemson, SC*

Clemson University

R.M. Cooper Library
Government Documents
Campus Box 343001
Clemson, SC 29634-3001
Telephone: 864-656-5168
Fax: 864-656-7608
Email: comforj@clemson.edu
Web: www.lib.clemson.edu/GovDocs/maps/index.htm
Personnel:
Responsible person: Jan Comfort, *email:* comforj@
    clemson.edu
Assistants: Carol Morgan, Library Specialist
Holdings:
Geographic strengths: South Carolina
Special collections: Sanborn Fire Insurance maps (on-
    line) for South Carolina
Map depositories and percentages: USGS topos
    (100%), USGS geology maps (75%), USGS other
    (50%), NOAA, GPO, CIA, National Forest Service,
    NIMA topos, NIMA nautical, NIMA aeronautical,
    BLM, State
40,000 printed maps
200 manuscript maps
72 raised relief maps
700 microfiche
50 gazetteers
50 CD-ROMs
Chronological coverage:
    1900–1939: 24%
    1940–present: 75%
Average budget over the last 5 years: $1,000
Access:
Collection is open to the public
Reference questions per year: 300
Answers email questions
Patrons per month: 30
Hours:
    Monday–Friday: 24 hours
    Saturday–Sunday: 10 A.M.–midnight
    Total hours per week opened: 148
Maps circulate
Circulation policies apply
    Map circulation duration: 2 days
    Number of maps circulated annually: 200
Geographic Information Systems:
Plotter available
Collection services:
Maps cataloged: 90%
Maps classified: 90%
Maps in OPAC: 90%
Classification schemes: LC, SuDocs, Local
Cataloging utilities: OCLC, Marcive

Catalog accessibility: online
Preservation techniques: encapsulation
Physical facilities:
Internet access available
Square footage: 1,000
Number of map cases: 50
Linear book shelving: 100 ft.
Copying facilities available: copier, microform copier, scanner, large-format copier and color copier available for a fee at the nearby Architecture Branch Library

442 *Columbia, SC*

Richland County Public Library

Walker Local History Room
1431 Assembly Street
Columbia, SC 29201
Telephone: 802-929-3402
Web: www.richland.lib.sc.us
Personnel:
Responsible person: Sarah S. Benson, *email:* sbenson@richland.lib.sc.us
FTE professionals: 1   *FTE para-professionals:* 1
Holdings:
Geographic strengths: Columbia, Richland County, South Carolina
Special collections: South Carolina topographic maps
1,020 printed maps
10 aerial photos
Access:
  Hours:
    Monday–Thursday: 9 A.M.–9 P.M.
    Friday–Saturday: 9 A.M.–6 P.M.
    Sunday: 2 P.M.–6 P.M.
Collection services:
Maps classified: 5%
Classification schemes: Other (card file finding aid)
Physical facilities:
Maps in separate area
Public computers: 2
Map cases: 1

443 *Columbia, SC*

South Carolina Department of Archives and History

Reference Services
8301 Parklane Road
Columbia, SC 29223
Telephone: 803-896-6104
Fax: 803-896-6198
Email: tuttle@scdah.state.sc.us
Web: www.state.sc.us/scdah
Personnel:
Responsible person: Charles H. Lesser, Accessions Archivist, *email:* lesser@scdah.state.sc.us

FTE professionals: 0.05
Holdings:
Geographic strengths: South Carolina
Special collections: Manuscript plats for South Carolina Land Grants, 1730-1895
Subject strengths: agriculture, archaeology, early cartography, modern cartography, city, economic geography, forestry, genealogy, geodetic surveys, geology, historical geography, hydrology, industries, land ownership, land use, military, mineral resources, political geography, railroads, roads, soil, waterways
1,500 printed maps
150,300 manuscript maps
15 wall maps
350 microfilms
15 printed atlases
Chronological coverage:
  Pre-1800: 40%
  1800–1899: 45%
Access:
Collection is paged
Answers email questions
Patrons per month: 835
Hours:
  Monday–Friday: 8:45 A.M.–4:45 P.M.
  Total hours per week opened: 40
Geographic Information Systems:
GIS services available by appointment
Scans maps for patrons
Collection services:
Maps cataloged: 0.6%
Maps in OPAC: 0.4%
Classification schemes: Local
Cataloging utilities: Local
Catalog accessibility: cards
Preservation techniques: encapsulation, deacidification, lamination
Items that have gone through the preservation process: 0.1%
Physical facilities:
Internet access available
Number of map cases: 17
Linear book shelving: 20 ft.
Copying facilities available: copier, microform copier

444 *Columbia, SC*

University of South Carolina

South Caroliniana Library
Published Materials, founded 1940
910 Sumter Street
Columbia, SC 29208
Telephone: 803-777-3132
Fax: 803-777-5747

Email: rcopp@gwm.sc.edu
Web: www.sc.edu/library/socar
Personnel:
Responsible person: Roberta V. Copp, Curator of Published Materials, *email:* rcopp@gwm.sc.edu
Assistants: Thelma Hayes, LTA; Joshua Vassallo
Number of student workers hours per week: 50
Holdings:
Geographic strengths: South Carolina, Southeast
Special collections: Kendall Collection, Sanborn Fire Insurance maps, Unpublished Sanborn Fire Insurance maps
Subject strengths: agriculture, archaeology, early cartography, modern cartography, climatology, city, economic geography, engineering, forestry, genealogy, geodetic surveys, geology, historical geography, hydrology, industries, land ownership, land use, map catalogs, map collecting, military, mineral resources, mining, nautical charts, oceanography, political geography, population, railroads, recreation, religion, roads, soil, travel books, vegetation, views, waterways
1,400 printed maps
50 manuscript maps
6 rolls microfilms
100 printed atlases
62 books
Chronological coverage:
Pre-1800: 20%
1800–1899: 40%
1900–1939: 25%
1940–present: 15%
Average budget over the last 5 years: $100
On-going publications: Caroliniana Columns; Program of the Annual Meeting of the University South Caroliniana Society
Access:
Maps in separate area
Collection is paged
Reference questions per year: 500
Answers email questions
Patrons per month: 560
Hours:
Monday: 8:30 A.M.–5 P.M.
Tuesday: 8:30 A.M.–8 P.M.
Wednesday: 8:30 A.M.–5 P.M.
Thursday: 8:30 A.M.–8 P.M.
Friday: 8:30 A.M.–5 P.M.
Saturday: 9 A.M.–1 P.M.
Sunday: closed
Total hours per week opened: 48.5
Geographic Information Systems:
No GIS services available
Scans maps for patrons
Collection services:

Maps cataloged: 0.95%
Maps classified: 0.95%
Maps in OPAC: 0.1%
Classification schemes: Dewey, Local
Cataloging utilities: OCLC, RLG, Local
Catalog accessibility: online, cards
Preservation techniques: encapsulation, deacidification, cartex
Items that have gone through the preservation process: 0.75%
Physical facilities:
No Internet access
Square footage: 1,156
Number of map cases: 20
Linear book shelving: 90 ft.
Linear atlas shelving: 15 ft.
Other map storage: 1 rolled map shelf
Copying facilities available: copier, large-format copier, microform copier, overhead scanner

445 *Columbia, SC*

University of South Carolina

Thomas Cooper Library
Map Library, founded 1897
Columbia, SC 29208
Telephone: 803-777-2802
Fax: 803-777-4661
Email: davidmcq@sc.edu
Web: www.sc.edu/library/maps.html
Personnel:
Responsible person: David C. McQuillan, Map Librarian, *email:* davidmcq@sc.edu
Assistants: Ross Taylor, Map Library Manager; Chris Hare, Digital Services Librarian
Number of student workers hours per week: 50
Holdings:
Geographic strengths: Columbia, South Carolina, Southeast, United States, World
Subject strengths: aerial photos, aeronautical, city, geology, nautical charts, raised relief models, recreation, roads, soil, travel books, views, Globes
Map depositories and percentages: USGS topos (100%), USGS geology maps (100%), USGS other (100%), Department of Transportation, NOAA, GPO, CIA, National Forest Service, NIMA topos, NIMA nautical, NIMA aeronautical, BLM, State
265,000 printed maps
100 wall maps
250 raised relief maps
125,000 aerial photos
400 gazetteers
3,500 printed atlases
2,100 books
250 CD-ROMs

30 computer programs
Collecting digital data
Chronological coverage:
  1900–1939: 20%
  1940–present: 75%
Average budget over the last 5 years: $500

Access:

Maps in separate area
Collection is paged
Maps off site: 10%
Reference questions per year: 2,000
Answers email questions
Patrons per month: 65

Hours:

Monday–Friday: 8 A.M.–5 P.M.
Saturday–Saturday: closed
Total hours per week opened: 37.5

Geographic Information Systems:

GIS services available by appointment
GIS software: ArcView
GIS assistance available for Census mapping
Scans maps for patrons

Collection services:

Maps cataloged: 40%
Maps classified: 90%
Maps in OPAC: 70%
Datasets are cataloged
Classification schemes: LC
Cataloging utilities: OCLC
Catalog accessibility: online
Preservation techniques: encapsulation
Items that have gone through the preservation process:
  10%

Physical facilities:

Internet access available
Square footage: 3,500
Number of map cases: 250
Number of vertical files (file cabinets): 60
Linear book shelving: 438 ft.
Linear atlas shelving: 195 ft.
Copying facilities available: copier, color copier, microform copier

446 *Conway, SC*

Coastal Carolina University

Kimbel Library
P.O. Box 261954
Conway, SC 29528
Telephone: 843-349-2414
Fax: 843-349-2412
Web: www.coatsal.edu/library

Personnel:

Responsible person: Peggy Bates, *email:* peggyb@
coastal.edu

FTE para-professionals: 0.5

Holdings:

Geographic strengths: South Carolina, North Carolina
Subject strengths: nautical charts, recreation
Map depositories: USGS topos, GPO, NIMA nautical
1,268 printed maps
10 aerial photos
10 satellite images
100 printed atlases
173 books
Chronological coverage:
  1900–1939: 10%
  1940–present: 90%
Average budget over the last 5 years: $500

Access:

Collection is open to the public
Reference questions per year: 50

Hours:

Monday–Friday: 8 A.M.–9 P.M.
Saturday: 9 A.M.–5 P.M.
Sunday: 1 P.M.–9 P.M.
Total hours per week opened: 81
Maps circulate
Circulation policies apply
  Map circulation duration: 3 weeks
  Book circulation duration: 3 weeks
  Number of maps circulated annually: 25
  Number of books circulated annually: 75
Interlibrary loan available

Geographic Information Systems:

No GIS services available

Collection services:

Maps cataloged: 10%
Maps classified: 100%
Maps in OPAC: 10%
Classification schemes: LC, SuDocs
Cataloging utilities: OCLC
Catalog accessibility: online
Items that have gone through the preservation process:
  1%

Physical facilities:

Internet access available
Square footage: 80
Linear book shelving: 10 ft.
Linear atlas shelving: 36 ft.
Copying facilities available: copier, microform copier

447 *Georgetown, SC*

Georgetown County Library

405 Cleland Street
Georgetown, SC 29440
Telephone: 843-545-3300
Fax: 843-545-3395
Web: www.gcpl.lib.sc.us

Personnel:

Responsible person: James Carolina

FTE professionals: 1

Holdings:

Geographic strengths: Georgetown County

Special collections: Early 18th century Land Grants and Rice Plantation Deeds with maps attached (primary source material: hand-drawn manuscripts, not printed items), Sanborn Fire Insurance maps of Georgetown, South Carolina

50 printed maps

Access:

Hours:

Monday–Friday: by appointment

Collection services:

Maps cataloged: 0%

Maps classified: 0%

Maps in OPAC: 0%

Physical facilities:

Maps in separate area

Notes: From early 18th century to the late 19th century, Georgetown County, South Carolina, was the center of the nation's rice plantation industry. For further details, see *The History of Georgetown County, South Carolina* by George C. Rogers, Jr., University of South Carolina Press, 1970.

448 *Greenville, SC*

Furman University

James B. Duke Library

Government Document Map Collection

3300 Poinsett Highway

Greenville, SC 29613

Telephone: 864-294-2260

Email: libby.young@furman.edu

Web: library.furman.edu

Personnel:

Responsible person: Libby Young, Government Documents Librarian, *email:* libby.young@furman.edu

Assistants: Lola Bradley, Documents Assistant

FTE professionals: 0.5   *FTE para-professionals:* 0.5

Holdings:

Geographic strengths: United States

Map depositories and percentages: USGS topos (100%), GPO, CIA

90,000 printed maps

Access:

Collection is open to the public

Reference questions per year: 25

Hours:

Monday–Thursday: 8 A.M.–1 A.M.

Friday: 8 A.M.–6 P.M.

Saturday: 10 A.M.–5 P.M.

Sunday: noon–1 A.M.

Geographic Information Systems:

No GIS services available

Number of public GIS workstations: 10

Collection services:

Maps cataloged: 100%

Maps in OPAC: 100%

Classification schemes: SuDocs

Cataloging utilities: Marcive

Catalog accessibility: online

Physical facilities:

Internet access available

Number of map cases: 43

Copying facilities available: copier, microform copier

449 *Greenville, SC*

Greenville County Library System

South Carolina Room, Government Documents Section

25 Heritage Green Place

Greenville, SC 29601

Telephone: 864-242-5000

Fax: 864-232-9656

Web: www.greenvillelibrary.org

Personnel:

Responsible person: Roger Wellington, Head of South Carolina Room, *email:* Rwellington@infoave.net

Assistants: Jimmy Smith, Government Documents Librarian

FTE professionals: 1   *FTE para-professionals:* 1

Holdings:

Geographic strengths: South Carolina

Map depositories: USGS topos, CIA

1,000 printed maps

3 globes

100 atlases

50 books

Access:

Hours:

Monday–Friday: 9 A.M.–9 P.M.

Saturday: 9 A.M.–6 P.M.

Sunday: 2 P.M.–6 P.M.

Collection services:

Maps cataloged: 100%

Maps classified: 100%

Maps in OPAC: 100%

Classification schemes: SuDocs, Dewey

Physical facilities:

Public computers: 100

Map cases: 3

Vertical files: 1

450 *Laurens, SC*

Laurens County Library

Laurens County Historical Room

1017 West Main Street

Laurens, SC 29360

Telephone: 864-984-0596

Fax: 864-984-0598
Email: bcooper@lcpl.org
Web: www.lcpl.org
Personnel:
Responsible person: Elaine Martin, *email:* emartin@
lcpl.org
FTE professionals: 0.75   *FTE para-professionals:* 0.25
Holdings:
Geographic strengths: Laurens County, South Carolina
Special collections: Sanborn Fire Insurance maps for
the cities of Clinton and Laurens, SC (1884–1930)
(microfilm), first official highway map of South Carolina (1916), 1907 Nash map of Laurens County, SC,
1775 Mouzon map, 1883 Kyzer and Hellams map of
Laurens County SC, map of the Town of Laurens SC
by C.L. Fike D.S. (1882–1883), Baptist Map of the
State of South Carolina by Rev. C. C. Brown (1895),
map of Greenwood County SC by William H. Yeldell
and W. J. Kird (1898), General Highway Map of
Laurens County (1957), Map of the County of Spartanburg (1869, Map of Greenville County (Jan
1917), Land Grant Maps of parts of Chester, Fair-
field, Greenville, Laurens, Newberry, Spartanburg
and Union Counties in S. C., George Hunter's Map
of the Cherokee Country and the path thereto in 1730
120 printed maps
75 aerial photos
2 atlases
30 books
2 CD-ROMs
Access:
Hours:
Monday–Tuesday: 9 A.M.–8:30 P.M.
Wednesday: 9 A.M.–5 P.M.
Thursday: 9 A.M.–8:30 P.M.
Friday: 9 A.M.–5 P.M.
Saturday: 9 A.M.–1 P.M.
Sunday: closed
Collection services:
Maps cataloged: 100%
Maps classified: 35%
Maps in OPAC: 35%
Classification schemes: Dewey, Local
Physical facilities:
Maps in separate area
Map cases: 2
Vertical files: 6
Notes: Our local history collection mainly is composed of
books and printed files. However, there are some maps
that are historical and important to the local area.

451 *Rock Hill, SC*

Winthrop University

Dacus Library
Government Documents

Oakland Avenue
Rock Hill, SC 29733
Telephone: 803-323-2322
Fax: 803-323-2215
Web: www.winthrop.edu/dacus/About/govdoc.htm
Personnel:
Responsible person: Jackie McFadden, *email:*
mcfaddenj@winthrop.edu
Assistants: Patti Stafford
FTE professionals: 1   *FTE para-professionals:* 1
Holdings:
Geographic strengths: South Carolina, North Carolina
Map depositories: USGS topos, CIA
2,710 printed maps
2 globes
455 atlases
54 books
Access:
Hours:
Monday–Thursday: 8 A.M.–midnight
Friday: 8 A.M.–6 P.M.
Saturday: noon–6 P.M.
Sunday: 1 P.M.–midnight
Collection services:
Maps cataloged: 100%
Maps classified: 100%
Maps in OPAC: 90%
Classification schemes: LC, SuDocs
Physical facilities:
Public computers: 42
Map cases: 5

452 *Spartanburg, SC*

Spartanburg County Public Library

Reference Department
151 South Church Street
Spartanburg, SC 29306
Telephone: 864-596-3505
Fax: 864-596-3518
Email: jaynem@infodepot.org
Web: www.infodepot.org/govdoc.htm
www.infodepot.org/kroom.htm
Personnel:
Responsible person: Jayne Moorman, *email:* jaynem@
infodepot.org
Assistants: Lisa Landrum, Reference Clerk; Dalila
Gomes, Technical Services Assistant
Holdings:
Geographic strengths: Spartanburg County, South
Carolina
Special collections: Sanborn Fire Insurance maps,
Spartanburg County historical maps
Subject strengths: historical geography, military, min-
eral resources, nautical charts, recreation, soil, travel
books

Map depositories: USGS topos, USGS geology maps, GPO, CIA, National Forest Service, State

860 printed maps

17 printed atlases

Chronological coverage:
  1940–present: 90%

Access:

Collection is open to the public

Answers email questions

Hours:

Monday–Friday: 9 A.M.–9 P.M.

Saturday: 9 A.M.–6 P.M.

Sunday: 1:30 P.M.–6 P.M.

Total hours per week opened: 73.5

Collection services:

Maps classified: 100%

Classification schemes: SuDocs, Local

Cataloging utilities: OCLC

Catalog accessibility: online, printout

Physical facilities:

Internet access available

Number of public computers: 21

Number of vertical map cases: 3

Number of microform readers: 10

Copying facilities available: copier, microform copier

453 *Brookings, SD*

South Dakota State University

Hilton M. Briggs Library

Box 2115

Brookings, SD 57007-1098

Telephone: 605-688-5576

Fax: 605-688-5133

Web: www3sdstate.edu/academics/library

Personnel:

Responsible person: Nancy Marshall, Documents Librarian, *email:* nancy_marshall@sdstate.edu

Holdings:

Geographic strengths: United States

Special collections: Fire Underwriter's Inspection Bureau maps, Sanborn Fire Insurance maps, South Dakota Geological Survey maps

Subject strengths: agriculture, soil

Map depositories and percentages: USGS topos (100%), GPO, CIA, National Forest Service, NIMA topos

78,600 printed maps

1,400 printed atlases

Chronological coverage:
  1940–present: 90%

Access:

Collection is open to the public

Reference questions per year: 75

Answers email questions

Hours:

Monday–Friday: 8 A.M.–midnight

Saturday: noon–9 P.M.

Sunday: 1 P.M.–midnight

Maps circulate
  Number of maps circulated annually: 1,500

Interlibrary loan available

Geographic Information Systems:

No GIS services available

Collection services:

Maps cataloged: 15%

Maps classified: 40%

Datasets are cataloged

Classification schemes: LC, SuDocs

Cataloging utilities: OCLC

Catalog accessibility: online

Preservation techniques: encapsulation

Physical facilities:

Internet access available

Copying facilities available: copier, microform copier

454 *Pierre, SD*

South Dakota State Archives

900 Governors Drive

Pierre, SD 57501

Telephone: 605-773-3804

Fax: 605-7736041

Email: archref@state.sd.us

Web: www.sdhistory.org/arc/archives.htm

Personnel:

Responsible person: Chelle Somsen, *email:* Chelle.Somsen@state.sd.us

Holdings:

Geographic strengths: South Dakota, Dakota Territory

Special collections: Sanborn Fire Insurance maps, Fire Underwriters Insurance maps, Missouri River, General Land Office Survey Boundary maps of South Dakota, Quadrangle maps, Department of Transportation Highway maps, South Dakota Railroad maps

Subject strengths: aerial photos, agriculture, climatology, city, forestry, hydrology, land ownership, land use, mineral resources, mining, railroads, recreation, roads, soil, vegetation, views, waterways

Map depositories and percentages: BLM

5,615 printed maps

1,000 manuscript maps

15 microfilms

200 aerial photos

235 printed atlases

Chronological coverage:
  1800–1899: 20%
  1900–1939: 30%
  1940–present: 50%

Access:

Collection is paged
Reference questions per year: 60
Answers email questions
Hours:
Monday–Friday: 9 A.M.–4:30 P.M.
Total hours per week opened: 37.5
Geographic Information Systems:
No GIS services available
Scans maps for patrons
Collection services:
Classification schemes: LC
Cataloging utilities: OCLC
Catalog accessibility: online
Preservation techniques: encapsulation, deacidification
Physical facilities:
No Internet access
Square footage: 7,000
Number of map cases: 310
Linear atlas shelving: 63 ft.
Copying facilities available: copier, microform copier

455 *Rapid City, SD*

South Dakota School of Mines and Technology

Devereaux Library
501 E St Joseph St
Rapid City, SD 57701-3995
Telephone: 605-394-2419
Fax: 605-394-1256
Web: www.sdln.net
Personnel:
Responsible person: email: library.reference@sdsmt.edu
Holdings:
Geographic strengths: Black Hills, South Dakota
Subject strengths: geology, land use, mineral resources, mining
Map depositories: USGS topos, USGS geology maps, USGS other, BLM
7,400 printed maps
21 gazetteers
64 printed atlases
440 books
Chronological coverage:
1900–1939: 30%
1940–present: 50%
Access:
Collection is open to the public
Reference questions per year: 20
Answers email questions
Patrons per month: 15
Hours:
Total hours per week opened: 98
Maps circulate
Circulation policies apply
Map circulation duration: 4 weeks

Book circulation duration: 4 weeks
Number of maps circulated annually: 25
Number of other items circulated annually: 500
Interlibrary loan available
Geographic Information Systems:
No GIS services available
Collection services:
Maps cataloged: 100%
Maps classified: 100%
Maps in OPAC: 100%
Classification schemes: LC, SuDocs
Cataloging utilities: OCLC, Local
Catalog accessibility: online
Preservation techniques: lamination
Physical facilities:
No Internet access
Linear book shelving: 132 ft.
Linear atlas shelving: 36 ft.
Copying facilities available: copier, microform copier

456 *Vermillion, SD*

University of South Dakota

I.D. Weeks Library
414 East Clark Street
Vermillion, SD 57059
Telephone: 605-677-5371
Fax: 605-677-5488
Web: www.usd.edu/library/idweeks.cfm
Personnel:
Responsible person: John Van Balen, *email:* vanbalen@usd.edu
Holdings:
Geographic strengths: South Dakota, Northern Great Plains
Subject strengths: early cartography, modern cartography, city, geodetic surveys, geology, historical geography, hydrology, land ownership, land use, map catalogs, mineral resources, mining, political geography, population, roads, soil
Map depositories: USGS topos, USGS geology maps, GPO, CIA, State
7,000 printed maps
Chronological coverage:
1940–present: 99%
On-going publications: Historical Maps in the Richardson Archives, I.D. Weeks Library; Dakota Place Names. Geographical Names on 18th Century Maps.
Access:
Collection is partially open to the public
Answers email questions
Patrons per month: 10
Hours:
Total hours per week opened: 90
Maps circulate

Circulation policies apply
  Map circulation duration: 2 weeks
  Atlas circulation duration: 4 weeks
  Book circulation duration: 4 weeks
Interlibrary loan available

Geographic Information Systems:
No GIS services available
Number of public GIS workstations: 95
Scans maps for patrons

Collection services:
Classification schemes: LC, SuDocs
Cataloging utilities: OCLC
Catalog accessibility: online
Preservation techniques: encapsulation, deacidification

Physical facilities:
Internet access available
Copying facilities available: copier, large-format copier, microform copier

---

457 *Chattanooga, TN*

Chattanooga–Hamilton County Bicentennial Library

Local History Map Collection
1001 Broad Street
Chattanooga, TN 37402
Telephone: 423-757-5317
Email: library@lib.chattanooga.gov
Web: www.lib.chattanooga.gov

Personnel:
Responsible person: Mary Helms, Local History Department Head, *email:* helms-m@mail.chattanooga.gov
Assistants: Kathleen Conway, Library Assistant

Holdings:
Geographic strengths: Chattanooga, Hamilton County, Tennessee, Georgia, Alabama
Special collections: Sanborn Fire Insurance maps
Subject strengths: city, genealogy, geospatial data, historical geography, roads
1,476 printed maps
12 wall maps
25 microfilms
149 aerial photos
10 gazetteers
10 printed atlases
25 books
Chronological coverage:
  1800–1899: 15%
  1900–1939: 20%
  1940–present: 60%

Access:
Collection is partially open to the public
Reference questions per year: 350
Answers email questions

Hours:
Monday–Thursday: 9 A.M.–9 P.M.

Friday–Saturday: 9 A.M.–6 P.M.
Sunday: 2 P.M.–6 P.M.
Total hours per week opened: 66–70

Geographic Information Systems:
Number of public GIS workstations: 6
Scans maps for patrons

Collection services:
Maps cataloged: 100%
Catalog accessibility: cards
Preservation techniques: encapsulation, deacidification
Items that have gone through the preservation process: 20%

Physical facilities:
Internet access available
Copying facilities available: copier, microform copier

---

458 *Chattanooga, TN*

Tennessee Valley Authority

Map and Photo Records
1101 Market Street
MR 5E
Chattanooga, TN 37402
Telephone: 423-751-8362
Fax: 423-499-6319
Email: maps2@tva.gov
Web: maps.tva.com

Personnel:
Responsible person: Raymond A. Mitchell, Project Specialist, *email:* ramitchell@tva.gov
Assistants: Peggy Cooper, Geo. Technician
FTE para-professionals: 25
Number of student workers hours per week: 20

Holdings:
Geographic strengths: Tennessee Valley
Subject strengths: aerial photos, aeronautical, agriculture, archaeology, early cartography, modern cartography, caves, city, engineering, forestry, geodetic surveys, geology, geospatial data, historical geography, hydrology, land ownership, land use, map catalogs, map collecting, mineral resources, mining, nautical charts, political geography, projections, railroads, raised relief models, recreation, roads, satellite imagery, soil, travel books, vegetation
Map depositories and percentages: USGS topos (15%), USGS geology maps, USGS other, National Forest Service, NIMA topos, State
200,000 printed maps
900 manuscript maps
40 raised relief maps
2,000,000 aerial photos
25 gazetteers
70 printed atlases
45 books

Collecting digital data
Chronological coverage:
   1900–1939: 10%
   1940–present: 90%
Average budget over the last 5 years: $40,000

Access:
Maps in separate area
Collection is partially open to the public
Maps off site: 25%
Reference questions per year: 2,000
Answers email questions
Patrons per month: 20

Hours:
   Total hours per week opened: 32
Maps circulate
Circulation policies apply
Interlibrary loan available

Geographic Information Systems:
GIS services available by appointment
Number of GIS stations (monitored): 10
GIS assistance available for Census mapping, geocoding, and image analysis
Plotter available
Scans maps for patrons

Collection services:
Maps cataloged: 70%
Maps classified: 15%
Classification schemes: Local
Cataloging utilities: Local
Catalog accessibility: online, printout
Preservation techniques: deacidification, lamination

Physical facilities:
Internet access available
Square footage: 3,200
Number of staff computers: 10
Number of vertical map cases: 30
Number of vertical files (file cabinets): 40
Linear book shelving: 400 ft.
Linear atlas shelving: 50 ft.
Number of light tables: 20
Copying facilities available: copier, color copier, large-format copier

459 *Clarksville, TN*

Austin Peay State University

Felix G. Woodward
Information Services
601 East College Street
Clarksville, TN 37044
Telephone: 931-221-7346
Fax: 931-221-7296
Email: berge@apsu.edu
Web: library.apsu.edu/
Personnel:

Responsible person: Elaine Berg, Librarian, *email:*
   berge@apsu.edu
Assistants: Charles McWhorter, Library Associate
FTE professionals: 0.05   *FTE para-professionals:* 0.05

Holdings:
Geographic strengths: Tennessee, Kentucky
Map depositories: USGS
1,701 printed maps
2 globes
50 atlases
1 CD-ROM

Access:
Hours:
   Monday–Friday: 7:30 A.M.–11 P.M.
   Saturday: 10 A.M.–5 P.M.
   Sunday: 10 A.M.–10 P.M.

Collection services:
Maps cataloged: 3%
Maps classified: 100%
Maps in OPAC: 3%
Classification schemes: LC, SuDocs

Physical facilities:
Public computers: 42
Map cases: 4

460 *Cookeville, TN*

Tennessee Technological University

Angelo and Jennette Volpe Library and Media Center
1100 North Peachtree Avenue
Cookeville, TN 38505
Telephone: 931-372-3326
Fax: 931-372-6112
Web: www.tntech.edu/govpub/
Personnel:

Responsible person: Regina Lee, Head of Government
   Publications, Maps and Microforms, *email:*
   rlee@tntech.edu
Assistants: Randall Raper, Library Assistant III
FTE professionals: 0.1   *FTE para-professionals:* 0.2

Holdings:
Geographic strengths: Tennessee, surrounding States
Subject strengths: topographic
Map depositories and percentages: USGS topos (20%),
   USGS geology maps (10%), USGS other (20%),
   NOAA, GPO, CIA, National Forest Service, NIMA
   topos, NIMA nautical, BLM
61,000 printed maps
20 satellite images
15 gazetteers
100 printed atlases
50 books
50 CD-ROMs
Chronological coverage:
   1940–present: 99%

Average budget over the last 5 years: $100

On-going publications: In-house list of some special collections Tennessee soil surveys, USGS miscellaneous Investigations

Access:

Collection is open to the public

Maps off site

Reference questions per year: 50

Answers email questions

Hours:

Monday–Friday: 7:45 A.M.–midnight

Saturday: 10 A.M.–6 P.M.

Sunday: 1 P.M.–midnight

Total hours per week opened: 94

Maps circulate

Circulation policies apply

  Map circulation duration: 2 weeks

  Number of maps circulated annually: 50

  Number of books circulated annually: 50

Interlibrary loan available

Geographic Information Systems:

No GIS services available

Number of public GIS workstations: 25

Collection services:

Maps classified: 100%

Classification schemes: LC, SuDocs, other (alphabetical, scale, special collection name)

Cataloging utilities: OCLC, DDM2, GPO

Catalog accessibility: online, cards

Items that have gone through the preservation process: 0.1%

Physical facilities:

No Internet access

Square footage: 1,400

Number of map cases: 63

Number of vertical files (file cabinets): 15

Linear book shelving: 50 ft.

Linear atlas shelving: 20 ft.

Number of microform readers: 10

Copying facilities available: copier, microform copier

461 *Johnson City, TN*

East Tennessee State University

Charles C. Sherrod Library

Documents/Law/Maps Department

P.O. Box 78665

Johnson City, TN 37614

Telephone: 423-439-5334

Fax: 423-439-5674

Web: www.etsu.edu/etsu/libraries.asp

Personnel:

Responsible person: Stephen A. Patrick, *email:* patricks@mail.etsu.edu

Assistants: Mike Willis, Library Assistant

FTE para-professionals: 0.5

Holdings:

Geographic strengths: United States, World

Map depositories: USGS topos, CIA, National Forest Service, BLM

82,000 printed maps

3 globes

50 atlases

100 books

35 active serials

50 CD-ROMs

Access:

Hours:

Monday–Thursday: 10 A.M.–8 P.M.

Friday–Saturday: 10 A.M.–6 P.M.

Sunday: 2 P.M.–8 P.M.

Collection services:

Maps classified: 100%

Maps in OPAC: 10%

Classification schemes: SuDocs

Physical facilities:

Public computers: 2

Map cases: 77

Vertical files: 10

Notes: The only maps housed in the documents/law/maps department are the USGS topos and other maps distributed by GPO. Atlases and globes are housed in reference department and serials are housed in the periodicals/microforms department. This does not include information on the historical collection of maps found in the Archives of Appalachia, located on our campus.

462 *Knoxville, TN*

Knox County Public Library

East Tennessee History Center

Calvin M. McClung Historical Collection, founded 1921

314 West Clinch Avenue

Knoxville, TN 37902-2313

Telephone: 865-215-8801

Fax: 865-215-8810

Email: mcclung@knoxlib.org

Web: www.knoxlib.org

Personnel:

Responsible person: Steve Cotham, Manager, *email:* scotham@knoxlib.org

Assistants: Sue Klispch, Technical Services Librarian; Martha Rosson, Reference Librarian

Holdings:

Geographic strengths: Knoxville, East Tennessee

Special collections: Sanborn Fire Insurance maps of Knoxville and East Tennessee, Knoxville/Knox County Planning Commission maps

Subject strengths: aerial photos, city, genealogy, geology, historical geography, land use, map catalogs, military, railroads, recreation, roads, soil, travel books

2,570 printed maps

25 wall maps

30 aerial photos

12 gazetteers

40 printed atlases

Chronological coverage:
1800–1899: 13%
1940–present: 79%

Average budget over the last 5 years: $1000

Access:

Maps in separate area
Collection is paged
Reference questions per year: 150
Answers email questions
Patrons per month: 1,000

Hours:
Monday–Tuesday: 9 A.M.–8:30 P.M.
Wednesday–Saturday: 9 A.M.–5 P.M.
Sunday: 1 P.M.–5 P.M.
Total hours per week opened: 60.5
Circulation policies apply

Geographic Information Systems:
Scans maps for patrons

Collection services:
Maps cataloged: 100%
Maps classified: 100%
Classification schemes: Dewey
Cataloging utilities: OCLC
Catalog accessibility: online, cards
Preservation techniques: encapsulation, deacidification

Physical facilities:
No Internet access
Square footage: 300
Linear book shelving: 42 ft.
Linear atlas shelving: 42 ft.
Copying facilities available: copier, color copier, large-format copier, microform copier

Notes: This response refers only the historical collection, not the Reference Department of Lawson McGhee Library, the main branch.

---

463 *Knoxville, TN*

Knoxville/Knox County Metropolitan Planning Commission

Library
Founded 1956
400 Main Street
Suite 403
Knoxville, TN 37902
Telephone: 865-215-2500
Fax: 865-215-2068

Email: gretchen.beal@knoxmpc.org
Web: www.knoxmpc.org

Personnel:

Responsible person: Gretchen F. Beal, *email:* gretchen.beal@knoxmpc.org

Assistants: Tim Kuhn, GIS Administrator

Holdings:

Geographic strengths: Knoxville, Knox County, Tennessee

Subject strengths: aerial photos, agriculture, caves, city, economic geography, forestry, geology, geospatial data, hydrology, industries, land ownership, land use, mineral resources, population, projections, railroads, raised relief models, recreation, roads, soil, vegetation, views, waterways, historic sites and districts; zoning, land use, city plans

Collecting digital data

Chronological coverage:
1940–present: 100%

Access:
Collection is open to the public
Maps off site: 60%
Reference questions per year: 150
Answers email questions

Hours:
Monday–Friday: 8 A.M.–4:30 P.M.
Total hours per week opened: 37.5

Geographic Information Systems:
GIS services available by appointment
GIS software: ArcView, Intergraph
GIS assistance available for Census mapping

Physical facilities:
Internet access available
Copying facilities available: copier, large-format copier, microform copier, plotter

Notes: The collection of 500 maps is exclusively in digital format print-on-demand copies are available for a fee.

---

464 *Knoxville, TN*

United States Department of Interior, Office of Surface Mining

Knoxville Field Office Geographic Information System (KFO GIS)
530 Gay Street SW
Suite 500
Knoxville, TN 37902
Telephone: 865-545-4103 x134
Fax: 865-545-4111
Email: bcard@osmre.gov

Personnel:

Responsible person: Bill Card, Geographer, *email:* bcard@osmre.gov

Assistants: Jo Gault, Geographic Information System Program Specialist

FTE professionals: 2

Holdings:

Geographic strengths: Tennessee

Special collections: Mining operations maps of permitted coal-mining operations within Tennessee (maintained in permit application files), digital environmental databases of geology, surface water, and groundwater attributes within the Tennessee coalfield, aerial photographs of the coalfield of Tennessee (1984), digital images of scanned underground mine maps of Tennessee.

1,100 printed maps

10,200 aerial photos

Access:

Hours:

Monday–Friday: 8 A.M.–4:30 P.M.

Collection services:

Maps cataloged: 0%

Maps classified: 0%

Maps in OPAC: 0%

Physical facilities:

Maps in separate area

Notes: The mining operations maps we have are obtained from an applicant after the review and approval of a proposed coal-mining operation. Digital spatial datasets are created from these and other hardcopy sources for use in computer software applications to support analysis of potential environmental impacts of coal-mining operations. Tabular environmental data, such as geology, surface water, and groundwater attributes in approved permit applications are entered into a digital database. These digital datasets are created as resources are made available. Digital copies of the datasets are available to the public. Requests for digital datasets should be addressed to Bill Card, or sent by e-mail to bcard@osmre.gov.

---

465 *Knoxville, TN*

University of Tennessee

Hoskins Library

Map Library, founded 1989

1401 Cumberland Avenue

Knoxville, TN 37996-4006

Telephone: 865-974-4315

Fax: 865-974-3925

Email: maplib@utk.edu

Web: www.lib.utk.edu/~cic/

Personnel:

Responsible person: Travis Dolence, Map/GIS Librarian, *email:* dolence@utk.edu

Assistants: Eric Arnold, Departmental Supervisor

Number of student workers hours per week: 40

Holdings:

Geographic strengths: Tennessee, United States

Subject strengths: aeronautical, modern cartography, city, geology, geospatial data, map catalogs, nautical charts, projections, raised relief models, recreation, roads

Map depositories and percentages: USGS topos (100%), USGS geology maps (100%), Department of Transportation, NOAA, GPO, CIA, National Forest Service, NIMA topos, NIMA nautical, NIMA aeronautical, BLM

350,000 printed maps

20 wall maps

239 raised relief maps

10 globes

56 gazetteers

546 printed atlases

1,033 books

1,002 CD-ROMs

Collecting digital data

Chronological coverage:

Pre-1800: <1%

1900–1939: 15%

1940–present: 80%

Average budget over the last 5 years: $8,000

Access:

Maps in separate area

Collection is open to the public

Reference questions per year: 350

Answers email questions

Patrons per month: 689

Hours:

Monday–Friday: 9 A.M.–5:30 P.M.

Saturday–Saturday: closed

Total hours per week opened: 42.5

Maps circulate

Circulation policies apply

Map circulation duration: 4 weeks

Atlas circulation duration: 4 weeks

Number of maps circulated annually: 3,197

Interlibrary loan available

Geographic Information Systems:

GIS services available in an open environment

GIS software: ArcGIS

General GIS questions answered

Plotter available

Scans maps for patrons

Collection services:

Maps cataloged: 20%

Maps classified: 80%

Maps in OPAC: 20%

Classification schemes: LC

Cataloging utilities: OCLC

Catalog accessibility: online

Preservation techniques: encapsulation

Items that have gone through the preservation process: 5%

Physical facilities:
Internet access available
Square footage: 7,000
Number of map cases: 205
Number of vertical files (file cabinets): 32
Linear book shelving: 150 ft.
Linear atlas shelving: 300 ft.
Copying facilities available: copier, large-format copier

466 *Knoxville, TN*

University of Tennessee

Special Collections, Hoskins Library
1401 Cumberland Avenue
Knoxville, TN 37996-4000
Telephone: 865-974-4480
Fax: 865-974-0560
Email: special@aztec.lib.utk.edu
Web: www.lib.utk.edu/spcoll
Personnel:
Responsible person: Anne Bridges, *email:* abridges@utk.edu
Assistants: Aaron Purcell; Nick Wyman; Bill Eigelsbach; Holly Adams; Rodney Jones; Erin Lawrimore
Number of student workers hours per week: 10
Holdings:
Geographic strengths: Tennessee, Great Smoky Mountains, Southern Appalachia
Special collections: Sanborn Fire Insurance maps of Tennessee
Subject strengths: aeronautical, early cartography, modern cartography, city, economic geography, historical geography, industries, land ownership, land use, military, mineral resources, political geography, population, railroads, recreation, roads, travel books, zoogeography
7,000 printed maps
10 wall maps
25 printed atlases
Chronological coverage:
    1800–1899: 45%
    1900–1939: 45%
On-going publications: Library Development Review
Access:
Collection is paged
Answers email questions
Hours:
    Monday–Friday: 9 A.M.–5:30 P.M.
    Saturday–Saturday: closed
    Total hours per week opened: 42.5
Geographic Information Systems:
Scans maps for patrons
Collection services:
Maps cataloged: 95%

Classification schemes: Local
Catalog accessibility: cards
Preservation techniques: encapsulation
Items that have gone through the preservation process: 75%
Physical facilities:
Internet access available
Number of map cases: 15
Copying facilities available: copier, large-format copier, microform copier

467 *Memphis, TN*

Memphis/Shelby County Public Library and Information Center

Memphis and Shelby County Room
3030 Poplar Avenue
Memphis, TN 38111
Telephone: 901-415-2742
Fax: 901-323-7981
Email: hisref@memphis.lib.tn.us
Web: www.memphislibrary.org
Personnel:
Responsible person: Robert Cruthirds, Map Librarian, *email:* cruthirdsr@memphis.lib.tn.us
Number of volunteer hours per month: 10
Holdings:
Geographic strengths: Memphis, Shelby County, Tennessee
Subject strengths: city, genealogy, historical geography, land ownership, military, political geography, roads, travel books, waterways
Map depositories and percentages: USGS topos (15%), CIA
825 printed maps
45 manuscript maps
150 gazetteers
250 printed atlases
1,200 books
Chronological coverage:
    1800–1899: 57%
    1900–1939: 23%
    1940–present: 17%
Average budget over the last 5 years: $500
Access:
Maps in separate area
Collection is paged
Reference questions per year: 2,500
Answers email questions
Patrons per month: 100
Hours:
    Monday–Friday: 9 A.M.–9 P.M.
    Saturday: 9 A.M.–6 P.M.
    Sunday: 1 P.M.–5 P.M.

Total hours per week opened: 70

Geographic Information Systems:

No GIS services available

Collection services:

Maps cataloged: 90%

Maps in OPAC: 90%

Classification schemes: SuDocs, Local

Cataloging utilities: Local

Catalog accessibility: online

Preservation techniques: encapsulation, deacidification

Physical facilities:

Internet access available

Square footage: 3,200

Number of public computers: 26

Number of map cases: 75

Linear book shelving: 72 ft.

Linear atlas shelving: 24 ft.

Number of microform printers: 10

Copying facilities available: copier, microform copier

468 *Memphis, TN*

University of Memphis

McWherter Library

Map Library

126 Ned R. McWherter Library

Memphis, TN 38152

Telephone: 901-678-2206

Fax: 901-678-8218

Web: exlibris.memphis.edu

Personnel:

Responsible person: Mary Freilich, *email:* freilich@ memphis.edu

Assistants: Larry Williams, Library Assistant

FTE professionals: 1   *FTE para-professionals:* 1

Holdings:

Map depositories: USGS topos, Department of Transportation, NOAA, CIA, National Forest Service, NGA nautical, NGA aeronautical

6,000 printed maps

100 aerial photos

1 globe

50 atlases

200 books

Access:

Hours:

Monday–Friday: 7:30 A.M.–midnight

Saturday: 10 A.M.–6 P.M.

Sunday: 1 P.M.–10 P.M.

Items circulate

Interlibrary loan available

Collection services:

Maps cataloged: 0%

Maps classified: 0%

Maps in OPAC: 0%

Classification schemes: SuDocs

Physical facilities:

Maps in separate area

Map cases: 32

Vertical files: 9

469 *Memphis, TN*

University of Memphis

McWherter Library

Special/Mississippi Valley Collections, founded 1965

126 Ned R. McWherter Library

Memphis, TN 38152

Telephone: 901-678-2210

Fax: 901-678-8218

Email: efrank@memphis.edu

Web: exlibris.memphis.edu

Personnel:

Responsible person: Ed Frank, Curator of Special Collections, *email:* efrank@memphis.edu

Holdings:

Geographic strengths: Deep South, Lower Mississippi Valley

Subject strengths: early cartography, historical geography, railroads, roads, waterways

1,000 printed maps

50 printed atlases

Chronological coverage:

Pre-1800: 10%

1800–1899: 40%

1900–1939: 40%

1940–present: 10%

Access:

Maps in separate area

Collection is paged

Answers email questions

Hours:

Monday–Friday: 8 A.M.–4:30 P.M.

Sunday: 1 P.M.–5 P.M.

Total hours per week opened: 46.5

Number of maps circulated annually: 120

Geographic Information Systems:

No GIS services available

Collection services:

Maps cataloged: 50%

Maps classified: 50%

Maps in OPAC: 50%

Classification schemes: Local

Cataloging utilities: OCLC

Catalog accessibility: online

Preservation techniques: encapsulation, deacidification

Items that have gone through the preservation process: 90%

Physical facilities:

Internet access available
Square footage: 200
Copying facilities available: copier
Notes: Map collection is a small part of Special Collections/ Mississippi Valley Collections holdings. All four Special/ MVC staff assist patrons in locating map resources.

470 *Nashville, TN*

Tennessee State Library and Archives

Tennessee State Library and Archives
Map Collection
403 Seventh Avenue North
Nashville, TN 37243
Telephone: 615-741-2764
Fax: 615-532-2472
Email: reference@state.tn.us
Web: www.state.tn.us/sos/statelib
Personnel:
Responsible person: email: reference@state.tn.us
Holdings:
Geographic strengths: Tennessee, Southeast
Subject strengths: agriculture, city, economic geography, forestry, geodetic surveys, geology, land ownership, land use, mineral resources, mining, political geography, population, railroads, recreation, roads, soil, waterways
2,500 printed maps
500 manuscript maps
Chronological coverage:
  Pre-1800: 11%
  1800–1899: 30%
  1900–1939: 31%
  1940–present: 28%
Access:
Collection is open to the public
Reference questions per year: 1,050
Answers email questions
Patrons per month: 25
Hours:
  Monday–Saturday: 8 A.M.–6 P.M.
  Total hours per week opened: 60
Geographic Information Systems:
No GIS services available
Scans maps for patrons
Collection services:
Maps cataloged: 90%
Maps classified: 100%
Maps in OPAC: 35%
Classification schemes: Local
Cataloging utilities: OCLC, Local
Catalog accessibility: online, cards
Preservation techniques: encapsulation, deacidification
Items that have gone through the preservation process:
  80%

Physical facilities:
Internet access available
Copying facilities available: copier, large-format copier, microform copier, photographic prints

471 *Nashville, TN*

Vanderbilt University

Stevenson Science and Engineering Library
Map Room, founded 1965
419 21st Avenue South
Nashville, TN 37240
Telephone: 615-322-2775
Fax: 615-343-7249
Email: sciref@vanderbilt.edu
Web: www.library.vanderbilt.edu/science/maps.html
Personnel:
Responsible person: Richard Stringer-Hye, Geology Librarian, Library Technology Coordinator, *email:* richard.s.stringer-hye@vanderbilt.edu
FTE professionals: 0.25
Number of student works: 1
Number of student workers hours per week: 10
Holdings:
Geographic strengths: Tennessee, Southeast
Map depositories and percentages: USGS topos (100%), USGS geology maps (100%), USGS other (100%), Department of Transportation, NOAA, GPO, State
120,000 printed maps
100 manuscript maps
15 wall maps
25 raised relief maps
10 gazetteers
100 printed atlases
20 books
100 CD-ROMs
10 computer programs
Collecting digital data
Chronological coverage:
  1900–1939: 10%
  1940–present: 80%
Average budget over the last 5 years: $1,000
Access:
Maps in separate area
Collection is open to the public
Maps off site
Reference questions per year: 100
Answers email questions
Patrons per month: 20
Hours:
  Monday–Friday: 24 hour access
  Saturday: 9 A.M.–10 P.M.
  Sunday: noon–midnight
  Total hours per week opened: 140+

Maps circulate
Circulation policies apply
  Map circulation duration: 2 weeks
  Atlas circulation duration: 2 weeks
  Number of maps circulated annually: 600
Interlibrary loan available

Geographic Information Systems:
GIS services available in an open environment
GIS software: ArcGIS
Scans maps for patrons

Collection services:
Classification schemes: LC, SuDocs, Dewey
Cataloging utilities: OCLC
Catalog accessibility: online
Preservation techniques: encapsulation, lamination

Physical facilities:
Internet access available
Square footage: 1,500
Number of map cases: 40
Number of vertical files (file cabinets): 15
Linear atlas shelving: 60 ft.
Other map storage: 2 rolled map cases
Copying facilities available: copier, microform copier

472 *Abilene, TX*

Abilene Christian University

Brown Library
Texas Topographic Map Collection, founded 1999
221 Brown Library
Abilene, TX 79601-9208
Telephone: 325-674-2316
Fax: 325-674-2202
Email: bakerl@acu.edu
Web: www.acu.edu/academics/library

Personnel:
Responsible person: Laura Baker, Government Documents Librarian, *email:* bakerl@acu.edu
Assistants: Martha Ketchersid, Government Documents Assistant
FTE professionals: 0.25 *FTE para-professionals:* 0.12
Number of student workers hours per week: 0.12

Holdings:
Geographic strengths: Texas
Special collections: Historic topographic maps of Texas (1800s to early 1900s)
Subject strengths: historical geography, topographic features and elevation
Map depositories and percentages: USGS topos, USGS geology maps (25%), CIA, National Forest Service, NIMA topos
14,000 printed maps
Chronological coverage:
  1940–present: 90%

Access:

Collection is open to the public
Reference questions per year: 50
Answers email questions

Hours:
Monday–Friday: 8 A.M.–midnight
Saturday: 9 A.M.–6 P.M.
Sunday: 1 P.M.–5 P.M., 7 P.M.–midnight
Total hours per week opened: 89.5

Geographic Information Systems:
No GIS services available
Scans maps for patrons

Collection services:
Maps cataloged: 50%
Maps classified: 80%
Maps in OPAC: 50%
Classification schemes: SuDocs, Dewey, Local
Cataloging utilities: OCLC
Catalog accessibility: online, local shelflist

Physical facilities:
Internet access available
Number of map cases: 20
Copying facilities available: copier, color copier, microform copier

Notes: Our most substantial map collection is of printed Texas 7.5 minute topographic maps. We are a federal depository and selectively acquire other depository maps.

473 *Abilene, TX*

Hardin–Simmons University

Rupert and Pauline Richardson Library
Williams Map Collection, founded 1975
2200 Hickory Street
Abilene, TX 79698
Telephone: 325-670-1239
Fax: 325-677-8351
Email: chamner@hsutx.edu
Web: rupert.alc.org/library/

Personnel:
Responsible person: Carol Hamner, Librarian, *email:* chamner@hsutx.edu
FTE professionals: 2
Number of student workers hours per week: 15

Holdings:
Subject strengths: city, historical geography, land ownership, military, political geography
1,500 printed maps
14 wall maps
Chronological coverage:
  1800–1899: 18%
  1900–1939: 68%
  1940–present: 11%

Access:
Maps in separate area
Collection is partially open to the public

Answers email questions

Hours:
Monday–Friday: 2 P.M.–5 P.M.
Total hours per week opened: 15

Geographic Information Systems:
No GIS services available

Collection services:
Maps cataloged: 0.5%
Maps classified: 0.5%
Maps in OPAC: 0.5%
Classification schemes: LC
Cataloging utilities: OCLC, RLG, Local
Catalog accessibility: online
Preservation techniques: encapsulation, lamination
Items that have gone through the preservation process: 0.7%

Physical facilities:
No Internet access
Copying facilities available: copier, color copier, large-format copier, microform copier

474 *Abilene, TX*

Hardin–Simmons University

Richardson Library
Government Documents, founded 1940
2200 Hickory
Abilene, TX 79698
Telephone: 325-670-1521
Email: jeffries@hsutx.edu
Web: rupert.alc.org/library/

Personnel:
Responsible person: Scott Jeffries, *email:* jeffries@hsutx.edu
Number of student workers hours per week: 30

Holdings:
Geographic strengths: Texas, Oklahoma, New Mexico, Southwest
Subject strengths: aeronautical, agriculture, modern cartography, celestial, climatology, city, geodetic surveys, geology, geospatial data, historical geography, map catalogs, mineral resources, population, projections, roads, satellite imagery, soil, vegetation, views, waterways
Map depositories and percentages: USGS topos (25%), USGS geology maps (25%), USGS other (25%), NOAA, GPO, CIA, National Forest Service, BLM, State, United Nations
650 printed maps
Chronological coverage:
1940–present: 80%

Access:
Collection is open to the public
Reference questions per year: 34
Answers email questions

Patrons per month: 25

Hours:
Monday–Friday: 7:30 A.M.–10:30 P.M.
Saturday: 11 A.M.–5 P.M.
Sunday: 1 P.M.–5 P.M.
Total hours per week opened: 75

Geographic Information Systems:
No GIS services available

Collection services:
Maps in OPAC: 15%
Classification schemes: SuDocs
Cataloging utilities: OCLC
Catalog accessibility: online
Preservation techniques: lamination
Items that have gone through the preservation process: 12%

Physical facilities:
Internet access available
Copying facilities available: copier, microform copier

475 *Angleton, TX*

Brazoria County Historical Museum

Adriance Research Library
100 East Ceder
Angleton, TX 77515
Telephone: 979-864-1591
Fax: 979-864-1217
Web: www.bchm.org

Personnel:
Responsible person: Michael J. Bailey, Curator, *email:* curator@bchm.org

Holdings:
Geographic strengths: Coastal Texas
Subject strengths: aerial photos, aeronautical, agriculture, archaeology, biology, early cartography, modern cartography, city, engineering, genealogy, geology, historical geography, land ownership, land use, military, nautical charts, population, railroads, roads, satellite imagery, soil, travel books, vegetation, views, 19th-century survey maps and survey notes
Map depositories and percentages: USGS topos, USGS geology maps (0.2%), NOAA, GPO, BLM, State
1,800 printed maps
200 manuscript maps
45 wall maps
100 aerial photos
25 satellite images
Chronological coverage:
Pre-1800: 10%
1800–1899: 60%
1900–1939: 15%
1940–present: 15%

Access:
Maps in separate area

Collection is partially open to the public
Reference questions per year: 300
Answers email questions
Hours:
  Total hours per week opened: 46
Geographic Information Systems:
No GIS services available
Scans maps for patrons
Collection services:
Maps cataloged: 75%
Maps classified: 50%
Maps in OPAC: 50%
Catalog accessibility: printout
Preservation techniques: encapsulation
Items that have gone through the preservation process:
  25%
Physical facilities:
No Internet access
Copying facilities available: copier, scanner, large
  printer

476 Arlington, TX

University of Texas, Arlington

Library
Information Services
702 College Street
P.O. Box 19497
Arlington, TX 76019
Telephone: 817-272-7514
Fax: 817-272-3593
Email: lindsey@uta.edu
Web: www.uta.edu/library
Personnel:
Responsible person: Thomas Lindsey, Social Science and
  Government Documents Librarian, *email:* lindsey@
  uta.edu
FTE professionals: 0.1
Holdings:
Geographic strengths: Southwest, Gulf Coast, United
  States
Special collections: Sanborn Fire Insurance maps of
  Texas (online)
Subject strengths: modern cartography, climatology,
  city, geology, land use, population, recreation, soil
Map depositories and percentages: USGS topos
  (85%), USGS geology maps (10%), USGS other,
  CIA, BLM
13,000 printed maps
114 printed atlases
Chronological coverage:
  1940–present: 100%
Average budget over the last 5 years: $200
Access:
Collection is open to the public

Answers email questions
Hours:
  Monday–Thursday: 7 A.M.–midnight
  Friday: 7 A.M.–8 P.M.
  Saturday: 9 A.M.–8 P.M.
  Sunday: 9 A.M.–midnight
  Total hours per week opened: 94
Maps circulate
Circulation policies apply
  Map circulation duration: 3 weeks
  Number of maps circulated annually: 100
Interlibrary loan available
Geographic Information Systems:
GIS services available by appointment
Number of public GIS workstations: 40
GIS assistance available for Census mapping, geocod-
  ing, and image analysis
GIS service available through Information Literacy De-
  partment
Plotter available
Scans maps for patrons
Collection services:
Maps cataloged: 90%
Maps classified: 100%
Maps in OPAC: 90%
Datasets are cataloged
Classification schemes: LC, SuDocs
Cataloging utilities: OCLC
Catalog accessibility: online
Physical facilities:
Internet access available
Square footage: 1,500
Number of public computers: 40
Number of map cases: 155
Number of vertical files (file cabinets): 13
Linear atlas shelving: 162 ft.
Copying facilities available: copier, color copier, large-
  format copier, microform copier

477 Arlington, TX

University of Texas, Arlington

Library
Special Collections, founded 1974
702 College Street
Arlington, TX 76019-0497
Telephone: 817-272-3393
Fax: 817-272-3360
Email: goodwin@uta.edu
Web: libraries.uta.edu/SpecColl
Personnel:
Responsible person: Kit Goodwin, *email:* goodwin@
  uta.edu
Number of student workers hours per week: 18
Holdings:

Geographic strengths: Texas, Gulf of Mexico, Southwest, Mexico, Western Hemisphere, World

Special collections: Sanborn Fire Insurance maps, FEMA, topographic, National Geographic, aerial photos, border maps, pocket maps

Subject strengths: aerial photos, aeronautical, agriculture, early cartography, modern cartography, celestial, climatology, city, economic geography, forestry, genealogy, geodetic surveys, geology, historical geography, hydrology, land ownership, land use, language, map catalogs, map collecting, military, mineral resources, mining, nautical charts, oceanography, political geography, population, projections, railroads, raised relief models, recreation, religion, roads, satellite imagery, soil, travel books, vegetation, views, waterways

Map depositories and percentages: USGS topos (12%), USGS geology maps (10%), Department of Transportation, NOAA, CIA, National Forest Service, State

15,000 printed maps
100 wall maps
7,200 microfilms
350 aerial photos
30 globes
75 gazetteers
2,400 printed atlases
12 active serials

Chronological coverage:
Pre-1800: 20%
1800–1899: 30%
1900–1939: 40%
1940–present: 10%

Average budget over the last 5 years: $25,000

On-going publications: Our publications: *Compass Rose.* Occasional papers: articles appearing in *Heritage Magazine, The Neatline, Imago Mundi, The Map Collector, Mercator's World.*

Access:
Maps in separate area
Collection is paged
Reference questions per year: 1,300
Answers email questions
Patrons per month: 20
Hours:
Monday–Saturday: 9 A.M.–5 P.M.
Sunday: closed
Total hours per week opened: 40
Geographic Information Systems:
No GIS services available
Scans maps for patrons
Collection services:
Maps cataloged: 99%
Maps in OPAC: 20%
Classification schemes: Local
Cataloging utilities: OCLC, Local
Catalog accessibility: online, fiche, cards

Preservation techniques: encapsulation, deacidification
Items that have gone through the preservation process: 100%

Physical facilities:
Internet access available
Number of map cases: 142
Number of vertical map cases: 21
Linear book shelving: 167 ft.
Linear atlas shelving: 260 ft.
Other map storage: 96 cubes for rolled maps
Copying facilities available: copier, color copier, microform copier, scanner, photographic reproductions

478 *Austin, TX*

Texas State Library and Archives

Historic Map Collection
P.O. Box 12927
Austin, TX 78711-2927
Telephone: 512-463-5480
Fax: 512-463-5430
Email: archinfo@tsl.state.tx.us
Web: www.tsl.state.tx.us/arc/maps/index.html

Personnel:
Responsible person: Laura Saegert, Map Archivist, *email:* lsaegert@tsl.state.tx.us
FTE professionals: 1

Holdings:
Geographic strengths: Texas
Special collections: A.R. Roessler Collection (military routes during Civil War), US Coastal Survey maps (1850s, 1930s, 1970s, 1990s), Texas State Highway county maps (1940, 1961, 1970s, 1990s)
8,000 printed maps
25 atlases

Access:
Hours:
Monday–Friday: 8 A.M.–5 P.M.
Collection services:
Maps classified: 90%
Classification schemes: Local
Physical facilities:
Public computers: 2
Map cases: 25

479 *Austin, TX*

Texas State Library and Archives

Reference/Documents
1201 Brazos
Austin, TX 78701
Telephone: 512-463-5455
Fax: 512-463-5430
Email: reference.desk@tsl.state.tx.us
Web: www.tsl.state.tx.us

Personnel:
Responsible person: Sue Troyan, Reference/Documents Librarian, *email:* stroyan@tsl.state.tx.us
Holdings:
Map depositories: CIA, National Forest Service
3,000 printed maps
Access:
Hours:
Monday–Friday: 8 A.M.–5 P.M.
Items circulate
Interlibrary loan available
Collection services:
Classification schemes: SuDocs
Physical facilities:
Public computers: 3
Map cases: 1

480 *Austin, TX*

University of Texas, Austin

Nettie Lee Benson Latin American Collection
Rare Books and Manuscripts Division
The General Libraries
Austin, TX 78713-8916
Telephone: 512-495-4520
Fax: 512-495-4568
Email: blac@lib.utexas.edu
Web: www.lib.utexas.edu/benson/
Personnel:
Responsible person: Christian Kelleher, Archivist, *email:* kelleher@mail.utexas.edu
Assistants: Michael Hironymous, Carol Russell, Carmen Sacomani
FTE professionals: 1.5   *FTE para-professionals:* 2
Holdings:
Geographic strengths: Mexico, Central America, South America, Caribbean
Special collections: Relaciones Geograficas: 37 "pinturas" from the collection of Joaquín García Icazbalceta, Manuel E. Gondra collection
17,000 printed maps
4 aerial photos
10 atlases
250 books
70 active serials
Access:
Hours:
Monday–Friday: 9 A.M.–5 P.M.
Collection services:
Maps cataloged: 95%
Maps classified: 5%
Maps in OPAC: 5%
Classification schemes: LC
Physical facilities:

Public computers: 2
Map cases: 27

481 *Austin, TX*

University of Texas, Austin

Perry–Castañeda Library
Map Collection
Austin, TX 78713
Telephone: 512-495-4275
Fax: 512-495-4296
Email: www.lib.utexas.edu/services/reference/email.html
Web: www.lib.utexas.edu/
Personnel:
Responsible person: Paul Rascoe, *email:* http://www.lib.utexas.edu/services/reference/email.html
Assistants: James Wieferman
FTE professionals: 0.5
Number of student workers hours per week: 32
Holdings:
Geographic strengths: United States, Mexico, Europe
Subject strengths: aerial photos, aeronautical, modern cartography, city, economic geography, forestry, geodetic surveys, historical geography, land use, language, map catalogs, military, nautical charts, oceanography, political geography, population, projections, railroads, raised relief models, recreation, religion, roads, satellite imagery, soil, views, waterways
Map depositories and percentages: USGS topos (100%), USGS other (75%), Department of Transportation, NOAA, GPO, CIA, National Forest Service, NIMA topos, NIMA nautical, NIMA aeronautical, BLM, State
250,000 printed maps
12 wall maps
25 raised relief maps
100 microfiche
150 aerial photos
250 satellite images
20 globes
350 gazetteers
700 printed atlases
35 books
650 CD-ROMs
Chronological coverage:
1900–1939: 10%
1940–present: 88%
Average budget over the last 5 years: $5,000
Access:
Maps in separate area
Collection is open to the public
Maps off site
Reference questions per year: 1,500
Answers email questions

Patrons per month: 750

Hours:

Monday–Friday: 7 A.M.–2 A.M.

Saturday: 9 A.M.–midnight

Sunday: noon–2 A.M.

Total hours per week opened: 125

Maps circulate

Circulation policies apply

Map circulation duration: 2 weeks

Number of maps circulated annually: 125,000

Number of books circulated annually: 10

Interlibrary loan available

Geographic Information Systems:

No GIS services available

Collection services:

Maps cataloged: 100%

Maps classified: 100%

Maps in OPAC: 100%

Classification schemes: LC, SuDocs, Local

Cataloging utilities: OCLC, Local

Catalog accessibility: online

Preservation techniques: encapsulation, lamination, edging

Items that have gone through the preservation process: 10%

Physical facilities:

No Internet access

Square footage: 6,910

Number of map cases: 865

Number of vertical files (file cabinets): 18

Linear book shelving: 125 ft.

Linear atlas shelving: 1,100 ft.

Copying facilities available: copier, microform copier

---

482 *Austin, TX*

University of Texas, Austin

Walter Geology Library

Tobin Map Collection, founded 1957

GEO 4.202-S5438

Austin, TX 78712-1101

Telephone: 512-495-4680

Fax: 512-495-4102

Email: georequests@lib.utexas.edu

Web: www.lib.utexas.edu/geo

Personnel:

Responsible person: Dennis Trombatore, Geology Librarian, *email:* drtgeol@mail.utexas.edu

Assistants: Carol Russell, Map Library Assistant

FTE para-professionals: 0.5

Number of student workers hours per week: 7

Holdings:

Geographic strengths: United States, North America, Mexico, Italy, Australia, South Africa

Special collections: U.S. Geological Survey series maps

Subject strengths: geology, hydrology, mineral resources

Map depositories and percentages: USGS topos, USGS geology maps (100%)

45,578 printed maps

200 satellite images

Chronological coverage:

1940–present: 95%

Average budget over the last 5 years: $4,000

Access:

Collection is open to the public

Maps off site

Reference questions per year: 365

Answers email questions

Patrons per month: 45

Hours:

Monday–Thursday: 8 A.M.–10 P.M.

Friday: 8 A.M.–6 P.M.

Saturday: noon–5 P.M.

Sunday: 2 P.M.–10 P.M.

Total hours per week opened: 79

Maps circulate

Circulation policies apply

Map circulation duration: 2 weeks

Number of maps circulated annually: 2,700

Interlibrary loan available

Geographic Information Systems:

No GIS services available

Collection services:

Maps cataloged: 95%

Maps classified: 95%

Maps in OPAC: 95%

Classification schemes: LC

Cataloging utilities: OCLC

Catalog accessibility: online

Preservation techniques: encapsulation, edging

Items that have gone through the preservation process: 10%

Physical facilities:

Internet access available

Square footage: 1,400

Number of map cases: 44

Number of vertical files (file cabinets): 35

Other map storage: 1 rolled map case

Copying facilities available: copier

Notes: Atlas shelving, public computers and copiers are close by in the main reading room of the geology library

---

483 *Canyon, TX*

West Texas A&M University

Cornette Library

P.O. Box 60748

Canyon, TX 79016

Telephone: 806-651-2205
Fax: 806-651-2213
Web: www.wtamu.edu/library/documents/docsmaps
.shtml
Personnel:
Responsible person: Laura Sare, Documents Librarian,
email: lsare@mail.wtamu.edu
Number of student workers hours per week: 90
Holdings:
Geographic strengths: Texas, Oklahoma, Colorado,
Kansas, New Mexico
Subject strengths: soil
Map depositories and percentages: USGS topos (10%),
GPO, CIA, BLM
2,820 printed maps
50 CD-ROMs
Chronological coverage:
1940–present: 94%
Access:
Collection is open to the public
Reference questions per year: 10
Answers email questions
Hours:
Total hours per week opened: 91
Maps circulate
Circulation policies apply
Map circulation duration: 3 weeks
Book circulation duration: 3 weeks
Number of other items circulated annually: 422
Interlibrary loan available
Geographic Information Systems:
No GIS services available
Collection services:
Maps cataloged: 0.1%
Maps classified: 0.5%
Maps in OPAC: 0.1%
Classification schemes: SuDocs
Cataloging utilities: OCLC
Catalog accessibility: online, cards
Preservation techniques: encapsulation
Items that have gone through the preservation process:
0.01%
Physical facilities:
Internet access available
Square footage: 2,214
Number of map cases: 12
Copying facilities available: copier, microform copier

484 *College Station, TX*

Texas A&M University

Sterling C. Evans Library
Maps/GIS Department, founded 1972
College Station, TX 77845-5000

Telephone: 979-845-1024
Fax: 979-845-6238
Email: rwarner@tamu.edu
Web: library.tamu.edu/
Personnel:
Responsible person: Richard L. Warner, *email:*
rwarner@tamu.edu
Number of student works: 14
Number of student workers hours per week: 176
Holdings:
Geographic strengths: Texas, Mexico, Central Amer-
ica, South America
Special collections: Al Stonestreet Parks, Recreation,
and Travel Collection, Brazos County Aerial Photographs
Subject strengths: aerial photos, aeronautical, agriculture, early cartography, modern cartography, celestial, climatology, city, economic geography, engineering, forestry, genealogy, geodetic surveys,
geology, geospatial data, historical geography, hydrology, industries, land ownership, land use, language, map catalogs, map collecting, military, mineral resources, mining, nautical charts, oceanography,
political geography, population, projections, railroads, raised relief models, recreation, religion,
roads, satellite imagery, soil, travel books, vegetation, views, waterways, topographic
Map depositories and percentages: USGS topos
(100%), USGS geology maps (100%), USGS other
(75%), Department of Transportation, NOAA, GPO,
CIA, National Forest Service, NIMA topos, NIMA
nautical, NIMA aeronautical, BLM, State, United
Nations
210,000 printed maps
77,500 manuscript maps
250 wall maps
55 raised relief maps
3,000 microfiche
2,500 aerial photos
150 satellite images
25 globes
20 gazetteers
1,500 printed atlases
500 manuscript atlases
2,000 books
1,000 CD-ROMs
10 computer programs
Collecting digital data
Chronological coverage:
1800–1899: 10%
1900–1939: 25%
1940–present: 60%
Average budget over the last 5 years: $8,000
Access:
Maps in separate area

Collection is open to the public
Reference questions per year: 10,092
Answers email questions
Patrons per month: 750
Hours:
    Monday–Friday: 8 A.M.–11 P.M.
    Saturday: 1 P.M.–5 P.M.
    Sunday: noon–11 P.M.
    Total hours per week opened: 85
Maps circulate
Circulation policies apply
    Map circulation duration: 2 weeks
    Atlas circulation duration: 2 weeks
    Book circulation duration: 2 weeks
    Number of maps circulated annually: 3,326
    Number of books circulated annually: 672
    Number of other items circulated annually: 500
Interlibrary loan available
Geographic Information Systems:
GIS services available by appointment
GIS software: ArcView
GIS assistance available for Census mapping
Basic ArcView 3.2 tutorial available
Scans maps for patrons
Collection services:
Maps cataloged: 75%
Maps classified: 95%
Maps in OPAC: 75%
Datasets are cataloged
Classification schemes: LC, SuDocs, Local
Cataloging utilities: OCLC, Local
Catalog accessibility: online
Preservation techniques: encapsulation, deacidification, lamination, edging
Items that have gone through the preservation process: 10%
Physical facilities:
No Internet access
Square footage: 2,500
Number of map cases: 168
Number of vertical files (file cabinets): 150
Linear book shelving: 500 ft.
Linear atlas shelving: 75 ft.
Number of stereoscopes: 15
Copying facilities available: copier, microform copier, scanner

485 *Dallas, TX*

Dallas Public Library

J. Eric Jonsson Central Library
Government Information Center/Map Collection, founded 1922
1515 Young Street

Dallas, TX 75201
Telephone: 214-670-1468
Fax: 214-670-1451
Email: government@dallaslibrary.org
Web: www.dallaslibrary.org/CGI/maps.htm
Personnel:
Responsible person: Darlene Brimmage, Map Specialist, *email:* dbrimmage@dallaslibrary.org
Assistants: Johanna Johnson, Manager
FTE professionals: 0.5   *FTE para-professionals:* 1.5
Holdings:
Geographic strengths: Texas, Arkansas, Louisiana, New Mexico, Oklahoma
Special collections: US city street maps, USGS geology series, topographic maps of Texas, Arkansas, Colorado, Louisiana, New Mexico, Oklahoma, Mexico 1:50,000, Mexico geology, County highway map of Texas, Arkansas, Louisiana, New Mexico, Oklahoma, Flood Insurance Rate Maps and Wetand Inventory of Dallas County, ONC navigation maps of Atlantic and Gulf Coast, Zoning maps of Dallas County
Subject strengths: city, geology, mineral resources, nautical charts, political geography, recreation, roads, soil
Map depositories and percentages: USGS topos (95%), USGS geology maps (90%), USGS other
60,000 printed maps
300 microfiche
346 microfilms
100 aerial photos
230 gazetteers
900 printed atlases
2,000 books
11 inactive serials
Chronological coverage:
    1940–present: 99%
Average budget over the last 5 years: $6,000
Access:
Collection is open to the public
Reference questions per year: 75
Answers email questions
Patrons per month: 40
Hours:
    Monday–Thursday: 9 A.M.–9 P.M.
    Friday–Saturday: 9 A.M.–5 P.M.
    Sunday: 1 P.M.–5 P.M.
    Total hours per week opened: 68
Maps circulate
Circulation policies apply
    Map circulation duration: 3 weeks
    Atlas circulation duration: 3 weeks
    Book circulation duration: 3 weeks
    Number of maps circulated annually: 4,800
    Number of books circulated annually: 1,225

Interlibrary loan available

Geographic Information Systems:

No GIS services available

Number of public GIS workstations: 14

Collection services:

Maps cataloged: 25%

Maps in OPAC: 25%

Classification schemes: LC, SuDocs, Dewey, Local

Cataloging utilities: OCLC

Catalog accessibility: online

Preservation techniques: encapsulation

Items that have gone through the preservation process: 1%

Physical facilities:

Internet access available

Square footage: 8,000

Number of public computers: 14

Number of map cases: 86

Number of vertical files (file cabinets): 32

Linear book shelving: 273 ft.

Linear atlas shelving: 490 ft.

Copying facilities available: copier, microform copier

486 *Dallas, TX*

Dallas Public Library

Texas/Dallas History and Archives Division
1515 Young Street
Dallas, TX 75201
Telephone: 214-670-1435
Fax: 214-670-1437
Web: dallaslibrary.org/ctx/ctx.htm

Personnel:

Responsible person: Michael C. Miller, *email:* mmiller@dallaslibrary.org

Holdings:

Geographic strengths: Dallas, Texas

Special collections: Murphy and Bolanz Block and Addition maps of Dallas County, Sanborn Fire Insurance maps of Texas, Dallas city maps, Dallas County aerial photographs

Subject strengths: aerial photos, city, land ownership, roads

4,000 printed maps

3,600 manuscript maps

30 wall maps

100,000 microfiche

75 microfilms

3,000 aerial photos

400 printed atlases

15 manuscript atlases

250 books

Chronological coverage:

1800–1899: 10%

1900–1939: 15%

1940–present: 74%

On-going publications: Collection indexes

Access:

Collection is paged

Answers email questions

Hours:

Monday–Thursday: 9 A.M.–9 P.M.

Friday–Saturday: 9 A.M.–5 P.M.

Sunday: 1 P.M.–5 P.M.

Total hours per week opened: 68

Geographic Information Systems:

Scans maps for patrons

Collection services:

Maps cataloged: 75%

Classification schemes: Local

Catalog accessibility: printout, MS Access/SQL database

Preservation techniques: encapsulation, deacidification

Items that have gone through the preservation process: 30%

Physical facilities:

Internet access available

Linear atlas shelving: 150 ft.

Number of microform readers: 12

Copying facilities available: copier, large-format copying available off site

487 *Dallas, TX*

Southern Methodist University

DeGolyer Library
Historic Map Collection
P.O. Box 750396
Dallas, TX 75275
Telephone: 214-768-4284
Fax: 214-768-1565
Email: bhuseman@smu.edu
Web: www.smu.edu/cul/degolyer

Personnel:

Responsible person: Ben Huseman, Curator, *email:* bhuseman@smu.edu

Assistants: Russell Martin, Director

FTE professionals: 3

Holdings:

Geographic strengths: Texas, Trans-Mississippi West, North America, New Spain, Mexico

Special collections: B. B. Barr and John N. Rowe Collection of Historic Maps Relating to Texas (1555–1950s)

900 printed maps

1 globe

40 atlases

3,000 books

Access:
  Hours:
    Monday–Friday: 9 A.M.–5 P.M.
  Collection services:
    Maps cataloged: 0.125%
    Maps in OPAC: 0.125%
    Classification schemes: LC
Physical facilities:
  Maps in separate area
  Map cases: 3
Notes: The great strength of the collection is in the number of maps in rare books, dating from the 16th to the 19th centuries. In addition to the geographical regions listed above, the collection's strengths are in exploration and travel and in railroads, the latter with a worldwide focus. Although citations for most of the books are available online, often proper descriptions of the maps they contain are not.

488 *Dallas, TX*

Southern Methodist University

Edwin J. Foscue Map Library
Founded 1942
6425 North Ownby Drive
Dallas, TX 750375
Telephone: 214-768-2285
Fax: 214-768-4236
Email: dyoungbl@smu.edu
Web: www.su.edu/cul/maps
Personnel:
  Responsible person: Maps and GIS Specialist, *email:* dyoungbl@smu.edu
  Number of student workers hours per week: 20
Holdings:
  Geographic strengths: United States, Europe, Russia
  Special collections: World War II captured German maps, World War II US maps and posters, International ARCO collection geology maps
  Subject strengths: aerial photos, aeronautical, archaeology, early cartography, modern cartography, city, economic geography, geodetic surveys, geology, geospatial data, historical geography, hydrology, map catalogs, military, mineral resources, mining, nautical charts, political geography, projections, railroads, raised relief models, recreation, roads, satellite imagery, soil, vegetation, views, waterways, zoogeography
  Map depositories and percentages: GPO
260,000 printed maps
20 wall maps
3,000 aerial photos
500 satellite images
110 gazetteers

400 printed atlases
650 books
15 CD-ROMs
Collecting digital data
Chronological coverage:
  1940–present: 90%
Average budget over the last 5 years: $2,000
Access:
  Maps in separate area
  Collection is open to the public
  Reference questions per year: 100
  Answers email questions
  Patrons per month: 30
  Hours:
    Monday–Friday: 8 A.M.–7 P.M.
    Saturday–Sunday: by appointment
    Total hours per week opened: 55
  Maps circulate
  Circulation policies apply
    Map circulation duration: 3 weeks
    Number of maps circulated annually: 25
Geographic Information Systems:
  GIS services available by appointment
  GIS software: Arc-View 8, MapViewer
  GIS assistance available for geocoding
  Plotter available
Collection services:
  Maps cataloged: 97%
  Maps classified: 95%
  Datasets are cataloged
  Classification schemes: LC
  Cataloging utilities: OCLC
  Catalog accessibility: online, cards
  Preservation techniques: encapsulation, deacidification
  Items that have gone through the preservation process: 10%
Physical facilities:
  Internet access available
  Square footage: 1,512
  Number of map cases: 26
  Linear book shelving: 60 ft.
  Linear atlas shelving: 20 ft.
  Copying facilities available: copier, microform copier
Notes: Additional Contact, Joe Milazzo, GIRM Librarian, 214-768-2561

489 *Denton, TX*

University of North Texas

Willis Library
Map Collection
P.O. Box 305190
Denton, TX 76203-5190
Telephone: 940-565-2870

Fax: 940-565-2599
Email: www.library.unt.edu/govinfo/help/govref.html
Web: www.library.unt.edu/govinfo/
Personnel:
Responsible person: Arlene Weible, *email:* aweible@
library.unt.edu
Assistants: Valerie Glenn, Documents Librarian
FTE professionals: 0.5   *FTE para-professionals:* 0.5
Holdings:
Geographic strengths: Texas, Southwest
Map depositories: USGS topos, CIA, National Forest
Service, BLM
19,850 printed maps
10 atlases
100 CD-ROMs
Access:
Hours:
Monday–Thursday: 9 A.M.–9 P.M.
Friday–Saturday: 11 A.M.–4 P.M.
Sunday: 1 P.M.–9 P.M.
Items circulate
Collection services:
Maps cataloged: 50%
Maps classified: 95%
Maps in OPAC: 50%
Classification schemes: LC, SuDocs, Dewey, Local
Physical facilities:
Maps in separate area
Public computers: 5
Map cases: 44
Vertical files: 2

490 *El Paso, TX*

University of Texas, El Paso

500 West University
El Paso, TX 79968
Telephone: 915-747-6702
Fax: 915-747-5327
Email: rarney@utep.edu
Web: libraryweb.utep.edu
Personnel:
Responsible person: Roberta Arney, Head, Govern-
ment Documents/Maps, *email:* rarney@utep.edu
Assistants: Susana Rodriguez, Library Assistant
Number of student workers hours per week: 15
Holdings:
Geographic strengths: El Paso, Texas, Southwest,
Mexico
Special collections: INEGI maps of Mexico
Subject strengths: city, geology, hydrology, land use,
mineral resources, mining, railroads, recreation, roads
Map depositories and percentages: USGS topos (100%),
USGS geology maps (100%), USGS other (100%),
GPO, CIA, National Forest Service, BLM, State
180,000 printed maps

34 raised relief maps
100 microfiche
240 aerial photos
200 satellite images
60 gazetteers
64 printed atlases
30 books
350 CD-ROMs
55 computer programs
Chronological coverage:
1940–present: 94%
Average budget over the last 5 years: $500
Access:
Maps in separate area
Collection is open to the public
Reference questions per year: 300
Answers email questions
Patrons per month: 400
Hours:
Monday–Friday: 7:30 A.M.–10 P.M.
Saturday: 9 A.M.–6 P.M.
Sunday: noon–10 P.M.
Total hours per week opened: 96
Maps circulate
Circulation policies apply
Map circulation duration: 4 weeks
Book circulation duration: 4 weeks
Number of maps circulated annually: 1,500
Geographic Information Systems:
No GIS services available
Collection services:
Maps cataloged: 60%
Maps classified: 100%
Maps in OPAC: 60%
Datasets are cataloged
Classification schemes: SuDocs, Local
Cataloging utilities: OCLC
Catalog accessibility: online
Preservation techniques: encapsulation
Items that have gone through the preservation process:
30%
Physical facilities:
No Internet access
Square footage: 970
Number of map cases: 102
Number of vertical files (file cabinets): 144
Linear atlas shelving: 25 ft.
Copying facilities available: copier, color copier, mi-
croform copier, microcard digital computer

491 *Houston, TX*

Lunar and Planetary Institute

Center for Information and Research Services
3600 Bay Area Blvd
Houston, TX 77059

Telephone: 281-486-2182
Fax: 281-486-2186
Email: cirs2@lpi.usra.edu
Web: www.lpi.usra.edu/library
Personnel:
Responsible person: Mary Ann Hager, *email:* hager@lpi.usra.edu
Assistants: Stephen Tellier, Information Services Librarian
FTE professionals: 1   *FTE para-professionals:* 0.5
Holdings:
Geographic strengths: Planets, Solar System, Moon, Mars
Special collections: Lunar photography and cartography
2,000 printed maps
50 globes
50 atlases
2,000 CD-ROMs
Access:
Hours:
Monday–Friday: 8 A.M.–5 P.M.
Items circulate
Interlibrary loan available
Collection services:
Maps cataloged: 50%
Maps classified: 75%
Maps in OPAC: 50%
Classification schemes: LC, Local
Physical facilities:
Public computers: 2

492 *Houston, TX*

Rice University

Fondren Library
Government Publications and Microforms
6100 Main
Houston, TX 77005
Telephone: 713-348-5483
Fax: 713-348-5902
Email: govhelp@rice.edu
Web: www.rice.edu/fondren/gov/
Personnel:
Responsible person: Esther Crawford, Head of Government Publications and Microforms, *email:* crawford@rice.edu
Assistants: tbn, GIS/Data Center Coordinator
FTE professionals: 0.2   *FTE para-professionals:* 0.2
Holdings:
Geographic strengths: Houston, Harris County, Texas
Special collections: Sanborn Fire Insurance maps
Map depositories: USGS topos, CIA
26,700 printed maps
Access:
Hours:
Monday–Thursday: 8:30 A.M.–10 P.M.

Friday: 8:30 A.M.–6 P.M.
Saturday: 10 A.M.–6 P.M.
Sunday: noon–9 P.M.
Interlibrary loan available
Collection services:
Maps cataloged: 95%
Maps classified: 95%
Maps in OPAC: 95%
Classification schemes: LC, SuDocs
Physical facilities:
Maps in separate area
Public computers: 4
Map cases: 56
Vertical files: 4

493 *Lubbock, TX*

Texas Tech University

University Library
Government Documents Map Collection
18th and Boston
Lubbock, TX 79409-0002
Telephone: 806-742-2268
Fax: 806-742-1332
Email: bruce.sarjeant@ttu.edu
Web: library.ttu.edu/ul/maps/
Personnel:
Responsible person: Bruce Sarjeant, Maps/GIS Librarian, *email:* bruce.sarjeant@ttu.edu
Assistants: Minerva Alaniz, Specialist IV
Number of student workers hours per week: 15
Holdings:
Geographic strengths: Texas, South Plains
Map depositories and percentages: USGS topos (100%), USGS geology maps (100%), USGS other (100%), Department of Transportation, NOAA, GPO, CIA, National Forest Service, NIMA nautical, NIMA aeronautical, BLM, State, Texas State Documents
69,572 printed maps
22 wall maps
84 aerial photos
32 gazetteers
1,667 printed atlases
24 books
96 CD-ROMs
Collecting digital data
Chronological coverage:
1940–present: 90%
Average budget over the last 5 years: $1,500
On-going publications: Maps web page, *Guide to U.S. Map Resources.*
Access:
Collection is open to the public
Reference questions per year: 400
Answers email questions
Patrons per month: 75

Hours:
Monday–Friday: 7:30 A.M.–2 A.M.
Saturday: 10 A.M.–11 P.M.
Sunday: 10 A.M.–2 A.M.
Total hours per week opened: 119.5
Maps circulate
Circulation policies apply
    Map circulation duration: 3 weeks
Geographic Information Systems:
GIS services available by appointment
GIS software: ArcGIS Desktop
Number of public GIS workstations: 30
GIS assistance available for Census mapping, geocoding, and image analysis
Collection services:
Maps cataloged: 79.5%
Maps classified: 100%
Maps in OPAC: 79.5%
Classification schemes: LC, SuDocs, Local
Cataloging utilities: OCLC
Catalog accessibility: online
Preservation techniques: encapsulation, edging
Physical facilities:
Internet access available
Square footage: 3,024
Number of public computers: 30
Number of map cases: 59
Linear book shelving: 207 ft.
Linear atlas shelving: 252.5 ft.
Copying facilities available: copier, microform copier, microform scanner

494 *Nacogdoches, TX*

Stephen F. Austin University

Ralph W. Steen Library
Government Documents/Maps
P.O. Box 13055 SFA Station
Nacogdoches, TX 75963
Telephone: 936-468-1574
Fax: 936-468-4117
Web: libweb.sfasu.edu/subject/government/default.htm
Personnel:
Responsible person: Kayce Halstead, Reference Librarian, *email:* khalstea@sfasu.edu
Number of student workers hours per week: 10
Holdings:
Subject strengths: forestry, geology, hydrology, map catalogs, mineral resources, soil
Map depositories and percentages: USGS topos (14%), USGS geology maps (25%), USGS other, GPO, CIA, National Forest Service, BLM, State
30,000 printed maps
500 microfiche
30 aerial photos
10 gazetteers

100 printed atlases
Chronological coverage:
    1800–1899: 15%
    1940–present: 80%
Access:
Collection is open to the public
Reference questions per year: 50
Answers email questions
Hours:
Monday–Friday: 7 A.M.–1 A.M.
Saturday: 10 A.M.–6 P.M.
Sunday: noon–1 A.M.
Total hours per week opened: 108
Maps circulate
    Map circulation duration: 1 day
    Number of maps circulated annually: 30
Geographic Information Systems:
GIS services available in an open environment
Number of public GIS workstations: 130
GIS assistance available for Census mapping
Scans maps for patrons
Collection services:
Maps cataloged: 100%
Maps classified: 100%
Maps in OPAC: 50%
Classification schemes: LC, SuDocs, Local
Cataloging utilities: OCLC, Local
Catalog accessibility: online, cards
Preservation techniques: lamination
Physical facilities:
No Internet access
Number of vertical files (file cabinets): 10
Linear atlas shelving: 100 ft.
Copying facilities available: copier, microform copier, scanner

495 *Richardson, TX*

University of Texas, Dallas

Eugene McDermott Library
Founded 1983
P.O. Box 830643
MC33
Richardson, TX 75083-0643
Telephone: 972-883-2950
Fax: 972-883-2473
Email: Hillary.Campbell@utdallas.edu
Web: www.utdallas.edu/library
Personnel:
Responsible person: Hillary Campbell, Government Documents Librarian, *email:* Hillary.Campbell@ utdallas.edu
Assistants: Brenda Mahar, Government Documents Cataloger
Holdings:
Geographic strengths: Texas, Southwest

Subject strengths: geodetic surveys, geology, mineral resources, roads

Map depositories and percentages: USGS topos (35%), USGS geology maps (35%), USGS other (35%), GPO, CIA, National Forest Service, BLM, State

34,657 printed maps

130 wall maps

1,816 printed atlases

200 books

50 active serials

76 CD-ROMs

Chronological coverage:
1940–present: 99%

Access:

Collection is open to the public

Answers email questions

Hours:
Monday–Friday: 8 A.M.–midnight
Saturday: 10 A.M.–8 P.M.
Sunday: 1 P.M.–midnight

Maps circulate

Collection services:

Maps cataloged: 90%

Maps classified: 90%

Maps in OPAC: 90%

Classification schemes: LC, SuDocs

Cataloging utilities: OCLC

Catalog accessibility: online

Physical facilities:

Internet access available

Number of map cases: 40

Copying facilities available: copier, color copier, microform copier

496 *San Antonio, TX*

Daughters of the Republic of Texas Library

P.O. Box 1401
San Antonio, TX 78295
Telephone: 210-225-1071
Fax: 210-212-8514
Email: drtl@drtl.org
Web: www.drtl.org

Personnel:

Responsible person: Elaine Davis, Library Director, *email:* edavis@drtl.org

Holdings:

Geographic strengths: Texas

Subject strengths: early cartography, modern cartography, city, genealogy, historical geography, land ownership, railroads, roads, soil, travel books, waterways

500 printed maps

60 manuscript maps

10 raised relief maps

50 microfilms

80 active serials

90 inactive serials

10 CD-ROMs

Chronological coverage:
1800–1899: 75%
1900–1939: 20%

Access:

Collection is paged

Reference questions per year: 20

Answers email questions

Patrons per month: 140

Hours:
Monday–Saturday: 9 A.M.–5 P.M.
Total hours per week opened: 48

Geographic Information Systems:

No GIS services available

Collection services:

Maps cataloged: 60%

Maps classified: 60%

Maps in OPAC: 60%

Classification schemes: Dewey

Catalog accessibility: online

Preservation techniques: encapsulation

Items that have gone through the preservation process: 1%

Physical facilities:

Internet access available

Copying facilities available: copier

497 *San Antonio, TX*

Saint Mary's University

Blume Library
One Camino Santa Maria
San Antonio, TX 78228
Telephone: 210-436-3441
Fax: 210-436-3782
Email: kamen@stmarytx.edu
Web: library.stmarytx.edu/acadlib/doc/maps/mapintro.htm

Personnel:

Responsible person: Kathleen L. Amen, *email:* kamen@stmarytx.edu

Assistants: Christina Ramos, Documents Clerk

FTE professionals: 0.05   *FTE para-professionals:* 0.05

Holdings:

Map depositories: USGS topos, CIA

1,000 printed maps

100 atlases

800 CD-ROMs

Access:

Hours:
Monday–Friday: 8 A.M.–midnight
Saturday: 8 A.M.–5 P.M.
Sunday: 1 P.M.–1 A.M.

Items circulate

Interlibrary loan available

Collection services:

Maps cataloged: 25%

Maps classified: 100%

Maps in OPAC: 25%

Classification schemes: Local

Physical facilities:

Public computers: 20

Map cases: 1

Notes: Our collection is very small and, other than a few old *National Geographic* maps, probably contains nothing that most libraries do not have. The USGS maps that we receive are sent directly to our Earth Science Department for listing and storage.

498 *Waco, TX*

Baylor University

Moody Memorial Library

Government Documents

1312 South 3rd

Waco, TX 76798

Telephone: 254-710-2157

Fax: 254-710-3116

Web: www3.baylor.edu/library

Personnel:

Responsible person: Sinai Wood, *email:* Sinai_Wood@Baylor.edu

Assistants: Taylor Hendrix, Documents Assistant; Linda Mangum, Documents Assistant

FTE professionals: 1   *FTE para-professionals:* 3

Holdings:

Geographic strengths: Texas, Arkansas, Colorado, Louisiana, New Mexico, Oklahoma

Map depositories: USGS topos, CIA

4,815 printed maps

71 atlases

150 books

80 CD-ROMs

Access:

Hours:

Monday–Friday: 7:30 A.M.–10 P.M.

Saturday: 9 A.M.–10 P.M.

Sunday: 1 P.M.–1am

Items circulate

Interlibrary loan available

Collection services:

Maps cataloged: 90%

Maps classified: 90%

Maps in OPAC: 90%

Classification schemes: SuDocs

Physical facilities:

Maps in separate area

Public computers: 9

Map cases: 41

Vertical files: 7

499 *Logan, UT*

Utah State University

Merrill Library

Documents and Maps Department

University Hill

Logan, UT 84322-3000

Telephone: 435-797-2684

Fax: 435-797-2880

Email: steve.weiss@usu.edu

Web: library.usu.edu/Govdocs/index.html

Personnel:

Responsible person: John S. Walters, *email:* johwal@ngw.lib.usu.edu

Assistants: Stephen C. Weiss

Number of student workers hours per week: 20

Holdings:

Geographic strengths: United States

Special collections: National Flood Insurance Program maps for Idaho and Utah, Geological Society of America maps

Subject strengths: aerial photos, aeronautical, city, forestry, geology, hydrology, land ownership, land use, map catalogs, nautical charts, population, roads, soil, travel books

Map depositories and percentages: USGS topos (100%), USGS geology maps (100%), Department of Transportation, NOAA, GPO, CIA, National Forest Service, NIMA topos, NIMA nautical, NIMA aeronautical, BLM, State

91,395 printed maps

104 wall maps

16 raised relief maps

564 aerial photos

538 printed atlases

630 CD-ROMs

Chronological coverage:

1940–present: 100%

Average budget over the last 5 years: $500

Access:

Collection is partially open to the public

Maps off site: 20%

Reference questions per year: 1,825

Answers email questions

Patrons per month: 300

Hours:

Monday–Friday: 8 A.M.–5 P.M.

Total hours per week opened: 40

Geographic Information Systems:

GIS services available by appointment

GIS software: ArcView

GIS assistance available for Census mapping

Plotter available

Collection services:

Maps cataloged: 15%

Maps classified: 15%

Maps in OPAC: 15%

Classification schemes: LC, SuDocs

Cataloging utilities: OCLC

Catalog accessibility: online

Physical facilities:

No Internet access

Square footage: 2,080

Number of map cases: 37

Number of atlas stands: 14

Linear atlas shelving: 78 ft.

Copying facilities available: copier, large-format copier, microform copier, plotter, color printer

500 *Logan, UT*

Utah State University

Merrill Library

Special Collections

3000 Old Main Hill

Logan, UT 84322-3000

Telephone: 435-797-2663

Web: library.usu.edu

Personnel:

Responsible person: Robert Parson, Head, *email:* bobpar@ngw.lib.usu.edu

Assistants: Noel Carmack, Preservation Librarian

Holdings:

Geographic strengths: Northern Utah, Southeastern Idaho, Intermountain West

Subject strengths: aerial photos, aeronautical, agriculture, archaeology, biology, early cartography, modern cartography, climatology, city, economic geography, engineering, forestry, genealogy, geodetic surveys, geology, historical geography, hydrology, industries, land ownership, land use, map collecting, mineral resources, mining, political geography, population, projections, railroads, recreation, religion, roads, travel books, vegetation, views, waterways

2,191 printed maps

Chronological coverage:

1800–1899: 25%

1900–1939: 50%

1940–present: 25%

Access:

Maps in separate area

Collection is paged

Answers email questions

Hours:

Monday–Friday: 8 A.M.–5 P.M.

Total hours per week opened: 40

Geographic Information Systems:

Scans maps for patrons

Collection services:

Classification schemes: Local

Cataloging utilities: web

Preservation techniques: encapsulation, deacidification, lamination

Items that have gone through the preservation process: 80%

501 *Ogden, UT*

Weber State University

Stewart Library

2901 University Circle

Ogden, UT 84408-2901

Telephone: 801-626-6511

Fax: 801-626-7045

Email: refdesk@weber.edu

Web: library.weber.edu/ref/government/mapsguide.cfm

Personnel:

Responsible person: Kathy Payne, Head of Reference and Information Services, *email:* KLPayne@weber.edu

Assistants: Lonna Rivera, Government Documents Coordinator

FTE para-professionals: 0.1

Holdings:

Map depositories and percentages: USGS topos (100%), USGS geology maps (60%), USGS other (50%), GPO, CIA, National Forest Service, BLM, State

38,000 printed maps

10 gazetteers

486 printed atlases

205 books

Collecting digital data

Chronological coverage:

1800–1899: 0.012%

1900–1939: 0.005%

1940–present: 99.8%

Average budget over the last 5 years: $500

On-going publications: Map guide updated annually— http://library.weber.edu/ref/guides/subject/maps.cfm

Access:

Collection is open to the public

Reference questions per year: 300

Answers email questions

Patrons per month: 35

Hours:

Total hours per week opened: 101

Circulation policies apply

Map circulation duration: 3 days

Atlas circulation duration: 3 weeks

Book circulation duration: 3 weeks

Number of maps circulated annually: 98

Interlibrary loan available

Geographic Information Systems:

GIS services available by appointment

GIS software: Arcview
Number of public GIS workstations: 72
GIS assistance available for Census mapping, and geocoding

Collection services:
Classification schemes: LC, SuDocs, Dewey
Cataloging utilities: OCLC
Catalog accessibility: online
Preservation techniques: encapsulation, cartex
Items that have gone through the preservation process: 0.017%

Physical facilities:
Internet access available
Square footage: 516
Number of public computers: 103
Number of staff computers: 72
Number of map cases: 31
Number of vertical files (file cabinets): 10
Linear book shelving: 13 ft.
Linear atlas shelving: 40 ft.
Copying facilities available: copier, color copier, large-format copier, microform copier

502 *Provo, UT*

Brigham Young University

Harold B. Lee Library
Map Collection
2420 HBLL
Provo, UT 84602
Telephone: 801-422-6179
Fax: 801-422-0466
Web: www.lib.byu.edu

Personnel:
Responsible person: Jerry Adams, Map Librarian, *email:* jerry_adams@byu.edu
Assistants: Rick Grapes, Map Manager
Number of student workers hours per week: 19

Holdings:
Geographic strengths: Utah, Intermountain West, United States, United Kingdom, Germany
Subject strengths: genealogy, geology, historical geography
Map depositories and percentages: USGS topos (70%), USGS geology maps (10%), USGS other (20%), Department of Transportation, NOAA, GPO, CIA, National Forest Service, NIMA topos, NIMA nautical, NIMA aeronautical, BLM
205,000 printed maps
50 wall maps
240 raised relief maps
6150 microfiche
350 microfilms
1335 aerial photos

158 satellite images
17 globes
1,100 gazetteers
3,000 printed atlases
1,000 books
38 CD-ROMs
Chronological coverage:
  1900–1939: 19%
  1940–present: 75%
Average budget over the last 5 years: $7,600
On-going publications: 1) *Index of Atlases and Gazetteers in the Harold B. Lee Library* 2) *Index to Geologic Maps of Utah* 3) *Index of Central Intelligence Agency Maps Held by the Science/Map Reference Desk in the Harold B. Lee Library* 4) *A Collection of Map Series Indices Held in the Harold B. Lee Library. Map Collection* (2 volumes)

Access:
Collection is partially open to the public
Reference questions per year: 700
Answers email questions

Hours:
  Monday–Friday: 7 A.M.–midnight
  Saturday: 8 A.M.–midnight
  Sunday: closed
  Total hours per week opened: 101
Maps circulate
Circulation policies apply
  Map circulation duration: 3 weeks
  Atlas circulation duration: 3 weeks
  Book circulation duration: 3 weeks
Interlibrary loan available

Geographic Information Systems:
GIS services available in an open environment
GIS software: Arc View
Using ArcView 3.3 tutorial available

Collection services:
Maps cataloged: 98%
Maps classified: 75%
Maps in OPAC: 75%
Classification schemes: LC, SuDocs, Local
Cataloging utilities: OCLC, RLG
Catalog accessibility: online, cards
Preservation techniques: encapsulation

Physical facilities:
Internet access available
Square footage: 7,200
Number of map cases: 234
Number of vertical files (file cabinets): 56
Linear book shelving: 110 ft.
Linear atlas shelving: 83 ft.
Other map storage: 2 dictionary stands, 1 microform cabinet
Copying facilities available: copier, large-format copier

503 *Salt Lake City, UT*

Family History Library

35 North West Temple Street
Salt Lake City, UT 84150-3400
Telephone: 800-346-6044 and 801-240-2584
Fax: 801-240-3718
Web: www.familysearch.org
Holdings:
Special collections: Land Ownership maps, topographic maps of the United States, Mapa Polski (Taktczna), Karte des Deutschen Reichs, Militär—Landesaufnahme und Spezialkarte der österreichisch—ungarische Monarchie, Estados Unidos Mexicanos, maps of Poland, Lithuania and Russia, Nederland—series M 635-S, Crownland index sheets, Nova Scotia Province, Canada, Irish townland survey, Yugoslavia, Hungary, index to world maps, United States, Papua and New Guinea, Mexico air navigation maps, Atlas del plano catastral de la República Argentina
Subject strengths: city, genealogy, land ownership, political geography, roads, travel books
5,769 printed maps
271 manuscript maps
257 microfiche
531 microfilms
2,000 gazetteers
106 printed atlases
10 CD-ROMs
On-going publications: Research outlines: states provinces and counties
Access:
Collection is open to the public
Hours:
Monday: 8 A.M.–5 P.M.
Tuesday–Saturday: 8 A.M.–9 P.M.
Sunday: closed
Total hours per week opened: 74
Collection services:
Maps cataloged: 100%
Maps classified: 100%
Maps in OPAC: 100%
Classification schemes: Dewey, Local
Cataloging utilities: OLIB-Fretwell-Downing World View
Catalog accessibility: online, fiche, local network
Preservation techniques: encapsulation, deacidification, edging, heat set tissue repair
Items that have gone through the preservation process: 90%
Physical facilities:
Internet access available
Number of map cases: 12

Copying facilities available: copier, color copier, microform copier, microfilm scanner

504 *Salt Lake City, UT*

University of Utah

Marriott Library
Science and Engineering Map Collection
295 South 1500 East
Salt Lake City, UT 84112-0860
Telephone: 801-581-7533
Web: www.lib.utah.edu
Personnel:
Responsible person: Ken Rockwell, Map Librarian, *email:* ken.rockwell@library.utah.edu
Holdings:
Geographic strengths: United States, Middle East, Europe
Special collections: AMS topos (World War II)
Subject strengths: city, genealogy, geology, historical geography, mineral resources, recreation, roads
Map depositories: USGS topos, USGS geology maps, USGS other, Department of Transportation, NIMA nautical, State
235,000 printed maps
100 wall maps
30 raised relief maps
300 aerial photos
100 satellite images
60 gazetteers
1,400 printed atlases
100 books
Chronological coverage:
1940–present: 90%
Average budget over the last 5 years: $8,000
Access:
Collection is open to the public
Maps off site
Reference questions per year: 300
Answers email questions
Hours:
Monday–Friday: 7 A.M.–11 P.M.
Saturday: 9 A.M.–8 P.M.
Sunday: 11 A.M.–midnight
Total hours per week opened: 40
Maps circulate
Circulation policies apply
Map circulation duration: 60 days
Interlibrary loan available
Geographic Information Systems:
No GIS services available
Scans maps for patrons
Collection services:
Maps cataloged: 90%
Maps classified: 100%

Maps in OPAC: 90%
Classification schemes: LC
Cataloging utilities: OCLC
Catalog accessibility: online
Preservation techniques: encapsulation
Physical facilities:
Internet access available
Square footage: 4,000
Number of map cases: 189
Linear book shelving: 250 ft.
Linear atlas shelving: 300 ft.
Copying facilities available: copier, color copier, large-format copier

505 *Salt Lake City, UT*

University of Utah

Marriott Library
Special Collections
295 South 1500 East
Salt Lake City, UT 84112-0860
Telephone: 801-581-8863
Web: www.lib.utah.edu
Personnel:
Responsible person: Walter Jones, *email:* walter
.jones@library.utah.edu
Holdings:
Geographic strengths: Intermountain West
Special collections: Sanborn Fire Insurance maps, 19th-century Western surveys
Subject strengths: aerial photos, geology, historical geography, mineral resources, mining
26,000 printed maps
1,000 manuscript maps
10 wall maps
30 raised relief maps
2,000 aerial photos
250 printed atlases
Access:
Collection is paged
Answers email questions
Geographic Information Systems:
No GIS services available
Collection services:
Maps cataloged: 95%
Maps classified: 100%
Maps in OPAC: 95%
Classification schemes: LC
Cataloging utilities: OCLC
Catalog accessibility: online
Preservation techniques: encapsulation
Physical facilities:
No Internet access
Number of vertical map cases: 20
Copying facilities available: copier, large-format copier

506 *Salt Lake City, UT*

University of Utah

Marriott Library
Western Americana, founded 1969
295 South 1500 East
Salt Lake City, UT 84112-0860
Telephone: 801-581-8863
Fax: 801-585-3464
Email: sreiter@library.utah.edu
Web: www.lib.utah.edu/spc/wam/maps/Maphomepage
.html.
Personnel:
Responsible person: email: sreiter@library.utah.edu
FTE para-professionals: 7
Holdings:
Geographic strengths: Utah, Intermountain West
Special collections: Sanborn Fire Insurance maps
Subject strengths: aerial photos, agriculture, archaeology, biology, early cartography, modern cartography, climatology, city, economic geography, forestry, genealogy, geodetic surveys, geology, geospatial data, historical geography, hydrology, industries, land ownership, land use, language, map catalogs, military, mineral resources, mining, political geography, population, railroads, recreation, religion, roads, soil, travel books, vegetation, views, waterways, zoogeography
36,000 printed maps
10 wall maps
48 boxes microfilms
400 aerial photos
15 printed atlases
580 books
Chronological coverage:
1900–1939: 20%
1940–present: 79%
Access:
Maps in separate area
Collection is paged
Reference questions per year: 250
Answers email questions
Patrons per month: 10
Hours:
Monday–Friday: 8 A.M.–5 P.M.
Saturday: 9 A.M.–5 P.M.
Sunday: closed
Total hours per week opened: 57
Geographic Information Systems:
No GIS services available
Scans maps for patrons
Collection services:
Maps cataloged: 99%
Maps classified: 100%
Maps in OPAC: 100%

Datasets are cataloged
Classification schemes: LC, SuDocs, Dewey
Cataloging utilities: OCLC
Catalog accessibility: online
Preservation techniques: encapsulation
Items that have gone through the preservation process:
　30%
Physical facilities:
Internet access available
Square footage: 1,152
Number of map cases: 19
Number of vertical map cases: 19
Linear book shelving: 71 ft.
Other map storage: 9 rolled map boxes
Copying facilities available: copier, microform
　copier

507 *Salt Lake City, UT*

Utah Geological Survey

Utah Department of Natural Resources Library
1594 West North Temple
Salt Lake City, UT 84114-6100
Telephone: 801-537-3333
Fax: 801-537-3400
Email: mageyonetani@utah.gov
Web: dnrlibrary.state.ut.us/
Personnel:
Responsible person: Mage Yonetani, Librarian, *email:*
　mageyonetani@utah.gov
Holdings:
Geographic strengths: Utah
Subject strengths: aerial photos, modern cartography,
　city, economic geography, engineering, forestry, ge-
　ology, hydrology, map catalogs, mineral resources,
　mining, roads, soil, waterways
Map depositories and percentages: USGS topos,
　USGS geology maps, USGS other, State
2,000 printed maps
10 microfiche
10 microfilms
250 aerial photos
20 active serials
15 inactive serials
75 CD-ROMs
Chronological coverage:
　1900–1939: 30%
　1940–present: 70%
Access:
Collection is partially open to the public
Reference questions per year: 10
Answers email questions
Patrons per month: 115
Hours:

Monday–Friday: 7:30 A.M.–4:30 P.M.
Total hours per week opened: 40
Geographic Information Systems:
No GIS services available
Collection services:
Classification schemes: SuDocs, Dewey
Catalog accessibility: online
Physical facilities:
Internet access available
Linear book shelving: 30 ft.
Copying facilities available: copier, color copier, mi-
　croform copier

508 *Salt Lake City, UT*

Utah State Historical Society

Utah History Information Center
300 Rio Grande
Salt Lake City, UT 84101
Telephone: 801-533-3536
Fax: 801-533-3504
Email: swhetsto@utah.gov
Web: www.history.utah.gov
Personnel:
Responsible person: Susan Whetstone, Photograph/Map
　Curator, *email:* swhetsto@utah.gov
Holdings:
Geographic strengths: Utah, West, Mormon Trail
Special collections: Salt Lake County Surveyor map
　collection, Sanborn Fire Insurance maps, Denver and
　Rio Grande Railroad maps, County Plat maps, Road
　maps, National forests, USGS topographical maps,
　mining maps, Utah State maps, cities and towns
Subject strengths: aerial photos, aeronautical, agricul-
　ture, archaeology, early cartography, modern cartog-
　raphy, climatology, city, economic geography, engi-
　neering, forestry, genealogy, geodetic surveys,
　geology, historical geography, hydrology, industries,
　land ownership, land use, map catalogs, map collect-
　ing, military, mineral resources, mining, political ge-
　ography, population, projections, railroads, raised re-
　lief models, recreation, religion, roads, soil, travel
　books, vegetation, views
32,000 printed maps
3,500 manuscript maps
30 raised relief maps
500 aerial photos
50 printed atlases
Chronological coverage:
　1800–1899: 18%
　1900–1939: 30%
　1940–present: 50%
Access:
Maps in separate area

Collection is paged
Reference questions per year: 25
Answers email questions
Patrons per month: 700
Hours:
 Total hours per week opened: 35
Geographic Information Systems:
No GIS services available
Scans maps for patrons
Collection services:
Maps cataloged: 90%
Classification schemes: Dewey
Cataloging utilities: RLG
Catalog accessibility: printout
Preservation techniques: encapsulation
Items that have gone through the preservation process:
 90%
Physical facilities:
No Internet access
Square footage: 150
Number of map cases: 24
Linear atlas shelving: 60 ft.
Copying facilities available: copier, microform copier

509 *Burlington, VT*

University of Vermont

Bailey/Howe Library
Map Room, founded 1965
538 Main Street
Burlington, VT 05405-0036
Telephone: 802-656-2588
Fax: 802-656-4038
Email: wgill@uvm.edu
Web: library.uvm.edu/reference/maps.html
Personnel:
Responsible person: Bill Gill, Reference Specialist,
 email: wgill@uvm.edu
FTE professionals: 0.5   *FTE para-professionals:* 0.5
Number of student workers hours per week: 50
Holdings:
Geographic strengths: Vermont, United States, Canada
Special collections: Sanborn Fire Insurance maps, his-
 torical Vermont maps
Subject strengths: aerial photos, aeronautical, agricul-
 ture, biology, modern cartography, celestial, climatology, city, economic geography, forestry, geodetic
 surveys, geology, geospatial data, hydrology, industries, land use, map catalogs, military, mineral resources, mining, nautical charts, oceanography, political geography, population, projections, railroads,
 raised relief models, recreation, religion, roads,
 satellite imagery, soil, vegetation, views, waterways,
 zoogeography
Map depositories: USGS topos, USGS geology maps,
 USGS other, Department of Transportation, NOAA,

GPO, CIA, National Forest Service, NIMA topos,
NIMA nautical, NIMA aeronautical, BLM, State,
Canada
210,000 printed maps
10 raised relief maps
3,000 microfiche
25,000 aerial photos
1,000 satellite images
320 gazetteers
500 printed atlases
100 books
300 CD-ROMs
30 computer programs
Collecting digital data
Chronological coverage:
 1900–1939: 25%
 1940–present: 70%
Average budget over the last 5 years: $5,000
Access:
Maps in separate area
Collection is open to the public
Maps off site: 10%
Reference questions per year: 4,000
Answers email questions
Patrons per month: 350
Hours:
 Monday–Wednesday: 9 A.M.–9 P.M.
 Thursday: 9 A.M.–6 P.M.
 Friday: 9 A.M.–5 P.M.
 Saturday–Sunday: 1 P.M.–5 P.M.
 Total hours per week opened: 61
Maps circulate
Circulation policies apply
 Map circulation duration: 1 month
 Book circulation duration: 1 month
 Number of maps circulated annually: 400
 Number of books circulated annually: 25
Geographic Information Systems:
GIS services available in an open environment
GIS software: ESRI
GIS assistance available for Census mapping, geocod-
 ing, and image analysis
Scans maps for patrons
Collection services:
Maps cataloged: 95%
Maps classified: 100%
Maps in OPAC: 10%
Datasets are cataloged
Classification schemes: LC, SuDocs, Other (AGS)
Cataloging utilities: OCLC
Catalog accessibility: online, cards, printout
Preservation techniques: encapsulation, edging
Physical facilities:
Internet access available
Square footage: 3,000
Number of map cases: 120

Number of vertical files (file cabinets): 20
Linear book shelving: 125 ft.
Linear atlas shelving: 350 ft.
Copying facilities available: copier, microform copier, scanner, color printer

510 *Blacksburg, VA*

Virginia Tech

Newman Library
Instruction and Reference Department
Kent Street
Blacksburg, VA 24060
Telephone: 540-231-6181
Fax: 540-231-9263
Email: gisdata@vt.edu
Web: www.lib.vt.edu/subjects/maps/gis.html

Personnel:
Responsible person: Bruce Obenhaus, Government Information Specialist, *email:* obenhaus@vt.edu
Assistants: Edwin Brooks, Maps/GIS Assistant
FTE professionals: 0.25   *FTE para-professionals:* 1

Holdings:
Geographic strengths: Virginia
Map depositories: USGS topos, Department of Transportation, CIA, National Forest Service, NGA aeronautical
136,000 printed maps
20,000 aerial photos

Access:
Hours:
Monday–Friday: 7:30 A.M.–midnight
Saturday: 9 A.M.–6 P.M.
Sunday: noon–midnight

Collection services:
Maps cataloged: 10%
Maps classified: 10%
Maps in OPAC: 10%
Classification schemes: SuDocs

Physical facilities:
Public computers: 2
Map cases: 90
Vertical files: 25

511 *Bridgewater, VA*

Bridgewater College

Alexander Mack Memorial Library
402 East College Street
Bridgewater, VA 22812
Telephone: 540-828-5672
Fax: 540-828-5482
Email: rtout@bridgewater.edu
Web: www.bridgewater.edu/departments/library/govdocuments.html

Personnel:
Responsible person: Robert Tout, Documents Librarian, *email:* rtout@bridgewater.edu

Holdings:
Geographic strengths: Virginia, West Virginia, Maryland, North Carolina
Subject strengths: map catalogs, soil, waterways
Map depositories: USGS topos, GPO, CIA
2,500 printed maps
10 wall maps
100 aerial photos
50 printed atlases
Chronological coverage:
1940–present: 95%

Access:
Collection is open to the public
Answers email questions
Hours:
Monday–Thursday: 8 A.M.–11 P.M.
Friday: 8 A.M.–5 P.M.
Saturday: 9 A.M.–5 P.M.
Sunday: 1:30 P.M.–11 P.M.
Total hours per week opened: 85
Maps circulate
Circulation policies apply
Map circulation duration: 4 weeks
Book circulation duration: 4 weeks
Number of maps circulated annually: 10
Number of books circulated annually: 10
Interlibrary loan available

Geographic Information Systems:
No GIS services available

Collection services:
Maps cataloged: 10%
Maps in OPAC: 10%
Classification schemes: SuDocs, Dewey
Cataloging utilities: OCLC
Catalog accessibility: online, printout

Physical facilities:
Internet access available
Square footage: 100
Linear book shelving: 25 ft.
Linear atlas shelving: 10 ft.
Copying facilities available: copier

512 *Charlottesville, VA*

University of Virginia

Alderman Library
Geospatial and Statistical Data Center
P.O. Box 400129
Charlottesville, VA 22904-4129
Telephone: 434-982-2630
Fax: 434-924-1431
Email: geostat@virginia.edu
Web: fisher.lib.virginia.edu

Personnel:

Responsible person: Blair Tinker, Geographic Information Specialist, *email:* tinker@virginia.edu

Assistants: Donna Tolson, Associate Director; Haynes Earnhardt, Maps Service Specialist

FTE para-professionals: 0.5

Number of student workers hours per week: 20

Holdings:

Geographic strengths: Virginia, New York City, Barcelona, United States

Special collections: Sanborn Fire Insurance maps of Virginia, Charlottesville Sanborn (atlases)

Subject strengths: aerial photos, aeronautical, celestial, city, geology, geospatial data, hydrology, map catalogs, military, nautical charts, political geography, population, roads, Virginia GIS Data (County/City Planimetrics)

Map depositories and percentages: USGS topos (100%), USGS geology maps (100%), USGS other (100%), Department of Transportation, NOAA, GPO, CIA, National Forest Service, NIMA topos, NIMA nautical, NIMA aeronautical, BLM, State, United Nations, Census

150,000 printed maps

100 wall maps

1,842 microfiche

38 microfilms

5,000 aerial photos

200 satellite images

700 gazetteers

700 printed atlases

125 books

550 CD-ROMs

10 computer programs

Collecting digital data

Chronological coverage:

1900–1939: 10%

1940–present: 88%

Average budget over the last 5 years: $7,500

On-going publications: Website http://fisher.lib.virginia.edu

Access:

Maps in separate area

Collection is open to the public

Maps off site

Reference questions per year: 300

Answers email questions

Patrons per month: 300

Hours:

Monday–Thursday: 8 A.M.–midnight

Friday: 8 A.M.–8 P.M.

Saturday: 9 A.M.–8 P.M.

Sunday: 11 A.M.–midnight

Total hours per week opened: 94

Maps circulate

Circulation policies apply

Map circulation duration: 2 weeks

Atlas circulation duration: 3 weeks

Number of maps circulated annually: 792

Interlibrary loan available

Geographic Information Systems:

GIS services available by appointment

GIS software: ArcGIS 8x, ArcView 3x, MapInfo, Erdas Imagine, Census CD plus Maps, Map Publisher

Number of public GIS workstations: 22

Number of GIS stations (monitored): 22

GIS assistance available for Census mapping, geocoding, and image analysis

General GIS questions answered

Scans maps for patrons

Collection services:

Maps cataloged: 90%

Maps classified: 100%

Maps in OPAC: 85%

Datasets are cataloged

Classification schemes: LC, SuDocs, Local

Cataloging utilities: OCLC, RLG, Local

Catalog accessibility: online, fiche, printout

Preservation techniques: encapsulation, digitization/scanning

Physical facilities:

Internet access available

Square footage: 2,600

Number of public computers: 22

Number of map cases: 107

Linear book shelving: 40 ft.

Linear atlas shelving: 480 ft.

Number of microform readers: 15

Number of microform printers: 11

Copying facilities available: copier, color copier, microform copier, scanner

513 *Charlottesville, VA*

University of Virginia

Special Collections Department
Alderman Library
Charlottesville, VA 22904
Telephone: 434-924-3025
Fax: 434-924-4968
Email: mssbks@virginia.edu
Web: www.lib.virginia.edu

Personnel:

Responsible person: Michael Plunkett, Director, *email:* mssbks@virginia.edu

Holdings:

Geographic strengths: Virginia, United States

Special collections: Sanborn Fire Insurance maps, McGregor Collection

Subject strengths: aerial photos, early cartography, celestial, city, genealogy, historical geography, land ownership, land use, map catalogs, map collecting, military, mineral resources, mining, nautical charts, political geography, population, railroads, recreation, roads, travel books, waterways

Map depositories and percentages: USGS topos, USGS geology maps, NOAA, National Forest Service

700 printed maps

Chronological coverage:

Pre-1800: 70%

1800–1899: 20%

Access:

Maps in separate area

Collection is paged

Answers email questions

Hours:

Monday–Thursday: 9 A.M.–9 P.M.

Friday–Saturday: 9 A.M.–5 P.M.

Sunday: closed

Total hours per week opened: 56

Geographic Information Systems:

No GIS services available

Scans maps for patrons

Collection services:

Maps cataloged: 10%

Maps classified: 100%

Maps in OPAC: 10%

Classification schemes: LC, Local, Other (place)

Cataloging utilities: OCLC

Catalog accessibility: online, cards, printout

Preservation techniques: encapsulation, deacidification

Items that have gone through the preservation process: 80%

Physical facilities:

Internet access available

Other map storage: rolled map cases

Copying facilities available: copier, color copier, large-format copier, scanner

514 *Fairfax, VA*

George Mason University

Fenwick Library

Government Documents/Maps

4400 University Dr

Fairfax, VA 22030

Telephone: 703-993-2238

Fax: 703-993-2494

Web: library.gmu.edu/resources/govt/

Personnel:

Responsible person: Joy Suh, Government Documents/ Maps Librarian, *email:* hsuh1@gmu.edu

Assistants: Heather Leadingham, Government Documents Assistant

FTE professionals: 0.25   *FTE para-professionals:* 0.25

Holdings:

Geographic strengths: Virginia, Washington DC, Maryland, West Virginia, Mid-Atlantic

Special collections: Sanborn Fire Insurance of Virginia and Washington DC (microfilm)

Map depositories: USGS topos, Department of Transportation, NOAA, CIA, National Forest Service, NGA nautical, NGA aeronautical

70,000 printed maps

52 aerial photos

2 globes

122 atlases

100 books

17 active serials

20 CD-ROMs

Access:

Hours:

Monday–Friday: 7:30 A.M.–midnight

Saturday: 9 A.M.–9 P.M.

Sunday: 9 A.M.–midnight

Items circulate

Collection services:

Maps cataloged: 15%

Maps classified: 15%

Maps in OPAC: 15%

Classification schemes: LC, SuDocs

Physical facilities:

Maps in separate area

Public computers: 4

Map cases: 42

Vertical files: 5

515 *Fairfax, VA*

George Mason University

Fenwick Library

Special Collections and Archives, founded 1979

4400 University Drive

Fairfax, VA 22030

Telephone: 703-993-2220

Fax: 703-993-2255

Email: speccoll@gmu.edu

Web: www.gmu.edu/library/specialcollections

Personnel:

Responsible person: Lauren I. Glaettli, Reading Room Supervisor, *email:* speccoll@gmu.edu

Holdings:

Geographic strengths: Alexandria, Arlington, Fairfax, Fauquier, Loudoun, Prince William, Spotsylvania, Stafford counties, Virginia, Washington D.C.

Special collections: C. Harrison Mann, Charles Baptie Historic Aerial Photographs, Prince William County Aerial Photographs

Subject strengths: aerial photos, early cartography, city, historical geography, military, political geography, railroads, roads, views

300 printed maps

10 manuscript maps

1,000 aerial photos

25 printed atlases
Chronological coverage:
Pre-1800: 10%
1800–1899: 30%
1900–1939: 10%
1940–present: 50%
Average budget over the last 5 years: $10,000

Access:
Collection is open to the public
Reference questions per year: 25
Answers email questions
Patrons per month: 0.5

Hours:
Monday–Friday: 12:30 P.M.–5 P.M.
Saturday–Saturday: closed
Total hours per week opened: 22.5

Geographic Information Systems:
No GIS services available
Scans maps for patrons

Collection services:
Maps cataloged: 10%
Maps classified: 10%
Maps in OPAC: 10%
Classification schemes: LC
Cataloging utilities: OCLC
Catalog accessibility: online, printout
Preservation techniques: encapsulation, deacidification

Physical facilities:
Internet access available
Square footage: 53
Linear atlas shelving: 12 ft.
Copying facilities available: copier

516 *Fredericksburg, VA*

Mary Washington College

Simpson Library
1801 College Avenue
Fredericksburg, VA 22401
Telephone: 540-654-1148
Fax: 540-654-1067
Email: refdesk@mwc.edu
Web: www.library.mwc.edu/maps.html

Personnel:
Responsible person: Reference Department, *email:* refdesk@mwc.edu
Number of student workers hours per week: 25

Holdings:
Geographic strengths: Virginia, Maryland, West Virginia, North Carolina, Tennessee, Kentucky, Metropolitan Washington, D.C., Chesapeake Bay, Delaware, New York, Pennsylvania
Special collections: Sanborn Fire Insurance maps of Virginia

Subject strengths: agriculture, archaeology, economic geography, genealogy, geology, geospatial data, hydrology, land ownership, land use, map catalogs, mineral resources, mining, political geography, population, raised relief models, satellite imagery, soil, vegetation
Map depositories and percentages: USGS topos (20%), USGS geology maps (20%), USGS other, GPO, CIA, NIMA topos, BLM, State, United Nations
1,600 printed maps
Chronological coverage:
1940–present: 100%
Average budget over the last 5 years: $700

Access:
Collection is open to the public
Answers email questions

Hours:
Total hours per week opened: 92
Book circulation duration: 5 weeks
Interlibrary loan available

Geographic Information Systems:
GIS services available in an open environment
Number of public GIS workstations: 30
Scans maps for patrons

Collection services:
Maps cataloged: 100%
Maps classified: 100%
Maps in OPAC: 100%
Datasets are cataloged
Classification schemes: LC, SuDocs
Cataloging utilities: OCLC
Catalog accessibility: online
Preservation techniques: encapsulation
Items that have gone through the preservation process: 20%

Physical facilities:
Internet access available
Square footage: 100
Linear book shelving: 50 ft.
Linear atlas shelving: 50 ft.
Copying facilities available: copier, color copier, microform copier

517 *Reston, VA*

United States Geological Survey, Reston

Library
Cartographic Information Services, founded 1881
950 National Center
12201 Sunrise Valley Drive
Reston, VA 20192
Telephone: 703-648-4302
Fax: 703-648-6373
Email: library@usgs.gov

Web: library.usgs.gov/
Personnel:
Responsible person: Robert A. Bier, Jr., Chief, Cartographic Information Services, *email:* rbier@usgs.gov
Number of student workers hours per week: 10
Number of volunteer hours per month: 10
Holdings:
Geographic strengths: United States
Special collections: USGS Topographic Map Archive
Subject strengths: modern cartography, caves, geology, geospatial data, historical geography, hydrology, mineral resources, mining, projections, raised relief models, soil
Map depositories and percentages: USGS topos (99%), USGS geology maps (99%), USGS other (99%), NOAA, CIA, NIMA nautical, BLM, State, Canada
562,000 printed maps
25 wall maps
200 raised relief maps
1,300 microfiche
480 microfilms
500 satellite images
20 globes
1,000 gazetteers
1,000 printed atlases
Collecting digital data
Chronological coverage:
1900–1939: 37%
1940–present: 60%
On-going publications: New Acquisitions (Web—Library Home Page). Includes all material added to the library including maps.
Access:
Collection is open to the public
Reference questions per year: 1,500
Answers email questions
Patrons per month: 200
Hours:
Monday–Friday: 8 A.M.–4 P.M.
Total hours per week opened: 40
Maps circulate
Circulation policies apply
Map circulation duration: 1 month
Atlas circulation duration: 1 month
Book circulation duration: 1 month
Number of maps circulated annually: 2,500
Interlibrary loan available
Geographic Information Systems:
GIS services available in an open environment
GIS software: ArcView
Number of public GIS workstations: 11
Collection services:
Maps cataloged: 75%
Maps classified: 75%
Maps in OPAC: 75%

Datasets are cataloged
Classification schemes: Other (USGS)
Cataloging utilities: OCLC
Catalog accessibility: online, cards
Items that have gone through the preservation process: 25%
Physical facilities:
Internet access available
Square footage: 8,500
Number of map cases: 790
Linear atlas shelving: 900 ft.
Other map storage: rolled map storage, various methods
Copying facilities available: copier, color copier, large-format copier, microform copier, large-format scanners

518 *Richmond, VA*

Library of Virginia

Archival and Information Services Division/Map Collection
Founded 1911
800 East Broad Street
Richmond, VA 23227
Telephone: 804-692-3888
Fax: 804-692-3556
Web: www.lva.lib.va.us
Personnel:
Responsible person: Marianne M. McKee, Senior Research Archivist and Map Specialist, *email:* mmckee@lva.lib.va.us
Holdings:
Geographic strengths: Virginia, East, Southeast
Special collections: Board of Public Works manuscript maps, Chesapeake and Ohio Railroad maps, Sanborn Fire Insurance maps of Virginia, Voorhees Collection of early maps
Subject strengths: early cartography, city, geology, historical geography, land ownership, military, mineral resources, railroads, roads, waterways
Map depositories: USGS topos, CIA, State, Virginia Department of Mineral Resources
45,000 printed maps
1,500 manuscript maps
20 wall maps
975 microfiche
54 microfilms
14 gazetteers
60 printed atlases
200 books
Chronological coverage:
1800–1899: 14%
1900–1939: 45%
1940–present: 40%

On-going publications: Maps Relating to Virginia in the Virginia State Library and other Departments of the Commonwealth (1914); A Description of the Country; Virginia's Cartographers and their Maps (1975); Virginia in Maps; Four Centuries of Settlement, Growth, and Development (2000)

Access:

Collection is open to the public

Reference questions per year: 1,100

Answers email questions

Patrons per month: 65

Hours:

Tuesday–Saturday: 9 A.M.–4:30 P.M.

Sunday: closed

Total hours per week opened: 37.5

Geographic Information Systems:

No GIS services available

Scans maps for patrons

Collection services:

Maps cataloged: 90%

Maps classified: 90%

Maps in OPAC: 10%

Classification schemes: LC, Other (modified Dewey)

Cataloging utilities: OCLC, Local

Catalog accessibility: online, cards

Preservation techniques: encapsulation, deacidification, acid-free 20-pt. folder stock with mylar sheet attached

Items that have gone through the preservation process: 50%

Physical facilities:

No Internet access

Square footage: 900

Number of map cases: 22

Linear book shelving: 32 ft.

Other map storage: 20 cases in stacks

Copying facilities available: copier, color copier, microform copier, scanners

Notes: We have about 5,000–6,000 maps in our core historical collection, but the percentages are based on the 45,000 number (many topos). We have a roped-off specific area and large tables where we serve the maps and a reference desk, but it's not a separate room. We are a depository for CIA maps, but they are with documents, not with the map collection.

519 *Richmond, VA*

University of Richmond

Boatwright Library
Government Documents Collection, founded 1900
1 Westhampton Way
Richmond, VA 23173
Telephone: 804-289-8851
Fax: 804-287-1840

Email: kweimer@richmond.edu
Web: oncampus.richmond.edu/is/library/govdocs/govinfo.html

Personnel:

Responsible person: Keith Weimer, Government Information Librarian, *email:* kweimer@richmond.edu

Assistants: Mark Burdette, Government Information Associate

Number of student workers hours per week: 27

Holdings:

Geographic strengths: Virginia, North Carolina, Maryland, West Virginia

Subject strengths: historical geography

Map depositories: USGS topos, USGS geology maps, USGS other, GPO, CIA, Census, Defense, Interior

2,595 printed maps

Chronological coverage:

1900–1939: 0.5%

1940–present: 98.5%

Access:

Collection is open to the public

Reference questions per year: 50

Answers email questions

Hours:

Total hours per week opened: 169

Geographic Information Systems:

GIS assistance available for Census mapping, geocoding, and image analysis

Collection services:

Maps cataloged: 60%

Maps classified: 100%

Maps in OPAC: 60%

Classification schemes: SuDocs

Cataloging utilities: OCLC

Catalog accessibility: online, shelf list

Physical facilities:

Internet access available

Copying facilities available: copier, color copier, large-format copier, microform copier

Notes: Our map collection is a subset of our federal depository collection, and is housed as part of the depository collection.

520 *Williamsburg, VA*

College of William and Mary

Earl Gregg Swem Library
Geology Department Library
P.O. Box 8795
Williamsburg, VA 23187-8795
Telephone: 757-221-2094
Fax: 757-221-2093
Email: kaberq@wm.edu
Web: swem.wm.edu/guide/geology/index.html

Personnel:

Responsible person: Karen Berquist, Library Specialist, *email:* kaberq@wm.edu

Assistants: Patricia Van Zandt, Science Librarian

FTE professionals: 1   *FTE para-professionals:* 1

Holdings:

Geographic strengths: Virginia

Map depositories: USGS

27,132 printed maps

972 aerial photos

25 atlases

30 books

210 CD-ROMs

Access:

Hours:

Monday–Friday: 8 A.M.–5 P.M.

Interlibrary loan available

Collection services:

Maps cataloged: 90%

Maps classified: 90%

Maps in OPAC: 90%

Classification schemes: LC, SuDocs

Physical facilities:

Public computers: 1

Map cases: 21

521 *Williamsburg, VA*

Colonial Williamsburg Foundation

301 First Street

Williamsburg, VA 23185

Telephone: 757-229-1000

Email: mpritchard@cwf.org

Web: www.colonialwilliamsburg.org

Personnel:

Responsible person: Margaret Beck Pritchard, *email:*
mpritchard@cwf.org

Assistants: Laura Pass Barry

FTE professionals: 2   *FTE para-professionals:* 0

Holdings:

Geographic strengths: Colonial America

500 printed maps

10 globes

40 atlases

200 books

4 active serials

Access:

Hours:

Monday–Friday: by appointment

Interlibrary loan available

Collection services:

Maps cataloged: 100%

Maps in OPAC: 50%

Classification schemes: LC

522 *Anacortes, WA*

Anacortes Museum

1305 8th Street

Anacortes, WA 98221

Telephone: 360-293-1915

Fax: 360-293-1929

Email: museum@cityofanacortes.org

Web: www.anacorteshistorymuseum.org

Personnel:

Responsible person: Garry Cline, Director, *email:*
museum@cityofanacortes.org

FTE para-professionals: 1.3

Holdings:

Geographic strengths: Fidalgo Island, Guemes Island

Special collections: Sanborn Fire Insurance maps
(1890–1925)

Subject strengths: early cartography, city, industries,
land ownership, land use, railroads, waterways

1,000 printed maps

Chronological coverage:

1800–1899: 20%

1900–1939: 50%

1940–present: 30%

Access:

Maps in separate area

Collection is open to the public

Answers email questions

Hours:

Monday–Friday: 1 P.M.–5 P.M.

Total hours per week opened: 12

Geographic Information Systems:

Scans maps for patrons

Collection services:

Maps cataloged: 100%

Classification schemes: Local

Physical facilities:

No Internet access

Square footage: 64

Number of map cases: 55

Number of vertical files (file cabinets): 28

Copying facilities available: copier, microform copier

523 *Bellingham, WA*

Western Washington University

Huxley Map Library

Founded 1957

AH 101

516 High Street

Bellingham, WA 98225-9085

Telephone: 360-650-3272

Fax: 360-650-7702

Email: jcollins@wwu.edu

Web: www.ac.wwu.edu/~maplib/

Personnel:

Responsible person: Janet R. Collins, Map Librarian, *email:* jcollins@wwu.edu

Number of student workers hours per week: 40

Holdings:

Geographic strengths: Pacific Northwest, Alaska, Canada, Pacific Rim

Special collections: Historical aerial photographs of Whatcom County, Orthophotomaps produced by Washington State DNR, Historical T-sheets of region produced by U.S. Coast and Geodetic Survey

Subject strengths: aerial photos, aeronautical, geospatial data, map catalogs, nautical charts, raised relief models, soil

Map depositories and percentages: USGS topos (100%), USGS geology maps (100%), USGS other (100%), NOAA, GPO, CIA, National Forest Service, NIMA topos, NIMA nautical, NIMA aeronautical, BLM, Canada (topographic maps)

246,800 printed maps

396 wall maps

162 raised relief maps

31,000 aerial photos

124 satellite images

55 globes

313 gazetteers

1,138 printed atlases

438 CD-ROMs

Chronological coverage:

1900–1939: 18%

1940–present: 80%

Average budget over the last 5 years: $1,200

Access:

Collection is open to the public

Answers email questions

Patrons per month: 350

Hours:

Monday: 9 A.M.–4 P.M.

Tuesday: 9 A.M.–1 P.M.

Wednesday: 9 A.M.–4 P.M.

Thursday: 9 A.M.–1 P.M.

Friday: 9 A.M.–4 P.M.

Total hours per week opened: 31

Maps circulate

Circulation policies apply

Map circulation duration: 1 day

Atlas circulation duration: 1 day

Book circulation duration: 1 day

Geographic Information Systems:

GIS services available in an open environment

GIS software: Arcview

Scans maps for patrons

Collection services:

Maps classified: 90%

Datasets are cataloged

Classification schemes: LC, Local

Cataloging utilities: Local

Catalog accessibility: online, cards

Preservation techniques: encapsulation

Items that have gone through the preservation process: 1%

Physical facilities:

Internet access available

Square footage: 4,206

Number of map cases: 225

Number of vertical files (file cabinets): 32

Linear book shelving: 214 ft.

Linear atlas shelving: 436 ft.

Copying facilities available: copier

524 *Bremerton, WA*

Kitsap County Historical Society

280 4th Street

Bremerton, WA 98337

Telephone: 360-479-6226

Fax: 360-415-9294

Email: kchsm@telebyte.net

Web: www.waynes.net/kchsm/

Personnel:

Responsible person: Pamela Kruse-Buckingham, Director, *email:* kchsm@telebyte.net

Assistants: Carolyn McClurkan, Archivist

Number of volunteer hours per month: 12

Holdings:

Geographic strengths: Kitsap County, Washington State

Special collections: Assessor maps, Assessor Photos, Land Title County Section maps for Kitsap County, Land Title County Recorded Land Documents for Kitsap County

Subject strengths: aerial photos, agriculture, archaeology, biology, early cartography, modern cartography, climatology, city, economic geography, engineering, forestry, genealogy, geodetic surveys, geology, historical geography, hydrology, land ownership, land use, mineral resources, mining, nautical charts, political geography, population, projections, railroads, recreation, roads, soil, travel books, vegetation, views, waterways, plat maps

2,000 printed maps

Chronological coverage:

1800–1899: 10%

1900–1939: 35%

1940–present: 50%

Access:

Maps in separate area

Collection is open to the public

Reference questions per year: 77

Answers email questions
Patrons per month: 25
Hours:
Tuesday–Saturday: 9 A.M.–5 P.M.
Total hours per week opened: 40
Geographic Information Systems:
No GIS services available
Scans maps for patrons
Collection services:
Maps cataloged: 75%
Maps classified: 50%
Preservation techniques: encapsulation, lamination, flat acid-free storage
Items that have gone through the preservation process: 100%
Physical facilities:
No Internet access
Copying facilities available: copier

525 *Cheney, WA*

Eastern Washington University

JFK Library
Maps
816 F Street
100 LIB
Cheney, WA 99004
Telephone: 509-359-2263
Fax: 509-359-6456
Web: www.library.ewu.edu/collections/maps.html
Personnel:
Responsible person: Sue Anderson, Acquisitions Librarian, *email:* sanderson@ewu.edu
Assistants: Jonathan Potter, Reference and Instruction Librarian; Karen Schatz, Cataloging Assistant
FTE professionals: 0.025   *FTE para-professionals:* 0.05
Holdings:
Geographic strengths: Washington State, Idaho
Special collections: Sanborn Fire Insurance maps, War Department Railroad Survey maps (1850s), county atlases
Map depositories: USGS topos, Department of Transportation, NOAA, CIA, National Forest Service, NGA nautical, BLM
7,489 printed maps
131 aerial photos
2 globes
175 atlases
65 CD-ROMs
Access:
Hours:
Monday–Thursday: 7:30 A.M.–11 P.M.
Friday: 7:30 A.M.–6 P.M.
Saturday: 10 A.M.–6 P.M.

Sunday: 1 P.M.–11 P.M.
Items circulate
Interlibrary loan available
Collection services:
Maps cataloged: 90%
Maps classified: 100%
Maps in OPAC: 90%
Classification schemes: LC, SuDocs
Physical facilities:
Map cases: 9
Notes: Hours vary when classes are not in session.

526 *Ellensburg, WA*

Central Washington University

James E. Brooks Library
Documents, Maps and Microforms
400 East University Way
Ellensburg, WA 98926-7548
Telephone: 509-963-1541
Fax: 509-963-3684
Email: bachb@cwu.edu
Web: www.lib.cwu.edu/documents/
Personnel:
Responsible person: Thomas Yeh, Professor and Head, *email:* yeht@cwu.edu
Assistants: Brian P. Bach, Map Specialist
FTE professionals: 0.5   *FTE para-professionals:* 0.75
Holdings:
Geographic strengths: Kittitas County, Central Washington State, Washington State
Special collections: Sanborn Fire Insurance maps (microfilm), Northwestern states, Civil War atlas, early USGS folios
Map depositories: USGS topos, Department of Transportation, NOAA, CIA, National Forest Service, NGA nautical, NGA aeronautical, BLM
88,383 printed maps
4,500 aerial photos
4 globes
95 atlases
400 books
3 active serials
20 CD-ROMs
Access:
Hours:
Monday–Thursday: 8 A.M.–10 P.M.
Friday: 8 A.M.–9 P.M.
Saturday: noon–9 P.M.
Sunday: 1 P.M.–10 P.M.
Items circulate
Interlibrary loan available
Collection services:
Maps cataloged: 15%

Maps classified: 95%
Maps in OPAC: 15%
Classification schemes: LC, SuDocs, Local, Other (microfilm accession number)
Physical facilities:
Maps in separate area
Public computers: 2
Map cases: 21
Vertical files: 8

527 *Fox Island, WA*

Fox Island Historical Society

Map Room, founded 1970
1017 9th Avenue
Fox Island, WA 98333
Telephone: 253-549-2461
Email: museum@foxisland.net
Web: foxisland.net
Personnel:
Responsible person: Hannah Jay, *email:* museum@foxisland.net
Number of volunteer hours per month: 10
Holdings:
Geographic strengths: Fox Island
Subject strengths: aerial photos, aeronautical, early cartography, modern cartography, city, engineering, land ownership, land use, raised relief models, recreation, roads
100 printed maps
Chronological coverage:
1800–1899: 20%
1900–1939: 70%
1940–present: 10%
Access:
Maps in separate area
Collection is partially open to the public
Answers email questions
Patrons per month: 50
Geographic Information Systems:
No GIS services available
Collection services:
Maps cataloged: 25%
Classification schemes: Local
Cataloging utilities: Local
Catalog accessibility: local database
Preservation techniques: deacidification, cartex, lamination
Items that have gone through the preservation process: 30%
Physical facilities:
No Internet access
Square footage: 80
Linear book shelving: 50 ft.
Linear atlas shelving: 50 ft.
Copying facilities available: copier

528 *Olympia, WA*

Evergreen State College

Daniel J. Evans Library
Government Documents/Maps
2700 Evergreen Parkway NW
Mailstop L-2300
Olympia, WA 98505
Telephone: 360-867-6251
Fax: 360-866-6790
Email: govdocs@evergreen.edu
Web: www.evergreen.edu/library/govdocs/index.html
Personnel:
Responsible person: Carlos A. Diaz, Government Documents Specialist, *email:* diazc@evergreen.edu
FTE para-professionals: 1
Holdings:
Geographic strengths: Washington State, Alaska, California, Montana, Idaho, Oregon, Pacific Northwest, British Columbia
Special collections: 19th century annual reports of the USGS topos, USDA, soil surveys, the Bureau of American Ethnology
Map depositories: USGS topos, Department of Transportation, NOAA, CIA, National Forest Service, NGA nautical, NGA aeronautical, BLM
30,000 printed maps
3 globes
Access:
Hours:
Monday–Thursday: 8:30 A.M.–10:45 P.M.
Friday: 8:30 A.M.–6:45 P.M.
Saturday: 10:30 A.M.–6:15 P.M.
Sunday: noon–10:45 P.M.
Items circulate
Interlibrary loan available
Collection services:
Maps cataloged: 95%
Maps classified: 100%
Maps in OPAC: 95%
Classification schemes: LC, SuDocs
Physical facilities:
Maps in separate area
Public computers: 3
Map cases: 14
Vertical files: 11

529 *Olympia, WA*

Washington State Department of Ecology

P.O. Box 47600
Olympia, WA 98504-7600
Telephone: 360-407-6000
Web: www.ecy.wa.gov/services/gis/maps/maps.htm
Personnel:

Responsible person: Mike Woodall, *email:* miwo461@ecy.wa.gov

Holdings:

Geographic strengths: Washington State

Subject strengths: aerial photos, biology, climatology, city, economic geography, forestry, geospatial data, hydrology, industries, land ownership, land use, political geography, population, railroads, raised relief models, recreation, roads, vegetation, waterways, latitude/longitude, township/range/section

1,000 printed maps

Collecting digital data

Chronological coverage:

1940–present: 100%

Access:

Answers email questions

Notes: This is a GIS web-based map collection of pdf-formatted theme maps and GIS web browser applications.

530 *Olympia, WA*

Washington State Department of Natural Resources

Public Land Survey Office
P.O. Box 47060
Olympia, WA 98504-7060
Telephone: 360-902-1190
Fax: 360-902-1191
Email: janet.phillips@wadnr.gov
Web: www.dnr.wa.gov/htdocs/plso/

Personnel:

Responsible person: Gwen Roy, PLS, *email:* gwen.roy@wadnr.gov

Assistants: Ted Smith, LSIT; Janet Charles-Foutch, Engineering Aide Research Specialist; Mary Zuris, Engineering Aide; Doug Popwell, Engineering Aide; Bob Danielson, Engineering Aide; Beth Watkins, Scanner Operator

Holdings:

Geographic strengths: Washington State

Special collections: Records of the following surveyors/companies: Jesse Allen, Charles McKay Anderson, Al Bell, Black Diamond Historical Museum, D. Bosworth, Phillip Botch, Henry Brooks, Grant Chandler, Malcolm Edwards, Jack Eller, Ruskin Fisher, Henry Gile, M.E. Halvorsen, J.L. Henderson, Edward Hobson, Gary Holmvig, Blaine McGillicudy, Robert McKiddy, Gilbert McMaster, James McPherson, John Meehan, L.A. Nicholson, Ken Oyler, Robert Powell, George Raper, T.A. Rixon, George Robertson, Mason County Logging Company, Mayr Brothers Logging Company, Murray and McCormick, Newell Gossett and Walsh, Palmer Coking Coal Company, Pope and Talbot indexes, Scott Paper Company, Roy Storey, Whitacre Engineering, Milwaukee Railroad R/W plats, Milwaukee Railroad

fieldbooks, R/W plats for all active and some inactive railroads in Washington State, Everett and Monte Cristo Railroad, U.S. Navy railroad—Shelton to Bangor, SP&S Railroad in Klickitat County

Subject strengths: geodetic surveys

400,000 printed maps

Chronological coverage:

1900–1939: 10%

1940–present: 85%

Access:

Maps in separate area

Collection is open to the public

Reference questions per year: 10,000

Answers email questions

Patrons per month: 100

Hours:

Monday–Friday: 8 A.M.–4:30 P.M.

Total hours per week opened: 40

Geographic Information Systems:

No GIS services available

Scans maps for patrons

Collection services:

Maps cataloged: 50%

Maps in OPAC: 100%

Datasets are cataloged

Classification schemes: Other (Public Land Survey System)

Catalog accessibility: online, fiche, cards, printout

Physical facilities:

Internet access available

Square footage: 2,300

Number of vertical files (file cabinets): 20

Other map storage: aperture card cabinets

Copying facilities available: copier, color copier, large-format copier, microform copier, large-format scanner

531 *Olympia, WA*

Washington State Department of Natural Resources, Division of Geology and Earth Resources

Washington Geology Library
1111 Washington Street SE
MS 47007
Room 173
Olympia, WA 98504-7007
Telephone: 360-902-1473
Fax: 360-902-1785
Email: lee.walkling@wadnr.gov
Web: www.dnr.wa.gov/geology/mapindex.htm

Personnel:

Responsible person: Lee Walkling, Librarian, *email:* lee.walkling@wadnr.gov

Holdings:

Geographic strengths: Washington State

Subject strengths: early cartography, modern cartography, caves, city, geology, mineral resources, mining, soil

Map depositories and percentages: USGS topos (95%), USGS geology maps (95%), National Forest Service

2,000 printed maps

10 gazetteers

10 printed atlases

Chronological coverage:
1940–present: 92%

Average budget over the last 5 years: $1,000

On-going publications: http://www.dnr.wa.gov/geology

Access:

Collection is open to the public

Reference questions per year: 2,000

Answers email questions

Hours:

Total hours per week opened: 30

Geographic Information Systems:

No GIS services available

Scans maps for patrons

Collection services:

Maps cataloged: 50%

Maps classified: 50%

Maps in OPAC: 50%

Catalog accessibility: online

Physical facilities:

No Internet access

Square footage: 300

Linear book shelving: 2,000 ft.

Copying facilities available: copier, large-format copier

Notes: We are open to the public. Our material does not circulate. We only collect material on Washington geology. We are not a branch of the Washington State Library.

532 *Olympia, WA*

Washington State Library

P.O. Box 42460

Olympia, WA 98504-2460

Telephone: 866-538-4996

Fax: 360-586-7575

Web: www.secstate.wa.gov/library/

Personnel:

Responsible person: Diane Hutchins, *email:* dhutchins@secstate.wa.gov

Assistants: Carol Estep, Library Information Associate; Ingrid Morley, Library Information Assistant

FTE para-professionals: 0.5

Holdings:

Geographic strengths: Washington State, Alaska

Special collections: Sanborn Fire Insurance maps, Washington Survey Field Notes, General Land Office Plats for Washington State, historic maps of Washington Territory/State

Map depositories: USGS topos, NOAA, National Forest Service, NGA nautical, BLM

22,400 printed maps

2 globes

158 atlases

Access:

Hours:

Monday–Friday: 8 A.M.–5 P.M.

Items circulate

Interlibrary loan available

Collection services:

Maps cataloged: 50%

Maps in OPAC: 50%

Classification schemes: SuDocs, Dewey, Local

Physical facilities:

Maps in separate area

Public computers: 6

Map cases: 4

Notes: Washington State Library houses all federal maps for Washington and Alaska, plus all NOAA and US Forest Service maps. We send to Evergreen State College all other BLM and USGS maps, plus all CIA maps. We send to the University of Washington all Department of Transportation maps, all NIMA aeronautical , and all other NIMA nautical charts.

533 *Port Townsend, WA*

Jefferson County Historical Society

Research Center

Map Collection

13692 Airport Cutoff Road (Hwy 19)

Port Townsend, WA 98368

Telephone: 360-379-6673

Email: jchsresearch@olypen.com

Web: www.jchsmuseum.org

Personnel:

Responsible person: Victoria A. Davis, *email:* jchsresearch@olypen.com

Number of volunteers: 20

Number of volunteer hours per month: 200

Holdings:

Geographic strengths: Jefferson County, Washington State

Special collections: Sanborn Fire Insurance maps of Port Townsend Washington

Subject strengths: aerial photos, city, land ownership, nautical charts

474 printed maps

Chronological coverage:
1800–1899: 25%
1900–1939: 20%
1940–present: 50%

Access:

Collection is open to the public

Answers email questions
Patrons per month: 162
Hours:
　　Total hours per week opened: 25
Geographic Information Systems:
No GIS services available
Collection services:
Maps cataloged: 100%
Cataloging utilities: Past Perfect
Catalog accessibility: online, printout
Preservation techniques: encapsulation
Physical facilities:
Internet access available
Copying facilities available: copier, microform copier
Notes: Map collection is part of entire collection and not treated separately.

534 *Pullman, WA*

Washington State University

Owen Science and Engineering Library
P.O. Box 643200
Pullman, WA 99164
Telephone: 509-335-2674
Fax: 509-335-2534
Email: owenref@wsu.edu
Web: www.wsulibs.wsu.edu/science/owen.htm
Personnel:
Responsible person: Rosemary Streatfeild, Science Librarian and Maps Coordinator, *email:* streatfe@wsu.edu
FTE professionals: 0.2　*FTE para-professionals:* 0.05
Holdings:
Geographic strengths: Washington State, Idaho, Oregon, Alaska
Map depositories: USGS topos, National Forest Service
16,000 printed maps
5 globes
200 atlases
Access:
Hours:
　　Monday–Friday: 7:45 A.M.–10:45 P.M.
　　Saturday: noon–5:45 P.M.
　　Sunday: 9 A.M.–10:45 P.M.
Items circulate
Collection services:
Maps cataloged: 65%
Maps in OPAC: 90%
Classification schemes: LC, SuDocs
Physical facilities:
Maps in separate area
Public computers: 1
Map cases: 22
Vertical files: 14

535 *Seattle, WA*

National Oceanic and Atmospheric Administration

NOAA Seattle Library
7600 Sand Point Way NE
Seattle, WA 98115
Telephone: 206-526-6241
Fax: 206-526-4535
Email: seattle.library@noaa.gov
Web: www.wrclib.noaa.gov
Personnel:
FTE professionals: 1
Holdings:
Geographic strengths: West Coast, Pacific Rim
Special collections: Historic U.S. Coast and Geodetic Survey Hydrographic Surveys of U.S. West Coast
Map depositories: Department of Transportation, NOAA
1,000 printed maps
4 globes
250 atlases
100 CD-ROMs
Access:
Hours:
　　Monday–Friday: 8:30 A.M.–4:30 P.M.
Collection services:
Maps cataloged: 80%
Maps in OPAC: 80%
Classification schemes: LC, Local
Physical facilities:
Public computers: 3
Map cases: 36
Vertical files: 4

536 *Seattle, WA*

Seattle Public Library

History/Travel, Maps Department and the Seattle Collection
1000 4th Avenue
Seattle, WA 98104
Telephone: 206-386-4636
Fax: 206-386-4632
Email: htm@spl.org
Web: www.spl.org
Personnel:
Responsible person: Mary H. Douglass, *email:* mary.douglass@spl.org
FTE professionals: 0.5　*FTE para-professionals:* 0.25
Holdings:
Geographic strengths: Seattle, King County, Washington State
Special collections: local history, Seattle/King County street and regional maps, Kroll real estate atlases, Sanborn Fire Insurance maps

Map depositories: USGS topos, NOAA, CIA, National Forest Service

35,000 printed maps

1 globe

500 atlases

250 books

2 active serials

50 CD-ROMs

Access:

Hours:

Monday–Wednesday: 10 A.M.–8 P.M.

Thursday–Saturday: 10 A.M.–6 P.M.

Sunday: 1 P.M.–5 P.M.

Items circulate

Interlibrary loan available

Collection services:

Maps cataloged: 10%

Maps classified: 85%

Maps in OPAC: 5%

Classification schemes: SuDocs, Dewey, Local

Physical facilities:

Public computers: 1

Map cases: 25

Vertical files: 6

537 *Seattle, WA*

University of Washington

Suzzallo/Allen Library

Map Collection and Cartographic Information Services, founded 1970

Box 352900

Seattle, WA 98195

Telephone: 206-543-9392

Fax: 206-685-8049

Email: maplib@u.washington.edu

Web: www.lib.washington.edu/maps

Personnel:

Responsible person: Anne Zald, Head, *email:* zald@u.washington.edu

Assistants: Matthew Parsons, Map Librarian

FTE para-professionals: 0.5

Number of student workers hours per week: 45

Number of volunteer hours per month: 25

Holdings:

Geographic strengths: Washington State

Special collections: Sanborn Fire Insurance maps

Subject strengths: aerial photos, geology, geospatial data

Map depositories and percentages: USGS topos (100%), USGS geology maps (100%), USGS other (100%), Department of Transportation, NOAA, GPO, CIA, National Forest Service, NIMA topos, NIMA nautical, NIMA aeronautical, BLM

267,059 printed maps

32 raised relief maps

5,602 microfiche

320 microfilms

80,827 aerial photos

83 satellite images

439 gazetteers

3,888 printed atlases

210 books

1,283 CD-ROMs

Collecting digital data

Chronological coverage:

1900–1939: 10%

1940–present: 89%

Average budget over the last 5 years: $33,000

Access:

Maps in separate area

Collection is partially open to the public

Reference questions per year: 5,224

Answers email questions

Hours:

Monday–Thursday: 9 A.M.–8 P.M.

Friday: 9 A.M.–5 P.M.

Saturday: 1 P.M.–5 P.M.

Sunday: closed

Total hours per week opened: 56

Maps circulate

Circulation policies apply

Map circulation duration: 4 weeks

Atlas circulation duration: 4 weeks

Book circulation duration: 4 weeks

Number of maps circulated annually: 18,748

Number of books circulated annually: 749

Number of other items circulated annually: 11,017

Interlibrary loan available

Geographic Information Systems:

GIS services available in an open environment

GIS software: ArcGIS, ArcView, ArcInfo

GIS assistance available for Census mapping

Data discovery and retrieval assistance available

Collection services:

Maps cataloged: 80%

Maps classified: 100%

Maps in OPAC: 80%

Datasets are cataloged

Classification schemes: LC

Cataloging utilities: OCLC

Catalog accessibility: online

Preservation techniques: encapsulation

Items that have gone through the preservation process: 5%

Physical facilities:

Internet access available

Square footage: 6,000

Number of map cases: 214
Number of vertical files (file cabinets): 40
Linear book shelving: 441 ft.
Linear atlas shelving: 1,104 ft.
Other map storage: atlas shelving used for storage of sheet map sets (2,340 linear feet), 3 media cabinets for CDs/diskettes
Copying facilities available: copier, microform copier, 11"-×-17" copies (b&w) can be made using copier in map collection; 8.5"-×-14" flat-bed scanner available in map collection

538 *Seattle, WA*

University of Washington

Suzzallo/Allen Library
Special Collections
Box 352900
Seattle, WA 98195
Telephone: 206-543-1929
Fax: 206-543-1931
Email: speccoll@u.washington.edu
Web: www.lib.washington.edu/specialcoll

Personnel:
Responsible person: Carla Rickerson, Head, *email:* crick@u.washington.edu
Assistants: Kristen Kinsey, Photo and Graphics Specialist
Number of student workers hours per week: 35

Holdings:
Geographic strengths: Seattle, Washington, Oregon, Alaska, Pacific Northwest
Special collections: Sanborn Fire Insurance maps for Seattle, Plat atlases for Seattle, published maps of the Ancient World, early printed maps (13th–18th centuries), Explorer's atlases, with concentration in Pacific Northwest maritime and overland exploration
Subject strengths: early cartography, city, forestry, historical geography, land ownership, land use, railroads, roads, travel books, views, waterways, growth and environmental change in Washington state in the 19th century
4,660 printed maps
85 manuscript maps
15 wall maps
358 aerial photos
45 gazetteers
494 printed atlases
30 manuscript atlases
Chronological coverage:
Pre-1800: 20%
1800–1899: 55%
1900–1939: 20%

1940–present: 5%
Average budget over the last 5 years: $1,000

Access:
Collection is paged
Answers email questions
Patrons per month: 515

Hours:
Monday–Tuesday: 10 A.M.–5 P.M.
Wednesday: 10 A.M.–8 P.M.
Thursday–Friday: 10 A.M.–5 P.M.
Saturday: 1 P.M.–5 P.M.
Sunday: closed
Total hours per week opened: 35

Geographic Information Systems:
No GIS services available

Collection services:
Maps cataloged: 60%
Maps classified: 100%
Maps in OPAC: 60%
Classification schemes: LC, Dewey
Cataloging utilities: OCLC
Catalog accessibility: online
Preservation techniques: encapsulation, deacidification, paper repair, digitization, photocopying
Items that have gone through the preservation process: 95%

Physical facilities:
Internet access available
Square footage: 198
Number of map cases: 23
Linear atlas shelving: 301 ft.
Other map storage: framed maps (5 linear feet)
Copying facilities available: copier, microform copier

Notes: In addition to the Sanborn Fire Insurance Maps for Seattle, there is microfilm of the Sanborn Fire Insurance Maps (complete set) housed in the microforms/newspapers division of the Suzzallo/Allen Library. Those microfilms are not accounted for in this submission, although they are available to library users.

539 *Tacoma, WA*

University of Puget Sound

Collins Memorial Library
1500 North Warner
Tacoma, WA 98416-1012
Telephone: 253-879-3669
Fax: 253-879-3670
Email: libref@ups.edu
Web: library.ups.edu/research/govt/about.htm

Personnel:
Responsible person: Lori Ricigliano, Associate Director, *email:* ricigliano@ups.edu

Assistants: Marlene West, Documents Specialist
FTE professionals: 1   *FTE para-professionals:* 1
Holdings:
  Geographic strengths: Pacific Northwest, California, Colorado, Arizona, Utah, New Mexico
  Map depositories: USGS topos, CIA
  6,000 printed maps
  152 atlases
  905 books
  36 CD-ROMs
Access:
  Hours:
    Monday–Thursday: 7:45 P.M.–2 A.M.
    Friday: 7:45 A.M.–6 P.M.
    Saturday: 9 A.M.–9 P.M.
    Sunday: 9 A.M.–2 A.M.
  Items circulate
  Interlibrary loan available
Collection services:
  Maps cataloged: 60%
  Maps classified: 20%
  Maps in OPAC: 60%
  Classification schemes: LC, SuDocs, Other (subject)
Physical facilities:
  Public computers: 7
  Map cases: 123
  Vertical files: 1

540 *Walla Walla, WA*

Whitman College

Penrose Library
345 Boyer Ave
Walla Walla, WA 99362
Telephone: 509-527-5191
Fax: 509-526-4785
Web: www.whitman.edu/penrose/departments.html
Personnel:
  Responsible person: Joe Drazan
Holdings:
  Geographic strengths: Pacific Northwest
  Map depositories and percentages: USGS topos, USGS geology maps
  15,000 printed maps
Access:
  Collection is open to the public
  Maps off site; *Percentage offsite:* 10%
Collection services:
  Cataloging utilities: OCLC
Physical facilities:
  Copying facilities available: microform copier
Notes: Perhaps 90% of the maps we have are USGS Topos, and Geologicals (MF, GQ, I, etc). Up-to-date holdings are listed under "Special Collections" on the library's webpage

541 *Morgantown, WV*

West Virginia University

Downtown Campus Library
Map Room
P.O. Box 6069
Morgantown, WV 26506
Telephone: 304-293-4040 x4039
Fax: 304-293-6923
Web: www.libraries.wvu.edu/downtown/maps.htm
Personnel:
  Responsible person: email: cchang@wvu.edu
  Assistants: Rhett Bailey, Library Technical Assistant
  FTE para-professionals: 1
Holdings:
  Geographic strengths: United States
  Special collections: USGS topographic maps
  Map depositories: USGS topos, Department of Transportation, NOAA, CIA, National Forest Service, NGA nautical, NGA aeronautical, BLM
  78,100 printed maps
Access:
  Hours:
    Monday–Friday: 9 A.M.–5:30 P.M.
  Items circulate
  Interlibrary loan available
Collection services:
  Maps classified: 100%
  Classification schemes: SuDocs
Physical facilities:
  Maps in separate area
  Public computers: 2
  Map cases: 54
  Vertical files: 18

542 *Beloit, WI*

Beloit College

Col. Robert Morse Library
731 College Street
Beloit, WI 53511
Telephone: 608-363-2230
Fax: 608-363-2487
Web: www.beloit.edu/~libhome
Personnel:
  Responsible person: email: thostens@beloit.edu
  FTE professionals: 0.1   *FTE para-professionals:* 0.2
Holdings:
  Geographic strengths: United States
  Map depositories and percentages: USGS topos (80%), USGS geology maps (80%), USGS other, GPO, CIA, BLM, State
  74,500 printed maps
  114 printed atlases

50 books
Chronological coverage:
1940–present: 100%
Access:
Collection is open to the public
Reference questions per year: 10
Answers email questions
Hours:
Total hours per week opened: 97
Maps circulate
Circulation policies apply
Map circulation duration: 4 weeks
Book circulation duration: 4 weeks
Number of maps circulated annually: 202
Geographic Information Systems:
No GIS services available
Collection services:
Maps cataloged: 10%
Maps classified: 100%
Maps in OPAC: 10%
Datasets are cataloged
Classification schemes: SuDocs, Dewey, Local
Cataloging utilities: OCLC
Catalog accessibility: online, cards
Physical facilities:
No Internet access
Square footage: 900
Number of map cases: 74
Number of vertical files (file cabinets): 14
Linear atlas shelving: 87 ft.
Copying facilities available: copier, microform copier
Notes: Our map collection is generally integrated into our entire collection, so some of the statistics (books) are not broken out. We do not have equipment (work stations, PCs, Microform readers/printer) specifically designated for use with the map collection.

543 *Eau Claire, WI*

University of Wisconsin, Eau Claire

William D. McIntyre Library
Depository Library Map Collection
Park and Garfield Streets
Eau Claire, WI 54702-4004
Telephone: 715-836-3859
Fax: 715-836-2906
Email: library.reference@uwec.edu
Web: www.uwec.edu/Library/gp/govpub2.html#MAP
Personnel:
Responsible person: Leslie Foster, Head of Government Publications, *email:* fosterla@uwec.edu
FTE professionals: 0.1 *FTE para-professionals:* 0.1
Holdings:
Geographic strengths: United States, Canada

Special collections: Canadian topographical maps
Map depositories and percentages: USGS topos (100%), GPO, CIA, National Forest Service, BLM, State
100,000 printed maps
50 CD-ROMs
Chronological coverage:
1940–present: 100%
Access:
Maps in separate area
Collection is open to the public
Reference questions per year: 60
Patrons per month: 10
Hours:
Total hours per week opened: 108
Maps circulate
Circulation policies apply
Map circulation duration: 4 weeks
Number of maps circulated annually: 100
Interlibrary loan available
Geographic Information Systems:
No GIS services available
Collection services:
Maps cataloged: 35%
Maps classified: 35%
Maps in OPAC: 35%
Classification schemes: SuDocs
Cataloging utilities: OCLC
Catalog accessibility: online
Preservation techniques: lamination
Items that have gone through the preservation process: 1%
Physical facilities:
No Internet access
Number of map cases: 70
Copying facilities available: copier, microform copier
Notes: Maps are available on a self-service basis and may be checked out whenever the library is open.

544 *Green Bay, WI*

University of Wisconsin, Green Bay

Cofrin Library
Founded 1936
2420 Nicolet Drive
Green Bay, WI 54311-7001
Telephone: 920-465-2303
Fax: 920-465-2388
Email: refdesk@uwgb.edu
Web: www.uwgb.edu/library/
Personnel:
Responsible person: Joan M. Robb, *email:* robbj@uwgb.edu
Assistants: Anne Kasuboski, Reference Coordinator; Debra Strelka, Coordinator of Library Processing

FTE professionals: 0.02 *FTE para-professionals:* 0.0125

Number of student workers hours per week: 0.5

Holdings:

Geographic strengths: Wisconsin

Special collections: Sanborn Fire Insurance maps

Subject strengths: political geography

Map depositories and percentages: USGS topos (27%), USGS geology maps (25%), USGS other (48%), Department of Transportation, NOAA, GPO, CIA, National Forest Service, NIMA topos, NIMA nautical, NIMA aeronautical, BLM, State, United Nations

57,550 printed maps

10 microfiche

20 satellite images

49 gazetteers

257 printed atlases

Chronological coverage:

Pre-1800: 0.5%

1800–1899: 10%

1900–1939: 20%

1940–present: 69.5%

Average budget over the last 5 years: $700

Access:

Collection is open to the public

Reference questions per year: 50

Answers email questions

Hours:

Monday–Thursday: 8 A.M.–11 P.M.

Friday: 8 A.M.–5:30 P.M.

Saturday: 10 A.M.–6 P.M.

Sunday: 1 P.M.–11 P.M.

Total hours per week opened: 87.5

Geographic Information Systems:

No GIS services available

Collection services:

Maps cataloged: 90%

Maps classified: 90%

Maps in OPAC: 80%

Classification schemes: LC, SuDocs

Cataloging utilities: OCLC

Catalog accessibility: online, cards

Physical facilities:

Internet access available

Square footage: 500

Number of map cases: 38

Linear atlas shelving: 202 ft.

Copying facilities available: copier, large-format copier, microform copier, scanner, microcard printer

545 *La Crosse, WI*

La Crosse Public Library

800 Main Street

La Crosse, WI 54601

Telephone: 608-789-7122

Fax: 608-789-7161

Email: refdesk@lacrosse.lib.wi.us

Web: www.lacrosselibrary.org

Personnel:

Responsible person: Darcy Johnson Skinna, Associate Reference Librarian and Anita Taylor Doering, Archivist, *email:* d.skibba@lacrosse.lib.wi.us and a.doering@lacrosse.lib.wi.us

Number of student workers hours per week: 1

Holdings:

Geographic strengths: La Crosse County, Wisconsin, Minnesota

Special collections: Sanborn Fire Insurance maps of La Crosse and Onalaska, bird's-eye views of La Crosse, Wisconsin

Subject strengths: city, genealogy, land ownership, political geography, railroads, recreation, roads, soil, views

Map depositories: USGS topos, GPO, CIA, National Forest Service, State

1,500 printed maps

20 microfilms

20 aerial photos

44 gazetteers

253 printed atlases

Chronological coverage:

1800–1899: 30%

1900–1939: 40%

1940–present: 100%

Average budget over the last 5 years: $150

Access:

Maps in separate area

Collection is paged

Answers email questions

Hours:

Monday–Friday: 9 A.M.–9 P.M.

Saturday: 9 A.M.–5 P.M.

Sunday: 1 P.M.–5 P.M.

Total hours per week opened: 68

Maps circulate

Circulation policies apply

Map circulation duration: 1 week

Atlas circulation duration: 3 weeks

Book circulation duration: 3 weeks

Geographic Information Systems:

GIS services available in an open environment

GIS software: Terrain Navigator

Number of public GIS workstations: 30

Collection services:

Maps cataloged: 80%

Maps classified: 100%

Maps in OPAC: 100%

Datasets are cataloged

Classification schemes: LC, SuDocs, Dewey, Local

Cataloging utilities: OCLC, Marcive

Catalog accessibility: online

Preservation techniques: encapsulation, deacidification, lamination

Physical facilities:

Internet access available

Square footage: 50

Number of microform readers: 12

Copying facilities available: copier, color copier, microform copier

Notes: We have two maps collections—one maintain in the archives room that stays in the room and another collection in the Reference Area which some can be checked-out and housed differently.

546 *La Crosse, WI*

University of Wisconsin, La Crosse

Murphy Library

1631 Pine Street

La Crosse, WI 54601

Telephone: 608-785-8505

Fax: 608-785-8639

Web: www.uwlax.edu/murphylibrary/

Personnel:

Responsible person: Michael Current, Government Information Public Services Librarian, *email:* current .mich@uwlax.edu

Assistants: Mary Baldwin, Library Services Assistant Senior

Holdings:

Geographic strengths: Wisconsin

Map depositories and percentages: GPO

4,800 printed maps

100 microfiche

55 printed atlases

12 CD-ROMs

Access:

Collection is open to the public

Hours:

Monday–Friday: 7:40 A.M.–midnight

Saturday: 11 A.M.–6 P.M.

Sunday: noon–midnight

Total hours per week opened: 92

Maps circulate

Circulation policies apply

Map circulation duration: 30 days

Book circulation duration: 30 days

Interlibrary loan available

Geographic Information Systems:

GIS services available in an open environment

GIS software: ArcExplorer, ArcView, Census Mapper, Landview IV

Number of public GIS workstations: 50

GIS assistance available for Census mapping

Collection services:

Maps cataloged: 40%

Maps classified: 40%

Maps in OPAC: 40%

Classification schemes: LC, SuDocs

Cataloging utilities: OCLC

Catalog accessibility: online

Physical facilities:

Internet access available

Number of public computers: 50

Number of staff computers: 50

Number of microform readers: 10

Copying facilities available: copier, microform copier

Notes: Most of UW-L's maps are in the Geography Department rather than Murphy Library. These were not taken into account. Most maps in Murphy Library are currently folded and shelved in government documents stacks. A majority of our maps are not cataloged.

547 *Madison, WI*

University of Wisconsin, Madison

Arthur H. Robinson Map Library

Founded 1967

550 North Park Street

Madison, WI 53706

Telephone: 608-262-1471

Email: maplib@geography.wisc.edu

Web: www.geography.wiscedu/maplib/

Personnel:

Responsible person: Jaime Martindale, Map/GIS Librarian, *email:* martindale@wisc.edu

Number of student workers hours per week: 20

Number of volunteer hours per month: 16

Holdings:

Geographic strengths: Madison, Dane County, Madison, Wisconsin, United States

Special collections: Approximately 250,000 photos, Wisconsin Historic Aerial Photography

Subject strengths: aerial photos, aeronautical, agriculture, archaeology, biology, early cartography, modern cartography, caves, celestial, climatology, city, economic geography, engineering, forestry, genealogy, geodetic surveys, geology, geospatial data, historical geography, hydrology, industries, land ownership, land use, language, map catalogs, military, mineral resources, mining, nautical charts, oceanography, political geography, population, projections, railroads, raised relief models, recreation, religion, roads, satellite imagery, soil, travel books, vegetation, views, waterways

Map depositories and percentages: USGS topos (100%), USGS geology maps (100%), USGS other (100%), Department of Transportation, NOAA, GPO, CIA, National Forest Service, NIMA topos, NIMA nautical, NIMA aeronautical, BLM, State, United Nations

280,000 printed maps

400 wall maps

50 raised relief maps
5,000 microfiche
500 microfilms
250,000 aerial photos
5,000 satellite images
15 globes
150 gazetteers
50 printed atlases
500 books
700 CD-ROMs
35 computer programs
Collecting digital data
Chronological coverage:
   1800–1899: 10%
   1900–1939: 20%
   1940–present: 70%
Average budget over the last 5 years: $5,000
Access:
Collection is open to the public
Maps off site
Reference questions per year: 600
Answers email questions
Patrons per month: 60
Hours:
Total hours per week opened: 20
Maps circulate
Circulation policies apply
Map circulation duration: 2 weeks
Book circulation duration: 4 weeks
Number of maps circulated annually: 5,000
Number of books circulated annually: 2,000
Number of other items circulated annually: 9,000 (aerial photos)
Interlibrary loan available
Geographic Information Systems:
GIS services available by appointment
GIS assistance available for Census mapping, geocoding, and image analysis
Scans maps for patrons
Collection services:
Maps cataloged: 90%
Maps classified: 65%
Maps in OPAC: 50%
Datasets are cataloged
Classification schemes: LC, SuDocs, Local
Cataloging utilities: OCLC
Catalog accessibility: online, cards
Preservation techniques: encapsulation, deacidification, cartex, lamination, edging
Items that have gone through the preservation process: 10%
Physical facilities:
Internet access available
Number of map cases: 120
Number of vertical map cases: 30

Number of vertical files (file cabinets): 55
Linear book shelving: 15 ft.
Copying facilities available: copier, large-format copier, microform copier

548 *Madison, WI*

University of Wisconsin, Madison

Geology and Geophysics Library
Founded 1974
1215 West Dayton Street
Madison, WI 53706-1692
Telephone: 608-262-8956
Fax: 608-262-0693
Email: geolib@library.wisc.edu
Web: www.geology.wisc.edu/library/
Personnel:
Responsible person: Marie Dvorzak, *email:* mdvorzak@library.wisc.edu
Holdings:
Geographic strengths: United States
Subject strengths: geology, hydrology, mineral resources
2,888 printed maps
185 printed atlases
Chronological coverage:
   1940–present: 95%
Access:
Collection is open to the public
Answers email questions
Hours:
   Monday–Friday: 8:30 A.M.–9 P.M.
   Saturday: 10 A.M.–4 P.M.
   Sunday: 1 P.M.–5 P.M.
   Total hours per week opened: 68.5
Maps circulate
Circulation policies apply
   Map circulation duration: 4 weeks
   Atlas circulation duration: 4 weeks
   Book circulation duration: 4 weeks
   Number of maps circulated annually: 200
Interlibrary loan available
Geographic Information Systems:
No GIS services available
Collection services:
Maps cataloged: 100%
Maps classified: 100%
Maps in OPAC: 100%
Classification schemes: LC
Cataloging utilities: OCLC
Catalog accessibility: online
Physical facilities:
No Internet access
Copying facilities available: copier, microform copier

549 *Madison, WI*

Wisconsin Historical Society

Library/Archives Division
Map Collection
816 State Street
Madison, WI 53706
Telephone: 608-264-6458
Fax: 608-264-6472
Email: gestrey@whs.wisc.edu
Web: www.wisconsinhistory.org/archives/maps/access
.html

Personnel:

Responsible person: Geraldine Strey, *email:* gestrey@
whs.wisc.edu
FTE professionals: 0.5

Holdings:

Geographic strengths: Midwest, United States, North
America
Special collections: Sanborn Fire Insurance maps, Wisconsin bird's-eye views, Wisconsin Land ownership
maps and atlases
Subject strengths: archaeology, early cartography,
modern cartography, city, genealogy, historical geography, land ownership, land use, map collecting,
railroads, recreation, roads, vegetation, views, waterways, Sanborn Insurance Company maps for
Wisconsin
15,000 printed maps
500 manuscript maps
25 wall maps
50 gazetteers
1,500 printed atlases
250 books
Chronological coverage:
Pre-1800: 10%
1800–1899: 70%
1900–1939: 10%
1940–present: 10%
Average budget over the last 5 years: $750

Access:

Maps in separate area
Collection is paged
Reference questions per year: 250
Answers email questions
Patrons per month: 125
Hours:
Monday–Friday: 8 A.M.–5 P.M.
Saturday: 9 A.M.–4 P.M.
Total hours per week opened: 47

Geographic Information Systems:
No GIS services available
Scans maps for patrons

Collection services:
Maps cataloged: 10%

Maps classified: 100%
Classification schemes: LC, Local
Cataloging utilities: OCLC
Catalog accessibility: online, cards
Preservation techniques: encapsulation, deacidification

Physical facilities:
Square footage: 700
Number of map cases: 90
Linear book shelving: 36 ft.
Linear atlas shelving: 500 ft.
Copying facilities available: copier, microform

550 *Milwaukee, WI*

Milwaukee Public Library

814 West Wisconsin Avenue
Milwaukee, WI 53233
Telephone: 414-286-3000
Fax: 414-286-2137
Web: www.mpl.org

Personnel:

Responsible person: Carolyn Colwell, *email:* ccolwe@
mpl.org

Holdings:

Geographic strengths: Milwaukee, Wisconsin, Great
Lakes
Special collections: Fire Insurance Atlases for Milwaukee (1876–1962), Great Lakes nautical charts, Milwaukee Road Railroad maps
Subject strengths: aerial photos, city, genealogy, land
ownership, nautical charts, railroads, recreation,
roads, soil, views
Map depositories and percentages: USGS topos
(100%), Department of Transportation, NOAA,
GPO, CIA, National Forest Service, NIMA nautical,
NIMA aeronautical, BLM, State
30,000 printed maps
2,000 printed atlases
Chronological coverage:
1900–1939: 45%
1940–present: 50%
Average budget over the last 5 years: $11,000

Access:

Collection is partially open to the public
Reference questions per year: 1,000
Patrons per month: 10
Hours:
Monday–Saturday: 9 A.M.–5:30 P.M.
Sunday: 1 P.M.–5 P.M.
Total hours per week opened: 64
Book circulation duration: 3 weeks

Geographic Information Systems:
No GIS services available

Collection services:

Maps cataloged: 95%
Maps classified: 95%
Maps in OPAC: 95%
Classification schemes: LC, SuDocs
Cataloging utilities: OCLC
Catalog accessibility: online
Preservation techniques: encapsulation

Physical facilities:

Number of map cases: 15
Copying facilities available: copier, color copier, microform copier

551 *Milwaukee, WI*

University of Wisconsin, Milwaukee

American Geographical Society Library, founded 1851
2311 East Hartford Avenue
Milwaukee, WI 53211
Telephone: 414-229-6282
Fax: 414-229-3624
Email: agls@uwm.edu
Web: www.uwm.edu/Libraries/AGSL/index.html

Personnel:

Responsible person: Christopher Baruth, PhD, *email:* cmb@uwm.edu
Assistants: Susan Peschel, Senior Academic Librarian; Jovanka Ristic, Senior Reference Academic Librarian; Patti Day, Senior Digital Spatial Data Reference Librarian; Angie Cope, Cartographic Materials Catalog Academic Librarian
FTE para-professionals: 1.5
Number of student workers hours per week: 90
Number of volunteer hours per month: 25

Holdings:

Geographic strengths: Milwaukee region, Wisconsin, East, Canada, North America, South America, Africa, Asia, Australia, Polar regions
Special collections: Sanborn Fire Insurance maps, European topographic maps pre and post WW I and WW II, early U.S. Western photography including Timothy O'Sullivan, U.S. County Atlases (historical), international geographic journals
Subject strengths: aerial photos, aeronautical, early cartography, modern cartography, celestial, climatology, city, economic geography, forestry, genealogy, geology, geospatial data, historical geography, hydrology, land ownership, land use, map collecting, military, mineral resources, nautical charts, political geography, population, projections, railroads, recreation, roads, satellite imagery, soil, travel books, vegetation, waterways, zoogeography, topographic coverage of the world—current and historical
Map depositories and percentages: USGS topos (95%), USGS geology maps (95%), USGS other (95%), Department of Transportation, NOAA, GPO, CIA, Na-

tional Forest Service, NIMA topos, NIMA nautical, NIMA aeronautical, BLM, United Nations
490,000 printed maps
200 manuscript maps
400 wall maps
50 raised relief maps
150 microfilms
83 globes
100 gazetteers
9,208 printed atlases
3,000 CD-ROMs
37,914 computer programs
Collecting digital data
Chronological coverage:
  1800–1899: 20%
  1900–1939: 38%
  1940–present: 38%
On-going publications: CGP (Current Geographical Publications) online in 2004. AGSL Special Publications

Access:

Collection is partially open to the public
Reference questions per year: 2,800
Answers email questions
Patrons per month: 1,000

Hours:

Monday–Friday: 8 A.M.–4:30 P.M.
Total hours per week opened: 42.5
Maps circulate
Circulation policies apply
  Book circulation duration: 1 month
  Number of maps circulated annually: 20
Interlibrary loan available

Geographic Information Systems:

GIS services available by appointment
GIS software: ArcGIS, FME, Blue Marble, Mapitude, Business Analyst, Geolytics, Map Point 2001
GIS assistance available for Census mapping, geocoding, and image analysis
Plotter available
Scans maps for patrons

Collection services:

Maps cataloged: 99%
Maps classified: 99%
Maps in OPAC: 50%
Datasets are cataloged
Classification schemes: LC, Other (AGS)
Cataloging utilities: OCLC
Catalog accessibility: online, cards, various databases (Access, Excel, etc) for unique photo, slide, digital collections
Preservation techniques: encapsulation, deacidification, edging, archival mending tape, mounting on linen

Physical facilities:

Internet access available
Square footage: 15,000

Number of staff computers: 11
Number of map cases: 980
Number of vertical files (file cabinets): 120
Linear book shelving: 25,000 ft.
Linear atlas shelving: 1,300 ft.
Other map storage: archival boxes, slide drawers, custome-made wooden shelves, framed items hanging on walls, secure vertical vault
Number of stereoscopes: 20
Number of microform readers: 6
Copying facilities available: copier, color copier, large-format copier, microform copier, large-format scanner off site

Notes: Air photos digital = 12,000; print = 13,000. Satellite images digital = 1,269; remotely sensed images (landsat film) = 98,000; print landsat = 500

552 *Oshkosh, WI*

Oshkosh Public Library

106 Washington Avenue
Oshkosh, WI 54901-4985
Telephone: 920-236-5205
Fax: 920-236-5227
Email: munroe@oshkoshpubliclibrary.org
Web: www.oshkoshpubliclibrary.org
Personnel:
Responsible person: Janice Dibble, Head of Reference, *email:* dibble@oshkoshpubliclibrary.org
Assistants: Mara Munroe, Nancy Gall
Holdings:
Geographic strengths: Oshkosh, Winnebago County
Special collections: Winnebago County plat maps
1,000 printed maps
64 aerial photos
Access:
Hours:
Monday–Friday: 9 A.M.–9 P.M.
Saturday: 9 A.M.–5 P.M.
Sunday: noon–6 P.M.
Collection services:
Maps cataloged: 0%
Maps classified: 0%
Maps in OPAC: 0%
Physical facilities:
Map cases: 3

553 *Oshkosh, WI*

University of Wisconsin, Oshkosh

Department of Geology
Founded 1965
800 Algoma Boulevard
Oshkosh, WI 54901
Telephone: 920-424-2268
Fax: 920-424-0240

Personnel:
Responsible person: Tom Suszek MS, *email:* suszek@uwosh.edu
Holdings:
Geographic strengths: Wisconsin
Special collections: Wisconsin USGS topographic maps
Subject strengths: geology
5,000 printed maps
100 wall maps
Chronological coverage:
1900–1939: 10%
1940–present: 89%
Access:
Maps in separate area
Collection is partially open to the public
Hours:
Monday–Friday: 9 A.M.–3 P.M.
Geographic Information Systems:
No GIS services available
Collection services:
Maps cataloged: 90%
Classification schemes: Other (place)
Physical facilities:
No Internet access
Square footage: 400
Number of map cases: 25
Number of vertical files (file cabinets): 10
Linear book shelving: 50 ft.

554 *Oshkosh, WI*

University of Wisconsin, Oshkosh

Polk Library
Government Documents Collection
800 Algoma Boulevard
Oshkosh, WI 54901
Telephone: 920-424-7305
Fax: 920-424-2175
Email: watkins@uwosh.edu
Web: www.uwosh.edu/library/depts/docs/gov.html
Personnel:
Responsible person: Michael P. Watkins, *email:* watkins@uwosh.edu
FTE professionals: 0.1
Holdings:
Geographic strengths: Wisconsin, Minnesota, Illinois, Iowa, Michigan, United States
Special collections: Sanborn Fire Insurance maps of Central Wisconsin
Subject strengths: aerial photos, aeronautical, agriculture, geology, geospatial data, hydrology, land ownership, land use, map catalogs, military, mineral resources, nautical charts, political geography, population, satellite imagery, soil, waterways
Map depositories and percentages: USGS topos (10%), USGS geology maps (100%), USGS other (100%),

GPO, CIA, National Forest Service, NIMA topos, NIMA aeronautical, BLM, State

1,300 printed atlases

12 active serials

24 inactive serials

Chronological coverage:
 1940–present: 94%

Access:

Maps in separate area

Collection is open to the public

Reference questions per year: 63

Answers email questions

Hours:

Monday–Thursday: 7:45 A.M.–midnight

Friday: 7:45 A.M.–4:30 P.M.

Saturday: 1 P.M.–6 P.M.

Sunday: 1:30 P.M.–10 P.M.

Total hours per week opened: 87

Maps circulate

Circulation policies apply

 Map circulation duration: 3 weeks

 Book circulation duration: 3 weeks

 Number of maps circulated annually: 83

 Number of books circulated annually: 87

Interlibrary loan available

Geographic Information Systems:

GIS services available by appointment

GIS software: Geolytics

GIS assistance available for Census mapping

Scans maps for patrons

Collection services:

Maps cataloged: 20%

Maps classified: 100%

Maps in OPAC: 20%

Datasets are cataloged

Classification schemes: LC, SuDocs

Cataloging utilities: OCLC

Catalog accessibility: online, cards, USGS indexes

Physical facilities:

Internet access available

Square footage: 224

Number of map cases: 24

Copying facilities available: copier, color copier, large-format copier, microform copier, scanner

555 *Sheboygan, WI*

Mead Public Library

710 North 8th Street

Sheboygan, WI 53081

Telephone: 920-459-3400 x3438

Fax: 920-459-4336

Web: www.esls.lib.wi.edu

Personnel:

Responsible person: Robert Thomes, *email:* rthomes@ esls.lib.wi.us

FTE professionals: 1

Holdings:

Geographic strengths: Wisconsin, United States

Special collections: Wisconsin topographic maps, Sanborn Fire Insurance maps of the city of Plymouth, city of Sheboygan Falls, city of Sheboygan, Sheboygan, Wisconsin (1950–1970)

1,939 printed maps

4 globes

80 atlases

Access:

Hours:

Monday–Saturday: 8 A.M.–5 P.M.

Sunday: 1 P.M.–5 P.M.

Items circulate

Collection services:

Maps cataloged: 20%

Maps classified: 100%

Maps in OPAC: 20%

Classification schemes: Dewey, Local

Physical facilities:

Public computers: 46

Map cases: 2

Vertical files: 11

556 *Stevens Point, WI*

University of Wisconsin, Stevens Point

Learning Resources Center (LRC)

UWSP Map Center

Science Building

Stevens Point, WI 54481

Telephone: 715-346-2629

Fax: 715-346-3372

Email: geoggeol@uwsp.edu

Web: www.uwsp.edu/geo/Internet/geog_geol_resources .html

Personnel:

Responsible person: Dr. Keith Rice, *email:* krice@ uwsp.edu

FTE professionals: 0   *FTE para-professionals:* 0

Holdings:

Geographic strengths: Portage County, Central Wisconsin, Wisconsin

Special collections: maps of Wisconsin cities, historic railroad maps of Wisconsin, Great Lakes Surveys and U.S. River Surveys, Wisconsin Lake Survey Maps, Wisconsin Department of Transportation maps

Map depositories: USGS topos, NOAA, NGA nautical, NGA aeronautical, BLM

38,000 printed maps

1,200 aerial photos
25 atlases
320 books
6 active serials
450 CD-ROMs
Access:
Items circulate
Collection services:
Maps cataloged: 70%
Maps classified: 20%
Maps in OPAC: 0%
Classification schemes: LC, SuDocs, Local
Physical facilities:
Map cases: 76
Vertical files: 6

557 *Superior, WI*

University of Wisconsin, Superior

Jim Dan Hill Library
Lake Superior Maritime Collections
Box 2000
Superior, WI 54880
Telephone: 715-394-8343
Fax: 715-394-8462
Web: library.uwsuper.edu
Personnel:
Responsible person: Laura Jacobs, Archivist, *email:* ljacobs@uwsuper.edu
Assistants: Ella Cross, Head Reference
FTE professionals: 1
Holdings:
Geographic strengths: North Western Wisconsin, Northern Minnesota, Great Lakes
Special collections: Great Lakes, especially Lake Superior, historic working charts and surveys of Lake Superior ports (especially Duluth, Minnesota/Superior, Wisconsin) by the US Army Corps of Engineers' Duluth, Minnesota office
Map depositories: USGS topos, NOAA, NGA nautical
1,100 printed maps
110 aerial photos
1 globe
50 atlases
35 books
Access:
Hours:
Monday–Friday: 9 A.M.–4 P.M.
Collection services:
Maps in OPAC: 1%
Classification schemes: LC, SuDocs, Local
Physical facilities:
Public computers: 2
Map cases: 5

558 *Casper, WY*

Natrona County Public Library

307 East 2nd Street
Casper, WY 82601
Telephone: 307-237-4935
Fax: 307-266-3734
Email: afrench@will.state.wy.us
Web: www.library.natrona.net
Personnel:
Responsible person: Amber French, Government Documents, *email:* afrench@will.state.wy.us
FTE para-professionals: 1
Holdings:
Geographic strengths: Wyoming
Special collections: Sanborn Fire Insurance maps of Casper Wyoming, Wyoming 7.5' topos, Wyoming, Casper
Map depositories: USGS topos, National Forest Service, BLM
3,036 printed maps
Access:
Hours:
Monday–Thursday: 10 A.M.–7 P.M.
Friday–Saturday: 10 A.M.–5 P.M.
Sunday: 1 P.M.–5 P.M.
Items circulate
Interlibrary loan available
Collection services:
Maps cataloged: 50%
Maps classified: 50%
Maps in OPAC: 50%
Classification schemes: LC, SuDocs
Physical facilities:
Maps in separate area
Public computers: 8
Map cases: 8
Vertical files: 3

559 *Cheyenne, WY*

Wyoming State Library

Statewide Information Services
2301 Capitol Avenue
Cheyenne, WY 82002
Telephone: 307-777-6333
Fax: 307-777-5920
Email: refdesk@state.wy.us
Web: www-wsl.state.wy.us
Personnel:
Responsible person: Venice Beske, Manager, Statewide Information Services, *email:* vbeske@state.wy.us
Assistants: Emily Sieger, State Government Information Coordinator

Holdings:

Geographic strengths: Wyoming

Map depositories: Department of Transportation, NOAA, CIA, National Forest Service, BLM

3,000 printed maps

3,000 aerial photos

10 atlases

10 books

2 active serials

200 CD-ROMs

Access:

Hours:

Monday–Friday: 8 A.M.–5 P.M.

Items circulate

Interlibrary loan available

Collection services:

Maps cataloged: 30%

Maps classified: 25%

Maps in OPAC: 30%

Classification schemes: LC, SuDocs, Local

Physical facilities:

Public computers: 3

Map cases: 4

Vertical files: 3

560 *Cheyenne, WY*

Wyoming State Parks and Cultural Resources Department

Wyoming State Archives

2301 Central Avenue

Cheyenne, WY 82002

Telephone: 307-777-7036

Fax: 307-777-7044

Email: wyarchive@state.wy.us

Web: wyoarchives.state.wy.us/

Personnel:

Responsible person: Cindy Brown, *email:* cbrown1@state.wy.us

FTE professionals: 0.2

Holdings:

Geographic strengths: Wyoming

Special collections: LC Bishop Trail Maps, Sanborn Fire Insurance maps, birds-eye view maps, Wyoming State Engineer Historical maps, Wyoming Public Lands Commissioner maps

8,400 printed maps

1,000 aerial photos

30 atlases

3 CD-ROMs

Access:

Hours:

Monday–Friday: 8 A.M.–4:45 P.M.

Collection services:

Maps cataloged: 95%

Maps classified: 70%

Maps in OPAC: 95%

Classification schemes: Local

Physical facilities:

Maps in separate area

Public computers: 1

Map cases: 26

561 *Laramie, WY*

University of Wyoming

Brinkerhoff Earth Resources Information Center

Department 3006

1000 University Avenue

Laramie, WY 82071

Telephone: 307-766-3374

Fax: 307-766-6679

Email: sscott@uwyo.edu

Web: www-lib.uwyo.edu/uwlibs/geo.htm

Personnel:

Responsible person: Sally J. Scott, Department Head, *email:* sscott@uwyo.edu

Assistants: Diane Trotter, Access Services Manager; Marilee Ohnstad, Circulation/Map Assistant

Number of student workers hours per week: 84

Holdings:

Geographic strengths: Wyoming, Rocky Mountain region

Special collections: Wyoming Aerial Photos, Yellowstone Fire Area Aerial Photos

Subject strengths: aerial photos, geology

Map depositories and percentages: USGS topos, USGS geology maps, USGS other, Department of Transportation, National Forest Service, BLM, State

235,750 printed maps

93,653 aerial photos

326 gazetteers

454 printed atlases

59 books

Average budget over the last 5 years: $750

Access:

Collection is open to the public

Answers email questions

Hours:

Monday–Thursday: 8 A.M.–9 P.M.

Friday: 8 A.M.–5 P.M.

Saturday–Sunday: noon–5 P.M.

Total hours per week opened: 71

Maps circulate

Circulation policies apply

Map circulation duration: 4 weeks

Book circulation duration: 4 weeks

Interlibrary loan available

Geographic Information Systems:

GIS services available in an open environment

Collection services:

Maps classified: 100%

Classification schemes: LC, SuDocs

Cataloging utilities: OCLC

Catalog accessibility: online

Preservation techniques: encapsulation, lamination

Physical facilities:

Internet access available

Square footage: 2,124

Number of map cases: 115

Number of vertical files (file cabinets): 24

Linear atlas shelving: 206 ft.

Copying facilities available: copier, large-format copier, microform copier

562 *Laramie, WY*

University of Wyoming

Libraries

Grace Raymond Hebard Collection, founded 1998

1000 East University Avenue

Laramie, WY 82071

Telephone: 307-766-6245

Fax: 307-766-3062

Email: thert@uwyo.edu

Web: www-lib.uwyo.edu/uwlibs/hebard_maps.htm

Personnel:

Responsible person: Tamsen Hert, Wyoming Bibliographer, *email:* thert@uwyo.edu

Holdings:

Geographic strengths: Wyoming, Yellowstone National Park, Grand Teton National Park

Special collections: Wyoming Sanborn Fire Insurance maps, Wyoming State Highway maps, USGS topographic maps of Wyoming

Subject strengths: agriculture, archaeology, biology, caves, climatology, city, economic geography, engineering, forestry, geodetic surveys, geology, historical geography, hydrology, industries, land ownership, land use, military, mineral resources, mining, political geography, population, projections, railroads, recreation, roads, satellite imagery, soil, travel books, vegetation, views, waterways, Overland Trail; Exploration routes

Map depositories and percentages: State

3,000 printed maps

Chronological coverage:

1800–1899: 33%

1900–1939: 34%

1940–present: 33%

Average budget over the last 5 years: $750

Access:

Maps in separate area

Collection is paged

Answers email questions

Hours:

Monday–Friday: 8 A.M.–5 P.M.

Saturday: 11 A.M.–5 P.M.

Total hours per week opened: 46

Interlibrary loan available

Geographic Information Systems:

No GIS services available

Scans maps for patrons

Collection services:

Maps cataloged: 100%

Maps classified: 100%

Maps in OPAC: 100%

Classification schemes: LC, SuDocs

Cataloging utilities: OCLC

Catalog accessibility: online

Preservation techniques: encapsulation

Physical facilities:

Internet access available

Copying facilities available: copier, large-format copier

Notes: The Grace Raymond Hebard Collection is the Wyoming research library for the University of Wyoming Libraries. Historic and current Wyoming maps were added to this collection in 1998. The Grace Raymond Hebard Collection, while a library "branch" is housed in the American Heritage Center. Staff there retrieve the materials upon request (the American Heritage Center is the archives for the University but is separate from the Libraries). The map collection is just part of the much larger collection of all materials printed about Wyoming (state).

563 *Riverton, WY*

Central Wyoming College

Library

2660 Peck Avenue

Riverton, WY 82501

Telephone: 307 855-2141

Fax: 307-855-2094

Email: cdeering@cwc.edu

Web: www.cwc.edu/student_services/library/index.php

Personnel:

Responsible person: Carol Deering, Director of Library Services, *email:* cdeering@cwc.edu

Holdings:

Geographic strengths: Wyoming

Map depositories: USGS topos, CIA

2,000 printed maps

Access:

Hours:

Monday–Thursday: 8 A.M.–9 P.M.

Friday: 8 A.M.–5 P.M.

Saturday: noon–4 P.M.

Items circulate

Interlibrary loan available

Collection services:
Maps cataloged: 80%
Maps classified: 80%
Classification schemes: SuDocs, Local
Physical facilities:
Public computers: 30
Map cases: 4

564 *Rock Springs, WY*

Western Wyoming Community College

Hay Library
2500 College Drive
Box 473
Rock Springs, WY 82902
Telephone: 307-382-1700
Fax: 307-382-7665
Web: www.wwcc.wy.edu/library
Personnel:
Responsible person: Sharon Dolan, *email:* sdolan@wwcc.cc.wy.us
Holdings:
Geographic strengths: Wyoming, West, Central America, Mexico, South America, Middle East
Subject strengths: aerial photos, aeronautical, agriculture, archaeology, early cartography, modern cartography, celestial, climatology, city, economic geography, forestry, geodetic surveys, geology, geospatial data, historical geography, hydrology, industries, land ownership, land use, language, mineral resources, mining, nautical charts, oceanography, political geography, population, projections, railroads, recreation, roads, satellite imagery, soil, travel books, vegetation, waterways

Map depositories and percentages: USGS topos (30%), USGS geology maps (15%), USGS other, Department of Transportation, CIA, National Forest Service, BLM, State, United Nations
6,000 printed maps
Access:
Maps in separate area
Reference questions per year: 1,100
Answers email questions
Hours:
Total hours per week opened: 73
Maps circulate
Circulation policies apply
  Map circulation duration: 1 week
  Book circulation duration: 1 month
Interlibrary loan available
Geographic Information Systems:
GIS services available in an open environment
Number of public GIS workstations: 15
GIS assistance available for Census mapping, and geocoding
Scans maps for patrons
Collection services:
Maps cataloged: 90%
Datasets are cataloged
Classification schemes: LC, SuDocs, Dewey
Cataloging utilities: OCLC, Local
Catalog accessibility: online
Preservation techniques: cartex, lamination, edging
Items that have gone through the preservation process: 50%
Physical facilities:
No Internet access
Copying facilities available: copier, color copier, microform copier

Appendix A

Original Announcement of the Opening of the Survey

Fill out a survey and win one of 2 $100 gift certificates from a national map dealer!!

The Map and Geography Roundtable (MAGERT) of the American Library Association is pleased to announce the opening of the survey whose results will be used to create the 3rd Edition of the *Guide to U.S. Map Resources*. The first edition was published in 1986, and the second in 1990 (974 collections participated). In the last 13 years there have been significant changes in the map library community. The 3rd Edition is long overdue and your help is needed.

All libraries in the United States and its territories with collections of over 1,000 maps, or with collections of significant research, or historic value are asked to participate. MAGERT's goal is to compile a comprehensive guide. This will be accomplished only with YOUR help. Libraries will need to complete the official survey. The official survey is exclusively available on the web at:

http://www.mines.edu/library/maproom/forms/US_guide_survey.html

Completed paper copies of the survey will also be accepted via US mail or fax by the editor (see contact information below). The Survey will take approximately 10 to 40 minutes to finish. It is acceptable to approximate figures or leave answers blank, particularly if the maps are dispersed throughout your institution.

Please forward this message on to institutions you believe should be included in the *Guide*.

The Survey itself will begin October 15, 2003 and close **January 31, 2004**.

After the closing of the survey, two libraries completing the survey will be chosen at random and each awarded a gift certificate from a national map dealer in the amount of $100.

Christopher J.J. Thiry, Map Librarian at The Colorado School of Mines, is the editor of this edition. Approximately 30 other people will act as regional editors.

Once again, the survey can be found at:

http://www.mines.edu/library/maproom/forms/US_guide_survey.html

For more information or questions, please contact:
Christopher J.J. Thiry, editor
Map Librarian
Colorado School of Mines
303-273-3697
cthiry@mines.edu

Appendix B
"Long Survey"

(Print version adapted by Linda Zellmer.)

We would appreciate your cooperation filling out this form. It takes approximately 10 to 30 minutes to finish this survey. Please complete this form and submit it by AS SOON AS POSSIBLE.

It is acceptable to approximate figures or leave answers blank, particularly if the maps are dispersed throughout your institution.

The Map and Geography Roundtable (MAGERT) of the American Library Association published the first edition in 1986, and the second in 1990 (974 collections participated). In the last 13 years there have been significant changes in the map library community. The 3rd Edition is long overdue and your help is needed. Christopher J.J. Thiry, map librarian at The Colorado School of Mines, is the editor of this edition. Approximately 30 other people will act as regional editors.

All libraries in the United States and its territories with collections of over 1,000 maps, or with collections of significant research, or historic value are asked to participate. MAGERT's goal is to compile a comprehensive guide. This will be accomplished only with YOUR help.

I. Institutional Information

Provide information specifically about the map collection.

Do the answers to this survey reflect a single map collection within an institution or maps throughout an entire institution?

Select one: Single Collection within an Institution
                Maps throughout an Entire Institution

Type of Institution   Academic   Public   Private   State   Federal   Other

Institution name:

Library name:

Division/map collection name:

Year separate map collection created (if known):

Address:

State:

Zip Code:

Telephone:

Fax:

Map collection e-mail address:

URL of Web page:

II. Staff

Identify all professional staff working in the map collection.

Responsible/Head person, title:

Hours per week this individual works in map collection:

Email:

Other full-time employees, titles:

What is the total number of persons assigned to the map collection during the year in FTE equivalents:

Professionals FTE:

Paraprofessionals FTE

Number of student workers:

Number of hours during the school year per week of student workers:

Number of volunteers:

Number of hours per month of volunteers:

III. Collection Area Strengths

*Identify major areas of specialization. Please list only those areas for which you have **SUBSTANTIAL** collections, whether it be a continent, individual country, or local area.*

Geographical strengths:

Subject Strengths

Identify major subject specializations. Please choose or list only those subjects for which you have SUBSTANTIAL collections of at least regional significance:

Aerial Photographs
Aeronautical charts
Agriculture
Archaeology
Biology
Cartography, early
Cartography, modern
Caves and caving
Celestial (including the Planets and the Moon)
Climatology
City
Economic geography
Engineering
Forestry
Genealogy
Geodetic surveys
Geology
Geospatial data
Historical geography

Hydrology
Industries
Land ownership
Land use
Language
Map/Atlas catalogs
Map collecting
Military geography
Mineral resources
Mining
Nautical charts
Oceanography
Political geography
Population
Projections
Railroads
Raised relief models
Recreation (including fishing, hiking, skiing, etc.)
Religion
Roads
Satellite imagery
Soils
Travel/guide books
Vegetation
Views (including bird's-eye views)
Waterways
Zoogeography
Other:

Special Collections

Identify those "special" collections within a collection (i.e. Sanborn Fire Insurance maps, Kohl Collection of American exploration). Please list only significant collections.

Map Depositories

Identify only those categories of maps that you receive on automatic sending. Indicate the percentage of those categories you receive:

US Geological Survey (topos) US Geological Survey (geology) US Geological Survey (other) Dept. of Transportation (including FAA aeronautical charts) NOAA (nautical charts) GPO (general) CIA US Forest Service NIMA (topos) NIMA (nautical charts) NIMA (aeronautical charts) BLM State United Nations Other depository categories:

Holdings

Number of printed maps:
Number of manuscript maps:
Number of raised relief maps:
Number of microfiche:
Number of microfilms:
Number of aerial photographs:
Number of satellite images:
Number of globes:
Number of gazetteers:
Number of printed atlases:
Number of manuscript atlases:

Number of books (map and cartographic materials only) (excluding atlases and gazetteers):
Number of serials titles (active) (map and cartographic materials only):
Number of serials titles (inactive) (map and cartographic materials only):
Number of CD-ROMs (map and cartographic materials only):
Number of computer programs:
Name of GIS programs available in map collection:

Is your collection actively collecting digital geospatial data? Yes No

Chronological coverage (percentage):
MUST ADD UP TO 100!

Pre-1800:
1800–1899:
1900–1939:
1940–

What is the AVERAGE annual acquisitions budget for the map collection over the last 5 years?
$

IV. Readers' Services

Please identify policies related to access and use of your map collection.

Open Partially Open Paged

Are parts of the map collection stored off site?   Yes   No

If yes, what percentage:

Hours map collection open:
Monday–Friday
Saturday
Sunday
Total number of hours per week:

Number of map reference questions answered per year:

Does the map collection respond to questions via email?   Yes   No

Average number of patron visits per month:

Do items in the collection circulate?   Yes   No

In general, what is the duration for checked out materials?

Does this apply to your collection?   Yes   No

Duration items circulate:
Maps:
Atlases:
Books:

Average annual circulation:
Maps

Books
Other

Are your items available through interlibrary loan?   Yes   No

Copying facilities in the library building: (choose all that apply)
None   Copier   Color copier   Oversize copier   Microform printer   Other:

Does the library scan items for patrons?   Yes   No

Is there internet access in the map collection?   Yes   No

Number of public workstations:

Geographic Information Services (GIS)

None   Open   Environment (not monitored)   By Appointment (monitored)

Number of GIS workstations:
Not monitored:
Monitored:

GIS assistance for: (choose all that apply)
Census mapping   Geocoding   Image analysis   Other:

Is there a plotter available for public use?   Yes   No

V. Collection Services

Identify the amount of bibliographic control of and access to the map collection.

Percentage of collection cataloged:

Percentage of collection classified:

Percentage of holdings in local online catalog:

Are datasets cataloged?   Yes   No

Classification used: (choose all that apply)
Library of Congress   SuDocs   Dewey   Local   Other:

Bibliographic utility used (choose all that apply):
OCLC   RLG   Local   Other:

Catalog format (choose all that apply):
Online   Fiche or film   Cards   Printout   Other:

Preservation techniques used (choose all that apply):
Encapsulation   Deacidification   Cartex   Lamination   Edging   Other:

Percentage of collection that has gone through a preservation process:

VI. Physical Facilities

Identify the floor space and equipment dedicated to the use of the map collection.

Are the maps in a separate room?   Yes   No

Square footage:

Number of Public Computers:
Number of Staff computers:
Number of Public printers:
Number of Map cases:
Number of Vertical map cases:
Number of File Cabinets:
Number of Atlas stands:
Book shelving (in linear feet):
Atlas shelving (in linear feet) (i.e. shelving of books lying flat):

List other map storage facilities (e.g. rolled map cases):

Number of Stereoscopes:
Number of Microform readers:
Number of Microform printers:
Number of Light tables:

VII. Publications

Identify publications describing the map collection or parts thereof.

On-going serial publications such as acquisition lists, newsletters, bibliographies, etc.:

Make a copy of this completed form for your records. The compilers thank you for completing this questionnaire, and appreciate your time and effort to provide up-to-date information. We are trying to make this *Guide* as complete as possible, therefore if you know of other collections of maps in your institution or local area, please ask them to fill out this form and submit it.

Person completing survey:
Institution:
Telephone number:
E-mail address:
Date:

Any additional comments?

Appendix C

"Short Survey"

(Print version adapted by Linda Zellmer.)

We would appreciate your cooperation filling out this form. It takes approximately 5 to 10 minutes to finish this survey. Please complete this form and submit it by AS SOON AS POSSIBLE.

It is acceptable to approximate figures or leave answers blank, particularly if the maps are dispersed throughout your institution.

The Map and Geography Roundtable (MAGERT) of the American Library Association published the first edition in 1986, and the second in 1990 (974 collections participated). In the last 13 years, there have been significant changes in the map library community. The 3rd Edition is long overdue and your help is needed. Christopher J.J. Thiry, map librarian at The Colorado School of Mines, is the editor of this edition. Approximately 30 other people will act as regional editors.

All libraries in the United States and its territories with collections of over 1,000 maps, or with collections of significant research, or historic value are asked to participate. MAGERT's goal is to compile a comprehensive guide. This will be accomplished only with YOUR help.

I. Institutional Information

Provide information specifically about the map collection.

Type of Institution   Academic   Public   Private   State   Federal   Other

Institution name:

Library name:

Division/map collection name:

Address:

State:

Zip Code:

Telephone:

Fax:

Map collection e-mail address:

URL of Web page:

II. Staff

Identify all professional staff working in the map collection.

Responsible/Head person, title:

Email:

Other full-time employees, titles:

What is the total number of persons assigned to the map collection during the year in FTE equivalents:

Professionals FTE: Paraprofessionals FTE

III. Collection Area Strengths

*Identify major areas of specialization. Please list only those areas for which you have **SUBSTANTIAL** collections whether it be a continent, individual country, or local area.*

Geographical strengths:

Special Collections

Identify those "special" collections within a collection (i.e. Sanborn Fire Insurance maps, Kohl Collection of American exploration). Please list only significant collections.

Map Depositories

Identify only those categories of maps that you receive on automatic sending:

US Geological Survey   Dept. of Transportation (including FAA aeronautical charts)   NOAA (nautical charts)
CIA   US Forest Service   NIMA (nautical charts)   NIMA (aeronautical charts)   BLM

Holdings

Number of printed maps:
Number of aerial photographs:
Number of globes:
Number of printed atlases:
Number of books (map and cartographic materials only) (excluding atlases):
Number of serials titles (map and cartographic materials only):
Number of CD-ROMs (map and cartographic materials only):

IV. Readers' Services

Please identify policies related to access and use of your map collection.

Hours map collection open:
Monday–Friday
Saturday
Sunday

Do items in the collection circulate?   Yes   No

Are your items available through interlibrary loan?   Yes   No

V. Collection Services

Identify the amount of bibliographic control of and access to the map collection.

Percentage of collection cataloged:

Percentage of collection classified:

Percentage of holdings in local online catalog:

Classification used: (choose all that apply)
Library of Congress   SuDocs   Dewey   Local   Other:

VI. Physical Facilities

Identify the floor space and equipment dedicated to the use of the map collection.

Are the maps in a separate room?   Yes   No

Number of Public Computers:
Number of Map cases:
Number of File Cabinets:

Make a copy of this completed form for your records. The compilers thank you for completing this questionnaire, and appreciate your time and effort to provide up-to-date information. We are trying to make this *Guide* as complete as possible, therefore if you know of other collections of maps in your institution or local area, please ask them to fill out this form and submit it.

Person completing survey:
Institution:
Telephone number:
E-mail address:
Date:

Any additional comments?

Appendix D

Totals of Map Holdings by Institution

All types of maps (printed, manuscript, wall, relief models, etc.) are totaled. The numbers in parentheses refer to the accession numbers used in this book.

All libraries (564 total):

1.	Library of Congress (125)	4,842,700
2.	National Archives and Records Administration (243)	3,000,000
3.	Boston Public Library (251)	1,400,000
4.	University of California, Los Angeles (58)	613,512
5.	United States Geological Survey (517)	562,225
6.	University of Florida (135)	513,857
7.	State Archives of Michigan (271)	500,030
8.	University of Wisconsin, Milwaukee (551)	490,000
9.	University of California, Santa Barbara (88)	464,800
10.	New York Public Library (343)	429,035
11.	University of Chicago (166)	410,849
12.	University of Illinois, Urbana-Champaign (178)	403,400
13.	Harvard University (254)	401,000
14.	University of Georgia (141)	400,750
15.	University of Maryland, College Park (245)	400,140
16.	Washington State Department of Natural Resources (530)	400,000
17.	University of California, Berkeley (46)	377,102
18.	University of Tennessee (465)	350,259
19.	Pennsylvania State University (427)	350,000
20.	University of Minnesota (281)	335,534
21.	University of Kansas (210)	333,599
22.	University of Michigan (263)	329,320
23.	Kentucky Division of Mines and Minerals (220)	327,000
24.	State University of New York, Buffalo (339)	320,420
25.	Louisiana State University (227)	312,232
26.	University of Idaho (159)	300,000
27.	Western Illinois University (170)	300,000
28.	Illinois State University (171)	300,000
29.	Indiana State University (196)	290,400
30.	University of Wisconsin, Madison (547)	280,450
31.	University of Alabama (8)	278,689
32.	University of North Carolina, Chapel Hill (352)	271,370
33.	Stanford University (91)	270,485
34.	University of Washington (537)	267,091
35.	University of South Carolina (445)	265,350
36.	Southern Methodist University (488)	260,020
37.	University of Texas, Austin (481)	250,037
38.	Southern Illinois University, Carbondale (160)	249,704
39.	Western Washington University (523)	247,358
40.	University of Oregon (400)	246,243
41.	University of Arizona (32)	238,525

42. University of Wyoming (561)	235,750
43. University of Utah (504)	235,130
44. Yale University (119)	226,125
45. Arizona State University (28)	213,630
46. University of Vermont (509)	210,010
47. University of Montana (299)	209,035
48. Johns Hopkins University (242)	208,150
49. Brigham Young University (502)	205,000
50. Purdue University (198)	201,000
51. Tennessee Valley Authority (458)	200,940
52. Colorado School of Mines (109)	200,803
53. Northwestern University (169)	200,770
54. Indiana University, Bloomington (182)	200,020
55. University of Nebraska, Lincoln (312)	200,000
56. Ohio State University (383)	200,000
57. Dartmouth College (325)	196,528
58. Georgia Institute of Technology (144)	193,060
59. University of Connecticut (121)	190,058
60. University of Colorado, Boulder (95)	190,010
61. University of Iowa (205)	188,427
62. San Francisco Public Library (79)	188,139
63. University of Texas, El Paso (490)	180,034
64. University of Illinois, Chicago (167)	179,000
65. Syracuse University (346)	175,100
66. Oregon State University (399)	170,000
67. Cleveland Public Library (378)	165,040
68. University of Hawai'i at Manoa (154)	164,000
69. Miami University (391)	152,105
70. South Carolina Department of Archives and History (443)	151,815
71. University of Virginia (512)	150,100
72. U.S. Geological Survey (105)	150,000
73. Southern Illinois University Edwardsville (168)	146,500
74. University of Nevada, Reno (321)	139,000
75. University of California, Santa Cruz (89)	138,098
76. San Diego State University (71)	138,000
77. Virginia Tech (510)	136,000
78. University of Toledo (394)	135,035
79. Free Library of Philadelphia (421)	135,025
80. Duke University (356)	134,074
81. University of California, Davis (51)	130,581
82. University of Cincinnati (376)	130,100
83. Saint Louis Public Library (292)	125,020
84. Western Carolina University (355)	124,019
85. California State University, Fresno (52)	122,450
86. Southwest Missouri State University (295)	121,043
87. Minot State University (369)	120,837
88. University of Arkansas (35)	120,150
89. Vanderbilt University (471)	120,140
90. Kansas State University (212)	120,010
91. Ohio University (372)	120,000
92. Ball State University (193)	118,023
93. Columbia University (342)	116,500
94. University of Massachusetts, Amherst (249)	115,000
95. Indiana State Library (190)	113,135

96. Washington University (294)	113,000
97. Iowa State University (199)	105,289
98. Emory University (143)	105,000
99. East Carolina University (360)	103,000
100. Enoch Pratt Free Library (241)	102,000
101. University of California, San Diego (55)	101,100
102. Augustana College (174)	100,800
103. East View Cartographic, Inc. (279)	100,500
104. University of California, Riverside (67)	100,040
105. University of Delaware (122)	100,000
106. Michigan Technological University (267)	100,000
107. Minneapolis Public Library (280)	100,000
108. University of Missouri, Rolla (291)	100,000
109. Saint Louis University (293)	100,000
110. Rutgers, The State University of New Jersey (329)	100,000
111. New Mexico State Library (334)	100,000
112. North Dakota State University (368)	100,000

Academic libraries (331 total):

1. University of California, Los Angeles (58)	613,512
2. University of Florida (135)	513,857
3. University of Wisconsin, Milwaukee (551)	490,000
4. University of California, Santa Barbara (88)	464,800
5. University of Chicago (166)	410,849
6. University of Illinois, Urbana-Champaign (178)	403,400
7. Harvard University (254)	401,000
8. University of Georgia (141)	400,750
9. University of Maryland, College Park (245)	400,140
10. University of California, Berkeley (46)	377,102
11. University of Tennessee (465)	350,259
12. Pennsylvania State University (427)	350,000
13. University of Minnesota (281)	335,534
14. University of Kansas (210)	333,599
15. University of Michigan (263)	329,320
16. State University of New York, Buffalo (339)	320,420
17. Louisiana State University (227)	312,232
18. Illinois State University (171)	300,000
19. Western Illinois University (170)	300,000
20. University of Idaho (159)	300,000
21. Indiana State University (196)	290,400
22. University of Wisconsin, Madison (547)	280,450
23. University of Alabama (8)	278,689
24. University of North Carolina, Chapel Hill (352)	271,370
25. Stanford University (91)	270,485
26. University of Washington (537)	267,091
27. University of South Carolina (445)	265,350
28. Southern Methodist University (488)	260,020
29. University of Texas, Austin (481)	250,037
30. Southern Illinois University, Carbondale (160)	249,704
31. Western Washington University (523)	247,358
32. University of Oregon (400)	246,243
33. University of Arizona (32)	238,525
34. University of Wyoming (561)	235,750
35. University of Utah (504)	235,130

36. Yale University (119)	226,125
37. Arizona State University (28)	213,630
38. University of Vermont (509)	210,010
39. University of Montana (299)	209,035
40. Johns Hopkins University (242)	208,150
41. Purdue University (198)	201,000
42. Colorado School of Mines (109)	200,803
43. Northwestern University (169)	200,770
44. Indiana University, Bloomington (182)	200,020
45. Ohio State University (383)	200,000
46. University of Nebraska, Lincoln (312)	200,000
47. Dartmouth College (325)	196,528
48. Georgia Institute of Technology (144)	193,060
49. University of Connecticut (121)	190,058
50. University of Colorado, Boulder (95)	190,010
51. University of Iowa (205)	188,427
52. University of Texas, El Paso (490)	180,034
53. University of Illinois, Chicago (167)	179,000
54. Syracuse University (346)	175,100
55. Oregon State University (399)	170,000
56. University of Hawai'i at Manoa (154)	164,000
57. Miami University (391)	152,105
58. University of Virginia (512)	150,100
59. Southern Illinois University Edwardsville (168)	146,500
60. University of Nevada, Reno (321)	139,000
61. University of California, Santa Cruz (89)	138,098
62. San Diego State University (71)	138,000
63. Virginia Tech (510)	136,000
64. University of Toledo (394)	135,035
65. Duke University (356)	134,074
66. University of California, Davis (51)	130,581
67. University of Cincinnati (376)	130,100
68. Western Carolina University (355)	124,019
69. California State University, Fresno (52)	122,450
70. Southwest Missouri State University (295)	121,043
71. Minot State University (369)	120,837
72. University of Arkansas (35)	120,150
73. Vanderbilt University (471)	120,140
74. Ohio University (372)	120,000
75. Ball State University (193)	118,023
76. Columbia University (342)	116,500
77. University of Massachusetts, Amherst (249)	115,000
78. Washington University (294)	113,000
79. Iowa State University (199)	105,289
80. Emory University (143)	105,000
81. East Carolina University (360)	103,000
82. University of California, San Diego (55)	101,100
83. Augustana College (174)	100,800
84. University of California, Riverside (67)	100,040
85. North Dakota State University (368)	100,000
86. Rutgers, The State University of New Jersey (329)	100,000
87. Saint Louis University (293)	100,000
88. University of Missouri, Rolla (291)	100,000
89. Michigan Technological University (267)	100,000
90. University of Delaware (122)	100,000

Federal institutions (20 total):

1. Library of Congress (125)	4,842,700
2. National Archives and Records Administration (243)	3,000,000
3. United States Geological Survey (517)	562,225
4. Tennessee Valley Authority (458)	200,940
5. U.S. Geological Survey (105)	150,000
6. State Library of Ohio (385)	90,600
7. National Archives and Records Administration, Rocky Mountain Region (104)	48,000

Other institutions (25 total):

1. Academy of Natural Sciences (420)	25,000
2. Minnesota Historical Society (287)	19,277
3. Ohio Historical Society (382)	14,000
4. New York Historical Society (344)	11,500
5. Mystic Seaport (117)	10,000
6. World Bank (128)	9,600
7. American Antiquarian Society (260)	9,500

Private institutions (34 total):

1. East View Cartographic, Inc. (279)	100,500
2. National Geographic Society (126)	45,000
3. Dayton Society of Natural History (387)	25,000
4. Oregon Historical Society (408)	25,000
5. Historical Society of Pennsylvania (422)	11,000
6. Family History Library (503)	6,040
7. Maine Historical Society (237)	5,500

Public libraries (94 total):

1. Boston Public Library (251)	1,400,000
2. New York Public Library (343)	429,035
3. Brigham Young University (502)	205,000
4. San Francisco Public Library (79)	188,139
5. Cleveland Public Library (378)	165,040
6. Free Library of Philadelphia (421)	135,025
7. Saint Louis Public Library (292)	125,020
8. Kansas State University (212)	120,010
9. Enoch Pratt Free Library (241)	102,000
10. Minneapolis Public Library (280)	100,000
11. Chicago Public Library (164)	94,200
12. Denver Public Library (102)	85,000
13. Buffalo and Erie County Public Library (338)	80,135
14. Los Angeles Public Library (56)	80,110
15. Toledo-Lucas County Public Library (393)	75,000
16. Dallas Public Library (485)	60,000
17. Omaha Public Library (316)	57,344
18. Seattle Public Library (536)	35,000
19. Milwaukee Public Library (550)	30,000

State institutions (60 total):

1. State Archives of Michigan (271)	500,030
2. Washington State Department of Natural Resources (530)	400,000
3. Kentucky Division of Mines and Minerals (220)	327,000
4. South Carolina Department of Archives and History (443)	151,815
5. Indiana State Library (190)	113,135

6. New Mexico State Library (334)   100,000
7. Arizona State Library, Archives and Public Records (22)   86,249
8. California State Library (69)   80,000
9. Arkansas State Library (37)   60,000
10. Bemidji State University (274)   48,182
11. Library of Virginia (518)   46,520
12. Illinois State Archives (175)   40,000
13. Utah State Historical Society (508)   35,530
14. Connecticut State Library (115)   24,550
15. Illinois State Geological Survey (161)   24,010
16. Washington State Library (532)   22,400

Aerial photographs and satellite images:

1. National Archives and Records Administration (243)   18,000,000
2. University of California, Santa Barbara (88)   4,400,000
3. Tennessee Valley Authority (458)   2,000,000
4. University of Oregon (400)   550,000
5. University of Minnesota (281)   410,569
6. University of Florida (135)   302,935
7. University of Illinois, Urbana-Champaign (178)   259,700
8. University of Wisconsin, Madison (547)   255,000
9. University of Georgia (141)   225,500
10. Purdue University (198)   150,000
11. University of Iowa (205)   146,305
12. University of South Carolina (445)   125,000
13. University of Kansas (210)   122,613
14. Louisiana State University (227)   108,424
15. University of California, Santa Cruz (89)   96,386
16. University of Wyoming (561)   93,653
17. University of Hawai'i at Manoa (154)   90,475
18. Southern Illinois University, Carbondale (160)   85,239
19. University of Washington (537)   80,910
20. Syracuse University (346)   80,010
21. University of Alabama (8)   78,260
22. University of California, Davis (51)   76,000
23. University of Nebraska, Kearney (303)   70,050
24. University of California, Berkeley (46)   69,528
25. Auburn University (1)   55,223
26. Southwest Missouri State University (295)   55,000
27. Connecticut State Library (115)   53,000
28. Colorado School of Mines (109)   46,767
29. Western Washington University (523)   31,124
30. East View Cartographic, Inc. (279)   31,000
31. University of Vermont (509)   26,000
32. University of California, Berkeley (47)   25,000
33. Minnesota State University, Mankato (278)   24,010
34. Arizona State University (28)   20,575
35. Virginia Tech (510)   20,000
36. Illinois State University (171)   20,000
37. University of Arizona (32)   19,200
38. California State University, Fresno (52)   16,386
39. University of Colorado, Boulder (95)   15,050
40. Pennsylvania Historical and Museum Commission (416)   15,000
41. Geological Survey of Alabama (6)   12,200
42. Western Illinois University (170)   12,000

43. Oregon State University (399)   11,000
44. U.S. Department of Interior, Office of Surface Mining (464)   10,200
45. University of Connecticut (121)   10,130
46. University of California, San Diego (55)   10,100
47. Pikes Peak Library District (98)   10,000
48. National Archives and Records Administration, Pacific Region-
    San Francisco (70)   10,000

Appendix E
Library/Institution Index

This is a comprehensive alphabetic index of all of the institutions. The numbers in parentheses refer to the accession numbers used in this book.

Abilene Christian University (472)
Brown Library
Texas Topographic Map Collection
221 Brown Library
Abilene, TX 79601-9208
Phone: 325-674-2316
Fax: 325-674-2202
Web: www.acu.edu/academics/library

Academy of Natural Sciences (420)
Ewell Sale Stewart Library
James Bond Map Room
1900 Benjamin Franklin Parkway
Philadelphia, PA 19103
Phone: 215-299-1040
Fax: 215-299-1144
Web: www.acnatsci.org/library

Adler Planetarium and Astronomy Museum (163)
History of Astronomy Research Center
1300 South Lake Shore Drive
Chicago, IL 60605
Phone: 312-322-0594
Fax: 312-341-9935
Web: www.adlerplanetarium.org

Alabama Department of Archives and History (5)
P.O. Box 300100
624 Washington Avenue
Montgomery, AL 36130
Phone: 334-242-4363
Fax: 334-240-3433
Web: www.archives.state.al.us

Alaska Division of Geological and Geophysical Surveys (12)
Library
3354 College Road
Fairbanks, AK 99709-3707
Phone: 907-451-5020
Fax: 907-451-5050
Web: www.dggs.dnr.state.ak.us

Alaska Resources Library and Information Services (ARLIS) (9)
3211 Providence Drive
Suite 111
Anchorage, AK 99508
Phone: 907-272-7547
Fax: 907-271-4742
Web: www.arlis.org

Alaska State Library (14)
Historical Collections
P.O. Box 110571
Juneau, AK 99811-0571
Phone: 907-465-2925
Fax: 907-465-2990
Web: www.library.state.ak.us/hist/hist.html

American Alpine Club (108)
Henry S. Hall, Jr. Library
710 Tenth Street
Suite 15
Golden, CO 80401
Phone: 303-384-0112
Fax: 303-384-0113
Web: www.americanalpineclub.org/knowledge/
aaclibrary.asp

American Antiquarian Society (260)
185 Salisbury Street
Worcester, MA 01609
Phone: 508-755-5221
Fax: 508-753-3311
Web: www.americanantiquarian.org

American Historical Society of Germans from Russia (304)
631 D Street
Lincoln, NE 68502-1199
Phone: 402-474-3363
Web: www.ahsgr.org

Anacortes Museum (522)
1305 8th Street
Anacortes, WA 98221
Phone: 360-293-1915
Fax: 360-293-1929
Web: www.anacorteshistorymuseum.org

Anderson County Public Library (434)
South Carolina Room
300 North McDuffie Street
Anderson, SC 29621
Phone: 864-260-4500
Fax: 864-260-4098
Web: www.andersonlibrary.org

Appalachian State University (347)
Department of Geography and Planning
Boone, NC 28618
Phone: 828-262-3000
Fax: 828-262-3067
Web: www.geo.appstate.edu

**Arizona Department Mines
and Mineral Resources** (21)
Arizona Mines and Mineral Resource Library
1502 West Washington
Phoenix, AZ 85007
Phone: 602-255-3795
Fax: 602-255-3777
Web: www.admmr.state.az.us

Arizona Geological Survey (29)
416 West Congress
Tucson, AZ 85701
Phone: 520-770-3500
Fax: 520-770-3505
Web: www.azgs.az.gov

**Arizona State Library,
Archives and Public Records** (22)
Arizona State Library Law and Research Division
Map Collection
1700 West Washington
Phoenix, AZ 85007
Phone: 602-542-4343
Fax: 602-542-4400
Web: www.lib.az.us

Arizona State Museum (30)
Arizona State Museum Archives
University of Arizona
Tucson, AZ 85721-0026
Phone: 520-621-2970
Fax: 520-621-2976
Web: www.statemuseum.arizona.edu/library

Arizona State University (27)
Hayden Library
Arizona Historical Foundation
P.O. Box 871006
Tempe, AZ 85287-1006
Phone: 480-966-8331
Fax: 480-966-1077
Web: www.arizonahistoricalfoundation.org

Arizona State University (28)
Noble Science and Engineering Library
Map Collection
P.O. Box 871006
Tempe, AZ 85287-1006
Phone: 480-965-3582
Fax: 480-965-0883
Web: www.asu.edu/lib/hayden/govdocs/maps/
mapcoll.htm

Arizona Western College (33)
Academic Library
P.O. Box 929
Yuma, AZ 85366
Phone: 928-344-7777
Fax: 928-344-7751
Web: www.azwestern.edu/library/

Arkansas Geological Commission (36)
Geological Library
3815 West Roosevelt Road
Little Rock, AR 72204
Phone: 501-296-1877
Fax: 501-663-7360
Web: www.state.ar.us/agc/agc.htm

Arkansas State Library (37)
Document Services
One Capitol Mall
Little Rock, AR 72201
Phone: 501-682-2869
Fax: 501-681-1532
Web: www.asl.lib.ar.us

Arkansas Tech University (40)
Pendergraft Library and Technology Center
305 West Q Street
Russellville, AR 72801
Phone: 479-968-0289
Fax: 479-964-0559
Web: library.atu.edu

Atlanta-Fulton Public Library (142)
Central Library
Special Collections/Georgia Local and Family History
One Margaret Mitchell Square
Atlanta, GA 30303

Phone: 404-730-1896-or-1897
Fax: 404-730-1895
Web: www.af.public.lib.ga.us./central/gagen/index.html

Auburn University (1)
Auburn University Library
231 Mell Street
Auburn University, AL 36849-5606
Phone: 334-844-1759
Fax: 334-844-4461
Web: www.lib.auburn.edu/govdocs/

Augusta State University (146)
Reese Library
2500 Walton Way
Augusta, GA 30904-2200
Phone: 706-737-1748
Fax: 706-667-4415
Web: www.aug.edu

Augustana College (174)
Thomas Tredway Library
Loring Map Collection
639 38th Street
Rock Island, IL 61201
Phone: 309-794-7318
Fax: 309-794-7564
Web: www.augustana.edu/library

Austin Peay State University (459)
Felix G. Woodward
Information Services
601 East College Street
Clarksville, TN 37044
Phone: 931-221-7346
Fax: 931-221-7296
Web: library.apsu.edu/

Ball State University (193)
Bracken
Geospatial Center and Map Collection
University Libraries
Muncie, IN 47306
Phone: 765-285-1097
Fax: 765-285-2644
Web: www.bsu.edu/library/collections/gcmc

Baylor University (498)
Moody Memorial Library
Government Documents
1312 South 3rd
Waco, TX 76798
Phone: 254-710-2157
Fax: 254-710-3116
Web: www3.baylor.edu/library

Beaufort County Public Library System (435)
Beaufort Branch
South Carolina Room
311 Scott Street
Beaufort, SC 29902
Phone: 843-525-4064
Web: www.bcgov.net/bftlib/normal.htm

Beloit College (542)
Col. Robert Morse Library
731 College Street
Beloit, WI 53511
Phone: 608-363-2230
Fax: 608-363-2487
Web: www.beloit.edu/~libhome

Bemidji State University (274)
Map Library
HS 244, Bemidji State University
Bemidji, MN 56601
Phone: 218-755-2804
Fax: 218-755-2822
Web: www.bemidjistate.edu/library

Berea College (218)
Hutchins Library
Berea, KY 40404
Phone: 850-985-3172
Web: www.berea.edu/hutchinslibrary

Berkeley Public Library (43)
2090 Kittredge Street
Berkeley, CA 94704
Phone: 510-981-6148
Fax: 510-981-6246
Web: www.berkeleypubliclibrary.org

Birmingham Public Library (2)
Linn-Henley Research Library
Rucker Agee Map Collection
2100 Park Place
Birmingham, AL 35203-2794
Phone: 205-226-3665
Fax: 205-226-3663
Web: www.bplonline.org

Blue Mountain Community College Library (403)
Map Collection
2411 NW Carden Ave
Pendleton, OR 97801
Phone: 541-278-5915
Fax: 541-276-6119
Web: www.bluecc.edu/library

Boise State University (156)
Albertsons Library
Hollenbaugh Map Collection

1910 University Drive
Boise, ID 83725
Phone: 208-426-1264
Web: library.boisestate.edu/Maps/

Boston Athenaeum (250)
10 1/2 Beacon Street
Boston, MA 02108
Phone: 617-227-0270
Fax: 617-227-5266
Web: bostonathenaeum.org

Boston College (258)
Thomas P. O'Neill Jr. Library
Catherine O'Connor Library
381 Concord Road
Weston, MA 02493
Phone: 617-552-8300
Fax: 617-552-8388
Web: www.bc.edu/libraries/centers/weston/

Boston Public Library (251)
Boston Public Library
Norman Leventhal Map Center
Copley Square
Boston, MA 02116
Phone: 617-536-5400
Web: www.bpl.org

Bostonian Society (252)
Bostonian Society Library and Special Collections
206 Washington Street
Boston, MA 02109
Phone: 617-720-1713 x12
Fax: 617-720-3289
Web: www.bostonhistory.org

Boulder Public Library (94)
Carnegie Branch Library for Local History
Map Collection
1125 Pine Street
Boulder, CO 80302
Phone: 303-441-3110
Fax: 720-406-7452
Web: www.boulder.lib.co.us

Bowling Green State University (373)
Jerome Library
Government Documents
Ridge Street
Bowling Green, OH 43403
Phone: 419-372-2142
Fax: 419-372-7996
Web: www.bgsu.edu/colleges/library/services/govdocs/
index.html

Bradley University (173)
Cullom-Davis Library
1501 West Bradley Avenue
Peoria, IL 61625
Phone: 309-677-2840
Fax: 309-677-2558
Web: library.bradley.edu

Brazoria County Historical Museum (475)
Adriance Research Library
100 East Ceder
Angleton, TX 77515
Phone: 979-864-1591
Fax: 979-864-1217
Web: www.bchm.org

Bridgewater College (511)
Alexander Mack Memorial Library
402 East College Street
Bridgewater, VA 22812
Phone: 540-828-5672
Fax: 540-828-5482
Web: www.bridgewater.edu/departments/library/
govdocuments.html

Brigham Young University (502)
Harold B. Lee Library
Map Collection
2420 HBLL
Provo, UT 84602-
Phone: 801-422-6179
Fax: 801-422-0466
Web: www.lib.byu.edu

Brigham Young University—Hawai'i Campus (155)
Joseph F. Smith Library
55-220 Kulanui Street
Laie, HI 96762
Phone: 808-293-3884
Fax: 808-293-3877

Broer Map Library (120)
74 Hampden Road
Somers, CT 06071
Phone: 413-221-4642
Web: www.broermaps.org/

Bryn Mawr College (414)
Collier Science Library
Geologic Map Library
101 North Merion Avenue
Bryn Mawr, PA 19010
Phone: 610-526-7462
Web: www.brynmawr.edu/geology

Buffalo and Erie County Public Library (338)
Central Library
Humanities and Social Sciences
1 Lafayette Square
Buffalo, NY 14203
Phone: 716-858-8900
Fax: 716-858-6211
Web: www.buffalolib.org

Bureau of Land Management,
Juneau—John Rishel Information Center (11)
100 Savikko Road
Douglas, AK 99824
Phone: 907-364-1553
Fax: 907-364-1574
Web: juneau.ak.blm.gov/library/library.html

California Academy of Sciences (72)
J.W. Mailliard, Jr. Library
Donald C. Heckman Memorial Map Collection
55 Concourse Drive
Golden Gate Park
San Francisco, CA 94118
Phone: 415-750-7102
Fax: 415-750-7106
Web: www.calacademy.org/research/library/

California Historical Society (73)
North Baker Research Library
678 Mission Street
San Francisco, CA 94105
Phone: 415-357-1848
Fax: 415-357-1850
Web: www.californiahistoricalsociety.org

California Institute of Technology (64)
Geological and Planetary Sciences Library
Map Room
Geology Library 100-23
Pasadena, CA 91125
Phone: 626-395-6699
Fax: 626-568-0935
Web: library.caltech.edu

California Polytechnic State University (86)
Robert E. Kennedy Library
Library—Reference Department
San Luis Obispo, CA 93407
Phone: 805-756-2649
Web: www.lib.calpoly.edu

California State Library (68)
California History Section
900 N Street
Room 200

Sacramento, CA 95814
Phone: 916 654-0176
Fax: 916 654-8777
Web: www.library.ca.gov

California State Library (69)
Government Publications Section
914 Capitol Mall
Sacramento, CA 95814
Phone: 916-654-0069
Fax: 916-653-6114
Web: www.library.ca.gov

California State University, Chico (49)
Meriam Library
Maps
400 West First Street
Chico, CA 95926
Phone: 539-898-5710
Fax: 530-898-4443
Web: www.csuchioco.edu/lbib/maps/maps-page1.html

California State University, Fresno (52)
Henry Madden Library
Map Library
5200 West Barton Avenue
M/S ML34
Fresno, CA 93740-8014
Phone: 559-278-2405
Fax: 559-278-6952
Web: www.lib.csufresno.edu/subjectresources/maps/

Campbell University (348)
Carrie Rich Memorial Library
Government Documents
227 Main Street
Buies Creek, NC 27506
Phone: 910-893-1465
Fax: 910-893-1470
Web: www.lib.campbell.edu

Carleton College (283)
Laurence McKinley Gould Library
Map Collection
One North College Street
Northfield, MN 55057
Phone: 507-646-4260
Fax: 507-646-4087
Web: www.carleton.edu/campus/library/collections/
overview.html#maps

Case Western Reserve University (377)
Kelvin Smith Library
11055 Euclid Avenue
Cleveland, OH 44106

Phone: 216-368-6511
Fax: 216-368-3669
Web: library.case.edu/ksl/index.html

Catawba College (365)
Corriher-Linn-Black Library
2300 West Innes Street
Salisbury, NC 28144
Phone: 704-637-4379
Fax: 704-637-4304
Web: www.lib.catawba.edu

Central Arkansas Library System (38)
Main Library
Reference Services
100 Rock Street
Little Rock, AR 72201
Phone: 501-918-3000
Fax: 501-376-1830
Web: www.cals.lib.ar.us

Central Michigan University (272)
Charles V. Park Library
300 East Preston Street
Mount Pleasant, MI 48859
Phone: 989-774-3414
Fax: 989-774-1350
Web: www.cmich.edu/libraries.htm

Central Washington University (526)
James E. Brooks Library
Documents, Maps and Microforms
400 East University Way
Ellensburg, WA 98926-7548
Phone: 509-963-1541
Fax: 509-963-3684
Web: www.lib.cwu.edu/documents/

Central Wyoming College (563)
Library
2660 Peck Avenue
Riverton, WY 82501
Phone: 307 855-2141
Fax: 307-855-2094
Web: www.cwc.edu/student_services/library/index.php

Charleston County Public Library (436)
Main Library
68 Calhoun Street
Charleston, SC 29401
Phone: 843-805-6930
Fax: 843-727-6752
Web: www.ccpl.org

Charleston Library Society (437)
164 King Street
Charleston, SC 29401

Phone: 843-723-9912
Fax: 843-723-3500

Charleston Museum (438)
Archives
360 Meeting Street
Charleston, SC 29403
Phone: 843-722-2996
Fax: 843-722-1784
Web: www.charlestonmuseum.org

Chattanooga-Hamilton County Bicentennial Library (457)
Local History Map Collection
1001 Broad Street
Chattanooga, TN 37402
Phone: 423-757-5317
Web: www.lib.chattanooga.gov

Chicago Public Library (164)
Harold Washington Library Center
Government Publications Department
400 South State Street
Chicago, IL 60605
Phone: 312-747-4508
Fax: 312-747-4516
Web: chipublib.org

Cincinnati Museum Center (374)
Cincinnati Historical Society Library
1301 Western Avenue
Cincinnati, OH 45203
Phone: 513-287-7030
Fax: 513-287-7095
Web: www.cincymuseum.org

Citadel Military College (439)
Daniel Library
171 Moultrie Street
Charleston, SC 29409
Phone: 843-953-2569
Fax: 843-953-5190
Web: www.citadel.edu/library/

City of Mesa Library (20)
64 East First Street
Mesa, AZ 85201
Phone: 480-644-2207
Web: www.mesalibrary.org

Claremont University Center, Claremont Colleges (50)
Honnold/Mudd Library
800 North Dartmouth Ave
Claremont, CA 91711
Phone: 909-621-8045

Fax: 909-621-8681
Web: libraries.claremont.edu/hm

Clemson University (441)
R.M. Cooper Library
Government Documents
Campus Box 343001
Clemson, SC 29634-3001
Phone: 864-656-5168
Fax: 864-656-7608
Web: www.lib.clemson.edu/GovDocs/maps/index.htm

Cleveland Public Library (378)
Map Collection
325 Superior Avenue
Cleveland, OH 44114
Phone: 216-623-2880
Fax: 216-902-4978
Web: www.cpl.org

Cleveland State University (379)
Library
2121 Euclid Avenue
Cleveland, OH 44114
Phone: 216-687-2475
Fax: 216-687-9380
Web: www.ulib.csuohio.edu

Coastal Carolina University (446)
Kimbel Library
P.O. Box 261954
Conway, SC 29528
Phone: 843-349-2414
Fax: 843-349-2412
Web: www.coatsal.edu/library

College of William and Mary (520)
Earl Gregg Swem Library
Geology Department Library
P.O. Box 8795
Williamsburg, VA 23187-8795
Phone: 757 221-2094
Fax: 757 221-2093
Web: swem.wm.edu/Guide/Geology/index.html

Colonial Williamsburg Foundation (521)
301 First Street
Williamsburg, VA 23185
Phone: 757-229-1000
Web: www.colonialwilliamsburg.org

Colorado College (97)
Tutt Library
Government Documents/Maps
1021 North Cascade Avenue
Colorado Springs, CO 80903

Phone: 719-389-6660
Fax: 719-389-6082
Web: www2.coloradocollege.edu/Library/

Colorado Historical Society (100)
Stephen H. Hart Library
1300 Broadway
Denver, CO 80224
Phone: 303-866-4600
Fax: 303-866-5739
Web: www.coloradohistory.org

Colorado School of Mines (109)
Arthur Lakes Library
Map Room
1400 Illinois
Golden, CO 80401
Phone: 303-273-3697
Fax: 303-273-3199
Web: www.mines.edu/library/maproom

Colorado State Archives (101)
1313 Sherman Street
Room 1B-20
Denver, CO 80203
Phone: 303-866-2550
Fax: 303-866-2257
Web: www.colorado.gov/dpa/doit/archives/geography
.htm

Colorado State University (107)
Morgan Library
Karen W. Jacob Map Collection
Fort Collins, CO 80523-1019
Phone: 970-491-1836
Fax: 970-491-5817
Web: lib.colostate.edu

Columbia River Inter-Tribal Fish Commission (404)
StreamNet Library
729 NE Oregon St, Ste 190
Portland, OR 97232
Phone: 503-731-1304
Fax: 503-731-1260
Web: www.fishlib.org

Columbia University (342)
Lehman Library
Map Collection
420 West 118th St
New York, NY 10027
Phone: 212-854-5664
Fax: 212-854-1365
Web: www.columbia.edu/cu/lweb/indiv/lehman/guides/
maps.html

Columbus Metropolitan Library (380)
Biography, History and Travel Division
96 South Grant Avenue
Columbus, OH 43215
Phone: 614-645-2710
Fax: 614-645-2051
Web: www.columbuslibrary.org

Connecticut Historical Society Library (114)
1 Elizabeth Street
Hartford, CT 06105
Phone: 860-236-5621
Fax: 860-236-2664
Web: www.chs.org

Connecticut State Library (115)
Connecticut State Library
History and Genealogy Unit
231 Capitol Avenue
Hartford, CT 06106
Phone: 860-757-6580
Fax: 860-757-6677
Web: www.cslib.org

Contra Costa County Library (65)
Central Library
1750 Oak Park Boulevard
Pleasant Hill, CA 94523-4497
Phone: 925-646-6434
Fax: 925-646-6040
Web: ccclib.org

Cornell University (340)
John M. Olin Library
Map and Geospatial Information Collection
Ithaca, NY 14853-5301
Phone: 607-255-7557
Fax: 607-255-9346
Web: www.library.cornell.edu/okuref/maps/map.htm

Dallas Public Library (485)
J. Eric Jonsson Central Library
Government Information Center/Map Collection
1515 Young Street
Dallas, TX 75201
Phone: 214-670-1468

Dallas Public Library (486)
Texas/Dallas History and Archives Division
1515 Young Street
Dallas, TX 75201
Phone: 214-670-1435
Fax: 214-670-1437
Web: dallaslibrary.org/ctx/ctx.htm

Fax: 214-670-1451
Web: www.dallaslibrary.org/CGI/maps.htm

Dartmouth College (325)
Baker/Berry Library
Evans Map Room
HB 6025
Hanover, NH 03755
Phone: 603-646-2579
Fax: 603-646-3628
Web: www.dartmouth.edu/~maproom/

Dartmouth College (326)
Kresge Physical Sciences Library
6115 Fairchild Center
Hanover, NH 3755
Phone: 603-646-3563
Fax: 603-646-3681
Web: www.dartmouth.edu/~krescook/index.shtml

Daughters of the Republic of Texas Library (496)
P.O. Box 1401
San Antonio, TX 78295
Phone: 210-225-1071
Fax: 210-212-8514
Web: www.drtl.org

David Rumsey Collection (74)
Cole Valley
San Francisco, CA 94117
Phone: 415-386-1750
Fax: 415-386-1781
Web: www.davidrumsey.com

Dayton Metro Library (386)
215 East Third Street
Dayton, OH 45402
Phone: 937-227-9500
Fax: 937-227-9548
Web: www.daytonmetrolibrary.org

Dayton Society of Natural History (387)
Library and Map Collection
2600 DeWeese Parkway
Dayton, OH 45414
Phone: 937-275-7431
Fax: 937-275-5811
Web: www.boonshoftmuseum.org

Denison University (389)
William Howard Doane Library
Geology Department/Government Documents
Granville, OH 43023
Phone: 740-587-5644
Fax: 740-587-6285
Web: www.denison.edu/library

Denver Public Library (102)
Central Branch
Government Publications/GOVPUBS Maps
10 West 14th Avenue Parkway
Denver, CO 80204-2731
Phone: 720-865-1721
Fax: 720-865-1785
Web: www.denverlibrary.org

Denver Public Library (103)
Western History Collection
10 West 14th Avenue Parkway
Denver, CO 80204
Phone: 720-865-1821
Fax: 720-865-1880
Web: www.denver.lib.co.us

DePauw University (187)
Prevo Science Library
602 South College
Greencastle, IN 46135
Phone: 765-658-4306
Web: www.depauw.edu/library

District of Columbia Public Library (123)
Martin Luther King Jr Memorial Library
Washingtoniana Division #307
901 G Street NW
Washington, DC 20001
Phone: 202-727-1213
Fax: 202-727-1129
Web: www.dclibrary.org

Doane College (300)
Perkins Library
Vertical Files
1014 Boswell Avenue
Crete, NE 68333
Phone: 402-826-8567
Fax: 402-826-8199
Web: www.doane.edu/library_new/index.asp

Douglas County Historical Society Library (315)
Library/Archives Center
Historical maps
5730 North 30th Street
Omaha, NE 68111
Phone: 402-451-1013
Fax: 402-453-9448
Web: www.omahahistory.org

Duke University (356)
Perkins Library
Public Documents and Maps Department
025 Perkins Library

Durham, NC 27708-0177
Phone: 919-660-5851
Fax: 919-684-2855
Web: docs.lib.duke.edu/maps/

Duke University (357)
Rare Book, Manuscript, and Special Collections Library
Map Collection
Box 90185
Durham, NC 27708-0185
Phone: 919-660-5822
Fax: 919-660-5934
Web: scriptorium.lib.duke.edu

Earlham College (195)
Wildman Science Library
P.O. Box 72
Richmond, IN 47374
Phone: 765-983-1245
Web: www.earlham.edu/~libr/wildman/

East Carolina University (360)
Joyner Library
Government Documents and Microforms
E. 5th Street
Greenville, NC 27858-4353
Phone: 252-328-0238
Fax: 252-328-2271
Web: www.lib.ecu.edu/govdoc/index.html

East Tennessee State University (461)
Charles C. Sherrod Library
Documents/Law/Maps Department
P.O. Box 78665
Johnson City, TN 37614
Phone: 423-439-5334
Fax: 423-439-5674
Web: www.etsu.edu/etsu/libraries.asp

East View Cartographic, Inc. (279)
Corporate Library
3020 Harbor Lane North
Minneapolis, MN 55447-8956
Phone: 763-550-0965
Fax: 763-559-2931
Web: www.cartographic.com

Eastern Illinois University (162)
Booth Library
Government Documents
600 Lincoln Avenue
Charleston, IL 61920
Phone: 217-581-6072
Fax: 217-581-6066
Web: www.library.eiu.edu

Eastern Kentucky University (226)
John Grant Crabbe Library
University Archives Map Collection
521 Lancaster Avenue
Richmond, KY 40475
Phone: 859-622-1792
Fax: 859-622-1174
Web: www.library.eku.edu/collections/sca/

Eastern Michigan University (273)
Bruce T. Halle Library
Maps
Ypsilanti, MI 48197
Phone: 734-487-0020 x2115, x2116
Fax: 734-487-8861
Web: www.emich.edu/halle

Eastern Oregon University (402)
Pierce Library
1 University Boulevard
La Grande, OR 97850
Phone: 541-962-3546
Fax: 541-962-3335
Web: pierce.eou.edu

Eastern Washington University (525)
JFK Library
Maps
816 F Street, 100 LIB
Cheney, WA 99004
Phone: 509-359-2263
Fax: 509-359-6456
Web: www.library.ewu.edu/collections/maps.html

Emory University (143)
Robert W. Woodruff Library
540 Asbury Circle
Atlanta, GA 30322
Phone: 404 727-6875
Web: web.library.emory.edu/subjects/maps/maps.html

Emporia State University (207)
William Allen White Library
Information and Instructional Services
1200 Commercial
Campus Box 4051
Emporia, KS 66801
Phone: 620-341-5207
Fax: 620-341-5997
Web: www.emporia.edu/libsv

Emporia State University (208)
William Allen White Library
Physical Science Division/Geology Map Library
1200 Commercial

Campus Box 4051
Emporia, KS 66801
Phone: 620-341-5207
Fax: 620-341-5997
Web: www.emporia.edu/earthsci/amber/maplibrary
.htm

Enoch Pratt Free Library (240)
Maryland Department/Map Collection
400 Cathedral Street
Baltimore, MD 21201
Phone: 410-396-5468
Fax: 410-396-9537
Web: www.epfl.net/slrc/md/

Enoch Pratt Free Library (241)
Social Science and History Department
400 Cathedral Street
Baltimore, MD 21201
Phone: 410-396-5320
Fax: 410-396-1413
Web: www.epfl.net

Evergreen State College (528)
Daniel J. Evans Library
Government Documents/Maps
2700 Evergreen Parkway NW
Mailstop L-2300
Olympia, WA 98505
Phone: 360-867-6251
Fax: 360-866-6790
Web: www.evergreen.edu/library/govdocs/index.html

Family History Library (503)
35 North West Temple Street
Salt Lake City, UT 84150-3400
Phone: 800-346-6044; 801-240-2584
Fax: 801-240-3718
Web: www.familysearch.org

Flagstaff City-Coconino County Public Library (16)
Main Library
300 West Aspen Avenue
Flagstaff, AZ 86001
Phone: 928-779-7670
Fax: 928-774-9573
Web: flagstaffpubliclibrary.org

Flint District Library (265)
Flint Public Library
Maps
1026 East Kearsley
Flint, MI 48502
Phone: 810-232-7111
Fax: 810-249-2635
Web: www.flint.lib.mi.us

Florida Atlantic University (129)
S.E. Wimberly Library
777 Glades Road
Boca Raton, FL 33431
Phone: 561-297-3760
Fax: 561-338-3863
Web: www.fau.edu/library

Folger Shakespeare Library (124)
201 East Capitol Street SE
Washington, DC 20003
Phone: 202-544-4600
Fax: 202-675-0313
Web: www.folger.edu

Fort Hays State University (209)
Forsyth Library
600 Park Street
Hays, KS 67601
Phone: 785-628-4340
Fax: 785-628-4096
Web: www.fhsu.edu/forsyth_lib

Fort Lewis College (106)
John F. Reed Library and the Center
   for Southwest Studies
Map Collection
Fort Lewis College
Durango, CO 81303
Phone: 247-7551
Web: library.fortlewis.edu/reference/mapgovweb/maps
   .html
   swcenter.fortlewis.edu/SpecialCollections.htm#
   Guides

Fox Island Historical Society (527)
Map Room
1017 9th Avenue
Fox Island, WA 98333
Phone: 253-549-2461
Web: foxisland.net

Franklin and Marshall College (418)
Martin Library of the Sciences
P.O. Box 3003
Lancaster, PA 17604
Phone: 717-291-3843
Fax: 717-291-4088
Web: library.fandm.edu

Free Library of Philadelphia (421)
Map Collection
1901 Vine Street
Philadelphia, PA 19103-1189
Phone: 215-686-5397

Fax: 215-563-3628
Web: www.library.phila.gov

Frostburg State University (246)
Lewis J. Ort Library
User Services Division
1 Stadium Drive
Frostburg, MD 21532
Phone: 301-687-4887
Fax: 301-687-7069
Web: www.frostburg.edu/dept/library/library.htm

Furman University (448)
James B. Duke Library
Government Document Map Collection
3300 Poinsett Highway
Greenville, SC 29613
Phone: 864-294-2260
Web: library.furman.edu

Geological Survey of Alabama (6)
Library
P.O. Box 869999
Tuscaloosa, AL 35486-6999
Phone: 205-247-3634
Fax: 205-349-2861
Web: www.gsa.state.al.us

George Mason University (514)
Fenwick Library
Government Documents/Maps
4400 University Dr
Fairfax, VA 22030
Phone: 703-993-2238
Fax: 703-993-2494
Web: library.gmu.edu/resources/govt/

George Mason University (515)
Fenwick Library
Special Collections and Archives
4400 University Drive
Fairfax, VA 22030
Phone: 703-993-2220
Fax: 703-993-2255
Web: www.gmu.edu/library/specialcollections

Georgetown County Library (447)
405 Cleland Street
Georgetown, SC 29440
Phone: 843-545-3300
Fax: 843-545-3395
Web: www.gcpl.lib.sc.us

Georgia College and State University (149)
Ina Dillard Russell Library
CBX 043

Milledgeville, GA 31061
Phone: 478-445-4047
Fax: 478-445-6847
Web: library.gcsu.edu

Georgia Institute of Technology (144)
Library and Information Center
Special Formats and Maps Department
704 Cherry Street
Atlanta, GA 30332-0900
Phone: 404-385-0226
Fax: 404-894-8190
Web: www.library.gatech.edu

Georgia Southwestern State University (140)
James Earl Carter Library
800 Wheatley Street
Americus, GA 31709
Phone: 229-931-2259
Fax: 229-931-2265
Web: www.gsw.edu/~library/

Georgia State University (145)
University Library
Information Services Department
100 Decatur Street SE
Atlanta, GA 30303-3202
Phone: 404-463-9934
Fax: 404-651-4315
Web: www.library.gsu.edu/maps

Grand Rapids Public Library (266)
Grand Rapids History and Special Collections Center
(GRHSCC)
111 Library Street NE
Grand Rapids, MI 49503
Phone: 616-988-5400
Fax: 616-988-5421
Web: www.grpl.org

Grand Valley State University (261)
James H. Zumberge Library
1 Campus Drive
Allendale, MI 49401
Phone: 616-331-3500
Web: www.gvsu.edu/library/govdoc

Greensboro Public Library (358)
North Carolina Collection
219 North Church Street
Greensboro, NC 27402-3178
Phone: 336-335-5430
Fax: 336-335-5416
Web: www.greensborolibrary.org

Greenville County Library System (449)
South Carolina Room—Government Documents
Section
25 Heritage Green Place
Greenville, SC 29601
Phone: 864-242-5000
Fax: 864-232-9656
Web: www.greenvillelibrary.org

Grinnell College (202)
Burling Library
1111 6th Avenue
Grinnell, IA 50112
Phone: 641-269-4234
Fax: 641-269-4283
Web: www.lib.grin.edu/Places/govdocs/

Gustavus Adolphus College (289)
Bob Moline Map Library
800 W College Avenue
Saint Peter, MN 56082
Phone: 507-933-7313
Fax: 507-933-7041
Web: www.gustavus.edu/library

Hanover College (188)
Duggan Library
P.O. Box 287
Hanover, IN 47243
Phone: 812-866-7165
Fax: 812-866-7172
Web: www.hanover.edu/Library

Hardin-Simmons University (474)
Richardson Library
Government Documents
2200 Hickory
Abilene, TX 79698
Phone: 325-670-1521
Web: rupert.alc.org/library/

Hardin-Simmons University (473)
Rupert and Pauline Richardson Library
Williams Map Collection
2200 Hickory Street
Abilene, TX 79698
Phone: 325-670-1239
Fax: 325-677-8351
Web: rupert.alc.org/library/

Harvard University (254)
Pusey Library
Harvard Map Collection
Cambridge, MA 02138
Phone: 617-495-2417

Fax: 617-496-0440
Web: hcl.harvard.edu/maps

Hawai'i State Archives (152)
Map Collection
Iolani Palace Grounds
Honolulu, HI 96813
Phone: 808-586-0329
Fax: 808-586-0330
Web: statearchives.lib.Hawaii.edu/

Hawai'i State Public Library System (153)
Hawai'i and Pacific Section
478 South King Street
Honolulu, HI 96813
Phone: 808-586-3535
Fax: 808-586-3586
Web: www.Hawaii.gov/hidocs

Heidelberg College (392)
Beeghly Library
10 Greenfield Street
Tiffin, OH 44883
Phone: 419-448-2104
Fax: 419-448-2578
Web: www.heidelberg.edu/offices/library

Historical Museum of Southern Florida (136)
Charlton W. Tebeau Research Library
101 West Flagler Street
Miami, FL 33130
Phone: 305-375-1492
Fax: 305-372-6313
Web: www.historical-museum.org

Historical Society of Cheshire County (327)
246 Main Street
PO Box 803
Keene, NH 3431
Phone: 603-352-1895
Web: www.hsccnh.org

Historical Society of Pennsylvania (422)
Library Division
Archives
1300 Locust Street
Philadelphia, PA 19107
Phone: 215-732-6200
Fax: 215-732-2680
Web: www.hsp.org

Historical Society of Western Pennsylvania (424)
1212 Smallman Street
Pittsburgh, PA 15222
Phone: 412-454-6364

Fax: 412-454-6028
Web: www.pghhistory.org

History San Jose (82)
Research Library
1650 Senter Road
San Jose, CA 95112-2599
Phone: 408-287-2290
Fax: 408-287-2291
Web: www.historysanjose.org/research/library

Humboldt State University (41)
University Library
1 Harpst Street
Arcata, CA 95521
Phone: 707-442-3418
Fax: 707-442-4900
Web: library.humboldt.edu/infoservices/atmapcoll.htm

Idaho State Historical Society (157)
Historical Library and State Archives
450 North Fourth Street
Boise, ID 83702
Phone: 208-334-3356
Fax: 208-334-3198
Web: www.idahohistory.net/library_archives.html

Illinois Institute of Technology (165)
Paul V. Galvin Library
Government Documents
35 West 33rd Street
Chicago, IL 60616
Phone: 312-567-3614
Fax: 312-567-3955
Web: www.gl.iit.edu/govdocs/

Illinois State Archives (175)
Illinois State Archives
MC Norton Building
Springfield, IL 62756
Phone: 217-782-3501
Fax: 217-524-3930
Web: www.cyberdriveillinois.com

Illinois State Geological Survey (161)
Library and Map Room
615 East Peabody Drive
Champaign, IL 61820
Phone: 217-333-5110
Fax: 217-333-2830
Web: www.isgs.uiuc.edu/library/index.html

Illinois State Library (176)
300 South Second Street
Springfield, IL 62701

Phone: 217-782-5823
Fax: 217-557-6737
Web: www.cyberdriveillinois.com/library/isl/ref/islmaps
   .html

Illinois State University (171)
Milner Library
Social Sciences Division
Campus Box 8900
Normal, IL 61790-8900
Phone: 309-438-3486
Fax: 309-438-3676
Web: www.mlb.ilstu.edu

Illinois Valley Community College (172)
Jacobs Library
815 North Orlando Smith Avenue
Oglesby, IL 61348
Phone: 815 224-0306
Fax: 815 224-9147
Web: www.ivcc.edu/library

Indiana Historical Society (189)
William Henry Smith Memorial Library
450 West Ohio Street
Indianapolis, IN 46202-3269
Phone: 317-232-1879
Fax: 317-234-0169
Web: www.indianahistory.org

Indiana State Library (190)
140 North Senate Avenue
Indianapolis, IN 46204-2296
Phone: 317-232-3685
Fax: 317-232-3728
Web: www.statelib.lib.in.us

Indiana State University (196)
Geography, Geology and Anthropology Department
   Map Library
Science 151, Indiana State University
Terre Haute, IN 47809
Phone: 812-237-2266
Web: lib.indstate.edu

Indiana University, Bloomington (181)
Geography and Map Library
701 East Kirkwood, 015 Student Building
Bloomington, IN 47405
Phone: 812-855-1108
Web: www.indiana.edu/~libgm

Indiana University, Bloomington (182)
Geology Library
1001 East Tenth Street
Bloomington, IN 47405-1405
Phone: 812-855-1494

Fax: 812-855-6614
Web: www.libraries.iub.edu

Indiana University, Bloomington (183)
Government Information, Microforms,
   and Statistical Services
1320 East 10th Street,
c264 IUB Main Library
Bloomington, IN 47405
Phone: 812-855-6924
Fax: 812-855-3460
Web: www.indiana.edu/~libgpd

Indiana University, Northwest (186)
Library
Government Publications Department
3400 Broadway
Gary, IN 46408
Phone: 219-980-6608
Fax: 219-980-6558
Web: www.iun.edu/~lib

Indiana University-Purdue University,
Fort Wayne (185)
Helmke Library
Geosciences Department Map Collection, SB230
2101 East Coliseum Boulevard
Fort Wayne, IN 46805
Phone: 260-481-6514
Fax: 260-481-6509
Web: www.lib.ipfw.edu

Indiana University-Purdue University,
Indianapolis (192)
University Library
775 West Michigan Street
Indianapolis, IN 46202-5195
Phone: 317-274-8278
Fax: 317-278-2300
Web: www.ulib.iupui.edu

Indianapolis-Marion County Public Library (191)
Library
40 East Street Clair Street
Indianapolis, IN 46202
Phone: 317-269-1700
Fax: 317-268-5229
Web: imcpl.org

Iowa State University (199)
Parks Library
Map Room
281 Parks Library, Iowa State University
Ames, IA 50011-2140
Phone: 515-294-3956
Fax: 515-294-5525
Web: www.lib.iastate.edu/libinfo/dept/maproom.html

Iron Range Research Center (275)
Maps
801 SW Highway 169
Suite 1
Chisholm, MN 55719
Phone: 218-254-7959
Fax: 218-254-7971
Web: www.ironrangeresearchcenter.org

Jefferson County Historical Society (533)
Research Center
Map Collection
13692 Airport Cutoff Road (Hwy 19)
Port Townsend, WA 98368
Phone: 360-379-6673
Web: www.jchsmuseum.org

Jefferson County Public Library (111)
Lakewood Library
Government Documents
10200 West 20th Avenue
Lakewood, CO 80215
Phone: 303-232-9507
Fax: 303-275-2234
Web: jefferson.lib.co.us

Johns Hopkins University (242)
Eisenhower Library
Government Publications/Maps/Law Library
3400 North Charles Street
Baltimore, MD 21212
Phone: 410-516-8360
Fax: 410-516-6029
Web: www.library.jhu.edu/gpml/

Johnson County Library (213)
9875 West 87th Street
Overland Park, KS 66212
Phone: 913-495-2400
Fax: 913-495-9104
Web: www.jocolibrary.org

Kalamazoo Public Library (268)
Central Branch
Adult Services/History Room
315 South Rose St
Kalamazoo, MI 49009
Phone: 269-553-7801
Fax: 269-342-0414
Web: www.kpl.gov

Kansas State Historical Society (215)
Center for Historical Research
Library and Archives Division
6425 SW 6th Avenue
Topeka, KS 66615-1099

Phone: 785-272-8681 x116
Fax: 785-272-8682
Web: www.kshs.org

Kansas State University (212)
Hale Library
Government Publications Division
Manhattan, KS 66502-1200
Phone: 785-532-7448
Fax: 785-532-6144
Web: www.lib.ksu.edu/depts/govpubs/mainmap.html

Kentucky Division of Mines and Minerals (220)
Mine Map Information Center
Mine Map Repository
P.O. 2244
Frankfort, KY 40601
Phone: 502-573-0140
Web: minemaps.ky.gov

Kentucky Historical Society (221)
Thomas D. Clark Library and Special Collections
Special Collections
100 West Broadway
Frankfort, KY 40601
Phone: 502-564-1792
Fax: 502-564-4701
Web: history.ky.gov/

Kern County Library (42)
Beale Memorial Library
Geology-Mining-Petroleum Room
701 Truxtun Avenue
Bakersfield, CA 93301
Phone: 661-868-0783
Web: www.kerncountylibrary.org

Ketchikan Public Library (15)
Adult Division
629 Dock Street
Ketchikan, AK 99901
Phone: 907 225 3331
Fax: 907-225 0153
Web: www.firstcitylibraries.org

Kitsap County Historical Society (524)
280 4th Street
Bremerton, WA 98337
Phone: 360-479-6226
Fax: 360-415-9294
Web: www.waynes.net/kchsm/

Knox County Public Library (462)
East Tennessee History Center
Calvin M. McClung Historical Collection
314 West Clinch Avenue
Knoxville, TN 37902-2313

Phone: 865-215-8801
Fax: 865-215-8810
Web: www.knoxlib.org

**Knoxville/Knox County
Metropolitan Planning Commission** (463)
Planning Commission Library
400 Main Street
Suite 403
Knoxville, TN 37902
Phone: 865-215-2500
Fax: 865-215-2068
Web: www.knoxmpc.org

Kutztown University (417)
Rohrbach Library
Maps Department
15200 Kutztown Road
Building 5
Kutztown, PA 19530
Phone: 610-683-4813
Web: www.kutztown.edu/library/maps.htm

La Crosse Public Library (545)
800 Main Street
La Crosse, WI 54601
Phone: 608-789-7122
Fax: 608-789-7161
Web: www.lacrosselibrary.org

Laboratory of Anthropology (333)
Laboratory of Anthropology Library
Archeological Records Management System
708 Camino Lejo
Santa Fe, NM 87503
Phone: 505-476-1275
Fax: 505-476-1320
Web: potsuii.arms.state.nm.us

Laurens County Library (450)
Laurens County Historical Room
1017 West Main Street
Laurens, SC 29360
Phone: 864-984-0596
Fax: 864-984-0598
Web: www.lcpl.org

Lehigh University (413)
Fairchild Martindale Library
Government Documents
8A East Packer Avenue
Bethlehem, PA 18015
Phone: 610-758-5337
Web: www.lehigh.edu/library

Lewis and Clark College (405)
Aubrey Watzek Library
Special Collections
0615 SW Palatine Hill Road
Portland, OR 97219
Phone: 503-768-7254
Fax: 5037687282
Web: www.lclark.edu/~archives/specialcollections

Library Company of Philadelphia (423)
Print and Photograph Department
1314 Locust Street
Philadelphia, PA 19107
Phone: 215-546-8229
Fax: 215-546-5167
Web: www.librarycompany.org

Library of Congress (125)
Geography and Map Division
101 Independence Avenue SE
Madison Building
Room LM B01
Washington, DC 20540-4650
Phone: 202-707-6277
Fax: 202-707-8531
Web: www.loc.gov/rr/geogmap/

Library of Michigan (270)
Public Services
702 West Kalamazoo
Lansing, MI 48909
Phone: 517-373-1300
Fax: 517-373-5853
Web: michigan.gov/libraryofmichigan

Library of Virginia (518)
Archival and Information Services Division/
  Map Collection
800 East Broad Street
Richmond, VA 23227
Phone: 804-692-3888
Fax: 804-692-3556
Web: www.lva.lib.va.us

Lincoln City Libraries (305)
136 S 14th St
Lincoln, NE 68508
Phone: 402-441-8530
Fax: 402-441-8534
Web: www.lcl.lib.ne.us

Loras College (201)
Library
1450 Alta Vista
Dubuque, IA 52001

Phone: 563-588-7042
Fax: 563-588-7292
Web: www.loras.edu/~LIB/

Los Angeles Public Library (56)
Richard J. Riordan Central Library
History and Genealogy Department
630 West 5th Street
Los Angeles, CA 90065
Phone: 213-228-7414
Fax: 213-228-7409
Web: www.lapl.org/guides/map_coll.html

Louisiana State University (227)
Cartographic Information Center
313 Howe-Russell Building
Baton Rouge, LA 70803
Phone: 225-578-6247
Fax: 225-578-4420
Web: www.cic.lsu.edu

Louisiana State University (228)
Hill Memorial Library
Special Collections
Louisiana State University
Baton Rouge, LA 70803
Phone: 225-578-6551
Fax: 225-578-9425
Web: www.lib.lsu.edu/special

Louisiana State University (229)
Troy H. Middleton Library
Government Documents/Microforms Department
53 Middleton
Baton Rouge, LA 70803
Phone: 225-578-2570
Fax: 225-578-6535
Web: www.lib.lsu.edu/govdocs

Louisiana Tech University (233)
Prescott Memorial Library
Everett Street at the Columns
Ruston, LA 71272
Phone: 318-257-4989
Fax: 318-257-2579
Web: www.latech.edu/tech/library/maps.htm

Loveland Public Library (112)
Map Vertical File
300 North Adams
Loveland, CO 80537
Phone: 970-962-2402
Fax: 970-962-2905
Web: www.ci.loveland.co.us/library

Loyola Marymount University (57)
Charles Von der Ahe Library
Department of Archives and Special Collections
One LMU Drive
MS 8200
Los Angeles, CA 90045-2659
Phone: 310-338-3048
Fax: 310-338-5895

Lunar and Planetary Institute (491)
Center for Information and Research Services
3600 Bay Area Blvd
Houston, TX 77059
Phone: 281-486-2182
Fax: 281-486-2186
Web: www.lpi.usra.edu/library

Maine Historical Society (237)
Research Library
489 Congress Street
Portland, ME 04101
Phone: 207-774-1822
Fax: 207-775-4301
Web: www.mainehistory.org

Maine Maritime Academy (234)
Nutting Memorial Library
Battle Avenue
Castine, ME 04420
Phone: 207-326-2265
Fax: 207-326-2261
Web: bell.mma.edu/~library

Maricopa County Assessor's Office (23)
Parcel Maps
301 West Jefferson Street Ste 330
Phoenix, AZ 85003
Phone: 602-3721627
Fax: 602-5063394
Web: www.maricopa.gov/assessor/gis

Mary Washington College (516)
Simpson Library
1801 College Avenue
Fredericksburg, VA 22401
Phone: 540-654-1148
Fax: 540-654-1067
Web: www.library.mwc.edu/maps.html

Massachusetts Institute of Technology (255)
Science Library
Map Collection
14S-134
77 Massachusetts Avenue
Cambridge, MA 02139-4307

Phone: 617-253-5685
Web: libraries.mit.edu/science

McNeese State University (230)
Frazar Memorial Library
Government Documents Department
300 Beauregard Drive
Lake Charles, LA 70609
Phone: 337-475-5736
Fax: 337-475-5719
Web: library.mcneese.edu/depts/docs/index.htm

Mead Public Library (555)
710 North 8th Street
Sheboygan, WI 53081
Phone: 920-459-3400 x3438
Fax: 920-459-4336
Web: www.esls.lib.wi.edu

**Memphis/Shelby County Public Library
and Information Center** (467)
Memphis and Shelby County Room
3030 Poplar Avenue
Memphis, TN 38111
Phone: 901-415-2742
Fax: 901-323-7981
Web: www.memphislibrary.org

Miami University (391)
Brill Science Library
Map Collections
Oxford, OH 45056
Phone: 513-529-1726
Fax: 513-529-1736
Web: www.lib.muohio.edu/external

Miami-Dade Public Library System (137)
Main Library
Social Science and the Florida Room
101 West Flagler Street
Miami, FL 33130
Phone: 305-375-5575
Fax: 305-375-3048
Web: www.mdpls.org

Michigan State University (264)
Main Library
Map Library
100 Library W308
East Lansing, MI 48854
Phone: 517-432-6277
Web: www.lib.msu.edu/coll/main/maps/index.htm

Michigan Technological University (267)
J.R. Van Pelt Library
Map Room

1400 Townsend Drive
Houghton, MI 49931
Phone: 906-487-2698
Fax: 906-487-2357
Web: www.lib.mtu.edu

Middle Georgia Archives (148)
Washington Memorial Library
Middle Georgia Archives Map Collection
1180 Washington Avenue
Macon, GA 31201
Phone: 478-744-0820
Fax: 478-744-0893
Web: www.co.bibb.public.lib.ga.us

Midland Lutheran College (301)
Earth Science Department
900 North Clarkson
Fremont, NE 68025
Phone: 402-941-6328
Web: www.mlc.edu/library

Mill Valley Public Library (60)
Lucretia Little History Room
375 Throckmorton Avenue
Mill Valley, CA 94941
Phone: 415-389-4292-x104
Web: www.millvalleylibrary.org

Milwaukee Public Library (550)
814 West Wisconsin Avenue
Milwaukee, WI 53233
Phone: 414-286-3000
Fax: 414-286-2137
Web: www.mpl.org

Minneapolis Public Library (280)
300 Nicollet Mall
Minneapolis, MN 55401
Phone: 612-630-6000
Fax: 612-630-6220
Web: www.mplib.org

Minnesota Geological Survey (286)
2642 University Avenue West
Saint Paul, MN 55114-1057
Phone: 612-627-4780
Fax: 612-627-4778
Web: www.geo.umn.edu/mgs/

Minnesota Historical Society (287)
Library and Archives
345 Kellogg Boulevard West
Saint Paul, MN 55102-1906
Phone: 651-296-2143
Fax: 651-297-7436
Web: www.mnhs.org

Minnesota State University, Mankato (278)
Memorial Library
P.O. Box 8419
Mankato, MN 56002-8419
Phone: 507-389-5952
Fax: 507-389-5155
Web: www.lib.mnsu.edu

Minot State University (369)
Gordon B. Olson Library
Government Documents and Maps
500 University Avenue W
Minot, ND 58707
Phone: 701-858-3200
Fax: 701-858-3581
Web: www.minotstateu.edu/library/

Missouri Southern State University, Joplin (290)
George A. Spiva Library
Tri-State Mining Collection
3950 East Newman Road
Joplin, MO 64801
Phone: 417-625-9552
Fax: 417-625-9734
Web: www.mssu.edu/spivalib

Mohave Museum of History and Art (19)
400 West Beale Street
Kingman, AZ 86401
Phone: 928-753-3195
Fax: 928-718-1562
Web: www.mohavemuseum.org

Montana Historical Society (298)
Research Center
225 North Roberts
P.O. Box 201201
Helena, MT 59620
Phone: 406-444-2681
Fax: 406-444-5297
Web: www.montanahistoricalsociety.org

Montana State University, Bozeman (296)
Roland R. Renne Library
P.O. Box 173320
Bozeman, MT 59717-3320
Phone: 406-994-3171
Fax: 406-994-2851
Web: www.lib.montana.edu

Montana Tech of the University of Montana (297)
Library
1300 West Park Street
Butte, MT 59701
Phone: 406-496-4281
Fax: 406-496-4133
Web: www.mtech.edu/library

Monterey Public Library (61)
California History Room
Map Collection
625 Pacific Street
Monterey, CA 93940
Phone: 831-646-3741
Fax: 831-646-5618
Web: www.co.monterey.ca.us/library

Montgomery College (247)
Department of Applied Technology
Applied Geography
51 Mannakee Street
Rockville, MD 20850
Phone: 301-251-7614
Fax: 301-279-5001
Web: www.montgomerycollege.edu/library

Moravian Archives (367)
457 South Church Street
Winston-Salem, NC 27101
Phone: 336-722-1742
Fax: 336-725-4514
Web: MoravianArchives.org

Moravian College (411)
Earth Science Collection
1200 Main Street
Bethlehem, PA 18018-6650
Phone: 610-861-1440
Fax: 610-625-7918
Web: home.moravian.edu/users/phys/mejjg01/interests/
apparatus_pages/map_shelving.htm

Moravian College (412)
Reeves Library
1200 Main Street
Bethlehem, PA 18018
Phone: 610-861-1540
Fax: 610-861-1577
Web: home.moravian.edu/public/reeves

Morehead State University (225)
Camden-Carroll Library
Morehead, KY 40351
Phone: 606-783-5491
Fax: 606-783-2799
Web: www.moreheadstate.edu/library/

Multnomah County Library (406)
Central Library
801 SW 10th Avenue
Portland, OR 97205
Phone: 503-988-5728
Fax: 503-988-5226
Web: www.multcolib.org

Mystic Seaport (117)
G.W. Blunt White Library
Charts and Maps Collection
75 Greenmanville Avenue
Mystic, CT 06355
Phone: 860-572-0711
Fax: 860-572-5394
Web: schooner.mysticseaport.org

National Archives and Records Administration (243)
Special Media Archives Services Division
Cartographic Section
8601 Adelphi Road
Room 3320
College Park, MD 20740-6001
Phone: 301-837-0564
Fax: 301-837-3622
Web: www.archives.gov

**National Archives and Records Administration,
Pacific Region, San Francisco** (70)
1000 Commodore Drive
San Bruno, CA 94066
Phone: 650-238-3501
Fax: 650-238-3510
Web: www.archives.gov/facilities/ca/san_francisco.html

**National Archives and Records Administration,
Rocky Mountain Region** (104)
P.O. Box 25307
Building 48
Denver Federal Center
Denver, CO 80225
Phone: 303-407-5740
Fax: 303-407-5707
Web: www.archives.gov/facilities/rocky_mountain_
region.html

National Geographic Society (126)
Harold A. Hanson Map Library
National Geographic Maps
1145 17th Street NW
Washington, DC 20036
Phone: 202-857-7083
Web: www.nationalgeographic.com

**National Oceanic and
Atmospheric Administration** (535)
NOAA Seattle Library
7600 Sand Point Way NE
Seattle, WA 98115
Phone: 206-526-6241
Fax: 206-526-4535
Web: www.wrclib.noaa.gov

Natrona County Public Library (558)
307 East 2nd Street
Casper, WY 82601
Phone: 307-237-4935
Fax: 307-266-3734
Web: www.library.natrona.net

Nebraska Department of Natural Resources (306)
Data Bank
Information Technology Division
301 Centennial Mall South
Lincoln, NE 68509
Phone: 402-471-2363
Fax: 402-471-2900
Web: www.dnr.state.ne.us

Nebraska Department of Roads (307)
GIS Map Library
P.O. Box 94759
Lincoln, NE 68509
Phone: 402-479-4550
Fax: 402-479-3884
Web: nebraskatransportation.org/maps/

Nebraska Library Commission (308)
Nebraska Publications Clearinghouse
1200 N Street
Suite 120
Lincoln, NE 68508
Phone: 402-471-2045
Fax: 402-471-2083
Web: www.nlc.state.ne.us/docs/clear.html

Nebraska State Historical Society (309)
Library/Archives
P.O. Box 82554
1500 R Street
Lincoln, NE 68501
Phone: 402-471-4786
Fax: 402-471-8922
Web: www.nebraskahistory.org

Nederlof Historical Library (48)
P.O.Box 130880
Carlsbad, CA 92013-0880
Phone: 760-634-2960
Fax: 760-635-8641

Nevada County Library System (62)
Doris Foley Library for Historic Research
Map Collection
211 North Pine Street
Nevada City, CA 95959
Phone: 530-265-4606
Fax: 530-478-9751
Web: new.mynevadacounty.com/library/

Nevada Historical Society (320)
1650 North Virginia Street
Reno, NV 89503
Phone: 775-688-1190
Fax: 775-688-2917
Web: www.nevadaculture.org

Nevada State Library and Archives (319)
100 North Stewart Street
Carson City, NV 89701-4285
Phone: 775-684-3310
Fax: 775-684-3371
Web: dmla.clan.lib.nv.us/docs/nsla/archives/

New Albany-Floyd County Public Library (194)
180 West Spring Street
New Albany, IN 47150
Phone: 812-949-3527
Fax: 812-949-3733
Web: www.nafcpl.lib.in.us

New Castle Public Library (419)
207 East North Street
New Castle, PA 16101
Phone: 724-658-6659
Fax: 724-658-9012
Web: www.newcastle.lib.pa.us

New Hampshire Historical Society (322)
The Tuck Library
Special Collections
30 Park Street
Concord, NH 03301
Phone: 603-228-6688
Fax: 603-224-0463
Web: www.nhhistory.org

New Haven Colony Historical Society (118)
Whitney Library
114 Whitney Avenue
New Haven, CT 06510
Phone: 203-562-4183, x15
Fax: 203-562-2002

New Mexico State Library (334)
1209 Camino Carlos Rey
Santa Fe, NM 87507
Phone: 505-476-9702
Fax: 505-476-9703
Web: www.stlib.state.nm.us/

New Mexico Tech, New Mexico Bureau of Geology and Mineral Resources (336)
Geological Information Center Library
801 Leroy Place
Socorro, NM 87801

Phone: 505-835 5322
Fax: 505-835 6333
Web: www.geoinfo.nmt.edu/data/home.html#gic

New York Historical Society (344)
Library
2 West 77th Street
New York, NY 10024
Phone: 212-485-9225
Fax: 212-875-1591
Web: www.nyhistory.org

New York Public Library (343)
Humanities and Social Sciences Library
Map Division
5th Ave and 42nd Street Room 117
New York, NY 10018
Phone: 212-930-0587
Fax: 212-930-0027
Web: www.nypl.org/research/chss/map/map.html

Norfolk Public Library (314)
Norfolk Public Library
Reference Department
308 Prospect Avenue
Norfolk, NE 68701
Phone: 402-844-2100
Fax: 402-844-2102
Web: www.ci.norfolk.ne.us/library

North Carolina Department Office of Archives and History (361)
State Archives of North Carolina
4614 Mail Service Center
Raleigh, NC 27699-4614
Phone: 919-807-7310
Fax: 919-733-1354
Web: www.ah.dcr.state.nc.us/sections/archives/arch/
default.htm

North Carolina Geological Survey (362)
1612 Mail Service Center
Raleigh, NC 27699-1612
Phone: 919-715-9718
Fax: 9190733-0900
Web: www.geology.enr.state.nc.us

North Carolina State University (363)
D.H. Hill Library
2205 Hillsborough Street
Campus Box 7111
Raleigh, NC 27695-7114
Phone: 919-515-2935
Fax: 919-515-8264
Web: http://www.lib.ncsu.edu/risd/govdocs

North Carolina State University (364)
Natural Resources Library
Jordan Hall Room #1102
2800 Faucette Drive
Campus Box 7114
Raleigh, NC 27615
Phone: 919-515-2306
Fax: 919-515-7802
Web: www.lib.ncsu.edu/natural/

North Dakota State University (368)
Library
P.O. Box 5599
Fargo, ND 58105-5599
Phone: 701-231-8863
Fax: 701-231-7138
Web: www.lib.ndsu.nodak.edu

Northern Arizona University (17)
Cline Library
Map Collection
P.O. Box 6022
Flagstaff, AZ 86011
Phone: 928-523-6805
Fax: 928-523-3770
Web: www.nau.edu/library

Northern Arizona University (18)
Cline Library
Special Collections and Archives Department
Box 6022
Flagstaff, AZ 86011-6022
Phone: 928-523-5551
Fax: 928-523-3770
Web: www.nau.edu/library/speccoll

Northern Kentucky University (222)
Steely Library
Map Collection
Louie B. Nunn Drive
Highland Heights, KY 40199-6101
Phone: 859-572-5456
Fax: 859-572-5390
Web: library.nku.edu/welcome.html

Northwestern University (169)
Main Library (Evanston Campus)
Government Publications and Maps Department
1970 Campus Drive
Evanston, IL 60202
Phone: 847-491-3130
Fax: 847-491-8306
Web: www.library.northwestern.edu/govpub/

Oakland Public Library (63)
125 14th Street
Oakland, CA 94612

Phone: 510-238-3136
Fax: 510-238-2125
Web: www.oaklandlibrary.org/Seasonal/Sections/amhl
.html#maps

**Office of Surface Mining Reclamation
and Enforcement** (429)
Anthracite (Coal) Mine Map Repository
Branch of Anthracite-MMR
7 North Wilkes-Barre Boulevard
Suite 308
Wilkes-Barre, PA 18702-5293
Phone: 570-830-1400
Fax: 570-830-1421
Web: mmr.osmre.gov

Ohio Department of Natural Resources (381)
Division of Geological Survey
4383 Fountain Square Drive
Columbus, OH 43224
Phone: 614-265-6576
Fax: 614-447-1918
Web: www,dnr.ohiodnr.com/geosurvey/

Ohio Historical Society (382)
1982 Velma Avenue
Columbus, OH 43211-2497
Phone: 614-297-2510
Fax: 614-297-2546
Web: www.ohiohistory.org

Ohio State University (383)
Orton Memorial Library of Geology
180 Orton Hall
155 South Oval Drive
Columbus, OH 43210
Phone: 614-292-2428
Web: www.lib.ohio-state.edu/geoweb/

Ohio State University (384)
William Oxley Thompson (Main) Library
Map Room
211 Main Library
1858 Neil Avenue Mall
Columbus, OH 43210
Phone: 614-688-8774
Fax: 614-292-7859
Web: library.osu.edu/sites/maps/

**Ohio State University, Newark and
Central Ohio Technical College** (390)
Newark Campus Library
1179 University Dr.
Newark, OH 43055
Phone: 740-366-9307
Fax: 740-366-9264
Web: www.newarkcampus.org/library

Ohio University (372)
Alden Library
Government Documents and Maps Collection
Park Place
Athens, OH 45701
Phone: 740-593-2718
Fax: 740-593-2719
Web: www.library.ohiou.edu/libinfo/depts/maps/
index.htm

Omaha Public Library (316)
W. Dale Clark Library
Business, Science, Technology
215 South 15th Street
Omaha, NE 68102-1629
Phone: 402-444-4817
Fax: 402-444-4585
Web: www.omaha.lib.ne.us

**Oregon Department of Geology
and Mineral Industries** (407)
800 NE Oregon Street #28
Portland, OR 97232
Phone: 503-731-4100
Fax: 503-731-4066
Web: www.oregongeology.com

Oregon Historical Society (408)
Research Library
Maps Collection
1200 S.West Park Avenue
Portland, OR 97205
Phone: 503-306-5240
Fax: 503-219-2040
Web: www.ohs.org

Oregon Institute of Technology (401)
Library
Maps
3201 Campus Dr.
Klamath Falls, OR 97601
Phone: 541-885-1772
Fax: 541-885-1777
Web: www.oit.edu/lbry

Oregon State Library (410)
250 Winter St NE
Salem, OR 97301
Phone: 503-378-4277 x236
Fax: 503-588-7119
Web: www.oregon.gov/osl

Oregon State University (399)
The Valley Library
Map Collection
121 The Valley Library

Corvallis, OR 97331-4501
Phone: 541-737-7295
Fax: 541-737-8224
Web: osulibrary.oregonstate.edu/research/guides/maps/
maproom.htm

Oshkosh Public Library (552)
106 Washington Avenue
Oshkosh, WI 54901-4985
Phone: 920-236-5205
Fax: 920-236-5227
Web: www.oshkoshpubliclibrary.org

Otterbein College (395)
Courtright Memorial Library
1 Otterbein College
Westerville, OH 43081
Phone: 614-823-1027
Fax: 614-823-1921
Web: library.otterbein.edu

Palace of the Governors (335)
Angélico Chávez History Library
Map Collection
120 Washington Avenue
Santa Fe, NM 87501
Phone: 505-476-5090
Fax: 505-476-5053
Web: www.palaceofthegovernors.org/library.html

Pennsylvania Department of Education (415)
Bureau of State Library of Pennsylvania
Maps Collection
333 Market Street
Harrisburg, PA 17126-1745
Phone: 717-783-5950
Fax: 717-787-9127
Web: www.statelibrary.state.pa.us

**Pennsylvania Historical and
Museum Commission** (416)
Pennsylvania State Archives
Division of Archives and Manuscripts
350 North Street
Harrisburg, PA 17120-0090
Phone: 717-783-3281
Fax: 717-787-4822
Web: www.phmc.state.pa.us/bah/dam/mg/mg11.htm

Pennsylvania State University (426)
Fletcher L. Byrom Earth and Mineral Sciences Library
105 Deike Building
University Park, PA 16802
Phone: 814-865-9517
Fax: 814-865-1379
Web: www.libraries.psu.edu/emsl/

Pennsylvania State University (427)
University Libraries
Maps Library
001 Paterno Library
University Park, PA 16802
Phone: 814-863-0094
Fax: 814-863-3560
Web: www.libraries.psu.edu/maps

Penobscot Marine Museum (239)
Stephen Phillips Memorial Library
P.O. Box 498
9 Church Street
Searsport, ME 04974
Phone: 207-548-2529 x212
Fax: 207-548-2520
Web: www.penobscotmarinemuseum.org

Phoenix Public Library (24)
Burton Barr Central Library
1221 North Central Avenue
Phoenix, AZ 85004
Phone: 602-262-4636
Fax: 602-261-8751
Web: www.phxlib.org

Pikes Peak Library District (98)
Carnegie Library
Special Collections
20 North Cascade Avenue
Colorado Springs, CO 80903
Phone: 719-531-6333 x2253
Fax: 719-389-8161
Web: ppld.org

Pittsburg State University (214)
Leonard H. Axe Library
Government Documents
1605 South Joplin
Pittsburg, KS 66762
Phone: 620-235-4889
Fax: 620-235-4090
Web: library.pittstate.edu

Portland State University (409)
Millar Library
P.O. Box 1151
Portland, OR 97207-1151
Phone: 503-725-5874
Fax: 503-725-4524
Web: www.lib.pdx.edu/resources/maps_collection/index.
html

Pratt Institute (337)
Library
200 Willoughby Avenue

Brooklyn, NY 11205
Phone: 718-636-3704
Fax: 718-399-4220
Web: lib.pratt.edu/public

Presidio Trust (75)
34 Graham Street
San Francisco, CA 94129
Phone: 415-561-5343
Web: www.presidio.gov

Princeton University (330)
Library
Historic Maps Collection
One Washington Road
Princeton, NJ 08544
Phone: 609-258-3166
Fax: 609-258-2324
Web: www.princeton.edu/~rbsc/department/maps

Providence Public Library (431)
225 Washington Street
Providence, RI 02903
Phone: 401-455-8000
Web: provlib.org

**Public Library of
Charlotte-Mecklenburg County** (353)
North Carolina Room Map Collection
310 N. Tryon Street
Charlotte, NC 28202
Phone: 704-336-2980
Fax: 704-336-6236
Web: www.plcmc.org

**Public Library of Cincinnati
and Hamilton County** (375)
History Department Map Collection
800 Vine Street
Cincinnati, OH 45230
Phone: 513-369-6905
Fax: 513 369-3123
Web: www.cincinnatilibrary.org

Pueblo City-County Library District (113)
Robert Hoag Rawlings Public Library
Western Research Map Collection
100 East Abriendo Avenue
Pueblo, CO 81004
Phone: 719-562-5626
Fax: 719-553-0327
Web: www.pueblolibrary.org

Purdue University (198)
Earth and Atmospheric Sciences (EAS) Library
EAS Map Room

Civil Engineering Building Room 2253
West Lafayette, IN 47907
Phone: 765-494-0202
Web: www.lib.purdue.edu/eas/inmaps.html

Queens Borough Public Library (341)
Long Island Division
89-11 Merrick Boulevard
Jamaica, NY 11432
Phone: 1-718-990-0770
Fax: 718-658-8342
Web: queenslibrary.org

Rhode Island College (432)
James P. Adams Library
600 Mount Pleasant Avenue
Providence, RI 2908
Phone: 401-456-8125
Fax: 401-456-1915
Web: www.ric.edu/adamslibrary

Rhode Island Historical Society (433)
Graphics Collections
121 Hope Street
Providence, RI 02906
Phone: 401-273-8107 x20 or x21
Fax: 401-274-6852
Web: www.rihs.org/libraryhome.htm

Rice University (492)
Fondren Library
Government Publications and Microforms
6100 Main
Houston, TX 77005
Phone: 713-348-5483
Fax: 713-348-5902
Web: www.rice.edu/fondren/gov/

Richland County Public Library (442)
Walker Local History Room
1431 Assembly Street
Columbia, SC 29201
Phone: 802-929-3402
Web: www.richland.lib.sc.us

Rutgers University, Camden Campus (328)
Paul Robeson Library
300 North 4th Street
Camden, NJ 8101
Phone: 856-225-6034
Fax: 856-225-6428
Web: www.libraries.rutgers.edu/rul/libs/robeson_lib

Rutgers, The State University of New Jersey (329)
Library of Science and Medicine
165 Bevier Rd

Piscataway, NJ 08854-8009
Phone: 732-445-2895
Fax: 732-44-5806
Web: www.libraries.rutgers.edu/rul/index.shtml

Saint Cloud State University (284)
James W. Miller Learning Resources Center
Government Documents/Maps
720 4th Avenue S
Saint Cloud, MN 56301
Phone: 320-308-2063
Fax: 320-308-4778
Web: lrts.stcloudstate.edu

Saint John's University (276)
Alcuin Library
Collegeville, MN 56321
Phone: 320-363-2122
Fax: 320-363-2126
Web: www.csbsju.edu/library

Saint Louis Public Library (292)
1301 Olive Street
Saint Louis, MO 63103
Phone: 314-241-2288
Fax: 314-539-0393
Web: www.slpl.lib.mo.us

Saint Louis University (293)
Pius XII Memorial Library
3650 Lindell Blvd
Saint Louis, MO 63108
Phone: 314-977-3590
Web: www.slu.edu/libraries/pius/

Saint Mary's University (497)
Blume Library
One Camino Santa Maria
San Antonio, TX 78228
Phone: 210-436-3441
Fax: 210-436-3782
Web: library.stmarytx.edu/acadlib/doc/maps/mapintro
.htm

Saint Paul Public Library (288)
Central Library
90 West 4th Street
Saint Paul, MN 55102
Phone: 651-266-7000
Fax: 651-266-7011
Web: www.sppl.org

Samford University (3)
Library
800 Lakeshore Drive
Birmingham, AL 35229

Phone: 205-726-2749
Fax: 205-726-2642
Web: library.samford.edu

San Diego State University (71)
Library and Information Access
5500 Campanile Drive
San Diego, CA 92182
Phone: 619-594 -6724
Fax: 619-594-3270
Web: infodome.sdsu.edu/research/guides/maps/index
.shtml

**San Francisco Maritime
National Historical Park** (76)
J Porter Shaw Library
Building E Fort Mason Center
San Francisco, CA 94123
Phone: 415-561-7030
Web: www.nps.gov/safr/local/lib/libtop.html

San Francisco Municipal Railway (77)
Library
1145 Market Street
Suite 402
San Francisco, CA 94103-1545
Phone: 415-934-3977
Fax: 415-934-5747

San Francisco Public Library (78)
General Collections Department
100 Larkin Street
San Francisco, CA 94102
Phone: 415-557-4401
Fax: 415-437-4831
Web: www.sfpl.org

San Francisco Public Library (79)
Government Information Center
100 Larkin Street
San Francisco, CA 94102
Phone: 415-557-4500
Fax: 415-557-4475
Web: sfpl4.sfpl.org/librarylocations/main/gic/gic.htm

San Francisco State University (80)
Alfred Rockwell Sumner Memorial Map Library
1600 Holloway Avenue
HSS 289
San Francisco, CA 94132
Phone: 415-338-1145
Fax: 415-338-6243
Web: bss.sfsu.edu/geog/maplib.htm

San Francisco State University (81)
J. Paul Leonard Library
Government Publications/Maps Department

1630 Holloway Avenue
San Francisco, CA 94132
Phone: 415-338-6953
Fax: 415-338-1504
Web: www.library.sfsu.edu/servcoll/maps.html

San Jose State University (83)
Department of Geology
San Jose, CA 95192-0102
Phone: 408-924-5050
Fax: 408-924-5053
Web: www.geosun.sjsu.edu

San Jose State University (84)
Dr. Martin Luther King Jr. Library
1 Washington Square
San Jose, CA 95192-0028
Phone: 408-808-2000
Web: www.sjlibrary.org

San Leandro Public Library (85)
Map File
300 Estudillo Avenue
San Leandro, CA 94577
Phone: 510-577-3971
Fax: 510-577-3987
Web: www.ci.san-leandro.ca.us/sllibrary.html

San Mateo County History Museum (66)
Archives
777 Hamilton Street
Redwood City, CA 94063
Phone: 650-299-0104 x22
Fax: 650-299-0141
Web: www.sanmateocountyhistory.com

Sandia National Laboratories (331)
Technical Library
P.O. Box 5820, MS 0899
Albuquerque, NM 87185
Phone: 505-845-8287
Fax: 505-844-3143
Web: infoserve.sandia.gov/

Santa Barbara Museum of Natural History (87)
Library
2559 Puesta del Sol Road
Santa Barbara, CA 93105
Phone: 805-682-4711
Fax: 805-569-3170
Web: www.sbnature.org/library/index.htm

Sara Hightower Regional Library (150)
Rome-Floyd County Public Library
Special Collections
205 Riverside Parkway
Rome, GA 30161

Phone: 706-236-4607
Fax: 706-236-4605
Web: www.floyd.public.lib.ga.us

Scripps Institution of Oceanography (54)
University of California, San Diego
Map and Chart Collection
8755 Biological Grade
La Jolla, CA 92093
Phone: 858-534-1228
Fax: 858-534-5269
Web: scilib.ucsd.edu/sio/guide/map.html

Seattle Public Library (536)
History/Travel, Maps Department
and the Seattle Collection
1000 4th Avenue
Seattle, WA 98104
Phone: 206-386-4636
Fax: 206-386-4632
Web: www.spl.org

Sharlot Hall Museum (25)
Archives
415 West Gurley Street
Prescott, AZ 86301
Phone: 928-445-3122
Fax: 928-776-9053
Web: www.sharlot.org/archives

Sioux City Public Library (206)
529 Pierce Street
Sioux City, IA 51101-1203
Phone: 712-255-2933 x221
Fax: 712-279-6432
Web: www.siouxcitylibrary.org

Smithsonian Institution (248)
National Anthropological Archives
4210 Silver Hill Road
Suitland, MD 20746
Phone: 301-238-2873
Fax: 301-238-2883
Web: www.nmnh.si.edu/naa

Smithsonian Institution (127)
Regional Planetary Image Facility
Planetary Maps
6th and Independence Avenue, SW
Washington, DC 20560
Phone: 202-633-2480
Fax: 202-786-2566
Web: www.nasm.si.edu/research/ceps/imagery.cfm

Sonoma County Library (90)
3rd and E Street
Santa Rosa, CA 95404

Phone: 707-545-0831
Fax: 707-575-0437
Web: www.sonomalibrary.org

**South Carolina Department
of Archives and History** (443)
Reference Services
8301 Parklane Road
Columbia, SC 29223
Phone: 803-896-6104
Fax: 803-896-6198
Web: www.state.sc.us/scdah

South Carolina Historical Society (440)
100 Meeting Street
Charleston, SC 29401
Phone: 843-723-3225
Fax: 843-723-8584
Web: www.schistory.org

South Dakota School of Mines and Technology (455)
Devereaux Library
501 E St Joseph St
Rapid City, SD 57701-3995
Phone: 605-394-2419
Fax: 605-394-1256
Web: www.sdln.net

South Dakota State Archives (454)
900 Governors Drive
Pierre, SD 57501
Phone: 605-773-3804
Fax: 605-7736041
Web: www.sdhistory.org/arc/archives.htm

South Dakota State University (453)
Hilton M. Briggs Library
Box 2115
Brookings, SD 57007-1098
Phone: 605-688-5576
Fax: 605-688-5133
Web: www3.sdstate.edu/academics/library/

Southeastern Oklahoma State University (396)
Henry G. Bennett Memorial Library
1405 North 4th Avenue
PMB 4105
Durant, OK 74701
Phone: 580-745-2935
Fax: 580-745-7463
Web: www.sosu.edu/govdocs/govdoc%20home.html

Southern Illinois University, Carbondale (160)
Morris Library
Map Library
605 Agriculture Drive
Carbondale, IL 62901-6636

Phone: 618-453-2705
Fax: 618-453-2704
Web: www.lib.siu.edu/hp/divisions/sci/maplib.shtml

Southern Illinois University, Edwardsville (168)
Lovejoy Library
Map Library
P.O. Boz 1063
Edwardsville, IL 62026-2063
Phone: 618-650-2632
Fax: 618-650-2717
Web: www.library.siue.edu/lib/

Southern Methodist University (487)
DeGolyer Library
Historic Map Collection
P.O. Box 750396
Dallas, TX 75275
Phone: 214-768-4284
Fax: 214-768-1565
Web: www.smu.edu/cul/degolyer/

Southern Methodist University (488)
Edwin J. Foscue Map Library
6425 North Ownby Drive
Dallas, TX 750375
Phone: 214-768-2285
Fax: 214-768-4236
Web: www.su.edu/cul/maps

Southwest Missouri State University (295)
Duane G. Meyer Library
Maps
901 South National #175
Springfield, MO 65804
Phone: 417-836-4534
Fax: 417-836-6799
Web: library.smsu.edu/meyer/maps/index.shtml

Spartanburg County Public Library (452)
Reference Department
151 South Church Street
Spartanburg, SC 29306
Phone: 864-596-3505
Fax: 864-596-3518
Web: www.infodepot.org/govdoc.htm; www.infodepot
.org/kroom.htm

Springfield City Library (257)
220 State St
Springfield, MA 01103
Phone: 413-263-6828
Web: www.springfieldlibrary.rg

Stanford University (91)
Branner Earth Sciences Library and Map Collections
Mitchell Earth Sciences Building

397 Panama Mall
Stanford, CA 94305
Phone: 650-725-1103
Fax: 650-725-2534
Web: www-sul.stanford.edu/depts/branner/brief_map
.html

Stanford University (92)
Green Library
Historic Map Collection
Department of Special Collections
    and University Archives
Green Library
Stanford, CA 94305
Phone: 650-725-1022
Fax: 650-723-8690
Web: www-sul.stanford.edu/depts/spc/maps/index.html

State Archives of Michigan (271)
P.O. Box 30740
Lansing, MI 48909
Phone: 517-373-1408
Fax: 517-241-1658
Web: www.michigan.gov/statearchives

**State Historical Society of Iowa,
Department of Cultural Affairs** (203)
State Historical Society of Iowa, Iowa City
Special Collections/Map Collection
402 Iowa Avenue
Iowa City, IA 52240
Phone: 319-335-3916
Fax: 319-335-3935
Web: www.iowahistory.org

State Library of Massachusetts (253)
341 State House
Boston, MA 02139
Phone: 617-727-2590
Fax: 617-727-9730
Web: www.mass.gov/lib

State Library of Ohio (385)
Government Information Services
274 East First Avenue
Columbus, OH 43201
Phone: 614-644-7051
Fax: 614-752-9178
Web: winslo.state.oh.us

State University of New York, Buffalo (339)
Arts and Sciences Libraries
Map Collection
Capen Hall
Buffalo, NY 14260-1672
Phone: 716-645-2947
Fax: 716-645-3710

Web: ublib.buffalo.edu/libraries/asl/maps/map_room
.html

State University of West Georgia (147)
Irvine Sullivan Ingram Library
1600 Maple Street
Carrollton, GA 30118
Phone: 770-830-2357
Fax: 770-836-6626
Web: www.westga.edu/~library/

Stearns History Museum (285)
Research Center and Archives
235 33rd Avenue South
Saint Cloud, MN 56301
Phone: 320 253-8424
Fax: 320 253-2172
Web: www.stearns-museum.org

Stephen F. Austin State University (494)
Ralph W. Steen Library
Government Documents/Maps
P.O. Box 13055 SFA Station
Nacogdoches, TX 75963
Phone: 936-468-1574
Fax: 936-468-4117
Web: libweb.sfasu.edu/subject/government/default.htm

Stetson University (133)
duPont-Ball Library
Government Documents Department
421 North Woodland Boulevard
DeLand, FL 32723
Phone: 386-822-7185
Fax: 386-740-3626
Web: www.stetson.edu/library/

Stony Brook University (345)
Melville Library
Map Collection
Stony Brook, NY 11790
Phone: 631-632-71
Web: www.sunysb.edu/library/ldmaps.htm

Syracuse University (346)
Maps and Government Information
Room 358
Bird Library
Syracuse, NY 13244
Phone: 315-443-4176
Fax: 315-443-9510
Web: libwww.syr.edu/information/mgi/index.html

Tennessee State Library and Archives (470)
Map Collection
403 Seventh Avenue North
Nashville, TN 37243

Phone: 615-741-2764
Fax: 615-532-2472
Web: www.state.tn.us/sos/statelib

Tennessee Technological University (460)
Angelo and Jennette Volpe Library and Media Center
1100 North Peachtree Avenue
Cookeville, TN 38505
Phone: 931-372-3326
Fax: 931-372-6112
Web: www.tntech.edu/govpub/

Tennessee Valley Authority (458)
Map and Photo Records
1101 Market Street
MR 5E
Chattanooga, TN 37402
Phone: 423-751-8362
Fax: 423-499-6319
Web: maps.tva.com

Texas A&M University (484)
Sterling C. Evans Library
Maps/GIS Department
College Station, TX 77845-5000
Phone: 979-845-1024
Fax: 979-845-6238
Web: library.tamu.edu/

Texas State Library and Archives (478)
Historic Map Collection
P.O. Box 12927
Austin, TX 78711-2927
Phone: 512-463-5480
Fax: 512-463-5430
Web: www.tsl.state.tx.us/arc/maps/index.html

Texas State Library and Archives (479)
Reference/Documents
1201 Brazos
Austin, TX 78701
Phone: 512-463-5455
Fax: 512-463-5430
Web: www.tsl.state.tx.us

Texas Tech University (493)
University Library
Government Documents Map Collection
18th and Boston
Lubbock, TX 79409-0002
Phone: 806-742-2268
Fax: 806-742-1332
Web: library.ttu.edu/ul/maps/

Toledo-Lucas County Public Library (393)
Main Library
325 Michigan Street

Toledo, OH 43624
Phone: 419-259-5207
Web: www.toledolibrary.org

Trinity College (116)
Watkinson Library
300 Summit Street
Hartford, CT 06106
Phone: 860-297-2268
Fax: 860-297-2251
Web: www.trincoll.edu/depts/library/watkinson/

Tucson-Pima Public Library (31)
Joel D. Valdez Main Library
Reference Department
101 North Stone Avenue
Tucson, AZ 85701
Phone: 520-791-4393
Web: www.tppl.org

United Society of Shakers (235)
Shaker Library
Map Collection
707 Shaker Road
New Gloucester, ME 04260
Phone: 207-926-4597
Web: www.shaker.lib.me.us

United States Army Corps of Engineers, NOD (231)
Library and Map Collection
IMO
704 Leale Avenue
New Orleans, LA 70118-3651
Phone: 504-862-1775
Fax: 504-862-1721

United States Department of the Interior, Minerals Management Service (232)
Library
1201 Elmwood Park Boulevard
New Orleans, LA 70123
Phone: 504-736-2521
Fax: 504-736-2525
Web: www.mms.gov/library

United States Department of Interior, Office of Surface Mining (464)
Knoxville Field Office Geographic Information System (KFO GIS)
530 Gay Street SW
Suite 500
Knoxville, TN 37902
Phone: 865-545-4103 x134
Fax: 865-545-4111
Web: library.uwsuper.edu

United States Geological Survey, Denver (105)
Central Region Library
Box 25046 Federal Center
Mail Stop 914
Denver, CO 80225
Phone: 303-236-1000
Fax: 303-236-0015
Web: library.usgs.gov

United States Geological Survey, Menlo Park (59)
Library
345 Middlefield Road
MS 955
Menlo Park, CA 94025
Phone: 650-329-5027
Fax: 650-329-5132
Web: library.usgs.gov

United States Geological Survey, Reston (517)
Library
Cartographic Information Services
950 National Center
12201 Sunrise Valley Drive
Reston, VA 20192
Phone: 703-648-4302
Fax: 703-648-6373
Web: library.usgs.gov/

University of Akron (370)
Bierce Library
Map Collection
Akron, OH 44325-1707
Phone: 330-972-8176
Fax: 330-972-7225
Web: www.uakron.edu/libraries/ul/subjects/look4maps .html

University of Akron (371)
Department of Geography and Planning
Map Room
Akron, OH 44325-5005
Phone: 330-972-7620
Fax: 330-972-6080
Web: www.uakron.edu/libraries

University of Alabama (8)
Map Library
P.O. Box 870322
Tuscaloosa , AL 35487
Phone: 205-348-6028
Web: maplibrary.ua.edu

University of Alabama (7)
W. S. Hoole Special Collections Library
Box 870266
Tuscaloosa, AL 35487-0266

Phone: 205-348-0500
Fax: 205-348-1699
Web: www.lib.ua.edu/libraries/hoole/

University of Alaska, Anchorage (10)
UAA/APU Consortium Library
3211 Providence Drive
Anchorage, AK 99508
Phone: 907-786-1825
Fax: 907-786-1834
Web: www.lib.uaa.alaska.edu

University of Alaska, Fairbanks (13)
Elmer E. Rasmuson Library
Documents and Maps Collection
P.O. Box 756817
Fairbanks, AK 99775-6817
Phone: 907-474-7624
Fax: 907-474-1155
Web: www.uaf.edu/library

University of Arizona (32)
Library
1510 East University
Tucson, AZ 85721
Phone: 520-621-6441
Fax: 520-621-9733
Web: www.library.arizona.edu

University of Arkansas (35)
University Libraries
Government Documents/Map Collection
365 North Ozark Avenue
Fayetteville, AR 72701
Phone: 479-575-5516
Fax: 479-575-6656
Web: libinfo.uark.edu/gis/

University of Arkansas, Little Rock (39)
Ottenhimer Library
2801 South University Avenue
Little Rock, AR 72204
Phone: 501-569-8806
Fax: 501-569-3017
Web: library1.ualr.edu

University of California, Berkeley (44)
Bancroft Library
Map Collection
Berkeley, CA 94720
Phone: 510-642-6481
Fax: 510-642-7589

University of California, Berkeley (45)
Department of Geography
Map Collection

507 McCone Hall #4740
Berkeley, CA 94720
Phone: 510-642-4368
Fax: 510-642-3370
Web: geography.berkeley.edu

University of California, Berkeley (46)
Earth Sciences and Map Library
50 McCone Hall
Berkeley, CA 94720-6000
Phone: 510-642-2997
Fax: 510-643-6576
Web: www.lib.berkeley.edu/EART/

University of California, Berkeley (47)
Water Resources Center Archives
410 O'Brien Hall
Berkeley, CA 94720-1718
Phone: 510-642-2666
Fax: 510-642-9143
Web: www.lib.berkeley.edu/WRCA/

University of California, Davis (51)
Peter J. Shields Library
Government Information and Maps
100 NW Quad
Davis, CA 95616
Phone: 530-752-1689
Fax: 530-752-3148
Web: www.lib.ucdavis.edu/govdoc/MapCollection/
map_about.html

University of California, Irvine (53)
Langson Library
P.O. Box 19557
Irvine, CA 92623-9557
Phone: 949-824-7290
Fax: 949-824-3644
Web: www.lib.uci.edu/libraries/collections/gis.html

University of California, Los Angeles (58)
Young Research Library
Henry J Bruman Map Collection
Room A4510
P.O. Box 951575
Los Angeles, CA 90095-1575
Phone: 310-825-1088
Fax: 310-825-6795
Web: www.library.ucla.edu/libraries/yrl/referenc/rco/
geographic.htm

University of California, Riverside (67)
Science Library
Information Services/Map Collection
P. O. Box 5900
Riverside, CA 92517

Phone: 909-787-6423
Fax: 909-787-6378
Web: library.ucr.edu/?view=collections/maps/

University of California, San Diego (55)
Social Sciences and Humanities Library
9500 Gilman Drive 0175R
La Jolla, CA 92093
Phone: 858-534-1248
Fax: 858-534-7548
Web: govinfo.ucsd.edu/maps/index.html

University of California, Santa Barbara (88)
Davidson Library
Map and Imagery Laboratory
University of California, Santa Barbara
Santa Barbara, CA 93106-9010
Phone: 805-893-2779
Fax: 805-893-8799
Web: www.sdc.ucsb.edu

University of California, Santa Cruz (89)
Science and Engineering Library
Map Room
1156 High Street
Santa Cruz, CA 95064
Phone: 831-459-2364
Fax: 831-459-4187
Web: library.ucsc.edu/maps/

University of Central Arkansas (34)
Torreyson Library
Archives Map Collection
201 Donaghey
Conway, AR 72035
Phone: 501-450-3418
Fax: 501-450-5208
Web: www.uca.edu

University of Central Oklahoma (397)
Max Chambers Library
Map Collection
100 North University
Edmond, OK 73034
Phone: 405-974-2906
Fax: 405-974-3806
Web: www.ucok.edu

University of Chicago (166)
Joseph Regenstein Library
Map Collection
1100 East 57th Street
Chicago, IL 60637
Phone: 773-702-8761

Fax: 773-702-6623
Web: www.lib.uchicago.edu/e/su/maps

University of Cincinnati (376)
Geology/Physics Library
Willis G. Meyer Map Collection
240 Braunstein Hall, M.L. 0153
Cincinnati, OH 45221
Phone: 513-5561324
Fax: 513-5561930
Web: www.libraries.uc.edu/libraries/geol-phys/home
  .html

University of Colorado, Boulder (95)
Jerry Crail Johnson Earth Sciences and Map Library
184 UCB
Boulder, CO 80309
Phone: 303-492-7578
Fax: 303-735-4879
Web: www-libraries.colorado.edu/ps/map/

University of Colorado, Boulder (96)
University Libraries
Archives
184 UCB
Boulder, CO 80309-0184
Phone: 303-492-7242
Fax: 303-492-3960
Web: www-libraries.colorado.edu/ps/arv/frontpage.htm

University of Colorado, Colorado Springs (99)
Kraemer Family Library
1420 Austin Bluffs Parkway
Colorado Springs, CO 80918
Phone: 719-262-3295
Fax: 719-528-5227
Web: web.uccs.edu/library/

University of Connecticut (121)
Homer Babbidge Library
Map and Geographic Information Center
369 Fairfield Road
Storrs, CT 06269-0584
Phone: 860-486-4589
Fax: 486-4100
Web: magic.lib.uconn.edu/

University of Delaware (122)
Hugh M. Morris Library
Map Room
181 South College Avenue
Newark, DE 19717-526
Phone: 302-831-6664
Fax: 302-831-1046

Web: www.lib.udel.edu/ud/digital/microcopy/gis/ and www.lib.udel.edu/ud/spec/findaids/hist_map/index.htm

University of Evansville (184)
Libraries
1800 Lincoln Avenue
Evansville, IN 47722
Phone: 812-479-2482
Fax: 812-471-6996
Web: libraries.evansville.edu/

University of Florida (134)
George A. Smathers Libraries
Historical Florida Map Collection
Department of Special and Area Studies Collections
2nd Floor
Library East
Gainesville, FL 32611
Phone: 352-392-9075
Web: web.uflib.ufl.edu/spec/pkyonge/index. html

University of Florida (135)
George A. Smathers Libraries
Map and Imagery Library
P.O.Box 11701
110 Marston Science Library
Gainesville, FL 32611-7011
Phone: 352-392-2825
Fax: 352-392-4787
Web: web.uflib.ufl.edu/maps

University of Georgia (141)
Libraries
Map Collection
Athens, GA 20602
Phone: 706-542-0690
Fax: 706-542-6523
Web: www.libs.uga.edu/maproom/index.html

University of Guam (151)
Robert F. Kennedy Memorial Library
Government Documents
UOG Station
Mangilao, GU 96923
Phone: 671-735-2321
Fax: 671-734-6882
Web: www.uog.edu/rfk/

University of Hawai'i at Manoa (154)
Hamilton Library
Map Collection
2550 McCarthy Mall
Honolulu, HI 96822

Phone: 808-956-6199
Fax: 808-956-5968
Web: libweb.Hawaii.edu/libdept/maps/index.html

University of Idaho (159)
Library
Government Documents Department
Box 442353
Moscow, ID 83844-2353
Phone: 208-885-6344
Fax: 208-885-6817
Web: www.insideidaho.org

University of Idaho (158)
Library
Reference Department
Box 442350
Moscow, ID 83844-2350
Phone: 208-885-6584
Fax: 208-885-6718
Web: www.lib.uidaho.edu OR www.insideidaho.org

University of Illinois, Chicago (167)
Richard J. Daley Library
Map Section
801 South Morgan Street
Chicago, IL 60607
Phone: 312-996-2738
Fax: 312-413-0424
Web: map pages under revision and will have a new URL; library homepage at www.uic.edu/depts/library/

University of Illinois, Urbana-Champaign (177)
Illinois Historical Survey
1408 West Gregory Drive
Urbana, IL 61801
Phone: 217-333-1777
Web: www.library.uiuc.edu/ihx

University of Illinois, Urbana-Champaign (178)
Map and Geography Library
418 Library
MC-522
1408 West Gregory Drive
Urbana, IL 61801
Phone: 217-333-0827
Fax: 217-333-2214
Web: www.library.uiuc.edu/max

University of Illinois, Urbana-Champaign (179)
Rare Book and Special Collections Library
1408 West Gregory Drive
Room 346
Urbana, IL 61801

Phone: 217-333-3777
Fax: 217-333-2214
Web: www.library.uiuc.edu/rbx/

University of Iowa (204)
Geoscience Library
136 Trowbridge Hall
Iowa City, IA 52242
Phone: 319-335-3084
Fax: 319-335-3419
Web: www.lib.uiowa.edu/geoscience

University of Iowa (205)
Libraries
Map Collection
3111 Main Library
Iowa City, IA 52242-1420
Phone: 319-335-5920
Fax: 319-335-5900
Web: www.lib.uiowa.edu/maps

University of Kansas (210)
Anschutz Library
Thomas R. Smith Map Collections
1301 Hoch Auditoria Drive
Lawrence, KS 66045
Phone: 785-864-4420
Fax: 785-864-4420
Web: www2.lib.ku.edu/mapscoll/

University of Kansas (211)
Kenneth Spencer Research Library
Special Collections
1450 Poplar Lane
Lawrence, KS 66045-7616
Phone: 785-864-4334
Fax: 785-864-5803
Web: spencer.lib.ku.edu/sc/index.htm

University of Kentucky (223)
Pirtle Geological Sciences Library and Map Collection
410 King Library Addition
Lexington, KY 40506-0039
Phone: 859-257-5730
Fax: 859-323-3225
Web: www.uky.edu/Libraries

University of Louisville (224)
Ekstrom Library
2301 S Third Street
Louisville, KY 40292
Phone: 502-852-6747
Fax: 502-852-8736
Web: library.louisville.edu/ekstrom/collections/maps.htm

University of Maine (236)
Raymond H. Fogler Library
Government Documents and Microforms Department
Fogler Library
Orono, ME 04469-5729
Phone: 207-581-1680
Fax: 207-581-1653
Web: www.library.umaine.edu/govdoc/default.htm

University of Maryland, College Park (244)
Hornbake Library
Maryland Map Collection
College Park, MD 20742
Phone: 301-410-9212
Fax: 301-314-2709
Web: www.lib.umd.edu/RARE/MarylandCollection/
   Maps/MdMaps.html

University of Maryland, College Park (245)
McKeldin Library
Government Documents and Maps
4118 McKeldin Library
College Park, MD 20742
Phone: 301-405-9165
Fax: 301-314-5651
Web: www.lib.umd.edu/gov/maproom.html

University of Massachusetts, Amherst (249)
W. E. B. Du Bois Library
Map Collection
154 Hicks Way
Amherst, MA 01003
Phone: 413-545-2397
Fax: 413-545-1399
Web: www.library.umass.edu/maps/index/html

University of Massachusetts, Dartmouth (256)
Library
Map Collection
285 Old Westport Road
Dartmouth, MA 02747
Phone: 508-999-8886
Fax: 508-999-9240
Web: www.lib.umassd.edu/Reference/Maps.html

University of Memphis (468)
McWherter Library
Map Library
126 Ned R. McWherter Library
Memphis, TN 38152
Phone: 901-678-2206
Fax: 901-678-8218
Web: exlibris.memphis.edu

University of Memphis (469)
McWherter Library
Special/Mississippi Valley Collections
126 Ned R. McWherter Library
Memphis, TN 38152
Phone: 901-678-2210
Fax: 901-678-8218
Web: exlibris.memphis.edu

University of Miami (130)
Otto G. Richter Library
Archives and Special Collection Department
1300 Memorial Drive
Coral Gables, FL 33124-0320
Phone: 305-284-3247
Fax: 305-284-4027
Web: www.library.miami.edu/archives/intro.html

University of Miami (131)
Otto G. Richter Library
Cuban Heritage Collection
1300 Memorial Drive
Coral Gables, FL 33124-0320
Phone: 305-284-4008
Fax: 305-284-4901
Web: www.library.miami.edu/umcuban/cuban.html

University of Miami (132)
Otto G. Richter Library
Government Information and
    Special Formats Department
1300 Memorial Drive
Coral Gables, FL 33124-0320
Phone: 305-284-3155
Fax: 305-284-4027
Web: www.library.miami.edu/library/mapcollection.html

University of Miami (138)
Rosenstiel School of Marine and
    Atmospheric Science Library
4600 Rickenbacker Causeway
Miami, FL 33149-1098
Phone: 305-361-4060
Fax: 305-361-9306
Web: www.rsmas.miami.edu/support/lib/

University of Michigan (262)
Bentley Historical Library
1150 Beal Avenue
Ann Arbor, MI 48109-2113
Phone: 734-764-3482
Fax: 734-936-1333
Web: www.umich.edu/~bhl

University of Michigan (263)
Map Library
Hatcher Graduate Library 825
Ann Arbor, MI 48109-1205
Phone: 734-764-0407
Fax: 734-763-5080
Web: www.lib.umich.edu/maplib

University of Minnesota (281)
O.M. Wilson Library
John R. Borchert Map Library
309 19th Avenue South
Minneapolis, MN 55455
Phone: 612-624-4549
Fax: 612-626-9353
Web: map.lib.umn.edu

University of Minnesota (282)
Science and Engineering Library
Geologic Map Collection
206 Walter Library
117 Pleasant Street SE
Minneapolis, MN 55455
Phone: 612-624-0224
Web: sciweb.lib.umn.edu/subject/earthsci.html

University of Minnesota, Duluth (277)
Library
416 Library Drive
Duluth, MN 55812-3001
Phone: 218-726-8100
Fax: 218-726-6205
Web: www.d.umn.edu/lib/

University of Missouri, Rolla (291)
Curtis Laws Wilson Library
A.C. Spreng Map Room
1870 Miner Circle
Rolla, MO 65409
Phone: 573-341-4007
Fax: 573-341-4233
Web: campus.umr.edu/library

University of Montana (299)
Maureen and Mike Mansfield Library
Documents/Maps Division
32 Campus Drive
Missoula, MT 59812-9936
Phone: 406-243-6866
Web: www.lib.umt.edu

University of Nebraska, Kearney (302)
Calvin T. Ryan Library
Government Documents Department

2508 11th Avenue
Kearney, NE 68849-2240
Phone: 308-865-8542
Fax: 308-865-8722
Web: www.unk.edu/acad/library/gov_doc/about.htm

University of Nebraska, Kearney (303)
Geography Map Library
Department of Geography
Kearney, NE 68849
Phone: 308-865-8682

University of Nebraska, Lincoln (310)
Conservation and Survey Division/SNR
102 Nebraska Hall
Lincoln, NE 68588-0517
Phone: 402-472-7523 or 402-472-3471
Fax: 402-472-4542
Web: csd.unl.edu/csd.htm

University of Nebraska, Lincoln (311)
C.Y. Thompson Library
East Campus
38th and Holdrege Streets
Lincoln, NE 68583-0717
Phone: 402-472-4407
Fax: 402-472-7005
Web: www.unl.edu/libr/libs/cyt

University of Nebraska, Lincoln (312)
Geology Library
10 Bessey Hall
Lincoln, NE 68588-0344
Phone: 402-472-2653
Web: www.unl.edu/libr/libs/geol/geol.html

University of Nebraska, Lincoln (313)
Love Memorial Library
Map Collection
Lincoln, NE 68588-4100
Phone: 402-472-3545
Fax: 402-472-2534
Web: www.unl.edu/libr/gis/

University of Nebraska, Omaha (317)
Department of Geography-Geology
Omaha, NE 68182-0199
Phone: 402-554-3586

University of Nebraska, Omaha (318)
University Library
Government Documents
6001 Dodge Street
Omaha, NE 68182
Phone: 402-554-2225

Fax: 402-554-3215
Web: library.unomaha.edu

University of Nevada, Reno (321)
DeLaMare Library
Mary B. Ansari Map Library
MS 262
Reno, NV 89557
Phone: 775-784-6945 x230
Fax: 775-784-6949
Web: www.delamare.unr.edu/Maps/

University of Nevada, Reno (322)
Getchell Library
Special Collections and Archives Department
1664 North Virginia Street
Reno, NV 89557-0044
Phone: 775-784-6500 x327
Fax: 775-784-4529
Web: www.library.unr.edu/specoll

University of New Hampshire (324)
Dimond Library
Government Documents/Map Room
18 Library Way
Durham, NH 03824
Phone: 603-862-1777
Fax: 603-862-3403
Web: docs.unh.edu

University of New Mexico (332)
Centennial Science and Engineering Library
Map and Geographic Information Center
   (aka The Map Room)
UNMGL/CSEL MSC05 3020 1
Albuquerque, NM 87131-0001
Phone: 505-277-5738
Fax: 505-277-0702
Web: elibrary2.unm.edu/csel

University of North Carolina, Chapel Hill (349)
Academic Affairs Library
North Carolina Collection
CB #3930
Wilson Library
Chapel Hill, NC 27514-8890
Phone: 919-962-1172
Fax: 919-962-4452
Web: www.lib.unc.edu/ncc

University of North Carolina, Chapel Hill (350)
Geological Sciences Library
CB #3315
Mitchell Hall
Chapel Hill, NC 27516

Phone: 919-962-2386
Fax: 919-966-4519
Web: www.lib.unc.edu/geolib/

University of North Carolina, Chapel Hill (351)
John N. Couch Biology Library
Botany Section
CB #3280
Coker Hall
Chapel Hill, NC 27599-3280
Phone: 919-962-3783
Fax: 919-843-8393
Web: wwww.lib.unc.edu/biology

University of North Carolina, Chapel Hill (352)
Wilson Library
Davis Reference/Maps Collection
CB#3928
Wilson Library
Chapel Hill, NC 27514-8890
Phone: 919-962-3028
Fax: 919-962-4452
Web: www.lib.unc.edu/maps and www.lib.unc.edu

University of North Carolina, Charlotte (354)
J. Murrey Atkins Library
9201 University City Boulevard
Charlotte, NC 282223
Phone: 704-687-3601
Fax: 704-687-3050
Web: library.uncc.edu/

University of North Carolina, Greensboro (359)
Jackson Library
Reference Department
P.O. Box 26170
Greensboro, NC 27402-6170
Phone: 336-334-5419
Fax: 336-334-5097
Web: library.uncg.edu

University of North Carolina, Wilmington (366)
William Madison Randall Library
601 South College Road
Wilmington, NC 28403-5616
Phone: 910-962-3270
Fax: 910-962-3078
Web: library.uncwil.edu

University of North Texas (489)
Willis Library
Map Collection
P.O. Box 305190
Denton, TX 76203-5190
Phone: 940-565-2870

Fax: 940-565-2599
Web: www.library.unt.edu/govinfo/

University of Northern Colorado (110)
James A. Michener Library
Campus Box 48
Greeley, CO 80639
Phone: 970-351-2671
Fax: 970-351-2963
Web: www.unco.edu/library/

University of Northern Iowa (200)
Rod Library
Documents and Maps Collection
1227 West 27th Street
Cedar Falls, IA 50613-3675
Phone: 319-273-2838
Fax: 319-273-2913
Web: www.library.uni.edu/gov/

University of Oregon (400)
Knight Library
Document Center
1299 University of Oregon
Eugene, OR 97403-1299
Phone: 541-346-4565
Fax: 541-346-1958
Web: libweb.uoregon.edu/map/

University of Pittsburgh (425)
Hillman Library
Map Collection
3960 Forbes Avenue
Pittsburgh, PA 15260
Phone: 412-648-7726; 412-648-7730
Fax: 412-648-7733
Web: www.library.pitt.edu/libraries/maps/maps.html

University of Puget Sound (539)
Collins Memorial Library
1500 North Warner
Tacoma, WA 98416-1012
Phone: 253-879-3669
Fax: 253-879-3670
Web: library.ups.edu/research/govt/about.htm

University of Rhode Island (430)
University Library
Government Publications
15 Lippitt Road
Kingston, RI 02881
Phone: 401-874-2606
Fax: 401-874-4608
Web: www.uri.edu/library/

University of Richmond (519)
Boatwright Library
Government Documents Collection
1 Westhampton Way
Richmond, VA 23173
Phone: 804-289-8851
Fax: 804-287-1840
Web: oncampus.richmond.edu/is/library/govdocs/
govinfo.html

University of South Alabama (4)
Library
307 University Boulevard
Mobile, AL 36688-0002
Phone: 251-460-7024
Fax: 251-461-1628
Web: library.southalabama.edu

University of South Carolina (444)
South Caroliniana Library
Published Materials
University of South Carolina Horseshoe
Columbia, SC 29208
Phone: 803-777-3132
Fax: 803-777-5747
Web: www.sc.edu/library/socar

University of South Carolina (445)
Thomas Cooper Library
Map Library
Columbia, SC 29208
Phone: 803-777-2802
Fax: 803-777-4661
Web: www.sc.edu/library/maps.html

University of South Dakota (456)
I.D. Weeks Library
414 East Clark Street
Vermillion, SD 57059
Phone: 605-677-5371
Fax: 605-677-5488
Web: www.usd.edu/library/idweeks.cfm

University of South Florida (139)
Tampa Library
Reference/Documents—Map Collection
4202 East Fowler Avenue
LIB 122
Tampa, FL 33620-5400
Phone: 813-974-2729
Fax: 813-974-9875
Web: www.lib.usf.edu/tampa/govdocs/

University of Southern Maine (238)
Glickman Family Library
Osher Map Library and Smith Center
for Cartographic Education

P.O. Box 9301
Portland, ME 04104-9301
Phone: 207-780-4850
Fax: 207-780-5310
Web: www.usm.maine.edu/maps

University of Tennessee (465)
Hoskins Library
Map Library
1401 Cumberland Avenue
Knoxville, TN 37996-4006
Phone: 865-974-4315
Fax: 865-974-3925
Web: www.lib.utk.edu/~cic/

University of Tennessee (466)
Special Collections—Hoskins Library
1401 Cumberland Avenue
Knoxville, TN 37996-4000
Phone: 865-974-4480
Fax: 865-974-0560
Web: www.lib.utk.edu/spcoll

University of Texas, Arlington (476)
Library
Information Services
702 College Street
P.O. Box 19497
Arlington, TX 76019
Phone: 817-272-7514
Fax: 817-272-3593
Web: www.uta.edu/library

University of Texas, Arlington (477)
Library
Special Collections
702 College Street
Arlington, TX 76019-0497
Phone: 817-272-3393
Fax: 817-272-3360
Web: libraries.uta.edu/SpecColl

University of Texas, Austin (480)
Nettie Lee Benson Latin American Collection
Rare Books and Manuscripts Division
The General Libraries
Austin, TX 78713-8916
Phone: 512-495-4520
Fax: 512-495-4568
Web: www.lib.utexas.edu/benson/

University of Texas, Austin (481)
Perry-Castañeda Library
Map Collection
Austin, TX 78713
Phone: 512-495-4275

Fax: 512-495-4296
Web: www.lib.utexas.edu/

University of Texas, Austin (482)
Walter Geology Library
Tobin Map Collection
GEO 4.202-S5438
Austin, TX 78712-1101
Phone: 512-495-4680
Fax: 512-495-4102
Web: www.lib.utexas.edu/geo

University of Texas, Dallas (495)
Eugene McDermott Library
P.O. Box 830643
MC33
Richardson, TX 75083-0643
Phone: 972-883-2950
Fax: 972-883-2473
Web: www.utdallas.edu/library

University of Texas, El Paso (490)
500 West University
El Paso, TX 79968
Phone: 915-747-6702
Fax: 915-747-5327
Web: libraryweb.utep.edu

University of Toledo (394)
William S. Carlson
Map Collection
2801 West Bancroft Street
Toledo, OH 43606-3390
Phone: 419-530-2865
Fax: 419-530-2542
Web: www.cl.utoledo.edu

University of Tulsa (398)
McFarlin Library
2933 East 6th Street
Tulsa, OK 74104-3123
Phone: 918-631-2874
Fax: 918-631-3791
Web: www.lib.utulsa.edu/govdocs/maps.htm

University of Utah (504)
Marriott Library
Science and Engineering Map Collection
295 South 1500 E.
Salt Lake City, UT 84112-0860
Phone: 801-581-7533
Web: www.lib.utah.edu

University of Utah (505)
Marriott Library
Special Collections
295 South 1500 E.

Salt Lake City, UT 84112-0860
Phone: 801-581-8863
Web: www.lib.utah.edu

University of Utah (506)
Marriott Library
Western Americana
295 South 1500 E.
Salt Lake City, UT 84112-0860
Phone: 801-581-8863
Fax: 801-585-3464
Web: www.lib.utah.edu/spc/wam/maps/Maphomepage
.html

University of Vermont (509)
Bailey/Howe Library
Map Room
538 Main Street
Burlington, VT 05405-0036
Phone: 802-656-2588
Fax: 802-656-4038
Web: library.uvm.edu/reference/maps.html

University of Virginia (512)
Alderman Library
Geospatial and Statistical Data Center
P.O. Box 400129
Charlottesville, VA 22904-4129
Phone: 434-982-2630
Fax: 434-924-1431
Web: fisher.lib.virginia.edu

University of Virginia (513)
Special Collections
Alderman Library
Charlottesville, VA 22904
Phone: 434-924-3025
Fax: 434-924-4968
Web: www.lib.virginia.edu

University of Washington (537)
Suzzallo/Allen Library
Map Collection and Cartographic Information Services
Box 352900
Seattle, WA 98195
Phone: 206-543-9392
Fax: 206-685-8049
Web: www.lib.washington.edu/maps

University of Washington (538)
Suzzallo/Allen Library
Special Collections
Box 352900
Seattle, WA 98195
Phone: 206-543-1929
Fax: 206-543-1931
Web: www.lib.washington.edu/specialcoll

University of Wisconsin, Eau Claire (543)
William D. McIntyre Library
Depository Library Map Collection
Park and Garfield Streets
Eau Claire, WI 54702-4004
Phone: 715-836-3859
Fax: 715-836-2906
Web: www.uwec.edu/Library/gp/govpub2.html#MAP

University of Wisconsin, Green Bay (544)
Cofrin Library
2420 Nicolet Drive
Green Bay, WI 54311-7001
Phone: 920-465-2303
Fax: 920-465-2388
Web: www.uwgb.edu/library/

University of Wisconsin, La Crosse (546)
Murphy Library
1631 Pine Street
La Crosse, WI 54601
Phone: 608-785-8505
Fax: 608-785-8639
Web: www.uwlax.edu/murphylibrary

University of Wisconsin, Madison (547)
Arthur H. Robinson Map Library
550 North Park Street
Madison, WI 53706
Phone: 608-262-1471
Web: www.geography.wisc.edu/maplib

University of Wisconsin, Madison (548)
Geology and Geophysics Library
1215 West Dayton Street
Madison, WI 53706-1692
Phone: 608-262-8956
Fax: 608-262-0693
Web: www.geology.wisc.edu/library/

University of Wisconsin, Milwaukee (551)
American Geographical Society Library
2311 East Hartford Avenue
Milwaukee, WI 53211
Phone: 414-229-6282
Fax: 414-229-3624
Web: www.uwm.edu/Libraries/AGSL/index.html

University of Wisconsin, Oshkosh (553)
Department of Geology
800 Algoma Boulevard
Oshkosh, WI 54901
Phone: 920-424-2268
Fax: 920-424-0240

University of Wisconsin, Oshkosh (554)
Polk Library
Government Documents Collection
800 Algoma Boulevard
Oshkosh, WI 54901
Phone: 920-424-7305
Fax: 920-424-2175
Web: www.uwosh.edu/library/depts/docs/gov.html

University of Wisconsin, Stevens Point (556)
Learning Resources Center (LRC)
UWSP Map Center
Science Building
Stevens Point, WI 54481
Phone: 715-346-2629
Fax: 715-346-3372
Web: www.uwsp.edu/geo/internet/geog_geol_resources
.html

University of Wisconsin, Superior (557)
Jim Dan Hill Library
Lake Superior Maritime Collections
Box 2000
Superior, WI 54880
Phone: 715-394-8343
Fax: 715-394-8462
Web: library.uwsuper.edu

University of Wyoming (561)
Brinkerhoff Earth Resources Information Center
Department 3006
1000 University Avenue
Laramie, WY 82071
Phone: 307-766-3374
Fax: 307-766-6679
Web: www-lib.uwyo.edu/uwlibs/geo.htm

University of Wyoming (562)
Libraries
Grace Raymond Hebard Collection
1000 East University Avenue
Laramie, WY 82071
Phone: 307-766-6245
Fax: 307-766-3062
Web: www-lib.uwyo.edu/uwlibs/hebard_maps.htm

Urbana Free Library (180)
Champaign County Historical Archives
201 South Race Street
Urbana, IL 61801
Phone: 217-367-0807
Fax: 217-367-4061
Web: urbanafreelibrary.org/archives.htm

Utah Geological Survey (507)
Utah Department of Natural Resources Library
1594 West North Temple
Salt Lake City, UT 84114-6100
Phone: 801-537-3333
Fax: 801-537-3400
Web: dnrlibrary.state.ut.us/

Utah State Historical Society (508)
Utah History Information Center
300 Rio Grande
Salt Lake City, UT 84101
Phone: 801-533-3536
Fax: 801-533-3504
Web: www.history.utah.gov

Utah State University (499)
Merrill Library
Documents and Maps Department
University Hill
Logan, UT 84322-3000
Phone: 435-797-2684
Fax: 435-797-2880
Web: library.usu.edu/Govdocs/index.html

Utah State University (500)
Merrill Library
Special Collections
3000 Old Main Hill
Logan, UT 84322-3000
Phone: 435-797-2663
Web: library.usu.edu

Valparaiso University (197)
Christopher Center for Library
and Information Resources
1410 Chapel Drive
Valparaiso, IN 46383
Phone: 219 464-5771
Fax: 219 464-5792
Web: www.valpo.edu/library/map

Vanderbilt University (471)
Stevenson Science and Engineering Library
Map Room
419 21st Avenue South
Nashville, TN 37240
Phone: 615-322-2775
Fax: 615-343-7249
Web: www.library.vanderbilt.edu/science/maps.html

Ventura County Museum of History and Art (93)
Research Library
100 E. Main Street
Ventura, CA 93001

Phone: 805-653-0323
Fax: 805-653-5267
Web: www.vcmha.org

Virginia Tech (510)
Newman Library
Instruction and Reference Department
Kent Street
Blacksburg, VA 24060
Phone: 540-231-6181
Fax: 540-231-9263
Web: www.lib.vt.edu/subjects/maps/gis.html

Washington State Department of Ecology (529)
P.O. Box 47600
Olympia, WA 98504-7600
Phone: 360-407-6000
Web: www.ecy.wa.gov/services/gis/maps/maps.htm

**Washington State Department
of Natural Resources** (530)
Public Land Survey Office
P.O. Box 47060
Olympia, WA 98504-7060
Phone: 360-902-1190
Fax: 360-902-1191
Web: www.dnr.wa.gov/htdocs/plso/

**Washington State Department of Natural Resources,
Division of Geology and Earth Resources** (531)
Washington Geology Library
1111 Washington Street SE, MS 47007, Room 173
Olympia, WA 98504-7007
Phone: 360-902-1473
Fax: 360-902-1785
Web: www.dnr.wa.gov/geology/mapindex.htm

Washington State Library (532)
PO Box 42460
Olympia, WA 98504-2460
Phone: 866-538-4996
Fax: 360-586-7575
Web: www.secstate.wa.gov/library/

Washington State University (534)
Owen Science and Engineering Library
P.O. Box 643200
Pullman, WA 99164
Phone: 509-335-2674
Fax: 509-335-2534
Web: www.wsulibs.wsu.edu/science/owen.htm

Washington University (294)
Earth and Planetary Sciences Library
One Brookings Drive
Saint Louis, MO 63130

Phone: 314-935-5406
Fax: 314-935-4800
Web: library.wustl.edu

Weber State University (501)
Stewart Library
2901 University Circle
Ogden, UT 84408-2901
Phone: 801-626-6511
Fax: 801-626-7045
Web: library.weber.edu/ref/government/mapsguide.cfm

West Chester University (428)
Francis Harvey Green Library
Dr. Sandra F. Pritchard Mather and Dr. John Russell
  Mather Map Room.
29 West Rosedale Avenue
West Chester, PA 19383
Phone: 610-436-2869
Fax: 610-436-2251
Web: www.wcupa.edu/library.fhg/fhg_tour/maps.htm

West Texas A&M University (483)
Cornette Library
P.O. Box 60748
Canyon, TX 79016
Phone: 806-651-2205
Fax: 806-651-2213
Web: www.wtamu.edu/library/documents/docsmaps
  .shtml

West Virginia University (541)
Downtown Campus Library
Map Room
P. O. Box 6069
Morgantown, WV 26506
Phone: 304-293-4040 x4039
Fax: 304-293-6923
Web: www.libraries.wvu.edu/downtown/maps.htm

Western Carolina University (355)
Hunter Library
Map Room
176 Central Drive
Cullowhee, NC 28723
Phone: 828-227-3394
Fax: 828-227-7380
Web: www.wcu.edu/library/research/maps/index.htm

Western Illinois University (170)
Leslie F. Malpass Library
Government and Legal Information Unit
1 University Circle
Macomb, IL 61455

Phone: 309-298-2700
Fax: 309-298-2791
Web: www.wiu.edu/library/govpubs/maps/

Western Kentucky University (219)
Helm-Cravens Library
Maps and Atlases Collection
1 Big Red Way
Bowling Green, KY 42101-3576
Phone: 270-745-6125
Fax: 270-745-6175
Web: www.wku.edu/library

Western Michigan University (269)
Waldo Library
Map Department
1903 West Michigan Avenue
Kalamazoo, MI 49008
Phone: 269-387-5047
Web: www.wmich.edu/library/depts/maps/index.html

Western Washington University (523)
Huxley Map Library
AH 101
516 High Street
Bellingham, WA 98225-9085
Phone: 360-650-3272
Fax: 360-650-7702
Web: www.ac.wwu.edu/~maplib/

Western Wyoming Community College (564)
Hay Library
2500 College Drive
Box 473
Rock Springs, WY 82902
Phone: 307-382-1700
Fax: 307-382-7665
Web: www.wwcc.wy.edu/library

Whitman College (540)
Penrose Library
345 Boyer Ave
Walla Walla, WA 99362
Phone: 509-527-5191
Fax: 509-526-4785
Web: www.whitman.edu/penrose/departments.html

Wichita Public Library (216)
Reference Services Division
223 South Main Street
Wichita, KS 67202
Phone: 316-261-8500
Fax: 316-262-4540
Web: www.wichita.lib.ks.us

Appendix F
Names Index

This is a comprehensive personal name index for all responsible persons, and assistants. The numbers in parentheses refer to the accession numbers used in this book.

Rich Aarstad
Reference Historian
Montana Historical Society (298)
Research Center
225 North Roberts
P.O. Box 201201
Helena, MT 59620
Phone: 406-444-2681
Fax: 406-444-5297
Web: www.montanahistoricalsociety.org

Suzanne Adamko
National Archives and Records Administration (243)
Special Media Archives Services Division
Cartographic Section
8601 Adelphi Road
Room 3320
College Park, MD 20740-6001
Phone: 301-837-0564
Fax: 301-837-3622
Email: suzanne.adamko@nara.gov
Web: www.archives.gov

Holly Adams
University of Tennessee (466)
Special Collections—Hoskins Library
1401 Cumberland Avenue
Knoxville, TN 37996-4000
Phone: 865-974-4480
Fax: 865-974-0560
Web: www.lib.utk.edu/spcoll

Jerry Adams
Map Librarian
Brigham Young University (502)
Harold B. Lee Library
Map Collection
2420 HBLL
Provo, UT 84602-
Phone: 801-422-6179
Fax: 801-422-0466
Email: jerry_adams@byu.edu
Web: www.lib.byu.edu

Tina S. Agren
Librarian/Archivist
United Society of Shakers (235)
Shaker Library
Map Collection
707 Shaker Road
New Gloucester, ME 04260
Phone: 207-926-4597
Web: www.shaker.lib.me.us

Aric Ahrens
Government Documents Depository Coordinator
Illinois Institute of Technology (165)
Paul V. Galvin Library
Government Documents
35 West 33rd Street
Chicago, IL 60616
Phone: 312-567-3614
Fax: 312-567-3955
Email: ahrens@iit.edu
Web: www.gl.iit.edu/govdocs/

Cynthia Akers
Head of Information and Instructional Services
Emporia State University (207)
William Allen White Library
Information and Instructional Services
1200 Commercial, Campus Box 4051
Emporia, KS 66801
Phone: 620-341-5207
Fax: 620-341-5997
Email: akerscyn@emporia.edu

Cynthia Akers
Head of Information and Instruction, Associate Professor
Emporia State University (208)
William Allen White Library
Physical Science Division/Geology Map Library
1200 Commercial
Campus Box 4051
Emporia, KS 66801
Phone: 620-341-5207

Fax: 620-341-5997
Email: akerscyn@emporia.edu
Web: www.emporia.edu/earthsci/amber/maplibrary.htm

Minerva Alaniz
Specialist IV
Texas Tech University (493)
University Library
Government Documents Map Collection
18th and Boston
Lubbock, TX 79409-0002
Phone: 806-742-2268
Fax: 806-742-1332
Web: library.ttu.edu/ul/maps/

Jane Albrecht
Librarian
Bureau of Land Management, Juneau—
  John Rishel Information Center (11)
100 Savikko Road
Douglas, AK 99824
Phone: 907-364-1553
Fax: 907-364-1574
Email: jalbrech@ak.blm.gov
Web: juneau.ak.blm.gov/library/library.html

Steven Alcorta
Librarian II
Sonoma County Library (90)
3rd and E Street
Santa Rosa, CA 95404
Phone: 707-545-0831
Fax: 707-575-0437
Email: salcorta@sonoma.lib.ca.us
Web: www.sonomalibrary.org

Susan Alden
Archivist
Sharlot Hall Museum (25)
Archives
415 West Gurley Street
Prescott, AZ 86301
Phone: 928-445-3122
Fax: 928-776-9053
Email: susan@sharlot.org
Web: www.sharlot.org/archives

Michael Aldrich
Government Documents Librarian
State University of West Georgia (147)
Irvine Sullivan Ingram Library
1600 Maple Street
Carrollton, GA 30118
Phone: 770-830-2357

Fax: 770-836-6626
Email: maldrich@westga.edu
Web: www.westga.edu/~library/

Claire Alexander
Map Curator
Purdue University (198)
Earth and Atmospheric Sciences (EAS) Library
EAS Map Room
Civil Engineering Building
Room 2253
West Lafayette, IN 47907
Phone: 765-494-0202
Web: www.lib.purdue.edu/eas/inmaps.html

Heather Alexander
LA II
University of California, Santa Barbara (88)
Davidson Library
Map and Imagery Laboratory
Santa Barbara, CA 93106-9010
Phone: 805-893-2779
Fax: 805-893-8799
Web: www.sdc.ucsb.edu

David Allen
Librarian
Stony Brook University (345)
Mellville Library
Map Collection
Stony Brook, NY 11790
Phone: 631-632-71
Web: www.sunysb.edu/library/ldmaps.htm

Marcy M. Allen
Western Illinois University (170)
Leslie F. Malpass Library
Government and Legal Information Unit
1 University Circle
Macomb, IL 61455
Phone: 309-298-2700
Fax: 309-298-2791
Email: mm-allen@wiu.edu
Web: www.wiu.edu/library/govpubs/maps/

Peter Allen
Map Room Specialist
Dartmouth College (325)
Baker/Berry Library
Evans Map Room
HB 6025
Hanover, NH 03755
Phone: 603-646-2579
Fax: 603-646-3628
Web: www.dartmouth.edu/~maproom/

Rebecca Allen
Librarian II
City of Mesa Library (20)
64 East First Street
Mesa, AZ 85201
Phone: 480-644-2207
Email: rebecca.allen@cityofmesa.org
Web: www.mesalibrary.org

Brent Allison
Director
University of Minnesota (281)
O.M. Wilson Library
John R. Borchert Map Library
309 19th Avenue South
Minneapolis, MN 55455
Phone: 612-624-4549
Fax: 612-626-9353
Email: b-alli@umn.edu
Web: map.lib.umn.edu

Tanya Allison
Associate Professor and Program Coordinator
Montgomery College (247)
Department of Applied Technology
Applied Geography
51 Mannakee Street
Rockville, MD 20850
Phone: 301-251-7614
Fax: 301-279-5001
Email: tanya.allison@montgomerycollege.edu

Kathleen L. Amen
Saint Mary's University (497)
Blume Library
One Camino Santa Maria
San Antonio, TX 78228
Phone: 210-436-3441
Fax: 210-436-3782
Email: kamen@stmarytx.edu
Web: library.stmarytx.edu/acadlib/doc/maps/mapintro
.htm

John M. Anderson
Map Librarian and Director
Louisiana State University (227)
Cartographic Information Center
313 Howe-Russell Building
Baton Rouge, LA 70803
Phone: 225-578-6247
Fax: 225-578-4420
Email: janders@lsu.edu
Web: www.cic.lsu.edu

Marti Anderson
Archivist
Boulder Public Library (94)
Carnegie Branch Library for Local History
Map Collection
1125 Pine Street
Boulder, CO 80302
Phone: 303-441-3110
Fax: 720-406-7452
Email: andersonma@boulder.lib.co.us
Web: www.boulder.lib.co.us

Sue Anderson
Acquisitions Librarian
Eastern Washington University (525)
JFK Library
Maps
816 F Street
100 LIB
Cheney, WA 99004
Phone: 509-359-2263
Fax: 509-359-6456
Email: sanderson@ewu.edu
Web: www.library.ewu.edu/collections/maps.html

Judy Andrews
Coordinator for Government Information,
    Data Sets and Maps
Portland State University (409)
Millar Library
P.O. Box 1151
Portland, OR 97207-1151
Phone: 503-725-5874
Fax: 503-725-4524
Email: andrewsj@pdx.edu
Web: www.lib.pdx.edu/resources/maps_collection/index.
    html

Robert G. Anthony, Jr.
Curator
University of North Carolina, Chapel Hill (349)
Academic Affairs Library
North Carolina Collection
CB#3930
Wilson Library
Chapel Hill, NC 27514-8890
Phone: 919-962-1172
Fax: 919-962-4452
Email: nccref@email.unc.edu
Web: www.lib.unc.edu/ncc

Pamela Arbeeny
Fort Lewis College (106)
John F. Reed Library and the
    Center for Southwest Studies

Map Collection
Durango, CO 81303
Phone: 247-7551
Email: arbeeny_p@fortlewis.edu
Web: library.fortlewis.edu/reference/mapgovweb/maps
.html
swcenter.fortlewis.edu/SpecialCollections.htm#
Guides

HelenJane Armstrong
Map and Imagery Librarian
University of Florida (135)
George A. Smathers Libraries
Map and Imagery Library
P.O.Box 11701
110 Marston Science Library
Gainesville, FL 32611-7011
Phone: 352-392-2825
Fax: 352-392-4787
Email: hjarms@uflib.ufl.edu
Web: web.uflib.ufl.edu/maps

Roberta Arney
Head, Government Documents/Maps
University of Texas, El Paso (490)
500 West University
El Paso, TX 79968
Phone: 915-747-6702
Fax: 915-747-5327
Email: rarney@utep.edu
Web: libraryweb.utep.edu

Eric Arnold
Departmental Supervisor
University of Tennessee (465)
Hoskins Library
Map Library
1401 Cumberland Avenue
Knoxville, TN 37996-4006
Phone: 865-974-4315
Fax: 865-974-3925
Web: www.lib.utk.edu/~cic/

John G. Arrison
Penobscot Marine Museum (239)
Stephen Phillips Memorial Library
P.O. Box 498
9 Church Street
Searsport, ME 04974
Phone: 207-548-2529 x212
Fax: 207-548-2520
Web: www.penobscotmarinemuseum.org

Margaret Atwater-Singer
Reference/Instruction Librarian
University of Evansville (184)
Libraries

1800 Lincoln Avenue
Evansville, IN 47722
Phone: 812-479-2482
Fax: 812-471-6996
Email: ma35@evansville.edu
Web: libraries.evansville.edu/

Paul Atwood
Assistant Librarian
University of California, Berkeley (47)
Water Resources Center Archives
410 O'Brien Hall
Berkeley, CA 94720-1718
Phone: 510-642-2666
Fax: 510-642-9143
Web: www.lib.berkeley.edu/WRCA/

Jack August
Director
Arizona State University (27)
Hayden Library
Arizona Historical Foundation
P.O. Box 871006
Tempe, AZ 85287-1006
Phone: 480-966-8331
Fax: 480-966-1077
Email: jack.august@asu.edu
Web: www.arizonahistoricalfoundation.org

Brian P. Bach
Map Specialist
Central Washington University (526)
James E. Brooks Library
Documents, Maps and Microforms
400 East University Way
Ellensburg, WA 98926-7548
Phone: 509-963-1541
Fax: 509-963-3684
Web: www.lib.cwu.edu/documents/

Debra Bacon
Collection Assistant
Cornell University (340)
John M. Olin Library
Map and Geospatial Information Collection
Ithaca, NY 14853-5301
Phone: 607-255-7557
Fax: 607-255-9346
Web: www.library.cornell.edu/okuref/maps/map.htm

Jeremy Bailey
San Francisco State University (80)
Alfred Rockwell Sumner Memorial Map Library
1600 Holloway Avenue
HSS 289
San Francisco, CA 94132
Phone: 415-338-1145

Fax: 415-338-6243
Web: bss.sfsu.edu/geog/maplib.htm

Michael J. Bailey
Curator
Brazoria County Historical Museum (475)
Adriance Research Library
100 East Ceder
Angleton, TX 77515
Phone: 979-864-1591
Fax: 979-864-1217
Email: curator@bchm.org
Web: www.bchm.org

Rhett Bailey
Library Technical Assistant
West Virginia University (541)
Downtown Campus Library
Map Room
P. O. Box 6069
Morgantown, WV 26506
Phone: 304-293-4040 x4039
Fax: 304-293-6923
Web: www.libraries.wvu.edu/downtown/maps.htm

Diane Bain
Arizona Department Mines and Mineral Resources (21)
Library
1502 West Washington
Phoenix, AZ 85007
Phone: 602-255-3795
Fax: 602-255-3777
Web: www.admmr.state.az.us

Dennis Baird
Head of Reference Service
University of Idaho (159)
Library
Government Documents Department
Box 442353
Moscow, ID 83844-2353
Phone: 208-885-6344
Fax: 208-885-6817
Email: dbaird@uidaho.edu
Web: www.insideidaho.org

Laura Baker
Government Documents Librarian
Abilene Christian University (472)
Brown Library
Texas Topographic Map Collection
221 Brown Library
Abilene, TX 79601-9208
Phone: 325-674-2316
Fax: 325-674-2202
Email: bakerl@acu.edu
Web: www.acu.edu/academics/library

Mary Baldwin
Library Services Assistant Senior
University of Wisconsin, La Crosse (546)
Murphy Library
1631 Pine Street
La Crosse, WI 54601
Phone: 608-785-8505
Fax: 608-785-8639

Georgia B. Barnhill
Curator of Graphic Arts
American Antiquarian Society (260)
185 Salisbury Street
Worcester, MA 01609
Phone: 508-755-5221
Fax: 508-753-3311
Email: gbarnhill@mwa.org
Web: www.americanantiquarian.org

Bruce Barron
Government Documents Librarian
Florida Atlantic University (129)
S.E. Wimberly Library
777 Glades Road
Boca Raton, FL 33431
Phone: 561-297-3760
Fax: 561-338-3863

Laura Pass Barry
Colonial Williamsburg Foundation (521)
301 First Street
Williamsburg, VA 23185
Phone: 757-229-1000
Web: www.colonialwilliamsburg.org

Marvin Barton
University of Nebraska, Omaha (317)
Department of Geography-Geology
Omaha, NE 68182-0199
Phone: 402-554-3586

Christopher Baruth
University of Wisconsin, Milwaukee (551)
Libraries
American Geographical Society Library
2311 East Hartford Avenue
Milwaukee, WI 53211
Phone: 414-229-6282
Fax: 414-229-3624
Email: cmb@uwm.edu
Web: www.uwm.edu/Libraries/AGSL/index.html

Peggy Bates
Coastal Carolina University (446)
Kimbel Library
P.O. Box 261954
Conway, SC 29528

Phone: 843-349-2414
Fax: 843-349-2412
Email: peggyb@coastal.edu
Web: www.coatsal.edu/library

Ruth Bauer Anderson
Reference Archivist
Minnesota Historical Society (287)
Library and Archives
345 Kellogg Boulevard West
Saint Paul, MN 55102-1906
Phone: 651-296-2143
Fax: 651-297-7436
Email: ruth.anderso@mnhs.org
Web: www.mnhs.org

Norris Bazemore, Jr.
Reference/Map Librarian
Boise State University (156)
Albertsons Library
Hollenbaugh Map Collection
1910 University Drive
Boise, ID 83725
Phone: 208-426-1264
Email: nbazemor@boisestate.edu
Web: library.boisestate.edu/Maps/

Gretchen F. Beal
Knoxville/Knox County Metropolitan
   Planning Commission (463)
Planning Commission Library
400 Main Street
Suite 403
Knoxville, TN 37902
Phone: 865-215-2500
Fax: 865-215-2068
Email: gretchen.beal@knoxmpc.org
Web: www.knoxmpc.org

Jeffery S. Beam
University of North Carolina, Chapel Hill (351)
John N. Couch Biology Library
Botany Section
CB #3280 Coker Hall
Chapel Hill, NC 27599-3280
Phone: 919-962-3783
Fax: 919-843-8393
Web: wwww.lib.unc.edu/biology

Susan Beard
Government Information Specialist
Northern Arizona University (17)
Cline Library
Map Collection
P.O. Box 6022
Flagstaff, AZ 86011

Phone: 928-523-6805
Fax: 928-523-3770
Email: Susan.Beard@nau.edu

Margaret Beck Pritchard
Colonial Williamsburg Foundation (521)
301 First Street
Williamsburg, VA 23185
Phone: 757-229-1000
Email: mpritchard@cwf.org
Web: www.colonialwilliamsburg.org

Derrick Beckner
Library Supervisor
Pennsylvania State University (427)
University Libraries
Maps Library
001 Paterno Library
University Park, PA 16802
Phone: 814-863-0094
Fax: 814-863-3560
Web: www.libraries.psu.edu/maps

Jo Anne Beezley
Pittsburg State University (214)
Leonard H. Axe Library
Government Documents
1605 South Joplin
Pittsburg, KS 66762
Phone: 620-235-4889
Fax: 620-235-4090
Email: beezley@pittstate.edu

Wendy Begay
University of Arizona (32)
Library
1510 East University
Tucson, AZ 85721
Phone: 520-621-6441
Fax: 520-621-9733
Web: www.library.arizona.edu

Suzanne T. Bell
University of Guam (151)
Robert F. Kennedy Memorial Library
Government Documents
UOG Station
Mangilao, GU 96923
Phone: 671-735-2321
Fax: 671-734-6882
Email: stbell@uog9.uog.edu

Walfrid C. Benavente
Library Technician II
University of Guam (151)
Robert F. Kennedy Memorial Library

Government Documents
UOG Station
Mangilao, GU 96923
Phone: 671-735-2321
Fax: 671-734-6882

Gordon E. Bennett
University of Nebraska, Kearney (303)
Geography Map Library
Department of Geography
Kearney, NE 68849
Phone: 308-865-8682

Mary Bennett
Special Collections Coordinator
State Historical Society of Iowa,
    Department of Cultural Affairs (203)
Special Collections/Map Collection
402 Iowa Avenue
Iowa City, IA 52240
Phone: 319-335-3916
Fax: 319-335-3935
Email: bennettm@blue.weeg.uiowa.edu
Web: www.iowahistory.org

Sarah S. Benson
Richland County Public Library (442)
Walker Local History Room
1431 Assembly Street
Columbia, SC 29201
Phone: 802-929-3402
Email: sbenson@richland.lib.sc.us

Bob Bentz
Program Specialist
Office of Surface Mining Reclamation
    and Enforcement (429)
Anthracite (Coal) Mine Map Repository
Branch of Anthracite-MMR
7 North Wilkes-Barre Boulevard
Suite 308
Wilkes-Barre, PA 18702-5293
Phone: 570-830-1400
Fax: 570-830-1421
Web: mmr.osmre.gov

Elaine Berg
Librarian
Austin Peay State University (459)
Felix G. Woodward
Information Services
601 East College Street
Clarksville, TN 37044
Phone: 931-221-7346
Fax: 931-221-7296

Email: berge@apsu.edu
Web: library.apsu.edu/

Rita Berk
Library Director
Moravian College (412)
Reeves Library
1200 Main Street
Bethlehem, PA 18018
Phone: 610-861-1540
Fax: 610-861-1577
Email: berkr@moravian.edu

Rebecca Bernthal
Head Librarian
University of Nebraska, Lincoln (311)
C.Y. Thompson Library
38th and Holdrege Streets
East Campus
Lincoln, NE 68583-0717
Phone: 402-472-4407
Fax: 402-472-7005
Email: rbernthal1@unl.edu

Karen Berquist
Library Specialist
College of William and Mary (520)
Earl Gregg Swem Library
Geology Department Library
P.O. Box 8795
Williamsburg, VA 23187-8795
Phone: 757 221-2094
Fax: 757 221-2093
Email: kaberq@wm.edu
Web: swem.wm.edu/Guide/Geology/index.html

Kathleen Berry
Boston College (258)
Thomas P. O'Neill Jr. Library
Catherine O'Connor Library
381 Concord Road
Weston, MA 02493
Phone: 617-552-8300
Fax: 617-552-8388
Email: berryka@bc.edu
Web: www.bc.edu/libraries/centers/weston/

Marie Berry
Reference Librarian
Campbell University (348)
Carrie Rich Memorial Library
Government Documents
227 Main Street
Buies Creek, NC 27506
Phone: 910-893-1465

Fax: 910-893-1470
Email: berry@camel.campbell.edu
Web: www.lib.campbell.edu

David J. Bertuca
Map Librarian
State University of New York, Buffalo (339)
Arts and Sciences Libraries
Map Collection
Capen Hall
Buffalo, NY 14260-1672
Phone: 716-645-2947
Fax: 716-645-3710
Email: dbertuca@buffalo.edu
Web: ublib.buffalo.edu/libraries/asl/maps/map_room
    .html

Venice Beske
Manager, Statewide Information Services
Wyoming State Library (559)
Statewide Information Services
2301 Capitol Avenue
Cheyenne, WY 82002
Phone: 307-777-6333
Fax: 307-777-5920
Email: vbeske@state.wy.us
Web: www-wsl.state.wy.us

Robert A. Bier, Jr.
Chief, Cartographic Information Services
United States Geological Survey, Reston (517)
Reston Library
Cartographic Information Services
950 National Center
12201 Sunrise Valley Drive
Reston, VA 20192
Phone: 703-648-4302
Fax: 703-648-6373
Email: rbier@usgs.gov
Web: library.usgs.gov/

Ann Billesbach
Head of Reference
Nebraska State Historical Society (309)
Library/Archives
P.O. Box 82554
1500 R Street
Lincoln, NE 68501
Phone: 402-471-4786
Fax: 402-471-8922
Web: www.nebraskahistory.org

Debbie Binsfeld
Saint Cloud State University (284)
James W. Miller Learning Resources Center
Government Documents/Maps

720 4th Avenue South
Saint Cloud, MN 56301
Phone: 320-308-2063
Fax: 320-308-4778

Karen Blackman-Mills
District of Columbia Public Library (123)
Martin Luther King Jr. Memorial Library
Washingtoniana Division #307
901 G Street NW
Washington, DC 20001
Phone: 202-727-1213
Fax: 202-727-1129
Email: karen.blackman-mills@dc.gov
Web: www.dclibrary.org

Margaret Blackstone
Government Documents Librarian
Omaha Public Library (316)
W. Dale Clark Library
Business, Science, Technology
215 South 15th Street
Omaha, NE 68102-1629
Phone: 402-444-4817
Fax: 402-444-4585
Email: mblackstone@omaha.lib.ne.us
Web: www.omaha.lib.ne.us

Erin Blake
Curator of Art
Folger Shakespeare Library (124)
201 East Capitol Street SE
Washington, DC 20003
Phone: 202-544-4600
Fax: 202-675-0313
Web: www.folger.edu

Merrialyce Blanchard
Oregon State Library (410)
250 Winter Street NE
Salem, OR 97301
Phone: 503-378-4277 x236
Fax: 503-588-7119

Robert E. Blesse
Head, Special Collections and Archives Department
University of Nevada, Reno (322)
Getchell Library
Special Collections and Archives Department
1664 North Virginia Street
Reno, NV 89557-0044
Phone: 775-784-6500 x327
Fax: 775-784-4529
Email: blesse@unr.edu
Web: www.library.unr.edu/specoll

Tim Blevins
Manager
Pikes Peak Library District (98)
Carnegie Library
Special Collections
20 North Cascade Avenue
Colorado Springs, CO 80903
Phone: 719-531-6333 x2253
Fax: 719-389-8161
Email: tblevins@mail.ppld.org
Web: ppld.org

L. Nicole Blum
Assistant Archivist
Moravian Archives (367)
457 South Church Street
Winston-Salem, NC 27101
Phone: 336-722-1742
Fax: 336-725-4514
Web: MoravianArchives.org

Eileen Bolger
Director, Archival Operations
National Archives and Records Administration,
    Rocky Mountain Region (104)
P.O. Box 25307
Building 48
Denver Federal Center
Denver, CO 80225
Phone: 303-407-5740
Fax: 303-407-5707
Email: eileen.bolger@nara.gov
Web: www.archives.gov/facilities/rocky_mountain_
    region.html

Anthony Bliss
Curator of Rare Books
University of California, Berkeley (44)
Bancroft Library
Map Collection
Berkeley, CA 94720
Phone: 510-642-6481
Fax: 510-642-7589

Richard Boardman
Head
Free Library of Philadelphia (421)
Map Collection
1901 Vine Street
Philadelphia, PA 19103-1189
Phone: 215-686-5397
Fax: 215-563-3628
Email: boardmanr@library.phila.gov
Web: www.library.phila.gov

Mary Bogue
Library Manager
Earlham College (195)
Wildman Science Library
P.O. Box 72
Richmond, IN 47374
Phone: 765-983-1245
Web: www.earlham.edu/~libr/wildman/

Don Bonsteel
Librarian
Enoch Pratt Free Library (240)
Maryland Department/Map Collection
400 Cathedral Street
Baltimore, MD 21201
Phone: 410-396-5468
Fax: 410-396-9537
Email: bonsteel@epfl.net
Web: www.epfl.net/slrc/md/

Lori Boone
Library Technician
University of Alaska, Fairbanks (13)
Elmer E. Rasmuson Library
Documents and Maps Collection
P.O. Box 756817
Fairbanks, AK 99775-6817
Phone: 907-474-7624
Fax: 907-474-1155
Web: www.uaf.edu/library

Arlyn Booth
Map Coordinator
Illinois State Library (176)
300 South Second Street
Springfield, IL 62701
Phone: 217-782-5823
Fax: 217-557-6737
Email: abooth@ilsos.net
Web: www.cyberdriveillinois.com/library/isl/ref/islmaps
    .html

Maria Borysiewicz
Cataloging Librarian
American Alpine Club (108)
Henry S. Hall, Jr. Library
710 Tenth Street
Suite 15
Golden, CO 80401
Phone: 303-384-0112
Fax: 303-384-0113
Web: www.americanalpineclub.org/knowledge/
    aaclibrary.asp

Roseann Bowerman
Team Leader Arts and Sciences Team
Lehigh University (413)
Fairchild Martindale Library
Located in Government Documents
8A East Packer Avenue
Bethlehem, PA 18015
Phone: 610-758-5337
Email: rb04@lehigh.edu

Robert Boyce
Reference Librarian
Lincoln City Libraries (305)
136 S 14th St
Lincoln, NE 68508
Phone: 402-441-8530
Fax: 402-441-8534
Web: www.lcl.lib.ne.us

Katherine Bradley
Reference Librarian
Kern County Library (42)
Beale Memorial Library
Geology-Mining-Petroleum Room
701 Truxtun Avenue
Bakersfield, CA 93301
Phone: 661-868-0783
Email: katherine.bradley@kerncountylibrary.org
Web: www.kerncountylibrary.org

Lola Bradley
Documents Assistant
Furman University (448)
James B. Duke Library
Government Document Map Collection
3300 Poinsett Highway
Greenville, SC 29613
Phone: 864-294-2260

Laura Bramble
Central Library Director
Indianapolis-Marion County Public Library (191)
Central Library
40 East Street Clair Street
Indianapolis, IN 46202
Phone: 317-269-1700
Fax: 317-268-5229
Email: lbramble@imcpl.org
Web: imcpl.org

Randal Brandt
Head of Cataloguing
University of California, Berkeley (44)
Bancroft Library

Map Collection
Berkeley, CA 94720
Phone: 510-642-6481
Fax: 510-642-7589

Eleanor Brennan
Library Technician
West Chester University (428)
Francis Harvey Green Library
Dr. Sandra F. Pritchard Mather and
    Dr. John Russell Mather Map Room.
29 West Rosedale Avenue
West Chester, PA 19383
Phone: 610-436-2869
Fax: 610-436-2251
Web: www.wcupa.edu/library.fhg/fhg_tour/maps.htm

Patricia B.M. Brennan
Head of the Reference Department
Rhode Island College (432)
James P. Adams Library
600 Mount Pleasant Avenue
Providence, RI 2908
Phone: 401-456-8125
Fax: 401-456-1915
Email: pbrennan@ric.edu
Web: www.ric.edu/adamslibrary

Alvan Bregman
Rare Book Collections Librarian
University of Illinois, Urbana-Champaign (179)
Rare Book and Special Collections Library
1408 West Gregory Drive
Room 346
Urbana, IL 61801
Phone: 217-333-3777
Fax: 217-333-2214
Email: abregman@uiuc.edu
Web: www.library.uiuc.edu/rbx/

Mary Brewer
Arkansas State Library (37)
Document Services
One Capitol Mall
Little Rock, AR 72201
Phone: 501-682-2869
Fax: 501-681-1532
Email: Mbrewer@asl.li.ar.us
Web: www.asl.lib.ar.us

Anne Bridges
University of Tennessee (466)
Special Collections—Hoskins Library
1401 Cumberland Avenue
Knoxville, TN 37996-4000
Phone: 865-974-4480

Fax: 865-974-0560
Email: abridges@utk.edu
Web: www.lib.utk.edu/spcoll

Darlene Brimmage
Map Specialist
Dallas Public Library (485)
J. Eric Jonsson Central Library
Government Information Center/Map Collection
1515 Young Street
Dallas, TX 75201
Phone: 214-670-1468
Fax: 214-670-1451
Email: dbrimmage@dallaslibrary.org
Web: www.dallaslibrary.org/CGI/maps.htm

David F. Broer
Broer Map Library (120)
74 Hampden Road
Somers, CT 06071
Phone: 413-221-4642
Email: dave@broermaps.org
Web: www.broermaps.org/

Edwin Brooks
Maps/GIS Assistant
Virginia Tech (510)
Newman Library
Instruction and Reference Department
Kent Street
Blacksburg, VA 24060
Phone: 540-231-6181
Fax: 540-231-9263
Web: www.lib.vt.edu/subjects/maps/gis.html

Leonard L. Brooks
Director
United Society of Shakers (235)
Shaker Library
Map Collection
707 Shaker Road
New Gloucester, ME 04260
Phone: 207-926-4597
Email: brooks1@shaker.lib.me.us
Web: www.shaker.lib.me.us

Aimee Brown
Archivist
Iron Range Research Center (275)
Maps
801 SW Highway 169
Suite 1
Chisholm, MN 55719
Phone: 218-254-7959

Fax: 218-254-7971
Email: aimee.brown@ironworld.com
Web: www.ironrangeresearchcenter.org

Cindy Brown
Wyoming State Parks and
    Cultural Resources Department (560)
Wyoming State Archives
2301 Central Avenue
Cheyenne, WY 82002
Phone: 307-777-7036
Fax: 307-777-7044
Email: cbrown1@state.wy.us
Web: wyoarchives.state.wy.us/

Judy Brown
LA
Anderson County Public Library (434)
South Carolina Room
300 North McDuffie Street
Anderson, SC 29621
Phone: 864-260-4500
Fax: 864-260-4098
Web: www.andersonlibrary.org

Rusty Brown
LA IV
University of California, Santa Barbara (88)
Davidson Library
Map and Imagery Laboratory
Santa Barbara, CA 93106-9010
Phone: 805-893-2779
Fax: 805-893-8799
Web: www.sdc.ucsb.edu

Diane Browning
Map Assistant
Eastern Michigan University (273)
Bruce T. Halle Library
Maps
Ypsilanti, MI 48197
Phone: 734-487-0020 x2115, x2116
Fax: 734-487-8861

Judy Brueggen
Library Specialist II
Northern Kentucky University (222)
Steely Library
Map Collection
Louie B. Nunn Drive
Highland Heights, KY 40199-6101
Phone: 859-572-5456
Fax: 859-572-5390
Web: library.nku.edu/welcome.html

Carrie Brunsberg
Librarian II
Minneapolis Public Library (280)
300 Nicollet Mall
Minneapolis, MN 55401
Phone: 612-630-6000
Fax: 612-630-6220
Web: www.mplib.org

Jimmy Bryant
University of Central Arkansas (34)
Torreyson Library
Archives Map Collection
201 Donaghey
Conway, AR 72035
Phone: 501-450-3418
Fax: 501-450-5208
Email: Jimmyb@uca.edu
Web: www.uca.edu

Fritz Buckallew
Map Librarian
University of Central Oklahoma (397)
Max Chambers Library
Map Collection
100 North University
Edmond, OK 73034
Phone: 405-974-2906
Fax: 405-974-3806
Email: fbuckallew@ucok.edu
Web: www.ucok.edu

Cheryl Burden
Case Western Reserve University (377)
Kelvin Smith Library
11055 Euclid Avenue
Cleveland, OH 44106
Phone: 216-368-6511
Fax: 216-368-3669

Mark Burdette
Government Information Associate
University of Richmond (519)
Boatwright Library
Government Documents Collection
1 Westhampton Way
Richmond, VA 23173
Phone: 804-289-8851
Fax: 804-287-1840
Web: oncampus.richmond.edu/is/library/govdocs/
govinfo.html

William R. Burk
University of North Carolina, Chapel Hill (351)
John N. Couch Biology Library
Botany Section

CB #3280 Coker Hall
Chapel Hill, NC 27599-3280
Phone: 919-962-3783
Fax: 919-843-8393
Email: billburk@email.unc.edu
Web: wwww.lib.unc.edu/biology

Bridget Burke
Library Director
American Alpine Club (108)
Henry S. Hall, Jr. Library
710 Tenth Street
Suite 15
Golden, CO 80401
Phone: 303-384-0112
Fax: 303-384-0113
Web: www.americanalpineclub.org/knowledge/
aaclibrary.asp

Helen Burke
Government Documents Coordinator
Minneapolis Public Library (280)
300 Nicollet Mall
Minneapolis, MN 55401
Phone: 612-630-6000
Fax: 612-630-6220
Email: hburke@mplib.org
Web: www.mplib.org

Brandon Burnette
Government Documents/Reference Librarian
Southeastern Oklahoma State University (396)
Henry G. Bennett Memorial Library
1405 North 4th Avenue
PMB 4105
Durant, OK 74701
Phone: 580-745-2935
Fax: 580-745-7463
Email: bburnette@sosu.edu
Web: www.sosu.edu/govdocs/govdoc%20home.html

Clayton Burnham
Head of Davidson Library and MIL systems,
programmer III
University of California, Santa Barbara (88)
Davidson Library
Map and Imagery Laboratory
Santa Barbara, CA 93106-9010
Phone: 805-893-2779
Fax: 805-893-8799
Web: www.sdc.ucsb.edu

Valerie Burnie
Reference Librarian
Public Library of Charlotte-Mecklenburg County (353)
North Carolina Room Map Collection

310 North Tryon Street
Charlotte, NC 28202
Phone: 704-336-2980
Fax: 704-336-6236
Email: ncrstaff@plcmc.org
Web: www.plcmc.org

Laura Burns
Ohio University (372)
Alden Library
Government Documents and Maps Collection
Park Place
Athens, OH 45701
Phone: 740-593-2718
Fax: 740-593-2719
Web: www.library.ohiou.edu/libinfo/depts/maps/index
.htm

Mary Anne Burns Duffy
Document and Map Librarian
West Chester University (428)
Francis Harvey Green Library
Dr. Sandra F. Pritchard Mather and Dr. John Russell
Mather Map Room.
29 West Rosedale Avenue
West Chester, PA 19383
Phone: 610-436-2869
Fax: 610-436-2251
Email: mburnsduff@wcupa.edu
Web: www.wcupa.edu/library.fhg/fhg_tour/maps.htm

Michael Buscher
Collection Management Team Leader
Library of Congress (125)
Geography and Map Division
101 Independence Avenue SE
Madison Building
Room LM B01
Washington, DC 20540-4650
Phone: 202-707-6277
Fax: 202-707-8531
www.loc.gov/rr/geogmap/

Nic Butler
Archivist
South Carolina Historical Society (440)
100 Meeting Street
Charleston, SC 29401
Phone: 843-723-3225
Fax: 843-723-8584
Email: nic.butler@schistory.org
Web: www.schistory.org

Rebecca H. Byrum
Valparaiso University (197)
Christopher Center for Library
and Information Resources

1410 Chapel Drive
Valparaiso, IN 46383
Phone: 219 464-5771
Fax: 219 464-5792
Email: becky.byrum@valpo.edu
www.valpo.edu/library/map

Alexandra Cabreja
Library Technical Assistant
New York Public Library (343)
Humanities and Social Sciences Library
Map Division
5th Ave and 42nd Street
Room 117
New York, NY 10018
Phone: 212-930-0587
Fax: 212-930-0027
Web: www.nypl.org/research/chss/map/map.html

R. Brantley Cagle
Documents Librarian
McNeese State University (230)
Frazar Memorial Library
Government Documents Department
300 Beauregard Drive
Lake Charles, LA 70609
Phone: 337-475-5736
Fax: 337-475-5719
Email: governmentinfo@mcneese.edu
Web: library.mcneese.edu/depts/docs/index.htm

Ellen Calhoun
Documents Librarian
Rutgers, The State University of New Jersey (329)
Library of Science and Medicine
165 Bevier Rd
Piscataway, NJ 08854-8009
Phone: 732-445-2895
Fax: 732-44-5806
Email: calhoun@rci.rutgers.edu
Web: www.libraries.rutgers.edu/rul/index.shtml

Hillary Campbell
Government Documents Librarian
University of Texas, Dallas (495)
Eugene McDermott Library
P.O. Box 830643
MC33
Richardson, TX 75083-0643
Phone: 972-883-2950
Fax: 972-883-2473
Email: Hillary.Campbell@utdallas.edu
Web: www.utdallas.edu/library

James W. Campbell
Library Services Manager
New Haven Colony Historical Society (118)

Whitney Library
114 Whitney Avenue
New Haven, CT 06510
Phone: 203-562-4183, x15
Fax: 203-562-2002

Laura Campbell
Library Assistant/Public Service
University of California, Santa Cruz (89)
Science and Engineering Library
Map Room
1156 High Street
Santa Cruz, CA 95064
Phone: 831-459-2364
Fax: 831-459-4187
Web: library.ucsc.edu/maps/

Laurie Canepa
Federal Document Librarian
New Mexico State Library (334)
1209 Camino Carlos Rey
Santa Fe, NM 87507
Phone: 505-476-9702
Fax: 505-476-9703
Email: laurie@stlib.state.nm.us
Web: www.stlib.state.nm.us/

Bill Card
Geographer
United States Department of Interior,
    Office of Surface Mining (464)
Knoxville Field Office Geographic
    Information System (KFO GIS)
530 Gay Street SW
Suite 500
Knoxville, TN 37902
Phone: 865-545-4103 x134
Fax: 865-545-4111
Email: bcard@osmre.gov

Gary A. Carlson
Midland Lutheran College (301)
Earth Science Department
900 North Clarkson
Fremont, NE 68025
Phone: 402-941-6328

Jane Carlson
Library Assistant III
University of Iowa (205)
Map Collection
3111 Main Library
Iowa City, IA 52242-1420
Phone: 319-335-5920
Fax: 319-335-5900
Web: www.lib.uiowa.edu/maps

Noel Carmack
Preservation Librarian
Utah State University (500)
Merrill Library
Special Collections
3000 Old Main Hill
Logan, UT 84322-3000
Phone: 435-797-2663

James Carolina
Georgetown County Library (447)
405 Cleland Street
Georgetown, SC 29440
Phone: 843-545-3300
Fax: 843-545-3395

Rachel Carpenter
Reference and Government Documents Librarian
Rhode Island College (432)
James P. Adams Library
600 Mount Pleasant Avenue
Providence, RI 2908
Phone: 401-456-8125
Fax: 401-456-1915
Web: www.ric.edu/adamslibrary

Larry Carver
Head
University of California, Santa Barbara (88)
Davidson Library
Map and Imagery Laboratory
Santa Barbara, CA 93106-9010
Phone: 805-893-2779
Fax: 805-893-8799
Email: carber@library.ucsb.edu
Web: www.sdc.ucsb.edu

Clark E. Center, Jr.
Curator
University of Alabama (7)
W. S. Hoole Special Collections Library
Box 870266
Tuscaloosa, AL 35487-0266
Phone: 205-348-0500
Fax: 205-348-1699
Email: ccenter@bama.ua.edu
Web: www.lib.ua.edu/libraries/hoole/

Janet Charles-Foutch
Engineering Aide Research Specialist
Washington State Department of Natural Resources (530)
Public Land Survey Office
P.O. Box 47060
Olympia, WA 98504-7060
Phone: 360-902-1190
Fax: 360-902-1191
Web: www.dnr.wa.gov/htdocs/plso/

Martha Childers
Government Documents Librarian
Johnson County Library (213)
9875 West 87th Street
Overland Park, KS 66212
Phone: 913-495-2400
Fax: 913-495-9104
Email: childersm@jocolibrary.org
Web: www.jocolibrary.org

Donna Christian
Toledo-Lucas County Public Library (393)
Main Library
325 Michigan Street
Toledo, OH 43624
Phone: 419-259-5207

Gayle Christian
Government Information/Map Librarian
Georgia State University (145)
University Library
Information Services Department
100 Decatur Street SE
Atlanta, GA 30303-3202
Phone: 404-463-9934
Fax: 404-651-4315
Email: gchristian@gsu.edu
Web: www.library.gsu.edu/maps

Karen Ciccone
North Carolina State University (364)
Natural Resources Library
Jordan Hall Room #1102
2800 Faucette Drive, Campus Box 7114
Raleigh, NC 27615
Phone: 919-515-2306
Fax: 919-515-7802
Email: karen_ciccone@ncsu.edu
Web: www.lib.ncsu.edu/natural/

George C. Clark
Reference and Government Documents Librarian
Minot State University (369)
Gordon B. Olson Library
Government Documents and Maps
500 University Avenue W
Minot, ND 58707
Phone: 701-858-3200
Fax: 701-858-3581
Email: clark@minotstateu.edu
Web: www.minotstateu.edu/library/

Caroline Clark Hudson
Librarian Assistant
Maine Maritime Academy (234)
Nutting Memorial Library
Battle Avenue

Castine, ME 04420
Phone: 207-326-2265
Fax: 207-326-2261
Email: chudson@mma.edu

Richard Clement
Head of Special Collections
University of Kansas (211)
Kenneth Spencer Research Library
Special Collections
1450 Poplar Lane
Lawrence, KS 66045-7616
Phone: 785-864-4334
Fax: 785-864-5803
Email: rclement@ku.edu
Web: spencer.lib.ku.edu/sc/index.htm

Garry Cline
Director
Anacortes Museum (522)
1305 8th Street
Anacortes, WA 98221
Phone: 360-293-1915
Fax: 360-293-1929
Web: www.anacorteshistorymuseum.org

Leo Clougherty
Head
University of Iowa (204)
Geoscience Library
136 Trowbridge Hall
Iowa City, IA 52242
Phone: 319-335-3084
Fax: 319-335-3419
Email: leo-clougherty@uiowa.edu
Web: www.lib.uiowa.edu/geoscience

David A. Cobb
Harvard University (254)
Pusey Library
Harvard Map Collection
Cambridge, MA 02138
Phone: 617-495-2417
Fax: 617-496-0440
Email: cobb@fas.harvard.edu
Web: hcl.harvard.edu/maps

Janet R. Collins
Map Librarian
Western Washington University (523)
Huxley Map Library
AH 101
516 High Street
Bellingham, WA 98225-9085
Phone: 360-650-3272
Fax: 360-650-7702

Email: jcollins@wwu.edu
Web: www.ac.wwu.edu/~maplib/

Kay Collins
University of California, Irvine (53)
Langson Library
P.O. Box 19557
Irvine, CA 92623-9557
Phone: 949-824-7290
Fax: 949-824-3644
Web: www.lib.uci.edu/libraries/collections/gis.html

Carolyn Colwell
Milwaukee Public Library (550)
814 West Wisconsin Avenue
Milwaukee, WI 53233
Phone: 414-286-3000
Fax: 414-286-2137
Email: ccolwe@mpl.org
Web: www.mpl.org

Jan Comfort
Clemson University (441)
R.M. Cooper Library
Government Documents
Campus Box 343001
Clemson, SC 29634-3001
Phone: 864-656-5168
Fax: 864-656-7608
Email: comforj@clemson.edu
Web: www.lib.clemson.edu/GovDocs/maps/index.htm

Holli Connell
Office Associate
University of Alabama (7)
W. S. Hoole Special Collections Library
Box 870266
Tuscaloosa, AL 35487-0266
Phone: 205-348-0500
Fax: 205-348-1699
Web: www.lib.ua.edu/libraries/hoole/

Doug Conrads
Indiana State Library (190)
140 North Senate Avenue
Indianapolis, IN 46204-2296
Phone: 317-232-3685
Fax: 317-232-3728

Michael Constan
Reference Librarian
Multnomah County Library (406)
Central Library
801 SW 10th Avenue
Portland, OR 97205

Phone: 503-988-5728
Fax: 503-988-5226
Email: michael.constan@co.multnomah.or.us

Kathleen Conway
Library Assistant
Chattanooga-Hamilton County
   Bicentennial Library (457)
Local History Map Collection
1001 Broad Street
Chattanooga, TN 37402
Phone: 423-757-5317
Web: www.lib.chattanooga.gov

Karen S. Cook
Assistant Special Collections Librarian (Manuscripts)
University of Kansas (211)
Kenneth Spencer Research Library
Special Collections
1450 Poplar Lane
Lawrence, KS 66045-7616
Phone: 785-864-4334
Fax: 785-864-5803
Web: spencer.lib.ku.edu/sc/index.htm

Jim Coombs
Map Librarian
Southwest Missouri State University (295)
Duane G. Meyer Library
Maps
901 South National #175
Springfield, MO 65804
Phone: 417-836-4534
Fax: 417-836-6799
Email: jac324f@smsu.edu
Web: library.smsu.edu/meyer/maps/index.shtml

Leonard A. Coombs
University of Michigan (262)
Bentley Historical Library
1150 Beal Avenue
Ann Arbor, MI 48109-2113
Phone: 734-764-3482
Fax: 734-936-1333
Email: coombs@umich.edu
Web: www.umich.edu/~bhl

Carol Coon
Documents Manager
San Francisco Public Library (79)
Government Information Center
100 Larkin Street
San Francisco, CA 94102
Phone: 415-557-4500
Fax: 415-557-4475

Email: ccoon@sfpl.org
Web: sfpl4.sfpl.org/librarylocations/main/gic/gic.htm

Peggy Cooper
Geo. Technician
Tennessee Valley Authority (458)
Map and Photo Records
1101 Market Street, MR 5E
Chattanooga, TN 37402
Phone: 423-751-8362
Fax: 423-499-6319
Web: maps.tva.com

Angie Cope
Cartographic Materials Catalog Academic Librarian
University of Wisconsin, Milwaukee (551)
American Geographical Society Library
2311 East Hartford Avenue
Milwaukee, WI 53211
Phone: 414-229-6282
Fax: 414-229-3624
Web: www.uwm.edu/Libraries/AGSL/index.html

Dennis Copeland
Archivist
Monterey Public Library (61)
California History Room
Map Collection
625 Pacific Street
Monterey, CA 93940
Phone: 831-646-3741
Fax: 831-646-5618
Email: copeland@ci.monterey.ca.us

Bill Copeley
Librarian
New Hampshire Historical Society (322)
The Tuck Library
Special Collections
30 Park Street
Concord, NH 03301
Phone: 603-228-6688
Fax: 603-224-0463
Web: www.nhhistory.org

Roberta V. Copp
Curator of Published Materials
University of South Carolina (444)
South Caroliniana Library
Published Materials
910 Sumter Street
Columbia, SC 29208
Phone: 803-777-3132
Fax: 803-777-5747
Email: rcopp@gwm.sc.edu
Web: www.sc.edu/library/socar

Kathleen Correia
Supervising Librarian
California State Library (68)
California History Section
900 N Street
Room 200
Sacramento, CA 95814
Phone: 916 654-0176
Fax: 916 654-8777
Email: cslcal@library.ca.gov
Web: www.library.ca.gov

Barbara Costello
Documents Librarian
Stetson University (133)
duPont-Ball Library
Government Documents Department
421 North Woodland Boulevard
DeLand, FL 32723
Phone: 386-822-7185
Fax: 386-740-3626
Email: bcostell@stetson.edu

Steve Cotham
Manager
Knox County Public Library (462)
East Tennessee History Center
Calvin M. McClung Historical Collection
314 West Clinch Avenue
Knoxville, TN 37902-2313
Phone: 865-215-8801
Fax: 865-215-8810
Email: scotham@knoxlib.org
Web: www.knoxlib.org

Jackie Couture
University Records Officer
Eastern Kentucky University (226)
John Grant Crabbe Library
University Archives Map Collection
521 Lancaster Avenue
Richmond, KY 40475
Phone: 859-622-1792
Fax: 859-622-1174
Web: www.library.eku.edu/collections/sca/

Esther Crawford
Head of Government Publications and Microforms
Rice University (492)
Fondren Library
Government Publications and Microforms
6100 Main
Houston, TX 77005
Phone: 713-348-5483
Fax: 713-348-5902

Email: crawford@rice.edu
Web: www.rice.edu/fondren/gov/

Maria Luisa Crawford
Professor
Bryn Mawr College (414)
Collier Science Library
Geologic Map Library
101 North Merion Avenue
Bryn Mawr, PA 19010
Phone: 610-526-7462
Web: www.brynmawr.edu/geology

John A. Creaser
Information/Map Specialist
University of California, Berkeley (46)
Earth Sciences and Map Library
50 McCone Hall
Berkeley, CA 94720-6000
Phone: 510-642-2997
Fax: 510-643-6576
Email: jcreaser@library.berkeley.edu
Web: www.lib.berkeley.edu/EART/

Glen Creason
Map Librarian
Los Angeles Public Library (56)
Richard J. Riordan Central Library
History and Genealogy Department
630 West 5th Street
Los Angeles, CA 90065
Phone: 213-228-7414
Fax: 213-228-7409
Email: gcreaso@lapl.org
Web: www.lapl.org/guides/map_coll.html

C. Daniel Crews
Archivist
Moravian Archives (367)
457 South Church Street
Winston-Salem, NC 27101
Phone: 336-722-1742
Fax: 336-725-4514
Email: nblum@mcsp.org
Web: MoravianArchives.org

Joyce Crews
History Room Librarian
Mill Valley Public Library (60)
Lucretia Little History Room
375 Throckmorton Avenue
Mill Valley, CA 94941
Phone: 415-389-4292 x104
Email: jcrews@cityofmillvalley.org

John D. Crissinger
Ohio State University, Newark and
    Central Ohio Technical College (390)
Newark Campus Library
1179 University Dr.
Newark, OH 43055
Phone: 740-366-9307
Fax: 740-366-9264
Email: crissinger.5@osu.edu

Ella Cross
Head Reference
University of Wisconsin, Superior (557)
Jim Dan Hill Library
Lake Superior Maritime Collections
Box 2000
Superior, WI 54880
Phone: 715-394-8343
Fax: 715-394-8462
Web: library.uwsuper.edu

Roger Cross
Collection Development
Doane College (300)
Perkins Library
Vertical Files
1014 Boswell Avenue
Crete, NE 68333
Phone: 402-826-8567
Fax: 402-826-8199
Email: rcross@doane.edu
Web: www.doane.edu/library_new/index.asp

Yvonne Crumpler
Curator
Birmingham Public Library (2)
Linn-Henley Research Library
Rucker Agee Map Collection
2100 Park Place
Birmingham, AL 35203-2794
Phone: 205-226-3665
Fax: 205-226-3663
Email: yvonne@bham.lib.al.us
Web: www.bplonline.org

Robert Cruthirds
Map Librarian
Memphis/Shelby County Public Library
    and Information Center (467)
Memphis and Shelby County Room
3030 Poplar Avenue
Memphis, TN 38111
Phone: 901-415-2742
Fax: 901-323-7981

Email: cruthirdsr@memphis.lib.tn.us
Web: www.memphislibrary.org

Larry Cruse
Map Bibliographer
University of California, San Diego (55)
Social Sciences and Humanities Library
9500 Gilman Drive 0175R
La Jolla, CA 92093
Phone: 858-534-1248
Fax: 858-534-7548
Email: lcruse@ucsd.edu
Web: govinfo.ucsd.edu/maps/index.html

Michael Current
Government Information Public Services Librarian
University of Wisconsin, La Crosse (546)
Murphy Library
1631 Pine Street
La Crosse, WI 54601
Phone: 608-785-8505
Fax: 608-785-8639
Email: current.mich@uwlax.edu

Lawrence W. Currie
Associate Librarian for User Services
California Academy of Sciences (72)
J.W. Mailliard, Jr. Library
Donald C. Heckman Memorial Map Collection
55 Concourse Drive
Golden Gate Park
San Francisco, CA 94118
Phone: 415-750-7102
Fax: 415-750-7106
Email: lcurrie@calacademy.org
Web: www.calacademy.org/research/library/

Gwen Curtis
Map Collection Manager
University of Kentucky (223)
Pirtle Geological Sciences Library and Map Collection
410 King Library Addition
Lexington, KY 40506-0039
Phone: 859-257-5730
Fax: 859-323-3225
Email: gscurt00@uky.edu
Web: www.uky.edu/Libraries

Lori Curtis
Director Special Collections
University of Tulsa (398)
McFarlin Library
2933 East 6th Street
Tulsa, OK 74104-3123

Phone: 918-631-2874
Fax: 918-631-3791
Web: www.lib.utulsa.edu/govdocs/maps.htm

James G. Cusick
University of Florida (134)
George A. Smathers Library
Historical Florida Map Collection
Department of Special and Area Studies Collections
2nd Floor
Library East
Gainesville, FL 32611
Phone: 352-392-9075
Email: jamcusi@mail.uflib.ufl.edu
Web: web.uflib.ufl.edu/spec/pkyonge/index. html

Tom Cutshall
Map Cataloger
University of Georgia (141)
Libraries
Map Collection
Athens, GA 20602
Phone: 706-542-0690
Fax: 706-542-6523
Web: www.libs.uga.edu/maproom/index.html

Bob Danielson
Engineering Aide
Washington State Department of Natural Resources (530)
Public Land Survey Office
P.O. Box 47060
Olympia, WA 98504-7060
Phone: 360-902-1190
Fax: 360-902-1191
Web: www.dnr.wa.gov/htdocs/plso/

Steve Davenport
Reference Librarian
San Francisco Maritime National Historical Park (76)
J Porter Shaw Library
Building E Fort Mason Center
San Francisco, CA 94123
Phone: 415-561-7030
Email: steve_davenport@nps.gov
Web: www.nps.gov/safr/local/lib/libtop.html

Jeanne Davidson
Physical Sciences Librarian
Oregon State University (399)
The Valley Library
Map Collection
121 The Valley Library
Corvallis, OR 97331-4501
Phone: 541-737-7295

Fax: 541-737-8224
Email: jeanne.davidson@oregonstate.edu
Web: osulibrary.oregonstate.edu/research/guides/maps/
maproom.htm

Deniece Davis
Acquisitions/Documents Manager
Oregon Institute of Technology (401)
Library
Maps
3201 Campus Dr.
Klamath Falls, OR 97601
Phone: 541-885-1772
Fax: 541-885-1777
Web: www.oit.edu/lbry

Elaine Davis
Library Director
Daughters of the Republic of Texas Library (496)
P.O. Box 1401
San Antonio, TX 78295
Phone: 210-225-1071
Fax: 210-212-8514
Email: edavis@drtl.org
Web: www.drtl.org

Harry O. Davis
Map Librarian
Southern Illinois University, Carbondale (160)
Morris Library
Map Library
605 Agriculture Drive
Carbondale, IL 62901-6636
Phone: 618-453-2705
Fax: 618-453-2704
Email: hdavis@lib.siu.edu
Web: www.lib.siu.edu/hp/divisions/sci/maplib.shtml

Pat Davis
Government Documents Assistant
Campbell University (348)
Carrie Rich Memorial Library
Government Documents
227 Main Street
Buies Creek, NC 27506
Phone: 910-893-1465
Fax: 910-893-1470
Web: www.lib.campbell.edu

Victoria A. Davis
Jefferson County Historical Society (533)
Research Center
Map Collection
13692 Airport Cutoff Road (Hwy 19)
Port Townsend, WA 98368

Phone: 360-379-6673
Email: jchsresearch@olypen.com

Barbara J. Dawson
Cincinnati Museum Center (374)
Cincinnati Historical Society Library
1301 Western Avenue
Cincinnati, OH 45203
Phone: 513-287-7030
Fax: 513-287-7095
Email: bdawson@cincymuseum.org
Web: www.cincymuseum.org

Patti Day
Senior Digital Spatial Data Reference Librarian
University of Wisconsin, Milwaukee (551)
American Geographical Society Library
2311 East Hartford Avenue
Milwaukee, WI 53211
Phone: 414-229-6282
Fax: 414-229-3624
Web: www.uwm.edu/Libraries/AGSL/index.html

Lewis S. Dean
Geological Survey of Alabama (6)
Library
P.O. Box 869999
Tuscaloosa, AL 35486-6999
Phone: 205-247-3634
Fax: 205-349-2861
Email: ldean@gsa.state.al.us
Web: www.gsa.state.al.us

David Deckelbaum
Cartographic Information Librarian
University of California, Los Angeles (58)
Young Research Library
Henry J Bruman Map Collection
Room A4510
P.O. Box 951575
Los Angeles, CA 90095-1575
Phone: 310-825-1088
Fax: 310-825-6795
Email: ddeckelb@library.ucla.edu
Web: www.library.ucla.edu/libraries/yrl/referenc/rco/
geographic.htm

John Decker
Assistant Director—Archives
Stearns History Museum (285)
Research Center and Archives
235 33rd Avenue South
Saint Cloud, MN 56301
Phone: 320 253-8424
Fax: 320 253-2172

Email: johnd@stearns-museum.org
Web: www.stearns-museum.org

Carol Deering
Director of Library Services
Central Wyoming College (563)
Library
2660 Peck Avenue
Riverton, WY 82501
Phone: 307 855-2141
Fax: 307-855-2094
Email: cdeering@cwc.edu
Web: www.cwc.edu/student_services/library/index.php

Barbara DeFelice
Head Kresge Library
Dartmouth College (326)
Kresge Physical Sciences Library
6115 Fairchild Center
Hanover, NH 3755
Phone: 603-646-3563
Fax: 603-646-3681
Email: klr@dartmouth.edu
Web: www.dartmouth.edu/~krescook/index.shtml

John Delaney
Curator
Princeton University (330)
Library
Historic Maps Collection
One Washington Road
Princeton, NJ 08544
Phone: 609-258-3166
Fax: 609-258-2324
Email: delaney@princeton.edu
Web: www.princeton.edu/~rbsc/department/maps

Gary N. Denue
U.S. Documents/Map Librarian
Southern Illinois University Edwardsville (168)
Lovejoy Library
Map Library
P.O. Boz 1063
Edwardsville, IL 62026-2063
Phone: 618-650-2632
Fax: 618-650-2717
Email: gdenue@siue.edu

Esperanza B. deVarona
Department Head
University of Miami (131)
Otto G. Richter Library
Cuban Heritage Collection
1300 Memorial Drive
Coral Gables, FL 33124-0320
Phone: 305-284-4008

Fax: 305-284-4901
Email: edevaron@miami.edu

Carlos A. Diaz
Government Documents Specialist
Evergreen State College (528)
Daniel J. Evans Library
Government Documents/Maps
2700 Evergreen Parkway NW
Mailstop L-2300
Olympia, WA 98505
Phone: 360-867-6251
Fax: 360-866-6790
Email: diazc@evergreen.edu
Web: www.evergreen.edu/library/govdocs/index.html

Janice Dibble
Head of Reference
Oshkosh Public Library (552)
106 Washington Avenue
Oshkosh, WI 54901-4985
Phone: 920-236-5205
Fax: 920-236-5227
Email: dibble@oshkoshpubliclibrary.org
Web: www.oshkoshpubliclibrary.org

Lois Dickenson
Library Operations Assistant
Eastern Illinois University (162)
Booth Library
Government Documents
600 Lincoln Avenue
Charleston, IL 61920
Phone: 217-581-6072
Fax: 217-581-6066

Kathy Diehl
Manager 3rd Floor Reference
Indianapolis-Marion County Public Library (191)
Central Library
40 East Street Clair Street
Indianapolis, IN 46202
Phone: 317-269-1700
Fax: 317-268-5229
Web: imcpl.org

Kathleen Leles DiGiovanni
Librarian II
Oakland Public Library (63)
125 14th Street
Oakland, CA 94612
Phone: 510-238-3136
Fax: 510-238-2125
Email: amhl@oaklandlibrary.org
Web: www.oaklandlibrary.org/Seasonal/Sections/amhl
.html#maps

Patti Dittoe
Library Associate
Ohio State University (383)
Orton Memorial Library of Geology
180 Orton Hall
155 South Oval Drive
Columbus, OH 43210
Phone: 614-292-2428
Web: library.osu.edu/sites/geology

Janet B. Dixon
Geosciences Librarian
University of Arkansas (35)
University Libraries
Government Documents/Map Collection
365 North Ozark Avenue
Fayetteville, AR 72701
Phone: 479-575-5516
Fax: 479-575-6656
Email: jbdixon@uark.edu
Web: libinfo.uark.edu/gis/

Steve Doell
Historical Society of Western Pennsylvania (424)
1212 Smallman Street
Pittsburgh, PA 15222
Phone: 412-454-6364
Fax: 412-454-6028
Email: sdoell@hswp.org
Web: www.pghhistory.org

Rachel Doggett
Curator of Rare Books
Folger Shakespeare Library (124)
201 East Capitol Street SE
Washington, DC 20003
Phone: 202-544-4600
Fax: 202-675-0313
Web: www.folger.edu

Sharon Dolan
Western Wyoming Community College (564)
Hay Library
2500 College Drive, Box 473
Rock Springs, WY 82902
Phone: 307-382-1700
Fax: 307-382-7665
Email: sdolan@wwcc.cc.wy.us

Travis Dolence
Map/GIS Librarian
University of Tennessee (465)
Hoskins Library
Map Library
1401 Cumberland Avenue
Knoxville, TN 37996-4006

Phone: 865-974-4315
Fax: 865-974-3925
Email: dolence@utk.edu
Web: www.lib.utk.edu/~cic/

Michael Donnelly
Enoch Pratt Free Library (241)
Social Science and History Department
400 Cathedral Street
Baltimore, MD 21201
Phone: 410-396-5320
Fax: 410-396-1413
Email: ssh@epfl.net
Web: www.epfl.net

Marcy Donner
Reference Assistant
Norfolk Public Library (314)
Reference Department
308 Prospect Avenue
Norfolk, NE 68701
Phone: 402-844-2100
Fax: 402-844-2102
Web: www.ci.norfolk.ne.us/library

Carol Doyle
Head, Government Documents and Maps
California State University, Fresno (52)
Henry Madden Library
Map Library
5200 West Barton Avenue
M/S ML34
Fresno, CA 93740-8014
Phone: 559-278-2405
Fax: 559-278-6952
Email: carol_doyle@csufresno.edu
Web: www.lib.csufresno.edu/subjectresources/maps/

Bob Douglas
Professor of Geography
Gustavus Adolphus College (289)
Bob Moline Map Library
800 West College Avenue
Saint Peter, MN 56082
Phone: 507-933-7313
Fax: 507-933-7041
Email: bdouglas@gac.edu

Mary H. Douglass
Seattle Public Library (536)
History/Travel, Maps Department
and the Seattle Collection
1000 4th Avenue
Seattle, WA 98104
Phone: 206-386-4636
Fax: 206-386-4632

CB#3930
Wilson Library
Chapel Hill, NC 27514-8890
Phone: 919-962-1172
Fax: 919-962-4452
Web: www.lib.unc.edu/ncc

Bill Eigelsbach
University of Tennessee (466)
Special Collections—Hoskins Library
1401 Cumberland Avenue
Knoxville, TN 37996-4000
Phone: 865-974-4480
Fax: 865-974-0560
Web: www.lib.utk.edu/spcoll

Todd Ellison
Fort Lewis College (106)
John F. Reed Library and the
    Center for Southwest Studies
Map Collection
Durango, CO 81303
Phone: 247-7551
Email: arbeeny_p@fortlewis.edu
Web: library.fortlewis.edu/reference/mapgovweb/maps
    .html
    swcenter.fortlewis.edu/SpecialCollections.htm
    #Guides

Kevin Engel
Librarian
Grinnell College (202)
Burling Library
1111 6th Avenue
Grinnell, IA 50112
Phone: 641-269-4234
Fax: 641-269-4283
Email: engelk@grinnell.edu
Web: www.lib.grin.edu/Places/govdocs/

Kathryn Engstrom
Reference Team Leader
Library of Congress (125)
Geography and Map Division
101 Independence Avenue SE,
Madison Building
Room LM B01
Washington, DC 20540-4650
Phone: 202-707-6277
Fax: 202-707-8531
Web: www.loc.gov/rr/geogmap/

Lisa Ennis
Government Documents Librarian
Georgia College and State University (149)

Ina Dillard Russell Library
CBX 043
Milledgeville, GA 31061
Phone: 478-445-4047
Fax: 478-445-6847
Email: lisa.ennis@gcsu.edu

Doug Erickson
Head of Special Collections College Archivist
Lewis and Clark College (405)
Aubrey Watzek Library
Special Collections
0615 SW Palatine Hill Road
Portland, OR 97219
Phone: 503-768-7254
Fax: 5037687282
Email: dme@lclark.edu
Web: www.lclark.edu/~archives/specialcollections

Carol Estep
Library Information Associate
Washington State Library (532)
P.O. Box 42460
Olympia, WA 98504-2460
Phone: 866-538-4996
Fax: 360-586-7575
Web: www.secstate.wa.gov/library/

Andrea Faling
Associate Director, Library/Archives
Nebraska State Historical Society (309)
Library/Archives
P.O. Box 82554
1500 R Street
Lincoln, NE 68501
Phone: 402-471-4786
Fax: 402-471-8922
Web: www.nebraskahistory.org

Daniel Farnbach
Library Assistant
American Alpine Club (108)
Henry S. Hall, Jr. Library
710 Tenth Street
Suite 15
Golden, CO 80401
Phone: 303-384-0112
Fax: 303-384-0113
Email: serials@americanalpineclub.org
Web: www.americanalpineclub.org/knowledge/
    aaclibrary.asp

David Farrell
Acting University Archivist
University of California, Berkeley (44)

Bancroft Library
Map Collection
Berkeley, CA 94720
Phone: 510-642-6481
Fax: 510-642-7589

Jennifer Farrington
Senior Archivist
University of Florida (135)
George A. Smathers Libraries
Map and Imagery Library
P.O.Box 11701
110 Marston Science Library
Gainesville, FL 32611-7011
Phone: 352-392-2825
Fax: 352-392-4787
Web: web.uflib.ufl.edu/maps

Alan Ferg
Archivist
Arizona State Museum (30)
Archives
University of Arizona
Tucson, AZ 85721-0026
Phone: 520-621-2970
Fax: 520-621-2976
Email: ferg@email.arizona.edu
Web: www.statemuseum.arizona.edu/library

Adonna Fleming
Assistant Professor University Libraries
University of Northern Colorado (110)
James A. Michener Library
Campus Box 48
Greeley, CO 80639
Phone: 970-351-2671
Fax: 970-351-2963
Email: adonna.fleming@unco.edu

Robert Filipek
University of Minnesota (282)
Science and Engineering Library
Geologic Map Collection
206 Walter Library
117 Pleasant Street SE
Minneapolis, MN 55455
Phone: 612-624-0224
Web: sciweb.lib.umn.edu/subject/earthsci.html

Janice Fiorino
Map Library Assistant
Southern Illinois University, Carbondale (160)
Morris Library
Map Library
605 Agriculture Drive

Carbondale, IL 62901-6636
Phone: 618-453-2705
Fax: 618-453-2704
Web: www.lib.siu.edu/hp/divisions/sci/maplib.shtml

Stefan Firtko
Lehigh University (413)
Fairchild Martindale Library
Government Documents
8A East Packer Avenue
Bethlehem, PA 18015
Phone: 610-758-5337

Madge Fitak
Ohio Department of Natural Resources (381)
Division of Geological Survey
4383 Fountain Square Drive
Columbus, OH 43224
Phone: 614-265-6576
Fax: 614-447-1918
Email: madge.fitak@dnr.state.oh.us
Web: www.dnr.ohiodnr.com/geosurvey/

Betty Fitzgerald
Rhode Island Collection Librarian
Providence Public Library (431)
225 Washington Street
Providence, RI 02903
Phone: 401-455-8000

Geoffrey Forbes
Director of Operations
East View Cartographic, Inc. (279)
Corporate Library
3020 Harbor Lane North
Minneapolis, MN 55447-8956
Phone: 763-550-0965
Fax: 763-559-2931
Web: www.cartographic.com

Leslie Foster
Head of Government Publications
University of Wisconsin, Eau Claire (543)
William D. McIntyre Library
Depository Library Map Collection
Park and Garfield Streets
Eau Claire, WI 54702-4004
Phone: 715-836-3859
Fax: 715-836-2906
Email: fosterla@uwec.edu
Web: www.uwec.edu/Library/gp/govpub2.html#MAP

Patrick J. Fraker
Colorado Historical Society (100)
Stephen H. Hart Library

1300 Broadway
Denver, CO 80224
Phone: 303-866-4600
Fax: 303-866-5739
Email: patrick.fraker@chs.state.co.us
Web: www.coloradohistory.org

Ed Frank
Curator of Special Collections
University of Memphis (469)
McWherter Library
Special/Mississippi Valley Collections
126 Ned R. McWherter Library
Memphis, TN 38152
Phone: 901-678-2210
Fax: 901-678-8218
Email: efrank@memphis.edu

Greg Frazier
Government Documents Librarian
Providence Public Library (431)
225 Washington Street
Providence, RI 02903
Phone: 401-455-8000

Brian Freels-Stendel
GIS Librarian
University of New Mexico (332)
Centennial Science and Engineering Library
Map and Geographic Information Center
    (aka The Map Room)
UNMGL/CSEL MSC05 3020 1
Albuquerque, NM 87131-0001
Phone: 505-277-5738
Fax: 505-277-0702
Web: elibrary2.unm.edu/csel

Mary Freilich
University of Memphis (468)
McWherter Library
Map Library
126 Ned R. McWherter Library
Memphis, TN 38152
Phone: 901-678-2206
Fax: 901-678-8218
Email: freilich@memphis.edu

Amber French
Government Documents
Natrona County Public Library (558)
307 East 2nd Street
Casper, WY 82601
Phone: 307-237-4935
Fax: 307-266-3734
Email: afrench@will.state.wy.us
Web: www.library.natrona.net

Anna Friedman
Assistant Curator
Adler Planetarium and Astronomy Museum (163)
History of Astronomy Research Center
1300 South Lake Shore Drive
Chicago, IL 60605
Phone: 312-322-0594
Fax: 312-341-9935
Web: www.adlerplanetarium.org

Cynthia Froman
Library Associate I
New Albany-Floyd County Public Library (194)
180 West Spring Street
New Albany, IN 47150
Phone: 812-949-3527
Fax: 812-949-3733
Web: www.nafcpl.lib.in.us

Michael Fry
Librarian
University of Maryland, College Park (245)
McKeldin Library
Government Documents and Maps
4118 McKeldin Library
College Park, MD 20742
Phone: 301-405-9165
Fax: 301-314-5651
Web: www.lib.umd.edu/gov/maproom.html

Nancy Gall
Oshkosh Public Library (552)
106 Washington Avenue
Oshkosh, WI 54901-4985
Phone: 920-236-5205
Fax: 920-236-5227
Web: www.oshkoshpubliclibrary.org

Mary Garcia
Government Documents Librarian
Miami-Dade Public Library System (137)
Main Library
Social Science and the Florida Room
101 West Flagler Street
Miami, FL 33130
Phone: 305-375-5575
Fax: 305-375-3048
Email: garciam@mdpls.org
Web: www.mdpls.org

Dawn Gardner
Public Services Manager
Flagstaff City-Coconino County Public Library (16)
Main Library
300 West Aspen Avenue

Flagstaff, AZ 86001
Phone: 928-779-7670
Fax: 928-774-9573
Email: dgardner@fpl.lib.az.us
Web: flagstaffpubliclibrary.org

Sue Ann Gardner
University of Nebraska, Lincoln (313)
Love Memorial Library
Map Collection
Lincoln, NE 68588-4100
Phone: 402-472-3545
Fax: 402-472-2534
Email: sgardner2@unl.edu
Web: www.unl.edu/libr/gis/

Michael Garrett
Bemidji State University (274)
Map Library
HS 244
Bemidji, MN 56601
Phone: 218-755-2804
Fax: 218-755-2822
Email: mgarrett@bemidjistate.edu
Web: www.bemidjistate.edu/library

Jo Gault
Geographic Information System Program Specialist
United States Department of Interior, Office of Surface
  Mining (464)
Knoxville Field Office Geographic Information System
  (KFO GIS)
530 Gay Street SW
Suite 500
Knoxville, TN 37902
Phone: 865-545-4103 x134
Fax: 865-545-4111

Donna Gautier
Government Documents Associate
Georgia College and State University (149)
Ina Dillard Russell Library
CBX 043
Milledgeville, GA 31061
Phone: 478-445-4047
Fax: 478-445-6847

Julia Gelfand
University of California, Irvine (53)
Langson Library
P.O. Box 19557
Irvine, CA 92623-9557
Phone: 949-824-7290
Fax: 949-824-3644
Web: www.lib.uci.edu/libraries/collections/gis.html

Joseph Gerencher
Moravian College (411)
Earth Science Collection
1200 Main Street
Bethlehem, PA 18018-6650
Phone: 610-861-1440
Fax: 610-625-7918
Email: gerencher@moravian.edu
Web: home.moravian.edu/users/phys/mejjg01/
  interests/apparatus_pages/map_shelving.htm

Paige Gibbs
Librarian
University of Massachusetts, Dartmouth (256)
Library
Map Collection
285 Old Westport Road
Dartmouth, MA 02747
Phone: 508-999-8886
Fax: 508-999-9240
Email: pgibbs@umassd.edu
Web: www.lib.umassd.edu/Reference/Maps.html

Bill Gill
Reference Specialist
University of Vermont (509)
Bailey/Howe Library
Map Room
538 Main Street
Burlington, VT 05405-0036
Phone: 802-656-2588
Fax: 802-656-4038
Email: wgill@uvm.edu
Web: library.uvm.edu/reference/maps.html

Jim Gillispie
Head, Government Publications/Maps/Law Library
Johns Hopkins University (242)
Eisenhower Library
Government Publications/Maps/Law Library
3400 North Charles Street
Baltimore, MD 21212
Phone: 410-516-8360
Fax: 410-516-6029
Email: jeg@jhu.edu
Web: www.library.jhu.edu/gpml/

Caroline L. Gilson
Coordinator, Prevo Science Library
DePauw University (187)
Prevo Science Library
602 South College
Greencastle, IN 46135
Phone: 765-658-4306
Email: cgilson@depauw.edu

Lauren I. Glaettli
Reading Room Supervisor
George Mason University (515)
Fenwick Library
Special Collections and Archives
4400 University Drive
Fairfax, VA 22030
Phone: 703-993-2220
Fax: 703-993-2255
Email: speccoll@gmu.edu
Web: www.gmu.edu/library/specialcollections

Miriam Glanz
Library Specialist Senior
Arizona State University (28)
Noble Science and Engineering Library
Map Collection
P.O. Box 871006
Tempe, AZ 85287-1006
Phone: 480-965-3582
Fax: 480-965-0883
Web: www.asu.edu/lib/hayden/govdocs/maps/mapcoll
  .htm

Valerie Glenn
Documents Librarian
University of North Texas (489)
Willis Library
Map Collection
P.O. Box 305190
Denton, TX 76203-5190
Phone: 940-565-2870
Fax: 940-565-2599
Web: www.library.unt.edu/govinfo/

Beth Goble
Government Information Coordinator
Nebraska Library Commission (308)
Nebraska Publications Clearinghouse
1200 N Street
Suite 120
Lincoln, NE 68508
Phone: 402-471-2045
Fax: 402-471-2083
Email: bgoble@nlc.state.ne.us
Web: www.nlc.state.ne.us/docs/clear.html

Joan Goodbody
Government Documents Coordinator/
  Instruction/Reference Librarian
Michigan Technological University (267)
J.R. Van Pelt Library
Map Room
1400 Townsend Drive
Houghton, MI 49931

Phone: 906-487-2698
Fax: 906-487-2357
Email: goodbody@mtu.edu
Web: www.lib.mtu.edu

Angela M. Gooden
University of Cincinnati (376)
Geology/Physics Library
Willis G. Meyer Map Collection
240 Braunstein Hall
M.L. 0153
Cincinnati, OH 45221
Phone: 513-5561324
Fax: 513-5561930
Email: angela.gooden@uc.edu
Web: www.libraries.uc.edu/libraries/geol-phys/home
  .html

Kit Goodwin
University of Texas, Arlington (477)
Library
Special Collections
702 College Street
Arlington, TX 76019-0497
Phone: 817-272-3393
Fax: 817-272-3360
Email: goodwin@uta.edu
Web: Libraries.uta.edu/SpecColl

Dalila Gomes
Technical Services Assistant
Spartanburg County Public Library (452)
Reference Department
151 South Church Street
Spartanburg, SC 29306
Phone: 864-596-3505
Fax: 864-596-3518
Web: www.infodepot.org/govdoc.htm; www.infodepot
  .org/kroom.htm

Kenneth A. Grabach
Maps Librarian
Miami University (391)
Brill Science Library
Map Collections
Oxford, OH 45056
Phone: 513-529-1726
Fax: 513-529-1736
Email: grabacka@muohio.edu

Nicholas Graham
Head of Public Services
University of North Carolina, Chapel Hill (349)
Academic Affairs Library
North Carolina Collection

CB#3930
Wilson Library
Chapel Hill, NC 27514-8890
Phone: 919-962-1172
Fax: 919-962-4452
Web: www.lib.unc.edu/ncc

Rick Grapes
Map Manager
Brigham Young University (502)
Harold B. Lee Library
Map Collection
2420 HBLL
Provo, UT 84602-
Phone: 801-422-6179
Fax: 801-422-0466
Web: www.lib.byu.edu

Barbara Gray
Nevada State Library and Archives (319)
100 North Stewart Street
Carson City, NV 89701-4285
Phone: 775-684-3310
Fax: 775-684-3371
Web: dmla.clan.lib.nv.us/docs/nsla/archives/

Susan Greaves
Map and GIS Librarian
Cornell University (340)
John M. Olin Library
Map and Geospatial Information Collection
Ithaca, NY 14853-5301
Phone: 607-255-7557
Fax: 607-255-9346
Email: sjg4@cornell.edu
Web: www.library.cornell.edu/okuref/maps/map.htm

Nathaniel Grifin
United States Army Corps of Engineers, NOD (231)
Library and Map Collection
IMO
704 Leale Avenue
New Orleans, LA 70118-3651
Phone: 504-862-1775
Fax: 504-862-1721
Email: nathaniel.grifin@mvn02.usace.army.mil

Emily Grimshaw
Map Librarian
Gustavus Adolphus College (289)
Bob Moline Map Library
800 West College Avenue
Saint Peter, MN 56082
Phone: 507-933-7313
Fax: 507-933-7041

Jaci Groves
Library Assistant III
University of Nebraska, Lincoln (312)
Geology Library
10 Bessey Hall
Lincoln, NE 68588-0344
Phone: 402-472-2653
Web: www.unl.edu/libr/libs/geol/geol.html

Howard C. Grueneberg
Urbana Free Library (180)
Champaign County Historical Archives
201 South Race Street
Urbana, IL 61801
Phone: 217-367-0807
Fax: 217-367-4061
Email: hcgruen@hotmail.com

Mollie Gugler, Sr.
Library Analyst
Yavapai College (26)
Library
1100 East Sheldon Street
Prescott, AZ 86301
Phone: 928-776-2261
Fax: 928-776-2275
Email: mollie_gugler@yc.edu
Web: www.yc.edu/library.nsf

Frances Hager
Acquisitions Librarian
Arkansas Tech University (40)
Pendergraft Library and Technology Center
305 West Q Street
Russellville, AR 72801
Phone: 479-968-0289
Fax: 479-964-0559
Email: frances.hager@mail.atu.edu
Web: library.atu.edu

Mary Ann Hager
Lunar and Planetary Institute (491)
Center for Information and Research Services
3600 Bay Area Blvd
Houston, TX 77059
Phone: 281-486-2182
Fax: 281-486-2186
Email: hager@lpi.usra.edu

Greg Hajic
Programmer II
University of California, Santa Barbara (88)
Davidson Library
Map and Imagery Laboratory
Santa Barbara, CA 93106-9010

Phone: 805-893-2779
Fax: 805-893-8799
Web: www.sdc.ucsb.edu

Alison Halfmoon
Library Technician
Columbia River Inter-Tribal Fish Commission (404)
StreamNet Library
729 NE Oregon Street
Suite 190
Portland, OR 97232
Phone: 503-731-1304
Fax: 503-731-1260
Web: www.fishlib.org

Lucinda M. Hall
Reference Bibliographer for Geography and Maps
Dartmouth College (325)
Baker/Berry Library
Evans Map Room
HB 6025
Hanover, NH 03755
Phone: 603-646-2579
Fax: 603-646-3628
Email: lucinda.m.hall@dartmouth.edu
Web: www.dartmouth.edu/~maproom/

Kayce Halstead
Reference Librarian
Stephen F. Austin State University (494)
Ralph W. Steen Library
Government Documents/Maps
P.O. Box 13055 SFA Station
Nacogdoches, TX 75963
Phone: 936-468-1574
Fax: 936-468-4117
Email: khalstea@sfasu.edu
Web: libweb.sfasu.edu/subject/government/default.htm

Carol Hamner
Librarian
Hardin-Simmons University (473)
Rupert and Pauline Richardson Library
Williams Map Collection
2200 Hickory Street
Abilene, TX 79698
Phone: 325-670-1239
Fax: 325-677-8351
Email: chamner@hsutx.edu
Web: rupert.alc.org/library/

Dawn Hampton
Coordinator, Special Collections
Sara Hightower Regional Library (150)
Rome-Floyd County Public Library

Special Collections
205 Riverside Parkway
Rome, GA 30161
Phone: 706-236-4607
Fax: 706-236-4605
Email: hamptond@mail.floyd.public.lib.ga.us
Web: www.floyd.public.lib.ga.us

Amy Hankins
Maps Library Associate
Southwest Missouri State University (295)
Duane G. Meyer Library
Maps
901 South National #175
Springfield, MO 65804
Phone: 417-836-4534
Fax: 417-836-6799
Web: library.smsu.edu/meyer/maps/index.shtml

Matt Hannigan
3rd Floor Reference Librarian
Indianapolis-Marion County Public Library (191)
Central Library
40 East Street Clair Street
Indianapolis, IN 46202
Phone: 317-269-1700
Fax: 317-268-5229
Web: imcpl.org

Todd Hannon
Assistant Librarian
Columbia River Inter-Tribal Fish Commission (404)
StreamNet Library
729 NE Oregon Street
Suite 190
Portland, OR 97232
Phone: 503-731-1304
Fax: 503-731-1260
Web: www.fishlib.org

Joanne Hansen
Map Librarian
Eastern Michigan University (273)
Bruce T. Halle Library
Maps
Ypsilanti, MI 48197
Phone: 734-487-0020 x2115, x2116
Fax: 734-487-8861
Email: joanne.hansen@emich.edu

Tom Hardaway
Map Room Assistant
University of Georgia (141)
Libraries
Map Collection

Athens, GA 20602
Phone: 706-542-0690
Fax: 706-542-6523
Web: www.libs.uga.edu/maproom/index.html

Chris Hare
Digital Services Librarian
University of South Carolina (445)
Thomas Cooper Library
Map Library
Columbia, SC 29208
Phone: 803-777-2802
Fax: 803-777-4661
Web: www.sc.edu/library/maps.html

Faye Harkins
Archivist
Oregon State University (399)
The Valley Library
Map Collection
121 The Valley Library
Corvallis, OR 97331-4501
Phone: 541-737-7295
Fax: 541-737-8224
Web: osulibrary.oregonstate.edu/research/guides/maps/
maproom.htm

Elizabeth Harper
Reference/Documents Librarian
Montana Tech of the University of Montana (297)
Library
1300 West Park Street
Butte, MT 59701
Phone: 406-496-4281
Fax: 406-496-4133
Email: eharper@mtech.edu

Rollie Harper
Program Specialist
Office of Surface Mining Reclamation
  and Enforcement (429)
Anthracite (Coal) Mine Map Repository
Branch of Anthracite-MMR
7 North Wilkes-Barre Boulevard
Suite 308
Wilkes-Barre, PA 18702-5293
Phone: 570-830-1400
Fax: 570-830-1421
Web: mmr.osmre.gov

Amy Hartman
Toledo-Lucas County Public Library (393)
Main Library
325 Michigan Street
Toledo, OH 43624
Phone: 419-259-5207

Mark Harvey
Reference Archivist
State Archives of Michigan (271)
P.O. Box 30740
Lansing, MI 48909
Phone: 517-373-1408
Fax: 517-241-1658
Web: www.michigan.gov/statearchives

Joan Haskell
San Francisco Public Library (78)
General Collections Department
100 Larkin Street
San Francisco, CA 94102
Phone: 415-557-4401
Fax: 415-437-4831
Email: jhaskell@sfpl.org
Web: www.sfpl.org

Cory Hatch
Interim Curator
Arizona State University (27)
Hayden Library
Arizona Historical Foundation
P.O. Box 871006
Tempe, AZ 85287-1006
Phone: 480-966-8331
Fax: 480-966-1077
Web: www.arizonahistoricalfoundation.org

Thelma Hayes
LTA
University of South Carolina (444)
South Caroliniana Library
Published Materials
University of South Carolina Horseshoe
Columbia, SC 29208
Phone: 803-777-3132
Fax: 803-777-5747
Web: www.sc.edu/library/socar

David M. Hays
Archivist
University of Colorado, Boulder (96)
University Libraries
Archives
184 UCB
Boulder, CO 80309-0184
Phone: 303-492-7242
Fax: 303-492-3960
Web: www-libraries.colorado.edu/ps/arv/frontpage.htm

John Hébert
Library of Congress (125)
Geography and Map Division

101 Independence Avenue SE
Madison Building
Room LM B01
Washington, DC 20540-4650
Phone: 202-707-6277
Fax: 202-707-8531
Web: www.loc.gov/rr/geogmap/

Ann Hefferman
LA IV, Office Manager and Student Supervisor
University of California, Santa Barbara (88)
Davidson Library
Map and Imagery Laboratory
Santa Barbara, CA 93106-9010
Phone: 805-893-2779
Fax: 805-893-8799
Web: www.sdc.ucsb.edu

Naomi Heiser
Library Technician III
University of Colorado, Boulder (95)
Jerry Crail Johnson Earth Sciences and Map Library
Map Library
184 UCB
Boulder, CO 80309
Phone: 303-492-7578
Fax: 303-735-4879
Web: www-libraries.colorado.edu/ps/map/

David Heisser
Reference/Documents Librarian
Citadel Military College (439)
Daniel Library
171 Moultrie Street
Charleston, SC 29409
Phone: 843-953-2569
Fax: 843-953-5190
Email: David.Heisser@Citadel.edu
Web: www.citadel.edu/library/

Mary Helms
Local History Department Head
Chattanooga-Hamilton County
   Bicentennial Library (457)
Local History Map Collection
1001 Broad Street
Chattanooga, TN 37402
Phone: 423-757-5317
Email: helms-m@mail.chattanooga.gov
Web: www.lib.chattanooga.gov

Wendie Helms
Map Curator, GIS Coordinator
University of California, Riverside (67)
Science Library

Information Services / Map Collection
P. O. Box 5900
Riverside, CA 92517
Phone: 909-787-6423
Fax: 909-787-6378
Email: wendie@citrus.ucr.edu
Web: library.ucr.edu/?view=collections/maps/

Taylor Hendrix
Documents Assistant
Baylor University (498)
Moody Memorial Library
Government Documents
1312 South 3rd
Waco, TX 76798
Phone: 254-710-2157
Fax: 254-710-3116
Web: www3.baylor.edu/library

Bambi Hernandez
Library Assistant
Louisiana State University (229)
Troy H. Middleton Library
Government Documents/Microforms Department
53 Middleton
Baton Rouge, LA 70803
Phone: 225-578-2570
Fax: 225-578-6535
Web: www.lib.lsu.edu/govdocs

Heather Hernandez
Tech Services Librarian
San Francisco Maritime National Historical Park (76)
J Porter Shaw Library
Building E Fort Mason Center
San Francisco, CA 94123
Phone: 415-561-7030
Web: www.nps.gov/safr/local/lib/libtop.html

Tamsen Hert
Wyoming Bibliographer
University of Wyoming (562)
Libraries
Grace Raymond Hebard Collection
1000 East University Avenue
Laramie, WY 82071
Phone: 307-766-6245
Fax: 307-766-3062
Email: thert@uwyo.edu
Web: www-lib.uwyo.edu/uwlibs/hebard_maps.htm

Dave Heueisen
Technician
Pennsylvania Department of Education (415)
Bureau of State Library of Pennsylvania

Maps Collection
333 Market Street
Harrisburg, PA 17126-1745
Phone: 717-783-5950
Fax: 717-787-9127
Web: www.statelibrary.state.pa.us

John Hiett
Program Manager
Kentucky Division of Mines and Minerals (220)
Mine Map Information Center
Mine Map Repository
P.O. 2244
Frankfort, KY 40601
Phone: 502-573-0140
Email: john.hiett@ky.gov
Web: minemaps.ky.gov

Judy Hilkemann
Reference Supervisor
Norfolk Public Library (314)
Reference Department
308 Prospect Avenue
Norfolk, NE 68701
Phone: 402-844-2100
Fax: 402-844-2102
Web: www.ci.norfolk.ne.us/library

Chuck Hill
University Archivist
Eastern Kentucky University (226)
John Grant Crabbe Library
University Archives Map Collection
521 Lancaster Avenue
Richmond, KY 40475
Phone: 859-622-1792
Fax: 859-622-1174
Email: archives.library@eku.edu
Web: www.library.eku.edu/collections/sca/

Richard Hill
Head of Main Reading Room
Pennsylvania Department of Education (415)
Bureau of State Library of Pennsylvania
Maps Collection
333 Market Street
Harrisburg, PA 17126-1745
Phone: 717-783-5950
Fax: 717-787-9127
Email: rhill@state.pa.us
Web: www.statelibrary.state.pa.us

Michael Hironymous
University of Texas, Austin (480)
Nettie Lee Benson Latin American Collection

Rare Books and Manuscripts Division
The General Libraries
Austin, TX 78713-8916
Phone: 512-495-4520
Fax: 512-495-4568
Web: www.lib.utexas.edu/benson/

Doreen Hockenberry
Head
Ohio University (372)
Alden Library
Government Documents and Maps Collection
Park Place
Athens, OH 45701
Phone: 740-593-2718
Fax: 740-593-2719
Email: hockenbe@ohio.edu
Web: www.library.ohiou.edu/libinfo/depts/maps/index
.htm

Julie Hoff
Map Librarian
Arizona State Library, Archives and Public Records (22)
Law and Research Division
Map Collection
1700 West Washington
Phoenix, AZ 85007
Phone: 602-542-4343
Fax: 602-542-4400
Email: jhoff@lib.az.us
Web: www.lib.az.us

John Hoffmann
University of Illinois, Urbana-Champaign (177)
Illinois Historical Survey
1408 West Gregory Drive
Urbana, IL 61801
Phone: 217-333-1777
Email: jmhoffma@uiuc.edu

Marc Hofstadter
Librarian
San Francisco Municipal Railway (77)
Library
1145 Market Street, Suite 402
San Francisco, CA 94103-1545
Phone: 415-934-3977
Fax: 415-934-5747
Email: marc_hofstadter@ci.sf.ca.us

Laura Holden
Head of Genealogy and Local History
Anderson County Public Library (434)
South Carolina Room
300 North McDuffie Street

Anderson, SC 29621
Phone: 864-260-4500
Fax: 864-260-4098
Email: lholden@andersonlibrary.org
Web: www.andersonlibrary.org

Allyson Holliday
Library Assistant
University of Alabama (7)
W. S. Hoole Special Collections Library
Box 870266
Tuscaloosa, AL 35487-0266
Phone: 205-348-0500
Fax: 205-348-1699
Web: www.lib.ua.edu/libraries/hoole/

Jake Homiak
Director
Smithsonian Institution (248)
National Anthropological Archives
4210 Silver Hill Road
Suitland, MD 20746
Phone: 301-238-2873
Fax: 301-238-2883
Email: homiak.jake@nmnh.si.edu
Web: www.nmnh.si.edu/naa

Tony Hoskins
History, Genealogy and Archives Librarian
Sonoma County Library (90)
3rd and E Street
Santa Rosa, CA 95404
Phone: 707-545-0831
Fax: 707-575-0437
Web: www.sonomalibrary.org

Rhonda S. Houser
GIS and Data Services Specialist
University of Kansas (210)
Anschutz Library
Thomas R. Smith Map Collections
1301 Hoch Auditoria Drive
Lawrence, KS 66045
Phone: 785-864-4420
Fax: 785-864-4420
Web: www2.lib.ku.edu/mapscoll/

Ann Hudak
Assistant Curator
University of Maryland, College Park (244)
Hornbake Library
Maryland Map Collection
College Park, MD 20742
Phone: 301-410-9212
Fax: 301-314-2709

Web: www.lib.umd.edu/RARE/MarylandCollection/
Maps/MdMaps.html

Alice Hudson
Chief
New York Public Library (343)
Humanities and Social Sciences Library
Map Division
5th Ave and 42nd Street
Room 117
New York, NY 10018
Phone: 212-930-0587
Fax: 212-930-0027
Email: ahudson@nypl.org
Web: www.nypl.org/research/chss/map/map.html

Harvey Huie
Library Technical Assistant II
University of Illinois, Chicago (167)
Richard J. Daley Library
Map Section
801 South Morgan Street
Chicago, IL 60607
Phone: 312-996-2738
Fax: 312-413-0424
Web: www.uic.edu/depts/library/

Ben Huseman
Curator
Southern Methodist University (487)
DeGolyer Library
Historic Map Collection
P.O. Box 750396
Dallas, TX 75275
Phone: 214-768-4284
Fax: 214-768-1565
Email: bhuseman@smu.edu

Diane Hutchins
Washington State Library (532)
P.O. Box 42460
Olympia, WA 98504-2460
Phone: 866-538-4996
Fax: 360-586-7575
Email: dhutchins@secstate.wa.gov
Web: www.secstate.wa.gov/library/

Doris Hutson
Library Technician
Louisiana State University (229)
Troy H. Middleton Library
Government Documents/Microforms Department
53 Middleton
Baton Rouge, LA 70803
Phone: 225-578-2570

Fax: 225-578-6535
Web: www.lib.lsu.edu/govdocs

Jane Ingalls
Assistant Map Librarian
Stanford University (91)
Branner Earth Sciences Library and Map Collections
Mitchell Earth Sciences Building
397 Panama Mall
Stanford, CA 94305
Phone: 650-725-1103
Fax: 650-725-2534
Web: www-sul.stanford.edu/depts/branner/brief_map
    .html

Grace Ireland
Government Documents Assistant
Hanover College (188)
Duggan Library
P.O. Box 287
Hanover, IN 47243
Phone: 812-866-7165
Fax: 812-866-7172
Email: ireland@hanover.edu
Web: www.hanover.edu/Library

Sheri Irvin
Government Publications Librarian; Carrie Marsh,
    Special Collections Librarian
Claremont University Center, Claremont Colleges (50)
Honnold/Mudd Library
800 North Dartmouth Ave
Claremont, CA 91711
Phone: 909-621-8045
Fax: 909-621-8681
Email: sheri.irvin@libraries.claremont.edu

Solomon Isiorho
Associate Professor of Geosciences
Indiana University-Purdue University, Fort Wayne (185)
Helmke Library
Geosciences Department Map Collection
SB 230
2101 East Coliseum Boulevard
Fort Wayne, IN 46805
Phone: 260-481-6514
Fax: 260-481-6509
Email: isiorho@ipfw.edu
Web: www.lib.ipfw.edu

Jared Jackson
Library Specialist
Arizona State University (27)
Hayden Library
Arizona Historical Foundation

P.O. Box 871006
Tempe, AZ 85287-1006
Phone: 480-966-8331
Fax: 480-966-1077
Web: www.arizonahistoricalfoundation.org

Muriel M. Jackson
Archivist
Middle Georgia Archives (148)
Washington Memorial Library
Map Collection
1180 Washington Avenue
Macon, GA 31201
Phone: 478-744-0820
Fax: 478-744-0893
Web: www.co.bibb.public.lib.ga.us

Rob Jackson
Senior Collection Specialist
Denver Public Library (102)
Central Branch
Government Publications/GOVPUBS Maps
10 West 14th Avenue Parkway
Denver, CO 80204-2731
Phone: 720-865-1721
Fax: 720-865-1785
Web: www.denverlibrary.org

Laura Jacobs
Archivist
University of Wisconsin, Superior (557)
Jim Dan Hill Library
Lake Superior Maritime Collections
Box 2000
Superior, WI 54880
Phone: 715-394-8343
Fax: 715-394-8462
Email: ljacobs@uwsuper.edu
Web: library.uwsuper.edu

LaVonne Jacobsen
Collection Access and Management Services Division,
    Head
San Francisco State University (81)
J. Paul Leonard Library
Government Publications/Maps Department
1630 Holloway Avenue
San Francisco, CA 94132
Phone: 415-338-6953
Fax: 415-338-1504
Email: lavonne@sfsu.edu
Web: www.library.sfsu.edu/servcoll/maps.html

Robert Jacobson
Documents Associate
North Dakota State University (368)

Library
P.O. Box 5599
Fargo, ND 58105-5599
Phone: 701-231-8863
Fax: 701-231-7138
Web: www.lib.ndsu.nodak.edu

Tomas Jaehn
Curator
Palace of the Governors (335)
Angélico Chávez History Library
Map Collection
120 Washington Avenue
Santa Fe, NM 87501
Phone: 505-476-5090
Fax: 505-476-5053
Email: tjaehn@mnm.state.nm.us
Web: www.palaceofthegovernors.org/library.html

Jo Anne Jager
Southwest Librarian
New Mexico State Library (334)
1209 Camino Carlos Rey
Santa Fe, NM 87507
Phone: 505-476-9702
Fax: 505-476-9703
Web: www.stlib.state.nm.us/

Janice Jaguszewski
University of Minnesota (282)
Science and Engineering Library
Geologic Map Collection
206 Walter Library
117 Pleasant Street SE
Minneapolis, MN 55455
Phone: 612-624-0224
Email: j-jagu@umn.edu
Web: sciweb.lib.umn.edu/subject/earthsci.html

Cynthia Jahns
Head, Maps Unit
University of California, Santa Cruz (89)
Science and Engineering Library
Map Room
1156 High Street
Santa Cruz, CA 95064
Phone: 831-459-2364
Fax: 831-459-4187
Email: cjahns@ucsc.edu
Web: library.ucsc.edu/maps/

Mohammed Jaleel
District of Columbia Public Library (123)
Martin Luther King Jr Memorial Library
Washingtoniana Division #307

901 G Street NW
Washington, DC 20001
Phone: 202-727-1213
Fax: 202-727-1129
Web: www.dclibrary.org

Barbara Janis
Presidio Trust (75)
34 Graham Street
San Francisco, CA 94129
Phone: 415-561-5343
Email: bjanis@presidiotrust.gov

Paul Jasmer
Saint John's University (276)
Alcuin Library
Collegeville, MN 56321
Phone: 320-363-2122
Fax: 320-363-2126
Web: www.csbsju.edu/library

Hannah Jay
Fox Island Historical Society (527)
Map Room
1017 9th Avenue
Fox Island, WA 98333
Phone: 253-549-2461
Web: foxisland.net

Scott Jeffries
Hardin-Simmons University (474)
Richardson Library
Government Documents
2200 Hickory
Abilene, TX 79698
Phone: 325-670-1521
Email: jeffries@hsutx.edu
Web: rupert.alc.org/library/

Margaret D. Jenks
Oregon Department of Geology
   and Mineral Industries (407)
800 NE Oregon Street #28
Portland, OR 97232
Phone: 503-731-4100
Fax: 503-731-4066
Email: margi.jenks@dogami.state.or.us
Web: www.oregongeology.com

Erik Jensen
Library Assistant
Blue Mountain Community College Library (403)
Map Collection
2411 NW Carden Ave
Pendleton, OR 97801

Phone: 541-278-5915
Fax: 541-276-6119
Web: www.bluecc.edu/library

Larrisa John
Technical Service Librarian
Oregon Institute of Technology (401)
Library
Maps
3201 Campus Dr.
Klamath Falls, OR 97601
Phone: 541-885-1772
Fax: 541-885-1777
Web: www.oit.edu/lbry

Charles Johnson
Librarian
Ventura County Museum of History and Art (93)
Research Library
100 E. Main Street
Ventura, CA 93001
Phone: 805-653-0323
Fax: 805-653-5267
Email: library@vcmha.org
Web: www.vcmha.org

Jenny Marie Johnson
Map and Geography Librarian
University of Illinois, Urbana-Champaign (178)
Map and Geography Library
418 Library, MC-522
1408 West Gregory Drive
Urbana, IL 61801
Phone: 217-333-0827
Fax: 217-333-2214
Email: jmj@uiuc.edu
Web: www.library.uiuc.edu/max

John Johnson
Documents Reference Librarian
Kansas State University (212)
Hale Library
Government Publications Division
Manhattan, KS 66502-1200
Phone: 785-532-7448
Fax: 785-532-6144
Email: jlj@ksu.edu
Web: www.lib.ksu.edu/depts/govpubs/mainmap.html

Johanna Johnson
Manager
Dallas Public Library (485)
J. Eric Jonsson Central Library
Government Information Center/Map Collection
1515 Young Street

Dallas, TX 75201
Phone: 214-670-1468
Fax: 214-670-1451
Web: www.dallaslibrary.org/CGI/maps.htm

Leelyn Johnson
Reference/Federal Documents Coordinator
Library of Michigan (270)
Public Services
702 West Kalamazoo
Lansing, MI 48909
Phone: 517-373-1300
Fax: 517-373-5853
Email: ljohnson@michigan.gov
Web: michigan.gov/libraryofmichigan

Darcy Johnson Skinna
Associate Reference Librarian
La Crosse Public Library (545)
800 Main Street
La Crosse, WI 54601
Phone: 608-789-7122
Fax: 608-789-7161
Email: d.skibba@lacrosse.lib.wi.us
Web: www.lacrosselibrary.org

Carolyn Jones
Lab Tech II, Scanning Supervisor
University of California, Santa Barbara (88)
Davidson Library
Map and Imagery Laboratory
Santa Barbara, CA 93106-9010
Phone: 805-893-2779
Fax: 805-893-8799
Web: www.sdc.ucsb.edu

Jody Jones
Local History Specialist
Pikes Peak Library District (98)
Carnegie Library
Special Collections
20 North Cascade Avenue
Colorado Springs, CO 80903
Phone: 719-531-6333 x2253
Fax: 719-389-8161
Web: ppld.org

Rodney Jones
University of Tennessee (466)
Special Collections—Hoskins Library
1401 Cumberland Avenue
Knoxville, TN 37996-4000
Phone: 865-974-4480
Fax: 865-974-0560
Web: www.lib.utk.edu/spcoll

Walter Jones
University of Utah (505)
Marriott Library
Special Collections
295 South 1500 East
Salt Lake City, UT 84112-0860
Phone: 801-581-8863
Email: walter.jones@library.utah.edu

William A. Jones
California State University, Chico (49)
Meriam Library
Maps
400 West First Street
Chico, CA 95926
Phone: 539-898-5710
Fax: 530-898-4443
Email: bjones2@csuchico.edu
Web: www.csuchico.edu/lbib/maps/maps_page1.html

Jennifer Joseph
Reference/Government Documents Librarian
New Castle Public Library (419)
207 East North Street
New Castle, PA 16101
Phone: 724-658-6659
Fax: 724-658-9012
Email: librarianjen@msn.com
Web: www.newcastle.lib.pa.us

Donna Just
Government Documents Paraprofessional
Minot State University (369)
Gordon B. Olson Library
Government Documents and Maps
500 University Avenue W
Minot, ND 58707
Phone: 701-858-3200
Fax: 701-858-3581
Web: www.minotstateu.edu/library/

Jeffrey H. Kaimowitz
Trinity College (116)
Library
Watkinson Library
300 Summit Street
Hartford, CT 06106
Phone: 860-297-2268
Fax: 860-297-2251
Email: jeffrey.kaimowitz@trincoll.edu
Web: www.trincoll.edu/depts/library/watkinson/

Thomas Kallsen
Map Library Supervisor
University of Alabama (8)
Map Library

P.O. Box 870322
Tuscaloosa, AL 35487
Phone: 205-348-6028
Email: maplib@bama.ua.edu
Web: maplibrary.ua.edu

Nancy Kandoian
Senior Cataloger
New York Public Library (343)
Humanities and Social Sciences Library
Map Division
5th Ave and 42nd Street
Room 117
New York, NY 10018
Phone: 212-930-0587
Fax: 212-930-0027
Web: www.nypl.org/research/chss/map/map.html

Angela Kao
Archival Technician
University of Alabama (7)
W. S. Hoole Special Collections Library
Box 870266
Tuscaloosa, AL 35487-0266
Phone: 205-348-0500
Fax: 205-348-1699
Web: www.lib.ua.edu/libraries/hoole/

Anne Kasuboski
Reference Coordinator
University of Wisconsin, Green Bay (544)
Cofrin Library
2420 Nicolet Drive
Green Bay, WI 54311-7001
Phone: 920-465-2303
Fax: 920-465-2388
Web: www.uwgb.edu/library/

John Kawula
Government Documents and Maps Librarian
University of Alaska, Fairbanks (13)
Elmer E. Rasmuson Library
Documents and Maps Collection
P.O. Box 756817
Fairbanks, AK 99775-6817
Phone: 907-474-7624
Fax: 907-474-1155
Email: ffjdk@uaf.edu
Web: www.uaf.edu/library

Margit Kaye
Library Assistant
Yale University (119)
Sterling Memorial Library
Map Collection
130 Wall Street

P.O. Box 208240
New Haven, CT 06520
Phone: 203-432-1867
Fax: 203-432-8527
Web: www.library.yale.edu/MapColl

Kevin Keating
Reference Librarian
Alaska Resources Library and
  Information Services (ARLIS) (9)
3211 Providence Drive
Suite 111
Anchorage, AK 99508
Phone: 907-272-7547
Fax: 907-271-4742
Email: ankmk@uaa.alaska.edu
Web: www.arlis.org

Kevin Keating
Reference Librarian
University of Alaska, Anchorage (10)
UAA/APU Consortium Library
3211 Providence Drive
Anchorage, AK 99508
Phone: 907-786-1825
Fax: 907-786-1834
Email: ankmk@uaa.alaska.edu
Web: www.lib.uaa.alaska.edu

Diana J. Keith
University of Nebraska, Kearney (302)
Calvin T. Ryan Library
Government Documents Department
2508 11th Avenue
Kearney, NE 68849-2240
Phone: 308-865-8542
Fax: 308-865-8722
Email: keithdi@unk.edu
Web: www.unk.edu/acad/library/gov_doc/about.htm

Christian Kelleher
Archivist
University of Texas, Austin (480)
Nettie Lee Benson Latin American Collection
Rare Books and Manuscripts Division
The General Libraries
Austin, TX 78713-8916
Phone: 512-495-4520
Fax: 512-495-4568
Email: kelleher@mail.utexas.edu
Web: www.lib.utexas.edu/benson/

Colin Kelly
Map and Aerial Photography Technician
University of Oregon (400)
Knight Library

Document Center
1299 University of Oregon
Eugene, OR 97403-1299
Phone: 541-346-4565
Fax: 541-346-1958
Web: libweb.uoregon.edu/map/

Michael Kelly
Curator of Special Collections
Wichita State University (217)
Ablah Library
Department of Special Collections
1845 Fairmount
Wichita, KS 67260
Phone: 316-978-3590
Fax: 316-978-3048
Email: Michael.kelly@wichita.edu
Web: specialcollections.wichita.edu/collections/maps/
  index.asp

Phyllis Kendig
Government Documents Librarian
Saint Paul Public Library (288)
Central Library
90 West 4th Street
Saint Paul, MN 55102
Phone: 651-266-7000
Fax: 651-266-7011
Email: phyllis.kendig@ci.stpaul.mn.us
Web: www.sppl.org

Miriam L. Kennard
University of North Carolina, Chapel Hill (350)
Geological Sciences Library
CB #3315 Mitchell Hall
Chapel Hill, NC 27516
Phone: 919-962-2386
Fax: 919-966-4519
Email: kennard@email.unc.edu
Web: www.lib.unc.edu/geolib/

Melissa Kenney
Library Technical Assistant
Southern Illinois University Edwardsville (168)
Lovejoy Library
Map Library
P.O. Boz 1063
Edwardsville, IL 62026-2063
Phone: 618-650-2632
Fax: 618-650-2717

Martha Ketchersid
Government Documents Assistant
Abilene Christian University (472)
Brown Library
Texas Topographic Map Collection

221 Brown Library
Abilene, TX 79601-9208
Phone: 325-674-2316
Fax: 325-674-2202
Web: www.acu.edu/academic/library

Terry Ketelsen
State Archivist
Colorado State Archives (101)
1313 Sherman Street
Room 1B-20
Denver, CO 80203
Phone: 303-866-2550
Fax: 303-866-2257
Web: www.colorado.gov/dpa/doit/archives/geography
.htm

Kristen Kinsey
Photo and Graphics Specialist
University of Washington (538)
Suzzallo/Allen Library
Special Collections
Box 352900
Seattle, WA 98195
Phone: 206-543-1929
Fax: 206-543-1931
Web: www.lib.washington.edu/specialcoll

Jeffrey M. Kintop
Nevada State Library and Archives (319)
100 North Stewart Street
Carson City, NV 89701-4285
Phone: 775-684-3310
Fax: 775-684-3371
Email: jmkintop@clan.lib.nv.us
Web: dmla.clan.lib.nv.us/docs/nsla/archives/

Erin Kirchhoff
Cataloger
Indiana Historical Society (189)
William Henry Smith Memorial Library
450 West Ohio Street
Indianapolis, IN 46202-3269
Phone: 317-232-1879
Fax: 317-234-0169
Web: www.indianahistory.org

Lynne Kiviluoma
Department Head
Chicago Public Library (164)
Harold Washington Library Center
Government Publications Department
400 South State Street
Chicago, IL 60605

Phone: 312-747-4508
Fax: 312-747-4516
Web: chipublib.org

Hilary Kleckner
Library Assistant
Pennsylvania State University (427)
University Libraries
Maps Library
001 Paterno Library
University Park, PA 16802
Phone: 814-863-0094
Fax: 814-863-3560
Web: www.libraries.psu.edu/maps

George Klein
Toledo-Lucas County Public Library (393)
Main Library
325 Michigan Street
Toledo, OH 43624
Phone: 419-259-5207

Sue Klispch
Technical Services Librarian
Knox County Public Library (462)
East Tennessee History Center
Calvin M. McClung Historical Collection
314 West Clinch Avenue
Knoxville, TN 37902-2313
Phone: 865-215-8801
Fax: 865-215-8810
Web: www.knoxlib.org

Bob Knecht
Curator of Maps
Kansas State Historical Society (215)
Center for Historical Research
Library and Archives Division
6425 SW 6th Avenue
Topeka, KS 66615-1099
Phone: 785-272-8681 x116
Fax: 785-272-8682
Email: bknecht@kshs.org
Web: www.kshs.org

Kevin Knoot
Special Collections Archivist
State Historical Society of Iowa,
    Department of Cultural Affairs (203)
Special Collections/Map Collection
402 Iowa Avenue
Iowa City, IA 52240
Phone: 319-335-3916
Fax: 319-335-3935
Web: www.iowahistory.org

Matthew Knutzen
Assistant Chief
New York Public Library (343)
Humanities and Social Sciences Library
Map Division
5th Ave and 42nd Street
Room 117
New York, NY 10018
Phone: 212-930-0587
Fax: 212-930-0027
Web: www.nypl.org/research/chss/map/map.html

Jill Koelling
Curator of Visual Materials
Northern Arizona University (18)
Cline Library
Special Collections and Archives Department
Box 6022
Flagstaff, AZ 86011-6022
Phone: 928-523-5551
Fax: 928-523-3770
Web: www.nau.edu/library/speccoll

Chris Kollen
University of Arizona (32)
Library
1510 East University
Tucson, AZ 85721
Phone: 520-621-6441
Fax: 520-621-9733
kollenc@u.library.arizona.edu
Web: www.library.arizona.edu

Ed Krakora
Heidelberg College (392)
Beeghly Library
10 Greenfield Street
Tiffin, OH 44883
Phone: 419-448-2104
Fax: 419-448-2578
Email: ekrakora@heidelberg.edu

Tim Kreider
Technicians
Pennsylvania Department of Education (415)
Bureau of State Library of Pennsylvania
Maps Collection
333 Market Street
Harrisburg, PA 17126-1745
Phone: 717-783-5950
Fax: 717-787-9127
Web: www.statelibrary.state.pa.us

Mary Krick
Head Librarian
Illinois State Geological Survey (161)

Library and Map Room
615 East Peabody Drive
Champaign, IL 61820
Phone: 217-333-5110
Fax: 217-333-2830
Email: krick@isgs.uiuc.edu
Web: www.isgs.uiuc.edu/library/index.html

Pamela Kruse-Buckingham
Director
Kitsap County Historical Society (524)
280 4th Street
Bremerton, WA 98337
Phone: 360-479-6226
Fax: 360-415-9294
Email: kchsm@telebyte.net
Web: www.waynes.net/kchsm/

Tim Kuhn
GIS Administrator
Knoxville/Knox County Metropolitan
   Planning Commission (463)
Library
400 Main Street, Suite 403
Knoxville, TN 37902
Phone: 865-215-2500
Fax: 865-215-2068
Web: www.knoxmpc.org

Michael "Mick" Kuhns
Office of Surface Mining Reclamation
   and Enforcement (429)
Anthracite (Coal) Mine Map Repository
Branch of Anthracite-MMR
7 North Wilkes-Barre Boulevard
Suite 308
Wilkes-Barre, PA 18702-5293
Phone: 570-830-1400
Fax: 570-830-1421
Email: mkuhns@osmre.gov
Web: mmr.osmre.gov

Jessica Lacher-Feldman
Public and Outreach Services Librarian
University of Alabama (7)
W. S. Hoole Special Collections Library
Box 870266
Tuscaloosa, AL 35487-0266
Phone: 205-348-0500
Fax: 205-348-1699
Web: www.lib.ua.edu/libraries/hoole/

Carolyn Lafoon
Professional Librarian
Purdue University (198)

Earth and Atmospheric Sciences (EAS) Library
EAS Map Room
Civil Engineering Building
Room 2253
West Lafayette, IN 47907
Phone: 765-494-0202
Email: carolyn@purdue.edu
Web: www.lib.purdue.edu/eas/inmaps.html

Kathryn Lage
Map Librarian
University of Colorado, Boulder (95)
Jerry Crail Johnson Earth Sciences and Map Library
184 UCB
Boulder, CO 80309
Phone: 303-492-7578
Fax: 303-735-4879
Email: katie.lage@colorado.edu
Web: www-libraries.colorado.edu/ps/map/

Donnelly Lancaster
Archival Access Coordinator
University of Alabama (7)
W. S. Hoole Special Collections Library
Box 870266
Tuscaloosa, AL 35487-0266
Phone: 205-348-0500
Fax: 205-348-1699
Web: www.lib.ua.edu/libraries/hoole/

Thomas S. Land
Institutional Records Analyst
University of Alabama (7)
W. S. Hoole Special Collections Library
Box 870266
Tuscaloosa, AL 35487-0266
Phone: 205-348-0500
Fax: 205-348-1699
Web: www.lib.ua.edu/libraries/hoole/

Larry Landis
Archivist
Oregon State University (399)
The Valley Library
Map Collection
121 The Valley Library
Corvallis, OR 97331-4501
Phone: 541-737-7295
Fax: 541-737-8224
Web: osulibrary.oregonstate.edu/research/guides/maps/
maproom.htm

Lisa Landrum
Reference Clerk
Spartanburg County Public Library (452)

Reference Department
151 South Church Street
Spartanburg, SC 29306
Phone: 864-596-3505
Fax: 864-596-3518
Web: www.infodepot.org/govdoc.htm;
www.infodepot.org/kroom.htm

John Lannon
Curator of Maps
Boston Athenaeum (250)
10 1/2 Beacon Street
Boston, MA 02108
Phone: 617-227-0270
Fax: 617-227-5266
Email: lannon@bostonathenaeum.org
Web: bostonathenaeum.org

Mary Lynette Larsgaard
Assistant Head
University of California, Santa Barbara (88)
Davidson Library
Map and Imagery Laboratory
Santa Barbara, CA 93106-9010
Phone: 805-893-2779
Fax: 805-893-8799
Email: mary@sdc.ucsb.edu
Web: www.sdc.ucsb.edu

Cheryl Lauricella
Reference Specialist
Wright State University (388)
University Libraries
Colonel Glenn Highway
Dayton, OH 45435
Phone: 937-775-2925
Fax: 937-775-2356
Email: cheryl.lauricella@wright.edu
Web: www.libraries.wright.edu

Erin Lawrimore
University of Tennessee (466)
Special Collections—Hoskins Library
1401 Cumberland Avenue
Knoxville, TN 37996-4000
Phone: 865-974-4480
Fax: 865-974-0560
Web: www.lib.utk.edu/spcoll

Ngan Le
Library Assistant
University of California, San Diego (55)
Social Sciences and Humanities Library
9500 Gilman Drive 0175R
La Jolla, CA 92093

Phone: 858-534-1248
Fax: 858-534-7548
Web: govinfo.ucsd.edu/maps/index.html

Heather Leadingham
Government Documents Assistant
George Mason University (514)
Fenwick Library
Government Documents/Maps
4400 University Dr
Fairfax, VA 22030
Phone: 703-993-2238
Fax: 703-993-2494
Web: library.gmu.edu/resources/govt/

Regina Lee
Head of Government Publications,
   Maps and Microforms
Tennessee Technological University (460)
Angelo and Jennette Volpe Library and Media Center
1100 North Peachtree Avenue
Cookeville, TN 38505
Phone: 931-372-3326
Fax: 931-372-6112
Email: rlee@tntech.edu
Web: www.tntech.edu/govpub/

Charles H. Lesser
Accessions Archivist
South Carolina Department of
   Archives and History (443)
Reference Services
8301 Parklane Road
Columbia, SC 29223
Phone: 803-896-6104
Fax: 803-896-6198
Email: lesser@scdah.state.sc.us
Web: www.state.sc.us/scdah

Lori Lester
Documents Associate
State University of West Georgia (147)
Irvine Sullivan Ingram Library
1600 Maple Street
Carrollton, GA 30118
Phone: 770-830-2357
Fax: 770-836-6626
Web: www.westga.edu/~library/

Paul Leverenz
Scripps Institution of Oceanography (54)
University of California, San Diego
Map and Chart Collection
8755 Biological Grade
La Jolla, CA 92093

Phone: 858-534-1228
Fax: 858-534-5269
Email: pleverenz@ucsd.edu
Web: scilib.ucsd.edu/sio/guide/map.html

David Liberty
Library Technician
Columbia River Inter-Tribal Fish Commission (404)
StreamNet Library
729 NE Oregon Street
Suite 190
Portland, OR 97232
Phone: 503-731-1304
Fax: 503-731-1260
Web: www.fishlib.org

Craig S. Likness
Head, Archives and Special Collections
University of Miami (130)
Otto G. Richter Library
Archives and Special Collection Department
1300 Memorial Drive
Coral Gables, FL 33124-0320
Phone: 305-284-3247
Fax: 305-284-4027
Email: clikness@miami.edu

Sandy Lillydahl
Map Supervisor
University of Massachusetts, Amherst (249)
W.E.B. Du Bois Library
Map Collection
154 Hicks Way
Amherst, MA 01003
Phone: 413-545-2397
Fax: 413-545-1399
Email: slillydahl@library.umass.edu
Web: www.library.umass.edu/maps/index/html

Allison Limbrick Barkley
Assistant Coordinator
Sara Hightower Regional Library (150)
Rome-Floyd County Public Library
Special Collections
205 Riverside Parkway
Rome, GA 30161
Phone: 706-236-4607
Fax: 706-236-4605
Web: www.floyd.public.lib.ga.us

Peter Linberger
Business, Geography, and Maps Bibliographer
University of Akron (370)
Bierce Library
Map Collection

Akron, OH 44325-1707
Phone: 330-972-8176
Fax: 330-972-7225
Email: pl@uakron.edu
Web: www.uakron.edu/libraries/ul/subjects/look4maps
.html

Susan Linden
Librarian I
Loveland Public Library (112)
Map Vertical File
300 North Adams
Loveland, CO 80537
Phone: 970-962-2402
Fax: 970-962-2905
Email: lindes@ci.loveland.co.us

Thomas Lindsey
Social Science and Government Documents Librarian
University of Texas, Arlington (476)
Library
Information Services
702 College Street
P.O. Box 19497
Arlington, TX 76019
Phone: 817-272-7514
Fax: 817-272-3593
Email: lindsey@uta.edu
Web: www.uta.edu/library

Eric Lindstrom
Map Library Director
National Geographic Society (126)
Harold A. Hanson Map Library
National Geogrpahic Maps
1145 17th Street NW
Washington, DC 20036
Phone: 202-857-7083
Email: elindstr@ngs.org

Chiawen Liu
Assistant Librarian
Illinois State Geological Survey (161)
Library and Map Room
615 East Peabody Drive
Champaign, IL 61820
Phone: 217-333-5110
Fax: 217-333-2830
Web: www.isgs.uiuc.edu/library/index.html

Cheryl Livingston
Library Technician III
Colorado School of Mines (109)
Arthur Lakes Library
Map Room
1400 Illinois

Golden, CO 80401
Phone: 303-273-3697
Fax: 303-273-3199
Email: clivings@mines.edu
Web: www.mines.edu/library/maproom

Kay Logan-Peters
Chair of Access and Branch Services
University of Nebraska, Lincoln (312)
Geology Library
10 Bessey Hall
Lincoln, NE 68588-0344
Phone: 402-472-2653
Email: klogan-peters1@unl.edu
Web: www.unl.edu/libr/libs/geol/geol.html

Ed Lonergan
Documents Coordinator
Springfield City Library (257)
220 State St
Springfield, MA 01103
Phone: 413-263-6828
Email: elonergan@spfldlibmus.org

Karl Longstreth
Head and Map Librarian
University of Michigan (263)
Map Library
Hatcher Graduate Library 825
Ann Arbor, MI 48109-1205
Phone: 734-764-0407
Fax: 734-763-5080
Email: karleric@umich.edu
Web: www.lib.umich.edu/maplib

Art Louderback
Historical Society of Western Pennsylvania (424)
1212 Smallman Street
Pittsburgh, PA 15222
Phone: 412-454-6364
Fax: 412-454-6028
Web: www.pghhistory.org

Betsy Lowenstein
State Library of Massachusetts (253)
341 State House
Boston, MA 02139
Phone: 617-727-2590
Fax: 617-727-9730
Email: betsy.lowenstein@state.ma.us
Web: www.mass.gov/lib

Cynthia A. Luckie
Alabama Department of Archives and History (5)
P.O. Box 300100
624 Washington Avenue

Montgomery, AL 36130
Phone: 334-242-4363
Fax: 334-240-3433
cluckie@archives.state.al.us
Web: www.archives.state.al.us

Weina Luo
Senior Library Technical Assistant
Florida Atlantic University (129)
S.E. Wimberly Library
777 Glades Road
Boca Raton, FL 33431
Phone: 561-297-3760
Fax: 561-338-3863

Andra Lupardus
Documents/Periodicals Librarian
University of Tulsa (398)
McFarlin Library
2933 East 6th Street
Tulsa, OK 74104-3123
Phone: 918-631-2874
Fax: 918-631-3791
Email: ajl@utulsa.edu
Web: www.lib.utulsa.edu/govdocs/maps.htm

Deborah Lupo
LA II
University of California, Santa Barbara (88)
Davidson Library
Map and Imagery Laboratory
Santa Barbara, CA 93106-9010
Phone: 805-893-2779
Fax: 805-893-8799
Web: www.sdc.ucsb.edu

Becky Lutkenhaus
Documents and Maps Librarian
University of Northern Iowa (200)
Rod Library
Documents and Maps Collection
1227 West 27th Street
Cedar Falls, IA 50613-3675
Phone: 319-273-2838
Fax: 319-273-2913
Email: becky.lutkenhaus@uni.edu
Web: www.library.uni.edu/gov/

Doug Magee
Map Librarian
Public Library of Cincinnati and Hamilton County (375)
History Department Map Collection
800 Vine Street
Cincinnati, OH 45230
Phone: 513-369-6905
Fax: 513 369-3123

Email: doug.magee@cincinnatilibrary.org
Web: www.cincinnatilibrary.org

Patricia Magierski
Librarian I
Chicago Public Library (164)
Harold Washington Library Center
Government Publications Department
400 South State Street
Chicago, IL 60605
Phone: 312-747-4508
Fax: 312-747-4516
Web: chipublib.org

Brenda Mahar
Government Documents Cataloger
University of Texas, Dallas (495)
Eugene McDermott Library
P.O. Box 830643
MC33
Richardson, TX 75083-0643
Phone: 972-883-2950
Fax: 972-883-2473
Web: www.utdallas.edu/library

Michael Maher
Librarian
Nevada Historical Society (320)
1650 North Virginia Street
Reno, NV 89503
Phone: 775-688-1190
Fax: 775-688-2917
Email: mpmaher@clan.lib.nv.us
Web: www.nevadaculture.org

Lou Malcomb
Librarian for Geography and Map Library
Indiana University, Bloomington (181)
Geography and Map Library
701 East Kirkwood
015 Student Building
Bloomington, IN 47405
Phone: 812-855-1108
Email: malcomb@indiana.edu
Web: www.indiana.edu/~libgm

Lou Malcomb
Head Government Information,
    Microforms and Statistical Services
Indiana University, Bloomington (183)
Government Information, Microforms,
    and Statistical Services
1320 East 10th Street
c264 IUB Main Library
Bloomington, IN 47405
Phone: 812-855-6924

Fax: 812-855-3460
Email: malcomb@indiana.edu
Web: www.indiana.edu/~libgpd

Rebecca Malin
Documents Assistant
Contra Costa County Library (65)
Central Library
1750 Oak Park Boulevard
Pleasant Hill, CA 94523-4497
Phone: 925-646-6434
Fax: 925-646-6040
Web: ccclib.org

Linda Mangum
Documents Assistant
Baylor University (498)
Moody Memorial Library
Government Documents
1312 South 3rd
Waco, TX 76798
Phone: 254-710-2157
Fax: 254-710-3116
Web: www3.baylor.edu/library

Wendy Mann
Coordinator, Government Publications
University of Pittsburgh (425)
Hillman Library
University Library System Map Collection
3960 Forbes Avenue
Pittsburgh, PA 15260
Phone: 412-648-7726;-412-648-7730
Fax: 412-648-7733
Email: wendym@pitt.edu
Web: www.library.pitt.edu/libraries/maps/maps.html

Carrie Marsh
Special Collections Librarian
Claremont University Center, Claremont Colleges (50)
Honnold/Mudd Library
800 North Dartmouth Ave
Claremont, CA 91711
Phone: 909-621-8045
Fax: 909-621-8681
Email: carrie.marsh@libraries.claremont.edu

Nancy Marshall
Documents Librarian
South Dakota State University (453)
Hilton M. Briggs Library
Box 2115
Brookings, SD 57007-1098
Phone: 605-688-5576
Fax: 605-688-5133
Email: nancy_marshall@sdstate.edu

Elaine Martin
Laurens County Library (450)
Laurens County Historical Room
1017 West Main Street
Laurens, SC 29360
Phone: 864-984-0596
Fax: 864-984-0598
Email: emartin@lcpl.org
Web: www.lcpl.org

Russell Martin
Director
Southern Methodist University (487)
DeGolyer Library
Historic Map Collection
P.O. Box 750396
Dallas, TX 75275
Phone: 214-768-4284
Fax: 214-768-1565

Jaime Martindale
Map/GIS Librarian
University of Wisconsin, Madison (547)
Arthur H. Robinson Map Library
550 North Park Street
Madison, WI 53706
Phone: 608-262-1471
Email: martindale@wisc.edu

Debra Martzahn
Library Assistant
Grinnell College (202)
Burling Library
1111 6th Avenue
Grinnell, IA 50112
Phone: 641-269-4234
Fax: 641-269-4283
Web: www.lib.grin.edu/Places/govdocs/

Catherine Masi
Programmer III, Head of Operational
    Alexandria Digital Library
University of California, Santa Barbara (88)
Davidson Library
Map and Imagery Laboratory
Santa Barbara, CA 93106-9010
Phone: 805-893-2779
Fax: 805-893-8799
Web: www.sdc.ucsb.edu

Brenda Mathenia
Assistant Professor/Reference Librarian
Montana State University, Bozeman (296)
Roland R. Renne Library
The Libraries
P.O. Box 173320

Bozeman, MT 59717-3320
Phone: 406-994-3171
Fax: 406-994-2851
Email: mathenia@montana.edu
Web: www.lib.montana.edu

Eileen Mathias
Information Services Librarian
Academy of Natural Sciences (420)
Ewell Sale Stewart Library
James Bond Map Room
1900 Benjamin Franklin Parkway
Philadelphia, PA 19103
Phone: 215-299-1040
Fax: 215-299-1144
Email: mathias@acnatsci.org
Web: www.acnatsci.org/library

John Maxymuk
Rutgers University, Camden Campus (328)
Paul Robeson Library
300 North 4th Street
Camden, NJ 8101
Phone: 856-225-6034
Fax: 856-225-6428

Rebecca Mayne
Archivist
Grand Rapids Public Library (266)
Grand Rapids History and Special Collections Center
  (GRHSCC)
111 Library Street NE
Grand Rapids, MI 49503
Phone: 616-988-5400
Fax: 616-988-5421
Email: rmayne@grpl.org
Web: www.grpl.org

Paula Maynor
Sales Office Manager
North Carolina Geological Survey (362)
1612 Mail Service Center
Raleigh, NC 27699-1612
Phone: 919-715-9718
Fax: 9190733-0900
Email: paula.maynor@ncmail.net
Web: www.geology.enr.state.nc.us

Carol McAuliffe
Senior Library Technician
University of Florida (135)
George A. Smathers Libraries
Map and Imagery Library
P.O.Box 11701
110 Marston Science Library
Gainesville, FL 32611-7011

Phone: 352-392-2825
Fax: 352-392-4787
Web: web.uflib.ufl.edu/maps

Carolyn McClurkan
Archivist
Kitsap County Historical Society (524)
280 4th Street
Bremerton, WA 98337
Phone: 360-479-6226
Fax: 360-415-9294
Web: www.waynes.net/kchsm/

Cheryl McCoy
University Librarian
University of South Florida (139)
Tampa Library
Reference/Documents—Map Collection
4202 East Fowler Avenue
LIB 122
Tampa, FL 33620-5400
Phone: 813-974-2729
Fax: 813-974-9875
Email: cmccoy@lib.usf.edu
Web: www.lib.usf.edu/tampa/govdocs/

Shelly McCoy
Head, Digital User Services Department
University of Delaware (122)
Hugh M. Morris Library
Map Room
181 South College Avenue
Newark, DE 19717-526
Phone: 302-831-6664
Fax: 302-831-1046
Email: smccoy@udel.edu
Web: www.lib.udel.edu/ud/digital/microcopy/gis/ and
   www.lib.udel.edu/ud/spec/findaids/hist_map/
   index.htm

Karl McCreary
Archivist
Oregon State University (399)
The Valley Library
Map Collection
121 The Valley Library
Corvallis, OR 97331-4501
Phone: 541-737-7295
Fax: 541-737-8224
Web: osulibrary.oregonstate.edu/research/guides/maps/
   maproom.htm

Dylan McDonald
Archivist
Idaho State Historical Society (157)
Historical Library and State Archives

450 North Fourth Street
Boise, ID 83702
Phone: 208-334-3356
Fax: 208-334-3198
Web: www.idahohistory.net/library_archives.html

Michael McDonnell
Reference Librarian for Maps and Documents
Western Michigan University (269)
Waldo Library
Map Department
1903 West Michigan Avenue
Kalamazoo, MI 49008
Phone: 269-387-5047
Email: Michael.McDonnell@wmich.edu
Web: www.wmich.edu/library/depts/maps/index.html

Scott R. McEathron
Map Librarian
University of Kansas (210)
Anschutz Library
Thomas R. Smith Map Collections
1301 Hoch Auditoria Drive
Lawrence, KS 66045
Phone: 785-864-4420
Fax: 785-864-4420
Email: macmap68@ku.edu
Web: www2.lib.ku.edu/mapscoll/

Douglas McElrath
Curator of Marylandia and Rare Books
University of Maryland, College Park (244)
Hornbake Library
Maryland Map Collection
College Park, MD 20742
Phone: 301-410-9212
Fax: 301-314-2709
Email: dmcelrat@umd.edu
Web: www.lib.umd.edu/RARE/MarylandCollection/
  Maps/MdMaps.html

Jackie McFadden
Winthrop University (451)
Dacus Library
Government Documents
Oakland Avenue
Rock Hill, SC 29733
Phone: 803-323-2322
Fax: 803-323-2215
Email: mcfaddenj@winthrop.edu
Web: www.winthrop.edu/dacus/About/govdoc.htm

Tom McGarvin
Geologist
Arizona Geological Survey (29)

416 West Congress
Tucson, AZ 85701
Phone: 520-770-3500
Fax: 520-770-3505
Email: tom.mcgarvin@azgs.az.gov
Web: www.azgs.az.gov

Patrick McGlamery
University of Connecticut (121)
Homer Babbidge Library
Map and Geographic Information Center
369 Fairfield Road
Storrs, CT 06269-0584
Phone: 860-486-4589
Fax: 486-4100
Email: patrick.mcglamery@uconn.edu
Web: magic.lib.uconn.edu/

Susan McGlothlin
Library Specialist
Northern Arizona University (18)
Cline Library
Special Collections and Archives Department
Box 6022
Flagstaff, AZ 86011-6022
Phone: 928-523-5551
Fax: 928-523-3770
Web: www.nau.edu/library/speccoll

Eileen McGrath
Collection Management Librarian
University of North Carolina, Chapel Hill (349)
Academic Affairs Library
North Carolina Collection
CB#3930
Wilson Library
Chapel Hill, NC 27514-8890
Phone: 919-962-1172
Fax: 919-962-4452
Web: www.lib.unc.edu/ncc

Sharon McGuire
Senior Technician
University of Kentucky (223)
Pirtle Geological Sciences Library and Map Collection
410 King Library Addition
Lexington, KY 40506-0039
Phone: 859-257-5730
Fax: 859-323-3225
Web: www.uky.edu/Libraries

Mary McInroy
University of Iowa (205)
Map Collection
3111 Main Library

Iowa City, IA 52242-1420
Phone: 319-335-5920
Fax: 319-335-5900
Email: mary-mcinroy@uiowa.edu
Web: www.lib.uiowa.edu/maps

Marianne M. McKee
Senior Research Archivist and Map Specialist
Library of Virginia (518)
Archival and Information Services Division/
    Map Collection
800 East Broad Street
Richmond, VA 23227
Phone: 804-692-3888
Fax: 804-692-3556
Email: mmckee@lva.lib.va.us
Web: www.lva.lib.va.us

Connie McKnight
Manager, Reference and Reader Services
Sioux City Public Library (206)
529 Pierce Street
Sioux City, IA 51101-1203
Phone: 712-255-2933 x221
Fax: 712-279-6432
Email: cmcknight@siouxcitylibrary.org
Web: www.siouxcitylibrary.org

Clara McLeod
EPSc Librarian
Washington University (294)
Earth and Planetary Sciences Library
One Brookings Drive
Saint Louis, MO 63130
Phone: 314-935-5406
Fax: 314-935-4800
Email: cpmcleod@wulib.wustl.edu
Web: library.wustl.edu

Patrick McNally
Section Head
Hawai'i State Public Library System (153)
Hawai'i and Pacific Section
478 South King Street
Honolulu, HI 96813
Phone: 808-586-3535
Fax: 808-586-3586
Email: hslhp@libarieshawaii.org
Web: www.hawaii.gov/hidocs

David C. McQuillan
Map Librarian
University of South Carolina (445)
Thomas Cooper Library
Map Library

Columbia, SC 29208
Phone: 803-777-2802
Fax: 803-777-4661
Email: davidmcq@sc.edu
Web: www.sc.edu/library/maps.html

James McQuinn
Dayton Metro Library (386)
215 East Third Street
Dayton, OH 45402
Phone: 937-227-9500
Fax: 937-227-9548
Email: jmcquinn@daytonmetrolibrary.org
Web: www.daytonmetrolibrary.org

Charles McWhorter
Library Associate
Austin Peay State University (459)
Felix G. Woodward
Information Services
601 East College Street
Clarksville, TN 37044
Phone: 931-221-7346
Fax: 931-221-7296
Web: library.apsu.edu/

Jane Mears
LTA
Anderson County Public Library (434)
South Carolina Room
300 North McDuffie Street
Anderson, SC 29621
Phone: 864-260-4500
Fax: 864-260-4098
Web: www.andersonlibrary.org

Larry Mello
Senior Library Technical Assistant
Florida Atlantic University (129)
S.E. Wimberly Library
777 Glades Road
Boca Raton, FL 33431
Phone: 561-297-3760
Fax: 561-338-3863

Harry C. Meserve
San Jose State University (84)
Dr. Martin Luther King Jr. Library
1 Washington Square
San Jose, CA 95192-0028
Phone: 408-808-2000
Email: hmeserve@sjsu.edu

Joann Meyer
Douglas County Historical Society Library (315)
Library/Archives Center

Historical Maps
5730 North 30th Street
Omaha, NE 68111
Phone: 402-451-1013
Fax: 402-453-9448
Email: archivist@omahahistory.org
Web: www.omahahistory.org

Tom Mikula
Librarian I
Chicago Public Library (164)
Harold Washington Library Center
Government Publications Department
400 South State Street
Chicago, IL 60605
Phone: 312-747-4508
Fax: 312-747-4516
Web: chipublib.org

Bill Miller
Assistant to the Map Librarian
University of Connecticut (121)
Homer Babbidge Library
Map and Geographic Information Center
369 Fairfield Road
Storrs, CT 06269-0584
Phone: 860-486-4589
Fax: 486-4100
Web: magic.lib.uconn.edu/

Michael C. Miller
Dallas Public Library (486)
Texas/Dallas History and Archives Division
1515 Young Street
Dallas, TX 75201
Phone: 214-670-1435
Fax: 214-670-1437
Email: mmiller@dallaslibrary.org
Web: dallaslibrary.org/ctx/ctx.htm

Kathryn C. Millis
Coordinator, Reference and Government Documents
DePauw University (187)
Prevo Science Library
602 South College
Greencastle, IN 46135
Phone: 765-658-4306

Nancy Milnor
Library Director
Connecticut Historical Society Library (114)
1 Elizabeth Street
Hartford, CT 06105
Phone: 860-236-5621
Fax: 860-236-2664

Email: nancy_milnor@chs.org
Web: www.chs.org

Raymond A. Mitchell
Project Specialist
Tennessee Valley Authority (458)
Map and Photo Records
1101 Market Street
MR 5E
Chattanooga, TN 37402
Phone: 423-751-8362
Fax: 423-499-6319
Email: ramitchell@tva.gov
Web: maps.tva.com

Christopher H. Mixon
Curator
Auburn University (1)
Library
231 Mell Street
Auburn University, AL 36849-5606
Phone: 334-844-1759
Fax: 334-844-4461
Email: mixonch@auburn.edu
Web: www.lib.auburn.edu/govdocs/

Sallie Mock
Map Assistant
Public Library of Cincinnati and Hamilton County (375)
History Department Map Collection
800 Vine Street
Cincinnati, OH 45230
Phone: 513-369-6905
Fax: 513 369-3123
Web: www.cincinnatilibrary.org

Riley Moffat
Head of Reference
Brigham Young University—Hawai'i Campus (155)
Joseph F. Smith Library
55-220 Kulanui Street
Laie, HI 96762
Phone: 808-293-3884
Fax: 808-293-3877
Email: moffatr@byuh.edu

Norm Moline
Augustana College (174)
Thomas Tredway Library
Loring Map Collection
639 38th Street
Rock Island, IL 61201
Phone: 309-794-7318
Fax: 309-794-7564
Email: ggmoline@augustana.edu
Web: www.augustana.edu/library

Mary Morganti
Director of Library and Archives
California Historical Society (73)
North Baker Research Library
678 Mission Street
San Francisco, CA 94105
Phone: 415-357-1848
Fax: 415-357-1850
Email: mary@calhist.org
Web: www.californiahistoricalsociety.org

Ingrid Morley
Library Information Assistant
Washington State Library (532)
P.O. Box 42460
Olympia, WA 98504-2460
Phone: 866-538-4996
Fax: 360-586-7575
Web: www.secstate.wa.gov/library/

Sharon Morris
Assistant Head, Government Publications/
    Maps/Law Library
Johns Hopkins University (242)
Eisenhower Library
Government Publications/Maps/Law Library
3400 North Charles Street
Baltimore, MD 21212
Phone: 410-516-8360
Fax: 410-516-6029
Web: www.library.jhu.edu/gpml/

Cheryl Moten
Washington University (294)
Earth and Planetary Sciences Library
One Brookings Drive
Saint Louis, MO 63130
Phone: 314-935-5406
Fax: 314-935-4800
Web: library.wustl.edu

Linda Morton-Keithley
Administrator
Idaho State Historical Society (157)
Historical Library and State Archives
450 North Fourth Street
Boise, ID 83702
Phone: 208-334-3356
Fax: 208-334-3198
Email: lindamk@ishs.state.id.us
Web: www.idahohistory.net/library_archives.html

Aaron Mount
San Francisco State University (80)
Alfred Rockwell Sumner Memorial Map Library

1600 Holloway Avenue
HSS 289
San Francisco, CA 94132
Phone: 415-338-1145
Fax: 415-338-6243
Web: bss.sfsu.edu/geog/maplib.htm

Cheryl Mouton
San Leandro Public Library (85)
Map File
300 Estudillo Avenue
San Leandro, CA 94577
Phone: 510-577-3971
Fax: 510-577-3987
Email: cmouton@ci.san-leandro.ca.us

Heiko Muehr
Geography and Map Library Coordinator
Indiana University, Bloomington (181)
Geography and Map Library
701 East Kirkwood
015 Student Building
Bloomington, IN 47405
Phone: 812-855-1108
Web: www.indiana.edu/~libgm

Eric L. Mundell
Director, Printed Collections and Artifacts
Indiana Historical Society (189)
William Henry Smith Memorial Library
450 West Ohio Street
Indianapolis, IN 46202-3269
Phone: 317-232-1879
Fax: 317-234-0169
Email: emundell@indianahistory.org
Web: www.indianahistory.org

Mara Munroe
Oshkosh Public Library (552)
106 Washington Avenue
Oshkosh, WI 54901-4985
Phone: 920-236-5205
Fax: 920-236-5227
Web: www.oshkoshpubliclibrary.org

Linda Musser
Head
Pennsylvania State University (426)
Fletcher L. Byrom Earth and Mineral Sciences Library
105 Deike Building
University Park, PA 16802
Phone: 814-865-9517
Fax: 814-865-1379
Email: Lrm4@psu.edu
Web: www.libraries.psu.edu/emsl/

Fred Musto
Curator
Yale University (119)
Sterling Memorial Library
Map Collection
130 Wall Street
P.O. Box 208240
New Haven, CT 06520
Phone: 203-432-1867
Fax: 203-432-8527
Email: fred.musto@yale.edu
Web: www.library.yale.edu/MapColl

Sharron Nagel
University of Nebraska, Lincoln (311)
C.Y. Thompson Library
38th and Holdrege Streets
East Campus
Lincoln, NE 68583-0717
Phone: 402-472-4407
Fax: 402-472-7005

J. Larry Nederlof
Nederlof Historical Library (48)
P.O.Box 130880
Carlsbad, CA 92013-0880
Phone: 760-634-2960
Fax: 760-635-8641
Email: larryn@microseconds.com

Mary Nelson
Library Assistant
Wichita State University (217)
Ablah Library
Department of Special Collections
1845 Fairmount
Wichita, KS 67260
Phone: 316-978-3590
Fax: 316-978-3048
Web: specialcollections.wichita.edu/collections/maps/
index.asp

Glenn Neumann
Chicago Public Library (164)
Harold Washington Library Center
Government Publications Department
400 South State Street
Chicago, IL 60605
Phone: 312-747-4508
Fax: 312-747-4516
Email: gneumann@chipublib.org
Web: chipublib.org

John M. Newman
Manager
Columbus Metropolitan Library (380)

Biography, History and Travel Division
96 South Grant Avenue
Columbus, OH 43215
Phone: 614-645-2710
Fax: 614-645-2051
Email: jnewman@cml.library.org
Web: www.columbuslibrary.org

Linda Newman
Geoscience and Map Librarian
University of Nevada, Reno (321)
DeLaMare Library
Mary B. Ansari Map Library
DeLaMare Library
MS 262
Reno, NV 89557
Phone: 775-784-6945 x230
Fax: 775-784-6949
Email: lnewman@unr.edu
Web: www.delamare.unr.edu/Maps/

Elizabeth Nielsen
Senior Staff Archivist
Oregon State University (399)
The Valley Library
Map Collection
121 The Valley Library
Corvallis, OR 97331-4501
Phone: 541-737-7295
Fax: 541-737-8224
Web: osulibrary.oregonstate.edu/research/guides/maps/
maproom.htm

Carol Niemann
Student Supervisor
University of Nebraska, Lincoln (313)
Love Memorial Library
Map Collection
Lincoln, NE 68588-4100
Phone: 402-472-3545
Fax: 402-472-2534
Web: www.unl.edu/libr/gis/

Nyal Niemuth
Arizona Department Mines and Mineral Resources (21)
Arizona Mines and Mineral Resource Library
1502 West Washington
Phoenix, AZ 85007
Phone: 602-255-3795
Fax: 602-255-3777
Email: njn22r@hotmail.com
Web: www.admmr.state.az.us

Eric Nitschke
Reference Librarian
Emory University (143)

Robert W. Woodruff Library
540 Asbury Circle
Atlanta, GA 30322
Phone: 404 727-6875
Email: liben@emory.edu
Web: web.library.emory.edu/subjects/maps/maps.html

Charles Nodler
Archivist
Missouri Southern State University, Joplin (290)
George A. Spiva Library
Tri-State Mining Collection
3950 East Newman Road
Joplin, MO 64801
Phone: 417-625-9552
Fax: 417-625-9734
Email: nodler-c@mail.mssu.edu
Web: www.mssu.edu/spivalib

Michael M. Noga
Massachusetts Institute of Technology (255)
Science Library
Map Collection
14S-134
77 Massachusetts Avenue
Cambridge, MA 02139-4307
Phone: 617-253-5685
Email: mnoga@mit.edu

Karen Nordgren
Government Documents Librarian
Emporia State University (207)
William Allen White Library
Information and Instructional Services
1200 Commercial
Campus Box 4051
Emporia, KS 66801
Phone: 620-341-5207
Fax: 620-341-5997

Jane Norem
Librarian
Illinois Valley Community College (172)
Jacobs Library
815 North Orlando Smith Avenue
Oglesby, IL 61348
Phone: 815 224-0306
Fax: 815 224-9147
Email: jane_norem@ivcc.edu

Nicholas Noyes
Head of Library Services
Maine Historical Society (237)
Research Library
489 Congress Street
Portland, ME 04101

Phone: 207-774-1822
Fax: 207-775-4301
Email: nnoyes@mainehistory.org
Web: www.mainehistory.org

Bruce Obenhaus
Government Information Specialist
Virginia Tech (510)
Newman Library
Instruction and Reference Department
Kent Street
Blacksburg, VA 24060
Phone: 540-231-6181
Fax: 540-231-9263
obenhaus@vt.edu
Web: www.lib.vt.edu/subjects/maps/gis.html

Hillery Oberle
Maps Assistant Archivist
Arizona State University (28)
Noble Science and Engineering Library
Map Collection
P.O. Box 871006
Tempe, AZ 85287-1006
Phone: 480-965-3582
Fax: 480-965-0883
Email: hillery.oberle@asu.edu
Web: www.asu.edu/lib/hayden/govdocs/maps/mapcoll
.htm

Dan O'Canna
Tech III
Kentucky Division of Mines and Minerals (220)
Mine Map Information Center
Mine Map Repository
P.O. 2244
Frankfort, KY 40601
Phone: 502-573-0140
Web: minemaps.ky.gov

Jim O'Donnell
Geological and Planetary Sciences Librarian
California Institute of Technology (64)
Geological and Planetary Sciences Library
Map Room
Geology Library 100-23
Pasadena, CA 91125
Phone: 626-395-6699
Fax: 626-568-0935
Email: jimodo@caltech.edu
Web: library.caltech.edu

Lenora A. Oftedahl
StreamNet Regional Librarian;
Columbia River Inter-Tribal Fish Commission (404)
StreamNet Library

729 NE Oregon Street
Suite 190
Portland, OR 97232
Phone: 503-731-1304
Fax: 503-731-1260
Web: www.fishlib.org

Marilee Ohnstad
Circulation/Map Assistant
University of Wyoming (561)
Brinkerhoff Earth Resources Information Center
Department 3006
1000 University Avenue
Laramie, WY 82071
Phone: 307-766-3374
Fax: 307-766-6679
Web: www-lib.uwyo.edu/uwlibs/geo.htm

Maureen Olle
Government Information/Microforms Librarian
Louisiana State University (229)
Troy H. Middleton Library
Government Documents/Microforms Department
53 Middleton
Baton Rouge, LA 70803
Phone: 225-578-2570
Fax: 225-578-6535
Email: molle@lsu.edu
Web: www.lib.lsu.edu/govdocs

John Olson
Maps/GIS Librarian
Syracuse University (346)
Library
Maps and Government Information
Room 358
Bird Library
Syracuse, NY 13244
Phone: 315-443-4176
Fax: 315-443-9510
Email: jaolson@syr.edu
Web: libwww.syr.edu/information/mgi/index.html

Mary Ann O'Neil
Tucson-Pima Public Library (31)
Joel D. Valdez Main Library
Reference Department
101 North Stone Avenue
Tucson, AZ 85701
Phone: 520-791-4393
Email: moneil1@ci.tucson.az.us
Web: www.tppl.org

Camille O'Neill
Reference Librarian
Arizona Western College (33)

Academic Library
P.O. Box 929
Yuma, AZ 85366
Phone: 928-344-7777
Fax: 928-344-7751
Email: camille.oneill@azwestern.edu
Web: www.azwestern.edu/library/

Rachel Onuf
Director of Archives and Collections Management
Historical Society of Pennsylvania (422)
Library Division
Archives
1300 Locust Street
Philadelphia, PA 19107
Phone: 215-732-6200
Fax: 215-732-2680
Email: ronuf@hsp.org
Web: www.hsp.org

Mike Orwell
Reference Librarian
New Castle Public Library (419)
207 East North Street
New Castle, PA 16101
Phone: 724-658-6659
Fax: 724-658-9012
Web: www.newcastle.lib.pa.us

Betty Osborn
University of Central Arkansas (34)
Torreyson Library
University of Central Arkansas
Archives Map Collection
201 Donaghey
Conway, AR 72035
Phone: 501-450-3418
Fax: 501-450-5208
Web: www.uca.edu

Judith G. Otteman
Staff Assistant
University of Nebraska, Lincoln (310)
Conservation and Survey Division/SNR
102 Nebraska Hall
Lincoln, NE 68588-0517
Phone: 402-472-7523 or 402-472-3471
Fax: 402-472-4542
Email: jotteman1@unl.edu
Web: csd.unl.edu/csd.htm

Penny Pace-Cannon
Manager 4th Floor Reference
Indianapolis-Marion County Public Library (191)
Central Library
40 East Street Clair Street

Indianapolis, IN 46202
Phone: 317-269-1700
Fax: 317-268-5229
Web: imcpl.org

Philip J. Panum
Special Collections Librarian
Denver Public Library (103)
Western History Collection
10 West 14th Avenue Parkway
Denver, CO 80204
Phone: 720-865-1821
Fax: 720-865-1880
Email: ppanum@denver.lib.co.us
Web: www.denver.lib.co.us

Coleen Parmer
Bowling Green State University (373)
Jerome Library
Government Documents
Ridge Street
Bowling Green, OH 43403
Phone: 419-372-2142
Fax: 419-372-7996
Email: parmer@bgnet.bgsu.edu
Web: www.bgsu.edu/colleges/library/services/govdocs/
index.html

Abraham Parrish
GIS Specialist
Yale University (119)
Sterling Memorial Library
Map Collection
130 Wall Street
P.O. Box 208240
New Haven, CT 06520
Phone: 203-432-1867
Fax: 203-432-8527
Web: www.library.yale.edu/MapColl

Robert Parson
Head
Utah State University (500)
Merrill Library
Special Collections
3000 Old Main Hill
Logan, UT 84322-3000
Phone: 435-797-2663
Email: bobpar@ngw.lib.usu.edu

Jim Parsons
Associate Director for Public Services
Saint John's University (276)
Alcuin Library
Collegeville, MN 56321

Phone: 320-363-2122
Fax: 320-363-2126
Email: jparsons@csbsju.edu
Web: www.csbsju.edu/library

Kathy A. Parsons
Head Stacks and Service Desks
Iowa State University (199)
Parks Library
Map Room
281 Parks Library, Iowa State University
Ames, IA 50011-2140
Phone: 515-294-3956
Fax: 515-294-5525
Email: kap@iastate.edu
Web: www.lib.iastate.edu/libinfo/dept/maproom.html

Matthew Parsons
Map Librarian
University of Washington (537)
Suzzallo/Allen Library
Map Collection and Cartographic Information Services
Box 352900
Seattle, WA 98195
Phone: 206-543-9392
Fax: 206-685-8049
Email: parsonsm@u.washington.edu
Web: www.lib.washington.edu/maps

Sharon Partridge
Government Documents Librarian
Jefferson County Public Library (111)
Lakewood Library
Government Documents
10200 West 20th Avenue
Lakewood, CO 80215
Phone: 303-232-9507
Fax: 303-275-2234
Email: sharonp@jefferson.lib.co.us
Web: jefferson.lib.co.us

Stephen A. Patrick
East Tennessee State University (461)
Charles C. Sherrod Library
Documents/Law/Maps Department
P.O. Box 78665
Johnson City, TN 37614
Phone: 423-439-5334
Fax: 423-439-5674
Email: patricks@mail.etsu.edu

Kathy Payne
Head of Reference and Information Services
Weber State University (501)
Stewart Library

2901 University Circle
Ogden, UT 84408-2901
Phone: 801-626-6511
Fax: 801-626-7045
Email: KLPayne@weber.edu
Web: library.weber.edu/ref/government/mapsguide.cfm

Jennifer Pendergast
Library Technical Assistant
University of North Carolina, Chapel Hill (352)
Wilson Library
Davis Reference/Maps Collection
CB#3928
Chapel Hill, NC 27514-8890
Phone: 919-962-3028
Fax: 919-962-4452
Web: www.lib.unc.edu/maps and www.lib.unc.edu

Sara Penhale
Reference Librarian
Earlham College (195)
Wildman Science Library
P.O. Box 72
Richmond, IN 47374
Phone: 765-983-1245
Email: sarap@earlham.edu
Web: www.earlham.edu/~libr/wildman/

Harry Perkins
Maps/Government Documents Technician
Minnesota State University, Mankato (278)
Memorial Library
P.O. Box 8419
Mankato, MN 56002-8419
Phone: 507-389-5952
Fax: 507-389-5155

Joanne M. Perry
Maps Librarian and Head of
   Cartographic Information Services
Pennsylvania State University (427)
University Libraries
Maps Library
001 Paterno Library
University Park, PA 16802
Phone: 814-863-0094
Fax: 814-863-3560
Email: jup4@psulias.psu.edu
Web: www.libraries.psu.edu/maps

Gretchen Persohn
Head of Reference Services
State Library of Ohio (385)
Government Information Services
274 East First Avenue

Columbus, OH 43201
Phone: 614-644-7051
Fax: 614-752-9178
Email: gpersohn@sloma.state.oh.us
Web: winslo.state.oh.us

Susan Peschel
Senior Academic Librarian
University of Wisconsin, Milwaukee (551)
American Geographical Society Library
2311 East Hartford Avenue
Milwaukee, WI 53211
Phone: 414-229-6282
Fax: 414-229-3624
Web: www.uwm.edu/Libraries/AGSL/index.html

Carol Peterson
Archivist
San Mateo County History Museum (66)
Archives
777 Hamilton Street
Redwood City, CA 94063
Phone: 650-299-0104 x22
Fax: 650-299-0141
Email: carol@samhist.com
Web: www.sanmateocountyhistory.com

Karrie Peterson
North Carolina State University (363)
D.H. Hill Library
2205 Hillsborough Street
Campus Box 7111
Raleigh, NC 27695-7114
Phone: 919-515-2935
Fax: 919-515-8264
Email: karrie_peterson@ncsu.edu
Web: www.lib.ncsu.edu/risd/govdocs

Theresa Peterson
Map Librarian
Phoenix Public Library (24)
Burton Barr Central Library
1221 North Central Avenue
Phoenix, AZ 85004
Phone: 602-262-4636
Fax: 602-261-8751
Email: theresa.peterson@phxlib.org
Web: www.phxlib.org

Sylvia Pham
Reference and Maps Librarian
Kutztown University (417)
Rohrbach Library
Maps Department
15200 Kutztown Road

Building 5
Kutztown, PA 19530
Phone: 610-683-4813
Email: spham@kutztown.edu
Web: www.kutztown.edu/library/maps.htm

Dave Philbin
Mining Engineer
Office of Surface Mining Reclamation
   and Enforcement (429)
Anthracite (Coal) Mine Map Repository
Branch of Anthracite-MMR
7 North Wilkes-Barre Boulevard
Suite 308
Wilkes-Barre, PA 18702-5293
Phone: 570-830-1400
Fax: 570-830-1421
Web: mmr.osmre.gov

John C. Phillips
Map Librarian
University of Toledo (394)
William S. Carlson
Map Collection
2801 West Bancroft Street
Toledo, OH 43606-3390
Phone: 419-530-2865
Fax: 419-530-2542
Email: John.Phillips@toledo.edu
Web: www.cl.utoledo.edu

Pamela Piatchek
Library Specialist
Northern Arizona University (18)
Cline Library
Special Collections and Archives Department
Box 6022
Flagstaff, AZ 86011-6022
Phone: 928-523-5551
Fax: 928-523-3770
Web: www.nau.edu/library/speccoll

Carolyn M. Picciano
Library Specialist
Connecticut State Library (115)
History and Genealogy Unit
231 Capitol Avenue
Hartford, CT 06106
Phone: 860-757-6580
Fax: 860-757-6677
Email: cpicciano@cslib.org
Web: www.cslib.org

Layne Pierce
Reference Librarian
Lincoln City Libraries (305)

136 South 14th Street
Lincoln, NE 68508
Phone: 402-441-8530
Fax: 402-441-8534
Email: l.pierce@mail.lcl.lib.ne.us
Web: www.lcl.lib.ne.us

Linda Pine
Archivist
University of Arkansas, Little Rock (39)
Ottenhimer Library
2801 South University Avenue
Little Rock, AR 72204
Phone: 501-569-8806
Fax: 501-569-3017
Web: library1.ualr.edu

Keith Pitts
Cartographer
University of Akron (371)
Department of Geography and Planning
Map Room
Akron, OH 44325-5005
Phone: 330-972-7620
Fax: 330-972-6080
Email: kpitts@uakron.edu

Elissa Plank
Library Assistant
Louisiana State University (229)
Troy H. Middleton Library
Government Documents/Microforms Department
53 Middleton
Baton Rouge, LA 70803
Phone: 225-578-2570
Fax: 225-578-6535
Web: www.lib.lsu.edu/govdocs

Mark Plotkin
Librarian
Miami-Dade Public Library System (137)
Main Library
Social Science and the Florida Room
101 West Flagler Street
Miami, FL 33130
Phone: 305-375-5575
Fax: 305-375-3048
Web: www.mdpls.org

Daniel Plumlee
Equipment/Collections Manager
University of California, Berkeley (45)
Department of Geography
Map Collection
507 McCone Hall #4740
Berkeley, CA 94720

Phone: 510-642-4368
Fax: 510-642-3370
Email: dplum@socrates.berkeley.edu
Web: geography.berkeley.edu

Michael Plunkett
Director
University of Virginia (513)
Special Collections Department
Alderman Library
Charlottesville, VA 22904
Phone: 434-924-3025
Fax: 434-924-4968
Email: mssbks@virginia.edu
Web: www.lib.virginia.edu

Stephen Pomes
United States Department of the Interior,
    Minerals Management Service (232)
Minerals Management Service Library
1201 Elmwood Park Boulevard
New Orleans, LA 70123
Phone: 504-736-2521
Fax: 504-736-2525
Email: stephen.pomes@mms.gov

Doug Popwell
Engineering Aide
Washington State Department of Natural Resources (530)
Public Land Survey Office
P.O. Box 47060
Olympia, WA 98504-7060
Phone: 360-902-1190
Fax: 360-902-1191
Web: www.dnr.wa.gov/htdocs/plso/

Ed Poston
Reference and Instruction Librarian
Berea College (218)
Hutchins Library
Berea, KY 40404
Phone: 850-985-3172
Email: ed_poston@berea.edu
Web: www.berea.edu/hutchinslibrary

Jonathan Potter
Reference and Instruction Librarian
Eastern Washington University (525)
JFK Library
Maps
816 F Street, 100 LIB
Cheney, WA 99004
Phone: 509-359-2263
Fax: 509-359-6456
Web: www.library.ewu.edu/collections/maps.html

Celia D. Pratt
Map Librarian
University of North Carolina, Chapel Hill (352)
Wilson Library
Davis Reference/Maps Collection
CB#3928
Chapel Hill, NC 27514-8890
Phone: 919-962-3028
Fax: 919-962-4452
Email: cdpmaps@email.unc.edu
Web: www.lib.unc.edu/maps and www.lib.unc.edu

Leah Prescott
Manuscripts and Archives Librarian
Mystic Seaport (117)
G.W. Blunt White Library
Charts and Maps Collection
75 Greenmanville Avenue
Mystic, CT 06355
Phone: 860-572-0711
Fax: 860-572-5394
Email: leah.prescott@mysticseaport.org
Web: schooner.mysticseaport.org

Jennifer Price
Government Document Technical Assistant
Frostburg State University (246)
Lewis J. Ort Library
User Services Division
1 Stadium Drive
Frostburg, MD 21532
Phone: 301-687-4887
Fax: 301-687-7069
Web: www.frostburg.edu/dept/library/library.htm

Hallie Pritchett
Library Assistant III
University of Minnesota (281)
O.M. Wilson Library
John R. Borchert Map Library
309 19th Avenue South
Minneapolis, MN 55455
Phone: 612-624-4549
Fax: 612-626-9353
Web: map.lib.umn.edu

Mary Prophet
Deputy Library Director
Denison University (389)
William Howard Doane Library
Geology Department/Government Documents
Granville, OH 43023
Phone: 740-587-5644
Fax: 740-587-6285
Email: prophet@Denison.edu

Nancy Pugh
LTA, Maps/Fiche
University of South Alabama (4)
University Library
307 University Boulevard
Mobile, AL 36688-0002
Phone: 251-460-7024
Fax: 251-461-1628

Aaron Purcell
University of Tennessee (466)
Special Collections—Hoskins Library
1401 Cumberland Avenue
Knoxville, TN 37996-4000
Phone: 865-974-4480
Fax: 865-974-0560
Web: www.lib.utk.edu/spcoll

Devon Pyle-Vowles
Collections Manager
Adler Planetarium and Astronomy Museum (163)
History of Astronomy Research Center
1300 South Lake Shore Drive
Chicago, IL 60605
Phone: 312-322-0594
Fax: 312-341-9935
Email: astrohistory@adlernet.org
Web: www.adlerplanetarium.or

Richard Quartaroli
Special Collections Librarian
Northern Arizona University (18)
Cline Library
Special Collections and Archives Department
Box 6022
Flagstaff, AZ 86011-6022
Phone: 928-523-5551
Fax: 928-523-3770
Web: www.nau.edu/library/speccoll

Christina Ramos
Documents Clerk
Saint Mary's University (497)
Blume Library
One Camino Santa Maria
San Antonio, TX 78228
Phone: 210-436-3441
Fax: 210-436-3782
Web: library.stmarytx.edu/acadlib/doc/maps/mapintro
.htm

Roberta Y. Rand
Library Director
University of Miami (138)
Rosenstiel School of Marine and Atmospheric Science
   Library

4600 Rickenbacker Causeway
Miami, FL 33149-1098
Phone: 305-361-4060
Fax: 305-361-9306
Email: rrand@rsmas.miami.edu
Web: www.rsmas.miami.edu/support/lib/

Randall Raper
Library Assistant III
Tennessee Technological University (460)
Angelo and Jennette Volpe Library and Media Center
1100 North Peachtree Avenue
Cookeville, TN 38505
Phone: 931-372-3326
Fax: 931-372-6112
Web: www.tntech.edu/govpub/

Paul Rascoe
University of Texas, Austin (481)
Perry-Castañeda Library
Map Collection
Austin, TX 78713
Phone: 512-495-4275
Fax: 512-495-4296
Web: www.lib.utexas.edu/

Kevin Ray
Institutional Records Assistant
University of Alabama (7)
W. S. Hoole Special Collections Library
Box 870266
Tuscaloosa, AL 35487-0266
Phone: 205-348-0500
Fax: 205-348-1699
Web: www.lib.ua.edu/libraries/hoole/

Melissa Raymer
Federal/Maps Assistant
Duke University (356)
Public Documents and Maps Department
025 Perkins Library
Durham, NC 27708-0177
Phone: 919-660-5851
Fax: 919-684-2855
Web: docs.lib.duke.edu/maps/

Lisa Raymond
Catalog Librarian
Woods Hole Oceanographic Institution (259)
MBL/WHOI Library
Data Library and Archives
266 Woods Hole Road
MS8
Woods Hole, MA 02543
Phone: 508-289-2497

Fax: 508-289-2183
Email: lraymond@whoi.edu
Web: www.mblwhoilibrary.mbl.edu

Ilene Raynes
Library Technician III
University of Colorado, Boulder (95)
Jerry Crail Johnson Earth Sciences and Map Library
Map Library
184 UCB
Boulder, CO 80309
Phone: 303-492-7578
Fax: 303-735-4879
Web: www-libraries.colorado.edu/ps/map/

Mac Reed
Fort Hays State University (209)
Forsyth Library
600 Park Street
Hays, KS 67601
Phone: 785-628-4340
Fax: 785-628-4096
Email: mreed@fhsu.edu

Betsy Reese
Map Curator
Bryn Mawr College (414)
Collier Science Library
Geologic Map Library
101 North Merion Avenue
Bryn Mawr, PA 19010
Phone: 610-526-7462
Email: breese@brynmawr.edu
Web: www.brynmawr.edu/geology

Terry Reese
Cataloger
Oregon State University (399)
The Valley Library
Map Collection
121 The Valley Library
Corvallis, OR 97331-4501
Phone: 541-737-7295
Fax: 541-737-8224
Web: osulibrary.oregonstate.edu/research/guides/maps/
maproom.htm

Rebecca Reid-Johansson
Library Assistant
California State University, Fresno (52)
Henry Madden Library
Map Library
5200 West Barton Avenue M/S ML34
Fresno, CA 93740-8014
Phone: 559-278-2405

Fax: 559-278-6952
Web: www.lib.csufresno.edu/subjectresources/maps/

Susan Remer
Senior Librarian Technician
University of Florida (135)
George A. Smathers Libraries
Map and Imagery Library
P.O.Box 11701
110 Marston Science Library
Gainesville, FL 32611-7011
Phone: 352-392-2825
Fax: 352-392-4787
Web: web.uflib.ufl.edu/maps

Rebecca Renz
Senior Cataloger
Indiana Historical Society (189)
William Henry Smith Memorial Library
450 West Ohio Street
Indianapolis, IN 46202-3269
Phone: 317-232-1879
Fax: 317-234-0169
Web: www.indianahistory.org

Janice Rice
Microforms Coordinator
East Carolina University (360)
Joyner Library
Government Documents and Microforms
E. 5th Street
Greenville, NC 27858-4353
Phone: 252-328-0238
Fax: 252-328-2271
Web: www.lib.ecu.edu/govdoc/index.html

Keith Rice
University of Wisconsin, Stevens Point (556)
Learning Resources Center (LRC)
UWSP Map Center
Science Building
Stevens Point, WI 54481
Phone: 715-346-2629
Fax: 715-346-3372
Email: krice@uwsp.edu
Web: www.uwsp.edu/geo/internet/geog_geol_resources
.html

Judith Rice-Jones
Social Sciences Librarian
University of Colorado, Colorado Springs (99)
Kraemer Family Library
1420 Austin Bluffs Parkway
Colorado Springs, CO 80918
Phone: 719-262-3295

Fax: 719-528-5227
jricejon@uccs.edu
Web: web.uccs.edu/library/

Nancy Richard
Director of the Library and Special Collections
Bostonian Society (252)
Library and Special Collections
206 Washington Street
Boston, MA 02109
Phone: 617-720-1713 x12
Fax: 617-720-3289
Web: www.bostonhistory.org

Lori Ricigliano
Associate Director
University of Puget Sound (539)
Collins Memorial Library
1500 North Warner
Tacoma, WA 98416-1012
Phone: 253-879-3669
Fax: 253-879-3670
Email: ricigliano@ups.edu
Web: library.ups.edu/research/govt/about.htm

Kim Ricker
Graduate Assistant
University of Maryland, College Park (245)
McKeldin Library
Government Documents and Maps
4118 McKeldin Library
College Park, MD 20742
Phone: 301-405-9165
Fax: 301-314-5651
Web: www.lib.umd.edu/gov/maproom.html

Carla Rickerson
Head
University of Washington (538)
Suzzallo/Allen Library
Special Collections
Box 352900
Seattle, WA 98195
Phone: 206-543-1929
Fax: 206-543-1931
Email: crick@u.washington.edu
Web: www.lib.washington.edu/specialcoll

Noreen Riffe
Pueblo City-County Library District (113)
Robert Hoag Rawlings Public Library
Western Research Map Collection
100 East Abriendo Avenue
Pueblo, CO 81004
Phone: 719-562-5626

Fax: 719-553-0327
Email: noreen@pueblolibrary.org
Web: www.pueblolibrary.org

Dale B. Riordan
Science Librarian
Franklin and Marshall College (418)
Martin Library of the Sciences
P.O. Box 3003
Lancaster, PA 17604
Phone: 717-291-3843
Fax: 717-291-4088
Email: dale.riordan@fandm.edu
Web: library.fandm.edu

Jovanka Ristic
Senior Reference Academic Librarian
University of Wisconsin, Milwaukee (551)
American Geographical Society Library
2311 East Hartford Avenue
Milwaukee, WI 53211
Phone: 414-229-6282
Fax: 414-229-3624
Web: www.uwm.edu/Libraries/AGSL/index.html

Nancy Ritchey
Geoscience Library Assistant
University of Iowa (204)
Geoscience Library
136 Trowbridge Hall
Iowa City, IA 52242
Phone: 319-335-3084
Fax: 319-335-3419
Web: www.lib.uiowa.edu/geoscience

Lonna Rivera
Government Documents Coordinator
Weber State University (501)
Stewart Library
2901 University Circle
Ogden, UT 84408-2901
Phone: 801-626-6511
Fax: 801-626-7045
Web: library.weber.edu/ref/government/mapsguide.cfm

Terri J. Robar
Special Formats Librarian
University of Miami (132)
Otto G. Richter Library
Government Information and
    Special Formats Department
1300 Memorial Drive
Coral Gables, FL 33124-0320
Phone: 305-284-3155
Fax: 305-284-4027

Email: trobar@miami.edu
Web: www.library.miami.edu/library/mapcollection.html

Dawn Roberts
Natural Resource Technician
Alaska Division of Geological
    and Geophysical Surveys (12)
Library
3354 College Road
Fairbanks, AK 99709-3707
Phone: 907-451-5020
Fax: 907-451-5050
Email: dawn_roberts@dnr.state.ak.us
Web: www.dggs.dnr.state.ak.us

Joan M. Robb
University of Wisconsin, Green Bay (544)
Cofrin Library
2420 Nicolet Drive
Green Bay, WI 54311-7001
Phone: 920-465-2303
Fax: 920-465-2388
Email: robbj@uwgb.edu
Web: www.uwgb.edu/library/

Bertrand Robbins
Library Technician
Portland State University (409)
Millar Library
P.O. Box 1151
Portland, OR 97207-1151
Phone: 503-725-5874
Fax: 503-725-4524
Web: www.lib.pdx.edu/resources/maps_collection/
    index.html

Willard Rocer
Head of Genealogy
Middle Georgia Archives (148)
Washington Memorial Library
Map Collection
1180 Washington Avenue
Macon, GA 31201
Phone: 478-744-0820
Fax: 478-744-0893
Email: rockerw@mailb.bibb.public.lib.ga.us
Web: www.co.bibb.public.lib.ga.us

Ken Rockwell
Map Librarian
University of Utah (504)
Marriott Library
Science and Engineering Map Collection
295 South 1500 East
Salt Lake City, UT 84112-0860

Phone: 801-581-7533
Email: ken.rockwell@library.utah.edu

Pauline Roddan
Library Assistant III
University of California, Davis (51)
Peter J. Shields Library
Government Information and Maps
100 NW Quad
Davis, CA 95616
Phone: 530-752-1689
Fax: 530-752-3148
Web: www.lib.ucdavis.edu/govdoc/MapCollection/
    map_about.html

Susana Rodriguez
Library Assistant
University of Texas, El Paso (490)
500 West University
El Paso, TX 79968
Phone: 915-747-6702
Fax: 915-747-5327
Web: libraryweb.utep.edu

Paulette Rogers
Library Technician
Louisiana State University (229)
Troy H. Middleton Library
Government Documents/Microforms Department
53 Middleton
Baton Rouge, LA 70803
Phone: 225-578-2570
Fax: 225-578-6535
Web: www.lib.lsu.edu/govdocs

Steve Rogers
Map Librarian
Ohio State University (384)
William Oxley Thompson (Main) Library
Map Room
211 Main Library, 1858 Neil Avenue Mall
Columbus, OH 43210
Phone: 614-688-8774
Fax: 614-292-7859
Email: rogers.20@osu.edu
Web: library.osu.edu/sites/maps/

Hazel Romero
Library Assistant
Palace of the Governors (335)
Angélico Chávez History Library
Map Collection
120 Washington Avenue
Santa Fe, NM 87501
Phone: 505-476-5090

Fax: 505-476-5053
Web: www.palaceofthegovernors.org/library.html

Roseanne Rosenberg
Librarian
Mohave Museum of History and Art (19)
400 West Beale Street
Kingman, AZ 86401
Phone: 928-753-3195
Fax: 928-718-1562
Web: www.mohavemuseum.org

Martha Rosson
Reference Librarian
Knox County Public Library (462)
East Tennessee History Center
Calvin M. McClung Historical Collection
314 West Clinch Avenue
Knoxville, TN 37902-2313
Phone: 865-215-8801
Fax: 865-215-8810
Web: www.knoxlib.org

Gwen Roy
Washington State Department of Natural Resources (530)
Public Land Survey Office
P.O. Box 47060
Olympia, WA 98504-7060
Phone: 360-902-1190
Fax: 360-902-1191
Email: gwen.roy@wadnr.gov
Web: www.dnr.wa.gov/htdocs/plso/

Roxanne Roy
Administrative Assistant
Historical Society of Cheshire County (327)
246 Main Street
P.O. Box 803
Keene, NH 3431
Phone: 603-352-1895
Web: www.hsccnh.org

Lynn Rueff
Manager Indiana History
New Albany-Floyd County Public Library (194)
180 West Spring Street
New Albany, IN 47150
Phone: 812-949-3527
Fax: 812-949-3733
Email: lrueff@nafcpl.lib.in.us
Web: www.nafcpl.lib.in.us

Alan Rumrill
Director
Historical Society of Cheshire County (327)
246 Main Street

P.O. Box 803
Keene, NH 3431
Phone: 603-352-1895
Email: diresctor@hsccnh.org
Web: www.hsccnh.org

David M. Rumsey
President
David Rumsey Collection (74)
Cole Valley
San Francisco, CA 94117
Phone: 415-386-1750
Fax: 415-386-1781
Email: rumsey@luna-img.com
Web: www.davidrumsey.com

Evan Rusch
Government Documents/Instruction Librarian
Minnesota State University, Mankato (278)
Memorial Library
P.O. Box 8419
Mankato, MN 56002-8419
Phone: 507-389-5952
Fax: 507-389-5155
Email: evan.rusch@mnsu.edu

Carol Russell
University of Texas, Austin (480)
Nettie Lee Benson Latin American Collection
Rare Books and Manuscripts Division
The General Libraries
Austin, TX 78713-8916
Phone: 512-495-4520
Fax: 512-495-4568
Web: www.lib.utexas.edu/benson/

Carol Russell
Map Library Assistant
University of Texas, Austin (482)
Walter Geology Library
Tobin Map Collection
GEO 4.202-S5438
Austin, TX 78712-1101
Phone: 512-495-4680
Fax: 512-495-4102
Web: www.lib.utexas.edu/geo

Judy Ruttenberg
University of California, Irvine (53)
Langson Library
P.O. Box 19557
Irvine, CA 92623-9557
Phone: 949-824-7290
Fax: 949-824-3644
Web: www.lib.uci.edu/libraries/collections/gis.html

Marianne Ryan
University of Maryland, College Park (245)
McKeldin Library
Government Documents and Maps
4118 McKeldin Library
College Park, MD 20742
Phone: 301-405-9165
Fax: 301-314-5651
Email: mryan1@umd.edu
Web: www.lib.umd.edu/gov/maproom.html

Nancy Ryckman
Assistant Head Reference Librarian
University of North Carolina, Greensboro (359)
Jackson Library
Reference Department
P.O. Box 26170
Greensboro, NC 27402-6170
Phone: 336-334-5419
Fax: 336-334-5097
Email: nancy_ryckman@uncg.edu

Joyce Ryerson
Map Room Specialist
Dartmouth College (325)
Baker/Berry Library
Evans Map Room
HB 6025
Hanover, NH 03755
Phone: 603-646-2579
Fax: 603-646-3628
Web: www.dartmouth.edu/~maproom/

Carmen Sacomani
University of Texas, Austin (480)
Nettie Lee Benson Latin American Collection
Rare Books and Manuscripts Division
The General Libraries
Austin, TX 78713-8916
Phone: 512-495-4520
Fax: 512-495-4568
Web: www.lib.utexas.edu/benson/

Laura Saegert
Map Archivist
Texas State Library and Archives (478)
Historic Map Collection
P.O. Box 12927
Austin, TX 78711-2927
Phone: 512-463-5480
Fax: 512-463-5430
Email: lsaegert@tsl.state.tx.us
Web: www.tsl.state.tx.us/arc/maps/index.html

Lori Sailors
Federal Documents Librarian
Nebraska Library Commission (308)

Nebraska Publications Clearinghouse
1200 N Street
Suite 120
Lincoln, NE 68508
Phone: 402-471-2045
Fax: 402-471-2083
Web: www.nlc.state.ne.us/docs/clear.html

Theresa Salazar
Curator of Western Americana
University of California, Berkeley (44)
Bancroft Library
Map Collection
Berkeley, CA 94720
Phone: 510-642-6481
Fax: 510-642-7589

Catherine Sandler
Head Librarian
Charleston Library Society (437)
164 King Street
Charleston, SC 29401
Phone: 843-723-9912
Fax: 843-723-3500
Email: chasLIBSociety@aol.com

Carolyn Sanford
Head of Reference and Instruction,
    Documents Librarian, Map Librarian
Carleton College (283)
Laurence McKinley Gould Library
Map Collection
One North College Street
Northfield, MN 55057
Phone: 507-646-4260
Fax: 507-646-4087
Email: csanford@carleton.edu
Web: www.carleton.edu/campus/library/collections/
    overview.html#maps

Inanama Santos
Librarian
Chicago Public Library (164)
Harold Washington Library Center
Government Publications Department
400 South State Street
Chicago, IL 60605
Phone: 312-747-4508
Fax: 312-747-4516
Web: chipublib.org

Sarah Santos
Head
Government Documents
University of Arkansas (35)
Libraries

Government Documents / Map Collection
365 North Ozark Avenue
Fayetteville, AR 72701
Phone: 479-575-5516
Fax: 479-575-6656
Web: libinfo.uark.edu/gis/

Bruce Sarjeant
Maps/GIS Librarian
Texas Tech University (493)
University Library
Government Documents Map Collection
18th and Boston
Lubbock, TX 79409-0002
Phone: 806-742-2268
Fax: 806-742-1332
Email: bruce.sarjeant@ttu.edu
Web: library.ttu.edu/ul/maps/

Laura Sare
Documents Librarian
West Texas A&M University (483)
Cornette Library
P.O. Box 60748
Canyon, TX 79016
Phone: 806-651-2205
Fax: 806-651-2213
Email: lsare@mail.wtamu.edu
Web: www.wtamu.edu/library/documents/docsmaps
.shtml

Stefan Sarenius
Coordinator, Maps and Microforms
Western Michigan University (269)
Waldo Library
Map Department
1903 West Michigan Avenue
Kalamazoo, MI 49008
Phone: 269-387-5047
Email: Michael.McDonnell@wmich.edu
Web: www.wmich.edu/library/depts/maps/index.html

Robert Sathrum
Natural Resources Librarian
Humboldt State University (41)
University Library
1 Harpst Street
Arcata, CA 95521
Phone: 707-442-3418
Fax: 707-442-4900
Email: rls2@humboldt.edu
Web: library.humboldt.edu/infoservices/atmapcoll.htm

Robert Saunderson
Berkeley Public Library (43)
2090 Kittredge Street

Berkeley, CA 94704
Phone: 510-981-6148
Fax: 510-981-6246
Email: bos2@ci.berkeley.ca.us
Web: www.berkeley-public.org

Julie Sayles, Sr.
Library Technical Assistant
University of South Florida (139)
Tampa Library
Reference/Documents—Map Collection
4202 East Fowler Avenue
LIB 122
Tampa, FL 33620-5400
Phone: 813-974-2729
Fax: 813-974-9875
Web: www.lib.usf.edu/tampa/govdocs/

Karen Schatz
Cataloging Assistant
Eastern Washington University (525)
JFK Library
Maps
816 F Street, 100 LIB
Cheney, WA 99004
Phone: 509-359-2263
Fax: 509-359-6456
Web: www.library.ewu.edu/collections/maps.html

Paul Schlotthauer
Librarian/Assistant Professor
Pratt Institute (337)
Library
200 Willoughby Avenue
Brooklyn, NY 11205
Phone: 718-636-3704
Fax: 718-399-4220
Email: pschlott@pratt.edu
Web: lib.pratt.edu/public

Joseph Schneider
Government Documents Librarian
Augusta State University (146)
Reese Library
2500 Walton Way
Augusta, GA 30904-2200
Phone: 706-737-1748
Fax: 706-667-4415
Email: jschneider@aug.edu
Web: www.aug.edu

Alan Schuck
Information Technology Librarian
Arizona Western College (33)
Academic Library

P.O. Box 929
Yuma, AZ 85366
Phone: 928-344-7777
Fax: 928-344-7751
Web: www.azwestern.edu/library/

Vanette Schwartz
Social Sciences and Maps Librarian
Illinois State University (171)
Milner Library
Social Sciences Division
Campus Box 8900
Normal, IL 61790-8900
Phone: 309-438-3486
Fax: 309-438-3676
Email: vmschwa@ilstu.edu

Mary W. Scott
Librarian
Ohio State University (383)
Orton Memorial Library of Geology
180 Orton Hall
155 South Oval Drive
Columbus, OH 43210
Phone: 614-292-2428
Email: scott.36@osu.edu
Web: library.osu.edu/sites/geology

Peggy Scott
Documents Assistant
Bradley University (173)
Cullom-Davis Library
1501 West Bradley Avenue
Peoria, IL 61625
Phone: 309-677-2840
Fax: 309-677-2558
Email: scott @bumail.bradley.edu
Web: library.bradley.edu

Sally J. Scott
Department Head
University of Wyoming (561)
Brinkerhoff Earth Resources Information Center
Department 3006
1000 University Avenue
Laramie, WY 82071
Phone: 307-766-3374
Fax: 307-766-6679
Email: sscott@uwyo.edu
Web: www-lib.uwyo.edu/uwlibs/geo.htm

Tim Seaman
ARMS Program Manager
Laboratory of Anthropology (333)
Library

Archeological Records Management System
708 Camino Lejo
Santa Fe, NM 87503
Phone: 505-476-1275
Fax: 505-476-1320
Email: seaman@arms.state.nm.us
Web: potsuii.arms.state.nm.us

Susan Searcy
Nevada State Library and Archives (319)
100 North Stewart Street
Carson City, NV 89701-4285
Phone: 775-684-3310
Fax: 775-684-3371
Web: dmla.clan.lib.nv.us/docs/nsla/archives/

Sandy Seeley
Ohio University (372)
Alden Library
Government Documents and Maps Collection
Park Place
Athens, OH 45701
Phone: 740-593-2718
Fax: 740-593-2719
Web: www.library.ohiou.edu/libinfo/depts/maps/index
.htm

Marsha L. Selmer
Map Librarian
University of Illinois, Chicago (167)
Richard J. Daley Library
Map Section
801 South Morgan Street
Chicago, IL 60607
Phone: 312-996-2738
Fax: 312-413-0424
Web: www.uic.edu/depts/library/

Gail Sewell
Library Technical Associate
Catawba College (365)
Corriher-Linn-Black Library
2300 West Innes Street
Salisbury, NC 28144
Phone: 704-637-4379
Fax: 704-637-4304

Leslie Shahi
Physical Sciences Librarian responsible
for Earth and Environmental Sciences
Dartmouth College (326)
Kresge Physical Sciences Library
6115 Fairchild Center
Hanover, NH 3755
Phone: 603-646-3563

Fax: 603-646-3681
Web: www.dartmouth.edu/~krescook/index.shtml

Kathryn H. Shelton
Alaska State Library (14)
Historical Collections
P.O. Box 110571
Juneau, AK 99811-0571
Phone: 907-465-2925
Fax: 907-465-2990
Web: www.library.state.ak.us/hist/hist.html

Emily Shen-Torbik
Head Librarian
United States Geological Survey, Menlo Park (59)
Library
345 Middlefield Road
MS 955
Menlo Park, CA 94025
Phone: 650-329-5027
Fax: 650-329-5132
Email: eshen-torbik@usgs.gov
Web: library.usgs.gov

Michael Sherbon
Pennsylvania Historical and Museum Commission (416)
Pennsylvania State Archives
Division of Archives and Manuscripts
350 North Street
Harrisburg, PA 17120-0090
Phone: 717-783-3281
Fax: 717-787-4822
Email: msherbon@state.pa.us
Web: www.phmc.state.pa.us/bah/dam/mg/mg11.htm

Terri Sheridan
Librarian
Santa Barbara Museum of Natural History (87)
Library
2559 Puesta del Sol Road
Santa Barbara, CA 93105
Phone: 805-682-4711
Fax: 805-569-3170
Email: tsheridan@sbnature2.org
Web: www.sbnature.org/library/index.htm

David B. Shirley
Documents and Map Librarian
Central Michigan University (272)
Charles V. Park Library
300 East Preston Street
Mount Pleasant, MI 48859
Phone: 989-774-3414
Fax: 989-774-1350
Email: David.B.Shirley@cmich.edu

Brian Shovers
Reference Historian
Montana Historical Society (298)
Research Center
225 North Roberts
P.O. Box 201201
Helena, MT 59620
Phone: 406-444-2681
Fax: 406-444-5297
Email: bshovers@state.mt.us
Web: www.montanahistoricalsociety.org

Steve Shuman
Map Room Supervisor
Iowa State University (199)
Parks Library
Map Room
281 Parks Library
Ames, IA 50011-2140
Phone: 515-294-3956
Fax: 515-294-5525
Web: www.lib.iastate.edu/libinfo/dept/maproom
  .html

Emily Sieger
State Government Information Coordinator
Wyoming State Library (559)
Statewide Information Services
2301 Capitol Avenue
Cheyenne, WY 82002
Phone: 307-777-6333
Fax: 307-777-5920
Web: www-wsl.state.wy.us

Lena Simms
Library Assistant
Santa Barbara Museum of Natural History (87)
Library
2559 Puesta del Sol Road
Santa Barbara, CA 93105
Phone: 805-682-4711
Fax: 805-569-3170
Web: www.sbnature.org/library/index.htm

Lynn Simonelli
Curator of Anthropology/Collections Manager
Dayton Society of Natural History (387)
Library and Map Collection
2600 DeWeese Parkway
Dayton, OH 45414
Phone: 937-275-7431
Fax: 937-275-5811
Email: lsimonelli@boonshoftmuseum.org
Web: www.boonshoftmuseum.org

Jacquelyn Sims
Head of Library Information
Catawba College (365)
Corriher-Linn-Black Library
2300 West Innes Street
Salisbury, NC 28144
Phone: 704-637-4379
Fax: 704-637-4304
Email: jsims@catawba.edu

Kitty Siu
Library Assistant
Auburn University (1)
Library
231 Mell Street
Auburn University, AL 36849-5606
Phone: 334-844-1759
Fax: 334-844-4461
Web: www.lib.auburn.edu/govdocs/

Jeremy Skinner
Assistant Archivist
Lewis and Clark College (405)
Aubrey Watzek Library
Special Collections
0615 SW Palatine Hill Road
Portland, OR 97219
Phone: 503-768-7254
Fax: 5037687282
Web: www.lclark.edu/~archives/specialcollections

Alex Slater
Operations Manager
University of Kansas (210)
Anschutz Library
Thomas R. Smith Map Collections
1301 Hoch Auditoria Drive
Lawrence, KS 66045
Phone: 785-864-4420
Fax: 785-864-4420
Web: www2.lib.ku.edu/mapscoll/

Brenda J. Smith
Rare Imprints Cataloger
Kentucky Historical Society (221)
Thomas D. Clark Library and Special Collections
100 West Broadway
Frankfort, KY 40601
Phone: 502-564-1792
Fax: 502-564-4701
Web: history.ky.gov/

Charles H. Smith
Science Librarian
Western Kentucky University (219)

Helm-Cravens Library
Maps and Atlases Collection
1 Big Red Way
Bowling Green, KY 42101-3576
Phone: 270-745-6125
Fax: 270-745-6175
Email: charles.smith@wku.edu

Dawn Smith
Department Head, Reference and Government Documents
Florida Atlantic University (129)
S.E. Wimberly Library
777 Glades Road
Boca Raton, FL 33431
Phone: 561-297-3760
Fax: 561-338-3863
Email: dsmith@fau.edu

Jimmy Smith
Government Documents Librarian
Greenville County Library System (449)
South Carolina Room—Government Documents Section
25 Heritage Green Place
Greenville, SC 29601
Phone: 864-242-5000
Fax: 864-232-9656

Michael L. Smith
Northwestern University (169)
Main Library (Evanston Campus)
Government Publications and Maps Department
1970 Campus Drive
Evanston, IL 60202
Phone: 847-491-3130
Fax: 847-491-8306
Email: mls@northwestern.edu
Web: www.library.northwestern.edu/govpub/

Rebecca A. Smith
Curator of Research Materials
Historical Museum of Southern Florida (136)
Charlton W. Tebeau Research Library
101 West Flagler Street
Miami, FL 33130
Phone: 305-375-1492
Fax: 305-372-6313
Email: hasf@historical-museum.org
Web: www.historical-museum.org

Ted Smith
LSIT
Washington State Department of Natural Resources (530)
Public Land Survey Office
P.O. Box 47060

Olympia, WA 98504-7060
Phone: 360-902-1190
Fax: 360-902-1191
Web: www.dnr.wa.gov/htdocs/plso/

David Smolen
Special Collections Librarian
New Hampshire Historical Society (322)
The Tuck Library
Special Collections
30 Park Street
Concord, NH 03301
Phone: 603-228-6688
Fax: 603-224-0463
Email: dsmolen@nhhistory.org
Web: www.nhhistory.org

Elaine Smyth
Curator of Special Collections
Louisiana State University (228)
Hill Memorial Library
Special Collections
Baton Rouge, LA 70803
Phone: 225-578-6551
Fax: 225-578-9425
Email: esmyth@lsu.edu
Web: www.lib.lsu.edu/special

Helen Snow
North Carolina Librarian
Greensboro Public Library (358)
North Carolina Collection
219 North Church Street
Greensboro, NC 27402-3178
Phone: 336-335-5430
Fax: 336-335-5416
Email: helen.snow@greensboro-nc.gov
Web: www.greensborolibrary.org

Susan Snyder
Head of Public Services
University of California, Berkeley (44)
Bancroft Library
Map Collection
Berkeley, CA 94720
Phone: 510-642-6481
Fax: 510-642-7589
Email: ssnyder@library.berkeley.edu

Chelle Somsen
South Dakota State Archives (454)
900 Governors Drive
Pierre, SD 57501
Phone: 605-773-3804
Fax: 605-7736041

Email: Chelle.Somsen@state.sd.us
Web: www.sdhistory.org/arc/archives.htm

James O. Sorrell
Head, Archival Description Unit
North Carolina Department Office
    of Archives and History (361)
State Archives of North Carolina
4614 Mail Service Center
Raleigh, NC 27699-4614
Phone: 919-807-7310
Fax: 919-733-1354
Email: james.sorrell@ncmail.net
Web: www.ah.dcr.state.nc.us/sections/archives/arch/
    default.htm

Mary Spencer
Geology Library Manager
University of Kentucky (223)
Pirtle Geological Sciences Library and Map Collection
410 King Library Addition
Lexington, KY 40506-0039
Phone: 859-257-5730
Fax: 859-323-3225
Web: www.uky.edu/Libraries

Timothy Spindler
Reference and Information Technology Librarian
Rhode Island College (432)
James P. Adams Library
600 Mount Pleasant Avenue
Providence, RI 2908
Phone: 401-456-8125
Fax: 401-456-1915
Web: www.ric.edu/adamslibrary

Claudene Sproles
Government Documents Reference Librarian
University of Louisville (224)
Ekstrom Library
2301 S Third Street
Louisville, KY 40292
Phone: 502-852-6747
Fax: 502-852-8736
Email: caspro01@louisville.edu
Web: library.louisville.edu/ekstrom/collections/maps.htm

Patti Stafford
Winthrop University (451)
Dacus Library
Government Documents
Oakland Avenue
Rock Hill, SC 29733
Phone: 803-323-2322
Fax: 803-323-2215
Web: www.winthrop.edu/dacus/About/govdoc.htm

Richard W. Starbuck
Assistant Archivist
Moravian Archives (367)
457 South Church Street
Winston-Salem, NC 27101
Phone: 336-722-1742
Fax: 336-725-4514
Web: MoravianArchives.org

Kathryn Steadman
Head of Adult Services
Kalamazoo Public Library (268)
Central Branch
Adult Services/History Room
315 South Rose St
Kalamazoo, MI 49009
Phone: 269-553-7801
Fax: 269-342-0414
Email: Katy@kpl.gov
Web: www.kpl.gov

Bridgit Stearns
Ketchikan Public Library (15)
Adult Division
629 Dock Street
Ketchikan, AK 99901
Phone: 907 225 3331
Fax: 907-225 0153
Email: bridgits@firstcitylibraries.org
Web: www.firstcitylibraries.org

JoAnn Steiger
Reference Assistant
Norfolk Public Library (314)
Reference Department
308 Prospect Avenue
Norfolk, NE 68701
Phone: 402-844-2100
Fax: 402-844-2102
Web: www.ci.norfolk.ne.us/library

Rosemary Steinat
Data Manager
Smithsonian Institution (127)
Regional Planetary Image Facility
Planetary Maps
6th and Independence Avenue, SW
Washington, DC 20560
Phone: 202-633-2480
Fax: 202-786-2566
Web: www.nasm.si.edu/research/ceps/imagery.cfm

Errol Stevens
Loyola Marymount University (57)
Charles Von der Ahe Library

Department of Archives and Special Collections
One LMU Drive
MS 8200
Los Angeles, CA 90045-2659
Phone: 310-338-3048
Fax: 310-338-5895
Email: estevens@lmu.edu

Frank Stieber
Library Specialist Senior
Arizona State University (28)
Noble Science and Engineering Library
Map Collection
P.O. Box 871006
Tempe, AZ 85287-1006
Phone: 480-965-3582
Fax: 480-965-0883
Web: www.asu.edu/lib/hayden/govdocs/maps/mapcoll
.htm

Elizabeth Story
Ohio University (372)
Alden Library
Government Documents and Maps Collection
Park Place
Athens, OH 45701
Phone: 740-593-2718
Fax: 740-593-2719
Web: www.library.ohiou.edu/libinfo/depts/maps/index
.htm

Dewayne Stovall
Western Kentucky University (219)
Helm-Cravens Library
Maps and Atlases Collection
1 Big Red Way
Bowling Green, KY 42101-3576
Phone: 270-745-6125
Fax: 270-745-6175

Rosemary Streatfeild
Science Librarian and Maps Coordinator
Washington State University (534)
Owen Science and Engineering Library
P.O. Box 643200
Pullman, WA 99164
Phone: 509-335-2674
Fax: 509-335-2534
Email: streatfe@wsu.edu

Debra Strelka
Coordinator of Library Processing
University of Wisconsin, Green Bay (544)
Cofrin Library
2420 Nicolet Drive

Green Bay, WI 54311-7001
Phone: 920-465-2303
Fax: 920-465-2388
Web: www.uwgb.edu/library/

Geraldine Strey
Wisconsin Historical Society (549)
Library/Archives Division
Map Collection
816 State Street
Madison, WI 53706
Phone: 608-264-6458
Fax: 608-264-6472
Email: gestrey@whs.wisc.edu
Web: www.wisconsinhistory.org/archives/maps/access
.html

Richard Stringer-Hye
Geology Librarian, Library Technology Coordinator
Vanderbilt University (471)
Stevenson Science and Engineering Library
Map Room
419 21st Avenue South
Nashville, TN 37240
Phone: 615-322-2775
Fax: 615-343-7249
Email: richard.s.stringer-hye@vanderbilt.edu
Web: www.library.vanderbilt.edu/science/maps.html

Kathleen Stroud
Map/GIS Librarian
University of California, Davis (51)
Peter J. Shields Library
Government Information and Maps
100 NW Quad
Davis, CA 95616
Phone: 530-752-1689
Fax: 530-752-3148
Email: kpstroud@ucdavis.edu
Web: www.lib.ucdavis.edu/govdoc/MapCollection/
map_about.html

Jeanne A. Struna
Library Technician
Illinois Valley Community College (172)
Jacobs Library
815 North Orlando Smith Avenue
Oglesby, IL 61348
Phone: 815 224-0306
Fax: 815 224-9147

Lynne Stuart
Government Publications/Maps/Law Librarian
Johns Hopkins University (242)
Eisenhower Library

Government Publications/Maps/Law Library
3400 North Charles Street
Baltimore, MD 21212
Phone: 410-516-8360
Fax: 410-516-6029
Web: www.library.jhu.edu/gpml/

Joy Suh
Government Documents/Maps Librarian
George Mason University (514)
Fenwick Library
Government Documents/Maps
4400 University Dr
Fairfax, VA 22030
Phone: 703-993-2238
Fax: 703-993-2494
Email: hsuh1@gmu.edu
Web: library.gmu.edu/resources/govt/

Cheryl Sund
United States Geological Survey, Denver (105)
Central Region Library
Box 25046
Federal Center
Mail Stop 914
Denver, CO 80225
Phone: 303-236-1000
Fax: 303-236-0015
Email: csund@usgs.gov
Web: library.usgs.gov

Tom Suszek
University of Wisconsin, Oshkosh (553)
Department of Geology
800 Algoma Boulevard
Oshkosh, WI 54901
Phone: 920-424-2268
Fax: 920-424-0240
Email: suszek@uwosh.edu

Johnnie D. Sutherland
Curator of Maps
University of Georgia (141)
Libraries
Map Collection
Athens, GA 20602
Phone: 706-542-0690
Fax: 706-542-6523
Email: jsutherl@uga.edu
Web: www.libs.uga.edu/maproom/index.html

Katelyn Dyani Swan
Library Technical Specialist
University of Illinois, Urbana-Champaign (178)
Map and Geography Library

418 Library
MC-522
1408 West Gregory Dr.
Urbana, IL 61801
Phone: 217-333-0827
Fax: 217-333-2214
Web: www.library.uiuc.edu/max

Julie Sweetkind-Singer
GIS and Map Librarian
Stanford University (91)
Branner Earth Sciences Library and Map Collections
Mitchell Earth Sciences Building
397 Panama Mall
Stanford, CA 94305
Phone: 650-725-1103
Fax: 650-725-2534
Email: sweetkind@stanford.edu
Web: www-sul.stanford.edu/depts/branner/brief_map
.html

Rose Ann Taht
Denver Public Library (102)
Central Branch
Government Publications/GOVPUBS Maps
10 West 14th Avenue Parkway
Denver, CO 80204-2731
Phone: 720-865-1721
Fax: 720-865-1785
Email: rtaht@denver.lib.co.us
Web: www.denverlibrary.org

Vicki Tate
Head, Documents/Serials
University of South Alabama (4)
University Library
307 University Boulevard
Mobile, AL 36688-0002
Phone: 251-460-7024
Fax: 251-461-1628
Email: vtate@jaguar1.usouthal.edu

Anita Taylor Doering
Archivist
La Crosse Public Library (545)
800 Main Street
La Crosse, WI 54601
Phone: 608-789-7122
Fax: 608-789-7161
Email: a.doering@lacrosse.lib.wi.us
Web: www.lacrosselibrary.org

Helen Taylor
Processing Archivist
State Archives of Michigan (271)

P.O. Box 30740
Lansing, MI 48909
Phone: 517-373-1408
Fax: 517-241-1658
Web: www.michigan.gov/statearchives

Ross Taylor
Map Library Manager
University of South Carolina (445)
Thomas Cooper Library
Map Library
Columbia, SC 29208
Phone: 803-777-2802
Fax: 803-777-4661
Web: www.sc.edu/library/maps.html

Suzanne N. Taylor
Reference Librarian
Colorado State University (107)
Morgan Library
Karen W. Jacob Map Collection
Fort Collins, CO 80523-1019
Phone: 970-491-1836
Fax: 970-491-5817
Email: staylor@manta.colostate.edu

Stephen Tellier
Information Services Librarian
Lunar and Planetary Institute (491)
Center for Information and Research Services
3600 Bay Area Blvd
Houston, TX 77059
Phone: 281-486-2182
Fax: 281-486-2186

Wayne C. Temple
Illinois State Archives (175)
MC Norton Building
Springfield, IL 62756
Phone: 217-782-3501
Fax: 217-524-3930
Web: www.cyberdriveillinois.com

Yolanda Theunnissen
Curator
University of Southern Maine (238)
Glickman Family Library
Osher Map Library and Smith Center
for Cartographic Education
P.O. Box 9301
Portland, ME 04104-9301
Phone: 207-780-4850
Fax: 207-780-5310
Email: curator@usm.maine.edu
Web: www.usm.maine.edu/maps

Christopher J.J. Thiry
Map Librarian
Colorado School of Mines (109)
Arthur Lakes Library
Map Room
1400 Illinois
Golden, CO 80401
Phone: 303-273-3697
Fax: 303-273-3199
Email: cthiry@mines.edu
Web: www.mines.edu/library/maproom

Mark Thomas
Map and GIS Librarian
Duke University (356)
Perkins Library
Public Documents and Maps Department
025 Perkins Library
Durham, NC 27708-0177
Phone: 919-660-5851
Fax: 919-684-2855
Email: mark.thomas@duke.edu
Web: docs.lib.duke.edu/maps/

Robert Thomes
Mead Public Library (555)
710 North 8th Street
Sheboygan, WI 53081
Phone: 920-459-3400 x3438
Fax: 920-459-4336
Email: rthomes@esls.lib.wi.us

Thelma B. Thompson
Government Documents and Maps Librarian
University of New Hampshire (324)
Dimond Library
Government Documents/Map Room
18 Library Way
Durham, NH 03824
Phone: 603-862-1777
Fax: 603-862-3403
Email: thelmat@cisunix.unh.edu
Web: docs.unh.edu

Kathryn Thomas
Documents Librarian
North Dakota State University (368)
Library
P.O. Box 5599
Fargo, ND 58105-5599
Phone: 701-231-8863
Fax: 701-231-7138
Email: Kathryn.Thomas@ndsu.nodak.edu
Web: www.lib.ndsu.nodak.edu

Harvey Thorleifson
Director
Minnesota Geological Survey (286)
2642 University Avenue West
Saint Paul, MN 55114-1057
Phone: 612-627-4780
Fax: 612-627-4778
Email: thorleif@umn.edu
Web: www.geo.umn.edu/mgs/

Karen Thornton
Case Western Reserve University (377)
Kelvin Smith Library
11055 Euclid Avenue
Cleveland, OH 44106
Phone: 216-368-6511
Fax: 216-368-3669
Email: kat4@cwru.edu
Web: library.case.edu/ksl/index.html

Blair Tinker
Geographic Information Specialist
University of Virginia (512)
Alderman Library
Geospatial and Statistical Data Center
P.O. Box 400129
Charlottesville, VA 22904-4129
Phone: 434-982-2630
Fax: 434-924-1431
Email: tinker@virginia.edu
Web: fisher.lib.virginia.edu

Jocelyn Tipton
Government Documents Coordinator
Eastern Illinois University (162)
Booth Library
Government Documents
600 Lincoln Avenue
Charleston, IL 61920
Phone: 217-581-6072
Fax: 217-581-6066
Email: cfjtt@eiu.edu

Shah Tiwana
Librarian III
Chicago Public Library (164)
Harold Washington Library Center
Government Publications Department
400 South State Street
Chicago, IL 60605
Phone: 312-747-4508
Fax: 312-747-4516
Web: chipublib.org

Fort Wayne, IN 46805
Phone: 260-481-6514
Fax: 260-481-6509
Web: www.lib.ipfw.edu

Roberto Trujillo
Head, Department of Special Collections, Frances and
    Charles Field Curator of Special Collections
Stanford University (92)
Green Library
Historic Map Collection
Department of Special Collections
    and University Archives
Green Library
Stanford, CA 94305
Phone: 650-725-1022
Fax: 650-723-8690
Email: trujillo@stanford.edu
Web: www-sul.stanford.edu/depts/spc/maps/index.html

Grace Tucker
Head of Reference
Flint District Library (265)
Flint Public Library
Maps
1026 East Kearsley
Flint, MI 48502
Phone: 810-232-7111
Fax: 810-249-2635
Email: gtucker@flint.lib.mi.us
Web: www.flint.lib.mi.us

Lynn Turner
Library Technical Assistant
University of North Carolina, Chapel Hill (350)
Geological Sciences Library
CB #3315 Mitchell Hall
Chapel Hill, NC 27516
Phone: 919-962-2386
Fax: 919-966-4519
Web: www.lib.unc.edu/geolib/

Thomas Twiss
Government Information Librarian
University of Pittsburgh (425)
Hillman Library
University Library System Map Collection
3960 Forbes Avenue
Pittsburgh, PA 15260
Phone: 412-648-7726;-412-648-7730
Fax: 412-648-7733
Web: www.library.pitt.edu/libraries/maps/maps.html

Karen J. Underhill
Northern Arizona University (18)
Cline Library

Special Collections and Archives Department
Box 6022
Flagstaff, AZ 86011-6022
Phone: 928-523-5551
Fax: 928-523-3770
Email: karen.underhill@nau.edu
Web: www.nau.edu/library/speccoll

Michille Unrue
4th Floor Reference Librarian
Indianapolis-Marion County Public Library (191)
Central Library
40 East Street Clair Street
Indianapolis, IN 46202
Phone: 317-269-1700
Fax: 317-268-5229
Web: imcpl.org

Tim Utter
Cataloger
University of Michigan (263)
Map Library
Hatcher Graduate Library 825
Ann Arbor, MI 48109.1205
Phone: 734-764-0407
Fax: 734-763-5080
Web: www.lib.umich.edu/maplib

David Valentine
Programmer III
University of California, Santa Barbara (88)
Davidson Library
Map and Imagery Laboratory
Santa Barbara, CA 93106-9010
Phone: 805-893-2779
Fax: 805-893-8799
Web: www.sdc.ucsb.edu

Bee Valvo
Library Specialist
Northern Arizona University (18)
Cline Library
Special Collections and Archives Department
Box 6022
Flagstaff, AZ 86011-6022
Phone: 928-523-5551
Fax: 928-523-3770
Web: www.nau.edu/library/speccoll

John Van Balen
University of South Dakota (456)
I.D. Weeks Library
414 East Clark Street
Vermillion, SD 57059
Phone: 605-677-5371

Fax: 605-677-5488
Email: vanbalen@usd.edu
Web: www.usd.edu/library/idweeks.cfm

Fatemah Van Buren
Acting Head, Map Cataloger
University of California, Berkeley (46)
Earth Sciences and Map Library
50 McCone Hall
Berkeley, CA 94720-6000
Phone: 510-642-2997
Fax: 510-643-6576
Web: www.lib.berkeley.edu/EART/

Patricia Van Zandt
Science Librarian
College of William and Mary (520)
Earl Gregg Swem Library
Geology Department Library
P.O. Box 8795
Williamsburg, VA 23187-8795
Phone: 757 221-2094
Fax: 757 221-2093
Web: swem.wm.edu/Guide/Geology/index.html

Lesbia Varona
Collection Development Librarian
University of Miami (131)
Otto G. Richter Library
Cuban Heritage Collection
1300 Memorial Drive
Coral Gables, FL 33124-0320
Phone: 305-284-4008
Fax: 305-284-4901

Joshua Vassallo
University of South Carolina (444)
South Caroliniana Library
Published Materials
University of South Carolina Horseshoe
Columbia, SC 29208
Phone: 803-777-3132
Fax: 803-777-5747
Web: www.sc.edu/library/socar

Donna L. Vavrek
Documents/Reference Librarian
Louisiana Tech University (233)
Prescott Memorial Library
Everett Street at the Columns
Ruston, LA 71272
Phone: 318-257-4989
Fax: 318-257-2579
Email: dvavrek@library.latech.edu
Web: www.latech.edu/tech/library/maps.htm

Linda Vida
Director
University of California, Berkeley (47)
Water Resources Center Archives
410 O'Brien Hall
Berkeley, CA 94720-1718
Phone: 510-642-2666
Fax: 510-642-9143
Email: lvida@library.berkeley.edu
Web: www.lib.berkeley.edu/WRCA/

Jess Vogelsang
Library Specialist
Northern Arizona University (18)
Cline Library
Special Collections and Archives Department
Box 6022
Flagstaff, AZ 86011-6022
Phone: 928-523-5551
Fax: 928-523-3770
Web: www.nau.edu/library/speccoll

Larry Vos
Coordinator of Reference Services
Wichita Public Library (216)
Reference Services Division
223 South Main Street
Wichita, KS 67202
Phone: 316-261-8500
Fax: 316-262-4540
Email: lvos@wichita.gov

Barbara J. Walker
Georgia Institute of Technology (144)
Library and Information Center
Special Formats and Maps Department
704 Cherry Street
Atlanta, GA 30332-0900
Phone: 404-385-0226
Fax: 404-894-8190
Email: barbara.walker@library.gatech.edu

Lee Walkling
Librarian
Washington State Department of Natural Resources,
    Division of Geology and Earth Resources (531)
Washington Geology Library
1111 Washington Street SE
MS 47007
Room 173
Olympia, WA 98504-7007
Phone: 360-902-1473
Fax: 360-902-1785
Email: lee.walkling@wadnr.gov
Web: www.dnr.wa.gov/geology/mapindex.htm

Larry Walls
Library Assistant 2
State Library of Ohio (385)
Government Information Services
274 East First Avenue
Columbus, OH 43201
Phone: 614-644-7051
Fax: 614-752-9178
Web: winslo.state.oh.us

Dwight Walsh
Library Specialist
Citadel Military College (439)
Daniel Library
171 Moultrie Street
Charleston, SC 29409
Phone: 843-953-2569
Fax: 843-953-5190
Web: www.citadel.edu/library/

John S. Walters
Utah State University (499)
Merrill Library
Documents and Maps Department
University Hill
Logan, UT 84322-3000
Phone: 435-797-2684
Fax: 435-797-2880
Email: johwal@ngw.lib.usu.edu
Web: library.usu.edu/Govdocs/index.html

Richard L. Warner
Texas A&M University (484)
Sterling C. Evans
Maps/GIS Department
Sterling C. Evans Library, Maps
College Station, TX 77845-5000
Phone: 979-845-1024
Fax: 979-845-6238
Email: rwarner@tamu.edu
Web: library.tamu.edu/

Linda Warren
Cataloging/Government Documents Assistant
Heidelberg College (392)
Beeghly Library
10 Greenfield Street
Tiffin, OH 44883
Phone: 419-448-2104
Fax: 419-448-2578

Tommye Warren
Library Assistant
Montana State University, Bozeman (296)
Roland R. Renne Library

The Libraries
P.O. Box 173320
Bozeman, MT 59717-3320
Phone: 406-994-3171
Fax: 406-994-2851
Web: www.lib.montana.edu

Beth Watkins
Scanner Operator
Washington State Department of Natural Resources (530)
Public Land Survey Office
P.O. Box 47060
Olympia, WA 98504-7060
Phone: 360-902-1190
Fax: 360-902-1191
Web: www.dnr.wa.gov/htdocs/plso/

Michael P. Watkins
University of Wisconsin, Oshkosh (554)
Polk Library
Government Documents Collection
800 Algoma Boulevard
Oshkosh, WI 54901
Phone: 920-424-7305
Fax: 920-424-2175
Email: watkins@uwosh.edu
Web: www.uwosh.edu/library/depts/docs/gov.html

Ken Watson
Map Librarian
Eastern Oregon University (402)
Pierce Library
1 University Boulevard
La Grande, OR 97850
Phone: 541-962-3546
Fax: 541-962-3335
Email: kwatson@eou.edu

Lisa Watson
GIS/Map Library Assistant
East View Cartographic, Inc. (279)
Corporate Library
3020 Harbor Lane North
Minneapolis, MN 55447-8956
Phone: 763-550-0965
Fax: 763-559-2931
Web: www.cartographic.com

Sarah Weatherwax
Curator of Prints and Photographs
Library Company of Philadelphia (423)
Print and Photograph Department
1314 Locust Street
Philadelphia, PA 19107
Phone: 215-546-8229

Fax: 215-546-5167
Web: www.librarycompany.org

Debbie Weber
California State Library (69)
Government Publications Section
914 Capitol Mall
Sacramento, CA 95814
Phone: 916-654-0069
Fax: 916-653-6114
Email: dweber@library.ca.gov
Web: www.library.ca.gov

Michael Weber
Cataloging Librarian
Kutztown University (417)
Rohrbach Library
Maps Department
15200 Kutztown Road
Building 5
Kutztown, PA 19530
Phone: 610-683-4813
Web: www.kutztown.edu/library/maps.htm

Kathleen Weessies
Head
Michigan State University (264)
Main Library
Map Library
100 Library W308
East Lansing, MI 48854
Phone: 517-432-6277
Email: weessie2@msu.edu
Web: www.lib.msu.edu/coll/main/maps/index.htm

Arlene Weible
University of North Texas (489)
Willis Library
Map Collection
P.O. Box 305190
Denton, TX 76203-5190
Phone: 940-565-2870
Fax: 940-565-2599
Email: aweible@library.unt.edu
Web: www.library.unt.edu/govinfo/

Keith Weimer
Government Information Librarian
University of Richmond (519)
Boatwright Library
Government Documents Collection
1 Westhampton Way
Richmond, VA 23173
Phone: 804-289-8851
Fax: 804-287-1840

Email: kweimer@richmond.edu
Web: oncampus.richmond.edu/is/library/govdocs/
govinfo.html

Carla Weiss
Reference and Collection Development Librarian
Rhode Island College (432)
James P. Adams Library
600 Mount Pleasant Avenue
Providence, RI 2908
Phone: 401-456-8125
Fax: 401-456-1915
Web: www.ric.edu/adamslibrary

Stephen C. Weiss
Utah State University (499)
Merrill Library
Documents and Maps Department
University Hill
Logan, UT 84322-3000
Phone: 435-797-2684
Fax: 435-797-2880
Web: library.usu.edu/Govdocs/index.html

Todd Welch
Digital Access Librarian
Northern Arizona University (18)
Cline Library
Special Collections and Archives Department
Box 6022
Flagstaff, AZ 86011-6022
Phone: 928-523-5551
Fax: 928-523-3770
Web: www.nau.edu/library/speccoll

Roger Wellington
Head of South Carolina Room
Greenville County Library System (449)
South Carolina Room—Government Documents
Section
25 Heritage Green Place
Greenville, SC 29601
Phone: 864-242-5000
Fax: 864-232-9656
Email: Rwellington@infoave.net

Marlene West
Documents Specialist
University of Puget Sound (539)
Collins Memorial Library
1500 North Warner
Tacoma, WA 98416-1012
Phone: 253-879-3669
Fax: 253-879-3670
Web: library.ups.edu/research/govt/about.htm

Susan Westin
Oregon State Library (410)
250 Winter Street NE
Salem, OR 97301
Phone: 503-378-4277 x236
Fax: 503-588-7119
Email: susan.b.westin@state.or.us

Deborah Whalen
Special Collections Librarian
Eastern Kentucky University (226)
John Grant Crabbe Library
University Archives Map Collection
521 Lancaster Avenue
Richmond, KY 40475
Phone: 859-622-1792
Fax: 859-622-1174
Web: www.library.eku.edu/collections/sca/

Susan Whetstone
Photograph/Map Curator
Utah State Historical Society (508)
Utah History Information Center
300 Rio Grande
Salt Lake City, UT 84101
Phone: 801-533-3536
Fax: 801-533-3504
Email: swhetsto@utah.gov
Web: www.history.utah.gov

Diane White
Office Manager
American Historical Society of
   Germans from Russia (304)
631 D Street
Lincoln, NE 68502-1199
Phone: 402-474-3363
Web: www.ahsgr.org

James Wieferman
University of Texas, Austin (481)
Perry-Castañeda Library
Map Collection
Austin, TX 78713
Phone: 512-495-4275
Fax: 512-495-4296
Web: www.lib.utexas.edu/

Frank Wihbey
University of Maine (236)
Raymond H. Fogler Library
Government Documents and Microforms Department
Orono, ME 04469-5729
Phone: 207-581-1680

Fax: 207-581-1653
Email: frankw@umit.maine.edu
Web: www.library.umaine.edu/govdoc/default.htm

Nancy Wilkinson
Geography Department Chair
San Francisco State University (80)
Alfred Rockwell Sumner Memorial Map Library
1600 Holloway Avenue
HSS 289
San Francisco, CA 94132
Phone: 415-338-1145
Fax: 415-338-6243
Email: nancyw@sfsu.edu
Web: bss.sfsu.edu/geog/maplib.htm

Maureen Wilks
New Mexico Tech, New Mexico Bureau of Geology
   and Mineral Resources (336)
Geological Information Center Library
801 Leroy Place
Socorro, NM 87801
Phone: 505-835 5322
Fax: 505-835 6333
Email: mwilks@gis.nmt.edu
Web: www.geoinfo.nmt.edu/data/home.html#gic

Larry Williams
Library Assistant
University of Memphis (468)
McWherter Library
Map Library
126 Ned R. McWherter Library
Memphis, TN 38152
Phone: 901-678-2206
Fax: 901-678-8218

Nancy Williams
Library Assistant
Montana State University, Bozeman (296)
Roland R. Renne Library
The Libraries
P.O. Box 173320
Bozeman, MT 59717-3320
Phone: 406-994-3171
Fax: 406-994-2851
Web: www.lib.montana.edu

Pamela S. Williams
Frostburg State University (246)
Lewis J. Ort Library
User Services Division
1 Stadium Drive

Frostburg, MD 21532
Phone: 301-687-4887
Fax: 301-687-7069
Email: pwilliams@frostburg.edu
Web: www.frostburg.edu/dept/library/library.htm

Sandra Q. Williams
Saint Cloud State University (284)
James W. Miller Learning Resources Center
Government Documents/Maps
720 4th Avenue South
Saint Cloud, MN 56301
Phone: 320-308-2063
Fax: 320-308-4778
Email: sqwilliams@stcloudstate.edu

Virginia Williams
Cataloger
Frostburg State University (246)
Lewis J. Ort Library
User Services Division
1 Stadium Drive
Frostburg, MD 21532
Phone: 301-687-4887
Fax: 301-687-7069
Web: www.frostburg.edu/dept/library/library.htm

Mike Willis
Library Assistant
East Tennessee State University (461)
Charles C. Sherrod Library
Documents/Law/Maps Department
P.O. Box 78665
Johnson City, TN 37614
Phone: 423-439-5334
Fax: 423-439-5674

L. Wilson
Information Assistant
World Bank (128)
Library and Archives Development
1818 H Street
Washington, DC 20433
Phone: 202-473-8670
Fax: 202-522-1160
Email: lwilson@worldbank.org

Yvonne Wilson
University of California, Irvine (53)
Langson Library
P.O. Box 19557
Irvine, CA 92623-9557
Phone: 949-824-7290

Fax: 949-824-3644
Web: www.lib.uci.edu/libraries/collections/gis.html

Joseph M. Winkler
Manager, Research Collections
Saint Louis Public Library (292)
1301 Olive Street
Saint Louis, MO 63103
Phone: 314-241-2288
Fax: 314-539-0393
Email: jwinkler@slpl.lib.mo.us
Web: www.slpl.lib.mo.us

Mary E. Winter
Special Collections Branch Manager
Kentucky Historical Society (221)
Thomas D. Clark Library and Special Collections
100 West Broadway
Frankfort, KY 40601
Phone: 502-564-1792
Fax: 502-564-4701
Email: mary.winter@ky.gov
Web: history.ky.gov/

Christopher Winters
University of Chicago (166)
Joseph Regenstein Library
Map Collection
1100 East 57th Street
Chicago, IL 60637
Phone: 773-702-8761
Fax: 773-702-6623
Email: wintersc@uchicago.edu
Web: www.lib.uchicago.edu/e/su/maps

Lisa Wishard
Sandia National Laboratories (331)
Technical Library
P.O. Box 5820
MS 0899
Albuquerque, NM 87185
Phone: 505-845-8287
Fax: 505-844-3143
Email: lawisha@sandia.gov
Web: infoserve.sandia.gov/

Bonni Wittstadt
Maps and GIS Specialist
Johns Hopkins University (242)
Eisenhower Library
Government Publications/Maps/Law Library
3400 North Charles Street
Baltimore, MD 21212

Phone: 410-516-8360
Fax: 410-516-6029
Web: www.library.jhu.edu/gpml/

Heather Wolf
Curator of Manuscripts
Folger Shakespeare Library (124)
201 East Capitol Street SE
Washington, DC 20003
Phone: 202-544-4600
Fax: 202-675-0313
Web: www.folger.edu

Sinai Wood
Baylor University (498)
Moody Memorial Library
Government Documents
1312 South 3rd
Waco, TX 76798
Phone: 254-710-2157
Fax: 254-710-3116
Email: Sinai_Wood@Baylor.edu
Web: www3.baylor.edu/library

Mike Woodall
Washington State Department of Ecology (529)
P.O. Box 47600
Olympia, WA 98504-7600
Phone: 360-407-6000
Email: miwo461@ecy.wa.gov
Web: www.ecy.wa.gov/services/gis/maps/maps.htm

Jennifer Wrampe
Documents Assistant
Nebraska Library Commission (308)
Nebraska Publications Clearinghouse
1200 N Street
Suite 120
Lincoln, NE 68508
Phone: 402-471-2045
Fax: 402-471-2083
Web: www.nlc.state.ne.us/docs/clear.html

Mark Wurster
Library Technical Associate
Catawba College (365)
Corriher-Linn-Black Library
2300 West Innes Street
Salisbury, NC 28144
Phone: 704-637-4379
Fax: 704-637-4304

Mary T. Wyant
Map Librarian
University of New Mexico (332)
Centennial Science and Engineering Library

Map and Geographic Information Center
(aka The Map Room)
UNMGL/CSEL MSC05 3020 1
Albuquerque, NM 87131-0001
Phone: 505-277-5738
Fax: 505-277-0702
Email: mwyant@unm.edu
Web: elibrary2.unm.edu/csel

Nick Wyman
University of Tennessee (466)
Special Collections—Hoskins Library
1401 Cumberland Avenue
Knoxville, TN 37996-4000
Phone: 865-974-4480
Fax: 865-974-0560
Web: www.lib.utk.edu/spcoll

Philip A. Yannarella
Documents Librarian
Northern Kentucky University (222)
Steely Library
Map Collection
Louie B. Nunn Drive
Highland Heights, KY 40199-6101
Phone: 859-572-5456
Fax: 859-572-5390
Email: yannarella@exchange.nku.edu
Web: library.nku.edu/welcome.html

Thomas Yeh
Professor and Head
Central Washington University (526)
James E. Brooks Library
Documents, Maps and Microforms
400 East University Way
Ellensburg, WA 98926-7548
Phone: 509-963-1541
Fax: 509-963-3684
Email: yeht@cwu.edu
Web: www.lib.cwu.edu/documents/

Mage Yonetani
Librarian
Utah Geological Survey (507)
Utah Department of Natural Resources Library
1594 West North Temple
Salt Lake City, UT 84114-6100
Phone: 801-537-3333
Fax: 801-537-3400
Email: mageyonetani@utah.gov
Web: dnrlibrary.state.ut.us/

Margarita Yonezawa
Map Collection Assistant
University of California, Riverside (67)

Science Library
Information Services / Map Collection
P. O. Box 5900
Riverside, CA 92517
Phone: 909-787-6423
Fax: 909-787-6378
Web: library.ucr.edu/?view=collections/maps/

James Young
Chair and Associate Professor
Appalachian State University (347)
Department of Geography and Planning
Boone, NC 28618
Phone: 828-262-3000
Fax: 828-262-3067
Email: youngje@appstate.edu
Web: www.geo.appstate.edu

Libby Young
Government Documents Librarian
Furman University (448)
James B. Duke Library
Government Document Map Collection
3300 Poinsett Highway
Greenville, SC 29613
Phone: 864-294-2260
Email: libby.young@furman.edu

Susan Young
Cartographer Supervisor
Arkansas Geological Commission (36)
Geological Library
3815 West Roosevelt Road
Little Rock, AR 72204
Phone: 501-296-1877
Fax: 501-663-7360
Email: susan.young@mail.state.ar.us
Web: www.state.ar.us/agc/agc.htm

Carol Yuke
Documents Specialist
Contra Costa County Library (65)
Central Library
1750 Oak Park Boulevard
Pleasant Hill, CA 94523-4497
Phone: 925-646-6434
Fax: 925-646-6040
Email: cyuke@ccclib.org
Web: ccclib.org

Anne Zald
Head
University of Washington (537)
Suzzallo/Allen Library
Map Collection and Cartographic Information Services
Box 352900

Seattle, WA 98195
Phone: 206-543-9392
Fax: 206-685-8049
Email: zald@u.washington.edu
Web: www.lib.washington.edu/maps

Linda Zellmer
Head
Indiana University, Bloomington (182)
Geology Library
1001 East Tenth Street
Bloomington, IN 47405-1405
Phone: 812-855-1494
Fax: 812-855-6614
Email: lzellmer@indiana.edu

Miriam Zecharias
Government Documents Assistant
Augusta State University (146)
Reese Library
2500 Walton Way
Augusta, GA 30904-2200
Phone: 706-737-1748
Fax: 706-667-4415
Web: www.aug.edu

Xiao-Hong Zhang
GIS/Map Librarian
East View Cartographic, Inc. (279)
Corporate Library
3020 Harbor Lane North
Minneapolis, MN 55447-8956
Phone: 763-550-0965
Fax: 763-559-2931
Email: xzhang@cartographic.com
Web: www.cartographic.com

Sarah Ziegenbein
Central Arkansas Library System (38)
Main Library
Reference Services
100 Rock Street
Little Rock, AR 72201
Phone: 501-918-3000
Fax: 501-376-1830
Email: sarahz@cals.lib.ar.us
Web: www.cals.lib.ar.us

Georgianna Ziegler
Head of Reference
Folger Shakespeare Library (124)
201 East Capitol Street SE
Washington, DC 20003
Phone: 202-544-4600
Fax: 202-675-0313
Web: www.folger.edu

Jim Zimbelman
Smithsonian Institution (127)
Regional Planetary Image Facility
Planetary Maps
6th and Independence Avenue SW
Washington, DC 20560
Phone: 202-633-2480
Fax: 202-786-2566
Email: jrz@nasm.si.edu
Web: www.nasm.si.edu/research/ceps/imagery.cfm

Thomas R. Zogg
Geography Librarian
University of Minnesota, Duluth (277)
Library
416 Library Drive
Duluth, MN 55812-3001
Phone: 218-726-8100
Fax: 218-726-6205
Email: tzogg@d.umn.edu
Web: www.d.umn.edu/lib/

Erin Zolotukin-Ridgeway
Librarian I
Saint Paul Public Library (288)
Central Library
90 West 4th Street
Saint Paul, MN 55102
Phone: 651-266-7000
Fax: 651-266-7011
Web: www.sppl.org

Mary Zuris
Engineering Aide
Washington State Department of Natural Resources (530)
Public Land Survey Office
P.O. Box 47060
Olympia, WA 98504-7060
Phone: 360-902-1190
Fax: 360-902-1191
Web: www.dnr.wa.gov/htdocs/plso/

Appendix G

Geographic/Subject/Special Collection Index

This is a comprehensive index of the geographic, subject strengths, and special collections using accession numbers. Items are cross-referenced. Note: "U.S." is used for "United States," and "Aerial photos" is used for "Air photos."

Aerial photos:
Alabama: 1, 2, 4, 5, 6
Arizona: 17, 19, 20, 23, 24, 28, 30, 31
Arkansas: 36
California: 46, 47, 51, 52, 53, 55, 58, 59, 60, 62, 63, 67, 70, 80, 82, 88, 88, 89, 90, 93
Colorado: 94, 95, 96, 102, 103, 109
Connecticut: 115, 121
Florida: 130. 135, 137
Georgia: 141, 144, 150
Hawai'i: 152, 154, 155
Idaho: 158
Illinois: 160, 161, 164, 167, 175, 176, 180
Indiana: 181, 196
Iowa: 200, 203, 205
Kansas: 210, 212
Kentucky: 223
Louisiana: 227, 228, 231
Maine: 235, 236
Maryland: 240, 243, 246, 247, 248
Massachusetts: 251, 252, 254
Michigan: 265, 271
Minnesota: 275, 278, 281
Missouri: 290, 295
Montana: 299
Nebraska: 301, 306, 310, 313
New Hampshire: 324
New Mexico: 332
New York: 338, 339, 341, 343, 345, 346
North Carolina: 352, 357, 361, 365
North Dakota: 369
Ohio: 371, 378
Oregon: 400, 402, 407
Pennsylvania: 414, 421
Rhode Island: 433
South Carolina: 445
South Dakota: 454
Tennessee: 458, 462, 463
Texas: 475, 477, 481, 484, 486, 488
Utah: 499, 500, 505, 506, 507, 508
Vermont: 509

Virginia: 512, 513, 515
Washington: 523, 524, 527, 529, 533, 537
Wisconsin: 547, 550, 551, 554
Wyoming: 561, 564
Aerial photos, Arizona, historic:
Arizona: 28
Aerial photos, Asia, East:
Hawai'i: 154
Aerial photos, California:
California: 46, 59
Aerial photos, California, Eldorado National Forest (1937):
California: 80
Aerial photos, California, Fresno County:
California: 52
Aerial photos, California, Lassen National Forest (1937):
California: 80
Aerial photos, California, Orange County:
California: 53
Aerial photos, California, Santa Clara County:
California: 82
Aerial photos, California, Tahoe National Forest (1937):
California: 80
Aerial photos, Colorado (1938 to ~1970):
Colorado: 95
Aerial photos, Connecticut (1932 to 1995):
Connecticut: 115
Aerial photos, Florida:
Florida: 135
Aerial photos, Georgia:
Georgia: 141
Aerial photos, Georgia, Floyd County:
Georgia: 150
Aerial photos, Hawai'i:
Hawai'i: 154
Aerial photos, historic:
Virginia: 515
Aerial photos, Idaho, Northern (historic):
Idaho: 158

New York: 338
Bureau of American Ethnology Map Collection:
Maryland: 248
Washington: 528
Bureau of Soils:
Minnesota: 289
Burgess (Robert) Vegetation Map Collection:
New York: 346
Burma (Myanmar):
Minnesota: 279
Butchart (Harvey) Grand Canyon, Arizona hiking maps:
Arizona: 18
Butte County, California, historic:
California: 49
California:
Arizona: 30
California: 42, 44, 46, 47, 50, 52, 53, 56, 58, 61, 67, 68, 69, 73, 78, 80, 81, 82, 83, 84, 85, 87, 88, 89, 90 91
Oregon: 401
Washington: 528, 539
California, aerial photos:
California: 46, 59
California, agri-land surveys:
California: 51
California, Central Valley:
California: 51
California, Central:
California: 70
California, climate:
California: 59
California Coast:
California: 76
California Coastal Surveys:
California: 61
California, exploration:
California: 61
California, geology:
California: 59
California, Nevada County, mining:
California: 62
California, Northeastern:
California: 49
California, Northern:
California: 70
California, Northwestern:
California: 41
California, Sanborn Fire Insurance maps:
California: 46
California, Sanborn Fire Insurance maps (Library of Congress microfilm collection):
California: 56
California, soil surveys:
California: 59, 65
California, Southern:

California: 50, 71
California, Southern, surveys and tract maps:
California: 57
California, topos:
California: 56, 59
California, topos, historic:
California: 52
California, water:
California: 59
Cambodia:
Minnesota: 279
Cameroon:
Minnesota: 279
Camp Wheeler Military Map Collection:
Georgia: 148
Canada:
California: 91
Illinois: 171, 178
Indiana: 198
Maryland: 246
Michigan: 263, 264
Minnesota: 281
North Carolina: 356
North Dakota: 369
Ohio: 384
Utah: 503
Vermont: 509
Washington: 523
Wisconsin: 543, 551
Canada, Eastern:
Maine: 236
Canada, Northern:
Alaska: 13
Canada, topos:
Iowa: 205
Wisconsin: 543
Captured German maps:
Iowa: 205
Texas: 488
Captured Japanese maps:
Iowa: 205
Captured maps, German:
California: 46
Iowa: 205
Texas: 488
Captured maps, Japanese:
California: 46
Iowa: 205
Carey Act maps:
Idaho: 157
Caribbean:
Florida: 132, 134, 135, 136, 138
Texas: 480
CARTA—Antique maps of Africa and Latin America:
Florida: 135

Appendix H

Regional Federal Depository Libraries Index

This is an index, by state, to the Regional Federal Depository Libraries of the Federal Depository Library Program (FDLP). The four-digit numbers correspond to the library's depository number. The numbers in parentheses refer to the accession numbers used in this book.

Libraries not listed in this book: Detroit Public Library, University of Mississippi, Newark Public Library, New York State Library, University of North Dakota, Oklahoma Department of Libraries, and Oklahoma State Library.

ALABAMA
Auburn University at Montgomery 0008B (1)
Library
7440 East Drive
Montgomery, AL 36117-3596
Phone: 334-244-3653
Fax: 334-244-3720

University of Alabama 0012 (8)
Amelia Gayle Gorgas Library
Capstone Drive
Tuscaloosa, AL 35487-0266
Phone: 205-348-9355
Fax: 205-348-0760

ALASKA
Served by **Washington State Library** (532)

AMERICAN SAMOA
Served by the **University of Hawai'i** (154)

ARIZONA
Arizona State Library, Archives and Public 0022 (22)
Records, Law and Research Library
1700 West Washington
Phoenix, AZ 85007
Phone: 602-542-3701
Fax: 602-542-4400

ARKANSAS
Arkansas State Library 0036B (37)
One Capitol Mall
Little Rock, AR 72201-1081
Phone: 501-682-2326
Fax: 501-682-1532

CALIFORNIA
California State Library 0040 (69)
Government Publications Section

P.O. Box 942837
Sacramento, CA 94237-0001
Phone: 916-651-6799
Fax: 916-653-6114

COLORADO
University of Colorado, Boulder 0069 (95)
Norlin Library
1720 Pleasant Street
Boulder, CO 80309-0184
Phone: 303-492-4375
Fax: 303-492-1881

Denver Public Library 0071 (102)
10 West 14th Avenue Parkway
Denver, CO 80204-2731
Phone: 720-865-1728
Fax: 720-865-1785

CONNECTICUT
Connecticut State Library 0075 (115)
231 Capitol Avenue
Hartford, CT 06106
Phone: 860-757-6599
Fax: 860-757-6569

DELAWARE
Served by the **University of Maryland** (245)

DISTRICT OF COLUMBIA
Served by the **University of Maryland** (245)

FLORIDA
University of Florida 0103 (135)
George A. Smathers Libraries
L120 Marston Science Library
Gainesville, FL 32611-7011
Phone: 352-273-0374
Fax: 352-392-3357

GEORGIA
University of Georgia 0114 (141)
Ilah Dunlap Little Memorial Library
320 South Jackson Street
Athens, GA 30602-1641
Phone: 706-542-0664
Fax: 706-583-0268

GUAM
Served by the **University of Hawai'i** (154)

HAWAI'I
University of Hawai'i, Manoa 0129 (154)
Hamilton Library
2550 The Mall
Honolulu, HI 96822-2274
Phone: 808-956-2549
Fax: 808-956-5968

IDAHO
University of Idaho 0135 (159)
Library
Rayburn Street
Moscow, ID 83844-2353
Phone: 208-885-6344
Fax: 208-885-6817

ILLINOIS
Illinois State Library 0140 (176)
300 South 2nd Street
Springfield, IL 62701-1796
Phone: 217-524-4200
Fax: 217-524-0041

INDIANA
Indiana State Library 0170 (190)
140 North Senate Avenue
Indianapolis, IN 46204-2296
Phone: 317-232-3685
Fax: 317-232-3728

IOWA
University of Iowa 0189A (205)
University Libraries
100 Main Library
Iowa City, IA 52242-1420
Phone: 319-335-5925
Fax: 319-335-5900

KANSAS
University of Kansas 0199 (210)
Anschutz Library
1301 Hoch Auditoria Drive
Lawrence, KS 66045-7537
Phone: 785-864-4593
Fax: 785-864-5705

KENTUCKY
University of Kentucky 0208 (223)
William T. Young Library
1000 University Drive
Lexington, KY 40506-0456
Phone: 859-257-0500:2141
Fax: 859-257-0508

LOUISIANA
Louisiana State University, Baton Rouge 0222 (227)
Troy H. Middleton Library
Baton Rouge, LA 70803-3312
Phone: 225-578-7021
Fax: 225-578-9432

Louisiana Tech University 0230 (233)
Prescott Memorial Library
Everett Street at The Columns
Ruston, LA 71272-0046
Phone: 318-257-4989
Fax: 318-257-2579

MAINE
University of Maine, Orono 0235 (236)
Raymond H. Fogler Library
Orono, ME 04469-5729
Phone: 207-581-1681
Fax: 207-581-1653

MARYLAND
University of Maryland, College Park 0242 (245)
McKeldin Library
College Park, MD 20742-7011
Phone: 301-405-9169
Fax: 301-314-5651

MASSACHUSETTS
Boston Public Library 0268A (251
700 Boylston Street
Boston, MA 02116-0286
Phone: 617-536-5400 x2226
Fax: 617-859-2292

MICHIGAN
Michigan Department of History,
Arts and Libraries 0273 (270)
Library of Michigan
702 West Kalamazoo Street
Lansing, MI 48915-
Phone: 517-373-9489
Fax: 517-373-9438

Detroit Public Library 0275
5201 Woodward Avenue
Detroit, MI 48202-4007

Phone: 313-833-1443
Fax: 313-833-9709

MICRONESIA
Served by the **University of Hawai'i** (154)

MINNESOTA
University of Minnesota 0295 (281)
Government Publications Library
309 19th Avenue South
Minneapolis, MN 55455-0414
Phone: 612-626-7520
Fax: 612-626-9353

MISSISSIPPI
University of Mississippi 0312
J.D. Williams Library
Library Loop
University, MS 38677-9793
Phone: 662-915-7986
Fax: 662-915-7465

MISSOURI
University of Missouri, Columbia 0321
Elmer Ellis Library
Lowry Mall
Columbia, MO 65201-5149
Phone: 573-884-8123
Fax: 573-882-8044

MONTANA
University of Montana 0341 (299)
Mansfield Library
32 Campus Drive
Missoula, MT 59812-9936
Phone: 406-243-6800
Fax: 406-243-4067

NEBRASKA
University of Nebraska, Lincoln 0345 (313)
Don L. Love Memorial Library
13th and R Streets
Lincoln, NE 68588-4100
Phone: 402-472-4473
Fax: 402-472-5131

NEVADA
University of Nevada, Reno 0353 (321)
University Library
1664 North Virginia Street
Reno, NV 89557-0044
Phone: 775-784-6500 x309
Fax: 775-784-4398

NEW HAMPSHIRE
Served by the **University of Maine** (236)

NEW JERSEY
Newark Public Library 0376
5 Washington Street
Newark, NJ 07101-0630
Phone: 973-733-7812
Fax: 973-733-5648

NEW MEXICO
University of New Mexico 0383 (332)
Government Information/General Library
1 University of New Mexico
Albuquerque, NM 87131-0001
Phone: 505-277-7180
Fax: 505-277-4097

New Mexico State Library 0386 (334)
1209 Camino Carlos Rey
Santa Fe, NM 87507-5166
Phone: 505-476-9717
Fax: 505-476-9703

NEW YORK
New York State Library 0387
Cultural Education Center
Empire State Plaza
Albany, NY 12230-0001
Phone: 518-474-6280
Fax: 518-474-5786

NORTH CAROLINA
**University of North Carolina
at Chapel Hill** 0447 (352)
Walter Davis Library
208 Raleigh Street
Chapel Hill, NC 27514-8890
Phone: 919-962-1151
Fax: 919-962-5537

NORTH DAKOTA
North Dakota State University 0455 (368)
The Libraries
1201 Albrecht Boulevard
Fargo, ND 58105-5599
Phone: 701-231-8863
Fax: 701-231-7138

University of North Dakota 0456
Chester Fritz Library
3051 University Avenue
Grand Forks, ND 58203-9000
Phone: 701-777-4647
Fax: 701-777-4811

OHIO
State Library of Ohio 0460 (385)
Government Information Services

274 East 1st Avenue
Columbus, OH 43201
Phone: 614-995-0033
Fax: 614-752-9178

OKLAHOMA
Oklahoma Department of Libraries 0487
U.S. Government Information
Division
200 NE 18th Street
Oklahoma City, OK 73105-3298
Phone: 405-522-3327
Fax: 405-525-7804

Oklahoma State University 0488
Edmon Low Library
Stillwater, OK 74078-1071
Phone: 405-744-6546
Fax: 405-744-7579

OREGON
Portland State University 0506A (409)
Branford Price Millar Library
P.O. Box 1151
Portland, OR 97207
Phone: 503-725-4126
Fax: 503-725-4524

PENNSYLVANIA
State Library of Pennsylvania 0508 (415)
Forum Building
Room 220
333 Market Street
Harrisburg, PA 17126-1745
Phone: 717-787-2327
Fax: 717-783-2070

PUERTO RICO
Served by the **University of Florida** (135)

RHODE ISLAND
Served by the **Connecticut State Library** (115)

SOUTH CAROLINA
Clemson University 0560 (441)
Robert Muldrow Cooper Library
Campus Box 343001
Clemson, SC 29634-3001
Phone: 864-656-5168
Fax: 864-656-7608

University of South Carolina, Columbia 0562 (445)
Thomas Cooper Library
1322 Greene Street
Columbia, SC 29208

Phone: 803-777-1775
Fax: 803-777-9503

SOUTH DAKOTA
Served by the **University of Minnesota** (281)

TENNESSEE
University of Memphis 0590A (468)
126 Ned R. McWherter Library
Memphis, TN 38152-3250
Phone: 901-678-4566
Fax: 901-678-8218

TEXAS
**Texas State Library and
Archives Commission** 0591 (479)
1201 Brazos Street
Austin, TX 78701-1938
Phone: 512-463-5455
Fax: 512-463-5430

Texas Tech University 0614 (493)
Library
18th and Boston
Lubbock, TX 79409-0002
Phone: 806-742-2238:280
Fax: 806-742-1332

UTAH
Utah State University 0618 (500)
Merrill Library
University Hill
Logan, UT 84321-3000
Phone: 435-797-2683
Fax: 435-797-2880

VERMONT
Served by the **University of Maine** (236)

VIRGIN ISLANDS
Served by the **University of Florida** (135)

VIRGINIA
University of Virginia 0640 (512)
Alderman Library
160 McCormick Road
Charlottesville, VA 22904-4154
Phone: 434-924-4963
Fax: 434-924-1431

WASHINGTON
Washington State Library 0642 (532)
P.O. Box 42460
Olympia, WA 98504-2460
Phone: 360-704-5273
Fax: 360-586-7575

WEST VIRGINIA
West Virginia University 0653 (541)
  Downtown Campus Library
  1549 University Avenue
  Morgantown, WV 26506-6069
  Phone: 304-293-4040 x4037
  Fax: 304-293-6923

WISCONSIN
University of Wisconsin, Madison 0664 (547)
  Memorial Library
  728 State Street
  Madison, WI 53706-1494

Phone: 608-262-9852
Fax: 608-262-8569

Milwaukee Public Library 0670 (550)
  814 West Wisconsin Avenue
  Milwaukee, WI 53233-2385
  Phone: 414-286-2167
  Fax: 414-286-2798

WYOMING
Served by the **University of Colorado, Boulder** (95)

Appendix I
Depository Libraries Collections Index

This is a comprehensive index of the entries for institutions that receive items from the listed agencies via the Federal Depository Library Program (FDLP) using accession numbers.

Government Printing Office (GPO), general:

National Forest Service (NFS):

**National Geospatial Agency/National Imagery and
Mapping Agency/ Defense Mapping Agency
(NGA/NIMA/DMA), aeronautical:**

**National Geospatial Agency/National Imagery and
Mapping Agency/ Defense Mapping Agency
(NGA/NIMA/DMA), nautical:**

South Carolina: 441, 445, 446
Tennessee: 460, 465, 468
Texas: 481, 484, 493
Utah: 499, 502, 504
Vermont: 509
Virginia: 512, 514, 517
Washington: 523, 525, 526, 528, 532, 537
West Virginia: 541
Wisconsin: 544, 547, 550, 551, 556, 557

National Geospatial Agency/National Imagery and Mapping Agency/ Defense Mapping Agency (NGA/NIMA/DMA), topos:
Alaska: 13
Arizona: 22, 32, 33
Arkansas: 35
California: 41, 46, 50, 52, 55, 56, 58, 63, 69, 88, 89, 91
Colorado: 95, 102, 107, 109
Connecticut: 119, 121
District of Columbia: 125
Florida: 135
Georgia: 141
Hawai'i: 154, 155
Idaho: 158
Illinois: 160, 162, 164, 166, 167, 169, 174, 176
Indiana: 190
Kansas: 210
Kentucky: 219, 223, 224
Louisiana: 227
Maine: 234, 236
Maryland: 242, 243, 245, 246, 247
Massachusetts: 251, 254
Michigan: 263, 264, 265, 267, 272, 273
Minnesota: 278, 281
Missouri: 290, 295
Montana: 299
Nebraska: 302
Nevada: 321
New Hampshire: 325
New Jersey: 329
New Mexico: 332
New York: 338, 339, 340, 343, 345
North Carolina: 352, 355, 356
North Dakota: 368, 369
Ohio: 378, 391
Oregon: 409
Pennsylvania: 425
South Carolina: 441, 445
South Dakota: 453
Tennessee: 458, 460, 465
Texas: 472, 481, 484
Utah: 499, 502
Vermont: 509

Virginia: 512, 516
Washington: 523, 537
Wisconsin: 544, 547, 551, 554

National Oceanic and Atmospheric Administration (NOAA), nautical charts:
Alabama: 1, 4, 8
Alaska: 10, 13, 14
Arizona: 22, 28, 32
Arkansas: 35, 37
California: 41, 46, 47, 51, 52, 54, 56, 58, 59, 63, 64, 69, 71, 72, 79, 81, 88, 89
Colorado: 95, 102, 107, 111
Delaware: 122
District of Columbia: 125
Florida: 135, 138
Georgia: 141, 144, 145, 146
Hawai'i: 154, 155
Idaho: 158, 159
Illinois: 160, 164, 166, 169, 170, 174, 176, 178
Indiana: 182, 185, 190, 193, 196, 198
Iowa: 199, 205
Kansas: 210
Kentucky: 223
Louisiana: 227, 230, 233
Maine: 234, 236
Maryland: 241, 242, 243, 245, 247
Massachusetts: 250, 251, 254, 256, 258
Michigan: 261, 263, 264, 265, 267, 269, 270, 273
Minnesota: 277, 278, 281, 283, 289
Missouri: 295
Montana: 299
Nebraska: 313
Nevada: 321
New Hampshire: 324, 325
New Mexico: 332, 334
New York: 338, 339, 340, 343, 345, 346
North Carolina: 347, 352, 354, 360, 363, 366
Ohio: 372, 377, 378, 385, 394
Oregon: 399, 406, 409
Pennsylvania: 414, 415, 420, 421, 425, 427
Rhode Island: 430
South Carolina: 441, 445
Tennessee: 460, 465, 468, 471
Texas: 474, 475, 477, 481, 484, 493
Utah: 499, 502
Vermont: 509
Virginia: 512, 513, 514, 517
Washington: 523, 525, 526, 528, 532, 535, 536, 537
West Virginia: 541
Wisconsin: 544, 547, 550, 551, 556, 557
Wyoming: 559

U.S. Geological Survey (USGS), topos: